AN EARLY AND STRONG SYMPATHY

An Early and Strong Sympathy

The Indian Writings of William Gilmore Simms

 Edited by

John Caldwell Guilds
and Charles Hudson

Published by the University of South Carolina Press
for the South Caroliniana Library with the Assistance
of the Caroline McKissick Dial Publication Fund
and the University Caroliniana Society

© 2003 University of South Carolina

Published in Columbia, South Carolina, by the
University of South Carolina Press

Manufactured in the United States of America

07 06 05 04 03   5 4 3 2 1

Library of Congress Cataloging-in-Publication Data

Simms, William Gilmore, 1806–1870.
  An early and strong sympathy : the Indian writings of William Gilmore
  Simms / edited by John Caldwell Guilds and Charles Hudson.
      p. cm.
Includes bibliographical references and index.
  ISBN 1-57003-441-9 (alk. paper)
  1. Indians of North America—Literary collections. 2. Indians of
North America I. Guilds, John Caldwell, 1924– II. Hudson, Charles M.
III. South Caroliniana Library. IV. Title.
  PS2843.G83 2002
  818'.309—dc21
                                                    2002001044

Frontispiece Portrait of William McIntosh. Attributed to Nathan and Joseph Negus.
Alabama Department of Archives and History, Montgomery, Alabama.

An early and strong sympathy with the subject of the Red Men, in moral and literary points of view, have rendered me in some degree a fit person to insist upon their original claims and upon what is still due them by our race.

—SIMMS TO HENRY ROWE SCHOOLCRAFT, 1851

Contents

Poems

Appendix 1

PREFACE

AN EARLY AND STRONG SYMPATHY is a product of interdisciplinary research and scholarship. Early in the process of editing what he then called simply the "Indian book," John Guilds recognized that William Gilmore Simms's extraordinary achievement in portraying the American Indian could not be brought to light through the literary approach alone. That he found in Charles Hudson an enthusiastic and knowledgeable coeditor makes *An Early and Strong Sympathy* an anthology that speaks not only to Simms devotees but also to general readers, linguists, anthropologists, historians—indeed, to anyone interested in understanding the Native American in the context of emerging American civilization.

In selecting which of Simms's bountiful writings about North American Indians to include in *An Early and Strong Sympathy*, the editors were guided both by literary merit and by ethnohistorical significance. Any work possessing both of these distinctions was an obvious choice. But since belles lettres, with its primary aim to entertain, seeks ethnological authenticity only as a means to an end, if at all, and since expository writing, with its primary aim to inform, seldom seeks artistic excellence per se, one can only rarely expect to find both literary execution and anthropological expertise in a single work. Therefore, *An Early and Strong Sympathy* contains Indian tales and poems of literary worth that may be of less interest to students of anthropology; likewise, it contains prose writings of anthropological worth with less appeal to students of belles lettres. For example, "The Arm-Chair of Tustenuggee. A Tradition of the Catawba" is an excellent short story that contains no Catawba "tradition" of anthropological authenticity. On the other hand, "Oakatibbe, or, the Choctaw Sampson"—an expansion of the concise "Indian Sketch"—is significant for its iconoclastic discourse on ethnic issues, but this discourse obtrudes upon the crisp, taut narrative of the original. In "The Two Camps. A Legend of the Old North State," however, Simms blends literary craftsmanship and ethnological perspicacity, and the story achieves excellence by the criteria of anthropologists and literary scholars alike.

Except for Simms's trilogy of Indian novels (*The Yemassee, Vasconselos,* and *The Cassique of Kiawah*), *An Early and Strong Sympathy* presents every genre of Simms's writings about Native Americans—poetry, essays, histories, and letters in addition to short stories. Care has been taken, too, to choose works from every period of Simms's career, with selections stretching from 1826 to 1868 and including a long manuscript poem left unpublished at his death.

John Guilds wishes to express appreciation to the University of Arkansas for the support his research has consistently received; to the South Caroliniana Library for visiting Simms research professorships in the summers of 1995 and 1996; and to Wolfson College, Cambridge, where, as visiting fellow in 1999–2000, he worked on the final phases of this project. Individuals to whom he is indebted include Eric Roman and Sean Busick, his research assistants at the South Caroliniana Library; Allen Stokes, Thomas Johnson, and other staff members at the South Caroliniana; Susan Whitlow and Dwayne Coleman, graduate students at the University of Arkansas; and, most of all, Kevin Collins, his graduate research assistant at the University of Arkansas. As with all his endeavors, *An Early and Strong Sympathy* owes much to the encouragement, insight, and know-how of Gertrud Pickar Guilds.

Charles Hudson wishes to express his appreciation to the University of Georgia for support for research from his Franklin professorship and for a Teaching Replacement Unit from the Franklin College of Arts and Sciences for the fall of 1999.

The editors are grateful to the University Caroliniana Society for the subsidy in support of this book's publication by the University of South Carolina Press. Special thanks are due to managing editor Barbara Brannon for her skill and care in guiding a difficult manuscript through the press.

William Gilmore Simms and the Portrayal of the American Indian

～ *A Literary View*

John Caldwell Guilds

I

Until the renaissance of serious study of his writings beginning slightly more than a decade ago, William Gilmore Simms had been thought of primarily, and almost exclusively, as the most important literary representative of the mind of the Old South. If one wished to understand the thinking of the pre–Civil War plantation owner (so the corollary went), one must read Simms, whose writings accurately reflected the manners and mores of elitist white Southerners—a noblesse oblige mindset influenced by chivalry and anchored in belief in the inequality of races. Early scholarship on Simms helped to confirm the stereotype by applauding the sterling character of the man and blaming his shortcomings as a writer on the benighted society in which he lived. While purporting to exonerate Simms from personal liability, this scholarship nevertheless abounded with quotations illustrative of the racial bigotry of the time and place. My purpose is not so much to contest the validity of Simms scholarship before about 1988—or even to contest the notion that (like most nineteenth-century Europeans and Americans, both Northern and Southern) Simms held views on race now recognized as bigoted. But I think it is of utmost importance to see Simms as more than *just* a product of his culture—to see him as a complex iconoclast who, particularly on social issues concerning individuals with whom he was intimately connected, was a practitioner of pragmatic humanism in advance of its time.

Though a slaveholder who generally upheld the principles of the planter class, Simms trained himself to judge individuals—black, red, or white; male or female—on his personal experience with them, his knowledge of their ability, performance, and character. When his observations came in conflict with social, moral, or religious principles, Simms gave priority to his own judgment because he recognized that no rule could in reason be absolute. "The proof of the pudding," Simms might well have said with Lambert Strether, "is in the eating."* This open-mindedness, particularly in human relationships, enabled Simms to view life pragmatically as well as metaphysically. He tended to be humanistic in his assessment of an individual, particularly one he knew well; whereas in broad, multifaceted matters like politics or religion, he was more apt to adopt a philosophical position based on theory or principle. This generalization holds true for many aspects of Simms's thinking, but our focus here is on Simms's perception of American Indians and, more particularly, on his portrayal of them in his literary works.

Simms's interest in American Indians was aroused at an early age when, at seventeen or eighteen, he visited his father on his plantation near Columbia, Mississippi. The impressionable youth was fascinated with the vivid accounts of Indians related to him by his energetic and adventurous father, a gifted storyteller who "had [just] returned from a trip of three hundred miles into the heart of the Indian country."† But even more engrossing to the younger Simms were his own experiences among the Creeks and Choctaws when for several months he and his father rode together on horseback on the frontier of Alabama and Mississippi. In later years Simms's memories of the adventure were still vivid: "I have travelled, in early years, greatly in the South & South West on horseback, seeing the whole region from Carolina to Mississippi personally, and as far back as 1825 when ⅔ was an Indian Country; . . . I saw the red men in their own homes; could imitate them in speech; imitate the backwoodsmen, mountaineers, swamp suckers &c."‡ These early curiosity-arousing experiences served to direct Simms's attention even more to the frontier and

---

* Henry James, *The Ambassadors,* ed. Christopher Butler (Oxford and New York: Oxford University Press, 1985), 351.

† William Peterfield Trent, *William Gilmore Simms* (Boston: Houghton Mifflin, 1892), 15. There is a possibility that Simms's earliest visit to the Southwest came before the well-recorded one in 1824–25. See my note now entitled "A New Simms Essay of 1835 and Evidence of His Earliest Trip to the Southwest" (originally titled "A Note on Simms's Trips to the Southwest: How Early Was the First?") *Simms Review* 8 (winter 2000): 32–33.

‡ Simms to O. J. Victor, apparently some time in September 1859. See *The Letters of William Gilmore Simms,* ed. Mary C. Simms Oliphant, Alfred Taylor Odell, and T. C. Duncan Eaves (Columbia: University of South Carolina Press, 1952–56), 4:178; hereafter

the Indian, a scrutiny that eventually grew into the mature writer's fixation on them as appropriate and compelling subjects for art and literature.

Almost immediately upon his return to Charleston from his 1824–25 visit to his father, young Simms, in his first literary endeavor, the *Album**—a journal that he (and perhaps others) established—demonstrated that Native Americans and their fate still occupied his thoughts. His earliest published writing about Indians—a review of the anonymous *The Christian Indian; or Times of the First Settlers* (New York, 1825)—contains in the opening sentence what was to become a recurring theme in his later works: "The features of the North American Indians, as well as themselves, are rapidly becoming extinct."† The *Album* also includes Simms's "Letters from the West," which record firsthand encounters with the Choctaw Indians during a return visit to the Southwest frontier in early 1826. Simms's first published story about Indians came two years later—"Indian Sketch" (1828) was supposedly an eyewitness account of an incident revealing aspects of Choctaw tradition and character that baffle and astound the novice white observer. The earliest indication of Simms's skill and power in narration, "Indian Sketch" demonstrated that the portrayal of the Indian was a subject of literary potential for which by predilection and experience he was peculiarly suited. Unlike those who knew the Native American only through reading about the romanticized Noble Savage—or equally romanticized Ignoble Savage—Simms had seen Indians at first hand, had traveled among them, had heard their language, and had at least briefly witnessed the practice of their religion and ideology. That he had observed manners and morals that he found fascinating, if largely incomprehensible, made him curious to learn more about them. Seeking support for his firsthand observations, Simms became an avid reader of whatever he could find in print on the subject of Indians. Both his reading and his observations are manifest in his public and private writing during the late 1820s and throughout the 1830s.

Between 1826 and 1840 Simms published more than twenty pieces of imaginative literature dealing with Indians—thirteen poems, eight stories,

---

cited as *Letters. Letters* serves as copy-text for seven of the eight Simms letters to Henry Rowe Schoolcraft recorded below, 113–17.

* See John C. Guilds, "Simms's First Magazine: *The Album*," *Studies in Bibliography* 8 (1956): 169–83.

† *Album* 1 (27 August 1825): 65.

and *The Yemassee* (1835), the powerful novel that established him in the eyes of the nation as a worthy rival to Cooper in the portrayal of the conflict between the white and red races.* Five of the poems treat aspects of Indian history: "The Broken Arrow" (his first published poem on an Indian subject) and "The Love of Mackintosh" deal with the assassination of General William McIntosh, the Coweta chief accused of selling out to the whites; "Death of King Philip" and "Son of Philip" are based on the death of King Philip, or Metacom of Montaup; and "The Forest Maiden" is Simms's first use of the Pocahontas legend. Other early Indian poems of note are "The Green Corn Dance" and "The Indian Village," which combine the fervor of romanticism with the rigor of realism.

But it was in his short fiction that Simms was most imaginative in his treatment of Indian themes. *The Book of My Lady* (1833) alone contains three stories—"Haiglar. A Story of the Catawbas," "The Children of the Sun," and "Legend of Missouri: or, the Captive of the Pawnee"—in which Simms blends folklore and history, superstition and fact, in the narration of seemingly credible Indian legends that are more the product of imagination than of authentic Indian tradition. These stories reveal the creativity and the purpose of the writer: his ability to use specific details to lend credibility to stories that, if not ethnohistorically accurate, are yet sympathetic portrayals not only of Indian culture but also of individual Indians as intelligent human beings capable of love, compassion, and generosity as well as of self-interest and cruelty. Of greater literary distinction, however, are "Logoochie; or, the Branch of Sweet Water. A Legend of Georgia" and "The Cherokee Embassage," both of which were published in *Carl Werner* (1838). These well-written and imaginative stories demonstrate with wit and irony Simms's ever-increasing interest in the history, culture, and character of Native Americans and his mounting sympathy with their cause. Aware that his own knowledge of Indians was incomplete,† but confident that he had hit upon an overlooked vein of Americana worthy of celebration as an integral part of a national literature, Simms wrote

---

* For Simms's characterization of Indians in *The Yemassee*, see "Afterword," in *The Yemassee*, ed. John Caldwell Guilds (Fayetteville: University of Arkansas Press, 1994), 414–24.
† That Simms was aware of the general paucity of knowledge about Indians is indicated in his comment in 1837: "It will be understood, however, by the reader, that strict accuracy is not to be looked for in any narrative which relates to the history of our Indian tribes" ("'Thle-cath-cha,' or the 'Broken Arrow,' Being a few passages from Muscoghee History," *Southern Literary Journal* 4 [July 1837]: 394). Simms's knowledge of Indians,

on Indian themes with a fervor and intensity more in keeping with his conviction than his erudition.

By the 1840s, Simms had established himself not only as the leading novelist in the South but as a major figure on the national literary scene. His forte was the American frontier,* and almost inseparable from the frontier was the American Indian. Thus it is no surprise that his two most important books of the decade—*The Wigwam and the Cabin* and *Views and Reviews in American Literature, History and Fiction* (both 1845)—contain some of Simms's most distinguished writing about Native Americans. Six stories in his best collection of short fiction, *The Wigwam and the Cabin*, focus on Indian character and legend; and two of the essays in *Views and Reviews* bear directly on his theory of the importance of Indian themes in the creation of a national literature. In the preface to the 1856 edition of *The Wigwam and the Cabin*, Simms argued for the relevance and the authenticity of the subject matter of his stories:

> One word for the material of these legends. It is local, sectional—and to be *national* in literature, one must needs be *sectional*. No one mind can fully or fairly illustrate the characteristics of any great country; and he who shall depict one *section* faithfully, has made his proper and sufficient contribution to the great work of *national* illustration. I can answer for it, confidently, that these legends represent, in large degree, the border history of the south. I can speak with confidence of the general truthfulness of its treatment. I have seen the life—have *lived* it—and much of my material is the result of a very early personal experience. The life of the planter, the squatter, the Indian, and the negro—the bold and hardy pioneer, the vigorous yeoman—these are the subjects. In their delineation I have mostly drawn from living portraits, and, in frequent instances, from actual scenes and circumstances within the memories of man. (*Wigwam*, 4, 5)

---

however faulty it seems today, was comparable to that of many of even the most creditable white Indian scholars of his times.

* See John Caldwell Guilds and Caroline Collins, eds., *William Gilmore Simms and the American Frontier* (Athens: University of Georgia Press, 1997). It is interesting to note, however, that the focus of the novels Simms called his Border Romances was on the violent struggle between the legitimate white settlers of the frontier and lawless white renegades—Indians playing little or no part. But in many of his short stories, essays, and poems of the frontier, the Indian is a central figure—and, of course, in *The Yemassee, Vasconselos,* and *The Cassique of Kiawah*, the full-length novels on Indian themes. See the bibliography of Simms's Indian writings below, 593–601.

This is one of America's earliest and best definitions of what constitutes both literary realism and literary nationalism. But in advocating "general truthfulness" in literature, Simms also issued a caveat of great import to one examining his portrayal of the American Indian: "I need not apologize for the endeavor to cast over the actual that atmosphere from the realms of the ideal, which, while it constitutes the very element of fiction, is not inconsistent with intellectual truthfulness" (*Wigwam,* 5). In *Views and Reviews,* Simms expanded on the idea that—particularly in trying to capture the essence of Indian character—the author aiming for verisimilitude may legitimately use imagination to make historical subjects alive and vibrant to the reader if factual evidence is insufficient. In fact, according to Simms, art is superior to history because the creative imagination can bridge the gaps in meaning and understanding that factual history can only record and leave unfilled: "It is the artist who is the true historian. It is he who gives shape to the unhewn fact, who yields relation to the scattered fragments,—who unites the parts in a coherent dependency, and endows, with life and action, the otherwise lifeless automata of history. It is by such artists, indeed, that nations live" (*Views,* 36).

As early as 1839, Simms had written then Secretary of War Joel Roberts Poinsett that "a favorite purpose" of his mind was to "procure as many documents of an official character, relating to our Indians of North America, as it may be within the power of your department to dispense with," to help the writer in "a contemplated Literary labor" (*Letters* 5: 334–35). The late 1840s bear witness to Simms's concentrated effort to learn what he could about the Indian and his culture. In his "Personal and Literary Memorials," the unpublished 302–page manuscript in the Charles Carroll Simms Collection at the South Caroliniana Library of the University of South Carolina, Simms reveals, even more than in his published work, a worldview that is surprisingly cosmopolitan—even more surprising in that it is grounded in the parochialism of the nineteenth-century South.

Before examining evidence revealing Simms's serious study of Native Americans and his evolving enlightenment amidst a basic conservative philosophy, I should first describe the makeup of the document. Hardbound in leather and cloth, "Personal and Literary Memorials" is literally a notebook of Simms's memorabilia, containing clippings and illustrations; drafts of letters, poems, and stories; letters received by Simms; bank statements and drafts; aphorisms, both original and quoted; and jottings on various subjects—literary, historical, political, and personal. Simms's unusual method of preserving these memorabilia is in itself worthy of comment: Beginning with the first page—on which he wrote "Private. Personal and Literary Memorials. W. G. Simms. So. Caro."—Simms filled the first 165 pages of the notebook (designated Notebook I) with paste-ins and his own scribblings. At that point, though he was no more than halfway through the volume, Simms turned the book around and upside-down, inscribed a new title page almost identical to the first, and proceeded in the new direction to fill another 137 pages (Notebook II). Some autobiographical portions of "Personal and Literary Memorials" were quoted in William Peterfield Trent's biography of Simms in 1892, and somewhat more extensively in my biography a hundred years later. But the entire notebook—which is now being prepared for publication—will shed important light on Simms and his times.

Among the striking new perceptions of Simms afforded us by "Personal and Literary Memorials" is his enlightened and persistent pursuit of lore about Native Americans. What sparked my immediate interest was Simms's detailed note-taking, which attests to his close reading of William Bartram's *Travels through North and South Carolina, Georgia, East & West Florida,* first published in 1791 or 1792.* Starting on page 43 of Notebook I, Simms carefully transcribed "Notes from Bartram" (Simms's own label) until on page 87, he had completed the task of going through Bartram's book from beginning to end: his first notation is to "B.'s preface" (I, 43) about which Simms made extensive notes (as he did about almost every chapter); and his last is to "Waccamaw. [p.] 473" (I, 87). Though Simms's notes on Bartram include some on birds, flowers, reptiles, and wildlife in general, it is evident to a peruser of "Personal and Literary Memorials" that Simms was most fascinated by Bartram's observations about Indians. A good example: next to the notation "Indian wars, customs, character" (I, 71), he cited a specific passage in Bartram that helped formulate his own concept of Native Americans:

Bartram's Travels (1791) [213] the Indians make war against, kill and destroy their own species, and their motives spring from the same erroneous source as it does in all other nations of mankind; that is, the ambition of exhibiting to their fellows, a superior character of personal and national valour, and thereby immortalize themselves, by transmitting their

---

* It is interesting that in his novel *Cold Mountain* (1997), Charles Frazier has Inman reading Bartram's *Travels* and Ada reading "a novel of Simms."

names with honour and lustre to posterity; or in revenge of their enemy, for public or personal insults; or lastly, to extend the borders or boundaries of their territories: but I cannot find upon the strictest enquiry, that their bloody contests, this day as marked with deeper strains of inhumanity or savage cruelty, than what may be observed amongst the most civilized nations: they do indeed scalp their slain enemy, but they do not kill the females or children of either sex.*

Bartram's humanistic interpretation of the psychology and behavior of Native Americans helps to explain Simms's understanding of, and respect for, Indian character—an understanding and a respect that enabled him, better than any other American writer of his time, to portray Native Americans as complex human beings with strengths and weaknesses no different from those of whites. Following Bartram's lead, Simms was not content to characterize Native Americans generically; he attempted to individualize, making distinctions—rare among white observers—between tribes and nations, and among members of tribes. In all, in his published writings, Simms delineated—some in detail, some only in mention—no fewer than seventy Native American tribes or social groups, at least seven of which he read about in Bartram and cited in his two notebooks.

At about the time that Simms was reading (and taking notes on) Bartram's *Travels,* he was also engaged in one of his most ambitious poetic endeavors dealing with Indians: the long poem entitled "The Mountain Tramp. Tselica; A Legend of the French Broad," the manuscript of which has lain neglected, if not entirely forgotten, for more than a century and a half.† "The Mountain Tramp" is an excellent example of Simms's imaginative ability to create a

---

* Whether or not the observations of Bartram are ethnologically sound is not at issue here; the relevant fact is that his studies of the Indian led him to respect and admire the intelligence and character of the Native American. Bartram's scholarly conclusions confirmed in Simms his own views on Indians gained from actual experiences with them.

† The 94-page manuscript is dated "December 1849" in Simms's own hand; it now rests in the Charles Carroll Simms Collection. A very brief version—entitled "Tzelica, A Tradition of the French Broad"—was published in Simms's *Southern and Western Monthly Magazine and Review* in 1845 (and later in his 1853 *Poems*), but Simms was never able to find a publisher for "The Mountain Tramp." Another version of the manuscript, entitled "Tselica, An Indian Legend," is located in the Beinecke Library, Yale University.

dramatic Indian saga based on (in his words) "a tradition of the Cherokees" involving the French Broad River, whose "Indian name," according to Simms, is "Tselica." There is no evidence that the tale of Tselica, as told by Simms, is an authentic legend of the Cherokees; but in his depiction of the tragic love of Tselica and Ockwallee—members of mutually antagonistic tribes—Simms dramatically reveals in individual Indians the whole range of human emotions and traits—love and hate, passion and compassion, bravery and cowardice, generosity and greed, trustworthiness and treachery, kindness and cruelty. Consistently present in Simms's characterizations of Indians—before and after his note-taking on Bartram's *Travels*—are these seemingly contradictory characteristics that bind all people. Reading Bartram, then, perhaps did not *change* Simms's perception of Indians so much as it confirmed the appropriateness of his literary representation of them.

In the 1850s, Simms's interest in learning as much as he could about Indian culture is demonstrated by his relationship with Henry Rowe Schoolcraft, the foremost authority of his day. Simms, we know, first approached Schoolcraft as early as 1845, when he requested copies of *Oneota*,* for which he "had applied ... in vain to my book sellers" (*Letters* 2:102). That Simms "read [Schoolcraft] with exceeding interest" (*Letters* 2:103) is corroborated by his continued pursuit of the Indian scholar, not only as a contributor to the *Southern Quarterly Review* but also as a source of information and inspiration about the unwritten literature of Native Americans that both men cherished and admired for its artistic worth. In the most significant of his nine known letters to Schoolcraft, in March 1851, Simms apologized for his own inadequacy to undertake reviews of the former's scholarly writings on Indians but added: "I must endeavour, myself, to do you and the subject the utmost possible justice—for which be sure I have the most sincere anxiety, even though I lack the endowment. An early and strong sympathy with the subject of the Red Men, in moral and literary points of view, have rendered me in

---

Oneota, or The Red Race of America was first issued in eight numbers by Burgess, Stringer, and Co., New York, in 1844–45. An edition in one volume was published by Wiley and Putnam, New York and London, in 1845. In his 1845 letter, Simms had high praise for another of Schoolcraft's books: *Algic Researches, Comprising Inquiries Respecting the Mental Characteristics of North American Indians. First Series. Indian Tales and Legends*, 2 vols. (New York: Harper & Brothers, 1839).

some degree a fit person to insist upon their original claims and upon what is still due them by our race" (*Letters* 3:101).*

His connection with Schoolcraft serving as a stimulus, Simms heightened the use of Native American themes in his poetry and fiction. In the 1850s he revised and republished in rapid succession three long narrative poems dealing with Indian legends or traditions: "The Cassique of Accabee; A Legend of the Ashley River" (1853); "The Last Fields of the Biloxi; A Tradition of Louisiana" (1853), and "Pocahontas; A Legend of Virginia" (1854). In addition, he brought out three full-length volumes of fiction steeped in Indian lore and history: *The Lily and the Totem* (1850), a fictional history about the French and their troublesome relationship with Native Americans in sixteenth-century Florida; *Vasconselos. A Romance of the New World* (1853), a novel about Hernando de Soto and the Indians, also set in sixteenth-century Florida; and *The Cassique of Kiawah. A Colonial Romance* (1859), the excellent novel set amid the English settlers' war against (and eventual near extinction of) the Kiawah Indians. Even if he had written nothing else about Native Americans, these six works, written in the last decade before the Civil War, place him first among his contemporaries—and among the elite Euro-American writers of all ages—in treating Indian history, legend, and character, both in poetry and in prose.† But of course Simms wrote much more: his total treatment of Native Americans, it will later be demonstrated, exceeds that of any other creative writer of the nineteenth century—in depth, in frequency, in complexity, in comprehensiveness.

* Simms published in the *Southern Quarterly Review* three reviews of Schoolcraft—"History of the Indian Tribes" (1851), "Schoolcraft's American Letters" (1852), and "Schoolcraft—Letters on the Condition of the African Race" (1852). An earlier, longer essay, entitled "Literature and Art among American Aborigines" (1845), was ostensibly a review of Schoolcraft's Indian writings. In the latter essay Simms observed: "We commend to some of our clever compilers,—Mr. Griswold, for example—the plan of an Indian miscellany, in which close specimens of their oratory, their fable, their poetry,—shall appear together, in judicious opposition. The material for a goodly volume is abundant" (*Views and Reviews,* 142). Rufus W. Griswold was editor of three anthologies of American writers: *The Poets and Poetry of America* (1842), *The Prose Writers of America* (1847), and *The Female Poets of America* (1849).

† Though Cooper's popular collection of Leatherstocking Tales approaches the sheer bulk of Simms's novels and tales about Indians, Cooper wrote almost no criticism or history about Native Americans; and in poetry, no one comes close to rivaling Simms's output on Indian themes—with Longfellow and Bryant being his nearest competitors.

II

Simms recognized that the primeval forests were sacred to the Southeastern Indian's spirit and essential to his way of life. A recurring theme in his work is the conflict between the Indians' reverence for nature and the relentless encroachment on and exploitation of it by the European settler. The long and evocative description of the natural setting that opens *The Cassique of Kiawah* demonstrates Simms's literary craftsmanship on this theme in that it presents the still-unspoiled Carolina forest simultaneously as both a living, sanctified whole and as the locus of commodities waiting to be exploited. A simple sentence drawn from this opening description artfully establishes the dual nature of the place, while at the same time setting the novel's tone and introducing the central theme that pervades it: "The streams are full of fish, the forests of prey, the whole region a wild empire in which the redman still winds his way, hardly conscious of his white superior, though he already begins to feel the cruel moral presence, in the instinctive apprehensions of his progress" (13).

Simms deals in depth with the cultural differences that lead to a tragic conclusion of events: though the white man may indeed admire the beauty of the wilderness, he nevertheless regards it as a commodity to be put to use for the benefit of civilization; the red man, on the other hand, has a spiritual view of the virgin land that transcends materialism and calls for its being honored and protected. Thus, the achievement of one culture's goal calls for the obliteration of the other culture's: what in the white settlers' view is the proper and full use of the land can result in the displacement and the annihilation of the Indian's cultural ideals. An irony not lost upon Simms is that even the whites with characteristics and attitudes most like those of Indians—Daniel Nelson, the frontiersman/protagonist/narrator of "The Two Camps," or his counterpart in "The Mountain Tramp," the wily old hunter who demonstrates his love of the wilderness to his gentleman guest*—even those wise and

---

* The words of the backwoodsman Gowdey in *The Cassique of Kiawah* come close to recognizing nature as conceived by the naturalist Indian: "Men who live, like me, all their lives in the woods. . . . I'arn to love woods, and thicks, and trees, and rivers, and lakes; and they gits a quick ear for the cries of birds and beasts; and they sometimes finds company in very small and sometimes strange matters. The woods and trees, and even the waters, get to be friends after awhile; and you talks to them, and you think and believe that they talks back to you. . . . There's the company of blessed spirits, that are always about us,

knowledgeable stewards of the land contribute (with greater or lesser degrees of malice) to the takeover of Indian territory by white civilization—a movement so powerful that the end result is inevitable. In Simms's portrayal, the motivations of the two cultures are so different that, if each is true to its beliefs and modes of conduct, only the most powerful can prevail, to the utter destruction of the other—in the author's own words, "the life of civilization usurping the domain of the savage" (*Cassique of Kiawah*, 206). Thus, without condemning the settlers, with whom he identifies, Simms has sympathy with the heroic but doomed Indian, whose suffering and exploitation he recognizes as a vivid and tragic chapter in our national history. This current of meaning runs through not only "The Two Camps" and "The Mountain Tramp" but is also central to two of the trilogy of Indian novels—*The Yemassee* and *The Cassique of Kiawah*—as well as to a multitude of other poems and stories (e.g., "The Love of Mackintosh," "Death of King Philip," "The Cassique of Accabee," "The Indian Village," "Thlecathcha; or the Broken Arrow," "Missouri," "The Cherokee Embassage," "The Children of the Sun," "Logoochie," "Lucas de Ayllon," "Indian Sketch," "The Subaltern's Yarn," "Oakatibbe," "The Loves of the Driver," "The Legend of Guernache," "Haiglar," and "The Spectre Chief of Accabee," to name a few). These works bear witness to the genuineness of Simms's avowal to Schoolcraft of "strong sympathy with ... the Red Man" and recognition of injustices done to them at the hands of "our race." On the other hand, they also recognize that—despite the inevitability of white "progress"—Simms viewed the Indian as part of "us," and thought that an infusion of the Indian worldview would be helpful to the American character.

Closely allied to the theme of destruction of the natural environment and en masse displacement of Native Americans is the pernicious influence of white society on the individual Indian—resulting in degradation within his own social group. Occonestoga, the prodigal son in *The Yemassee,* and Oakatibbe, the improvident murderer in the story bearing his name, are prime examples of honorable Indians whose dissipation can be attributed directly to their involvement with European civilization. In *The Cassique of Kiawah*, the eventual alienation of young Iswattee from his father, Cussoboe, the

---

night and day, doing something—we don't know what or how—to help us, and keep our hearts up" (189–90).

Kiawah chief, can be traced to the well-meaning lad's adoption of some of the attitudes and ways of white society.* As elsewhere in his writings, in *Kiawah* Simms in his authorial voice presents both sides of the struggle between European settlers and Native Americans, pointing out that "most of the bloodshed along the frontiers was due to the gross incompetence of the white authorities," whose "blunders ... made the white race absolutely contemptible in the eyes of the savage" (135). Yet Simms also reveals that the philosophical goals of Edward Berkeley—described in his own words as "the gradual diversion of the tribes from barbarism to the civilizing tasks of culture"—represent, not reality, but false idealism like that of missionaries who believe it their responsibility to convert the world to their faith. Simms never disapproves of Edward Berkeley's idealism per se, but he clearly sees it as a mote in his eye that blinds him to the malicious intentions of others. Throughout, the irony in Simms's presentation is that the Indians—with their capacity for good as well as evil—initially received white settlers with openness and generosity until that trust was destroyed by association with European ideals and practices.

The narrative techniques of Simms's Indian writings highlight his themes in much the same way as a well-designed house enhances the beauty of its furnishings. Integral to the craftsmanship in his fiction and poetry about Native Americans is the use of realistic details. "The Narrative of Le Barbu," for instance, captures and holds the interest of the reader through its revelation of the details of everyday Indian life as observed by the omniscient author-narrator. "Le Barbu" features a striking example of another realistic technique, the candid portrayal of complex characters. Exceptional persons with myriad strengths and weaknesses abound in Simms's Indian writings, and the author's realistic delineation of them—red, white, and black; male and female—adds interest and substance to his subject matter.† In addition to Le Barbu, other exceptional and vividly drawn individuals in Simms's poems and stories about Indians are Mingo in "The Loves of the Driver," Combahee

---

* The recognition in Simms's fiction of such cultural dissociation presages a historical phenomenon: the similar social fragmentation in Indian society today.
† Simms recognized that the credibility of any piece of literature was enhanced by believable, realistic characterization, whatever the race, gender, or nationality of the character, and whatever the theme of the work.

in "Lucas de Ayllon," the chief of Accabee in "The Cassique of Accabee," Tsel-ica in "The Mountain Tramp," Cocalla in *Vasconselos,* Daniel Nelson in "The Two Camps," Sanutee and Matiwan in *The Yemassee,* Zulieme in *The Cassique of Kiawah,* and the narrator in "The Subaltern's Yarn." In many of these char-acterizations, Simms sprinkles dialogue with dialect or nonstandard Eng-lish—whether the Gullah of Mingo, the broken English of Oakatibbe, or the backwoods vernaculars of such characters as Daniel Nelson, the old hunter of "The Mountain Tramp," and the Kentuckian in "Missouri"—thereby adding an aura of reality to plots in which romanticism and realism vie for domin-ion. The portrayal of comparable imperfections in all of these groups serves to underline the humanity of all of them.

Another technique that recurs throughout the oeuvre of Simms—the use of history for the purposes of art—is employed consistently in his Indian writings. Certain of his stories, in fact, can best be classified as fictional his-tory; these works have frameworks of historical events and characters that the author brings to life by supplementing historical data with details of the imagination. An example is "Lucas de Ayllon" (subtitled "An Historical Nou-vellette"), the story of an actual Spanish explorer, but one that Simms embel-lished for dramatic and philosophical effect. Many of the stories in *The Lily and the Totem* meet the criteria of fictional history as well. Whereas in Simms's historical romances the protagonists are fictional, in *The Lily and the Totem* all characters are historical figures whose actions are based loosely on actual history. Simms's gift in making those historical characters come to life depends on his creation of fictional dialogues and episodes, an imaginative process designed to illustrate and expand the hard facts of history.*

Simms, it is important to note, frequently writes stories and poems about Indians that blend history, personal experience, and folklore or mythology (sometimes entirely invented). "The Arm-Chair of Tustenuggee," "Jocassée," "The Fields of Biloxi," and "The Children of the Sun" serve as good examples of this practice, which Simms adroitly defends in his seminal essay, "The Epochs and Events of American History, as Suited to the Purposes of Fic-tion." Simms adds plausibility to the mixture of art and history in writing

---

* In *The Lily and the Totem* three characters stand out in particular for their robustness and vitality—the aforementioned Le Barbu, Guernache, and Monaletta, Guernache's sensuous wife. Several of the stories—"The Legend of Guernache," "The Narrative of Le Barbu," and "Iracana"—move with a powerful sweep of narrative.

about Indians by focusing on the region of America that he knows best—the Southeast—with most of his narratives set between the Atlantic coast and the Mississippi River. But, perhaps aiming for a national readership, he occasionally stretches his vision to extend into the American West,* setting forth a romantic interpretation of the clash between the Pawnees and Omahas to which Simms attributes the naming of what is now the state of Missouri. Part of his purpose may have been to demonstrate his vastness—his expansiveness—so that, like Walt Whitman, he could say, "I am large ... I contain multitudes."† His vision, like Whitman's, was as boundless as was America's—and he wanted to convey a vibrant nationalism that carried him beyond his native region, the South, so frequently stereotyped even in his own time.

Motivated by the desire to be all-inclusive, Simms went far beyond stereotypes in portraying Indian social groups and even more so in portraying individuals. From an ethnohistorical point of view, he was frequently inaccurate in depicting tribal characteristics, but it is significant that he constantly sought valid information about the cultural and physical makeup of Native Americans—knowledge to be used in the creation of belles lettres. In an authorial aside in Vasconselos, Simms pointedly and sarcastically asked, "What fool was it who first thought that the red man lacked the sensibilities of humanity?" (476). In his portraits of individual Indians, Simms consistently humanized them by revealing in them passions, ideas, and deeds good and bad. Sanutee, Matiwan, Cocalla, the chief of Accabee, General McIntosh, Combahee, Tselica—red figures painted with overlapping characteristics of good and evil‡—match the complexity, intensity, and creativity of his best-drawn whites, like Nelson, and his best-drawn blacks, like Mingo. In short, Simms's Indian writings are strengthened by realistic, flesh-and-blood characterizations of human beings of all races and both sexes.

Another narrative technique at work in Simms's fiction dealing with Native Americans is the vision or dream sequence, which foreshadows the

---

* Discounted from this study of Simms's portrayal of Native Americans (or American Indians) are three works that deal with aborigines of the Caribbean or Central America: "A Legend of the Pacific" (1832), The Damsel of Darien (1839), and "The Maroon. A Legend of the Caribees" (1847).

† "Song of Myself," line 1316.

‡ Imagery is not widely utilized by Simms in his Indian tales. But two notable exceptions are "Haiglar," with its animal imagery, and "The Cherokee Embassage," with its gold-chain symbolism.

crucial action in both "The Two Camps" (in which Daniel Nelson experiences two prophetic visions) and "Legend of Missouri" (in which Enemoya learns through a dream about the danger threatening Missouri). Use of the oral storyteller who captivates his audience by his manner is another device employed by Simms in "The Two Camps" and "Jocassée"—in the latter of which the first-person narrator tells the story as it was related to him by another person. "The Mountain Tramp" also uses the oral storyteller technique in much of Part I but reverts to the omniscient narrator in Part II, perhaps with a resulting loss of verisimilitude.

Simms's fascination with Indians—to speculate for a moment—could be related at least in part to his natural literary affinity with their traditions: the symbolic dreams found in Simms's writings are matched in Native American folklore; and, perhaps even more significant, the oral storytelling tradition that Simms as an impressionable boy learned from his maternal grandmother (and later, as a young man, from his raconteur father) is the centerpiece of Indian oral literature. The transmission of Native American mythology from one generation to another by oral storytellers is strikingly similar in technique to Simms's "passing on" to readers his grandmother's tales of the Revolution and his father's accounts of frontier life in his Revolutionary War novels and stories, and in his Border Romances, respectively.

During the Civil War, it should be noted, Simms ceased to write about Indians. Beginning with secession, he was so preoccupied with political, economic, and military tragedy that he had neither sufficient time nor an appropriate mood for creative efforts on other matters. It is also true, of course, that the backlash of Northern sentiment against him as a slavehold-ing advocate of secession and the Confederacy deprived him of his publish-ers, almost all of whom were in the North. In fact, from 1861 to 1865, Simms published no books; and his only book-length works—*Paddy McGann; or Demon of the Stump* (a cleverly disguised political satire) in 1863, and his eyewitness account of the *Sack and Destruction of the City of Columbia, S.C.* in 1865—were published serially in Southern journals or newspapers. But shortly after the end of Civil War hostilities, Simms turned once again to Indian topics (perhaps partly because there was no longer a market for his novels about the antebellum South). Simms resorted to writing expanded ver-sions of earlier poems on Indian themes, and in the process he produced two of his very best poems—"Chilhowee, the Indian Village" and "Thlecathcha; or, the Broken Arrow" (both 1868). These accomplished poetic pieces, coupled with the two works left in manuscript at his death—the long narrative poem "The Mountain Tramp" and the magnificent tall tale "'Bald-Head Bill Bauldy,' and How He Went Through the Flurriday Campaign!"—demonstrate not only that in the last two years of his life Simms was at the peak of his prowess as a writer but also that, as a writer, he remained interested in the character, the philosophy, and the fate of the Native American.

All in all, Simms wrote more than a hundred literary pieces about Indians (poems, stories, essays, and novels). But that he wrote more about, thought more seriously about, and almost certainly knew (and cared) more about the American Indian than any other man of letters of the nineteenth century is one of the best-kept secrets in American literary history. Albert Keiser's early recognition that the treatment of the Indian by Simms was the most balanced and most accurate in American literature[*] makes the scholarly oversight of his important and extensive Indian writings even more puzzling.[†] Though other examples abound, nowhere is this gaping lacuna more dramatically revealed than in a recent edition (1998) of *The American Tradition in Literature,* a respected, widely used anthology published by McGraw-Hill: despite devoting a section to "the Native American Heritage" and including selections from Hopkins, Irving, Cooper, Sedgwick, Bryant, and Parkman, the editors fail even to mention Simms. Omission from anthologies (particularly those designed for classroom adoption) in which he has a legitimate place is more damaging to the reputation of an author than the mere absence of due recognition in literary criticism or history.

---

[*] Albert Keiser, *The Indian in American Literature* (New York: Oxford University Press, 1933), 154–74.

[†] Recent books that pay scant attention to Simms's treatment of Native Americans include Susan Scheckel, *The Insistence of the Indian: Race and Nationalism in Nineteenth-Century American Culture* (Princeton: Princeton University Press, 1998); Roy Harvey Pearce, *Savagism and Civilization: A Study of the Indian and the American Mind,* rev. ed. (Berkeley: University of California Press, 1988); Louise K. Barnett, *The Ignoble Savage: American Literary Racism, 1790–1890* (Westport, Conn.: Greenwood Press, 1975); and *The Frontier Experience and the American Dream,* ed. David Mogen, Mark Busby, and Paul Bryant (College Station: Texas A & M University Press, 1989. More encouraging is the fact that *The Native American in American Literature: A Selectively Annotated Bibliography,* compiled by Roger O. Rock (Westport Conn.: Greenwood Press, 1985) includes enough citations to Simms to suggest his importance.

The neglect by literary historians of Simms's writings on American Indians is better understood if put into the context of the longstanding scholarly neglect of the Southeastern Indians—a shameful oversight not seriously addressed until the publication of Charles Hudson's *The Southeastern Indians* in 1976. In the preface and introduction of his book, Hudson candidly and unequivocally acknowledged: "More than any of the native people of North America, the Southeastern Indians have been the victims of scholarly neglect. . . . All people have blind spots in their memory of the past, but the Southeastern Indians are victims of a virtual amnesia in our historical consciousness."* In his introductory essay to the present volume, Hudson comments on the widespread and pernicious side effects of this "amnesia" on the South as a whole, particularly in the public perception of Southern history and culture, not only by outsiders but even by Southerners themselves (see below, 34–35). In full agreement with this thesis was Donald Davidson, who in his penetrating essay introducing the first volume of Simms's *Letters* (1952), contended that, because the frontier of the Lower South is not known to Americans generally "in the same familiar way that the history of frontier Kentucky and Tennessee, the Ohio Valley, and the trans-Mississippi West is known," the actual frontier Simms knew and wrote about "has been overshadowed and virtually lost in our historical consciousness" (1:xxxvii–xxxviii). Thus, the lack of recognition of Simms's literary representation of the Indians seems part of a wider pattern of neglect and misconception: it is not merely that Simms the author has been marginalized or overlooked; it is that a whole frontier and a whole people (subjects of much of Simms's writing) have little or no presence in our historical consciousness.

The inadequate scholarly portrayal of Southeastern Indians until well into the twentieth century points up the obstacles Simms faced in his nineteenth-century efforts to incorporate their history and character into a national literature: the Indians that he knew best (and wrote about most) were not the Indians most prominent in white America's consciousness (nor was the frontier that he knew and wrote about the frontier of America's consciousness); the scholars Simms chose as his mentors were the best available, but because even their knowledge was flawed, incomplete, and frequently inaccurate (particularly with regard to Southeastern Indian culture), his study of them could

---

* Charles Hudson, *The Southeastern Indians* (Knoxville: University of Tennessee Press, 1976), vii, 3.

not and did not free him of misconceptions and errors. A further irony is that the insufficient and flawed depiction of Native Americans by historians and anthropologists of his time should have enhanced the significance of Simms's literary representation of them: his factual mistakes and cultural misunderstandings were often reflections of the scholarly record; yet his gift for literary realism, particularly to humanize Indian characters, added to his creative portrayals a verisimilitude that the scholarship lacked.

Though, as we have seen, he occasionally ventured west of the Mississippi River in his portrayals of Indians, Simms as a writer about Indians (like Simms as a writer about all mankind) was at his best when he wrote about what he knew best: the people, landscape, and history of his own region of the country. Thus, Simms's portrait of the American Indian was *largely* the portrait of the Southeastern Indian—despite the great diversity revealed in "Native Americans in the Writings of William Gilmore Simms" (Appendix 1, 573–87). Simms's awareness of the blind spots in his knowledge of Indian character, culture, and history partially accounts for his motivation at every opportunity to read, observe, and learn all he could about Indians. Though through reading and experience he became the foremost authority on Native Americans among America's writers of belles lettres, he never implied that his ever-growing knowledge of Indians was other than rudimentary; to the contrary, he repeatedly referred to the dearth of his understanding of a culture vastly different from his own. It was, it should be recalled, his *sympathy* (and the resultant desire for knowledge) that he emphasized in his letter to Schoolcraft that gives this book its title. Since Simms wrote specifically about the enslavement of Indians by Spaniards in "Lucas de Ayllon"—a scathing indictment of the inhumanity of slavery—one may wonder whether he had knowledge of the enslavement of Indians by early English settlers, particularly the Carolinians of the seventeenth and eighteenth centuries, one of the greatest transgressions against the Indians of the Southeast.* The validity of his claim of "an early and strong sympathy with the Red Man" is evidenced, however, by his condemnation of the white man's injustice to the aborigines and his recognition of the penance "still due them by our race." And with all his inaccuracies and misunderstandings about the culture of the Southeastern Indians, in portraying them sympathetically, Simms made

---

* The entire English-speaking world seems to have subscribed to the Black Legend, the theory that the Spanish were the cruelest and most malevolent of the early colonizers.

a contribution not only to literature but to our understanding of history as well. Significantly, he also presaged the sense of profound loss—a sense that dominated American scholarship in the twentieth century—that accompanied the tragic decline of Indian civilizations. Nowhere else in American letters is there a fuller and more fruitful picture of the aborigines of a large region of North America than in the prose and poetry of William Gilmore Simms.

Simms's focus on the South—like, for example, the focus of Hawthorne on New England—is consistent with his own thesis that the writer who "shall depict *one section* faithfully" contributes significantly to the creation of a distinctive national literature. And by filling in the gaps in history with creative imagination, Simms not only upheld his theory of the purpose of art, but he also, more importantly, gave the Cherokees, Choctaws, Catawbas, Yamasees,* Muscoghees, and other Southeastern Indians a place in the literature of a nation that had exploited and almost forgotten them.

Before entering into the joint enterprise responsible for making this book, as a literary scholar I knew the scope and the depth of Simms's prodigious writings about Native Americans, and I was amazed by what seemed to me his intricate knowledge of their character, history, and culture. Now, though still a novice in ethnohistory, I recognize that much of Simms's knowledge of Indians was flawed and incomplete, subject to at least some of the stereotyping he avidly sought to discredit. However, within the limits of nineteenth-century naiveté—even of anthropologists and ethnohistorians—the knowledge Simms *did* possess of Indian culture was impressive for a layman. But what is little less than astounding is his compulsion to know about Indians and to write about them with fervor and conviction. Despite my awareness now of the large gaps in Simms's comprehension of American Indians, what is still apparent to me is that in comparison with all other literary men of his age—including, of course, Cooper, universally recognized for his characterization of Native Americans—Simms wrote about Indians with more frequency, depth, and accuracy at least in part because he possessed more knowledge about them.

Elsewhere, I have observed that Simms "needs to be read to be appreciated, and he can be neither read nor appreciated unless his works are made available."[†]

---

* Though Simms in his novel and elsewhere used the spelling *Yemassees, Yamasees* is used here because it is the accepted spelling of the actual people.

† "Preface to the Arkansas Edition," *Guy Rivers: A Tale of Georgia* (Fayetteville: University of Arkansas Press, 1993), ix.

True of Simms's work as a whole, this statement is especially relevant with reference to his Indian writings—which until the publication of *An Early and Strong Sympathy* could be read only after tedious searching through numerous scattered sources. It is to be hoped that this book—the first attempt to select and collect in a single volume a representation of his Indian writings—will enable readers to judge for themselves the significance of Simms's vision of the American Indian. To Simms, representation of the Native American was indispensable—not only in recording an authentic and comprehensive history of our country, but also in creating an imaginative and distinctive national literature.

ᐧ᪻ *An Ethnohistorical View*

CHARLES HUDSON

MY PURPOSE HERE is to assess William Gilmore Simms's depiction of the American Indians. I shall do so, not as a literary scholar, but as one who has devoted his career to making sense out of the anthropology and ethnohistory of the Indians of the southeastern United States. Simms undertook to write a series of novels, stories, and poems depicting the vast canvas of American history, most particularly Southern history. His artistic vision was grand in scale, and his pursuit of it was tenacious.* He meant to celebrate the history of all the European nationalities who colonized America—the Spanish and the French as well as the English—and he meant to represent all of the varieties of people who played roles in this immense drama, black and Indian as well as white, from all walks of life.

That much of the American history depicted in Simms's stories, novels, and poems unfolded in the South should come as no surprise, for Simms was a Southerner, or, as he would say, a "Southron." But it is still not widely appreciated by Americans that much of the first period of American history, as delineated by Simms, from about 1497 to about 1607, played itself out in the region that was to become the American South. In comparison, the region that was to become the American North was arguably marginal during this time.

Moreover, important events in Simms's second and third periods of American history, from about 1608 to 1782, the era of colonial wars, occurred in the South. These events are well known to specialist scholars, but laymen are to this day relatively unaware of them. This is the period of time that Americans conceptualize as the frontier era, though few laymen imagine that much of importance took place in the South. More recently, social historians are inclined to describe the social system of the frontier era as made up of several loosely articulated ethnic and economic groups.† Although the American frontier was a social terrain that contained potent instabilities and yawning

---

* John Caldwell Guilds, *Simms: A Literary Life* (Fayetteville: University of Arkansas Press, 1992), 333–34.

† Colin G. Calloway, *New Worlds for All: Indians, Europeans, and the Making of Early America* (Baltimore: Johns Hopkins University Press, 1993), 1–7.

fissures, it was nonetheless a social world that was at least minimally intelligible to the people who lived in it.

One of the ironies of Simms's career is that his second and third periods of American history possibly had more palpability in the minds of early-nineteenth-century American intellectuals—partly through Simms's own efforts—than was later the case. There are at least three reasons for this historical amnesia. One is that Simms saw the frontier through the eyes of an elite member of the Old South, a social order that was rent asunder by the Civil War and whose institutions and mentalities were resoundingly discredited by a victorious North. The second is that the frontier in the North, and more particularly in the West, was subsequently mythologized as a conflict between whites and Indians. Blacks, and particularly black slaves, were left out of this mythical picture. A cast of whites and Indians more neatly fitted a central theme in the myth of the frontier: the triumph of civilization over savagery. And finally, the third reason Simms's frontier novels have been marginalized in modern times, even in the South, is that all things attending the Civil War and the social order that sponsored it became the overriding historical concern of Southerners and, hence, of Southern historians. In the wake of the Civil War, it was as if the South had hardly known an eighteenth century, much less a seventeenth or sixteenth century. As Simms realized, though, it had known all three. Thus, it has come about that libraries bulge with historical novels about the Northern and more particularly Western frontiers, and for a time so did film libraries. But aside from Simms's own work, relatively few novels have been written about the Southern frontier; and Mel Gibson's recent movie, *The Patriot*, is evidently the first commercially successful movie about the Southern frontier. Some would argue that even *The Patriot* falls short, because Southern speech is hardly in evidence in the film and because the character Gibson plays is such a nice guy that all of his black laborers are freedmen.

In all that Simms wrote about Indians, it must be kept in mind that he worked before the field of anthropology existed; hence, he had no conception of culture and its variability or of the evolution of various forms of social structure. He labored under the considerable handicap of lacking modern conceptual tools with which to distinguish among and compare peoples. What he had to think with was the now-discredited concept of *race*—that is, the assumption that people can be sorted out into relatively neat biological categories and that certain mental and physical capabilities and characteristics are necessarily entailed in one's racial identity. Simms even referred to the settlers of the Southern backcountry, predominantly immigrants from the border between England and Scotland, as the "Border race," as if they were a separate racial stock. Of course, such thinking was not confined to the South. In the nineteenth century the concept of race was pervasive in the English-speaking world and much more widely than that. It should be noted, however, that Simms was unusual for his time in being strongly of the opinion that Indians were not mentally inferior to whites. Part of his estimation of them rested on evidences of their verbal ability, particularly as shown in their recorded speeches.[*]

Beyond such racial characteristics, Simms tried to portray various Southeastern Indians in terms of their character, almost as if the various Indian societies could be described as persons writ large. For example, Simms asserts in "Haiglar" that eighteenth-century Catawbas, naturally warm and courageous, were "the most chivalrous of all the savage nations," and they had always been lively and steadfast friends of South Carolina; whereas the "Muscoghees" were sullen and ferocious, and the Cherokees had taken the most steps toward civilization.[†]

The attempt to define entire peoples in terms of their "national character" has a long history. The Indian agent Edmund Atkin and others used similar characterizations in the eighteenth century.[‡] Indeed, only a little more sophisticated were the characterizations of preliterate peoples by anthropologists Ruth Benedict and Margaret Mead in the twentieth century. Their only innovation was that they attempted to characterize various cultures using philosophical and psychological jargon.[§]

Since Simms claimed that his Indian writings represented historical actualities with some fidelity, we need to examine the quality of his sources of information. It falls into two main types: (1) information he acquired through firsthand observation from his travels in Indian country, along with secondhand information told him by people who were firsthand observers of Indians; and (2) published and perhaps some few manuscript sources.

---

[*] William Gilmore Simms, "Literature and Art among the American Aborigines," 140–41.

[†] Ibid., 137.

[‡] Edmund Atkin, *The Appalachian Indian Frontier: The Edmund Atkin Report and Plan of 1755*, ed. Wilbur Jacobs (Lincoln: University of Nebraska Press, 1967), 68–71.

[§] Ruth Benedict, *Patterns of Culture* (New York: Bantam Books, 1953), 72.

TRAVELS IN INDIAN COUNTRY

Simms made at least four trips into the Indian country where he could observe Indians in vivo, acquiring a kind of information that James Fenimore Cooper seems not to have had. Possibly his first and most formative visit came in 1824–25, when he traveled overland to visit his father on his plantation in Mississippi.* While there, he and his father rode about, visiting frontier settlements in Mississippi and Alabama. He appears to have made no written record of his travels and observations, but later he surely drew on his memory of these experiences.

On April 30, 1825, a party of Upper Creeks assassinated William McIntosh, an important Creek leader.† A few weeks later Simms passed near where this occurred, in the vicinity of present Columbus, Georgia, where he heard many stories and opinions about McIntosh. In a "public house" he saw a full-length oil painting of McIntosh considered by those who knew him to have been a good likeness.‡ Simms was fascinated with McIntosh, and in later years he wrote about him in both poetry and prose.

Simms may not have realized that the Indians he saw on his travels were a defeated and dispirited people. Travel through Creek country was somewhat dangerous, and travelers feared being robbed and killed both by Indians and by renegade whites. The Indians lived in villages well away from main thoroughfares; hence, one could not depend on them to supply necessities. Once when Simms paid an Indian full price for a small watermelon, a fellow traveler castigated him for not paying only half of what the man had asked, making it clear to Simms that it was white people, not Indians, who fixed prices. This fellow traveler told Simms that he had recently paid an Indian half price for a purchase, and when the Indian complained, the man had

---

* Guilds, *Simms,* 17. Guilds has recently advanced evidence of a possible fifth visit to the Indian country. Guilds, "A New Simms Essay of 1835 and Evidence of His Earliest Trip to the Southwest," *Simms Review* 8 (winter 2000): 32–33.

† Benjamin W. Griffith Jr., *McIntosh and Weatherford, Creek Indian Leaders* (Tuscaloosa: University of Alabama Press, 1988), 248–51.

‡ "Notes of a Small Tourist," #6. This painting, probably by Nathan Negus, is in the collection of the Alabama Department of Archives and History, Montgomery. See Jessie Poesch, *The Art of the Old South: Painting, Sculpture, Architecture and the Products of Craftsmen, 1560–1860* (New York: Harrison House, 1989), 170–71. The portrait serves as the frontispiece to this volume.

beaten him with a horsewhip. On another occasion the travelers crossed what had only recently been a toll bridge that some Indians had built across a troublesome creek. By the time Simms crossed the bridge, the whites had beaten off the Indians, and passage was free. The "Border race" lorded it over the Indians, and they could beat them with as much impunity as when they beat blacks. Such incidents, Simms said, occurred mostly when Indians were out traveling, away from the support of their fellows.*

On this same trip, a particularly revealing incident occurred after dinner late one afternoon when the travelers were far from any known settlement. They heard sounds they could not identify coming from a thick woods upstream from where they had camped. They could not make out whether the sounds were animal or human. Simms and some companions set out with their guns to discover the source of the sounds. As they crept silently through the woods, they found that the sounds came from an Indian "squaw and some half dozen naked urchins," playing in the stream. When Simms peeped over a log to see them, they spied him immediately, and without uttering a sound, they rushed from the stream and melted into the forest. One can surmise the fear they felt upon learning that they were being spied upon by armed white men. If Simms was discomfited by their fear, he does not say so. However, he does speculate on how this incident might later be the genesis of a myth told by the Indians about being stalked by a mysterious ogre while swimming, and he and his companions returned to camp laughing about the incident. Later they saw other Indians out foraging for wild food, always traveling in groups. Little wonder.

Though Simms had experiences with Indians unmatched by any other man of letters of his time, in the interest of perspective it must be pointed out that he never came close to attaining the standard of evidence modern anthropologists require of firsthand field observations. He was never a participant-observer. That is, there is no evidence that he ever gained any acceptance in a native society that would have permitted him to see the world from a native point of view, the yardstick by which modern anthropological field work is measured. He was always an outside observer.

On one of Simms's first two trips into Choctaw country, he witnessed or was told about an incident (discussed in some detail below) that proceeded from the most authentic piece of Southeastern Indian culture in all of his writings—an instance of blood revenge or *lex talionis*. Simms's description of

* William Gilmore Simms, "Sketches of Indian Character," 12.

the custom is accurate as far as it goes. But he had no way of knowing that blood revenge was not enforced by the Choctaws as a collectivity but by the clans on each other through the matrilineal kinship system that was so important in the social organization of the Choctaws and other Southeastern Indians; that is, every Choctaw had membership in a clan, and in only one clan, through his or her mother. And when a killing occurred, whether "accidental" or intentional, the clan of the dead person exacted revenge on the clan of the killer. They preferred to kill the killer, but any member of the killer's clan would satisfy the demand for vengeance. Despite his interest in Indian culture, Simms lacked the knowledge and skills to understand its complexities. He viewed it as an appropriate subject for belles lettres, not as an exotic human institution that begged for explanation.

WRITTEN SOURCES

The mature Simms had the good judgment to rely heavily on the writings of Henry Rowe Schoolcraft, the outstanding American Indian scholar of the mid-nineteenth century. In his 1845 review of Schoolcraft's *Oneota, or the Red Race in America* and *Algic Researches*, Simms set forth his fullest statement of his understanding of the American Indians.[*] From Simms's correspondence with Schoolcraft, it is clear that he respected the latter's scholarship and understanding of Indian culture. Simms was probably correct in assuming that Schoolcraft got some of his insights into the Indian point of view from his first wife, who was fully conversant in the Algonquian language of her mother.[†]

Simms particularly admired Schoolcraft for publishing the texts of Indian myths. Since hardly any information of this sort existed for Southeastern Indians in Simms's lifetime, he may very well have relied on Schoolcraft's mostly Northern Indian texts for insights into what he assumed was a generalized Indian mentality. Simms may also have gotten from Schoolcraft the first stirrings of a comparative framework for thinking about preindustrial societies. At the time of earliest European exploration, wrote Simms, the Indians of North America were roughly equivalent in complexity to Gauls, Goths, and Cimbrians. Nor did he judge the Saxons at the time of the Norman Conquest to be much superior to the Indians.[‡]

[*] Simms, "Literature and Art among the American Aborigines."
[†] Review of Mrs. Schoolcraft's *Letters on the Condition of the African Race* (1852).
[‡] "Literature and Art among the American Aborigines," 136–39.

He also held a then-popular notion that the Indians were latecomers to the Americas. An earlier race—probably white, he thought—had first reached the Americas and had built the high civilizations of Central and South America, as well as the mound-building civilizations of North America.* This myth of a mysterious non-Indian "race" of mound builders was not laid to rest until the end of the nineteenth century as one of the first major research efforts of the Bureau of American Ethnology.† Even earlier, the Savannah polymath Charles C. Jones Jr. had assembled evidence that the mounds had been built by none other than the Indians.‡ Curiously, even though Simms knew Jones, he seems to have not read his Indian writings, which may not have appealed to Simms because Jones was of a scientific rather than literary turn of mind.§

Simms was familiar with several of the more important late-eighteenth- and early-nineteenth-century historical works containing information on Indians, including works by Theodore Irving (nephew of Washington Irving), Alexander Hewatt, Thomas Jefferson, Robert Beverley, and Pierre de Charlevoix. More important, Simms was also familiar with several works by eighteenth-century and early-nineteenth-century writers who had firsthand knowledge of Indians, including Cadwallader Colden, John Heckewelder, John Lawson, James Adair, and Lewis Henry Morgan.‖

How closely Simms read some of these works is uncertain because he was, to say the least, not effusive in citing his sources. As an anthropologist, I regret that he seemed not to recognize the significance of Lewis Henry Morgan's *League of the Ho-de-sau-nee, or Iroquois* (1851), one of the premier anthropological works of the nineteenth century.# Not only was Morgan one

---

* Ibid., 136–37.

† Cyrus Thomas, *Report on the Mound Explorations,* 12th Annual Report of the Bureau of American Ethnology, 1890–91 (Washington, D.C.: G.P.O., 1894).

‡ Charles C. Jones Jr., *Antiquities of the Southern Indians, Particularly of the Georgia Tribes* (New York, 1873), 132–35.

§ I am grateful to John C. Guilds for bringing Simms's acquaintance with Jones information to my attention.

‖ "Literature and Art among the American Aborigines," 143–46.

Simms to Schoolcraft, 26 February 1852. Even his awareness of Morgan's "recently published" book (which he asked Schoolcraft to review) is indicative of Simms's desire to keep abreast of the field, but Simms commented to Schoolcraft: "The work seems to contain much material, but the author has shown himself a little too ambitious in its manufacture, and his speculations sometimes provoke a smile, showing no great philosophical depth" (*Letters* 3:166).

of the first Europeans to appreciate the importance of kinship systems among simple societies, but he also had attained important insights into matrilineal kinship, an institution as important for understanding Southeastern Indians as for the Iroquois. As with the writings of Charles C. Jones Jr., it may be that the complex technicalities of Morgan's analysis put Simms off.

In writing his *Vasconselos*, Simms drew on Theodore Irving's book *The Conquest of Florida by Hernando de Soto* (1851), and he may have drawn material from Irving in his "Lucas de Ayllon" as well. His citations make it clear that he relied heavily on Pierre de Charlevoix's *Journal of a Voyage to North-America* for the historical portion of *The Lily and the Totem*, and he claims that his narrative is based on the account of René de Laudonnière, perhaps a Hakluyt translation that he cites on several occasions.* Simms evidently read James Adair's *History of the American Indians*, because he cites him both silently and by name.† He realized that Adair was off the track in his attempt to explain the American Indians as having issued from Ancient Hebrews. Simms evidently drew on Adair's *History* in explaining that the Black Drink festival (the Green Corn Ceremony) was a general rite of purification for the Southeastern Indians.‡

Simms also had the perspicacity to read closely one of the premier eighteenth-century descriptions of Southeastern Indians, William Bartram's *Travels*.§ Simms drew his story "The Children of the Sun" from Bartram, who claimed to have heard from Creek Indians this story about a mysterious people of the Okefenokee Swamp. It must have been doubly interesting to Simms that these people were said to have been a remnant population of Yamasees.‖

HISTORICAL FICTION/FICTIONAL HISTORY

In his role as editor and critic, Simms was unusually forthcoming about his conception of the purpose and function of literature. In 1838 he wrote that

---

* W. G. Simms, *The Lily and the Totem* (New York, 1850), 10, 12, 31. Pierre de Charlevoix, *Journal of a Voyage to North-America*, 2 vols. (London, 1761). René de Laudonnière, *L'histoire notable de la Floride* (1586), translated by Richard Hakluyt in *Principal Navigations* (1600), 3:319–56.

† James Adair, *The History of the American Indians* (London, 1775).

‡ "Thle-cath-cha," 432.

§ Gregory A. Waselkov and Kathryn E. Holland Braund, eds., *William Bartram on the Southeastern Indians* (Lincoln: University of Nebraska Press, 1995).

‖ William Bartram, *Travels* (Philadelphia, 1791), 24–26.

literature is, or should be, the study of humans as moral agents acting within the constraints of history. Indians, he thought, were interesting to his readers because their "genius" was so different from that of other Americans. Their early history was very poorly known at the time, he wrote, and knowledge of their prehistory was virtually nonexistent, making Indians a fit subject for fiction.* That is, it was an opportunity for novelists to imaginatively fill in the gaps in historical knowledge. For the sake of his readers, his aim was to "raise the tune of history and warm it with hues of fancy." To a factual historical narrative, he promised to add fictional episodic matter.†

Historical fiction is, as the name implies, a mixed genre. The proportions of historical factualness to fictional creativity can vary markedly. As Simms matured as a writer, he endeavored—not always successfully—to make his work more historically accurate. By about 1842 he claimed to resort to fiction only to fill out deficiencies in the historical record. His fiction is always subordinate, he says, to historical fact. His ideal in writing was to make it possible for his reader to separate out what is certain from what is merely conjectural. The term *historical fiction* should be reserved for works that have a historical setting but whose content is fictional, or mostly fictional. In contrast, as John C. Guilds suggests in his essay above, we can use the term *fictional history* to refer to works that contain substantial historical content.

By these definitions, fidelity to the documentary record was not a priority in Simms's historical Indian fiction. His early novel *The Yemassee* has but a slender factual basis. This is even more the case with a class of stories and poems that might be called literary myths of place. One of his aims seems to have been to provide a kind of mythical charter for Indian place-names attached to creeks, rivers, and localities. This includes such works as "Logoochie," a myth of south Georgia; "Tselica," a myth of the French Broad River; "The Last Fields of the Biloxi"; and many others.

In "Logoochie," for example, Simms constructs a myth for south Georgia. This story is set in a time after the Indians have been driven out. Their gods still linger in the Okefenokee Swamp, but as whites begin to penetrate even there, the native gods become outcasts. Simms names two of these gods Satilla and Logoochie. Satilla he styles as the Mercury, or messenger god, of the Southern Indians, named after the Satilla River to the east of Okefenokee;

---

* W. G. Simms, "Customs and Peculiarities of the Indians," 431.
† Simms, *The Lily and the Totem*, iii–vii.

and Logoochie is perhaps named after the Withlacoochee River to the west of Okefenokee. In his story the gods call a conference in the swamp, but Logoochie, styled the trickster god, is absent, hiding from the others. Logoochie has something of the appearance of a pine tree, with scaly bark and a pine-knot head; his hair is ruffed out like a pine cone. Logoochie has remained behind on the St. Mary's River after the other native gods have departed to follow the Indians to the West. He plays pranks on the white frontiersmen, blunting their axes and hiding their possessions. He loves the smell of the tobacco smoke with which the frontiersmen, unwittingly, liberally regale him. Simms embroiders his myth with the love story of a sweet young thing—Mary Jones— and one Ned Johnson, who suffers from near terminal wanderlust.

Then, into St. Mary's sails a Yankee schooner, the *Smashing Nancy*, captained by Nicodemus Doolittle—"Old Nick"—by implication, the very devil himself. With the appearance of this ship, commerce and a connection to a larger world are established by the little village of St. Mary's. Ned, to the consternation of Mary, signs onto the crew of the *Smashing Nancy*. But it turns out that Mary is a favorite of Logoochie, who without her knowledge has done her many small favors over the years. As Mary takes a walk along the St. Mary's River, she happens upon Logoochie, writhing in pain from a thorn imbedded in his foot. Mary removes the offending thorn and tells Logoochie about her distress. He returns her favor by putting magical leaves and a berry into the water, and he tells her that if Ned would only drink from the river's water, her troubles would be over. When she contrives to walk along the river with Ned, she gives him a gourd dipper full of the water of the St. Mary's River. As he drinks the magic water, Ned immediately loses the itch to wander, and he strikes out for the Okefenokee to hide out from Old Nick, to whom he was legally obligated. (Seemingly, flight to the Okefenokee canceled all contracts, both Yankee and Satanic.) Logoochie takes his leave after this, going to the West to be with the Indians. But the spell he cast is still in effect on the waters of the St. Mary's. This story is strictly Simms's invention, reflecting nothing of authentic Southeastern Indian mythology.

In fact, there is hardly any authentic native culture in Simms's myths of place. In "The Children of the Sun," loosely based on a story in Bartram's *Travels*, two Creek adventurers paddle into the Okefenokee Swamp, not in a proper Southeastern dugout canoe, but in a birch bark canoe. Here they meet two "maidens of the Sun," members of mysterious group of remnant Yamasees, living in the Okefenokee. The maidens serve the warriors cocoa, oranges, and dates, none of which grow in the Okefenokee. They also served them cakes made of corn sweetened with sugar they could only have purchased in Charleston, which would have made the maidens' mystery status difficult to sustain.

Simms's fictional history sometimes falls short of his own standard. In his story "Lucas de Ayllon. A Historical Nouvellette," for example, the name of his central character should have been spelled "Vásquez de Ayllón," not "Velasquez de Ayllon," and while Ayllón, a Spanish official on Hispaniola did finance a slaving ship he sent on a raid to the Bahamas and from there to the South Carolina coast in 1521, he did not himself go on this raid. Ayllón did return to South Carolina in 1526, launching a colonizing venture, but there is little historical evidence on the details of his death. It is only known that he died of an unknown disease on October 18, 1526.* There is no evidence whatever that he was killed by Indians in a great act of revenge.

Almost all history in Simms's day was exemplar history, whose purpose was to promote morality and pride in one's own kind. The concepts of cultural relativity and ethnocentrism are quite modern, and Simms could therefore not have availed himself of them. He writes unapologetically as an elite, English-speaking son of colonists in the New World. For example, Simms fully subscribed to the Black Legend, the assumption that the Spanish had a monopoly on gratuitous cruelty. In "Lucas de Ayllon," he decries the Spanish practice of enslaving Indians, seemingly oblivious to the fact that English traders enslaved Indians by the thousands in the seventeenth- and eighteenth-century Southeast. The Black Legend also misleads him badly in *The Yemassee*, where he makes Spanish political machinations out to be the cause of the Yamasee war. In contrast, modern historians today argue that it was stimulated by the excesses of abusive, dishonest English traders and that their enslavement of Indians was certainly a contributing factor.[†]

Like most historians of his era, Simms had no framework for stepping back to view historical personages as actors in larger social and economic systems. He could not see Ayllón as a Spanish bureaucrat and adventurer in a particular era of the Spanish conquest of the Americas. Rather, for him Ayllón was a man with the "narrow and contracted soul of a miser,

---

* Paul E. Hoffman, *A New Andalucia and a Way to the Orient: The American Southeast during the Sixteenth Century* (Baton Rouge: Louisiana State University Press, 1991), 76.
† Verner W. Crane, *The Southern Frontier, 1670–1732* (Durham, N.C.: Duke University Press, 1928), 162–86.

incapable of noble thoughts or generous feelings. The love of gold was the settled passion of his heart, as it was too much the passion of his countrymen."

Similarly, Simms did not have benefit of modern conceptions of cultural
variability. When one examines his presentation of Indian beliefs, one finds
that they are in fact Christian and European beliefs dressed in colorful garb.
In "Lucas de Ayllon," for example, he writes that when Indian warriors
die, they are believed to go to eat "of honey in the golden tents of the Great
Spirit." The Southeastern Indians did have a conception of souls continuing
on in another life, but it was not an equivalent of the Judeo-Christian heaven,
and the Indian conception of an afterlife was not elaborated in their belief
system as it is in Christianity.*

Simms's implicit model for Indian political and kinship institutions is
that of European royalty. For example, in "Lucas de Ayllon," when his principal Indian chief Chiquola (after "Chicora," a sixteenth-century native society) dies, his widow Combahee (after the river) must choose a new husband.
When she does, the new husband, Edelano, thereby becomes the chief and is
automatically admitted to the elite circle of "heads and fathers of the tribe."
In fact, descent on the native South Carolina coast was probably matrilineal;
hence, Chiquola would have been succeeded by his sister's son or by some
other suitable matrilineal nephew.†

Of Simms's Indian writings, perhaps the ones that most accurately reflect
something genuine about Southeastern Indian culture are those based on the
previously mentioned incident of Choctaw blood revenge. Europeans who
witnessed this custom in action were astonished when they observed the
willingness with which a clan turned over one of its own for capital justice
as well as with the willingness with which a killer would go to his own death.
The native consideration was that if the killer were to evade death, then
someone else in his clan would have to die. Each clansman was quite aware
that if the killer did not pay with his life, then it could be *me* who pays with
my life, or else one of *my* beloved kinsmen. The Southeastern Indians never
forgave a killing, although they would sometimes accept a mediated payment
for the loss of one of their own.‡

---

* Charles Hudson, *The Southeastern Indians* (Knoxville: University of Tennessee Press,
1976), 171–72.
† Hudson, *Southeastern Indians,* 185–86, 206–9.
‡ Ibid., 230–32.

Ironically, this is the subject of Simms's very first Indian story—"Indian Sketch." He tells it in first person, and he does so persuasively. It is possible that he heard this story while in Mississippi, perhaps from the planter alluded to in the story. In "Indian Sketch," the narrator spends the night in a small inn run by a "mixed-blood." Someone in the inn tells the narrator a story about a murder, and he is surprised to learn that the killer is present in the room. "Indian Sketch" ends with the execution of the killer the next morning. To this account, Simms appended a poem on the same subject "by a native writer." In *The Book of My Lady*, published in 1833, Simms included a revision of this story as "The Choctaw Criminal," the only changes being to inflate the language, making it more florid. For example, "I ate my supper in silence" becomes "I partook of my repast in comparative silence." A revised version of the poem was again appended.

He used this same material yet again in *The Wigwam and the Cabin* in 1845 in his story "Oakatibbe, or the Choctaw Sampson." In this third version, he expands the story to carry a remarkable philosophical freight, and he gives the planter, who has recently moved to Mississippi, a name—Colonel Harris. It is in a conversation between the narrator and Colonel Harris that the story begins to unfold. Harris's cotton crop that year is so great that his slaves cannot pick it all, so he takes the unusual step of hiring some forty-five young Choctaws, mostly female, to help him. He pays his workers weekly, and each day they bring him the bag or basket of cotton they pick, which he weighs before computing each worker's due.

In this version, Simms uses the story as a vehicle of his conception of the frontier social order. Feeling superior to the Indians, the black slaves stand around with contemptuous grins as the cotton is weighed. Middle-aged Indian men, represented as too lazy to work themselves, also stand around, keeping track of the earnings of their female relatives. They want pay in the form of whiskey or in money with which they can buy whiskey. The narrator is skeptical of Colonel Harris's experiment: "Could a race, proud, sullen, incommunicative, wandering, be persuaded, even by gradual steps, and with the hope of certain compensation, to renounce the wild satisfaction afforded by their desultory and unrestrained mode of life?"

The narrator insists that money will not serve as an incentive for Indians to work, because the men will squander the money their women earn. The only way a "savage people" can be made to labor is by coercion. They must be taught obedience. They must be taught that they know nothing. They will never learn this lesson if they can, at any moment, quit work and walk away. Savages are like children, after all. God made the races different, says the narrator. Prejudice is natural, and barriers between the races have to be maintained. Inferior races should be brought into subjection where they can learn that they can win their sustenance through toil. This will reconcile them to their inferior position. If only the English colonists had conquered and subjugated the Indians, they would thereby have been integrated into our society. How long would it take? It took four hundred years to civilize the Hebrews; and it took perhaps half that for the Normans to civilize the Britons and Saxons. Because the English colonists had such a low population, the narrator says, they coddled the Indians. They gave them presents, signed treaties to acquire their land; and this made the Indians conceited and arrogant.

In the story, when the workers come in at the end of the day with their bags of cotton, a black female slave comes in with one to two hundred pounds of cotton, whereas Indian women average only forty-five pounds. Slim Sampson (the English name of Oakatibbe), one of the few mature Indian men who picks, comes in with 86 pounds. While the workers are weighing in, a middle-aged Indian man named Loblolly Jack makes a nuisance of himself. His wife and two daughters are among the workers, and he quarrels with Colonel Harris about whether his family got full credit for what they had picked. Slim Sampson and Loblolly Jack are at odds with each other, and they commence to fight. But Colonel Harris breaks it up. Later that evening, the narrator and Colonel Harris hear a death cry from the nearby shop of a trader, one who sells whiskey to the Indians. Soon after, they encounter Slim Sampson, who tells them that he has killed Loblolly Jack. Colonel Harris takes Slim Sampson in for the night. He talks him into fleeing for his life, to find refuge in the Indian Territory beyond the Mississippi River. The next morning, a crowd gathers at Colonel Harris's house. With Slim Sampson absent, the offended people demand satisfaction—a substitute for the killer would have to step forward to be executed. But into this tense scene, Slim Sampson at last comes riding up to do the honorable thing and go voluntarily to his death.

From the point of view of an anthropologist and ethnohistorian, "Caloya; or, the Loves of the Driver" is one of Simms's best Indian stories. This story is valuable not so much for what it says as for what it implies. It is a most interesting depiction of the social position of the Catawba Indians in the first third of the nineteenth century. It is an account of their bringing in their native pottery to sell on the streets of Charleston. They travel, not in a single body, but as families or small groups, dispersed in the manner of Gypsies so as not to incite anxiety and opposition among the whites. They travel down the Edisto River or else to the swamps at the head of Ashley River to visit favorite clay deposits, where they camp and make their pottery. They construct shelters out of poles with a bark covering, an ancient form of temporary shelter in the Southeast. According to Simms, old ladies in Charleston regarded Catawba pottery as the best ware for cooking okra soup. It is likely that neither Simms nor the old ladies of Charleston were aware that okra was a cultigen brought to South Carolina by slaves from Africa and that hence this culinary practice was not as ancient as they might have thought.

In the story Mingo, a black slave driver, plots in every way he can to win the affections of Caloya, a beautiful young Catawba woman married to Richard Knuckles, an aging Catawba man. The master of the plantation is Colonel Gillison, a young and rather distracted man who is too trusting of his driver. When measured against the norms of plantation society, Mingo is a flawed individual. He is excessively vain and uppity. He continually tries to advance himself beyond his station, and he bends or breaks the rules to do so. He tries to finesse a command of the English language he does not possess, and his fractured grammar and maladroit word choices make him appear ridiculous.

The degraded social position of the Catawbas is evident in Mingo's clearly regarding himself as superior to the Indians. He fully expects Indians to steal chickens and hogs from whites for their dinner table. This was the same onus, by the way, that whites in the Old South placed on blacks. Mingo is at pains to protect *his* plantation from such depredations. Mingo regards himself as superior to any Indian man, both as a worker and as a fighter. And he insists that blacks treat their women better than Indians do. Mingo was of the opinion that only Indian women were willing to work (an opinion likely shared by Simms himself).

For Knuckles's part, he claims to be superior to Mingo because he is free and Mingo is not. But Mingo replies that he does not depend on the labor of his woman and that he dresses decently, whereas Knuckles does not. A man is not free, says Mingo, unless he can fill his own stomach and put proper clothes on his own back.

In the denouement, Mingo and Knuckles get into a comic but grim fight, fully intending to kill each other. Both Caloya and Mingo's wife intercede, only to get into their own fight with each other. At the last moment, Colonel Gillison wakes up to his duty to attend to the affairs of his plantation and breaks up the fight before anyone is killed. He learns of Mingo's lies and transgressions, and he demotes him ingloriously to serve under a younger driver. Of all the principals in this story, only Caloya remains without blemish throughout.

SIMMS'S ELITE POINT OF VIEW

Well before the political divide that led to the Civil War, Simms saw himself as a spokesman on Indian affairs for the South. For example, in his review of James Buchanan's *Sketches of the History, Manners, and Customs of the North American Indians, with a Plan for Their Melioration* (1828), Simms criticized as mere enthusiasts those who wished to heighten sympathy for the Indians as an oppressed and suffering people. Merely raising money and sending out missionaries to the Indians, particularly when these missionaries had no command of native languages, would be to no avail, argued Simms. The American Indians, in his view, were like all other savages or barbarians, occupying a rung in the great chain of being intermediate between monkey at the bottom and civilized people at the top. Like other barbarians, Indians were "bold, warlike, and enterprising." They were patient and endured fatigue without complaint. In order to civilize them, one would first have to undo what savagery had done to them. Because of the supposed wandering habits of savages, it was impossible to send out missionaries in sufficient quantity to civilize them. Only a few Indian children could be educated in this way. And it had been Simms's observation that most such children were, in fact, the offspring of poor white fathers and Indian mothers, who were seldom married in the church.

Simms argued that white traders and squatters among the Indians, "however low themselves," had a more salutary effect on the Indians than did all the labors of the missionaries. Such people naturally felt superior to the Indians, kept aloof from them, built houses, and were farmers who went about in proper clothing. The whites would employ the Indians as laborers, and this would introduce civilized skills and desires among them. In time they would be absorbed into the larger economy, they would cease to hunt, they would learn to labor and farm as white men did, and they would thereby create for themselves new necessities.

In his review of James Buchanan's *Sketches of the History, Manners and Customs of the North American Indians* (pp. 7–19 below), Simms further argued that the

Indian character was ordinarily misrepresented in literature. Some represent the Indian character in terms as morally inflated as the Gaelic heroes in James Macpherson's Ossianic poems; others represent them as heroic warriors, disdaining civilized life. In contrast, others represent Indians as a race noted only for "habits of filth, drunkenness, and dishonesty" and as "cunning, sullen, cowardly, revengeful, and inhuman." But, Simms insists, Indians are not to be judged in terms of the outcasts one might see on the streets of Mobile. They are neither demigods nor brutes but, rather, a rude people who, though ignorant and unpolished, are highly intelligent. They are to be improved by degrees, first by teaching them practical skills and wants. This was to be done, not by forcing them to migrate west of the Mississippi River, but by incorporating them into the larger society a step at a time. Such a plan, he thought, would work if some way could be had of regulating the sale of alcohol, which was profoundly destructive to Indians.

CONCLUSION

Authors of historical fiction, and more particularly fictional history, are twice vulnerable. Their work is subject to changing literary sensibilities and tastes as well as to changes in the historical record and its interpretation. As an anthropologist and ethnohistorian, I have to say that for me, Simms's florid, allusive prose is an acquired taste. In Simms's successive reworking of the Choctaw blood revenge incident, for example, I prefer the plain, vigorous prose of his very first version. Each time he rewrote and recast it, he added romantic and philosophical encrustations onto the body of the story.

The historical record has grown by quantum leaps, and its interpretation has changed drastically since Simms's day. Exemplary history has few champions today, and many historians favor interpreting regional histories within the context of larger cultural and social histories. And yet, for all this, no man of letters has come forward to endeavor to improve upon what Simms attempted to do. Perhaps the real question should be whether we as a region and as a nation have gotten over the Civil War sufficiently to cast our eyes back to the three preceding centuries of Southern history. Is there anything in sixteenth-, seventeenth-, or eighteenth-century Southern history that appeals to the literary sensibilities of contemporary Americans? If a contemporary Simms were to reap the harvest of modern historical and anthropological researchers and to then depict through the storyteller's art this extinct landscape and its varied peoples, would anybody buy his books?*

As an anthropologist and ethnohistorian who has spent many years trying to squeeze enough information out of the surviving fragments of the Southeastern Indians' past to reconstruct something of their vast history, I have the greatest admiration for Simms's agenda for depicting this same history in fiction and poetry. I also admire the persistence and discipline with which he pursued his plan, filling in piece after piece of the picture.

* I have a more than theoretical interest in this question because both my wife and I have recently written fiction set in this time and place. Joyce's novel *Apalachee* (Athens: University of Georgia Press, 2000) is set in northern Florida, Georgia, and South Carolina in 1704–16. A significant part of her story takes place during the Yamasee War, only the second fictional retelling of it—so far as I am aware—since Simms's *The Yemassee*. (The other one is Herbert Ravenel Sass's *Emperor Brims* (New York: Doubleday, Doran, and Co., 1941). My own, *Conversations with the High Priest of Coosa* (Chapel Hill: University of North Carolina Press, 2003) attempts to do through fiction what cannot be done by using scientific or historical methodology—to reconstruct the belief system of a sixteenth-century Southeastern chiefdom. Neither of us, I hasten to add, consider ourselves to be in the same league as Simms.

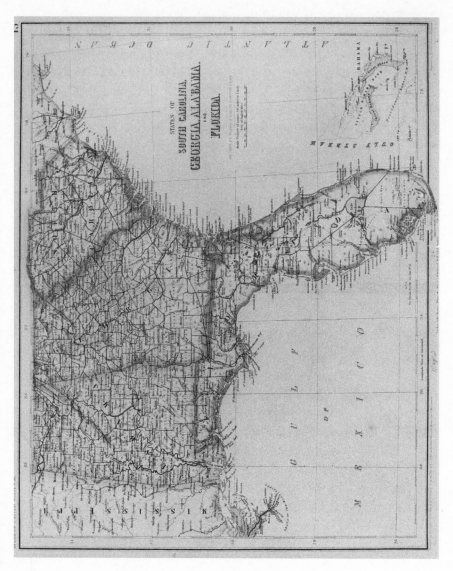

A Map of the States of South Carolina, Georgia, Alabama, and Florida, 1857. Courtesy of the South Caroliniana Library, University of South Carolina.

The Mountain Tramp

Tselica;

A Legend of the French Broad.

1

The sun that dries our lowland rills,
But warms th' Apalachian hills;
And he who stoops upon the plain,
By burning skies and airs oppressed,
There wins his manhood back again,
And feels new raptures fill his breast.
The sultry breath of lowland skies,
Burns never there the heart and eyes;
The fogs that from marshy tracts that spread,
And fill the soul with dreams of dead,
. . . . . cling above the plain, nor dare
The conflict with the mountain air,
Dispersed by . . . . . winds as wild as those,
That rouse the ocean's maddest throes,
And borne o'er billowy height, that brave
The skies more proudly than the wave.

Title page of "The Mountain Tramp. Tselica; A Legend of the French Broad" Courtesy of the South Caroliniana Library.

Statement of Editorial Principles

A FEW OBSERVATIONS regarding the current edition will be of help to the reader. In the case of writings published during the lifetime of Simms, his nineteenth-century spelling, capitalization, and punctuation have been preserved. Obvious typographical errors, omissions, or redundancies have been corrected; emendations throughout the volume are listed in the table of emendations (below, 589–90). With reference to proper nouns, Simms's various spellings have been retained unless otherwise noted. Simms's letters to Henry Rowe Schoolcraft are recorded exactly as he wrote them.

To provide as clear a text as possible, the editors have limited footnotes in the text to those written by Simms. (All of Simms's footnotes have been retained, and some of his headnotes have been recorded in full or in part.) To provide in a single, compact volume of representative writings that reveal the complexity of Simms's interest in the American Indian, the editors have been forced to observe rigid limitations in space, and the focus on the Indian takes precedence over other considerations. The best illustration of this focus is the three fictional histories drawn from *The Lily and the Totem*—"The Legend of Guernache," "The Narrative of Le Barbu," and "Iracana." Although a knowledge of French history is necessary for understanding some of the historical references, such knowledge is not essential to the reader's comprehension of the plot and its portrayal of Indian character and culture. (All interested readers are referred to *The Lily and the Totem* itself, in which Simms intersperses historical summaries among the fictional chapters—summaries too long for inclusion in the text of this anthology.)

The textual variation characteristic of nineteenth-century publication poses a special problem; author's intent has been the guiding principle in determining wording and punctuation for titles. Previously published poems conform, in indentations and punctuation, to copy-text. See 503–4 for the special set of editorial principles that apply only to the rough manuscript poem, "The Mountain Tramp."

AN EARLY AND STRONG SYMPATHY

ESSAYS AND LETTERS

THE FIRST WRITTEN EVIDENCE of William Gilmore Simms's interest in the Indian is provided by the series of "Letters from the West" he wrote for (and published in) *The Album* (1826), the Charleston literary journal of which he was one of the founding editors. In early 1826 young Simms, then nineteen, made his second (or possibly third) trip to the Southwest, to visit the plantation of his father near Columbia, Mississippi. Simms sailed from Charleston on 12 January 1826 to New Orleans, and from thence overland to Mobile, Alabama, and finally to Columbus, Mississippi. He wrote letters for publication at each stop, including two from Columbus, near the Alabama-Mississippi border. The second of the two appears in *An Early and Strong Sympathy*.

ᑌ *Letters from the West No. IV*

Columbus, April 12, 1826

MY DEAR _____,

I have but just returned from my excursion to Pearl River, of which I believe I previously have advised you; and now proceed, according to promise, to furnish you with a condensed view of my note book.

I left this place, after delaying a week or more for company, without any; but was fortunate enough to find the flat which transported me over the Tombigbee, or as it is more commonly called the *Bigbe*, already partially occupied. My fellow travellers were a gentleman and lady, the latter as Lord Byron aptly says, having arrived at "a certain age," so you see there was but little to be apprehended on my side. We immediately on landing entered the Choctaw Nation, and proceeded for the first day with little interruption and less variety.—The roads, from the excessive rains, were very bad. The swamps, as observed a negro, whom we questioned on the subject, were "knee deep to our horses chest," and the wading through water and slough not inconsiderable. The prairies, several of which we rode through, are beautiful and striking demonstrations of that wild waywardness that characterizes nature in some of her whims. A vast plain, about six miles, having scarcely a shrub, and covered with a carpet of green, interrupting the general monot-onous character of the forest. Yet encircled with thick groves of giant oaks scattered and dimly seen in the distances, strikes the eye not only as singular, but stupendous, in character. But the level of our first day's ride was consid-erably interrupted on the second, by a succession of rising hills almost approximating to mountains, where "distance lends enchantment to the view."

The addition of more company on our way, seemed to promise an increase to our enjoyments, and we certainly were not disappointed.

One of our companions was altogether an oddity. A Frenchman by birth; had been much of a traveler—but was altogether unacquainted with our pris-tine neighbors—and the sight of one of them appearing suddenly before him in the road, was sufficient to elicit from him

"Diable! Vat is dat?"

"Why that," said a rigid featured moralist, who had joined us at the same time, and was apparently disposed to make as much of the Frenchman's ignorance as possible, "that is an alligator, Monsuere." This was evidently an overstretch, and Monsieur cut his eyes sharply on the respondent but said nothing. "Is it not singular," said my former companion, "how those Indian horses will endure fatigue. A journey that one of our noblest steeds would sink under totally nerveless, will rather induce to their vigor, and the long gallop of that little tackey will be continued without interruption during the whole day and for weeks."

"Yes," said our new comer, whom I now observed, pretended somewhat to the character of a wit, "Yes, they are certainly a singularly fine animal; they do not hesitate to ascend rocks perfectly perpendicular, and the Indians fre-quently send them up the hickory trees for the purpose of gathering the nuts from them; and it is not uncommon where no rocks can be found for the owners to discharge their hoops to crack them on." We smiled—and the Frenchman betrayed his wonder by the wonted—"Diable." By this time the Indian, whom we soon discovered to be a Chief, by his scarlet cloak, cocked hat, plume and nose ring, and the other various concomitants to manly dis-play, approached us; and after the usual salutation, "How do?" our *jovial* companion desired to know how much ahead the traveller was who had passed yesterday. "Ek-sho," (gone away.)

"You one very fine hors, Monsieur," observed the little Frenchman, rather cautiously to the rover. "Yaow! chickamafena," (yes, very fine, good or great.) "Your chick-a," and the inquirer to himself half mutteringly, yet afraid to press the question to the Chief that presented itself to his mind. "He means," said the little man's tormentor, "that he should be good when fed on chickens." The Indian showed some dissent to this explanation and it was explained to the satisfaction of all. Whiskey, the staple of the country, and almost the only liquor drank, was produced from the saddle bags of one of the party, and after passing it round, we parted with our savage brother mutually satisfied.

Believe me, yours sincerely,

W.G.S.

"NORTH AMERICAN INDIANS," ostensibly a review of James Buchanan's *Sketches of the History, Manners and Customs of the North American Indians* (1828) was published in the opening number (September 1828) of the *Southern Literary Gazette,* a Charleston magazine Simms coedited with James Wright Simmons. In the essay, Simms voiced in great detail convictions that he was to repeat two months later in the story "Indian Sketch" (see below, 125–33).

∿ North American Indians (1828)

SKETCHES OF THE HISTORY, MANNERS AND CUSTOMS OF THE
NORTH AMERICAN INDIANS, WITH A PLAN FOR THEIR MELIORATION.
BY JAMES BUCHANAN, ESQ. 2 VOLS. PP. 338—NEW-YORK.

The author or rather compiler of the above mentioned sketches seems to us, to be one of those well-meaning, benevolent individuals who have been blessed with a large portion of human charity and good feeling, but with little of the foresight and reflection necessary for their proper guidance;— easily gulled with the extravagancies of others, on subjects little known and little examined into, and willing to believe as gospel all the representations of the idle, and all the theories and speculations of the ingenious and designing. Such a character is not uncommon in every community, and holding as it does, a situation, marked and aloof from the rest of society only by that peculiar disposition, which in fact gives it all the notoriety it acquires. Like Dr. Mitchell, it will bestow elaborate inquiry upon a head formed from a turnip, and like him, it possesses that claim upon public respect and esteem which arises solely from a knowledge of clever or humane intention: No farther.

It is the object of the author as set forth in his preface, to excite a general sympathy in behalf of an oppressed and suffering people, and, if possible, to direct the attention of the public to the proper investigation of a subject, which alledges to have been totally omitted in the catalogue of evils already provided for by the christian world, viz. The miserable condition of our North American Indians. It may be as well ere we advance any farther into the main body of the two volumes before us, to ask, if this be true? Is it true, that while the African and the Zealander and the Greenlander and the South Sea Savage, have been provided with lavish views of the principles of the church of Christ; while the bible has been sent to and expounded among them; while schools are directing the proper course of their understandings, and cloths and coverings are conspiring to warm and civilize them—is it true, we ask—that nothing has yet been done for the North American Indian? Has he been forgotten amid all the provisions of an enthusiastic zeal, which has called forth donations and charities with the tongues of demure and puritanical men, preaching women and prattling babes? For our own part, we had long ago been led to believe from what we have thought an extravagant rage upon this subject, that there was a great deal too much said, and (unlike the cases where too much is said) a great deal too much *done* for their civilization. To avoid being taken up rather shortly, by the professing christian for this apparent indisposition to the proper extension of the word of Christ, and the fruit of his interposition, among the Savage, we will go more largely into our own views upon the subject.

The grand object of all interference on the part of the civilized, in relation to those who are as yet in the land of darkness, is strictly speaking,—the bettering of their condition. By this is meant as well their physical as moral condition;—the requirements of the body and the wants of the mind. Nothing on the first blush of the proposition is seemingly easier than to determine, how these wants are to be satisfied. The only question apparently asked by those who desire this sort of thing, is—'how shall we get money?' It is never for a moment thought at all important to enquire what is the proper mode of civilization; or whether it will be even necessary that the savage should be first taught to understand your language before you address him on the subjects of revelation and the immortality of the soul. With a blind zeal worthy of the days of Peter the Hermit, and with all due reverence be it spoken, with all the *liberal disinterestedness* of that fanatical period, when Kings were content to be horseboys and warriors to assume the cowl and figure in the 'shaven crown of *proud humility*,' our modern enthusiasts, begin the work of improvement by gathering taxes throughout the land:—nothing is done by the spirit, and it has even grown into a fashion, (so little is cared for select capacities) that young men for whose labors and honesty experience has given no pledge, and time and trial no sanction, are reared to the vocation of the missionary as to a business; when, without any ordeal they are sent to strange countries, with a moral character yet to form, and without any of those restrictions, and, to speak plainly, those *eyes* upon them, which alone can confine them to a proper course and impose upon them a reasonable responsibility for the performance of a duty so highly sacred and important.

It is not our intention, however, to enter into any discussion as to the utility of these missions. Our object is only to show, as we have ourselves been led to believe, that there have been at different periods strenuous exertions, and not without wonderful success made to collect money in these very *benevolent and enlightened* States, with the avowed object of spreading the benefits of civilization among the different savage tribes still existing in our country. We are fully assured that it will be only necessary to advert to the subject, to refute, in the minds of the community, the erroneous impression of our author. That money has been collected to a vast amount, that monies are still daily collecting, that young men are regularly brought up to the business and serve a certain period of apprenticeship as in any other trade, and (considering the extent of mind usually employed for this purpose) we may say literally, any other handicraft; that they are sent among a people whose language in many instances they neither do understand, nor, save with an application not to be expected from young men, have any means of acquiring, even in many years, particularly from the want of books; and among a people whose only acquaintance with our language amounts to a disgraceful commentary upon their teachers, and a pledge of what may be reasonably expected from them in the future, being confined to a few such emphatic phrases, as 'money, whiskey,' &c.—that the results of their labors are only known from their own representations, and considering how much they are interested in these their general character may be guessed at—all these facts must be by this time generally well known. We introduce them at present barely to show that our author is clearly wrong in believing that nothing has been done for the Indians still lingering within our territorial limits—and satisfied with having, as we believe, pointed out the error in this comparatively immaterial portion of his work, we go on to subjects of infinitely more importance.

Proposing as we do, to consider the subject before us, solely with a view to utility and general benefit, it will be our first object to enquire into the actual condition of this wretched remnant of a people, by all accounts once so mighty and numerous. Looking at them as a vast assemblage constituting one community, however diversified by a difference in language, order and government, we can only distinguish a wandering horde of barbarians, like all other savages living in a condition, that with a modern author, presents us with a connecting link between the man and the monkey. Brutal in habit, and with a society, which has one feature in common with the brute, and with no other reason, they but herded together among their different species for security. This in fact constituted the various distinctions of nation, tribe and family. Each of these divisions having their separate head, uniting under one general government. And this is the precise situation in which they made their acquaintance with and were discovered by the first settlers. Yet they had many of those striking, and if the term may apply to a savage at all, those fine qualities which are well calculated to win the admiration while they excite the respect of the beholders. Like all other barbarians, they were bold, warlike, and enterprizing. Taught from their cradle in a tree, the virtues of patience in suffering, endurance in toil and fatigue, and triumph over torture and death, we can only regret that such good materials have been left to the management of the ignorant, the intolerant, the puritanical, or the cunning, for instruction and reform. It will be obvious to all not indisposed to reflection upon this subject, that a people such as we have briefly described, are not to be educated in the same manner, or confined to the same rules, as the youth already prepared or partially so, by the examples and customs daily exhibited around him. It will first be necessary to undo, with the savage all that has already been done. With that part of the present generation, already advanced in years or in the middle stages of life, it will easily be seen that the task must become one of considerable difficulty—perhaps wholly fruitless, as who shall hope, however sanguine his temperament, to obliterate the habits of thirty or forty years and replace them with others, foreign to the customs of his people, the spirit of his times, and decidedly at variance with those examples of the past, which with the illiterate and uninformed are more strong 'than fetters of brass, more enduring than habits of steel.' Supposing, however, as from the views and wishes of the time, there may be some reason for the supposition, that the old as well as the young may be gathered as 'brands from the burning,' and be made serviceable to themselves and at length able and honorable portions of the community, there seems to be a visible defect in the one plan already pursued in the furtherance of this object. Allowing, for the sake of argument, that the divines and teachers sent out for this purpose among the Indians, we will say of our sister state of Georgia—the lower Creeks or farther on to Florida, the Seminoles, &c. have all the necessary qualities of mind and intention, zeal and good fortune, in fact every thing that may be requisite to, and the absence of which might be fatal to the prosecution of this scheme. Suppose still farther—that the Indians themselves which is not often the case, and is certainly very unlikely, are favorable to the appearance of the good men among them, what number may we ask in the first place should we send out that the different bodies of Indians may be equally and sufficiently well supplied? The very few that we could by any possibility support among them would be barely sufficient for the bettering of the Coweta district. And surely the wandering habits of the Indians, denying them every thing like a certain or fixed habitation, would operate fatally to prevent any thing like that familiar and daily intercourse between the white man and themselves, which alone can bring the latter to the adoption of the habits and manners of the former. And before these habits are fixed upon them, before they are brought to close and certain labor, before their wandering inclinations are discarded, and the views, situations and customs of the whites are made perfectly familiar, not only to their understandings, but their very lives—it would be an excess of absurdity to endeavour to fix them in any distinct profession of moral or christian pursuit. These although not the only reasons which we might advance for our opinion that the Indians of North America are not to be civilized by the plans at present pursued, are sufficient in themselves to establish a bar to the object which ill-directed perseverance will combat in vain, and enterprize and zeal, however penetrating or able, will find insurmountable. The only benefit that can arise from the present endeavours of the Christian world, will be the education of some few of the Indian children:—this certainly is a considerable achievement, considering the difficulties already presented and still to be ascertained—difficulties only to be known from immediate intercourse with the people whom we would wish to enlighten. But from our own observation during a hasty journey through some of the nations falling under the cognizance of this article, as well as the accounts of the few, who in travelling among this people have thought them of sufficient importance for comment, we have been led to believe, and we now make the assertion, that these children are principally the children of white men of the lower orders, who by travelling among them for the purposes of trade are frequently won by a tendency to the same wandering habits to settle with and intermarry among them. In these marriages we allow that the rights and rites of the Church are most generally professedly disregarded. The forms in use are perhaps more simple and less refined than the leaping over the broomstick, splitting a willow wand; flagellating the back with a plum or hickory or supple-jack, or in fact any of the forms and ceremonies of marriage common among the savage tribes of the rest of the world. In the reform of this perni-cious practice we hope that the missionaries will do much; at least we think that much more may be done by them in this department of civilization, than in any other. But to return.

These white traders, however low themselves, have a natural desire that their children should be possessed of the advantages of that education which their remoteness from the habitations of the whites and perhaps their inabil-ity and want of means, would otherwise render a hopeless desire. But while we fully agree that these should not be denied the benefits of that charity which we in profession, at least, propose for the benefit of all, we must say that they constitute a different class of people, and from certain views which we shall proceed to exhibit should rather be considered wholly white, than mixed in the slightest degree. It will perhaps require no great exercise of thought to be satisfied, that the white man straggling among the Indians or any race who believe themselves inferior (and that they are inferior the North American Indians must feel from their relations to our government and people) will exercise a certain degree of authority, and in fact feel con-scious, however low among his fellows, that he is a superior among them. He will necessarily as the first step to ascendancy, keep himself in many particu-lars aloof from them. He will build himself a cabin. He will introduce habits of husbandry, and regular labor. The plough will in time, as his views extend and means increase, succeed the hoe. He wears (an important particular) clothes himself. His children (half-breeds) while playing among their savage brethren will have on breeches, while their playmates will present a less deli-cate exterior, and that too with a singular unconsciousness which to us, would present a feature of savage life far from uninteresting or unpleasant. There will be even among these children a marked deference shewn to him of white origin—he will be the lion among them. The breeches alone would create him so, and as children are apt at knowing the characters of those around them, he will feel his influence, and not be slow in exercising it. But his father will render the distinction more apparent. He will if able himself, learn his child to read. We all know the influence of letters. This influence is as well felt, though not as well understood by the savage as the citizen. In fact it is more acknowledged and worshipped from its rarity, and we would say, that learning would be rewarded with more respect, and did their capability warrant any such liberality, with more solid advantages by far, than with us. Thus is information conveyed, even by the humble and ignorant individual squatter. And we dare affirm that, spite of the pernicious custom of introducing whiskey among them by these traders, they in other respects do more real good to the condition, ay moral condition of the Indian, than does the missionary, who has one regular station but goes among them at set times, to explain subjects, the explanation of which is a deeper mystery to them. But the physical, as a first step to the moral condition of the savage, is improved by such an adventurer. When he settles, being generally without hands, he must employ them, and the Indians, are with his own assistance, the architects who frame his log house, build his outhouses, erect his fence, fell his trees, roll and burn his timber, and clear his land. This provides the savage, not only with food for the time but perhaps with corn for the winter. It also teaches him a habit of labor, which should be the elementary part of all education among savages, like ours, so little used to, and so perfectly unacquainted with it. He now builds for himself a more commodious and more decent hut; an enclosure is soon discovered springing up around it; a corn and then a ground nut patch appears—these become extended in time, as he discovers that the white man sells corn for money to the traveller, and that this money buys powder, shot, cloth, beads and other articles, which, however ignorant of before, he now finds he cannot do without. He also discovers that it is not necessary that he should be always hunting, and that he is no longer dependent on the precarious subsistence afforded by his rifle in the woods. He has corn at home, when he finds no venison abroad, and he discovers in the course of one season, that the regular labor of the field is an enjoyment, compared with the fatiguing difficulties of the hunt. And here let us assure the reader that it is not the love of hunting, but its necessity, that renders it the principal employment of an Indian's life. Unacquainted with agriculture and gleaning nothing from the earth but that which is spontaneous, we find them even feeding on weeds and acrid and bitter roots, when the deer and turkey are scarce in order to live. It is idle to say that they are too indolent to bestow the labor necessary for the production of corn and other articles of food, requiring very slight if any manual exertion, and rewarding them with plenty unknown before, even in greater fatigues and more intense anxieties. This idea is fully refuted by the fact, now well established, that, in the Western States, and we believe in some parts of East Florida, and Georgia, the Indians living in the neighborhood of the planters are regularly employed throughout the year to perform the same labors as the negro; while the women and children are occupied in the picking of cotton and such other lighter avocations as may best suit their less robust and active frames.

Nothing has been more misunderstood among us than the Indian character. Like other subjects of which little is known, and over which time has thrown an impenetrable mystery, Fancy has stept in to the aid of history, and tradition has dreamed until fact has lost its character and all become poetry. Were we to believe the fanciful accounts of some of our countrymen, from whom we should have expected different things, the Indian character very nearly resembles our own. At least in one important particular, the making of long talks and great speeches. From these, our writers on this subject have gathered so much, that the extravagant madness of Macpherson's illegitimate Ossian, has been fully equalled, if not surpassed. We in America, have certainly as much reason to contend in our several states for the birth place of our 'Walk in the Water,' 'Tecumtheh,' 'Little River,' 'Blackfoot' and 'Turkey' as ever the Irish and Scotch had to dispute the ownership of the Bard of Fingal. Unfortunately for the subjects of either controversy their merits if discovered at all were discovered too late to benefit them and we venture to express a belief, however heretical, that they were none of them worth the discussion. We have not even learned whether our President has ever invited one of these latter worthies to encounter him in a glass of strong water, and celebrate his 'Great Father' in an extemporaneous speech, written for him by some John Dunn Hunter. It is the fashion, in speaking of an Indian Chief to picture an Ulysses, strong at the bow and matchless in the chase, with the wisdom of Mentor, full of grace and elegance, and withal as figurative as a modern poet. He is brought before our fancy as a warrior who disdains the servile and slavish fashions of civilized life, roves like a giant in the woods, encountering (we have no lions, alas! in our country) bears and panthers, like another Orson at every turn; speaking elegies over them, and withal possessed of such beautiful, symmetric, yet Herculean organization, that we are perpetually with an Orlando or Troilus before us, instead of, as is most frequently the case, a thick tolerably well set, straight, bandy legged, sullen savage, his rifle slung upon his shoulder sauntering on through the woods, muttering when spoken to, a sullen 'How do?' and smacking his lips with 'whiskey berry good' after he has proved with a deep draught how well his actions mete out the honesty of his words: encountering when he can find no deer, nor bear, nor panther, the bristly boar of some neighbouring farmer, then sneaking through some by-way to his habitation, and venturing only in search of more meat when his last prize is entirely exhausted.

Other writers, and particularly some of late date have fallen into another extreme in discussing the merits of this people. They are represented to be a race only notorious for their habits of filth, drunkenness and dishonesty. They are shewn us as crowded upon the towns with all these several qualities momentarily exhibited before the eyes of the white community. They are described as cunning, sullen, cowardly, revengeful and inhuman; not to be trusted, and only docile and to be depended on, while it is in their interest to be so.*

With regard to the latter clause in this description, we fear that there are too many even among the civilized who are only to be depended on while it is their interest to be honest. That they are sullen, revengeful, and inhuman, but not cowardly, we are ready to admit—where have savages ever been known without these particular qualities? The habits of their lives, the customs of their people, and the perpetual wars of their tribes are circumstances well calculated to make them so. With regard to their habits of drunkenness, we think that the remark comes with as ill a grace from the American people as the books of the English upon the subject of slavery in America—as well might we put aconite into one's food and when he is perishing with the poison, reproach him for taking it. From the evil of drunkenness arises that of idleness, dishonesty and filth. It will be for us, as we have made them acquainted with the bane, to furnish them as speedily as convenient with the only antidote we know of—the education of the mind and the employment of the body.

But we are not disposed to admit that as a people they are of this character, or merit this description. We remember that the city of Mobile, about a couple of years since, was completely filled with these miserable wretches, in the most horrible state of degradation and drunkenness; lying about the

* [SIMMS'S NOTE] *American Quarterly Review,* No. 2 Art. Florida.

streets in numbers and perfectly nude, beggaring the town with an exhibition as disgusting to the sight as it was painful to the feelings of humanity. But we soon learned as well from the information of some of the citizens as from our own subsequent observation, that these were but outcasts from the tribe; and that we were not to judge from the few wretches before us, of a still numerous, and we regret to believe, still hardly treated people.*

The North American Indians, are strictly speaking, a rude and simple race. We will be understood as speaking of the different nations, and not of the struggling outcasts, who haunt the townships for liquor, and whom we allow to be possessed of all pernicious qualities uniformly consequent to such degradation. In regarding them, however, we must carefully avoid both of the extremes already briefly presented. We are neither to worship them as a race of demigods, nor on the other hand to despise them as a horde of brutes. As a simple people, we do not wish to be understood, as conveying that sense which belongs to the word as we frequently apply it to individuals. We are not at all disposed to look upon the Indian as a fool. We regard him rather as a rude, uninformed, and unpolished, but still, highly intellectual being: shrewd and if we are so compelled to term it, cunning in the extreme, from a habit of depending solely upon himself even from his childhood; a habit which we would willingly see more common among ourselves. Highly imitative in his character and closely observant, we may perceive from this simple feature, the feasibility of that plan which would give them employment among ourselves and by degrees, from our example convey to them our customs and pursuits. How else can the attention of a savage be fixed—not by abstract reasoning upon the duties of man to man, and man to God; but by bringing home to the practices of men at first, and teaching him, *not by words,* the duties which he owes to himself, then to his family as contributors to his happiness; then

---

* [Simms's note] That portion of the Nation of the lower Creeks in Georgia, known chiefly as the adherents of the celebrated Gen. M'Intosh (who, however friendly to the whites, was a traitor to his country, and was punished by his people according to his deserts) have been sent to some tract beyond or near the Red River by the Government of the United States. It may be as well to observe, that in the course of a short time it is but likely we shall hear of their final extermination by the more warlike and numerous tribes of Indians already occupying that district of country. This certainly is expected by those engaged in this transaction, as it was no doubt in the contemplation of Government, however unexpressed, by this cruel and mistaken policy to rid themselves of unprofitable neighbours and avoid all farther expenditure on their account.

to his people as contributors to his security; and finally to his Creator as the being who has endued him with a sense for enjoyment, a desire for security and the value of life, and for that capacity which makes him valuable to the community in which he lives in the same proportion as each individual is valuable to him.

It may be urged that this is impracticable from the nature of the Indian character. We say again that this character is generally unknown, and where it has been treated of, is mistaken. The very fact of their having adopted the dress and clothing of the white people; of their having in many instances hired themselves to the whites, and laboured honestly and assiduously; and a greater evidence of the influence of our customs, the drinking of whiskey and chewing tobacco, is sufficient to shew that if generally incorporated among us they would by sensible and rapid degrees adopt our rules of life, diet and language, and become in time valuable portions of our community. We have only to refer to the present character of the Cherokee Nation in immediate connection with the settled part of Georgia and Alabama for full establishment of our argument in favor of the influence of example arising from an immediate association of the savage with the civilized. If our sister State of Georgia instead of ridding themselves of this people as is their evident desire, we think that it would have been far better to have brought them more closely into contact with themselves. Thus, in the late Georgia purchase, the new settlers would have been comparatively too few to have found the Indians any incumbrance. There would have been enough land for the whites proposing to settle, and supposing the Indians did not immediately come into employment, there would have been sufficient hunting ground for their support, while time, necessity and a closer intimacy with the whites would gradually have undone those prejudices in favour of their wandering habits, which with most people is said to be the only bar to the progress of civilization among them. The adventurers upon this new country, like all other pioneers in the wilderness must be generally very poor. Without any assistance from the possession of negroes, an admirable and cheap substitute is presented in the class of people, that they injudiciously desire to be rid of. Unused to labor they may be clumsy and slow, but practice will soon create an ability which joined to the athletic and enduring character of the Indian will be more than sufficient for all the laborious duties incident to the agricultural profession. Besides this, the price of labour would be with them so moderate, as to be hardly felt by the employer; and where it became heavy an incorporation of interest would perhaps render the parties more earnest in exertion, and as a consequence, more successful in enterprize. There are but two evils which we can at this time foresee to the different parties in this connection. In the first place, the cupidity of the lower orders of the whites would no doubt find exercise and reward in furnishing the Indians with spiritous liquors, while the latter until the habits of the whites became familiar would practice many petty depredations upon the least protected of the settlers; who in revenge for the robbery of a henroost or pasture might take the life of the unfortunate depredator.

The former evil can only be remedied by municipal regulation. Let a law be enforced rendering it criminal for any person to sell liquor to an Indian, except for the purposes of sickness, and then in a certain limited quantity, with a penalty sufficiently heavy to be felt and feared. A regulation like this, though we feel assured that it would be inefficient altogether to destroy, would nevertheless prevent that public and open display and circulation of this dangerous article of trade which in a measure renders its use in the extreme, venial, and disregarded. The lower orders of people engaged in a contraband sale of the interdicted element, would be restrained in its exposure; and apprehension of the penalty, would at least render them so cautious when they did vend it, as in a measure to become of themselves, defenders of, while they infringed the law. The evil which presents itself next to our consideration is one, that like the former can only be partially avoided. There can be no civil regulation, beyond the local tribunals already established that can prevent, however it may punish, the instances of petty larceny that must be from the circumstances of the connection and the facilities afforded for its exercise, of frequent occurrence. The only means by which, as well for the prosperity of the settler, as for the benefit of the savage these thefts may be prevented, are the exercise of a watchfulness, which it is perhaps idle, to suggest to the losers; and the passive guard afforded by a strong and good fence, good dogs and solid houses. Above all, too much forebearance, in cases of punishment cannot be exercised towards this people. No moral restraints can be placed upon those who are unacquainted with the nature of moral obligation; and it would be cruel to punish men for an infringement of a law which is as new to them as the regulations exhibited upon the pillars of Caligula.

To return to the post, from which we first set out, we will but glance at the work, upon which we have grounded our observations. As we have said before, we believe the compiler of the two volumes before us to be a good and well meaning man—we only regret that good intention is so unfrequently allied to ability. The book in the first place is quite useless to the American public, being principally compiled from works already well known and in every body's hands. It is also compiled in very bad taste from the least interesting portions of the many idle and extravagant tomes which have been written upon this subject, consisting chiefly of speeches never spoken and treaties never kept. The plan for the amelioration of the condition of the Indians accompanying the work is a mere dream, and not a very reasonable one either. To say the least of it, the Sketches of the North American Indians are of no manner of use, gathered from bad sources,* and wretchedly dull.

FROM JANUARY 1830 TO JUNE 1832, Simms served as editor of the *Charleston City Gazette* (the newspaper that in 1831 opposed the locally popular doctrine of Nullification); and during his second year as editor, he wrote "Notes of a Small Tourist," a series of ten letters to the newspaper about his third (or fourth) trip to the Southwest. The sixth, seventh, and eighth of these letters— rich in Simms's observations about his encounters with Indians—appear below. The portrait of General McIntosh that Simms describes in the sixth letter is reproduced as the frontispiece of this volume.

᧦ *Notes of a Small Tourist*

No. 6

[March 31, 1831]

In Macon, from an interregnum in the departure of the Stage, I was compelled, however unwilling to remain a day. A pause like this may seem quite

---

* [SIMMS'S NOTE] For instance, John Dunn Hunter. For some account of this imposter, reference may be made to a late number of the *North American Review*. We do not know whether this man was most successful in gulling John Bull or in misrepresenting brother Jonathon's red brethren. The only objection we have to the article referred to, is that it gave too much importance to the miserable wretch who was its subject.

The old missionary Heckewelder, from whom Mr. Buchanan quotes largely, was we believe a very good old gentleman, who wrote and talked the public to death on the subject of the Indians. We say, that it is idle for these men to talk of the prospect of success in their labours, or to give any account of a people who are forever in the woods, and who have scarcely a fixed habitation beyond the whole range of their country.

too short to have been a subject of much inconvenience; but, really, all circumstances considered, preserve me from a country village, where all around you are strangers, and, from their characteristic inquisitiveness, perpetually in your way. I did what I could in such a situation, to make myself comfortable. I strolled to the printing offices generally, and learnt the news—such, at least, as it was possible in those parts to acquire. There are three newspapers (weeklies) already published in this place, of some seventeen-hundred inhabitants, and a fourth is about to be established. Macon is a place of some importance in these parts. It does no small share of business, and hopes have been, and are still entertained, that, ere long, it will become the capital of Georgia. It is said, with how much statistical correctness, I will not pretend to determine—the map not being by me—to be more clearly in the centre of the state, than Milledgeville; but I apprehend that the chief question, and that upon which the ultimate choice will in all cases be made to depend, will be, whether it is in the centre of the population, and of the wealthy portions of the country.—Are its facilities for business more or less great—are the lands contiguous, more or less productive—are the waters more frequent, and is the country better wooded, &c.? Of course the question will be chiefly: Is the interest of the legislative majority sustained or depressed by the transfer, and the vote may be ascertained accordingly. Our patriotism means neither more nor less, in nine cases out of ten, than to see that number one is provided for. Columbus, on the Chatahoochee, a place nearly, if not quite as large, as Macon, and quite certainly as promising, had I think when I trod the same site six years ago, no existence. It is now possessed of a considerable trade, and I was informed, about fifteen hundred inhabitants. It forms the late Indian boundary in that section, though by the removal of the Creeks into Alabama, it is no more contiguous to any of the tribes. A few scattered families, having no regular organization, inhabit still the neighborhood, but they are not of sufficient importance, to occasion much remark. It was at a public house in this place that I saw a full length portrait of the celebrated Indian Chief, William McIntosh, (the Broken Arrow) in the costume of a chief of his nation. The drawing is said to have been made from the life, and the Indians, I am told, consider the likeness good. The person of McIntosh was tall and gaunt, not over well made, that is to say, not such as we should select as a model, unless in an extra degree of good humor. Still it is good, and rather commanding than otherwise. My impressions on a survey of his face, were not favorable to the character of the chief. There is less of dignity than low cunning in his features—he was, I believe, a kind of Indian Van Buren, and was more of the intriguing and wily politician, than the free, frank, and generous warrior. He was a warrior, however, and the manner of his death, had something of the Roman in it. This does not say much for him I believe, as firmness and scorn of death are the characteristics of all our Indian tribes, and is not a subject of surprise, the nature of their education taken into consideration. In the instruction of the young, they are not unlike the sages of Laconia; and, indeed, were they not to make it a subject of national concern, the roving practices of their people, would in great measure, prepare the youth; for instances of hardihood and daring, by no means dishonoring the Spartan character. McIntosh, in the general expression of his countenance, its color &c. appears to me, less to resemble the Indian, than some of the bright mulattoes whom we hourly encounter in our streets. His face is not over long, but having high cheek bones, thinly coated with flesh, and narrowing considerably to the chin, it has an elongated air, that is anything but national. In general I think, the Indian face round and inexpressive. It is true, the expression of moody sullenness, which, in the nation, they carry perpetually about with them, must command attention; but in all other essential particulars, they seem to be rather dull, and unintelligent. The dress of the Chief is rich, in an aboriginal point of view. It consists of a turban—a la Turque—arranged with taste, and worn with hauteur. A hunting shirt, after the manner of the tribe, of some chequered stuff, bound at all points, with a white cotton fringe, which contrasts agreeably with the ground work, upon which it is laid. This is encircled round the waist, with a belt, thickly studded with beads of assorted colors. From his shoulders depends another belt of the same material, to which is attached a pouch, the contents of which are usually, the bowl of a pipe, tobacco, a knife, flints, &c. &c. His leggings and mocassins of finely dressed buck skin, are similarly embellished. His attitude is rather graceful, being in the act of speech—his left hand extended. The likeness was taken at some grand talk of the nation, in which McIntosh was rather active, and this accounts for the manner of his dress and corresponding attitude.

No. 7

[April, 1831]

Columbus is situated upon the Chatahooche river, a stream, which, upon entering the territory of Florida, becomes the Apalachicola. It is navigable for steamboats and schooners, to the former township, and perhaps beyond. A few miles above the site of Columbus, the river has a fall of considerable velocity—the cascade being, I am told, upwards of thirty feet. Passing it by night, I had no opportunity of seeing it, but its roarings were very distinctly heard. From this spot, Fort Mitchell, a frontier station, lies a distance of *nine* miles. It was in reaching this station and overcoming this brief distance, that we encountered, one of those little estoppels, which in a country like this, not unfrequently make their appearance, to relieve, as it were, the otherwise monotonous tedium of a quiet narrative journey. In doing this nine miles, we occupied the entire interim from seven of the evening, to three o'clock of the ensuing morning. About three or four miles after passing the river, our vehicle, "mired down," as the phrase goes, in the quagmire of a vehement watercourse; from which predicament, the united energies of passengers and drivers, were inadequate to its extrication.—A council of war having been called, it was determined to employ for a "consideration," the lingering moiety of a tribe of Indians, dwelling within a mile on the opposite side. One of the party, having deputed for this purpose, we were soon emboldened and encouraged by the appearance of some ten or a dozen of the greasy runagates—men and women—who without any ado, turned in hastily, but clumsily to their vocation—a black man, one of their own slaves, standing by all the while, directing their exertions, but offering not the slightest assistance himself. It is a matter of much surprise, how great is the influence which these slaves have over their masters. They defer to them in most particulars, and yield a marked deference, I am given to understand, to their opinions, even on matters of pressing importance. From what cause this arises, I do not pretend to conjecture—whether it is, that the natural indolence of temperament, commonly attributed to the Indian character, is willing to depute to the guardianship and direction of others, those matters which it would be laborious for themselves to perform, and which they can, without hesitation, compel their own slaves to undertake; or whether it is, that acknowledging, as they do, the superiority of the whites, they conceive that some portion of those faculties which imparted to them that superiority, must, necessarily, have been acquired by the negroes, from their connection, however subordinate, with them—I know not; but nevertheless such is truly the case. Among the Indians, the negroes gain caste; acquire authority and certainly great influence. They are not often ill treated—they grow in little time, as lazy as their masters; they dress immediately like them; they acquire the same sinister and sullen look with the Indians, and in all general respects, their manners and habits alone considered, they copy very closely after them. On the occasion under notice, we employed a negro—a slave, to get us out of the mud. He came on horseback, employed his master, for aught I know, certain it is, he employed the Indians, men and women—set them to work—told them what to do and coolly cheated them out of one half of the money after the duty was performed. Though stiffened with cold, knee deep in mud and water, and anxious to proceed, in fear of losing the next stage from Fort Mitchell to Montgomery, I could not help admiring the high degree of picturesque which entered into the scene around me. The shoutings of the Indians in self encouragement, and in their quick detached and fragmentary language—the cheerings of our own party—innumerable torches, scattered about the woods, and on the marge of the swollen waters—the rushing of the waters themselves—the neighing and struggling of the horses, up to their middles in the creek swamp—added to the cheerless and wild character of the prospect, and those associations, which sought in vain to reconcile, the present with the past fortunes and labors of the Indian tribes—all combined to give a graphic force to a picture, worthy of the pencil of Rembrandt. We got out with difficulty, and barely saved our distance, in reaching the next stage, a moment ere its departure.

No. 8

[April 2, 1831]

It was on this part of my journey, that I encountered Chief Tuskina, who has acquired no very small share of notoriety, from his stoppage of the United States Mail. This affair has been variously represented. The commonly received opinion among us, is, that Tuskina, with a small touch of patriotic fury, a little exaggerated by whiskey, denied the right of Uncle Sam, to ride over the territory of his fathers and his father's graves, and all that sort of thing. This opinion is the more prevalent, from the fuss kept up by the philanthropists, who, without knowing any thing about them, are eternally meddling in the concerns of the South; and who would make us believe, and probably believe themselves, that the Indian is a sort of Roman, having all the benefits(?) of modern civilization, relieved in its monotony and sameness by a little flourish of the romantic spirit of the middle ages. But, to those, who know any thing of the Indian character, as it is, without the glossings of such twiddle-twaddle as this, such notions are generated in the very extremest humbuggery. We say every thing of the North American, and in justice— 'nothing extenuate, nor set down aught in malice,' when we call him a mere savage, like all others, and no better than any savages, but a very few degrees removed from condition of the brute, and those few degrees, less in the habits and manners, than in the form and the necessities under which they have existence. But to return. The affair of Tuskina, as I learnt it from one of the stage drivers—a set of men, generally intelligent—appears to have been this:—Tuskina was desirous of communicating, by letter, with some one on the stage route, and deeming no difference to exist between the Post Office and the mail carrier, in the transmission of his letter, he determined with some forethought, to await the passage of the stage, at a particular point of the road, and thus, spare himself the inconvenience of a ride to any other more remote point of the compass. He did so accordingly and when the stage hove in sight, burdened as it was, and with wooden shoed rope dancer, Herr Cline, then on his way from Charleston to Orleans, he gave the driver the 'view hallo,' and required his pause. The driver was doubtless sulky and the rope dancer alarmed at a request, that perhaps sounded more like a command than any thing else, and no other notice was taken of Tusk, than an increased application of the whip to, and the additional speed of the horses. This the Indian, sullen by nature, insolvent by station, and probably roused and irritable by repeated application to the whiskey bottle, resented by actively springing forward, seizing the reins and exhibiting his weapons. The driver feared his immediate ferocity, Herr Cline his tribe, and the rest of the passengers doubtless shared indiscriminately of the feelings of these two, whom I have severally noticed, for their *distinguishment* in the world. There was doubtless something highly amusing in the predicament of the rope dancer. His wooden shoes, though actually on the stage, could not avail. His feets, (feet it should be written) could not extricate him, and the entire cavalcade, horses, drivers and actors were compelled to remain quiescent, under the bodily fear of the tomahawk of Tusky. At Mobile, Tuskina was tried for the offence and mulct in the penalty of one hundred dollars. This he is well able to pay, though, really, I do not think, the circumstances considered, that any Jury should have brought in other than nominal damages. He is stated to be worth some ten to fifteen thousand dollars in land and negroes, but under his excesses of life, this property is rapidly diminishing. He is a fine looking savage, has quite a martial, libertine cast of countenance. I should consider him an Indian Mark Antony. There is the martial and characteristic boldness of the soldier fitted in command—the cavalier, ease and freedom of one who could be tended also in the extreme. By the way, did you never remark that ferocity and much tenderness were to be found in most instances, strangely in unison. They seem to me, most commonly to go together with such men and women, as are most susceptible. I have found it so. Tuskina, has also, just such a bloated visage, as he would give, in our imagination, to the winebibber of the Triumvirate. His person is full, well made and manly. He is like the Indians, commonly too liberal in his libations, for his own good, so much I can say, from the passing glance afforded me, in a momentary pause, which he made beside our vehicle. He did not, however, seek to stop our progress, though I was almost tempted to desire it, to have obtained a better survey, and to have had some talk with him.

Montgomery, a town of some business in Alabama was the point we next made. It is situated upon the river Alabama, and possesses a steam boat trade to Mobile. The river is navigable for steam boats, some twelve or twenty miles higher up to the falls of Coosaw. Montgomery is by land, about one hundred and eighty miles above Mobile; by water, four hundred, more or less. It contains probably, fifteen hundred to two thousand inhabitants; a Court House, Post Office, and a few stores, having a decent capital. Two newspapers are published in the place, one of them the Alabama Journal, conducted by TURNER BYNUM, Esq. formerly of our city. The town is situated upon a bluff of some elevation above the river, and is reputed to be not unhealthy—a reputation which I should, from its locality, be greatly disposed to call in question.

Columbia, Miss. April 2.

DESPITE SMALL EFFORTS ON HIS PART to disguise his authorship, it can now be demonstrated that Simms was the writer of "Sketches of Indian Character," signed with the pseudonym "A Traveller" when first published in two installments in the *Southern Literary Journal* in 1835 and 1836.* "Number One" of "Sketches of Indian Character" appeared in *SLJ* 1 (October 1835): 101–7.

ᑯ *Sketches of Indian Character No. 1.*

It is now sixteen years since the writer left Charleston on an excursion of *recreation* in the then *wilderness* of the South-West. Some of your readers will

* See Guilds, "A New Simms Essay," *Simms Review* 8 (winter 2000): 32–33.

doubtless smile at the idea of such an expedition, but the truth is, I was born and brought up in the country, and though it has been my lot to pass my life amidst 'the busy haunts of men,' sedulously engaged in the active pursuits of business—my heart has never ceased to yearn after the simple pleasures of a country life. Whether it be the effect of early habits, or of a romantic disposition—whatever may be the cause—certain it is, that throughout the whole course of a long, active and laborious life, I have never lost my early relish for retirement. I can truly say of such pleasures, what the poet of sentiment and feeling so beautifully expresses, though in another sense,

"My heart, untravell'd, fondly turns to thee."

The beauties of nature have at all times possessed for me an indescribable charm. Not that I am fond of analyzing the various parts that make up the picture. Minute descriptions of rural scenery do not interest me deeply, and the course of my studies, as well as the business habits of life, have shut me out from the exquisite satisfaction, which must surely be derived, by every lover of nature, from a minute acquaintance with Natural History, Chemistry, and Botany—sciences, a thorough knowledge of which, the late Stephen Elliot used to say, "could beguile the most tedious journey, and strew the path of life with flowers." I mention these things merely to account, for what might otherwise be considered so *unaccountable,* that any man should voluntarily give up the comforts of a city life, to seek recreation in the wilderness. I will confess, however, that a desire to survey the *broad lands of Alabama* the *El Dorado* which was then opening golden visions to the longing eyes of our enterprising countrymen—an almost irresistible inclination too, to see, and become personally acquainted with, that hardy race of men THE PIONEERS of the wilderness—who, hovering on the borders of civilization, present in their character a rare combination of the vices as well as the virtues of civilized and savage life—but above all, an earnest wish to visit some of the INDIAN TRIBES, with a view to judge for myself, as to the true character and actual condition of that wonderful people, of whom in a few brief years nothing will be remembered but that they *once were*—all these had their influence in inducing me to undertake a journey, a few of the incidents of which I now propose to recal.

Escaping from the duties of a laborious profession, and casting care behind my back, I commenced my pilgrimage under a burning sun, in the latter part of July, and leaving Charleston, bent my way towards Augusta. It took me four days, not idly spent, to reach that city, then, as now, the abode of as many warm hearts and liberal minds, as are to be found in any part of the world. There were no rail roads then, and the man would have been pronounced an idle dreamer who had ventured to predict that the time would ever come when a traveler who had breakfasted in Charleston, should (as I have myself done) take his tea in Augusta, on the same day, cheered by the beams of the setting sun. It is not my purpose, however, to give my readers merely a personal narrative, nor to dwell on the every day scenes of domestic and social life, which render a tour through the Southern States so interesting and delightful to every traveler of liberal sentiments and refined feelings. My present business is with the *wilderness*—the red men of the forest, and the border race. Even of these, however, my sketches must necessarily be few and imperfect. With all the feelings of a school boy, who has escaped from the smoke of the city, and the dull monotony of his daily task, to sport in the green fields, animated by the recollections of his childhood, or, (to borrow the eloquent thought of John Randolph of Roanoke) "with the feelings of a man who retires from the cares of business and the bustle of the world, to muse on the beauties of nature beneath the shade of his patrimonial oaks"—did I plunge into the very depths of the forest, to luxuriate in pleasures of which a man born and brought up wholly in a city, cannot form even a conception. It is needless to say, that in such a frame of mind, I carried no sketch book, and took no notes. The very slight sketches therefore which I propose to give, and the anecdotes I am about to relate, it must be borne in mind by my readers, are drawn entirely from the stores of my very imperfect memory—and if they offer little of novelty, and are without startling incidents, I trust they will not be wholly uninteresting, especially, when it is remembered, that I do not propose, like many travellers, "to draw upon my imagination for my facts," but to give a simple history of events as they occurred, and a delineation of characters as they fell under my own observation, no farther colored than may be necessary to fill up the picture.

Passing rapidly through Georgia, *we* (for I had as a travelling companion a gentleman of fine sense and many accomplishments, who, like myself, was in pursuit of health and pleasure, recreation and instruction) we reached the country inhabited by the Creek Indians, then indiscriminately called the "Nation"—"the Creek Country"—and "the wilderness." A journey at that time from Fort Hawkins in Georgia, to Alabama, through the Creek Country, was deemed no inconsiderable undertaking, though it is now, I am informed, easily accomplished by the aid of a line of excellent four horse stages, in a day or two;—admirable accommodations being afforded by well kept public houses, stationed at convenient distances along the road;—nor since the celebrated adventure of HERR CLINE, who was forcibly arrested by a body of Indians, and if not actually robbed and murdered, was, I think, indebted in some way or other to *his art* for his safety—has any interruption been experienced by peaceable travellers. It was otherwise at the period of which I am writing. Travellers were then constantly interrupted, robberies were not infrequent, and murders were sometimes committed. These were always charged upon the Indians, but I was induced to believe, that not unfrequently, desperate criminals escaping from our penitentiaries, or otherwise fleeing from justice, sought refuge among the Indians, and continued there to practice with impunity the crimes which had driven them from civilized society. But however this may be, a journey through the Creek Country at that time, was regarded as a pretty serious business. There was not a public house, except THE AGENCY, where either accommodations or provisions could be procured. Indeed, there was not a single house of any description any where to be seen—and as the Indian *villages*—(and the Indians always live in villages, in this trait their character rather resembling the French peasantry as we see them in Canada, than our American borderers—with whom it is a maxim 'not to live within hearing of the barking of a neighbor's dog,') are far removed from the public highway, it was impossible for the traveller to derive his supplies from that source. I do not remember, in the whole course of my journey, to have met with but a single Indian on the road who offered any thing for sale, and he presented a small watermelon for which he asked the exorbitant price of half a dollar. A traveller who had casually fallen in with us at the time, advised us to take it from him, and to give him half price; and to induce us to do so, told us an anecdote, of his having the day before treated an Indian in that manner, and silenced his complaints with his horsewhip. This example however we felt no inclination to follow, and when we understood that the poor fellow had actually travelled thirty miles to find a market for this, perhaps the only product of his wretched garden, we paid him his full price, greatly to the dissatisfaction of our fellow-traveller, who openly reproached us with having violated that section of the *border code* which declares "that in dealing with Indians we must always *fix our own price*, and take care *never to give too much.*"

While relating this anecdote, I will tell another, illustrative of the treatment which the Indians at that time habitually received at the hands of the whites.

Coming to a rapid stream, which, with every fall of rain is so swollen as to be, for a short time, too deep to be forded, we found, to our surprise, that a rude bridge, evidently of Indian construction, had been thrown over it— a convenience to the traveller, which we observed no where else in the Indian country. Inquiring of our companion the history of this bridge, he informed us, that it had been built by the Indians, who had been in the habit of exacting a trifling toll, from those who found it necessary, when the streams were up, to pass over it; the emigrants had by common consent refused to pay the toll, and that the Indians charged with the duty of collecting it having been *beaten off*, it was now a *free bridge*.

I select these two incidents, out of many others with which I became acquainted, to show, that if there have sometimes been just cause of complaint against the violent conduct of the Indians, they are not altogether without excuse. Indeed, I was surprised to see, in how arbitrary and dictatorial a manner the white borderers lorded it over the Indians. An Indian—at least out of his own village—never thought of resisting a white man. On the highway, unless under the influence of liquor, they made no resistance, even when beaten without a cause. In this respect, I could perceive no difference between the Indians and the negroes. They would both receive the whip, from a passing traveller, without seeming even to feel the degradation; and if such treatment was ever revenged, it was in the Indian fashion—by waylaying the adversary, and making him the victim of an unseen hand. I am sorry to be compelled to raise so much of the veil of romance, with which our modern novelists have covered the Indian character. But I state facts; and will add, that on visiting, afterwards, the Catawba tribe of Indians in Lancaster district, in our own State, I found that this indifference to outrages upon their persons had long existed among them.

I do not know that the attempt was ever made by any white man, to illtreat an Indian, especially a chief, in an Indian village, or when surrounded by their own people; but when wandering abroad, in the open day, and out of the shelter of their forests, they always seem to me to be in the condition of animals cut off from a resort to their *instincts* for protection. Losing all confidence in their own resources, and feeling themselves defenceless, they at once become humble and powerless. That their character has undergone some change in this respect, cannot be doubted. But I have been assured by an officer, who has several times been engaged in battles with the Indians, (and among them, some of the fiercest and most uncontaminated tribes of the Northwest), that when driven from their fastnesses and brought into the open plain, however superior their numbers, they at once cease to resist— nay, I have been assured that a single horseman seen on a neighboring hill has put them to flight. An Indian, from whom an explanation of this fact was asked, merely replied '*de horse run.*' Black Hawk himself, whose exploits gave him, for a season, a reputation, as a hero, second only to that of Gen. Jackson (with whom, indeed, he fairly divided the public homage, when carried on a visit to New York), became crestfallen and spiritless the moment he emerged from his native forests.

But to return to my journey. Having laid in, on the borders, our supplies of provisions, including corn for our horses (which I well remember cost us three dollars a bushel—a fact worthy to be recorded), and having provided ourselves with a tent, to the use of which I had, during the late war, become somewhat accustomed, armed with a fowling piece and a pair of double-barrel pistols, we marched boldly into the wilderness. It was, I think, about midday of our second day's journey—an hour at which it was our habit to lay by for a couple of hours, to refresh our jaded horses and to cook our dinner, consisting of cold ham and bread, with a pair of boiled doves or partridges, which we were sportsmen enough generally to pick up on the way, washed down with a glass of wine, and when our wine was exhausted, a little brandy and water—that we had taken our seat at the foot of a tall oak, while a transparent stream dashed by our feet, that an incident occurred which occasioned some little excitement at the time, and which I will here relate, although not otherwise perhaps worthy of being recorded, as affording some insight into Indian character and manners. We were distant at least thirty miles from any residence whatever, a small Indian village on the Chattahouchie being the nearest known settlement. I had not seen a human face the whole day, except that of my friend, and the Carolina negro who accompanied us, and who was our hostler, butler, cook and body servant, and withal *a character* in his way, as worthy to be studied and described as any negro that has been immortalized in the pages of Cooper or our own Simms. While gazing with extreme intent upon the noble scenery by which we were surrounded, and, I grieve to add, ever and anon betraying the weakness of the flesh, by impatient glances at the culinary preparations of old Juba, which seemed to us to be characterised, by even more than his usual bustle and importance, that our attention was suddenly aroused by cries, of a character which defies all description. They seemed to proceed from a thick wood some short distance up the stream, and were heard only at intervals. But whether they were the notes of distress, the exclamations of despair, or of pleasure;—whether they were the cries of beasts, of men, or of devils, we were utterly unable even to conjecture. It has since seemed to me, that the height of the banks of the stream whence these sounds proceeded, and the dark deep swamp by which the spot was surrounded, might have so swelled the echoes, as to give to our minds an exaggerated impression of the sounds which fell upon our ears. We supposed the noise might proceed from wild cats or wolves; but the old negro insisted, that it was a combat among the panthers over a wounded deer. Adventurers as we were, however, it was not to be thought of, that this mystery should be left unexplored. If we were not, like Don Quixotte actually seeking for distressed damsels, to be delivered—yet *adventures,* of all kinds, seemed to fall fairly enough within the scope of our enterprise. We immediately therefore called a council of war, and the plan of the campaign was speedily arranged. Old Juba, to whom we gave one of the pistols (which seemed to afford him great consolation, though he certainly would not have known how to use it, on any emergency), was left as a rear guard, for the protection of the horses, baggage and camp equipage, and above all *the provisions,* with a strict charge on no account—to *let the fire go out;* I myself constituted the advance, armed with the fowling-piece, well charged with buckshot; while my friend, with the other pistol, formed a *corps-de-reserve.* Every thing being thus settled to our mutual satisfaction, I proceeded cautiously along the banks of the little stream, which was overshadowed by lofty trees, and tangled with underbrush—as most of our Southern streams are—towards the point whence these strange sounds proceeded. Having been a hunter, in my youth, somewhat skilled in *forest-craft,* which a quarter of a century ago was deemed an indispensible accomplishment of the sons of every low country planter, I was not ignorant of the stratagems necessary to cover my approach, towards a spot where game was expected to be found. Advancing always under cover of the shrubbery—at first erect, then stooping the body lower and lower, so as to form with the legs an angle, first obtuse, then a right, and then an acute angle, until the face is brought within a few inches of the ground, with the shoulders rounded into the form of the hump on the back of the buffalo— I finally sank down upon my hands and knees, and thus cautiously and slowly approached the desired spot. Immediately before me was a projecting bank, around which the current swept, forming above an extensive basin, which, from this point, was fairly overlooked. In the midst of a clump of low bushes, by which this spot was covered, stood an old black stump, from which extended the trunk of a fallen pine, the remains of one of those lords of the forest, which had fallen beneath the blast, like the mighty ones of the earth before the irresistible fury of those political elements, which has changed, and is still changing, the face of the world. For years, had the wandering savage built his rude hut of the bark of this noble tree, and cooked his game at the fire afforded by its decaying branches. Nothing now remained but its weather-beaten and blackened trunk. Keeping this as a breastwork, I crept on in silence to gain a shelter, from whence I expected to be able *to see without being seen,* intending, like every good partizan, to be then governed by circumstances. Having nearly reached the desired point, I deposited my hat upon the ground, examined the priming (percussion caps had not then been invented), and sinking down fairly upon my stomach, dragged myself along, in the manner practiced by riflemen, engaged in surprising an enemy's sentinel at the outpost, or what may imply still greater caution, like some old 'leather stocking' of our pine barrens, attempting to surprise an old buck at sunrise, on a cold December morning, while his antlers are high in the air, and he is *snuffing the approach of danger.* At length I reached the barrier, and prepared for the onset. I will confess, however, that, in creeping over the last hundred yards, my heart had begun to misgive me. Notwithstanding the deceiving sounds, greatly magnified doubtless by the echoes of the swamp, and the deathlike stillness of the surrounding forest, I began to suspect, that the strange noises which saluted my ears, resembled neither the bleating of deer, the barking of wolves, nor the caterwaulling of wild cats; but had rather some faint resemblance to the sound of human voices, strangely harsh and unnatural, it is true, but still not so much so, as entirely to banish the suspicion that they might proceed from such a source. I thought I could catch the cry of anger and indignation; then the voice of complaint; and, ever and anon, the joyous outbreak of revelry and laughter, strangely varied, however, from the coarse gutteral of authority, down to the 'childish treble' of sportive infancy. At one moment, I supposed the noise was not unlike those Babel sounds, which issue from a bevy of school boys, dashing (as we used to do sixty years since) into Cannon's millpond on a warm evening in July, to the great scandal of the town, frightening the horses, and making the welkin ring with their outcries.

On the whole, however, I rather thought that the sounds were exactly such as might proceed from a congregation of the Rev. Mr. Irving's transplanted to the wilderness, and all holding forth in their 'unknown tongue.' But what could bring *them* into the Creek country, or indeed any one else, except an Indian hunter in pursuit of game?—and it was certain there was no hunter here. Resolved to unravel the mystery, I passed the muzzle of the gun carefully over the log, and putting the butt to my shoulder, cautiously raised my head so as just to bring my eyes to the level of the upper part of the log. In an instant, in the twinkling of an eye, I became visible to the astonished group whom I had just surprised; consisting of an Indian squaw and some half a dozen naked urchins, who were sporting in the stream. In a moment all was hushed. With the quickness of thought they scampered up the bank, and catching up their garments, bounded with the velocity of affrighted deer into the forest, and disappeared. Not a word was uttered, not a cry of surprise or alarm escaped their lips, and so quickly did the whole party vanish, that the scene passed before my eyes like enchantment. I have often thought of the terrible tale which these simple children of the forest probably told, on their return home, of the white giant, armed with a huge rifle, who surprised, and would doubtless have murdered, scalped, and eaten them, but for the interposition of the Great Spirit; and it is not improbable that some sixty years hence, a traveller among the scattered remnant of the Creek tribe, *west of the Mississippi,* may find among its traditions the account of an Ogre, with great red eyes; a river demon, who haunts the streams of their 'father land,' frightening the women, and devouring the children. Heathen mythology has admitted river gods on less foundation: for I am free to confess, that my proceedings were very suspicious, and my manner of approach not at all calculated to present me in a friendly light, to the naked and defenceless beings, upon whose property I had intruded.

We not unfrequently came across, afterwards, small parties, composed of women and children, wandering in the woods, far from their homes; and we were told that it was their custom in the summer season, before the green corn feast; when, being *usually destitute of food,* they sought a precarious subsistence from the *berries* which are then found in the woods. Indians are seldom met alone, they even 'hunt in couples'—but the squaws are sufficiently independent to wander about in the forest for weeks together, attended only by their children, with not unfrequently an infant *at the back.* In the whole course of my travels, I do not remember to have met an Indian man or woman entirely alone. After this adventure, we returned to our *bivouac,* laughing over our disappointment; and dinner being soon served up upon a pine log, we fell to, with a glorious appetite, such as travellers in a wilderness can alone feel; and our taste for Indian adventures being whetted by the incident which I have related, we resolved at once to make a detour to the Indian village (called, I think, *Tallassee*) at the falls of the Tallapoosa, the known residence of the BIG WARRIOR, the celebrated king of the Upper Creeks.

Should the readers of this Journal take any interest in our travels, we shall invite them to accompany us, on our visit to this mighty chief, when we promise to give them some insight into the domestic economy, and the political institutions of the Indians, as they existed sixteen years ago.

A TRAVELLER.

THE PROSE "THLE-CATH-CHA" IS NOTABLE for its endeavor to provide posterity a readable, imaginatively conceived, realistically accurate written account imparting life and meaning to a portion of Native American history previously recorded only in the oral tradition. Throughout "Thle-cath-cha," Simms portrays historical figures—white and red—as fallible human beings; but the taut closing scene with Jackson and Weatherford—sensitive in its preservation of the sense of dignity and honor in both races—underscores Simms's sympathy for the inevitable yet unjust plight of the Muscoghees.

◌ *Thle-cath-cha. Being a few passages from Muscoghee History*

CHAPTER ONE

"Thle-Cath-Cha," or "The Broken Arrow," is, or was, the name of a large district of country once centrally situated in the territory formerly owned by the Creek or Muscoghee nation of Indians, and now forming one of the border counties in the State of Georgia. Its name may well be employed to designate the fortunes of a people whose numbers are daily diminishing, whose strength is departed, and whose name, once powerful above all of the forest tribes of the South, is now no longer associated with greatness or authority; but, in this narrative, we would rather couple the epithet of "the Broken Arrow," with the history of a Chief, who, for a long period of time, was the master spirit among his people, and whose erring aims and melancholy fall and fate, fairly entitle him to the appellation. The writer of this narrative happening a few weeks after the death of General William Mackintosh, the fifth Chief of Muscoghee, to pass through the nation in the immediate neighborhood of the place of his execution, had his attention necessarily drawn to a subject, then in the mouths of all around him, and upon which the general opinions were various and conflicting. Sundry little particulars which he picked up, as well from Indian as from white authorities, were carefully treasured up in his memory, and, subsequently, the possession of some public, but little read documents, which furnished him with additional material, enabled him to throw together the few following facts, which, in his humble opinion, form an exceedingly interesting passage in our domestic history. It will be understood, however, by the reader, that strict accuracy is not to be looked for in any narrative which relates to the history of our Indian tribes. Oral statements can never be so precise as written records, and depending as they must for their preservation upon the uncertain memorials of men, error becomes unavoidable even where the most conscientious principles govern the narrator. He trusts, however, that the leading facts which he now records will be found as free from vital imperfections as it is possible for such histories to be.

It will not be necessary to the comprehension of this brief narration, to go very deeply into the Muscoghee councils. Something, however, of past history, may be held necessary on the part of the reader, to enable him to judge correctly of the relative position of the parties,—the nation on one hand, and the Chief whom they executed on the other. The justice of their award, and the right which they had to inflict it, must result from the general institutions under which they lived. If these institutions were republican in their form and character, it must follow as inevitable, that the popular will, with certain modifications, must be the supreme law; and if it be that the law under which Mackintosh perished, was one well known to the victim as to the nation, and not one,—(as it is contended) *ex post facto,* and contemplative only of his conduct,—then, it equally follows that the nation simply avenged its own wrongs and maintained its integrity, in the execution, according to their summary forms, of an outlaw and a traitor. But let the facts speak for themselves; and without stopping to analyze the laws and institutions of a wandering people whose government must vary its forms according to the caprices of their existence, we will content ourselves with simply discovering as much of the truth as we can, leaving it to our readers, each to draw his own inference, as to the justice of the proceeding which we shall finally relate.

All the barbarians are descended from Gods of one sort or another, and it does not matter, knowing this common assumption, that we should search very deeply into the origin of any people. If they do not always set up so ambitious a pretension, they are, to say the least, all, more or less, the especial objects of care with some one or other benevolent deity. The Muscoghees had their Gods, and God-fathers, like all the rest, and the preliminary history of Greeke, Roman, Persian and Scythian, with here and there a slight change of name and attribute, will not improperly, answer for those who were quite as proud of their ancestors as any Roman of us all. They claim to have come from the chambers of the Sun himself, and always point to the west, as the region from which they sprang. Their progenitors, a people covered with hair, and who carried thunder and lightening in their hands, were evidently intended to be known as Gods. They were probably the most powerful Indian nation in North America; and a portion of their policy, which was strictly Roman in its character, contributed daily to make them more so. They incorporated with their own, on equal terms, the nations which they overcame, and hence the somewhat interesting fact, as it is one peculiar to their history, that their numbers are said to have almost doubled between the years 1730 and 1760. In 1775, their hunting grounds covered a region of country more than one hundred and eighty miles in length. They had more than fifty towns, and were subdivided into the tribes of Apalacheè, Alabama, Abecaw, Cowetaw, Conechaw, Coosaw, Cosawteè, Chochickhomaw, Natcheè, Ockmulgee, Oconee, Ockohoghee, Pachanee, Tensaw, Talepoosaw, Chatahoochee, Wetumpkee, and perhaps many others of which our early historians knew nothing. It is probable, indeed, that every town, with its hunting grounds around, constituted a distinct tribe, and had its several chiefs, or a single chief, all subject to the will of the great warrior of the nation. The territory originally claimed by the Muscoghees, extended from the Tombeckbe to the Atlantic, and from the extreme Western parts of Florida, to the thirty-fourth degree of North latitude; and their claim seems to have been generally undisputed among the other nations. It is more than probable, that their sway extended over South-Carolina, and certainly as far North as Beaufort, for even in the settlement of Georgia, though the number of their tribes had been then reduced, we found them in a conference with Mr. Oglethorpe, claiming from the Savannah river, and having their claim recognized by the Indians who then still dwelt in the neighborhood. The Indians of Yamacraw,—a tribe of South-Carolina Indians, and noted in our history as a distinct nation, confessed themselves, through Chief *Mico,* or Prince, Tomochichee, to be Creeks and they spoke the Muscoghee language.

When Mr. Oglethorpe first established his colony on the Savannah river, he deemed it prudent to conciliate this nation, and a solemn conference was held at one of the new houses to which he gave them a general invitation. They came from various quarters, and with many proofs of their number and power as a nation. The tribe, or town of Coweetaw, sent their *Mico* or King, a Chief named *Yahankakee,* and *Essaboo,* then Chief Warrior, the son of old Brim, whom the Spaniards called their Emperor. These were followed by ten attendants, eight of whom were men, and two women. The Cussetas sent *Cusseta,* their Mico, and Talchicahatchie, their head Warrior, with four attendants. The Osweechies sent Ogeesee, their war-king, Neath-louthee-ko and Ougachie, two head Chiefs, with three attendants. From the tribe of the Chechawees came Outh-letoee, their King, Thlantho-lookee, Figeer, Sootamilla, their war-chiefs, with three attendants. From the Echatees, came Chutabatchee, and *Robin* (the latter with the English name having been partly bred and wholly christened by the English) with four attendants. The tribe of Poloccucolee sent Chillattee, their head warrior with five attendants The Oconees sent Oneekechumpa, called by the English "Long-King," and Kooe-woo, a chief warrior. From the tribe of Eufalee came Tomaumi, a head warrior and three attendants.

Here we have the names of many tribes which are now unknown to the nation, though, in place of them, we have tribes at present existing, who were then unknown. It is not improbable that in fact the tribes are still the same, and merely change their names to that of some more popular chief than the rest; since, while the old names are lost to their own chronicles, it does not appear that the population undergoes any diminution. It may be, that some tribes wander away, and some, it seems, may be expatriated. One little passage in the conference which took place on this occasion between Oglethorpe and the Muscoghees, would seem, indeed, to afford a sufficient warrant for this conjecture.

In the progress of the speech of Oneekechumpa, or the Long king,—a very tall man,—who came as the representative of the Oconees, and was the spokesman of the nation,—he said, towards the conclusion,—that he "thanked him (the Governor, Oglethorpe) for his kindness to Tomochichee (who was Mico, or king of the Yamacraws) and his Indians, to whom he said he was related, and *though Tomochichee was banished from his nation*, yet he was a good man, and had been a great warrior; and it was for his wisdom and justice that the *banished men* had chosen him king," &c. When he had done speaking, Tomochichee, came in with the Yamacraw Indians, and making a low obeisance, said, "*I was a banished man, and I came here poor and helpless to look for good lands near the graves of my ancestors*," &c.

Here is the theme of a poem. What a moral interest may be made to gather about the mystery of this man's banishment, and that of his tribe. What could have been the offence of a tribe which could prompt the nation to strike them from their great family,—to blot them out of their memories, and expel them to seek their fortunes among strangers and enemies. An active and keen imagination may readily weave from this little doubt, a story of the most exciting and high moral interest. Indeed, this little anecdote alone, proves the possession of higher sensibilities on the part of the Aborigines than we have been willing heretofore to concede them. The very fact that banishment is considered a serious punishment, shows a degree of refinement in their sensibilities which will yield to the romancer, a sufficient warranty, for giving them those attributes of the feeling and thinking man, which, we have ever been but too ready to deny them.

The conference with Oglethorpe ended in a treaty, for the purposes of trade and general alliance. The traders were to carry goods into the nation which they were to sell at prices arranged by the treaty. Restitution and reparation were to be made on both sides for injuries; *but criminals were to be punished by English law*,—a wise provision, and one necessary to protect the whites against the practice among the savages which makes personal revenge a legal right, and justifies the extremity of punishment even against a wrong doer by accident. Trade was to be withdrawn from any Indian town which should offend against the treaty. The English to possess all lands not *used* by the Indians, reserving, however, to the nation such as it might desire, and the division of which, was to be agreed on between the *beloved men* of the two parties. Runaway negroes were to be brought back to the English, and the rewards of their captors were fixed, for every restored runaway, at four blankets, or two guns, or the value thereof in other goods,—and one blanket only, if the negro should happen to be killed in endeavoring to escape. "VI. and lastly, They promise, with straight hearts and love to their brother English, to give no encouragement to any other white people to settle here," &c. Such was the monopolizing selfishness of the trader. Competition would have cheapened the goods to the poor Indian, but would have lessened the profits to his generous white brother. As a fitting conclusion to this treaty, though sometime after, Oglethorpe carried Tomochichee, king of the Yamacraws to England, with Senawkie his wife, Toonakowee, his nephew, Hillispillee, a war Captain, with five other Indian Chiefs, and an Interpreter. They were introduced to the king at Kensington, to whom Tomochichee made a speech, and presented a bunch of eagle's feathers. In his speech he says,—

"I am come for the good of the whole nation called the Creeks. I am come over in my old days, though I cannot live to see the good myself. I am come for the good of the children of all of the nations of the Upper and Lower Creeks, that they may have knowledge of the English. These are the feathers of an eagle, the swiftest of birds, who flieth round all the nation. They are the sign of peace in our land, and I have brought them to leave them with you as a sign of everlasting peace," &c. "The words you say to me, I will say faithfully to all the kings of the Muscoghees."

Chapter Two

We concluded our last chapter of this narrative, by describing briefly the interview, which took place at Kensington, between his Britannic majesty, George the Second, and Tomochichi, the Mico or King of the Yamacraws; Senawkie, his wife; Toonakowee, the Prince, his nephew; Hillespillee, a war chief, and five other principal Indians of the same nation, who had been carried over to England by Oglethorpe. A treaty followed the interview, and certain rules were adopted, then and there, for the regulation of trade and traders among them, at their own suggestion; which, with partial modifications, have been continued to this day by our Government. Among these, they required that there should be but one Store House in each Indian town, for supplying their people; and that this should be under the direction of certain Trustees among the English, without whose license no white man was permitted to trade; and their goods were then only to be furnished at prices, which were to be arbitrarily fixed beforehand. An act was also prepared and adopted, for preventing the introduction of ardent spirits among them; but the insatiable appetites of the one people, and the no less insatiable cupidity of the other, soon rendered this salutary provision a mere dead letter in their chronicles. A law was also passed, prohibiting the introduction of slaves into the colony; but this, too, was soon made obsolete by the operation of influences beyond the control of a people, capricious like the Indians, and of adventurers so feeble, in physical respects if not in moral, as were all the early colonists. The chiefs gave, while in England, according to the account from which I quote, "Evident marks of their good sense, and of a sincere inclination to carry on a friendly correspondence between their nation and ours." Indeed, they were the lions of the season, and were quite as much subjects of wonder to the cockneys, as every thing they saw in Europe must have been of wonder to them. The nobility entertained them at their tables,—the crowd followed them in the streets, and flocked around them at public places, and the honor of shaking hands with the red sons of the forest was as eagerly sought by the English, as in modern times, and among ourselves, was the desire of grappling with the fingers of Lafayette. Twenty pounds sterling a week were allowed them for their support, while they remained in England; and when they left it, it is computed that they brought away presents of value to the amount of five hundred pounds beside. They remained four months in the immediate neighbourhood of the Court, which was then at Kensington; and it was the carriage of his majesty, that carried them to Gravesend to embark for Georgia. It is very doubtful whether this treatment, which was thought to be good policy at the time, did not spoil the savages, by the sudden importance to which it raised them. The disposition manifested to buy their favor, made them mercenaries, who were not unwilling to sell themselves to the highest bidder; as the spoils of the fields of Granson made the rude Swiss, who had been, while poor, the fearless asserters of their own freedom, the hirelings of Moloch throughout the European world. For a time, however, the effect of this treatment was beneficial to the colonists, and the Muscoghees were willing tributaries of the Georgians; though it was not long after this, that the latter sought in vain, to procure by purchase the lands which lie between Ebenezer and Briar Creek, then belonging to the Uchee tribe, whose subsequent settlements may be traced, step by step, as the whites advanced among them, 'till we find their latest *stakes,* five hundred miles distant from the first on the banks of the Chatahoochie.

But the policy of the English became that of the French and Spaniards, from the first named of which people they had borrowed it; and to conciliate, or in other words to buy up and to make the brute ferocity of the savages subservient to their national jealousies and trading interests, the Spaniards sent emissaries in all directions to tamper with the Muscoghees. Oglethorpe, advised of this, was compelled to the renewal of his efforts; and the better to defeat the schemes of his enemies, with a degree of intrepidity which deserves eulogium, he prepared to go himself into the heart of the savage country, and add to the value of his presents, the imposing influence of his personal appearance and address. His reputation, by this time, had become generally known among the Indians, and of this fact he seems to have been fully aware. Setting forth with several pack horses, laden with such goods as would best please the fancies and meet the wants of a savage people, he proceeded toward Cowetan, the chief town of the Muscoghees. There he met with a general assembly of the Creeks, Cherokees and Choctaws; and here we find sufficient evidence of a fact, which does not seem to have been often remarked, and which would indicate a striking degree of kindred, between these seemingly distinct people—namely, that in the grand councils of one nation, there are almost always present some counsellors from the rest, who speak, recommend and vote, precisely as if they were representatives of the people, in authority, with whom they appear only to have commission to confer. This, it is true, may be only a consequence of their primitive and simple habits of life; habits which lead them to reverence the wise of every nation, and persuade them to hear with patience, and regard with a yielding judgment, the persuasions and advice of those they esteem to be worthy of trust; and yet, I cannot help thinking, that these several people were originally members of the same family, distinct tribes, it may be, which from their increasing numbers and the remoteness of their settlements from each other, found it convenient to act independently, on all ordinary occasions of society;—the differences of their languages, from what I can learn, do not seem vital, and are not greater than the various dialects of most European people, where, though coming from a common stock, circumstances, climate, and an occasional encounter with strangers produce changes in sundry regions, which are insulated and remote from the centre, which, to the inartificial ear, will seem as utterly foreign to the parent language, as it is possible for one language to seem from another. One thing is certain, that among the three great Southern nations of Indians which still exist, there has been on most occasions of national interest, a general reference to the feelings and interests of each other, and most commonly a decided unanimity of sentiment and action.

At the interview which followed this visit of Oglethorpe, he was received with a great show of hospitality and friendship, smoked with them the pipe of peace, drank with them the *black*, or purifying drink, and made another treaty of amity and interest. By this treaty, the Indians "declared that all the dominions, territories and lands between the Savannah and St. John's Rivers, including all the Islands, from the St. John's to the Bay of Apalatchie, and therein to the mountains, do by ancient right, belong to the Muscoghee nation, &c." They confirmed all previous grants at the same time, and indicated the republican character of their social policy, by declaring themselves to hold their lands as *tenants,* or as *they* would phrase it, in more guarded language, proprietors in common.

This visit of Oglethorpe was timely, and the presents and arguments which he carried, were judicious and of excellent effect. The Muscoghees and Chickasaws sent a small force, the next year, to assist Oglethorpe, who commanded the combined troops of Carolina and Georgia in an unsuccessful and rather discreditable attack, which was made upon the Spanish fortress of St. Augustine; and it was on this occasion that the General gave great offence to his Indian allies, by suffering his humanity to get the better of a cooler policy. The Chickasaws slew a Spaniard, and as the account goes, cut off his head; perhaps they merely scalped him. But whether it was the head or scalp merely, which they brought to Oglethorpe as a trophy, it provoked him to an expression of abhorrence and disgust, which vexed and astonished them. Instead of giving them the rewards, which they had been taught by the practice of all their previous European employers to expect, he denounced them as "barbarous dogs," and bade them "begone from his sight." This offended their *amour propre* to such a degree, that they seized the earliest opportunity to desert them. It does not belong to our narrative to say further on the subject of this expedition, than that it was a most unfortunate failure, which entailed many dangers and a heavy debt on the two colonies engaged in it.

The indignity which Oglethorpe had put upon the Indians, by his scornful rejection of the trophy which they brought, was not, fortunately, resented universally among them, since we find a portion of the Yamacraw Creeks doing good service two years after, as allies of the General, in the able defence which he made of the colony against the Spaniards, where, defeating a force vastly superior to his own, he more than retrieved the reputation which he was supposed to have lost in the mis-managed expedition against St. Augustine. It was on this occasion that Toonakowee, the nephew of the Mico, Tomichichee, behaved with great personal bravery, slaying one of the Spanish captains, after he had been himself severely wounded in the right arm by his enemy. The Indians, as scouts and in ambuscades, contributed in no small degree to the singular success of the defence, made by Georgia on this occasion. Though the people of old Tomichichee had behaved thus bravely; and they furnished nearly one sixth of Oglethorpe's force,—the aged king did not live to witness their valor. He died on the 15th October, 1739, about four miles from Savannah at the advanced age of ninety-seven. He expressed indifference to his approaching fate, as he said he had survived the ability to go to war any more, and could do nothing, he well knew, to help the English, when the Spaniards, who were expected, should come against them. He exhorted his people to a faithful adherence to their friends, the Georgians, and made a last request that he might be buried among the English. This wish was complied with, and his body was interred with military honors in Percival square, where Oglethorpe ordered a suitable monument and inscription.

The next relation, in which we find the Muscoghees to the colonists of Georgia, was one far from being either so friendly or favorable. The circumstances, which we are now about to relate, form a curious episode in history of our sister State, and possess a singular interest, as well from the tragical consequences which had so nearly followed this occurrence, as from the ludicrous absurdity which pervaded their entire aspects. It appears, that among the colonists of Frederica there happened to be a divine, one Thomas Bosomworth, a preacher of the church of England and chaplain to Oglethorpe's English regiment. This person, whether from insanity or a wild ambition that looked exceedingly like it, projected a scheme for his own aggrandizement, which promised fair at one moment, to destroy the whole colony. One of the Indian chiefs or kings, as they were styled by courtesy, of the Muscoghee nation, named Malatchie, was made use of by the ambitious parson, who persuaded him to suffer himself to be formally crowned and anointed, in the European fashion, as the Emperor of all the Creeks. This, as there happened to be a large number of Indians, chiefs and others at Frederica, at this time, was a matter of little difficulty. The ignorant creatures, it is more than probable, knew not well the meaning of the ceremony, and wholly regardful of the good cheer that came with it, were not unwilling to have made a dozen Emperors. Whether the sacred unction was poured upon the head of Malatchie by the reverend chaplain, or by a less worthy personage, is not recorded. The publication of the proceedings, however, was sufficiently formal and formidable. The manifesto, which they put forth on the occasion, has been fortunately preserved, and may very well bear recital at length. It runs thus:

"Frederica, (Georgia,) Dec. 14, 1747.

"Know all men by these presents, that we, Simpeopy, war-king of the Cowetas; Thlockpalati, head warrior of the said town; Moxumgi, king of Etchitas (or, as now written, Hitchetas;) Iswige, head warrior of the Etchitas, and Actithilki, beloved man of the said town; Ciocolichee, king of Osuchee (Osweechee); Appalya and Ischabogy, beloved men of Nipkey; and Himmopacohi, warrior of said town; Tokeah, war-king of the Chehaws; Whyanneachee and Etowah, warriors of said town; Mahelabbi, beloved man of the Cussetahs, and Scheyah, warrior of said town; and Estcho-thalleatchi Yahulla (Yoholo) Mico of the Tuskigas; having full power by the laws of our nation, to conclude every thing for the towns we represent, do hereby acknowledge Malatchie Opya, Mico, to be our rightful and natural Prince. And we likewise, further acknowledge, that, by the laws of our nation, we think ourselves obliged to stand by, ratify and confirm, every act and deed of his, as much as if we ourselves were present; and we therefore make this public declaration to all subjects of the Crown of Great Britain, that Malatchie Opya, Mico, has full power and authority as our natural Prince, to transact all affairs of our nation, as firmly and fully to all intents and purposes, as we, the whole nation might or could do if present. In confirmation, &c."

This was signed in the presence of half a dozen white witnesses, proved by one of them, and put on record in the Secretary's office of South Carolina,—the document being as rigidly authenticated, as if it were of certain and unquestioned value. This rare fooling was not without its selfish and deliberate purposes, however visionary and absurd the whole matter may seem. Bosomworth who devised it, seems to have suffered from that form of madness, which exhibits still, in all its phases and fluctuations, a general aspect of narrow cunning, that invariably lets it down from its height, and shows its spots of earth, at the very time when it is about to seem least earthy. It is scarcely possible, when we consider his subsequent proceeding, to suppose for a moment, that he could be other than insane. Charity at least, would have us presume so. Having accomplished this matter to his own satisfaction, he next drew up a deed of conveyance in common form, by which the new made Emperor of the upper and lower Creeks, in consideration of "ten pieces of strand, twelve pieces of duffles, two hundred weight powder, two hundred weight lead, twenty guns, twelve pair of pistols and one hundred weight of vermillion," conveyed to Thomas Bosomworth, and Mary his wife, "all those tracts of land, known by the names of Hussopee or Ossabaw, Cowleygee or St.

Catharine's, and Sapelo Islands, with their appurtenances, &c; warranting and defending the same to the said Thomas and Mary, so long as the sun shall shine, or the waters run in the rivers,"—forever. Signed on the fourth day of the Windy Moon.—(14th December.)

Before the end of this farce, which had like to have been tragedy, can be recorded, it will be necessary that we should state a few particulars touching "Mary, his wife." She was an Indian woman, who was originally known among the whites as Mary Musgrove, subsequently as Mary Mathews, and lastly as Mary Bosomworth. She was a woman of some influence among the Creeks, and being intelligent, was singled out by Oglethorpe, at an early period in his treaties with the Indians, as an interpreter. He distinguished her by many favors; allowed her for her services one hundred pounds sterling per annum; and employed her as an agent and messenger to her nation and its several tribes. Bosomworth married this woman, accepted a grant of land from the Crown, and settled permanently in the province. Having procured his more extended grant from the new Emperor, he determined to assert his right to the lands which it conveyed; and in order to strengthen his claim, he circulated a report that "Mary, his wife," was an elder sister of Malatchie, and was descended from the Indian sovereign, who previously held dominion over all the Muscoghees. This done, Mary assumed the title of an Independent Princess, and became "Queen Mary." She disavowed all allegiance to the King of Great Britain or any other King; or any connection with him, other than such as should result from the formation of treaties and alliances. She next summoned a meeting of the Creeks, who attended in large numbers. To these she made a long speech, setting forth not only her novel claims, but also, with more effective art, the great injury which her subjects had sustained by the loss of their territories. She urged them to redress themselves by taking up arms. The influence of this woman provoked the Indians to fury; nor should this be a matter of surprise. It was the strict consequence of Oglethorpe's policy in employing her as a confidential emissary to her people, and in sending occasional and annual presents through her hands. This confidence endowed her with an influence, infinitely beyond any thing possessed by any individual of the nation. The warrior blessed and worshipped the hand, which gave him the rifle and the hatchet, the beads, the blanket, and the vermillion. To obey her, was to be favored; to offend, was to forfeit the luxuries which were most imposing to the savage eye and mind. The result of her speech was doubly overwhelming, as it was instantaneous.

The savages were fired at her alleged indignities and their own. They pledged themselves to a man, to perish in the recovery of their common rights. Thus prepared for all events, Queen Mary, escorted by a large body of the savages, upon whom she had so wrought, set forth for Savannah, to demand from the President's Council the restoration of her possessions; or, at least, the recognition of her claims. A herald was despatched in advance of the Royal progress, to communicate the tidings of its approach, announcing the assumption by the Queen of her throne, and formally demanding, that all her lands south of the Savannah, should be relinquished without loss of time. She threatened, in the event of refusal, to bring down upon the colony, the whole force of the two nations of Upper and Lower Creeks, as their rightful Queen.

The affair now began, in spite of all its absurdities, to put on a serious aspect. The foolish woman, was attended by a horde of savages, whom she had inflamed by her artful addresses beyond their own, and possibly, her control. The whole force of Savannah amounted in this emergency to but one hundred and seventy men. The President (Stephens) and his Council, began to be alarmed at these bold proceedings, and much embarrassment ensued accordingly in their deliberations. They dreaded, and with sufficient reasons, her influence over the Indians, which they very well knew; and felt themselves too weak to resolve upon any measure of audacity. It was hastily resolved to temporize with the pretender; to use soft and persuasive measures, until they could seize upon her person with safety. In the meanwhile, they were not neglectful of the necessary measures of defence. The neighboring militia were ordered to hold themselves in readiness to march to Savannah, and the town was in the best posture of defence. A messenger was sent to "Queen Mary" while she was yet several miles off, to demand if she were really serious in her pretensions, and to use every means of persuasion to divert her from her folly. But finding her inflexible, on the return of the messenger, the President resolved to receive the savages with a resolute countenance, and prepare for the last emergencies. The militia were ordered under arms, and as the Indians entered the town, Capt. Noble Jones, at the head of the cavalry, met them, and by a timely show of intrepidity and daring, he compelled them to ground and delivered up their arms. They submitted with great reluctance and entered the town unarmed. Bosomworth, in his canonical robes, with his Queen beside him, (it is not said what kind of robes she wore,) followed by the kings and chiefs, marched through the streets (20th July, 1749,) making a most formidable and frightful appearance. The inhabitants were struck with terror at the sight of this ferocious tribe. When they came to the parade, the militia were under orders to receive them, and gave them a ceremonious salute of fifteen cannon. They were then conducted to the house of the President, where a consultation ensued on the subject of the claims of Thomas, and Mary, his wife. From this conference they were excluded, and the Indian chiefs were called upon to declare their objects. But this they declined to do, unless through their Queen and usual interpreter. They said that "she should speak for them, and they would abide only by what she said. They had heard that the whites were to send her like a captive over the great waters, and hence their coming in such a body to protect their Queen; they were unwilling to lose her; they meant no harm, however, and demanded the restoration of their arms which Captain Jones had taken from them, &c." To this last demand the Council gave their consent; the arms were restored, but all ammunition was rigidly with-held from them. On the following day, after the Indians had received their instructions in secret from "Queen Mary," they marched through the streets in a tumultuous manner, and with a degree of sullen ferocity in their faces, which threatened mischief. The alarm of the inhabitants was renewed. The women and children, dreading every moment to be scalped and murdered, contributed greatly to the confusion; the men turned out *en masse,* and armed to the teeth in preparation; and a false report that was put in circulation, that some of the Indians had murdered President Stephens, nearly produced the catastrophe, which it was the earnest policy of the Georgians to avoid. It was with great difficulty, that the officers could keep their men from commencing the affair, by firing on the savages. Such a movement would have deluged the town with blood. A more peaceable policy succeeded better. Bosomworth, the true author of the mischief, was privately seized, and hurried into confinement. Like another Montezuma and Atabalipa, he was required in his own person to be the security for the good conduct of his subjects. "Queen Mary" became doubly frantic at this desecration of her husband's person, and denounced all manner of vengeance upon the colony; ordered all white persons to depart from her territories, cursed Oglethorpe and his fraudulent treaties, and with the fury of a demon, stamping the earth beneath her feet, swore by her Maker that the whole world should know, that the land was her own. The Council, finding that she kept the savages so much under her own eye, as to prevent any countervailing influence which they might employ, availed themselves of an opportunity to lay hands upon her sacred majesty, and put her into limbo along with her canonical husband. This done, the matter of conference and expostulation was found more easy. A feast was prepared for the chiefs and leading warriors. Persons acquainted with the Indian tongue were employed as interpreters, and through their medium, the design of Bosomworth and his wife, and certain portions of their history, of which the savages hitherto knew nothing, were revealed to them. They were told, that "Bosomworth had involved himself in heavy debts, chiefly to people in Carolina, (which it seems was the case,) and which he was utterly unable to pay, unless he could procure the lands from the Indians, and the presents which had been sent over to the King for their use only, and which, in all such matters heretofore, had been usually given them by 'Queen Mary' as Indian interpreter." It is, indeed, not improbable, that the employment of another agent than herself, in the distribution of these presents, was the true cause of her insane fury. The Council continued, by telling the now heedful auditory, that "these presents were theirs only," [It is not unlikely that they were apprized, that some even then awaited them.] "That they were intended by the King as a compensation for their services and fidelity during the war against their common enemy, the Spaniards; that the lands to which Bosomworth laid claim could not be surrendered, as they were reserved for their places of encampment, whenever they should visit their beloved friends in Savannah; that the three maritime Islands, so improvidently included in their grant to Bosomworth, were reserved for their hunting and fishing, when they should come to bathe in the salt waters, &c."

This conference seemed to have the desired effect. Many of the Chiefs declared that Bosomworth had deceived them; and even Malatchie, whom he had made emperor, renounced his relationship to Mary, "the Queen." Being asked why he had acknowledged her as a Queen of the great Creek nation, and surrendered his power to a despicable old woman, he replied in an answer, which opened the eyes of the whites more fully to their own impolitic proceedings. He said that the "whole nation acknowledged her as such, for that nobody could distribute the royal presents but herself, or some of her family heretofore." The President of Council answered this argument in the most effective manner, and closed the discussion, by proceeding to make in person, a general distribution of presents. While preparations were making for this distribution, the Council believing things to be now secure, imprudently suffered Malatchie, whose capriciousness of character was proverbial even among the Indians, at his own request, to see Bosomworth and wife, in their place of *retiracy;* and in this interview the arts of "Queen Mary" succeeded in undoing all that had been done. While the savages, gathered together, were actually receiving the gifts from the hands of the President, he came forth and addressed them in the language of hostility and hate. With a frowning visage and furious gestures, he delivered a speech, in which he repeated all the extravagant claims of Bosomworth and wife; declared that the lands were possessed by Mary, long before General Oglethorpe came to the country; that she was Queen and head of the Muscoghees; that by her consent only, were Englishmen first permitted to settle on them; that she was still their rightful owner; and that her words were those of three thousand warriors, who were now ready to raise the hatchet in defence of her rights. When he had concluded, he drew from his pocket a written paper, which he delivered to the President in confirmation of what he had said.

This production was evidently from the hands of Bosomworth, and served to convict him, more effectually, of disgraceful and dangerous designs. It contained a preamble reciting a great number of names of Indians, who were styled kings of the upper and lower Creek towns, and who were most probably their chief men and leaders. But two of these were present on this occasions. The speech of Malatchie formed the contents of the paper. The President answered Malatchie by a brief recital of their first acquaintance with Mary; this scrap of history may very well be given without much condensation:

"FRIENDS AND BROTHERS:—When Mr. Oglethorpe and his people first came to Georgia, they found Mary, then the wife of John Musgrove, living in a small hut at Yamacraw. He was a white trader, and had a license from the Governor of South Carolina, to trade with the Indians. Mary was then in a poor ragged condition, neglected and despised by your people; but Gen. Oglethorpe finding that she could speak both our languages, made her his interpreter between us, put good clothes on her, gave her presents, and made her a person of consequence. The people of Georgia thought well of her, and she was useful to them, until she married this man, Bosomworth. From that time on she has proved a liar and a cheat. She is no relative of Malatchie, as we all know; but the daughter of an Indian woman of no account, by a white husband. Gen. Oglethorpe bought no lands of her, for she had none to sell; he treated for them with the old and wise men of your nation. At that time, the Muscoghees had a great deal of land, of which they could make no use. They parted with a portion of it to their white friends, and were glad when we came among them to supply their wants."

After this preamble, which was doubtless strictly true, he proceeded to show, that the present discontents of their people had been infused into them by their pretended Empress, at the instigation of her white husband; that their object was purely selfish; that he, Bosomworth, had demanded from Council a third part of Royal bounty, which had been designed for the Indians only; and that it was his object, in truth, to rob them of their rights, and not to maintain them; that he had quarrelled with the Council of Georgia for rejecting his exorbitant demands, and hence his desire to make mischief, &c.

The effect of this conference was again pacific. The Indians declared their eyes to be opened, and talked in the usual figures, about chains of friendship, and the union of hearts and hands, and brethren. They begged that the pipe of peace might be brought; and the pipe of peace, as they well knew, never came unaccompanied by the jug of rum. This, too, made its appearance on the present occasion, and the hall of council became the hall of feasting. Liberal gifts, at the same time, of various commodities, ammunition excepted, were distributed among them, and they all seemed satisfied. While the President and Council were thus busy, and flattering themselves with the idea that their difficulties were happily over, "Queen Mary," who it seems had not been denied free access to the potent beverage, in which they were all indulging, escaping from her place of honorable restraint, rushed, perfectly drunk, into the midst of the assemblage, and flew at the President, whom she denounced as seeking to seduce her people from their allegiance. The worthy man, though utterly confounded, was probably not displeased that she limited her assault to the feminine weapon only; and however annoying that of itself might be to delicate ears, was content that she forebore the use of others, which might have been of more lasting detriment. He met her partially on her own ground, and replied as calmly as he could to her denunciations and assertions. This would have shown bad taste in President Stephens, had his audience been only Europeans. But the necessity of having the last word, among savages, is of no small importance; and for the honor of the colony, the President was resolved not to be outdone in eloquence. The Indians listened to the belligerents with faces of grave deliberation, until "Queen Mary," making a partial concession of the ground to her opponent, addressed herself to those who had fewer words than the President. The latter injudiciously threatened, if she did not keep her tongue, to put her again into confinement. This threat she repeated to Malatchie; with some gross exaggerations and harsh comments, and with so much art, that the capricious savage started to his feet; seized his arms; called upon his people to follow his example; dragged the "Queen" into the ring, which, at a signal, they formed around her; and with a tomahawk waving above the heads of each counsellor, they prepared to obey her command. Nothing less than instant death was expected by the counsellors; for an instant the triumph of "Queen Mary" seemed complete. But before her signal could be shown, or the word of slaughter spoken, Captain Jones, at the head of the guard, seasonably made his appearance, and with a promptness of resolve, which he had manifested once before in the same business, he overawed the aroused savages; and with a bold hand which they did not dare to arrest, he seized once more upon the factious woman, and carried her off to safe-keeping. The Indians submitted with sullen reluctance, and the task of soothing and reconciling them had to be begun anew. In this emergency, the President and Council were greatly assisted by a young warrior named Ellick, who was either less capricious, or more easily persuaded than the rest. It would seem that he disclosed to the whites, sundry of the intrigues and proceedings of Bosomworth, which had been kept secret by the rest; and it is more than probable, that he advised them to keep the two ringleaders, the Canon and the Empress, in solitary confinement, without communion with his people. This done, Ellick moved off to the nation in advance of his brethren. Finding that he was unable to see Bosomworth or Mary, and perhaps, that nothing more was to be got by delay, Malatchie and his savages followed in detached parties the steps of Ellick; and the people of Savannah tired out with constant duty, were at length fortunately relieved from an insurrection, no less strange in its origin, than threatening, at one time, in its aspects. Had Bosomworth been endowed with as much courage as art, his success must have been complete; and the affair must have terminated fatally for the infant settlement. He had only to surprise the magazine on his first arrival in Savannah; and provided with ammunition, his savages were in sufficient numbers, to have overpowered the militia, when a general massacre must have ensued. It may be added here, that Bosomworth and his wife went to England, where they urged their claim, which was litigated in the Courts for several years. To a considerable extent the decision was favorable to their claim. The Court of St. James granted them the Island of St. Catharine, and gave instructions at the same time, for the sale of the rest of the lands, the proceeds of which were applied to the extinction of their titles. Bosomworth took possession of the Island, where he resided for some years with "Queen Mary," who died in the process of time, like all other Queens. The husband, whose taste in wives seems to have been rather curious, subsequently married his chambermaid. The three lie buried in the same grave yard of St. Catharine's, and they are said to lie together without commotion.

We shall end our chapter with this episode, which, with a little ingenuity, might be worked with considerable effect into a story of those days. We commend it, with due respect, to the regards of the romancers.

Chapter Three

Though the Georgians were rescued from the immediate power of the Muscoghees, incited as they had been by Bosomworth and his wife, the release was temporary only, and the infant colony could not but tremble with frequent apprehensions, to reflect upon the immense power possessed by the neighbouring savages. To form some, though still an imperfect idea of the dangers to which they were subjected by this propinquity, we will quote a few lively passages from the Memorial of South Carolina to the Crown, setting forth its weakness and claiming assistance. "The Province of South Carolina," says the Memorial, "and the new colony of Georgia, are the Southern frontiers of all your majesty's dominions on the Continent of America; to the south and south-west of which is situate the strong castle of St. Augustine, garrisoned by four hundred Spaniards, who have several nations of Indians living under their subjection, besides several other small settlements and garrisons near the Apalachies, some of which are not eighty miles distant from the colony of Georgia. To the south-west and west of us, the French have already erected a considerable town near Fort Thoulouse on the Moville river, and several other forts and garrisons, some not above three hundred miles distant from our settlements; and at New Orleans, on the Mississippi river, since her late Majesty, Queen Anne's war, they have exceedingly increased their strength and traffic, and have won many forts and garrisons on both sides of that large river for several hundred miles. And since his most Christian majesty has taken out of the Mississippi company, the government of that country into his own hands, the French natives of Canada came down in shoals to settle all along that river, where many regular forces have been sent over by the King to strengthen the garrisons of those places; and according to our best and latest advices, they have kept five hundred men in pay, constantly employed as wood-rangers, to keep the neighbouring Indians in subjection, and prevent those more distant from disturbing the settlement. The management of the French has so well succeeded, that we are very well assured that they have wholly in their possession, and under their influence, the several numerous nations that are situate near the Mississippi; one of these, the Choctaws, comprising by estimation, about five thousand fighting men who were always deemed very warlike, lies on this side of the river, and not above four hundred miles from our settlements. Among these the French Europeans have been sent to settle, and are encouraged by their Priests and Missionaries to take Indian wives and use divers other alluring methods to attach the Indians to the French alliance. By which means the French have become thoroughly acquainted with the Indian way of warring and living in the woods, and have now a great number of white men among them able to perform a long march, with an army of Indians, upon any expedition. * * * They have already paved a way for a design of that nature by erecting a fort called Fort Albama, otherwise Fort Louis, in the middle of the Upper Creek nation, upon a navigable river leading to Moville, which is kept well garrisoned, and mounts fourteen pieces of cannon. They have already been stopped from building yet another nearer to us. The Creeks are a nation, very bold, active and daring, consisting of about thirteen hundred fighting men, and not above one hundred and fifty miles distant from the Choctaws. Though we have hitherto traded with, claimed and held them in our alliance, yet the French, on account of that fort, and a superior ability to make them liberal presents, having been for some time striving to gain them over, and have succeeded with some of the Creek towns. This nation, if it can be secured in your Majesty's interest, is the only nation which your Majesty's subjects can here depend upon, as their best barrier against any attempts either of the French or of their confederate Indians."

These passages present a hurried but lively picture of the face and occupants of the country. The latter extract testifies to the important influence of the Muscoghees among the neighbouring barbarians:—an influence scarcely reconcilable with the estimate put upon their numbers. That they numbered but thirteen hundred warriors is out of the question; they must have numbered five thousand at the least. But this difficulty is one natural enough in all estimates made by the whites of the population of the roving tribes with which they came in contact. The census was unknown to the savages themselves. The strength of the people was ascertained through the leaders only, and determinable only by their success. It was not asked how many men were in the war party, but what totem—what mocasin—what paint. Every petty chief had a mocasin peculiar to his clan, and his paint was a heraldic badge, which was as entirely exclusive as the coat of arms of the European noble-man. A chief was invited to the war party; it was not asked, and seldom known, what number of men he brought with him. Indeed, one of the great instruments of civilization in preventing wars has been the proper knowledge of numbers. When rival nations know where a majority lies, they are always sufficiently slow to offend it.

It is amusing enough, looking back over the passages just quoted, to observe how unwilling our people seem to have been to admit that they had less aptitude for securing the favor of the savages than their adversaries, the French. They ascribe the greater success of the latter in conciliating the Indians, to the overawing forts which they erected, and their superior ability in making presents;—as if they did not themselves sprinkle the country with forts from the Roanoke to the foot of the Apalachies, and were not drawing annually upon the British treasuries and their own for the purpose of mak-ing presents. The true secret of the French success is clear enough in their history, nor less so in the very narration in which this ludicrous complaint is made. The narrative says:—"Among whom and several other nations of Indians, the French Europeans have been sent to settle, whom the Priests and Missionaries encourage to take Indian wives, and use other alluring methods to attach to the French alliance. By which means, &c." The elastic character of the French people, even in destitution, their cheerfulness, love of music and dancing, and the ready accommodation of their own to the habits of strangers, furnish the true secret of their success. These characteris-tics were not a little strengthened by the religion which they professed and taught,—a religion highly imposing in its forms and ceremonies, and attrac-tive from the symbolic splendors which it employed to teach those mysteri-ous truths which an inferior people will seldom easily acquire from any other form of education. The English and their immediate descendants, were, on the other hand, inflexible to the last degree. Stern language and sudden blows were the agents of education among them, which they carried among their barbarous neighbours. They made no concessions to the simple and wander-ing habits of the savage. They had no toleration for the irregularities of a people never before restrained either by place or form. They applied the cus-toms of civilization as tests and standards to a people, which had never yet learned its rudiments, and forced the laws and penalties of European justice upon those, who, living chiefly in common, knew but little of mine and thine. Their punishments were prompt and sudden; their vengeance terrible, and urged with a puritanic vindictiveness which savored the spirit of Milton's curses. While the Frenchman, with a smile of good nature and extended hands, came to the savage as to an equal and slept in the corner of his hut, and took his wife from among the tribe, and adopted the totem, and went out as one of them in pursuit of the wild turkey and the bear; the Englishman approached him with coat buttoned to the chin, armed to the teeth with long sword and match-lock; a bible in one hand and a keg of Jamaica rum in the other. He put on an air of condescension at the interview, and his first demand was that the savages should avow allegiance to a king that they had never heard of, and swear fealty on the fat cheeks of the Elector of Hanover, glaring from a medal of shining copper. The very assumption of superiority was that which the proud and solemn savage, could tolerate least of all. Much of the speeches of the English he could not understand, and what he did understand, was not always inoffensive. He understood the Bible and King George while the keg of Jamaica rum was unexhausted, but no longer. He was not unwilling to be a pensioner, but we may boldly assert, that in no single instance, though our treaties represent them as numerous enough, was he willing to confess himself a subject. Why should he, and what an absurdity to make such a demand? Without making it, the French by a more artful, and may we say, without fear of contradiction, a more amiable policy, obtained all the substantial advantages which the English anticipated from theirs, and in a more complete degree. The difference between the two was every thing. The English claimed as conquerors,—the French as friends, and we cannot feel surprised when we behold the difference of their reception among all the savages. To this day, we learn from the Memoirs of General Harrison, that the Western Indians speak of the French with language of the deepest regret; and he adds, that were they sure of their return, they would freely rise in insurrection upon all the Anglo Saxon race. It will, perhaps, only be necessary here to say, that Fort St. Louis was placed at Mobile Bay, about the spot occupied by the present city of Mobile; and was not identical with the Fort Albama or Albamous, as stated in the quoted passages preceding. The Albamous fort upon the old maps occupied a place lying in the fork formed by the rivers Alabama and Tallapoosa, a site subsequently employed by us as Fort Jackson. Mobile, as we see, was written by the French Moville, or, more properly, Mauville; and the Indian tribe from which it received its name, a tribe most probably of the Chickasaws, was generally recognized as the most polished of all the Indian tribes of the south-west. The Mauville was, *par excellence*, the

Court language of that region. To illustrate more effectually what we have said of the great leading difference of character between the French and the English, producing the results of which the latter so bitterly complained, we will quote but a single passage farther. It belongs to the same memorial.— "The French at Moville, perceiving that they could not gain the Indians to their interest without buying their deer skins, which is the only commodity the Indians have to purchase necessaries with, and the French not being able to dispose of these skins, by reason of their having no vent for them in old France, have found means to encourage vessels from hence (Charleston) from New York, and other places which are not prohibited by the acts of trade; to truck those skins with them for Indian trading goods, especially the British woolen manufactures, which the French dispose of to the Creeks and Choctaws and other Indians, by which means the Indians are much more alienated from our interest; and on every occasion object to us, that the French can supply them with shrouds and blankets as well as the English, which would have the contrary effect, if they were wholly furnished with those commodities by your Majesty's subjects. If a stop were therefore put to that pernicious trade with the French, &c." Perhaps, there could not have been written a passage more highly eulogistic of the French mode of dealing with the Indians than that we have just read. They certainly were pursuing the very best mode of civilizing the savage, by appealing to his interests and stimulating his industry. It appears too that buying English goods, at an English market, they could yet undersell the British traders among the Indians. This must have been the case, else the Indians would never have given the preference to the French trade; since experience has sufficiently proved them to be as cunning in driving a bargain, as they are jealous of assumption, and distrustful to the last degree of imposition. The British memorialists modestly prayed to the King that the laws of trade,—those pernicious laws which so frequently defeat the energies of nations, and deprive trade of one of its greatest social advantages, an open market—should be so extended as to drive out all competition, and place the poor savages entirely at their mercy; a prayer to which the ruler has only too frequently hearkened, and the concession of which may fairly be assumed as the true cause of most of those bloody wars which the British colonist and his successor has been carrying on with the Indians for the last three hundred years.

On the occasion of Oglethorpe's visit to the Muscoghee nation at the head town of Coweta, glanced at in our last chapter, which had for its object the counteracting of the efforts of the French among the Indians, a treaty was made between the Muscoghees and the English, the importance of which was highly estimated by the latter. After enumerating the different and numerous tribes and principalities represented at this meeting, the treaty proceeds thus:—"The said estates being solemnly held, and opened at the great square of Coweta, and adjourned from thence to the town Cussitas; and the deputies having drank Black Drink together, according to the ancient custom of their nation, (being a religious form, transmitted down by their ancestors,) the whole estates declared by a general consent, without one negative, that they adhered in their ancient love to the King of Great Britain, and to their agreements made in the year 1739, &c.; and farther declared that all the dominions, territories and lands, from the river Savannah to the river St. John's, and all the islands between the said rivers; and from the river St. John's to the Bay of Apalachy, within which is all the Apalachy old fields; and from the said Bay of Apalachy to the mountains, *doth by ancient right belong to the Creek nation; and they have maintained possession of the said right, against all opposers by war; and can show the heaps of bones of their enemies slain by them in defence of the said lands.*" This clause partially determines their territorial boundaries. The festival of the "Black Drink," we may here add, is not merely a religious ritual. It is a wholesome physical policy which like many of those of the Jews, incorporated among the ceremonies of the church, had for its object nothing more than the purification of the animal. At one stated period of the year, when the fruits ripen, the different tribes assemble at a point sufficiently central, and celebrate the Green Corn Dance. The festival lasts usually for three days. In these three days they dance almost constantly, drinking at intervals of the Black Drink, which is a decoction of certain roots, having the effect of an emetic. They drink, dance, and vomit;—return to the decoction, and continue to drink and dance and vomit until the three days expire. The object seems to be a general purification of the people,—an object particularly important during our early vegetable season, and which is in use, to a certain extent, among the poor white people of our less healthy regions at the same period. The force of a religious ordinance seems to be necessary among all savage people, to impress the compliance with this policy upon them. They have other beverages of a more agreeable character, one of which is a mucilaginous drink made of dried corn; and it is more than probable that the wholesome and pleasant beer prepared from the sassafras root, which is so well known to us now, is a gift of Indian pharmacy.

The Muscoghees, according to the English account, seem to have been quite as much delighted with the visit of Oglethorpe and the subsequent treaty which he made with them, as the two colonies of South Carolina and Georgia certainly were. But these notions were, doubtlessly, mere illusions. The savages were pleased with the presents, the arms and the gewgaws, and while they lasted were faithful enough. But the latest gift worked a sudden forgetfulness of the past, and the new comer was most usually preferred to the preceding one. The Indians soon discovered from the solicitude of the whites,—English, Spanish and French,—that they, in fact, were the arbiters upon whom the safety and peace of the latter depended, and they were cunning enough to make the best market out of the several candidates. The French appear to have been the only people by whom they were moved, quite as much through the sentiments and the affections, as by the sordid interests which were too commonly employed for the temptation of their appetites or the subduing of their power. Perhaps it may be asserted with complete safety, that the French, in their dealings with the Indians, have quite as little to reproach themselves with as Penn and his associates, while their flexibility of habit and disposition made them companions more pleasing to the savage and more lastingly beloved.

In 1715 the Muscoghees joined the league with the Yemasee and other Indians, and invaded Carolina, but were defeated, and so severely scourged by the Carolinians, in several engagements, that they were glad to make peace. With the exception of occasional murders by small parties, they kept faithfully to their treaties; but still the whites distrusted them, and the colony of Georgia was founded by Carolina as a frontier for its protection from their incursions. In the dawn of the Revolution, and while the British fleet was preparing for its descent upon Charleston in 1776, their emissaries were busy exciting the Indians of the south and south-west, generally, to insurrection. The Cherokees prematurely commenced their work of massacre along the frontiers, but receiving a terrible chastisement from General Williamson, they were compelled to sue in the most submissive manner for peace. This timely punishment had an excellent effect upon their neighbours, and the Muscoghees remained quiet until the British had made themselves masters of the soil both of Carolina and Georgia. It was then impossible to forbear longer, and the invitation to join the British forces, and the temptation to plunder, brought thousands of them into the field. Of these, the Muscoghees were the most daring and active, and General Greene, then in command of the American army of the South, dispatched Wayne—mad Anthony—to encounter them. Wayne crossed into Georgia for this purpose, and with a small force fully executed the duty required from him. Vigilance, activity and bravery supplied the place of numbers, and so effectually did he maintain the barrier which he established between the Indian country and the lower parts of Georgia, that the savages found no avenue unguarded, none open to their approach. In their own words, "finding the path bloody and shut up," they began to return in small bodies to the nation. Several strong war parties of the Muscoghees alone remained, and with their accustomed tenacity, promised to do mischief, and required all the watchfulness of the experienced and brave chief opposed to them. Wayne was apprised of the approach among these war parties of the then famous warrior of the Creeks, Emistasego. Some time elapsed, however, and Wayne, watching with unrelaxing vigilance, remained without disturbance. He was then encamped on the Ogeechee road, four miles south-west of Savannah, having fixed upon that city the eye of the hawk, and meditating hourly to stoop upon the British who were crowded for shelter within its streets. At this time, with every avenue guarded, which might make his camp accessible, he yet found his precautions no security against the keen and subtle chief then in command of the Muscoghee warriors. Emistasego, at midnight, stole past the American Colonel, Clarke, who was expressly stationed to watch his coming from the west. He evaded spy and patrol and sentinel, and though the position which Wayne had taken, was chosen with the especial view of intercepting this very enemy, yet he gained the rear of the encampment without detection. Into the heart of the camp he led his party with equal impunity, and the only sentinel who started in alarm before him, he struck down with a sudden tomahawk. The first signal, announcing the presence of the enemy, was the terrific war-whoop. This was followed by a sharp, close fire upon the sleeping rearguard. Awaking, and finding the foe so much dreaded, close upon them, they fled to the cover of the houses. This left the artillery in possession of the savages, and to them, was convincing proof of their victory. Their exultation at possessing engines which are so greatly the object of an Indian's apprehensions, produced a pause in their progress, which, otherwise, must have led them to complete success. Had they pressed forward and prevented the rally of the Infantry, which they might easily have done, they must have routed the main body of the army before it could form. But not content with possession of the artillery, they lost the precious moment in an awkward effort to use it, and gave time to the flying troops to rally. Wayne was soon on horseback, his infantry formed, and the bayonet did its irresistible work upon the hitherto successful savages. They fled in confusion, but left Emistasego, their chief, some of their white allies, and about thirty of their warriors behind them on the field.

CHAPTER FOUR

It is a point of some importance in Muscoghee history, to be able to state, that from our first acquaintance with them, they occupied a territory, the limits of which were clearly designated by themselves, and seem generally to have been acknowledged by their neighbours. Their prowess in war may have been the reason for this tacit concession; but the first fact, it may be well to state, is not often the case with a barbarous people. They are seldom stationary, and invade and occupy the hunting lands of the neighbours whenever the game becomes scarce in their own. Some difficulties have arisen among our early geographers which a little attention to this fact might have obviated, and may still reconcile. They have found themselves frequently at a loss to detect the characteristics, and names and peculiarities, as described by preceding travellers among the Indians, and sometimes find them in absolute contrast with those which they themselves encounter in the same regions. This would be a matter of small difficulty if we would always recollect, that driving out the possessors of the soil, which they do constantly, the conquerors give it their own designations, and confer upon it all the distinctive peculiarities of their own nation. The name of the reigning Prince is frequently the name of the tribe,—that of the chief warrior distinguishes the war party under his command; and as these change their habitations, by choice or necessity, their names are eradicated by those who take their places. The American tribes were in constant motion, and it is more than probable, that when the Muscoghees are spoken of as a stationary people, nothing more is meant than that they confined themselves to certain geographical limits, which were sufficiently extensive to afford the means of subsistence to their hunters without rendering it necessary that they should invade their neighbours; and yet we have seen in the progress of this very narrative, that they sent out entire tribes, either in banishment as a punishment for some departure from their laws, or because of the great increase of their numbers,—this indeed, being the true history of the colonizing expeditions of most nations. The Yamacraws claim to have been a tribe of the Creeks; and Tomichichee, their mico, or chief, asserted himself to be a man banished from his people. The Muscoghees assert themselves to be an original, in other words, a pure, unmixed people. This matter is also a subject of very great doubt. It is very doubtful whether the race of Indians known to *us* now, are the descendants of those who raised the tumuli which are scattered over the face of the country. These tumuli seem altogether older than the people and as much beyond their capacity to raise, as are the thousand more imposing structures which are daily brought to light in our western and south-western forests. It is doubtful whether any of the Indians within the limits of the United States, bury in mounds at all at this moment; and it is not reasonable to think that a wandering people ever did so. The practice, in numberless instances, to the knowledge of the writer, is far otherwise now. It would be physically impossible, indeed, to bear the warrior engaged in a distant war, or in a forest hunt miles away from his hamlet, who happened to be slain, to a customary spot for burial; and it is in these expeditions that greater number of the savages perish. Besides, their villages have been generally of too temporary a character to have been intended for more than occasional abiding places during those intervals, in which they were spared from war and the chase for the repose and recreations of domestic life. The erection of these tumuli demanded too a greater amount of labor than the Indian was ever disposed to give to any object; and the race which devolved upon its women all its labor, and limited its agricultural efforts to the cultivation of a pitiable field of maize, was not likely to waste so much of it as these structures called for, on so useless an object as a dead warrior or a famished squaw. There is another and no less important objection to the belief, arising from its inconsistence with a practice better known to exist among them. This is the desire of concealing their dead from the vengeance of their enemies,—a desire which could not be more completely set at nought than by the ostentation of mound-burial. No scalp could possibly have been kept by its owner in a place so public as the tumulus; and wars, lacking all other provocation, would result continually from the mutual desecration of the several places of sepulture chosen by the rival nations of tribes. It cannot, however, be denied, that to a certain extent the Muscoghees were a stationary people. Tookanbatchie, one of their chief towns, in which they have held several conventions with the whites for the purpose of treaty-making, their tradition asserts to be that in which they first encountered the European for this same object. In an interview at Broken Arrow in 1824, the commissioners of the United States who were sent to treat with them for a further cession of their lands, having in the course of their speeches told them, (which was without question the truth) that they themselves were but usurpers of the soil, having come from the west and driven off the original proprietors, were told in reply, "that this was new to them." "*From all the traditions,*" said they, "*which have been handed down to us from our forefathers, we have been impressed with the belief that we are the original and sole proprietors of the soil;*"—and there is no evidence to the contrary. We have no reason to reject their belief, though there is much to throw suspicion upon it. None of their asservations are entirely to be relied on. Their speeches and letters are prepared for them by white men, most of whom are interested in keeping them where they are. These whites are generally from that class of borderers who acknowledge few of the obligations, as they know but few of the ties of civilized life. They enter the nation, take wives from among the tribe, possess themselves of lands, and from their superior intelligence, acquire influence enough among the savages to become their advisers, and in many instances their chiefs. These men, though self-banished from the dwellings of the whites, are not willing to remove utterly from their connection, and into a world consisting of savages only. They strenuously oppose, therefore, with all the cunning and steadiness of self-interest, every effort to persuade the Indians to a sale of their lands. They arm themselves with the conjectures and speculations of civilized men, to furnish weapons of defence in argument to the Indian; and thus it is that we have traditions of the past among this people, which have not, in numberless instances, even the air of *vraisemblance* to sustain them. It is, perhaps, utterly impossible, that any people to whom the rudiments of agricultural life are unknown, and who keep no cattle, can be a stationary people. Even herdsmen, in all primitive countries, are compelled to keep moving with the advancing seasons, and in search of pasturage. But, when first known to the European the Muscoghees were neither herdsmen nor agriculturalists. They were hunters of game, whom the constant use of arms in this pursuit made warriors; and who waged war in the defence of their own, or in invasion of other hunting lands than their own. War was the inevitable consequence of the collision of rival hunters. But to return:

In 1802, the Oconee River formed the eastern boundary of the Muscoghees, and the nation occupied about twenty millions of acres. Its population at this period is not exactly known. It may be estimated to have been thirty thousand or more; of these six or eight thousand may have been warriors. In that year by a treaty with the United States they made a cession of land for the benefit of Georgia, and in 1805, by another treaty, an additional territory; by these two conventions giving up nearly three millions of acres. So far, with few exceptions, from the Revolution down to the year 1812, their conduct had been comparatively pacific. Individuals had occasionally committed depredations upon the white settlers of Georgia and Alabama, occasionally stealing cattle, shooting hogs, and sometimes a traveller; but in these crimes the nation had taken no part, and in some instances had delivered up the criminals to punishment. But there was a moral groundswell upon the confines, arising from the continual struggle between civilized and barbarous life, which kept up a tacit hostility between the parties, even though positive blows were not the result. The vexing feeling of inferiority on the part of the savages,—the violent consciousness of superiority, and perhaps, a less elevated sentiment belonging to a mercenary desire for unemployed lands over which the Indian wandered, on the part of the whites, kept up by a sleepless jealousy between the two, which only waited a proper opportunity or some provocation more urgent than usual, to show itself in war. This was soon found when the long pending differences of the United States with Great Britain terminated in 1812, by the declaration of war on the part of the former. The emissaries of the latter nation, who have never been slow in such proceedings, availing themselves of the contest maintained by the Spaniards in certain stations on the Florida coast, penetrated into the country of the Creeks with the usual persuasives and arguments to Indian appetite; and in an evil hour for themselves, not less than for their neighbors, a majority of the nation put on red paint, and despatched the war club to their scattered partisans. The war club is not so much an effective instrument of battle, as a sign and symbol by which Indians who have resolved upon hostilities communicate their purpose to their allies. It is a stick varying from sixteen to twenty-four inches in length, painted red, sometimes sharpened at one end and terminating mace-like at the other; sometimes capped at one or both ends with a blade resembling a hatchet, formed in latter days of iron, but at the first period in Anglo-American history, of stone or flint. These are given into the hands of other runners before hostilities have commenced, who bear them to distant tribes, place them into the hands of other runners, who transmit them in like manner to tribes yet more distant, until the whole nation is aroused to an equal degree of preparedness and excitement. This custom resembles that of the burning brand among the early Scotch tribes, and is, indeed, the mode in use for conveying the signal of strife among all barbarous nations, being almost if not quite as rapid as the blaze from the headland heights, the "*beal*," or "bale-fire" of Ireland, and those employed by the Greeks in Homer's day, as beautifully described by Clytemnestra, in the opening of the 'Agamemnon' of Æschylus:

> "The fire, that from the height of Ida sent
> Its streaming light, as from the announcing flame
> Torch blazed to torch. First Ida to the steep
> Of Lemnos: Athos' sacred height received
> The mighty splendor, &c."

Only inferior to this startling and impressive incident, as coming after, and therefore, an imitation, is the beautiful passage in Scott's Lady of the Lake, descriptive of the like peculiarity among the Scotch:

> "Benledi saw the cross of fire;
> It glanced like lightning up Strath-Ire;—"
> —"Not faster o'er thy heathery braes
> Balquidder, speeds the midnight blaze,
> Rushing, in conflagration strong,
> Thy deep ravines and dells along,
> Wrapping the cliffs in purple glow,
> And reddening the dark lakes below;
> Nor faster speeds it, nor so far,
> As o'er thy heaths the voice of war!
> The signal roused to martial coil
> The sullen margin of Lockvoil,
> Waked still Loch Doine, and to the source
> Alarm'd, Balvaig, thy swampy course;
> Thence southward turned its rapid road
> Adown Strath-Gartney's valley broad,
> 'Till rose in arms each man might claim
> A portion in Clan-Alpine's name,
> From the gray sire, whose trembling hand
> Could hardly buckle on the brand,
> To the raw boy, whose shaft and bow
> Were yet scarce terror to the crow.
> Each valley, each sequestered glen,

Muster'd its little horde of men
That met, as torrents from the height
Of highland dales their streams unite,
Still gathering, as they pour along
A voice more loud, a tide more strong,
Till at the rendezvous they stood
By hundreds, prompt for blows and blood;
Each trained to arms since life began,
Owing no tie but to his clan,
No oath but by his Chieftain's hand,
No law, but Roderick Dhu's command."

The practice as prevailing among all our Indian tribes is not less available for the purposes of poetry, and we may confidently look for the day to arrive, when the Genius Loci will wed it to strains of immortality worthy of those of the divine minstrels to whom we have made brief reference. Nothing could well be made more picturesque, than the sudden and startling appearance of the grim warrior, silent and stern, gleaming with the frightful hues with which he colours himself for battle, rushing into the quiet village, amidst the reposing warriors, the toiling women, and the playful children, engaged in the sports of mimic strife, displaying his red brand aloft, while the warriors leap to arms, and the fierce whoop of war proclaims their immediate recognition of the signal, and their readiness to obey its summons. The scene is one alike worthy of poet and painter.

But the red-stick, (which usually confers its name upon all the warriors who grasp it,) is not merely a symbol. It is occasionally used in battle, when, having introduced confusion into the ranks of the enemy, nothing is more necessary than to pursue and destroy. It answers the purpose of the tomhag, and since the acquaintance of the Indians with the Europeans, is used only by those who have not been able to provide themselves with the hatchet, or who may have lost it in flight or battle. On the present occasion the red-stick was presented to the Muscoghees by no less a personage than the celebrated Tecumtheh. This great chief, who combining all the small subtlety of the savage with the extended views of the European, was the Metacom of the Western frontier, conceived the bold idea of concentrating all the Indian tribes in the limits of the United States in one concerted action against the whites. Having, with the aid of his brother, the Prophet Elkswatawha, stimulated his own people, the Shawanee, (or as I should write it, the Chowannee,) to the proper pitch of excitement, he next addressed himself to the Muscoghees as, probably, at once the most warlike and powerful of all the savage nations. He repaired to Tookanbatchie, in Georgia, sometime in the spring of 1812, and had several conferences with the chiefs. These were not as unanimous as he wished to find them. Two or three of them were decidedly friendly to the Americans, among these the warrior with whose fortunes and summary fate we propose to close this narrative—Thle-cath-cha, alias William Mackintosh, generally distinguished by the honorary title of General Mackintosh. Tecumtheh then passed from the Georgia tribes to those of Alabama with whom he was more successful. These acting upon their brethren in Georgia produced the effect, and something more than the effect which Tecumtheh desired. He, while arousing them to hostility, was careful in counselling them to keep up until a certain season all the pacific appearances, which he himself had so long and so cunningly maintained; but he had scarcely left the territory on his return to his own, than the torch which he had laid, broke out into a flame; and the young warriors in little squads, in which they pursued the common objects of hunters and warriors, proceeded to attack the frontier settlers, and committed several shocking murders within the limits of Tennessee and Georgia. An attempt on the part of Col. Hawkins, the agent for the United States among the Indians, to punish the murderers with death, served to complete what Tecumtheh had begun. The red-sticks flew to arms, and the peace-party then greatly in the minority, were compelled either to join their ranks, or take refuge in the few white military posts established on the frontiers by the whites, or in the white settlements of Georgia. Their numbers momently increased, and the elite of the nation were in little time prepared for the sanguinary war which was to follow.

To sound the war-whoop was to strike the blow. The action of the Indian warrior is a part of the resolve which prompts him; and once in the field the Muscoghees industriously employed themselves in seeking out their enemy. The campaign was commenced by one of their prophets, named Francis, seconded by a brave and noble warrior named Weatherford, who led a force of eight or nine hundred men down to Fort Mimms, a stockaded fort on the Tensau river about ten miles above Fort Stoddart, and some thirty-five miles below St. Stephen's, then a chief town on the Tombeckbe. The stockade was one of little or no strength; and had been hastily put up around the residence of one of the border settlers, whose name it received. The alarm had been given by some of the friendly Indians of the approach of the *red-sticks*, and the women and children of the vicinity to the number of one hundred and thirty were placed in it for safety. The fort was garrisoned by a detachment of "twelve months men," commanded by Major Beasly, who had been detached for this service by General Claiborne. These, with the men capable of bearing arms who lived in the neighborhood, amounted to one hundred and seventy, rank and file; a small force, scarcely equal to that led by the Indians, not experienced in war, and probably not sufficiently on their guard, having an enemy so wily in their vicinity. The remissness or obstinacy of the officer in command seems to have reached a criminal extent, as it appears that a negro had reported the presence of lurking Indians about the fort, and was punished for false information. At first the *red-sticks* made their approach with sufficient caution,—some days elapsed after reaching the neighbourhood before they commenced the attack. It is probable that this delay arose from prophetic intimation from Francis, whom they implicitly obeyed, and whose predictions they superstitiously confided in. But the storm broke at last over the devoted fort. On the morning of the 30th August, 1813, a little before day break, they commenced the attack with a force and fury calculated to strike terror into the hearts of those, who at this moment, though warned, were not sure of their propinquity. Instigated by exhortations of the Prophet who had assured them of victory, and promised them a thousand things besides, sublunary and eternal, they rushed to the assault. He led the assault in person with a confident zeal that showed an equal reliance upon his own predictions with that which he had impressed upon his followers. His assault was not less ably conceived than conducted. His force was divided into three bodies; one of these armed with axes, marched boldly up to the pickets in several places, and proceeded to hew them down. For the protection and covering of these, another stationed body kept up a continual fire on the defenders who made their appearance in conflict with the axemen; while a third party, in constant movement, encircled the fortress, availing itself of every opportunity for favorable assaults, and by their continual clamor, and dreadful cries, diverting and distracting the minds of the few and devoted defenders. When an axeman was shot down his place was instantly filled up and his axe employed by one of the battle division, until after continued efforts, a sufficient number of pickets was cut down to enable the assailants to effect an entrance. If the unfortunate commander of the stockade erred in the first instance by an excess of confidence either in his position, or in his faith in the pacific disposition of the Indians, it is due to his memory to say, that he strove to repair his error by an exhibition of bravery which has not often been exceeded. The moment that the pickets were forced he placed his own body in the breach, and his example was followed by a resolute troop, who like himself, were prepared for the worst. A dreadful conflict, hand to hand ensued, and overpowered by numbers, the brave commander perished with every man who stood beside him, not however, before they had sacrificed thrice their own number of the reckless savages. The women and children rushed for the block-house when the fate of their defenders was known, but numbers of them were overtaken and cut down before they could reach it. Nor were those who did so more fortunate. The cruel savages put fire to the building, and thrusting back the unhappy inmates as they sought to rush forth from the blazing timbers, they perished miserably among the burning ruins. But eight persons escaped from the fortress, and these only through the blind drunkenness of heart with which success had filled the savages. More than three hundred perished, of whom nearly two hundred were women and children, equally incapable of injury and defence. The Muscoghees paid dearly for their victory,—it having been ascertained that more than two hundred warriors were killed and full as many wounded.

Chapter Five

The campaign thus bloodily and successfully commenced by the Muscoghees, was continued with the utmost fury. The panic which their progress excited in the minds of the white borderers is beyond description. The poor wretches, acting without concert, and scattered over an extensive territory where unanimity was next to impossible, fled in small bodies with their little families to the nearest places of shelter. The stockade posts were generally abandoned in the night as no longer places of security, and the roads were covered by the despairing and confounded refugees, hurrying without thought, and enduring every sort of suffering and privation, in seeking to escape from their howling and triumphant enemy. They crowded upon the towns in neighbouring States, bringing terror and dismay wherever they came. The Muscoghees followed fast upon their heels. Their homes were no sooner abandoned than they were burnt—their blazing corn-fields frequently gave light to their flying footsteps, and the shot which destroyed their cattle often sounded in the ears. Many fell under the hatchets of the savages, who, scattering themselves in pursuit, left traces of their presence every where in blood.

But if the success of the Muscoghees so far, had intoxicated them, it had also the effect of rousing a spirit which it was utterly beyond their power to lay. On the receipt of the cruel intelligence in Tennessee, the militia of that State were summoned to the standard of a leader who may be termed, by excellence, the very master of Indian warfare. General Jackson, having the command, led them at once into the Muscoghee territories. In the meantime, the red-sticks or the war party of the Muscoghees, having driven out or destroyed all of the white settlements, turned upon the people of their own nation who had refused to espouse their cause. The peace party was under the direction of Chinnabee, a brave warrior and one of their chiefs, who imme-diately concentrated such a force as he could collect, of those who felt with him, at a fort near the Ten Islands on the Coosa river, to which his name was given. To this point the war party addressed themselves, and the steps of General Jackson were hurried by the intelligence that Chinnabee was in im-mediate danger from their leaguer. Shelocta the son of Chinnabee, was him-self despatched to the army of Tennessee to solicit immediate relief for his father. His entreaties were strengthened by the arrival, a few days after, of two runners sent by Path-killer, a chief of the Cherokees, who reached the camp bringing information that the Indians from nine of the hostile towns were assembling near the Ten Islands and threatening the several stations of the friendly Creeks and Cherokees in the same neighbourhood. Without provi-sions, Jackson pressed forward, dismissing the messengers of Path-killer with the cool and confident answer:—"Go back to the chief,—say, that the hostiles will not trouble him until they have first met with me; and that, I think, will put them out of the notion of fighting for sometime at least."

When arrived within a few miles of the Ten Islands the army was met by old Chinnabee, bringing with him two prisoners. It was then found that some of the advices which Jackson had received were untrue and the apprehensions of the peace party premature. The intelligence now brought was, that the enemy in considerable force had posted themselves at Tallushatchie, on the south side of the Coosa and about thirteen miles from the army. Gen. Coffee was despatched accordingly with nine hundred mounted men, forming a brigade, to attack and disperse them. Before this was done, Col. Dyer, who, on a march to the Ten Islands with a force of two hundred cavalry, had been sent against the town of Littafutchie which stands at the head of a creek called

Canoe Creek, which empties into the Coosa from the west, succeeded in destroying the town and making twenty-nine prisoners.

General Coffee under the guidance of friendly Indians, proceeded to the execution of his enterprise. Fording the Coosa at the Fish Dams, about four miles above the Islands, he encamped beyond it until the next day, when he renewed his march and pressed forward with all diligence upon the steps of the enemy. When within a mile and a half of the town of Tallushatchie, he formed his detachment into two divisions and directed their equal march, so that, on the union of their respective heads, the town might be completely environed. He was not suffered to carry out his plan, unnoticed, to completion. The Muscoghees were soon apprized of the approaching danger and began to prepare for action. Their drums were beaten and their yells and war-whoop added terror to the clamors of their music. The action was commenced about an hour after sunrise by two companies of spies and the commands of Captain Hammond and Lieutenant Patterson, which had passed, by instruction, within the circle of alignment in order to draw the Indians out of their fastnesses. The exhibition of their force, to the town, and the discharge of a few scattering shot, had the effect. The provocation was not to be withstood by the savages, who, with all their cunning, may be moved to indiscretion in war by a proper provocation of their impulses. They rushed forth in considerable numbers, and the companies of spies gave way under the impetuous violence of their charge. These were pursued until they reached the main body, which, opening a general fire upon the pursuers, charged in turn. The Muscoghees fighting bravely all the while, fled, though slowly, until they got behind the buildings or within them. An obstinate conflict now ensued. They maintained their ground, fighting desperately to the last, while they could lift a weapon or an arm, neither giving nor asking quarter. They were killed almost to a man, and, unhappily, some few of their women and children among them. From the manner in which they fought, huddled up together, this misfortune was unavoidable. Their loss was one hundred and eighty-six slain. There were eighty-four women and children taken captives. Of the Americans five were killed and forty-one wounded. Two were killed by arrows, which, on this occasion, formed a principal part of the arms of the Muscoghees; to these they resorted after the first fire of their pieces, which they threw aside until an opportunity was given for reloading them.

Meantime the hostile Muscoghees were busy. In great numbers they beleaguered a fort of the peace party called Talladega, and pressed it so closely that it was soon evident that it must fall into their hands. The army of Jackson was about thirty miles off from this station. He received the tidings by a runner, and with that decisive promptness which is, perhaps, one of the greatest excellencies of a warrior, he at once put his troops in motion for the scene of strife. To find the Indians embodied is the chief difficulty in this sort of warfare. The ease with which they can scatter and hide themselves and again unite at a signal, is the secret of their successful evasion, in most cases, of the arms of the conqueror. Leaving behind him his sick, wounded and baggage, with every thing not absolutely necessary, or which might obstruct the rapidity of his movement, he set out at midnight with twelve hundred infantry and eight hundred mounted gun-men and cavalry. The river, which, at the crossing place, was six hundred yards wide, was crossed by the army on horseback, each of the mounted men taking one of the foot soldiers behind him. Still, as the number of the latter greatly exceeded that of the former, it was necessary to send back the horses for the residue. This made the passage tedious. Several hours were consumed before it was completed. But this did not materially affect the rapidity of movement which Jackson had resolved upon. Though deprived of sleep and thus delayed, the army continued the march with animation, and by evening had arrived within six miles of the enemy. This forced march was of the most important consequence, since nothing could be more so than the protection of the Muscoghees who had declared for the whites, and whom the runners had represented to be in momentary peril of falling into the hands of their furious and embittered brethren. Yet, though marching with such rapidity, Jackson used the utmost circumspection to prevent surprise. He led his army, as was his constant habit, in three columns, which, by a speedy manœuvre, he might place in such a position as to resist attack from any quarter. His march was uninterrupted.

When he reached the neighbourhood of the Fort, he found the hostile Muscoghees posted in great force around, and within a quarter mile of, it. They numbered probably twelve hundred men, and were well disposed to annoy the Fort and defend themselves against the Americans. The quick military eye of General Jackson did not hesitate, however, to perceive the route which lay to victory, and his resolute mind at once proceeded to avail himself of it. He determined to lose no time in bringing the enemy to action. By four o'clock in the morning, the army, which had travelled thirty miles the day preceding, and that too without sleep the night before, was again in motion. At seven o'clock it was displayed in order of battle. At eight, the advance, having arrived within eighty yards of the enemy who were hidden in a thick shrubbery, covering the edge of a small rivulet, received their fire. This was returned with spirit, and the men pressing forward, the enemy was dislodged. This done, the advance fell back according to orders upon the centre. The Muscoghees now emerged from their covering, and, yelling furiously, rushed forward upon a brigade commanded by General Roberts, a few companies of which alarmed by their shouts and numbers, fled at the first fire. Jackson soon filled the chasm with a portion of his reserve. The militia seeing their places supplied, rallied, resumed their position in line, and joined in check-ing the advance of the hostiles. The action now became general and fierce along the line; but it was of no long duration. The onset of the Americans was terrible, the slaughter great, and in fifteen minutes after the armies had fairly joined; the Indians were flying in all directions. The plan of Jackson had been such that they were nearly environed. On the left, as they fled, they were met and driven back by the mounted riflemen, and, but for the halt of Bradley's regiment, which was directed to occupy the extreme right, and the too great circuit made by Colonel Allen who commanded one wing of the cavalry, they must have all perished or surrendered at discretion. The spaces left open by these failures enabled the survivors to escape from the enclosure. But they were closely pursued for three miles until they found shelter in the moun-tains. They left three hundred of their number upon the field of battle, and many more are supposed to have perished in the pursuit. Probably few of them escaped unhurt. Subsequently, they admitted a loss of six hundred warriors.

This was a terrible chastisement to the Muscoghees, but their battles had only begun. Another division of the American army under General White, about the same time, surprised one of their towns on the Tallapoosa river, slew sixty of their warriors and made prisoners of nearly three hundred. This event was followed by the invasion of a third army from Georgia under the command of General Floyd. He soon reached the two Autossee towns on the same river, which the Indians under the assurance of their Prophets, con-ceived to be not only sacred, but secure from the invasion of the whites. He attacked both of the towns at the same moment, and was resisted with uncommon bravery. It was only after a close and hard conflict of nearly three hours, that the Muscoghees were defeated and driven at the point of the bayonet into the forests. Their two towns were given to the flames and they lost two hundred warriors including the kings of Tallassee and Autossee. The month following was distinguished among the Muscoghees by another disaster of the same sort, and from a different quarter. Colonel Claiborne advanced upon them from Alabama, and coming suddenly upon the towns of Eccanachaca above the mouth of the Cahawba, upon the river of Alabama, he completely destroyed them and killed thirty of their warriors without the loss of a man.

One of the events above recorded must be regarded with particular regret. It is that of General White's attack of the Hillabee town on the Tallapoosa River. The Hillabee tribes had suffered severely, and principally by the victories of Jackson; and their emissaries, suing for peace, were in the camp of the latter when White's victory was obtained. They had asked peace from Jackson on his own terms, and he had specified its conditions. "They must afford evidence," said he, "of the sincerity of their professions for peace. They must restore the prisoners and the property they have taken from us,—they must restore the friendly Creeks; and the instigators of the war,—the murderers of our citizens must be surrendered." The latter demand, though untenable in the case of an independent nation, was yet reasonable enough in the case of a tributary. The effect of White's victory at this moment was a serious evil. The people of the Hillabee tribes believed themselves to be attacked by the army of Jackson, and when they found themselves assailed, as they imagined, by the chief who had promised them peace, they no longer entertained a hope of it,—they regarded the war as one of extermination; and in all their battles afterwards they neither asked quarter nor manifested the slightest disposition to receive it.

The various and severe losses of the nation in these several conflicts were yet not enough to subdue the spirit of the Muscoghee warriors. So far from their having this effect, the Indians seem only to have been stimulated by them into acts of newer daring or desperation. General Jackson was advancing to the relief of Fort Armstrong which was threatened by the warriors of no less than fifteen towns on the Tallapoosa, when they proceeded to attack him. But so excellent a warrior was not to be taken by surprise. He was ready for the attack which was made upon his left flank by the dawn of day. Their assault was furious, as is that of the Indian always. He springs like a tiger from his jungle, and failing in his first effort slinks back into cover waiting for newer opportunities. The Muscoghees were beaten off at all quarters, and after a severe but brief conflict, fled in every direction. They were chased about two miles and suffered considerable loss. But still they held their encampment, and General Coffee with four hundred men was despatched to destroy it. Having reconnoitred their position, he found it too strong for his force and returned to the main body for support. He had scarcely done so, when the Muscoghees renewed the assault with quite as much fury as before and with the same success. They were a second time beaten off, and the fugitives now took refuge on the margin of a reedy creek where they lay hidden. It was well that General Jackson, with consummate foresight, commanded his troops not to follow. The attack was but a feint,—the main attack was now made by the Muscoghees with greater judgment, and with their main force, which had been concealed before on the left of the army. They were met by Jackson in person who received them with a cool and immovable firmness which defied all their assaults. The battle was maintained by the assailants from behind logs, trees, shrubs, and indeed any thing that offered the slightest prospect of protection, with a tenacity that denoted no less resolution than hate. But they withered and fled before the charge, which was made under the lead of Col. Carroll. They fell in great numbers on the field and during the pursuit, but their loss was never correctly ascertained. This, however, did not end the sanguinary combat. The Muscoghees upon the right, whom General Coffee had driven into cover, were yet to be dispersed; and finding that this could not be done by assault without immediate danger, the General resolved upon a stratagem which had the desired result. He ordered his men to retire, and believing the movement to be a retreat, the warriors rushed from their hiding places, and with wild yells commenced pursuit. Their appearance was a signal to Coffee to wheel upon his own ground and contend with them on equal terms. The action had lasted an hour with great loss to both sides, and still the parties continued nearly equal. At this juncture Jackson, having dispersed the enemy upon the left, despatched a re-inforcement to his right which put an end to the battle. A dreadful slaughter followed, in which it is believed that scarce a warrior escaped. Thus ended a day of almost continual combat, which could not have terminated so favourably to the Americans but for the falling off of one of the Muscoghee tribes. The Cheallegreans were to have made one of the attacking parties which were to be three instead of two. This tribe, having passed that part of the army which they were to attack, without being seen, instead of doing so, kept on their way and retreated safely to their villages. The severe fighting to which the Americans were subjected from the action with the two divisions makes the inference fair, that it might not have been so easy to escape the concerted assault of the three.

Jackson having effected the object of his march, which was to make a diversion in favor of the Georgia army under General Floyd, who was carrying on his operations lower down on the Tallapoosa, began his return to the camp at the Ten Islands. This he continued without interruption the day following the fight at Emuckfau. Towards night he became convinced from certain signs that his inveterate enemies were in pursuit, and he immediately proceeded to throw up a breastwork. But the night wore away without disturbance. He had been too well provided for attack; and resolving to renew his march the next day, he concluded that the hostiles would prepare for him an ambuscade at the first fitting place and opportunity. There was a creek in his front which he had to cross, the banks of which being steep, rugged, and thickly covered with reeds and umbrage, seemed well calculated for ambush. A deep ravine running between two hills overgrown with brown sedge and shrubbery, led to this passage and increased its dangers. At midnight Jackson despatched a select corps of pioneers to find another route. This was done, and the head column of the army moved aside from the ambuscade, which had been admirably prepared for its reception. The army had reached a handsome slope of woodland leading to the new ford, the view of which was unobstructed, and sprinkled but not covered with reeds. The front-guards and a part of the columns with the wounded had passed, and the artillery was just entering the water, when the Indians, who, by this time, had discovered the alteration of the route, commenced a furious attack upon the rear. They were resisted with spirit by a company under the command of Captain Russell. Though assailed by a force so greatly its superior, it returned the fire, gradually retiring until it reached the rear-guard, which, according to previous instructions, was to face about in the event of attack and act as the advance, while the right and left columns, turning on their pivots so as to loop the enemy, would have rendered his destruction certain. But the onset of the Muscoghees was too sudden and severe to permit such a deliberate movement at such a moment. The rage and astonishment of Jackson was unspeakable, when, calculating on victory only, he beheld the right and left columns of the rear-guard, after a feeble effort at resistance, precipitately give way, bringing confusion where they fled, and obstructing the passage in their flight over which the main army had now to be re-crossed. Nothing but the determined valor of a few could have saved the army. Nearly the whole of the centre column followed the shameful example of the other two and precipitated itself into the creek, and not more than twenty persons remained to oppose the violence of the first assault. The artillery company of Lieutenant Armstrong, composed of young men of the first families, who had volunteered at the commencement of the campaign, formed themselves with their muskets before a piece of ordnance, and hastily dragged it from the creek to an eminence where they could play it to advantage. Here ensued an obstinate conflict. The possession of the piece was the object of the enemy who addressed their whole endeavours to this task. But the artillerists held their ground against the repeated charges of four times their number, and though suffering dreadful loss, yet effectually checked their advance. They preferred death to flight. Armstrong fell at the side of his piece, crying out where he lay: "Some of you must perish, but don't lose the gun." Many fell around him before Jackson could relieve the rest. This he did, after a few minutes, with complete effect. The Indians were defeated after a warm struggle, and fled, leaving behind them their blankets and every thing that could impede their flight. They were pursued for miles and dispersed. Their loss was great,— more than two hundred of those who went out to battle never returned to their homes. A few days only had elapsed after this event, when General Floyd, with the Georgia troops, was attacked in like manner, by warriors from the same gallant tribes, and though he defeated them with considerable loss, his own was proportionably great. Seventeen of his men were killed outright, and nearly one hundred and fifty wounded.

These severe chastisements, it might be supposed, would have brought the hostiles to their senses, but it only increased their desperation. They were reserved for punishments yet more terrible; and, strengthened by reinforcements, Jackson resumed the offensive. On 21st March, 1814, he set out for "Hickory Ground," where the Muscoghees were embodied in force. His entire force was about three thousand men. At ten o'clock on the morning of the 27th, he reached the villages of Tokopeka, where the warriors from the four neighbouring towns of Oakfuskie, Hillabee, Eufalee, and New Youcka, amounting to twelve hundred men or more, were in readiness awaiting his approach. Their position was admirably chosen for defense. It was naturally a fortress and their cabins had greatly strengthened it. Almost surrounded by the Tallapoosa, it received the shape of the horse-shoe from the turnings of the river, and from this physical feature it was called the Bend of the Horse Shoe. It was accessible only by the narrow neck of land that prevented its utter isolation. This neck was probably three hundred yards wide, and was secured with considerable art by the defenders, who had placed large timbers and trunks of trees horizontally upon each other, leaving open but a single place of entrance. From a double row of port-holes formed within it, they were enabled, while living in complete security themselves, to give the most admirable direction to their fire.

The arrangement of their force indicated the presence of superior military command, and required the utmost judiciousness in the conduct of any attack which could hope to be successful. It was obvious that an enemy so posted was fully equal to five times its number. But these preparations proved no discouragement to an assailant like Jackson. He, at once, proceeded to his own arrangements. General Coffee with the mounted Infantry and friendly Indians were despatched early in the morning with orders to gain the southern bank of the river, completely encircle the bend, and so manœvre as to divert, as far as he might, the Muscoghees from the point at which the main assault was intended to be made. One other object of this provision was to prevent the escape of the Indians in their canoes, with which it was understood that their side of the river was completely girdled, in readiness for use. Coffee soon executed his commission, and announced by signals his perfect readiness for action. Jackson meanwhile, with the rest of the army, took post directly in front of the breastwork. His cannon was planted upon an eminence about two hundred yards distant from it. His infantry and riflemen ensconced behind such shelter as the woods offered, were placed considerably nearer and within the point of effective operations. These were watchful as the Indians happened to show themselves from behind their works. The artillery opened its fire upon their defences, and though well served, was kept up for several minutes without making any impression, so admirably had the Indians sheltered themselves. But his preparations having been completed, Coffee in readiness, and the troops anxious for a charge, the Commander-in-chief gave orders for the assault. A fine spirit of emulation between the regulars and the militia exhibited itself in simultaneous expressions of impatience at the slow progress of the affair. They were led, the former by Col. Williams and Major Montgomery, and the latter by Col. Bunch. Rushing through a destructive fire, they soon reached the ramparts, and a close strife, hand to hand, ensued between the combatants, each contending for the possession of the port-holes. So close was the conflict that the balls from the rifles of the Muscoghees, were, in many instances, welded between the bayonets and muskets of the assailants. At this moment, the crisis of the action as it were, Major Montgomery of the Regulars leapt upon the breast-work, calling upon his men to follow. The next moment he was shot through the head and fell backward to the ground. But the troops had followed his lead in numbers,—the ramparts were generally scaled; and finding their post no longer tenable, the Muscoghees fell back among the brush and timber that thickly covered the peninsula, and renewed the combat. For a time their fire was galling and destructive; but a second charge again drove them backward, and being pressed, the only means left them of escape lay in their canoes. To these, therefore, they rushed, but only to discover new occasion for despair. The opposite banks were closely watched by the troops of Coffee, which stood waiting their approach. Dreading an encounter with fresh enemies, they turned upon their old ones, and leaping along the banks, or concealing themselves among the cliffs and steeps, which were covered every where with trees and umbrages, they carried on a desultory fight as opportunity offered for firing. General Jackson, seeing that however long the conflict might be delayed, their final destruction was yet inevitable, sent a flag with an interpreter, proposing a surrender. But the flag was fired upon in answer and one of the party wounded. The proposal may not have been properly explained, the proposition not understood; or, remembering the treatment of the Hillabee tribes on a previous occasion, which had been assailed by General Roberts while soliciting peace from Jackson, they may have despaired of any treaty with their vindictive enemy. Whatever may have been the motives for resistance, the consequences were sufficiently painful. They had a warrior opposed to them capable of driving them by strategy like their own from all their retreats. Lighted torches were thrown down the steeps,—the brush was ignited, and driven forth from their loop-holes and crannies, they darted out into the view of the watchful riflemen. The carnage continued until night separated the combatants, bringing that opportunity of escape to the surviving warriors which another hour of day-light would have utterly denied them. The village of Tokopeka which stood upon the peninsula, but at some distance from the fortifications, was destroyed by fire while the battle lasted, by a detachment from the brigade of Coffee. This event, by distracting the attention of the warriors from the assault in front, contributed in no small degree to the success of the assailants.

This battle annihilated the hopes of the hostile Muscoghees, even if it did not utterly annihilate their power. The best and most daring of their warriors were slain in the action. But few escaped the carnage. Of the killed, many were thrown into the river while the battle raged; many were drowned in flight, and nearly six hundred of them were left dead upon the ground. Three of their Prophets, dressed in the sacred garments, were among the slain. They had taken a conspicuous lead in the conflict, had howled, danced, exhorted, implored, and prayed, while it was in progress,—scarring their faces with sharp flints, and running fearlessly among the combatants with grimaces and contortions most frightful and disgusting to behold. To them may be attributed the continuance of the conflict when resistance became hopeless. The arts of deception have their phrenzy quite as often as the proselytes which they beguile. Monohoe, their chief Prophet, of great eminence for his divinations, was one of those who perished.

Many of the Muscoghees now applied for peace, particularly when they discovered that so far from being contented with the victories already won, their resolute conqueror was pressing into the very heart of the nation. But Jackson who knew the faithlessness of the tribes, doubting their sincerity, demanded, as a first condition, that they should bring Weatherford, their most able chief, as a captive to his camp, that he might suffer death for the conspicuous part which he had taken in the massacre at Fort Mimms. The bold savage waited not to be delivered, but without being personally known, fearlessly presented himself at the quarters of the General.

"Who are you?" demanded Jackson.

"Weatherford!—I am he who commanded at Fort Mimms."

"I commanded that you should be brought to me confined—bound," said Jackson.

"It did not need," was the calm reply, "I am in your power,—your soldiers are around me,—do with me as you please;—but give peace to my nation."

"Had they brought you to me bound, I should have known what to do with you," said Jackson, "You have murdered my people without cause."

"I am a warrior," replied the bold barbarian, "I fought like a warrior. I did my enemy all the harm I could, for he was my enemy. I fought him, and fought him without fear. If I had an army, I would fight him still; but I have none. I come for my nation,—they want peace;—you have killed all my warriors,—I can only weep like a woman."

The air of natural nobleness which spoke in the manner and the eye of the savage, not less than his language, was pleasing to his conqueror.

"I do not ask you to make peace," said Jackson,—"I have told your people my conditions. If they do not like them—go. I will take no advantage of your coming. Go to the war-party and resume your arms. I will seek you in the nation,—but if I take you captive, you shall die for your butcheries of my women and children."

"Ah!" was the melancholy answer of the savage, "it is well that you can talk to me such words. Where is my people,—who will you fight now? There was a day when I could have rejoiced to bring my warriors to meet you. But I have now no choice. I cannot speak life into the dead,—my warriors hear my words no longer. They lie at Talladega, at Tallushatchie, at Emuckfau, at Tokopeka. I have not come to you thoughtlessly. Whilst I could fight you I asked no peace. But I can fight you no longer. My people are gone,—I ask peace now for my nation. I am sorry for what is done,—I would keep from my nation worse calamities. It is from you that I ask for peace. If I had been left to fight with the Georgia army only, I would have raised my corn on one bank of the river and fought them on the other. It is you that have destroyed my nation. You are a brave man,—I rely upon your generosity. You will make no laws for a conquered people but such as are generous. Whatever you say they will submit to. It is folly to oppose you. If any of my people do oppose your laws, I, Weatherford, will bring them to obedience. The few who hold out must not sacrifice the country. Your talk is a good one,—my people shall listen to it."

"You shall go back to your people," was the reply of Jackson, "you shall persuade them to bury the hatchet. You shall carry them my terms of peace. You are a brave warrior,—you will not deceive me if I let you go."

"No!" was the prompt reply of the chief, putting his hand upon his breast as he spoke, "Weatherford will carry peace to his nation."

THOUGH SOMETIMES CALLED A STORY, "The Broken Arrow. An Authentic Passage from Unwritten American History" is (as the title indicates) expository, a combination of essay and history. Like "Thle-cath-cha," it reflects Simms's scholarly interest in Native American history, in this instance particularly that revolving around the exploits and assassination of William McIntosh, a topic Simms became fascinated with as a young man. Though the opening paragraph of "The Broken Arrow" is essentially repetitious of the opening paragraphs of "Thle-cath-cha," it is included here because of the insight it provides to Simms's initial and revised purposes.

ᴄᴡ *The Broken Arrow. An Authentic Passage from Unwritten American History*

By the author of "The Yemassee," "The Kinsman," etc.

["Thlecathcha," or the "Broken Arrow," is, or was, the very romantic name of a portion of country, lying in the Muscoghee territory, within the limits of Georgia. In this narrative, however, we have thought it not unseemly to apply this epithet to a chief, who, for a long period of time, was the master-spirit among his people, and whose erring aims, and melancholy fate, fairly deserve the appellation. The writer of this narrative, then a mere youth, happening, a few weeks after the assassination of General William Mackintosh, to pass through the nation in the immediate vicinity of the scene of execution, had his attention necessarily drawn to a subject which was then in the mouths of all around him, and upon which the general opinions were equally numerous and conflicting. In this manner he picked up, as well from Indian as from white authorities, sundry small particulars relating to the event. These were treasured in his memory, without effort; and, subsequently, the possession of certain documents—public, but little read or known—which furnished him with additional material—induced and enabled him to throw together the details which follow. These, in his opinion, form an exceedingly interesting passage in our unwritten domestic history, and may assist some more comprehensive chronicler, hereafter, in elaborating the train of events which are coupled with this, in the fortunes of the decaying people whom it mostly concerns. The reader will please to understand, however, that strict accuracy is not pretended to in regard to the minor details of this narrative. In the case of oral relations, depending, as they must, upon the uncertain memories of men—uncertain in the most tenacious instances—error becomes unavoidable, even where the spirit of the narrator is most conscientious. But the substantial truth of the leading events in this sketch,—the vital facts—may all be religiously relied on; and will be found freer from mistake of detail, and misconstruction of intention, than is commonly the case with what is usually called history. He may add, by way of further warning to the reader, of evil yet to come, that, by dipping thus deeply into the Indian chronicle, the author was insensibly beguiled farther than he originally designed to go, and before he well knew what he had done, had written out the whole known History of the Muscoghee Nation—gathered from its traditions and our chronicles, from the very moment, when, "covered with red hair, their gigantic ancestor, with thunder on his tongue, and a sheaf of lightening in his hand, sprang out of the chambers of the sun, in the west, and set forth on those conquests, turned eastward, which left his descendants in possession of their Apalachian hunting-grounds." But sufficient for the day is the evil thereof. At present, we will afflict the reader with a more brief, certain and matter-of-fact narrative.]

The war of 1812 with Great Britain brought, as is well known, the Creek nation of Indians into the field against us. Stimulated by the emissaries of the British, and bribed with their treasure, the bloody atrocities which they committed will long be remembered along the frontiers of the South and West. Scourged and humbled by the conduct and valor of that great man, Andrew Jackson,—the Indians sued for peace and obtained it; but only, among other conditions, by a large cession of their lands, the possession of which, by the whites along the borders, was justly esteemed necessary to their security and peace. This cession was followed, in 1818, by another, in which two other large tracts of territory were surrendered; and, by a treaty in 1821, a third cession made the Flint and Chatahooché rivers the Eastern boundary of the "nation." These subsequent cessions, it must be understood, were not granted by way of immunities. The lands were contracted and paid for, even liberally, in money and goods, at rates which would be considered monstrous by all European people, and infinitely beyond any measure of compensation, ever adopted by the early colonists in their transactions with the Indians.

But these cessions did not meet the emergencies of the whites. The great increase of our population, the certain result of institutions, which, like our own, enable man to assert his manhood, in the only christian and intellectual way,—carried the banner of civilization, day by day, still deeper into the forests. The red man, stationary but unperforming, impeded the progress which he refused to facilitate; and the urgent demands of the people of Georgia rendered it necessary that Government should make corresponding efforts to comply with their necessities. Accordingly, in the year 1822, Congress appropriated the sum of $30,000, for the purpose of defraying the expenses of such further conferences with the Indians as might accrue from bringing them together. It was desirable to extinguish utterly, their title,—desirable for many reasons—particularly to the people of Georgia, who felt all the inconvenience, annoyance and insecurity, which ensued from the proximity of a people so capricious and treacherous;—and, indeed, had the Government of the United States been true to itself, the close of the war of 1812, would have been signalized by the forcible transfer of the whole nation to the more congenial regions beyond the Mississippi. It was with some considerable reluctance, however, that Congress took the necessary steps to effect the same object, by treaty, in 1822. The immediate pressure of danger withdrawn, governments of the people are usually slow to provide against such evils as only threaten, or do not threaten—in the distance. The duty, solemnly assumed by the United States in 1802, by which it guarantied the early extinction of the Indian titles, was one, irksome on several accounts, to various portions and parties in the country—particularly in those portions where the measures resorted to, at an earlier period, were much more summary, and less equitable, for the attainment of a kindred object. The desire of Georgia was assumed to be one growing rather out of her cupidity, than because of any real annoyance or danger from the Indians. At all events, it is certain that the public mind in many parts of the Union was prepared to regard the proceeding with unfriendly eyes, and to address itself against it, with the most earnest opposition. False ideas of philanthropy prevailed, to bring about this feeling of hostility, with many, who failed to perceive that, though not actually engaged in war,—with arms in their hands, and fury in their hearts,—there was yet, and must be always, a tacit social warfare going on continually, between any two races, actually in contact, and differing so very materially in all moral and physical respects, as the red men and the white. These very differences produce dislikes, and the war of arms must ultimately ensue. The white man, conscious of intellectual and numerical superiority, will necessarily assert it; and the rugged savage sense of independence, to which the Indian is accustomed,—not to speak of his anti-social modes of thinking and feeling on almost all subjects connected with morals and property,—would render him at times a jealous, resentful and unsafe neighbor. The consequences of the propinquity of the two races would, to every thoughtful and inquiring mind, seem inevitable, and were so. But philanthropy does not behold its object with the eyes of philosophy; and the fanciful and lofty notions which prevailed among an educated and highly refined people, were made to apply, as governing moral standards, to the condition of a very barbarous one. The feelings which inspire our poetry, were assumed to fill the breasts of a people utterly insensible to all constituents of poetry, such portions alone excepted as possibly enter into the orgies and faith of the Scandinavian savage, or the Corinthian boor. It was assumed by Fancy—who sometimes puts on the habit, and looks grave, like Philosophy,—as a monstrous evil, that a people should be expelled from homes in which they had made no permanent habitation—which they had neither enriched by culture, nor made attractive by art or ingenuity. The changes were rung upon the deplorable cruelty which would drive them away from the contemplation of the graves of their fathers; and, from the expression of complaints like these, the wandering savage was, for the first time, instructed in the language of a suffering which he himself had never felt. The sympathy of the philanthropic among the whites, thus injudiciously and unreasonably expressed, rendered the Indians stubborn—nay, furnished them with the arguments, by which they met the wise provision which alone could protract the day of their utter extermination. Their writings were prepared by white men, squatters in the nation, who found their profit in baffling the designs of Government, and keeping the Indians in a state of partial dependence upon themselves. Their very chiefs and head men were either whites or descended from white men; and these, generally the most abandoned of their sort, were just as regardless of the sympathies with their own color, as they were indifferent to the interests of the poor savage. From their knowledge of the people whom they had abandoned, they infused arguments and opinions into the minds of those they served—such arguments as were gathered from the wild declamations of newspapers, or the yet more wild declamation of the uneducated Western preacher. These, too, sometimes took wives among them, acquired property in consequence, and, becoming thus stationary, were loth to abandon their comfortable quarters, to share the fortunes of the people with whom they had allied themselves. Such a feeling of reluctance, though natural enough to the individual white, was yet of small importance to the Indians, until he furnished the arguments which made it equally imposing to them. That the savages should choose white men to be their chiefs and counsellors, excludes obviously the recognition of any independent notions of their own on the subject of their policy as a community. Thoughtless and improvident, as are all people who have never been practised in the holy and blessing tasks of labor, they were incapable of discussing their own interests with any likelihood of just and beneficial results. Their nomadic life made them really indifferent to place, unless as readily affording them the game upon which they subsisted; and thus, feebler than children, the policy which rendered them a stationary people, in a region which had been almost denuded of all resources of this description,—unless coupled with the stern guardianship which would have subjected them to the methodical employments of industry—would have been one as destructive in the end to themselves, as it would have been adverse to every hope of keeping them pacific. The whole argument, on this subject, equally comprehensive and simple, is comprised in a nutshell, which any ordinary mind may crack at any moment. We will not pursue it here.

The effects of this meddlesome philanthropy soon made itself apparent, and has made itself felt in repeated and painful occurrences ever since. Under the appropriation of 1822, made by Congress for holding conferences with the Georgia Indians, the Commissioners of Government appointed to carry this object into effect, repaired first to the Cherokee Nation, sometime in the autumn of 1823; and submitted to the Chiefs of that nation certain proposals for the cession of their territory. But a more potential voice had anticipated them in their designs, and prepared the Indians against their application. Certain of the Cherokee chiefs were of white blood, had travelled among the whites, and gathered money and arguments, in liberal quantity, from the philanthropists in various parts of the Union. To the proposals of the Commissioners they returned a flat denial. The Cherokees, it may be well to state, had, by this time, made considerable advances, speaking with certain qualifications, in the arts of civilization—some few of them at least. Always a less wandering and less courageous people than the contemporaneous nations—regarded, with some contempt, as unmanly, by the Muscoghees, Chickasaws, Choctaws and Catawbas,—it was with them, a less difficult process, a less degrading transition, to pass from the hunter to the pastoral and agricultural life. Long before the American Revolution, they had achieved certain advances in these labors which had placed them in an attitude of superior civilization to their neighbors; and the severe punishments which they received from the Carolinians in 1761, by more effectually subduing whatever martial spirit they may have had, rendered the adoption among them of the preliminary arts of civilization, more desirable and more easy. Until late years, however, their progress had not gone much beyond the cultivation of adequate supplies of Indian Corn, and the most ordinary provisions. They had small herds of cattle, which relied entirely on the forest ranges for their pasturage. No portion of their provision was raised in reference to their cattle; even their favorite beast of burden,—the Cherokee pony—which has a reputation of its own for hardihood and activity, derived its food from the cane-top, from chance depradations upon the meanly enclosed fields,—from the woods at large,—or from any source but their masters. But the grand step which the

Cherokees had made, or were about to make, toward civilization, consisted in their having become stationary—in contracting their limits, the individual as the nation,—and this step was most probably forced upon them, by the pressure, on all sides, of the accumulating whites. Something, also, no doubt was due to the mixed blood of their chiefs and leading men, many of whom had received the benefits—important in the highest degree as well to them as to us,—of a grammar school education, and all of whom were in the habit of mingling, more or less, with the white population of the neighborhood. The women wove and spun a little. There was probably a blacksmith—a half-breed—among them; and, perhaps, they had a native carpenter, and others who professed a slight knowledge of other necessary mechanic arts. The nation possessed a newspaper, which, like many of our own, did an infinite deal of mischief in the hands of small politicians. A man of mixed blood, named Guess, the son of a white father and Indian mother—one of that class, which, for good or evil, will always have the most influence among the Indian tribes of our country—had derived enough from his Anglo-American origin, to effect an achievement upon which the philanthropists every where could declaim, *ad libitum,* as a proof of the national genius and its paramount resources. Like another Cadmus,—such was the bruit—he had evolved the characters which embodied to the eye the sounds known to the language of his people; and this invention was the great and conclusive argument, which, with the enthusiastic and visionary, proved every thing. The benefits of this discovery, whatever they might have been, ensued rather to the advantage of the whites and half-breeds, within the nation, than to the still miserable people whose concerns they mismanaged. At all events, under the circumstances in which the nation stood, swayed by whatever motives or opinions, the Cherokee Chiefs positively refused, on any terms, to accede to the wishes of the Government. It should not be forgotten, also, that these persons, by this time, had been taught by the cupidity of the white squatter, that "there was gold in the land, and that the gold of the land was good." Cupidity and treachery are probably the two most prominent characteristics of Indian education, or, in the Western dialect, of "Indian natur." Besides, they had heard exaggerated accounts of the hardships endured by that portion of their countrymen, who had already, years before, emigrated beyond the Mississippi— the poverty of the soil, the want of "lightwood," and the proximity of dangerous neighbors;—and they either really felt these as objections, or they made them appear so in their declamations.

It was on occasion of this projected treaty, that the services of the somewhat celebrated Muscoghee Chief, William Mackintosh,—otherwise "The Broken Arrow," were put in requisition by the whites; and he was persuaded by the Commissioners to visit the Cherokee nation with the view to the promotion, by his eloquence,—which was plausible and ingenious,—of the object which they had in contemplation. Mackintosh had acquired the confidence of the whites in the last war between them and his own people. He was of the minority who took sides against the "red sticks," and joined the army of Jackson in their extirpation. He did admirable service against them, and against the Seminoles, when Jackson pursued the fugitive Creeks, down into the very heart of that outlawed nation. He had risen into power among his own people after the peace; and, strengthened by the whites, to whom his attachments were almost wholly given—for he too, was in part descended of white parentage,—he, perhaps, wielded the nation almost entirely at his will. This amazing influence, it may be well, passingly, to intimate, was the true cause of the jealousy among his associate Chiefs, which contributed, in a great degree, to overthrow and destroy him. But we will not anticipate.

As an artful politician, an able orator, a well known leader among the Creeks, and highly esteemed among the Cherokees, from which nation he had chosen his wife, Mackintosh visited the latter people in order to urge upon them the sale of their territory. He appeared in their Councils, and, publicly, to their assemblies, and privately to individuals, boldly urged the various arguments which he thought would avail to effect his mission. It is a well known custom among the Chiefs of the Indian tribes, when at peace, to visit one another, and, as warriors and sages, to take part in the national deliberations, precisely as if the visitor were a citizen, and had equal interests with those among whom he came. This courtesy has been frequently extended by them to their white guests, to whose counsels they listen with becoming gravity, though, perhaps, always with that suspicious judgment, which never sleeps when in contact with a superior person or intellect. Confiding in the honor of their guest, however, they are not unwilling to avail themselves of his wisdom; and in times of doubt or danger, the Muscoghee Council listened gladly to the advice of the Sachem of Cherokee, and, in turn, the latter yielded a respectful ear to the instructive comment or sagacious judgment of the orator from Tookanbatchie. The appearance of William Mackintosh, therefore, before the Grand Council of the Cherokees, was neither a suspicious nor an unusual circumstance; but it is not improbable that, long before this period,

Mackintosh himself had begun to lose the confidence and the affections of this people. Their leaders were in fact so many rivals; and the very intimacy which the Creek Chief possessed among the whites, was necessarily unfavorable to his influence over those of his own complexion. Their deference in hearing his arguments, was accorded to their custom rather than to the particular speaker. They listened with patience, but their fears were aroused, and their indignation excited. There was yet another circumstance that tended to lessen the influence of the warrior. He had become a tradesman. He had thrown aside the tomahawk and taken up the day-book—he had left the forum for the counter;—and this change, acting upon a disposition which is represented to have been naturally mercenary—as probably is the case with all savages—contributed to debase his virtues in the vulgar mind, which, least of all, is apt to forgive the *auri sacra fames,* in the heart of him that aspires to its rule and management. We state the opinions entertained by his opponents, without meaning to vouch for their authenticity. It is not improbable that, educated among the whites,—partially a white himself,—a man of great sagacity and forethought,—he had received the conviction, which would infallibly occur to any mind familiar with the true character of his people, that their only hope of safety, as well as independence, lay in their absolute removal from all connection with the superior people. The true purposes of Mackintosh may not have been the less patriotic, because they were so little popular. My own opinion is that no rulers have ever been more selfish in their aims and performances, than the Indian Chiefs of our country in modern periods. Certainly, no people has ever been kept in a more squalid state of destitution than those over whom they hold the rule.

However equivocal may have been the motives of Mackintosh, he urged his arguments with the same zeal which he had ever shown as an ally of the American people. When his arguments failed, however, he committed himself and cause, by imprudently attempting to bribe certain of the most influential chiefs whom he had failed to convince. If they were dissatisfied by his previous efforts, they were now displeased. Besides, they were now able to crush him. He had furnished them the means to do so. They, accordingly, rejected his overtures with disdain, and denounced them. John Ross, the then President of the National Council, to whom he had submitted his proposals in writing, confronted him with them in open assembly of the chiefs, and denounced him as a traitor to his nation. The letter, written by the Cherokee chiefs, which discloses the perfidy of Mackintosh, to his own people, is worthy of perusal. It dates from "New Town," in the Cherokee nation, "October 24th, 1823." It is addressed to Big Warrior and Little Prince, the Head Chiefs of the Muscoghees, and runs thus:—

"FRIENDS AND BROTHERS:—We have this day gone through a painful and unpleasant ceremony. Your chief, William Mackintosh, arrived here soon after the commencement of the present council, accompanied by seven others of his countrymen, including his son and Interpreter. They were received by the General Council, as friends and brothers; an appropriation of money was made to procure forage for their horses. After having showed them every friendship, we did not expect that William Mackintosh had any ungenerous disposition towards the interest of the nation; but we were mistaken. We find that his visit here must have been entirely through speculative designs. He has used intriguing language with some of our chiefs, to yield the land to United States Commissioners, who are now here for that object; and has made promises of obtaining large sums of money for them, in which he proposed to share. His words, at first, were not taken notice of, but he still pursued the same course, and made a written communication to John Ross, the President of the national committee, on the subject; promising nineteen thousand dollars to be paid over to such individuals as *he* may think proper, in case of accession. He further stated, verbally, to some of our chiefs, that he had offered his whole country to the United States Commissioners, at two dollars per acre, and *suggested the idea of the Cherokees, Creeks, Choctaws and Chickasaws, all to surrender up their country, and emigrate west of the Mississippi River, and there to settle themselves under one government.* The letter aforesaid, has been exposed, and read in open council to-day, by John Ross, in the presence of William Mackintosh; and the General Council have decreed that William Mackintosh be, and he is hereby *discharged* from ever having a voice in our councils, hereafter, as a chief connected with this nation. Brothers," continues the letter of the Cherokee chiefs, "we are astonished at our brother's conduct in this place. We have lost all confidence in his fidelity; and advise you, as brothers, to keep a strict watch over his conduct, or he will ruin his nation."

This letter was signed by Pathkiller, the principal, and twenty-eight other chiefs.

The Muscoghees, thus forewarned of the probable dishonesty of one of their chiefs, became doubly suspicious of him; and, following the advice of the Cherokees, now maintained a more strict watch upon his proceedings than ever. For a long time previously, his great intimacy with the people, and some of the authorities of Georgia,—a state which, it was well known to the Indians, was exceedingly desirous of obtaining possession of their lands,— had alarmed their jealousy, and the mercenary disposition which Mackintosh had evinced as a retail trader in the nation, had contributed greatly to lessen him in their esteem as an individual. These suspicions, and their occasion, at length aroused the apprehensions of Mackintosh himself. He began to fear, not only the loss of his general influence, as a chief,—for he might be '*broken*' and deprived of his authority,—but he also saw that his personal safety was endangered. He became, accordingly, much more circumspect in his dealings with the white people, and more earnest in his assurances of fidelity to his own. But this was not enough for the jealous Muscoghees; and they proceeded to re-enact a law of their nation, made time out of mind "on the West Bank of the Ockmulge," which decreed "rope and gun"—in other words, death by shot or halter,—to any of their people who should propose the sale of any more of their lands to the whites, or seek, by any means, to impair the integrity of their existing title. In 1821, Mackintosh, with other leading chiefs, infringed this law by a treaty,—(pronounced illegal, but afterwards consented to by the rest,)—with the United States: and nearly incurred this penalty; 'till he showed them that the sale had become necessary, in order to meet the claims existing against the nation. Though this sale was concurred in, yet the penalty threatened against chiefs offending again in like manner, was solemnly re-enacted, on the present occasion; Mackintosh, himself, appearing as one of the advocates and signers of the law,—"which they then vowed to make permanent, as the only means of keeping their lands!" When the message of the Cherokees, denouncing Mackintosh, was brought to them, such was the excitement against him, that the law was again revived, or re-delivered to the people, at a place called Pole Cat Springs, and, as it is stated by his brother, and superior chiefs, revived by a proposition from himself. This movement was most probably designed to disarm their jealousy, and to disprove the presentations of these Cherokees. According to their statement, he made an eloquent speech, while moving the re-enactment, the better to enforce its provisions upon the minds of all present. He told them, "that the law was for the whole nation, without any exception; not for any persons in particular, but for all—*half breeds and all;* and even for the 'Little Prince' and 'Big Warrior'— their two principal chiefs." This law was to be rigidly enforced, for it ordained, among other provisions, that, if it should so happen, that the people of one town refused to prosecute and punish the offender, then 'law menders,' (executioners,) from the other towns were directed to do so;—and the property of him who violated the law was to be forfeited to those who enforced it by punishment. The re-enactment of this law, at the period referred to, and the stern decision of all chiefs upon it, contemplated, in particular, the case of Mackintosh, whose intrigues with the whites were now notorious,—whose mercenary character was odious,—and whose doubtful patriotism was more than suspected.

But with all this prejudice against him, in spite of these suspicions, the superior cunning of Mackintosh enabled him to maintain his position as a chief, and to influence the feelings and opinions of a very strong party in the nation. These, it is true, were a minority, and were chiefly confined to the towns in his own neighborhood; but their very compactness gave them an appearance of strength, which equally deceived the Indians and the Georgians,—leading the former to conduct their proceedings with a studious caution, which, if it made their operations slow, rendered them more certainly effectual;—and prompting the Georgians to assume, as they did most probably on the representations of Mackintosh himself, that he was not only stronger than he really was, but that in fact he wielded the real vote, and prompted the true voice and feelings of the nation. It is barely possible that Mackintosh deceived himself in like manner. At all events, this prevailing error led to the catastrophe which followed. It made his enemies circumspect, while it made him audacious; and it so far influenced the governor of Georgia, as to prompt his too active and open interference in the concerns of the nation,—a circumstance which, while it increased the apprehensions and indignation of the Indians, stimulated their hostility against the individual to whose false representations they ascribed the interference which they resented, as well as the mischiefs which they feared.

The effect of the communication from the Cherokees was very soon and strikingly made manifest to the commissioners who came to treat on the part of the United States. The Creeks resolutely answered "No!" to every application for the sale of their lands. Their councils were directed, and their reply signed by four chiefs, Mackintosh, (then also the speaker of the nation,) being one of them. In their reply, they allege that they are convinced that "their ruin must be the inevitable consequence of their removal beyond the Mississippi." The commissioners, not discouraged, renewed their efforts; and a long talk was addressed to the Indians, in council, the day following their refusal. This talk briefly sums up their history as far as it had connection with that of the whites,—insists upon the rights acquired by the latter from their conquest,— dwells upon the poverty of the Indians; their dependence and feebleness; and describes, truly, the destitution and miserable state in which they lived, in consequence of their stubborn continuance of the destructive life of the hunters, in a region already denuded of its primitive resources. The reply of the Indians, signed by the same chiefs as before—after giving their version of certain parts of their history, in which they differ from that given by the commissioners, ends by their returning the same repulsive answer; and, after several days of profitless negotiation,—profitless to both parties,—the proceedings were discontinued, and the Indians retired to their homes.

The commissioners alledge, and with strong probability in behalf of their convictions, that there was a secret agency at work against them, apart from that of the Cherokees, which brought about this effect. The Indians were, in fact, under the government of white men,—persons who drove a good business in the nation; and of squatters, who, having married Indian women, found it in their own most certain interest not only to keep where they were themselves, but to keep the Indians equally in the same moral and geographical position. The removal of the nation to the west, would suggest a necessity for their removal also; and the prospect of change alone, suggested by the probability of such an abridgement of their power as they were unwilling to contemplate; since it was very clear that their agency, in the affairs of the Indians, would be of far less importance to the latter when once they were withdrawn from all contact with the neighboring white settlements. The importance of the squatter to the Indian, was derived chiefly from the occasional intercourse of the savage with the settlers of the contiguous states. He drew up the accounts of the savages;—urged his claims, by writing either to Justice, Charity, or Favor;—sold and bought for him;—inspected the money which he received; wrote his memorials to Government;—and prepared his arguments, and furnished his histories,—as in the present instance,—when he met in council for the purpose of treating with the whites. In this way, a few white men of half breeds, possessed the most unqualified sway over the Indians. Their words were so many laws; and they employed their vast influence, most commonly, with a base and narrow reference to their own selfish interests and feelings, and not to the necessities or true policy of the ignorant barbarians who confided in them, and who knew not where else to turn for counsel. Even the messengers of the Gospel, the ministers of religion, were sometimes to be found among these perverse advocates. They, too, received their bias, against the removal of the Indians to a remoter region, from the consciousness of those superior toils to themselves, which such a removal would draw after it. Reasoning for the Indians, from that policy which undoubtedly would have been their own, they may be assumed, as they have been too frequently found, to be among the stumbling blocks in the way of Government, in all their efforts for removal and subsequent improvement of the tribes.

An attempt was renewed a few months after, to make a treaty for the desired object, at a place called Indian Springs. On this occasion, a large number of chiefs and head men attended;—and here again, as alleged, some secret management prevailed, if not entirely to baffle the execution of the treaty, at least to render its validity doubtful, and make its performance dangerous. A man named Hanbly, acting as one of the United States interpreters, and probably largely interested in keeping the Indians where they were, perceiving the progress of the commissioners toward the attainment of their object, alarmed the fears of certain of the chiefs, by assuring them that, if they did not fly, it was the intention of the whites to put them in prison. The savages, at this suggestion, took to the woods at midnight, and before the dawn of day, were distant twenty miles from the spot. It was conceived by those who were hostile to this treaty, that this would be a sufficient and sure mode for preventing its completion. In this, however, their policy was at fault. The influence of Mackintosh prevailed over those who remained, and the propositions of the commissioners were finally acceded to by himself and fifty-two others, all of whom, with the exception of himself, are represented as being inferior men among the nation; not chiefs,—of no general influence, and without any power either to make laws or conclude treaties. They were persons representing eight towns of the nation only, when the number of these towns was no less than fifty-six. When Mackintosh approached to sign the treaty, his hand was arrested by another chief, Opokbyobolo, who had stubbornly opposed it. This was now the speaker of the nation,—a man of comprehensive understanding, and an eloquent orator.

"Brother," he exclaimed, to Mackintosh, "what would you do? You are about to sell our country. You are in danger!"

The remonstrance was unavailing. A fatality attended the movements of Mackintosh, and the orator, with a look of warning, retired from the assembly. *He* had not signed the paper, nor had any of the principal chiefs, with the single exception of Mackintosh, who ranked as first chief, as the lowest among them. The rest, with all the subordinate chiefs and law-makers of the nation, embodied their objections to the treaty in a protest, which was immediately sent after it to Washington. The letter alleges the treachery of Mackintosh, and prays that the ratification of the treaty may be temporarily deferred, in order that time should be allowed to the Indians to deliberate, and to the Congress to inquire into the truth concerning the manner in which it was procured.

The prayer of the petitioners was not granted them. The treaty was ratified by the Senate of the United States, with the protesting memorial before them. Doubtlessly, they weighed the force of its arguments with a proper consideration—it is not easy to say, at this time, what varieties of suggestions, of a political kind, had force in prompting them to set aside the protest of the dissenting chiefs; and, with the conviction which we feel, that the substantial good of the poor Indians was really best consulted by the measure of their removal, we are unwilling to assert that the ratification of the treaty, by the Senate, was precipitate, still less unwise. Considering the Indian tribes of our country, with a due reference to their savage and immature condition,—their ferocity and inferior civilization,—it was, perhaps, an error in the first instance, to have ever treated with them on terms of equality. A comprehensive view of the relations existing between any two races in actual contact, suggests the religious duty of the superior to take the inferior under its guardianship,—to protect it from injustice, from cruelty and spoilation,—to teach, to guide, and to restrain it;—but, at all events, to do for it that which seems best for the preservation of peace and good will between the parties, and for the promotion of the moral and intellectual, as well as social progress of the minor and inferior race. A people like the North American Indians, in relation to the European colonists, were so many children only,—to be treated as children, and gradually lifted to the social eminences of civilization, by a hand equally firm and considerate. Any other process—that, in particular, which recognizes an equality of judgment and condition between them and the whites, which did not, and could not exist—was the very process most likely to result,—as it has resulted—in their overthrow and destruction. A like process of indulgence and deference, shown to our sons, would produce the same distressing consequences, even in the growing generations of the already superior race.

But, disquisition aside,—the evil was consummated. The Government of the United States recognized and ratified the treaty, as if made in good faith; and the distress and anger of the Indians, when apprized of it, were heightened to ferocity. Mackintosh became alarmed, and, conscious of his treachery, or perhaps warned of his danger by some friendly Indian, he fled within the limits of Georgia for safety. He sought Governor Troup, of that state, and declared his apprehensions. To calm his fears, and, possibly, at his own suggestion, the Governor dispatched one of his aides, Colonel Lamar—(the gentleman, we believe, who was late the President of Texas)—with a "talk" to the Indians of the nation, which was intended to soothe their anger, and disarm their hostility. We are not sure that this proceeding was a wise one,—at all events, we are persuaded that the talk itself was not a judicious one. Its language of expostulation and warning, was expressed in tones which too nearly resembled those of denunciation and threatening, to be very successful in soothing a highly exasperated people;—a people, too, who believed themselves to be sacrificed to the desires of the very party whose messenger had thus addressed them. But whatever might have been the real feelings of the Indian chiefs, they took care to express none other than that of peace. Being older politicians than Lamar, they found it easy to beguile his confidence; and he left them in the full conviction that Mackintosh might return to the nation in perfect safety. It was unfortunate that Mackintosh shared in this conviction. He did return, only to commit another indiscretion which revived and increased the ferocity of the Indians. He presumed upon the power,—assuming an authority to which he had no claim,—of granting the permission to Georgia, to make the survey of the ceded territory at an earlier period than had been specified in the treaty. It is probable that had he not taken this step, the Indians might have foreborne his punishment; and, taking counsel from their fears, and with some regard to their ancient veneration, have permitted him to go free, without attempting to enforce the extreme penalty which the violation of their laws had incurred. But this last proceeding, the precise tenor of which was not exactly understood among them, and the evils of which were represented by designing persons, as no less than the immediate dispossession of their lands, and the forfeiture of their slaves, stock, cattle and improvements, rendered them desperate, and left them without any restraints either of good will or prudence. Their excitement, as represented by the United States agent on the spot, was absolutely dreadful. The apprehensions of the whites, in and about the nation, were excited to such a degree, as to prompt their immediate flight; and every symptom was supposed to be shown, which would denote one of those bloody outbreaks of the savages, which could terminate only in the burning and massacre of the frontier. Meanwhile, lulled into a false security, Mackintosh remained in his fine dwelling on the Chatahoochie, where, amidst abundance of every kind—for he was wealthy—he either had no apprehensions of danger, or with ordinary Indian inflexibility, he contrived to conceal them.

The Chiefs, meanwhile, who were hostile to his course, were preparing themselves in secret, for the purpose of redressing the violated laws of their country. Having quieted the fears of the criminal, and beguiled him back to the nation, they were content that their proceedings should be slow in order that they should be effectual. They gathered in consultation only such of their number as could be thoroughly relied on. Their meeting took place at midnight, on the banks of a gloomy river. Every precaution seems to have been taken that their place of consultation, and purpose, should not be borne abroad. Their conference was rather as to the mode of carrying the punishment into effect, than of simply passing sentence. That seems to have been already done. The voice of the nation had condemned the offender. The judgment had been silently recorded in the bosoms of the great majority. The "Law Menders" simply met to arrange the manner of proceeding. The decree of "rope and gun" against William Mackintosh, was devolved for execution, upon certain chiefs of the Oakfuskies, Talladegas and Emuckfaus—tribes over which the influence of the criminal was too small to make it doubtful that they would perform the duty without favor or flinching, entrusted to their hands. From these tribes, a party of no less than four hundred warriors was made up, the direction of whose movement was assigned to the two Chiefs, Mad Wolf and Menawé, both of whom were supposed to regard Mackintosh with feelings of particular dislike and jealousy.

The victim, little dreading the fate which was at hand, remained with his family, and without a guard, at his dwelling on the Chatahoochie. His confidence in the assurances of protection from Georgia, and in the virtue of that "talk," which Colonel Lamar had borne to the hostile Chiefs,—with, possibly, not an unreasonable reliance on the strength of his ancient popularity in the nation,—rendered him less circumspect and acute than was his wont. Besides, he was naturally a brave man,—had acquired this reputation under the bravest of his own or of any time, (Jackson,)—and a sense of shame at the apprehensions which he had recently shown, and which was no doubt only the natural result of a superior sense of guilt, emboldened him to stay, and stimulated him to the opposite extreme of an unwise confidence in his fortunes. The Indian agent, (Col. Crowell,) ascribes this obtuseness entirely to the imprudent assurances of protection which he received from Georgia. He asserts, that, if Mackintosh had been left to himself, he would have baffled his enemies by flight. Delay was all that was necessary for his safety, and could he have avoided the danger, for the time, until the first fury of the Indians had overblown, it is probable that the execution of their judgment would have been foreborne for ever.

The "*Law Menders*," for such, in the dialect of the nation, is the very appropriate title given to those who are appointed for the punishment of "*Law-breakers*"—proceeded to their tasks with a settled and sufficient deliberation. Their approach to the dwelling of Mackintosh was timed to take place at midnight, or just before the dawn of day. The house was surrounded in profound secrecy, without occasioning the least alarm. When this was done, and the leaguer was believed to be complete, they despatched one Hutton, a white man, whom they had brought along with them for this purpose, with a message to the family of Mackintosh. Hutton was instructed to declare their purpose, which was the death of the offender only;—and to bring out, and send away in safety, any white person who might happen to be lodging there for the night. Nothing could more certainly declare the deliberation, calm resolution, and a considerate regard for their relations to the white people, and the consequences of offending them, than this proceeding—a proceeding scarcely to be expected from any, and least of all, from a savage people, while laboring under an excitement so extreme and universal. Hutton's mission being concluded, and himself with the whites withdrawn from the dwelling, they sounded the terrific war-whoop, and advanced resolutely to the work of death. The first purpose of Mackintosh was to defend himself. He had with him, in his house, his son, Chilly Mackintosh, and one or two other Indians, all of whom were determined men. His dwelling was strong, and the summons of Mad Wolf, which was distinctly audible amid the uproar, commanding him to "Come out like a man, and die by the laws he had himself made," was answered by defiance. But his assailants were not disposed to afford him a chance for fight, and soon made it apparent that no measure of valor, in actual conflict, could avail him. The torches blazed beneath his windows; the flames were already seizing upon the timbers of his dwelling, when he bade his son, with the other Indians, to fly and leave him to his fate.

They did so, and leaping through the windows, were permitted to escape;—a few shot being fired after them, less, perhaps, with a view to kill them, than to hasten their flight. Commissioned for the destruction of one offender, they confined their deadly attentions solely to him. Alone,—hopeless, but fearless, the beleaguered chief, like the wolf driven to his den, and rendered furious by the fire, rushed boldly to the entrance. It was probably an instinctive movement of his hand by which it grasped the rifle. He did not attempt to use it, and could have had no hope that its use, even if he brought down the most formidable enemy, could have availed to extricate him from the four hundred by whom he was environed. If he did not utterly despair—if his movements were not prompted solely by a desperate resolution to meet death with a fearless and characteristic defiance—then, he probably flattered himself with the hope, that his presence and his voice might arrest their purpose. His former popularity, at one time almost boundless, might linger still in their memories;—and never, among all his people, had they known an orator so silver-tongued, so persuasive, so captivating as himself. Could they but be brought to look and listen—hear his voice, feel his arguments, understand his reasoning,—or, possibly, behold the treasures which he could display before their eyes, to enforce his entreaty,—all might yet go well, and the danger would pass by. Such may have been his thoughts, such his hopes, and, possibly, such might have been his success, had he been suffered to address the multitude. But the chiefs who came against him also knew his resources, and dreaded his arts and powers of persuasion. They knew too well the danger of permitting him to exercise them. His lips were barely parted for speech,—the sounds of his voice just beginning to be heard—when they were stilled for ever by the rifle of Mad Wolf. The bullet penetrated the mouth of the speaker, and was the signal for a general discharge. Nearly two hundred bullets took effect in the body of the victim. His house was burnt to ashes, and his property distributed among the executioners, by the same law which called them into exercise, as the ministers of its justice.

"LITERATURE AND ART AMONG THE AMERICAN ABORIGINES" is Simms's seminal essay on the artistic aspirations and capabilities of Native Americans and the appropriateness of Indian history and legend as prime subjects in the creation of a distinctive national literature. Ostensibly a review of two books by Henry Rowe Schoolcraft, the essay first appeared in the *Southern and Western Monthly Review and Magazine* in 1845, before inclusion in *Views and Reviews in American Literature, History and Fiction*, First Series, later that year.

ᴄᴏ Literature and Art among the American Aborigines

I. ONEOTA, OR THE RED RACE OF AMERICA; THEIR HISTORY, TRADITIONS, CUSTOMS, POETRY, PICTURE WRITING, &C. BY HENRY R. SCHOOLCRAFT. NEW YORK: BURGESS, STRINGER & CO. 1845.

II. ALGIC RESEARCHES. BY HENRY R. SCHOOLCRAFT, 2 VOLS. HARPER & BROTHERS. NEW YORK [1839.]

The vitality of a people, their capacity to maintain themselves in recollection and to perpetuate a name through all the ordinary vicissitudes of empire, is in just proportion to their sensibilities; and these are shown in due degree with their susceptibility to the impressions of art. The highest manifestations of this susceptibility are those of invention—the faculty to combine and to compare, to adapt, endow, and, from the rude materials furnished by the experience of the nation, to extract its intellectual and moral resources, whether of pride or of pleasure, of triumph, or simple consolation. The humblest manifestation of this sensibility is that of music, since this is one of the most universal known to man, and may be entertained, even in large degree, by nations wholly barbarous in every other respect. There is, perhaps, no primitive people so very rude and wretched, as to be wholly without one or other of these manifestations. In all probability music is one of the first. If not exactly a substitute for thought—as one of the British poets would seem to affirm—it is yet apt to precede the toils of thought, and, possibly, to pave the way for it. Appealing directly to the sense, it serves to chasten and refine them, and, by subduing or mollifying the passions, it leaves the intellectual nature free to assert itself, and to maintain, by other processes the ascendancy which it thus acquires over the brutal. Other developments follow which are more or less modified according to the circumstances and condition of a country. These declare themselves, first, in rude attempts at material art; in outlines upon the wall; in figures wrought in clay; in uncouth attempts to connect narrative with music;—the germs, not to be overestimated in the analysis of a national mind, of its romance and poetry. These are all bald or copious, fluid or constrained, wild or soft, according to the necessities, the habits, and the climate of a people. Where the nation, either directly, or through individuals whom it sends forth, have contact with strangers who are superior to themselves in art and civilization, the exercise of a rude faculty of imitation necessarily precedes all native and original endeavour. Where this is not the case, the art springs, slowly and painfully, from the usages of the tribes, from their sports, their toils, their religion, the egotism of the individual, or the pride of the stock,—to all of which it imparts, or seeks to impart, by little and little, the attributes of form, grace, colour and dignity. At first, no higher object is aimed at than simply to reconcile the struggle and impatient nature, yearning for better things, to a fate which seems unavoidable, and to a toil which needs assuasion. The shepherd is thus taught to find a solace, and perhaps a charm, in his rustic and wretched life among the bleak passes of the Alps; persuaded by his Melibœus of a superior loveliness of a condition,—with crook, and pipe, and dog—from which he feels it impossible to escape;—and the squalid fisherman who draws his nets, and pursues his miserable occupation, along the gloomy edges of the northern seas, may well yield himself to those assurances of song which can only reconcile him to his own land and labour by disparaging those of other nations as more wretched still. And thus it is that the poet becomes the first minister of a people, either to find a solace for the present, or to provoke prouder and more attractive hopes in another and more fruitful condition. Thus it is that we have the pastoral and piscatory Muse,—the Muse of a humble nature and inferior pursuits—to which it seeks to impart beauty and a grace which nothing but the growing fancy, under this tutelage, enables the miserable labourer to behold. In this manner are the rude nomadic tribes hurried forward under the stimulating entreaties of the lyrist,—himself a hunter and a warrior,—to the invasion of distant forests. Thus the young savage grapples with the grizzly bear and confronts the she wolf in her den. War thus, is made to look lovely in spite of all its terrors; its dangers are wooed with the eager impetuosity of the bridegroom—its achievements form the objects of glory which a tribe most sedulously preserves for imitation—and the Bard justifies the crimes which are committed with this sanction—stimulates resentment, and impels the passions of the living to emulate, by similar atrocities, the terrible actions of the dead. The Greeks, sung by Homer, were neither more nor less than highwaymen and pirates;—the chiefs and demigods of the northern nations, honoured by Odin with highest places in Valhalla, were of the same kidney;—and both find their likeness in the hunter of the American forest—the dark, fierce, barbarian Choctaw or Cherokee—whom we are apt to consider nothing more than the barbarian. But he too had his song, his romances and his deities—good and evil—even as the Hellenes and the Northmen; and his deeds were just as deserving of these, of their Saemund and Melesigenes. That they would have found their poet and historian to have given them as admirable a record as any of those which recount the deeds of Greek and Trojans, was a certainty to have followed hard upon their progress to that degree of civilization which would have brought with it the higher efforts of invention. The Greeks had no Homer till their wanderings were over; and, with the concentration of their affections and their endowments upon a fixed abode, the American aboriginals would have then looked back upon the past, gathering up, with equal curiosity and industry, its wild fragmentary traditions. These, in process of years, they would have embodied in a complete whole, and we should then have been as rigidly fettered by its details as we are now by those of Livy and Herodotus. First, we should have had the crude ballads, the border minstrelsy, of the several tribes, descriptive of their wild and bloody encounters for favourite hunting grounds, or for revenge of a wrong done to the honour of a proud ambitious family. These would have been welded together by a better artist in a more refined period, and a still superior genius, seizing upon this labour as so much crude material, would have remodelled the action, improved upon the events, brought out the noble characters with more distinctness, adorned it with new fancies and episodes, and sent it forth to admiring posterity, stamped with his own unchallenged impress. The rough story from which he drew, would, in the course of a century, have been as completely forgotten as were the still ruder ballads from which that was originally wrought; and nothing would have remained to future history but the symmetrical narrative, too beautiful for fact, which we cannot willingly believe, yet know not how to deny—a work too rich for history, yet too true to art, to be approached with anything short of delight and veneration.

That those materials were in possession of the North American Indians,—that these results might have followed their amalgamation into one great family,—in a fixed abode—addressed to the pursuits of legitimate industry, and stayed from wandering either by their own internal progress, or by the coercion of a superior power—are conclusions not to be denied by those who have considered the character of this people. They had all the susceptibilities that might produce this history. Eager and intense in their feelings, lofty and courageous in spirit,—sensible in high degree to admiration,—ambitious of fame,—capable of great endurance, in the prosecution of an object, or in the eye of an adversary,—they were, at the same time, sensible to the domestic influences—were dutiful to the aged, heedful of the young,—rigid in their training and hopeful of their offspring,—with large faith in friendship,— large devotion to the gods,—not cold in their religion, and with an imagination which found spirits, divine and evil,—as numerous as those of the Greeks or Germans—in their groves, their mountains, their great oceans, their eternal forests, and in all the changes and aspects of their visible world. Their imaginations, which carried them thus far, to the creation of a vast pneumatology of their own, did not overlook the necessity of furnishing their spiritual agents with suitable attributes and endowments; and a closer inquiry than has yet been made into their mysteries, their faiths and fancies, will develop a scheme of singular imaginative contrivance, with wide spread ramifications, and distinguished by a boldness of conception, which will leave nothing wanting to him who shall hereafter contemplate a dream in midsummer for his Chickasah or Choctaw Oberon. These traits and characteristics of mind and temperament, constitute the literary susceptibilities of a people. These susceptibilities are the stuff out of which Genius weaves her best fabrics,—those which are most truthful, and most enduring, as most certainly native and original—to be wrought into symmetry and shape with the usual effects of time and civilization. Cultivation does not create, nor even endow the mind with its susceptibilities,—it simply draws them forth, into sight, and stimulates their growth and activity. Nor, on the other hand, does repose lose or forfeit the germinating property which lies dormant in the core. Like those flower seeds plucked from the coffin of the mummy of the Egyptian Pyramids, where they have lain sapless and seemingly lifeless for three thousand years,—they take root and flourish the moment that they feel the hand of the cultivator—springing into bud and beauty, as gloriously bright as the winged insect darting from his chrysalis cerements with the first glimpses of that warming sunlight which is kindred in its sympathy to the secret principle suspended in its breast. Time and change are necessary to these results. As the flower seed which had no light in the waxen grasp of Egyptian mortality, transferred to the sunny plains of Italy, or even nursed in the warm flower palaces of England, shoots out into instant vitality—so, the nature of the savage, sterile while traversing the wide prairies of Alabama, or ranging the desert slopes of Texas, subdued and fettered by the hand of civilization among the hills of Apalachy, becomes a Cadmus, and gives a written language to his hitherto unlettered people.* The most certain sources of a national literature, are to be found in the denseness of its population, in its readiness to encounter its own necessities—in other words, its willingness to labour in the domestic tendencies of the citizen—in the growth of intellectual wants—in the necessity of furnishing a stimulus to pampered and palsied appetites, and in the sympathy of the community, thus needing provocatives, with the talent which is required to provide them. These conditions obtained,—with the sensibilities already insisted upon,—and the literature of a people is a growth too natural in its rise, too gradual in its progress, to be traced easily in its transitions. All other conditions fulfilled, and its growth follows the requisitions of its people. In their summons, in their sympathy, the poet finds his birth and provocation. He scarcely asks their rewards. The eagerness of the Athenians after news—an eagerness which moves the patriotic indignation of the orator—was yet one of the prime sources of the popular intelligence—by which the orator himself obtained his audience—which furnished strings to the grand organ of Æschylus, and filled the mouth of the Bee of Colonus with that honey which other bees can find there still. To this very appetite, this thirsting for the novel, they owed the beginnings of their drama, and all their other glorious arts. The exquisite finish of their first conceptions, was the duty of successive periods. As invention began to stale, taste ripened into fastidiousness. The massive outline, wholly beyond human ability to rival or surpass, was left in its acknowledged supremacy; and Genius, exhausted in the struggle for original conquest, settled down to the perfection of details. This is a history. These are all achievements of the city, of the crowded mart, of struggling, toiling, conflicting masses. It is the progress of those masses, writing itself in stone, in tower, in temple, in all sorts of monuments. These are the signs of permanence, of a fixed condition, drawing resolutely from itself and from the narrow empire to which its domain is circumscribed. We can hope for nothing of this sort from a wandering people. They build no monuments, rear no temples, leave no proofs behind them that they ever had a faith, or an affection, a hero or a God! The hunter, and even the agricultural life, is necessarily thus sterile. Their capacities,—such as depend on the studious cultivation of their sensibilities,—are

* [SIMMS'S NOTE] The allusion here is to the invention of the Cherokee Alphabet by Gess, a half breed—an event quite as worthy of commemoration among his people, as the achievement of Cadmus was among the Greeks.

deadened and apathetic by disuse. But that we reason from first principles and just parallels, we have no right to know that they ever had sensibilities,—that they are not obtuse and incapable by nature,—an inferior order of creation having different uses, and a far inferior destiny. But we know better, and justly ascribe to pursuit and condition that which the unobserving judgment would refer to native incapacity. This sort of mental flexibility and aptitude, which, in a state of crowded society, is the necessary result of attrition with rival minds, conflicting temperaments, and continually arising necessities, yields, in their cases, to a cold shyness of character, a stern and jealous self-esteem, a hard and resolute reserve and haughty suspiciousness of mood, which leaves the individual wholly deficient in all the arts of conciliation. Confident in himself, his own strength and individuality, he lacks that love of approbation, that concern for the opinions of others, which is at the bottom of much of the ambition by which poet and painter are drawn to their tasks. He asks for no sympathy, does not expect it, perhaps scarcely cares for it in any degree. Is he not himself?—Equal to his own wants, fearless of foes, wholly indifferent of friends? It matters not much what you think of him, so that you do not question him. If he has a merit, a faculty, it is enough, for his own gratification, that he is conscious of its possession. He does not feel or find it necessary that you should quaff at his fountains. His light, if it burns at all, is carefully hidden beneath his own bushel. He has virtues, but they are not those which belong to, or spring from society. He is proud, and this protects him from meanness; generous, and capable of the most magnanimous actions; hospitable,—you shall share his bread and salt to his own privation,—loves liberty with a passion that absorbs almost all others—and brave—rushing into battle with the phrenzy of one who loves it—he prolongs the conflict, unhappily, long after mercy entreats to spare.

Such is the North American Indian. He probably bore an equivalent relation to the original possessors of this continent, with the barbarians of the Northern Hive to Italy, in the days of her luxurious decline. At the time of the discovery of America, he was very much the sort of savage that the historians represent the Gaul, the Goth, and Cimbrian to have been during the wars of Camillus and Catallus, of the Scipios and of Caius Marius. The Teutones—the great German family, with all its tribes—were all of this complexion;—neither braver, nor wiser, nor better, nor more skilful in the arts, nor possessed of a jot more imagination and letters, at the moment when they first became known to civilization. The Saxon Boor when first scourged by the Norman into manhood and stature, moral and physical, had given scarcely more proofs of intellectual endowment than the red men of the great Apalachian chain. He was a Christian, it is true, after a fashion; but Christianity is properly the religion of civilization, and he was not a civilized being—far less so, as we know, in the time of Rollo, than was the Mexican during the reign of Montezuma. Of all these nations, North and South, the North American Indian—keeping in mind the parallels of time already indicated—was probably the superior person. He was quite as valiant, quite as venturous— had probably overthrown the more civilized nations of Central and South America, and, as dim glimpses seem to assure us, had been the conqueror of a highly civilized and even white people in North America. He was fleet of foot, strong of frame, capable of great enterprises; of great powers of endurance; equally erect, large, and symmetrical—a model, according to West, for the conception of a god;*—and not without some few of the arts of civilization, whether acquired by conquest, or by his own unassisted genius. His bow and arrows, his war club, his canoes, his own garments and decorations, were wrought, not only with considerable dexterity and ingenuity, but with an eye to the beautiful and picturesque. He had a picture-writing like the Mexicans, and was not without very decided beginnings of a literature. This may have been rude enough,—not so rude, however, as we are accustomed to think it—but it is sufficient that he had made a beginning. His genius answered for the rest. This differed considerably in the several families. Among these, the Catawbas and the Natchez, seem to have been most distinguished for an elasticity and grace of manner, which separated them widely from the sullen and ferocious Muscoghee. The Cherokees, however, had taken the most certain steps toward civilization. Their structures were more permanent, their towns more populous, and a large portion of their people had engrafted the farmer upon the hunter life. The laws of nature are so mutually provocative, that one step cannot well be taken without another. The moment that the habitation and limits of the barbarian become circumscribed, he begins to labour. This is of necessity. The extension of the abodes

* [SIMMS'S NOTE] The reader need not be reminded of the famous anecdote of the American painter West, who, on seeing the statue of the Apollo Belvedere, exclaimed, "My God! how like a young Mohawk warrior!" The coincidence was not in the mere symmetry of frame. It was the eye, the breathing attitude—the mind and music in the air, action and expression.

of man, and the increase of his numbers, is fatal to the wild beast of the forest,—to the forest itself—and it becomes really easier to find food from labour, in the earth, than to wander remotely, into distant regions, to the probable encounter with superior enemies, furious at any intrusion upon their hunting grounds. This, in fact, was the secret cause of the moral improvement of the Cherokees. The Creeks boasted to have made women of them. They had whipt them into close limits, where they were compelled to labour,—and labour,—a blessing born of a penalty,—is the fruitful mother of all of the nobler exercises of humanity. Hence, the progress of the Cherokees—their farms, their cattle, their manufactures, their discovery of the alphabet, their schools, their constitution, and newspaper,—all the fruit of their subjection, by the Muscoghees and other nations, just before the first English settlements in Virginia and the Carolinas. Had these English settlements been such as a mighty nation should have sent forth—had the colonies been such as had issued from the fruitful ports of Carthage,—thirty thousand at a time, as were sent out by Hanno,—what would have been the effect upon the destinies of the red men of America. They would have been rescued from themselves and preserved,—a mighty nation, full of fire, of talent, of all the materials which ensure long life to the genius and the eminence of a race. The good people of England were not the morbid philanthropists that they have become in latter days—latter day saints, putting to the blush such poor pretenders as those who read the golden plates of Mormon, and look out for the fiery advents which disturb the dreams of Parson Miller. They would have subdued the aborigines, as William of Normandy subdued the Saxons. An European colony of ten thousand men would have done this. They would not have paltered with the ignorant savages, flattering their vanity in order to conciliate their prejudices and disarm their anger, as was done by the feeble settlers at James Town, and other places. They would have overrun them, parcelled them off in tens, and twenties, and hundreds, under strict task masters, and, by compelling the performance of their natural duties—that labour which is the condition of all human life,—would have preserved them to themselves and to humanity. Properly diluted, there was no better blood than that of Cherokee and Natchez. It would have been a good infusion into the paler fountain of Quaker and Puritan—the very infusion which would put our national vanity in subjection to our pride, and contribute to keep us as thoroughly independent of the mother country, in intellectual, as we fondly believe ourselves to be in political respects. But we are becoming too discursive.

Our imperfect knowledge of the Indian,—the terror that he inspired,—
the constant warfare between his race and our own—have embittered our
prejudices, and made us unwilling to see any thing redeeming either in his
character or intellect. We are so apt to think him no more than a surly savage, capable of showing nothing better than his teeth. The very mention of
his name, recalls no more grateful images than scalping knife and tomahawk;
and, shuddering at the revolting associations, we shut our eyes, and close our
ears, against all the proofs which declare his better characteristics. We are
unwilling to read his past as we are unable to control his future;—refuse to
recognize his sensibilities, and reject with scorn the evidence of any more
genial attributes, in his possession, which might persuade us to hope for him
in after days—for his natural genius and his real virtues—when, shut in by
the comparatively narrow empire which we have allotted him—barred from
expansion by the nations which are destined to crowd upon him on every
hand,—the people of Texas, of Oregon and Mississippi,—he will be forced to
throw aside the license of the hunter, and place himself, by a happy necessity,
within the traces of civilization.

Regarded without prejudice, and through the medium even of what we
most positively know of his virtues and his talents, and the North American
Indian was as noble a specimen of crude humanity as we can find, from history, any aboriginal people to have been. There is not the slightest reason to
suppose that he laboured under any intellectual deficiency. On the contrary,
the proofs are conclusive, that, compared with other nations—the early
Romans before their amalgamation with the great Tuscan family; the Jews
prior to the Egyptian captivity;—the German race to the time of Odoacer,—
the Saxon, to the period of the Heptarchy, and the Norman tribes in the reign
of Charlemagne;—he presented as high and sufficient proofs of susceptibility
for improvement and education, as any, the noblest stocks in our catalogue.
In some respects, indeed, the Indians show more impressively. The republican features in their society—their leagues for common defence and necessity, and the frequency of their counsels for the adjustment of subjects in
common—led to the growth of a race of politicians and orators, of whose
acuteness, excellent skill in argument, and great powers of elocution, the early
discoverers give us some of the most astonishing examples. The samples
of their eloquence which have come down to us, are as purely Attic as the
most severe critic could desire—bold, earnest, truthful—clear in style, closely
thought, keenly argued, conclusive in logic, and, in the highest degree,

impressive in utterance. That their action was admirable, and would have delighted Demosthenes, we know from authorities upon which we would as cheerfully rely as upon the assurances of the great Athenian orator himself. Now capacious and flowing, now terse and epigrammatic, adapting the manner to the matter, and both to the occasion,—sometimes smooth and conciliatory, anon searching and sarcastic—now persuasive and adroit, and again suddenly startling because of their vehement force and audacious imagery;— these were the acknowledged characteristics of their eloquence, which awed the most fearless spectator and would have done honour to the noblest senate. An eloquent people is capable of taking any place in letters—in mastering all forms of speech, in perfecting any species of composition—history, or poetry—the one faculty, indeed, somewhat implying all the rest, since to be a great orator, imagination must keep pace with thought,—and reason, and the capacity for historical narration, must contribute to the embodiment of the argument, to which a warm fancy must impart colour and animation, and which great energies of character must endow with force. All of these qualities and constituents were in possession of our aborigines. They had all the requisites, shown by their speeches only, even if there were no other proofs, for intellectual development in every species of literature. Tecumsah was a very great orator,—so was his brother, the prophet. The Cherokee, Attakullakullah, was one of the most persuasive and insinuating of speakers; and the renown of Logan, of the Shawanee, is already a proverb from the single speech preserved by Jefferson. Some of the sayings and orations of the Seminoles and Creeks, are equally remarkable for their significance and poetical beauty. Of the Six Nations we have numerous fragments, and the Catawbas had a reputation of this sort, among the tribes of the South, though but few specimens are preserved to us. Weatherford, who roused the Southern Indians to war, while Tecumsah and his brother were fomenting the western nations, was not inferior to either of these as a statesman and an orator. His speech to Jackson, when he surrendered himself, voluntarily, a willing sacrifice, in order that his country should obtain peace, is at once one of the most touching and manly instances of eloquence on record; and, in recent times, Osceola of the Seminoles, and Mooshalatubbee of the Choctaws—the one a bold, and the other an adroit speaker,—are proofs in point, showing that the faculty was not one to die utterly out in the emasculation of their several people. We should be pleased, did our space suffice, to give examples from each of these remarkable men. Enough to say, that they betrayed the possession of a power of logical thinking, lively fancy, subdued good taste, cool judgment, and lofty imagination, such as, addressed to literature, in a community even partially civilized, would have been worthy of all fame and honour in succeeding times. And that we should doubt or be insensible to this conclusion, is only to be accounted for by reference to our blinding prejudices against the race—prejudices which seem to have been fostered as necessary to justify the reckless and unsparing hand with which we have smitten them in their habitations, and expelled them from their country. We must prove them unreasoning beings, to sustain our pretensions as human ones—show them to have been irreclaimable, to maintain our own claims to the regards and respect of civilization.

We commend to some of our clever compilers,—Mr. Griswold, for example—the plan of an Indian miscellany, in which choice specimens of their oratory, their fable, their poetry,—shall appear together, in judicious opposition. The material for a goodly volume is abundant. Colden, Heckewelder, Adair, Jefferson, Hewett, Lawson, Duponceau, and many others, may be examined with this object; and, among recent writers, there is Mr. Schoolcraft,—a host in himself—whose passion for the subject will make him a willing contributor to any plan for doing it justice. Such a miscellany will prove the native North American to have been an artist, a poet, a painter, and a novelist. His abilities were not confined to oratory alone. His faculties were exercised in other kinds of composition. He was no barren churl—no sullen, unproductive savage—such as we are too willing to suppose him. He had the necessary sensibilities for literature, and was not wholly without the performance. His affections were deep and lively, and stimulated his genius to other utterances than those of the Council House. These sensibilities, though perhaps less nice and active than they would have been were he less the hunter—less fierce and intractable in war—were not utterly subdued by his more prevailing passions. His superstitions alone are in proof of his spiritual susceptibility. It has been commonly insisted that these were of a cold and brutal character, at best resembling those of the Northmen—a savage mythology, filled with gods like Odin and Thor,—bloody, dark, malignant, and gratified only by the most horrid rites and festivities. This is only true in part. They had gods of terror it is true, as the Etrurians had—but like these people and the Greeks, they had others of gentle and benignant influence, smiling, graceful, fantastic, who watched over the happier hours of the race, promoted their kindlier fortunes, and gave countenance to the better feelings and habits of the individual. Their pantheon was quite as well supplied as the Greek, though they had not lived long enough to have it arranged, and made immortal, by their dramatists and poets. They had their ruling, their un-known god—their good and evil genii—their demons of the elements—of earth and air, of fire and water, of hill and valley, and lake and wood; and the lively genius of the people, in moments of danger or delight, created new deities for the occasion, consecrating the hour and the place to that worship which had been ordained by their passing necessities or moods. For all of these they had names and veneration. Offices were assigned them, adapted, each, to their several attributes and station, the analysis of which constantly reminds you of those so common among the Germans, by means of which their modern writers have framed so many fanciful and delightful histories. The Kobalds, and Ondines, and Salamanders, might find their parallels among the personifications of the Indian—and their spirits of the mine and the river, of the forest and the mountain, bearing Indian epithets quite as musical as any in the language of the Teuton, attest all the preliminary con-ditions of an intellect that needed but little help from civilization to grow into a vast and noble literature. His gods were hostile or benignant, cold or affectionate, hateful to the sight and mind, or lovely to the imagination and the eye. He addressed them accordingly. To some he urged solicitations, and implored in song. Others he deprecated, and addressed in prayer and expos-tulation. He had his burnt offerings also, and no idea could have been more happy, than that of fumigating his deity with the smoke of that precious weed, whose aroma, so pleasant to himself, was to be extorted only by his own lips. The operation was thus never wholly in vain, whether the god accepted the sacrifice or not. The spirit of the cape and headland, of the battle and hunting ground, of peace, and war, and fortune; of love, and of hate;—com-manded thus his homage and received his devotions. Extraordinary events or achievements; a spot rendered peculiar by circumstance, or by its own aspect; the wild beast that baffled his skill, or the bird that appeared to him on frequent occasions, when he was troubled, or very joyful;—these were all fixed in recollection by some spiritual name and emblem. His omens were not a whit less picturesque, or imposing, less reasonable, or less impres-sive, than those of the Greeks and Romans. The vulture spoke to him in a language of command, as it did to the wolf-suckled children of Rhea Sylvia.

His prophets were quite as successful as the augur, Attius Navius, and practised, with equal success, the art of bringing the gods to a participation in the affairs of State. The favourable response cheered, and the unfriendly paralyzed his valour—and, altogether, with faith and veneration, the character of the North American Indian exhibited, not merely in common but in large degree, all of those moral and human sensibilities, out of which art has fashioned her noblest fabrics. The capacities and sensibilities were there, present, in mind and heart, waiting but the hour and the influence which come at length to every nation, thus endowed, which is permitted to survive long enough in independent career. Their growth and just development, must have followed the first steps of civilization. We have noted their oratory, and their spiritual exercises; but their songs must teach us something farther. What was the song of war, of victory, and the death song, but strains, each, like those of the Jews and the Northmen, on similar occasions, under similar exigencies, combining history with invocation. The exploits of their warriors, thus chaunted in the hearing of the tribe, and transmitted through successive generations, would, if caught up, and put in the fashion of a living language, be not unanalogous to those rude ballads, out of which Homer framed his great poem, and the German his Nibelungen Lied. They embodied the history of the race, with its groups of gallant warriors, and one great commanding figure in the foreground. If the chief filled the centre, emulous and admiring subordinates grew around him, and the correspondence of all furnished a complete history. How such a history, chaunted by a famous chief on his bed of death and glory, could be made to ring, trumpet like, in a modern ear, by such a lyre as Walter Scott. We should not need a Milton, or a Homer, for the performance. The material would have suited Scott's poetical genius better, perhaps, than that of better bards. And how rich must be that material! How wild were the conflicts of our Indians—how numerous—with what variety of foes, under what changing circumstances, and how individual always! What is there improbable in the notion that Powhatan, in his youth, was at the sacking and the conquest of some of the superior nations in the southwest—the Biloxi for example,—of whom the tradition goes that they were a rich and populous people, accomplished in the arts, who were overrun by an influx of strange barbarians and driven into the sea. His ancestors may have brought their legions to the conquest of Palenque—may have led the assault on the gloomy towers of Chi Chen—may have been the first to cross the threshold of those gloomy and terrible superstitions, whose altars have so strangely survived their virtues. It is a somewhat curious fact, in connection with this suggestion, that Opechancanough—a famous warrior—a man of very superior parts who usurped the sway of the Virginia Indians after the death of Powhatan, and probably disputed it while he lived—was described by them as having been the "Prince of a foreign nation,"—and as having "come to them a great way from the southwest." Beverly adds,—"And by their accounts, we suppose him to have come from the *Spanish Indians, somewhere near Mexico,* or the mines of St. Barbe:—but be that matter how it will, from that time (his usurpation) till his captivity, there never was the least truce between them and the English,"* We reserve to another paper our notice of the miscellany, by which the preceding remarks have been occasioned. Mr. Schoolcraft is an authority, in Indian history, upon which we are permitted to rely. He has passed more than thirty years of his life, chiefly in an official capacity, among the red men of the continent. He married an Indian woman of great intelligence and beauty, and was thus placed in a position to see her people, if we may so phrase it, without disguise. He was admitted to their privacy, and informed in their traditions and character. He has accordingly written, at frequent periods upon these subjects, and, we may add, exhibits no larger predilection in their behalf, than the proofs which he produces can fairly justify. A few years ago, he put forth two interesting volumes of Indian traditions, under the title of "Algic Researches." We doubt if the publication attracted much attention, though quite worthy to do so in the eyes of the student. The title probably discouraged the ordinary reader. Of the work before us, we are in possession of the first number only, though a second has recently been published. A detailed notice of these shall be given in future pages, when it will be seen that nothing has been urged in our text, whether for the capacities of the red men, or their actual performance, for which there is not good warranty in the records.

---

* [SIMMS's NOTE] Itopatin, the brother of Powhatan, succeeded to his empire, but was dispossessed by Opechancanough, who was remarkable for his talents, his address, his large stature, noble presence, and the terrors of his name. Here now is material for fiction. Why should not Opechancanough have been a prince in Mexico, flying from the Spaniards? Why should he not have been a captive to the sire of Powhatan, while he and the latter were yet children? How easy to form a romance upon this conjecture! How easy to convert his ceaseless struggle against the English invader into another story. Then, there is the overthrow of Itopatin—but—

IN ALL, IT IS KNOWN that Simms wrote nine letters to Henry Rowe School-craft, America's foremost authority on American Indians before the Civil War. Among the eight included in this volume is the letter of 18 March 1851 that provides the title and the epigraph for this anthology. The letter of 16 February 1851 is previously unpublished. The "Dr. Lieber" first referred to in Letter 3 is Francis Lieber (1800–1872), Berlin-born professor of history and political economy at South Carolina College; the "Gen H." referred to in Letter 7 is James Henry Hammond (1807–1864), Simms's closest friend and confidant. Another matter related to letter 7 concerns the Liège Lady," the second Mrs. Schoolcraft: in one of his reviews of Schoolcraft in *SQR*, Simms made a tactical error in stating that Schoolcraft "took his first wife out of the wigwam"—a blunder causing Schoolcraft's second wife (Mary Howard, a South Carolinian) to write to Simms to point out that her predecessor (Jane Johnston, the granddaughter of Waubojeeg, chief of the Ojibway tribe) was an educated woman (*Letters* 3: 176n). In letter 8, Simms mentions how he emended his mistake. This embarrassing episode does not detract from the fact that Simms was the first American novelist to take seriously the study of American Indian culture.

ᕈᕈ Letters to Henry Rowe Schoolcraft

To Henry Rowe Schoolcraft, 26 September 1845

LETTER 1

[c. September 26, 1845]

DEAR SIR

I am very anxious to procure the numbers of 'Oneota' after the first. I have applied for them in vain to my booksellers. May I beg that you will supply me if it be within your power. The first number I have, and have examined it with great pleasure. I have also,—and have read with exceeding great interest your Algic Researches.— Assist me, my dear Sir, to make my collection complete, and I shall be greatly pleased, hereafter, to requite you after the same fashion.

Very truly & respectfully & c.

W. Gilmore Simms
76 Eleventh Street. N. Y.

LETTER 2

Woodlands Feb 16 [1851]

DEAR SIR:

I have been for some time anxious to address you in order to solicit from you an occasional article, on Indian topics, for the Southern Quarterly Review, of which I have the present charge; but have been discouraged from doing so, from the inability of the publishers to compensate their contributors. Southern periodicals are rarely profitable concerns, and the Review, though largely circulating, is yet so badly paid, that its proprietors are necessarily needy and incapable of doing for authors what they would really most desire. I do not, under these circumstances, feel justified in soliciting a regular correspondence, but write now only to say how happy I should be to recieve from you any occasional article on subjects, such as the Indian, which I know you to pursue *con amore.* The S. Q. R., let me say, will for any such, always, afford a place, and your communication will always recieve prompt & respectful consideration from, dear Sir, yr. ob. svt.

W. Gilmore Simms

[Original in Library of Congress]

LETTER 3

Woodlands March 18. [1851]

DEAR SIR:

I cannot really regret that I cannot recieve an article from you on the subject of the Red Men, since I find you engaged on a copious history devoted to the same topic. Still I may be permitted to regret that there should be no other person equally competent to review your volume. Let me thank you for a present of the copy you design me. I have only recently written to Dr. Lieber, for a paper on the affairs of Germany; but as soon as I can hear from him, I will communicate your wish that he should take up your publication for the Review. Perhaps, a word from you to him, would determine him to do so, & I should be pleased, for the views you indicate that he should do so. Should he not, I must endeavour, myself, to do you and the subject the utmost possible justice—for which be sure I have the most sincere anxiety, even though I lack the endowment. An early and strong sympathy with the Red Men, in moral and literary points of view, have rendered me in some degree a fit person to insist upon their original claims and upon what is still due them by our race. I suppose we are both equally prepared to believe now, that they were an original race, and that God planted them independently in the hemisphere where we find them. If I may presume so far, let me beg that the copy of your work designed for me, be sent as soon as possible. Let one be sent also to Dr. Lieber. It will give me great pleasure to facilitate your circulation in the South, by appropriate hints to our Journalists.—

Yours very truly
W. Gilmore Simms

LETTER 4

Woodlands May 8. 1851

MY DEAR SIR:

I am in reciept of a copy of your volume for which please recieve my best acknowledgements. It is in truth a very splendid publication, and does honor to the liberality & munificence of Government. I shall acknowledge its reciept, and say thus much in our Critical Notices for July, but must leave the full review for a later period. In the meantime let me beg, as a favor to our Review, that, should there be any of your acquaintance, willing, & having the necessary ability for the purpose, you will not scruple to intimate to him that our pages will be open, from 30 to 40, to an examination of the merits of your publication. I say this, as, should Lieber decline—I shall write to him tomorrow—I know not to whom I shall turn for a proper article, such as your work deserves. I shall have, in short, without feeling quite at home with the subject, to undertake it myself, unless I am succored, in this way, from some unanticipated source. I have every disposition to do you justice, and I have a sincere sympathy for your subject; but have not made of it so close and critical a study as seems to be demanded for an elaborate and searching review. Let me add that it will heighten my satisfaction in procuring such a paper, if it should come to me sufficiently soon for publication in our July issue, in which I shall be able to find a place up to the 10th. Otherwise I should desire to make it an early article in our October issue. Failing all assistance from without, I shall address myself to the duty, and be ready I trust in the latter quarter of the year.—As yet, I have only been able to glance at your volume. I cannot guess how many volumes you design, but it seems to me that one of your objects should be to collect the reports of all witnesses, from the beginning of the era of certain discovery,—no matter how faulty subsequent experience shows them to have been. A series of running commentaries, as footnotes, can be made to correct mistakes, and clear up obscurities. If there be no stint of funds, we ought by all means to have grouped in one body the entire testimony on the subject of the Red Men, so that the future Artist, Critic and Historian, will be able to grasp at the same moment the whole amount of the material. Excuse the presumption which thus undertakes to suggest in a case in which your plans have already been (no doubt) well digested and ascribe it to my interest in your work, rather than to any impertinent desire to appear as an adviser. With very great respect, I am

dear Sir, Yr obliged
& obt. Servt.
W. Gilmore Simms

LETTER 5

Charleston, June 10. [1851]

DEAR SIR:

Lieber shrinks from the Review of your book fearing that it would lead him too far, & thus interfere with other labors which he has on hand. He tells me of a paper of his on the subject which has been republished in the Nat. Gazette or Intellig. If you can procure & send me this you will oblige me. Lieber speaks of your second vol. devoted to Indian Languages in a manner that leads me to suppose he will probably undertake the Review of that. It lies more certainly in his way. I have a brief notice of your publication in our July issue of the Quarterly, and shall make great efforts to prepare something more at length for the October; but as I have arranged to be absent at the north for two months this summer, and as we have already provided fully the material for Oct., it is possible that the paper will be delayed to January. This will not be too late, but will rather, I suspect be in the nick of time to exercise its effect on Congress. You will believe me, my dear sir, when I assure you of my great sympathy with your labors, & my sincere desire to promote them all I can. If an article can be furnished for me by Oct. I should exclude other matter to find for it a place. but where its preparation depends upon myself, a hundred labors supervene. The mere editorship of the contributions furnished me, is a sufficient labor for any one man, particularly in this most excruciating weather.—Squier's books I have not seen. I took for granted, when I saw the title of the last, that there would be much more of the fanciful than the philosophical in the plan.

Yours very truly
W. Gilmore Simms

P.S. I shall probably look in upon you in Washington some time in August.

LETTER 6

Charleston, Feb. 26, 1852

Henry R. Schoolcraft Esq.

DEAR SIR:

There is a book recently published, Morgan's League of the Iroquois—of which I should greatly like a review from your pen for the Southern Quarterly. The work seems to contain much material, but the author has shown himself a little too ambitious in its manufacture, and his speculations sometimes provoke a smile, showing no great philosophical depth. But this you will see readily for yourself. May I hope that you will find leisure for the performance.—I have been waiting on Dr. Bachman for the article on your great work, but not a syllable from him yet. You will percieve that I have noticed it, and your two octavos, briefly, but as fully as my space & leisure would allow. Suppose you inquire of Dr. B. in a casual epistle. Dr. Lieber has partly promised to review your second volume for us. When is that to appear?—I trust you keep well & vigorous. That you keep working I am sure. Pray do me the grace to remember me respectfully to Mrs. S.—

Yours Very truly

W. Gilmore Simms

LETTER 7

[April 14, 1852]

Henry R. Schoolcraft Esq.

MY DEAR SIR:

The Box with your second vol. has been recieved. I happened to be in the city at the moment of its arrival, and gave instructions to the Publishers in what way to dispose of the Copies, that excepted to Gen H. to whom they will write as to the best mode of conveying it safely. I will write to Lieber in the hope that he will (as he seemed to promise once) review it for our pages. I am in reciept of a letter from your *Liege* Lady, correcting some of the short comings in the Review. I enclose a note to her Ladyship. I note what you say of the Politicians, but truly, my dear Sir, I have learned well the maxim, that he who toucheth pitch is sure to be defiled. So I wash my hands of them.

Very truly but in great haste.

Yr obliged frd & Servt.

W. Gilmore Simms

Letter 8

Charleston, July 7. 1852.

Hon. Henry R. Schoolcraft.

Dear Sir:

I find that Lieber errs. Professor Miles regretfully but positively declines to write the Review of the Indian History. His hands he says are quite too full. Lieber has just gone North, with his head full of projects, and excusing himself from every possible task. Bachman is busy writing up the refutation of Luther in the Newspaper. My allies, confederates, contributors, appear to have left me every where in the lurch and I begin the October number of the Review this week with but a single article. Unless you can get me an article from some of your *confreres,* I shall have to undertake the Review myself at my first leisure; yet, when I shall again have leisure, God only knows. The d——d devil of the printing office is perpetually howling in my ears, in the language of that voice heard by the Apostle in Patmos, "Write!"—Do say to our princess, Madame S. that she will percieve in the July number of the Review, which will probably be out next week, that I have endeavoured to make the *amende honorable.* Present her with my best respects, and compliments.—By the way, could you not prompt young Lanman, with all the proper key notes & set him to work preparing a good review? With clues put into his hands, he might do the matter very well.

Yours truly & c

W. Gilmore Simms

When Simms was unsuccessful in persuading others (whom he thought better qualified) to write reviews of Schoolcraft's books on Native Americans for the *Southern Quarterly Review,* he as editor decided to undertake the task himself. His decision reflects his growing confidence in his own knowledge of Indian affairs as well as the high importance he attributed to the subject of Schoolcraft's scholarship.

୧୬ *Reviews of Henry Rowe Schoolcraft*

REVIEW OF *HISTORICAL AND STATISTICAL INFORMATION, RESPECTING THE HISTORY, CONDITION AND PROSPECTS OF THE INDIAN TRIBES OF THE UNITED STATES.* [FROM *SOUTHERN QUARTERLY REVIEW* IV, JULY 1851.]

This splendid volume must not be dismissed in a careless paragraph. It demands and deserves the most elaborate examination, such as will require time and compel study. At the moment, we can do little more than acknowledge its receipt. It is a publication, the design and execution of which are alike honourable to the republic and to those employed in the prosecution of its plan. No pains or money have been spared on it, and the result is a work, creditable, in high degree, to the munificence of the government, and to the state of art among us. It is worth much more, in a national point of view, than is usually achieved by an single session of Congress, consumed in no matter how many speeches. It is, mechanically, a beautiful specimen of book-making. The engravings are finely executed, and the letter-press is from the hands of an editor, than whom there is no one in the country more competent to the task of grouping the facts and elucidating the mysteries of Indian tradition and history. Mr. Schoolcraft has passed all his life in this employment. His experience in this field is, perhaps, far beyond that of any living man. His mind has been matured by study and devout research, and has been refined and sharpened for study by a proper education. We have, then, every guaranty that the work will prove worthy of the nation and honourable to the government. We shall examine it duly, at a future period, in regard to its intrinsic merits, as a critical history of the red men of America. The plan of this book is strictly national. It could only be achieved by a wealthy nation. To gather all the scattered proofs and traditions, in respect to the Indian races of America—to bring them together, in due relationship, for the future student—is to confer incalculable benefits upon science, history and art. There is another publication, in regard to our continent, which we should like to see the government undertake. This is collection of all voyages of original discovery to the New World, such as are scattered over hundreds of volumes, but little known, and which the student of history will need, for the proper analysis of facts in the discovery, colonization and progress of the States of America. Two volumes, such as the one before us, might be made to contain all this scattered material, and, with the aid of a competent editor, and copious notes, would contribute wonderfully to the success of those inquiries into our early history which are now pursued painfully, expensively, and with results always changing, in consequence of the impossibility of grasping all the authorities at the same moment. We shall return to this volume of Mr. Schoolcraft as soon as possible, satisfied that he has made of it a monument to his own zeal and industry, as well as to the perishing families of red men of America. We may add that the work contemplates other volumes, like the present. We know not how many. It should contain all records of authority, without mutilation, since no editor can know what portions of the chronicle or tradition will compel the consideration of art—will furnish his subject to the poet, the painter, the sculptor or the dramatist—and the highest value of history is in the use which is made of it by art. The errors and misconceptions of history are still portions of history, and are themselves not unfrequently seized upon by genius, for its most admirable imaginings, even as the chimerical terrors of the "still vexed Bermoothes"—the "Isle of Devils"—as described by early voyagers—have, in the hands of Shakespeare, taken shapes delightful to the heart and fancy—shapes of beauty, grace and wonder, such as have never been surpassed by any similar creations of art.

Review of *American Indians* and *Personal Memoirs.*
[From *Southern Quarterly Review* V, n.s., January 1852]

These are two great octavos, chiefly from the pen of a person who has probably enjoyed larger opportunities of knowing the red man, his nature, habits and history, than any other living man. Mr. Schoolcraft has spent some forty years of his life among the Indians of the North West. He has been variously a traveller, and long a resident among them. In the capacity of United States agent, he had singular opportunities of intercourse with them, and naturally acquired very considerable influence over them. In addition to these advantages, he was fortunate in another, which gave him a distinguished social position among the tribes. Adopting the old French custom, he took his first wife out of the wigwam,—a young damsel of one of the most distinguished families. This gave him the rank of a chief. His choice of a wife was particularly happy. She was a woman of quick mind, of a lively, intelligent genius, became an apt English pupil, and was soon enabled to teach her husband the mysteries of the laws, the language, and the traditions of her people. It follows from this, that, if any one person may be recognized as good authority in the affairs of the red man, Mr. Schoolcraft is that person. A man of quick intelligence himself, a devoted student, indefatigable in his studies, and rating them at a becoming valuation, he has acquired a vast body of material, such as has never been accumulated before by any single writer. His descriptions of the Indian character in general, of the warrior and chief, the hunt and the game, the family, the tribe, of war and council, are probably as accurate as we shall ever know. But his most valuable contribution to our resources is in what may be called the Literature of the Red Man. This volume contains a great variety of specimens of the Indian mind—its fancies, myths, traditions, legends and philosophies. Here is a complete body of mythology. Here are the narratives of the gods and good spirits, and demons, and nondescript beings, as attest the measure of the imagination of the red man, and show him in possession of the natural endowments, which, could he have been subdued and kept subordinate to a superior race, in familiar and daily contact, might have resulted in his preservation, as a people, and have enabled him to unfold the treasures of original intellect which he possessed. To the student, these volumes of Mr. Schoolcraft are a very precious acquisition. We regret that he had not made them into one, which he might easily have done by condensing his diary. A diary, well kept, by a man who is engaged in the struggles of the world, is no doubt a very interesting thing to posterity; but its publication requires selection, and the careful exclusion of what is merely passing and insignificant.

Stories

WRITTEN SHORTLY AFTER his 1824–25 visit to Mississippi, where he and his father rode on horseback among the Choctaws, "Indian Sketch" (1828), Simms's earliest fictional portrayal of the Native American, revolves around the difficulties that even intelligent Euro-Americans have in comprehending the complexities of Choctaw character and culture. Though rough in syntax, "Indian Sketch" is noteworthy for the narrative skill and power of its young author, particularly in the sparse, tightly woven final three paragraphs.

∾ Indian Sketch

During a short excursion, some years since in the Western country, I found, after a long and fatiguing ride over bad roads, on a hot and sultry day in June, that I was at length approaching something like a human settlement. The indication of the traces of human perseverance are to be met with in the wilderness some miles in advance of the habitations of the wanderers themselves. The long cross rail fence, the opening in the trees upon the sky, the clear whistle of the wind among the few remaining giants of the forest, and the distant hum of happy voices—together with the more clearly marked and intelligible lowing of cattle, neighing of horses, cackling of geese, and now and then the apparition of some bristly hog half wild and half tame, brushing suddenly by you, to your infinite alarm, particularly if night fall be at hand. Travelling, (as in all new countries, one must, if he wishes to travel without inconvenience from creeks running over their banks by frequent freshets, felled trees and often compelled to take a new road) on horseback, is calculated to render, after a long day's ride, the sight of a farm house one of those somethings in life, which, while we shall blush to give it the character or appellation of a pleasure, is nevertheless an object of no little moment and concern. I found the one to which I was fast approaching a perfect cure to my fatigue and ill-humour of the day. Whether it was that I had already begun to calculate on the smoking and enticing supper of fried bacon, eggs, fresh water trout, fresh butter, and round and glowing biscuits made of new Ohio flour—or that the natural tendency of the frame to repose and quietude, induced the feeling of gratitude and pleasure that I enjoyed, I leave to bookmen, apt at enquiries of this nature, to determine. Certain it was that I was more than pleased. I had ridden the whole day through a seemingly interminable forest, that, when I had emerged from the density of one seemed to show forth a denser and darker in which I had to embowel myself—that I had at length arrived safe at my resting place for the night, and all that was left for me to do, was to see my horse fed, rubbed down, and watered (a duty which no traveller ought to neglect) and to provide for the content and appetite of his equally hungering and jaded master. It required no great effort to make the inmates of this well stocked but humble cottage understand the nature of my wants, and provide for them accordingly, practised as they were, by an almost daily recurrence of similar duties. The supper table of neat pine was quickly furnished forth—a white cotton cloth with fringe from its sides a foot deep, was soon spread over it, and the rude but well relished dainties of country life were before me, and I nothing loth, ready for my repast.

I ate my supper in silence. My host was a half breed, who had married an Indian woman of the Nation (Choctaw) and under the sanction of the tribe, had commenced the business of Innkeeper upon their principal road. It is never the character of the Indian to be communicative; and nature has in this simple particular provided him with an education, which makes him more polite than the civilized man. His native independence and secluded and wandering habits, by removing him from the necessity of society, throws him upon himself, and his mind becomes actively employed, while his tongue may be said to slumber. The half-breed has so much of the aborigine still about him, that he partakes of nearly the same ascetic and taciturn disposition. His words are always significant and full of meaning—his looks are taught to have a language of their own for the better filling out and illustrating the brief and pithy accents of his speech. The Indian women are of a degraded *caste* in the opinion of the men. They are considered and used as mere beasts of burthen. Seldom, if ever admitted to the confidence of equality or affection, they are kept at a humble distance from their superiors, who assume to themselves in practice, the full supremacy as Lords of the creation. Nothing can be more amusing to one who is at all intimate with the Indian character, than the various pictures which are given of them by the Poet and the novelist. Nothing more idle and extravagant. The glory of the Indians (as they were) is the hunt and the battle field; and in robbing them of the extent of country sufficient for the one pursuit, and exercising such a powerful restraint upon them, as a ready and well-armed frontier, in the other, we seem to have robbed them of all of that pride, love of adventure and warlike enthusiasm, which is the only romance, the North American Indian ever had in his character.

As I have said, my supper was discussed in silent solemnity. My host sat before me at the head of the table, eating only occasionally. His consort, a large, strapping Indian woman *stood up behind* his chair and waiting upon us throughout the meal. The looks of both of them as well as of two young and tolerably well looking savages who sat in the corner of the room, seemed full of gravity and sadness. Although naturally gloomy and sullen, I could easily perceive that something unusual had taken place, and accordingly as soon as our repast was ended, after a preliminary compliment on my part of a twist of Tobacco, which seemed to have stirred up the spirit to an effort, I began my enquiries of the youngest of the group whom I soon ascertained to be the most communicative and intelligent. From him, I gathered the following interesting communication. There had been, it seems, (I use my own language, as his was broken and scarcely intelligible) a number of Indians, young men and women, employed by a neighbouring planter (a white man) to pick a quantity of cotton which he had on hand. For some days they pursued their labor, with diligence and assiduity, which, accustomed as we are to hear of the indisposition of the Indians to all manner of employment, except that of hunting, was, at least to me, new and interesting.

At length on the last day of the time for which they had been employed, the Planter, after rewarding them for their labor, produced the all inviting jug of whiskey—and placed it before them. This there was no withstanding. Those who had tasted the "Fire water" before, now set the example for those as yet ignorant of its perniciously seductive influence, and they all, with the exception of Mewanto became immediately intoxicated. This young man, who amidst the general example thus placed before him and from a society, than which, he could have no other restraint, could thus stoically resist, it must be supposed was a man of no ordinary strength of mind. He was in fact the pride of his people, and amidst their general depravity they felt the moral superiority of the man, and were "ashamed of their nakedness." Mewanto, had among the many who had bartered the higher energies of their original character, for sensual and momentary indulgence, one intimate, closely allied and dear friend, called Oolatibbe. He strove for a long while to prevent this young man from falling into the dangerous habits of his associates—but in vain. The prevalence of custom proved more effective than the advice and entreaties of friendship, and the youth, unaccustomed to the liquor, became in a short time deeply intoxicated. His friend, with some difficulty led him away from the small grove or thicket where the rest of the party were still carousing, and represented to him in the simple language of truth, the danger and the error of his present licentious and unhappy indulgence. He spoke with much warmth and a good deal of that native eloquence with which this people are said to be so admirable gifted—and I remember, my informant having used (for he adopted the figurative mode of speech so common, not only with them but every savage people) as the language of the young savage on this occasion, the following sentence. Alluding to the prostration of his people on the appearance of the whites, "that they had been as many as the leaves on the trees about them, but the white man had been the whirlwind that shook them down, and the remaining few were falling one by one, blighted and blasted by the cunning of their enemy, otherwise, wholly unable to remove them." The drunken man listened to him with a sort of stupid attention for some time, but at length suddenly starting back as if he had encountered some fearful object, he tore the knife from his belt, and before his friend could avoid the danger plunged it quickly into the bosom of Mewanto, who fell dead upon the spot.

He remained in a sort of stupor for a moment—but suddenly became sobered on the instant to behold with horror the dead body before him. A shriek or howl, which is indicative of some matter of death, and peculiar to the Indians, was the result of his first awakening to sensibility and reason. This, the rest of the Indians perfectly well understood, and it had the effect of bringing them all to their proper senses. A loud, wild, and melancholy cry was sent up in general by the party—the murderer preceding them to the great council of the nation. They placed no restraint whatever upon him— and without any compunction he voluntarily delivered himself up to the council and demanded to be led to death. "To-morrow," said my informant in conclusion, "he will be shot."* And where is he now, said I, anxious to gather from the youth as much more as possible, for his fit of talkativeness seemed to be nearly exhausted. "By your side," he returned. I started and

* For the full text of Simms's note see page 131.

beheld the same young man, whose countenance had first struck me while at the supper table. The question involuntarily arose and I asked with some astonishment—"and is he not confined—and will he not escape." "He cannot fly, for did he not help to make the law himself." Thus was the powerfully moral rule of all christian denominations, "Do not unto others what you would not others should do unto you," fairly and honestly obeyed on the most trying occasion in the annals of humanity, as if it had been one of the simplest duties of the domestic hearth.

I was curious to witness the final termination of this, to me, wonderful characteristic of a people, whom we have learned to despise, before we have been taught to understand. I turned round and fixed my gaze upon the condemned. What could a spectator, unacquainted with the circumstances, have met with there. Nothing of the precise and awful matter of fact, that connected itself with the fortunes and life of the object of observation. I addressed him—I brought him to the subject so deeply interesting to himself. He spoke of it, as of those common occurrences which we often speak of unconsciously. He took up the handle of a tomahawk and employed himself in carving upon it, a space for a bit of flattened silver which he labored to introduce into it. He spoke in detached sentences, during this little effort. In reply to a question which I put, touching the commission of the crime, and whether he was conscious that he was doing it or not, he replied—"Yes—he knew it all—he knew it was the one of himself, the best part—but he had put on a horrible shape and the evil one darkened his eye sight—that while he struck the blow, he knew perfectly well that it was his friend he struck, but that he was made to do it."

We conversed at intervals till a late hour—he seemed to sing at times or rather muttered a few broken catches of song, monotonous and highly solemn—at length, the rest having withdrawn, he threw himself upon a bear skin before the door, and I attended the little boy, who was with difficulty aroused from a deep sleep, to my chamber, which he pointed out.

It may be supposed, I slept little that night. I was filled with thoughts of the strange obedience which this ignorant savage manifested to his rude and barbarous, but really equitable laws. The highest moral obligation however instructing him, "that he must not expect others to do, what he would not do himself."

The next morning, a large crowd had assembled within and around the house in which I slept. I rose and went to the window. The open space in front of the house was covered with the Indians. A great deal of excitement seemed to run through them all. I dressed myself as quickly as possible and went down among them. They were crowded in the house as well as in the area before it. I looked about for the principal in this extraordinary spectacle —his were the only features unmoved in the assembly. He seemed busily employed in gathering up sundry little articles as well of ornament as necessity in the Indian's life. His dress seemed more studied—it consisted of a pair of pantaloons, seemingly much worn, and probably the cast off donation of some passing traveller. There was a buckskin hunting shirt on him, with several falling capes, all thickly covered with fringe, a belt of wampum, studded with beads of various colours, tolerably well arranged, encircled his waist— while his legs, which were well formed, were admirably fitted by a pair of leggings loaded with beads. Several other little ornaments were thrown about him, particularly over his neck and shoulders.

A difference in sentiment seemed to operate upon, and form a division among the assembled multitude, an air of anger, impatience and exultation, fully indicated the friends of the deceased thirsting for the blood of his murderer—while an appearance of sadness and concern, pointed out those who were most tenderly disposed toward him. At length, the victim himself made the first signal of preparation. He arose, and giving to a little boy who followed him, a bundle which he had been making up of beads, hatchets, arrow heads, knives, tobacco-pouch and some other little things, he led the way. I joined in the mournful procession. Our way led through a long grove of stunted pines—at the end of which we were met, and accompanied by three men appointed as his executioners, who were armed with rifles, which they wore under the left arm.

Never did I behold a man with a step so firm on any occasion, or head so unbent—a countenance so unmoved, and yet without any of the effort common to most men who endeavor to assume an aspect of heroism upon an event so trying. He walked as to a victory. The triumphal arch seemed above him, and instead of an ignominious death, a triumph over a thousand hearts seemed depicted before him.

The grave was in sight. I watched his brow attentively. I felt myself shudder and grow pale, but saw no change in him. He began a low song, apparently consisting of monosyllables only. He grew more impassioned—more deeply warm. I could not understand a single word he uttered—but, even though he stood as firm, proud and unbending as a Roman might be supposed to have stood, as if he disdained the addition of action to his words, the cadence, the fall, the melody and wild intonation of this high-souled savage's voice was to me an active eloquence, which I could not misunderstand. He paused at length. Then moving with an even pace, he took his place at the head of the grave prepared for him—beckoned the boy near, who had followed him, with the simple utensils of savage life, and when he had retired, motioned the executioners. I saw them prepare their rifles, and take their aim—I looked upon the features of the victim—they were steady and calm— I turned my head away with a strange sickness. I heard the single report of the three rifles, and when I turned my eye on the spot so lately occupied by the unfortunate victim of an infatuation, which has slain more than the sword, they were slowly shovelling the earth into the grave of the murderer.

[SIMMS'S NOTE] *We annex a poem by a native writer upon this subject, which (as we believe it has never been quoted before) may serve as an apt illustration of this article.*

> At midnight did the Chiefs convene,
> With many a shriek of wild alarm,
> 'Till solemn silence hushed the scene,
> As in prophetic charm;
> When, wild the cry of horror broke,
> And thus a dark brow'd warrior spoke
>
> "I come to die—no vain delay,
> Nor trembling pulse unnerves my soul;
> Ye fellow Chiefs, prepare the way—
> Let death's dark clouds about me roll;
> My bosom feels alone life's dread—
> There is no feeling with the dead!
>
> Our tribe has lost its bravest steel—
> 'Tis well the scabbard follow too,
> Since life no longer can reveal
> Aught that can glad my view:
> From its own home, I madly tore
> The jewel, that my bosom wore.

He cross'd me in my hour of wrath,
And still with cruel love pursued—
An evil spirit dimn'd my path,
A film o'erspread my gaze—I view'd
No more, the friend I lov'd so well,
But some insatiate foe from hell!

My hand had grasp'd its kindred knife,
A struggle, and I heard a cry—
It was the shriek of parting life,
For it is hard to die,
A friend or kindred soul to leave—
Now, there are none, for me will grieve!

Too late, too late I knew my friend,
Too late, had wish'd the deed undone!
'Twere vain, my bosom's grief to blend
With tears, that can restore me none,
(Tho' in unending streams they fell)
Of all the friend, I loved so well.

Far, wand'ring on the distant hills,
Yet watching for the morning's dawn,
His spirit lingers near the rills,
Now anxious to be gone:
And only waits my kindred shade,
To bear it to the grave I made.

His hatchet seen in gleaming light,
When first the warhoop's cry is heard,
I've placed to meet his walking sight,
When carols first the morning bird!
Nor did my bosom's care forget,
His rifle, knife and calumet!

Prepare the grave, I long to fly,
To that far distant realm of bliss,
Where nought can dim the spirit's eye,
Or, lead the heart like this;
Where, morning owns no clouded shade
And life is light, and undecay'd.

Oh, brother, whom I madly slew,
Then shall our kindred spirits join;
At morn the red-deer's path pursue—
At eve the tented camp entwine;
Close atone time the mutual eye,
And on one blanket's bosom, lie."

No longer spoke the Warrior Chief,
But sullen sternness clothed his brow,
Whilst fate and anguish, fix'd and brief,
Proclaim'd him—ready now!
No counsel spoke—no pray'r was made—
No pomp—no mock'ry—no parade.

He walk'd erect, unaw'd, unbound;
He stood upon the grave's dread brink,
And look'd with careless eye around;
Nor did his spirit shrink,
The deadly rifle's aim to greet,
His bosom long'd its death to meet.

A moment's pause—no sound was heard;
He gazed—then with unchanging look,
He spoke in pride, the signal word,
With which the valley shook—
And when the smoke had cleared away,
The dark-eyed Chief before me lay.

IN "LEGEND OF MISSOURI" (originally, the main title was simply "Missouri"), Simms moves west of the Mississippi River to depict the brutal warfare between the Omahas and the Pawnees that is destructive to both tribes. The story exemplifies Simms's theme that despite their nobility—sense of honor, passion for freedom, capacity for love, natural eloquence of expression, bravery in battle, and moral commitment to purpose—Native Americans were doomed to tragic extinction by the encroachment of white civilization.

∾ Legend of Missouri: or, the Captive of the Pawnee

> "A token from the spirit land—
> A hallowed gift from fairy hand;
> A withered leaf, a flower whose stem,
> Thus broke, we liken unto them.
> A rainbow hue, that now appears,
> Then melts away, like hope, in tears."

The Pawnees and the Omahas were neighboring nations, and perpetually at war with one another. A deadly hostility, increased by every contest, existed between them; and it became evident that no cessation of war could be hoped for, from the inextinguishable hatred of either people, unless in the total annihilation of one or the other, or, more probably of both. They were equally numerous, equally brave, equally cunning and cautious; equally matched, indeed, in almost every respect. The advantage obtained by either side, was most generally trifling, and the victor had but little to boast. Sheer exhaustion, and the necessity of a breathing spell alone, sometimes interposed to give them "a task of peace," and, in a pause from hostility, to allow them to rebuild their broken lodges, and provide materials for sustenance and war. The original causes of this vindictive spirit might not well be ascertained at the date of our story, so remote had been its origin. Antiquity had, in some degree, to each generation consecrated the strife, and given it sanctity; and one of the first lessons taught, accordingly, to the Pawnee and Omaha boy, was to learn how to strike and scalp and circumvent the national enemy, and transmit the same vindictive lesson to his descendants in turn.

Such was the condition of things at the period of which we speak. The autumn campaign was about to be begun, and the Pawnee-loups, before setting upon the war path, held a solemn feast and council, in order to determine upon the most advisable plans, and to obtain the sanction of the Great Spirit, as ascertained by his priests. It is useless to dwell, even for a moment, upon the many horrid rites which attended and characterised this festival. The American reader, with few exceptions, is familiar with the long details of that barbarous mummery, in which, on these occasions, the savages indulge; without any seeming meaning, and scarcely with any regular design in view. It is enough to say, that on this event, nothing was omitted from the festival, at all calculated, in the mind of the savage, to give it an air of the most imposing solemnity. The priests divined and predicted general success —taking care, however, as in the case of most other prophets, to speak in language sufficiently vague to allow of its adaptation to any circumstances— or resting solely on those safe predictions, which commonly bring about their own verification. They did not, however, confine themselves to prophesying the event of the war—they counselled the course to be pursued, and the plans to be adopted, and, with too dictatorial a manner to be resisted or rejected. Among other of their predictions, they declared that victory should now rest with that nation who took and put to death the first prisoner by the fire torment—a favourite punishment with the Indians, as affording a trial of the courage and firmness of the captive. Such a prediction as this, though seemingly barbarous and cruel, was in reality of a tendency highly merciful, and more than any other measure calculated to arrest the wanton fury of warfare, which is so much the characteristic of the savage. All unnecessary risk was avoided; and the object now, with the Pawnees, was how to obtain a captive from the enemy, without endangering the freedom of their own people. The subtlety of the Indian, notoriously great, was not long wanting in a stratagem to bring about its object. They effected their designs, and procured their captive without loss or exposure to themselves.

The Omahas were not unconscious or unadvised of the goings on of their enemies. They too had their grand council, and made their preparations for the autumn war path. Their warriors had assembled at different points, and both nations, about the same moment, had sallied forth from their lodges. It was not the intention of the Pawnees to proceed to extremities at the outset. With a degree of caution, which, to them, was highly unusual, and which awakened the surprise of their opponents, they contented themselves with patroling their towns and villages, making no overtures of combat, and seemingly bent only on defending their country from attack. In vain, provoked beyond all patience by this shyness, did the young brave of the Omahas sally forth in sight of the watchful Pawnees; daring them to combat, assailing them with all manner of reproachful taunt, and denouncing them as mere women, and degenerate from their ancestors. Though feeling all this sorely, and scarcely able to command the natural temper of the nation, the Pawnees still contrived to be quiet in the meanwhile, blindly relying on the prediction of their priests, and satisfied that success alone lay in the counsels which they had given them.

The Omaha village was one of the most beautiful that can be imagined, in the verge and limit of a southern country, which boasts an almost perpetual spring. Their principal settlement was upon a small island, embosomed in a broad and glassy lake, which empties into the river Platte. There was no approach to it but by boats, and no invader could make his appearance within gunshot, without being at once perceptible from all parts of the secluded and quiet island. There every thing wore the smooth and soothing features of a perpetual summer. The flowers were lengthened in life and strengthened with odour, and the breeze, from the broad prairies, in crossing over the little lake, lost all its sharpness and rigour, and retained only its balm and sweetness.

The secluded character of this situation—its remoteness from the enemies' country, and the great and unalloyed security, which, in all their wars, it had heretofore enjoyed, had served to make the Omahas relax somewhat in the vigilance, with which, at one time, they had been accustomed to guard and watch over so exquisite a spot. But a few warriors, principally infirm, remained on the island; the residue being either out on the war path, or engaged in the sports of the chase—it being the custom, arising from the necessity of the thing, thus to employ one portion of the people in procuring, and another defending, the sustenance and provisions of their community. If the cunning Pawnees did not exactly know of this fact, they at least suspected it; and while the great body of their warriors contrived to keep in check, and exercise the unconscious Omahas, a small, but selected band, had been despatched by a circuitous route, with the daring intention of making a descent upon the defenceless village, and taking a captive, no matter of what sex or condition, in order to secure for their nation the full benefit of the prediction of their prophets.

There was among the Omaha warriors, a youth, scarcely attained to manhood, than whom a braver or more daring man the nation did not possess. Though young, he had been often engaged in conflict, and had acquired a name among his tribe, which placed him among the foremost in war, and won for him the respect of the most aged in the solemn deliberations of the council. Brave though he was, however, and stern and terrible among his enemies, the young Enemoya was not insensible to the tender passion. He had already told his love to the gentle Missouri, the loveliest and liveliest maiden of his tribe, and upon his return from the present expedition, she was to leave her own and take up her abode in the lodge of Enemoya.

Many were the thoughts of Enemoya—while, day after day, he watched, without any prospect of action, the motions of the Pawnees—on the subject of his love, and of the hour of his return. Of the spoils, which he would bear home as a trophy of his victory, and a pledge of his affections, and of the happiness which would make all his life before him, like the flower of the prairie, that expands its leaves during the day for the reception of the sunshine, which at evening it shuts up nor allows to escape. He dreamt, as the young heart always dreams when love is the subject; and in his dreamings he grew impatient of the war, which kept him from the maid of his bosom, and gave him no spoils to take home to her. Finding it impossible to provoke a fight, the Omahas began to direct their attention to the sports of the forest, and contenting themselves with throwing, in the manner of their enemies, a line of observation and guard between the assailable points of their country, and the usual war paths of the Pawnees; the one half of them set seriously to work, to add to the stock of venison which was to supply their nation. Not so with Enemoya. Denied to come to battle with his enemies, he forbore to join in the chase, but taking his arms along with him, he stole away from his associates, and took the path back to the little island and the beautiful Missouri. To the light-footed warrior, pursuing the direct course, the journey was not long in consummation; and in the course of a few days, we find him on the borders of the placid lake, which lay, like a slumbering and glad spirit, unmoved and untroubled before him. He paused but for an instant, to take from the branch on which it hung, the clear and yellow gourd, and to drink from the sweet waters; then stepping into the light "dug-out," or canoe, which stood ready on its margin, he struck out the paddle alternately upon either side, and it shot rapidly towards the island. Enemoya did not remark any peculiarity in the village while crossing; for his mind was filled with that dreamy contemplation, which, directed only to, and absorbed in but one subject, effectually excluded and shut out every other; but as he approached, and when his bark struck the smooth and silvery beach, he became conscious of an unusual degree of quietude and gloom, for which he knew not how to account. There were but few persons to be seen, and their looks were downcast, and grave in the extreme, and indicative of some terrible disaster. He soon learned the worst from those he encountered. The Pawnees, in a strong body, had unexpectedly made a descent upon them, and after putting to death the few who continued to resist, had borne off as captives, several of their maidens, among whom the horror-stricken Enemoya heard the name of his Missouri. After a moment of stupid desolation, he rushed to the point of land whence the descent was made, hurriedly enquired into its several particulars, learned the course taken by the ravishers, and without hesitation, set off in the pursuit.

The headlong Enemoya went on without other delay than was necessary to discern the tracks left behind by the departing enemy. Under any other lighter circumstances the free step of Enemoya would have made him fearful as a pursuer, but an added facility and lightness of foot grew out of the fury and the frenzy of his heart. Passion and despair seemed to have provided him with wings, and he evidently gained upon his enemy. Every step he took freshened their tracks to his eye, and new hopes were aroused and multiplied in his heart. At midnight of the second day of his pursuit he came suddenly, (and by a bend made by a broad river shooting obliquely from his path, which had heretofore run beside it,) upon the blaze of a large camp-fire. Such a prospect would have cheered the white man, but it had no such effect upon the Indian. He knew that the enemy for whom he sought would raise no such beacon for his guidance; but he hesitated not to approach the fire, around which a group of white men were seated, partaking of a rude repast, which they had just prepared. The savage was not ignorant of the civilised; and the intercourse of Enemoya with the fur traders, in which business his nation largely dealt, had even given him some knowledge of the language. They started to their arms, and demanded his business. It was soon revealed, and with a degree of warmth and passion, which, as it was supposed to be uncommon with the Indian character, surprised them. They heard his story, and immediately gave him intelligence of the party which he pursued. They were a party of settlers from Kentucky, who had drawn stakes, and were now on the look-out for a new whereabout, in which they might replant them. They were a hardy set of adventurers, and as they sat around their blazing fires, while their wives were preparing their repasts, the young warrior, for the first time, conceived the idea of craving their co-operation in the rescue of the fair Missouri. Such leagues were not unfrequent between the settlers and the proprietors, and in this way, in most cases, as in the history of the downfall of the Roman empire, those who came as allies remained as conquerors. Having, by joint effort, destroyed one tribe, it was no difficult matter for the auxiliaries to turn upon those they had succoured, and in their weakened condition, as little difficult to overpower them. This, indeed, is in most part, the history of American sway in the valley of the Mississippi. The squatters heard his prayer with attention, and found their account in it. They determined to assist him, and making a hasty but hearty supper, they somewhat varied their original line of march, and joined in the pursuit.

It was not long before the pursuers came upon the certain and sure signs of the enemy. The eye of Enemoya soon perceived, and his quick and awakened spirit did not delay in pointing them out. He knew the country, its bearings and character, and taking them to a turn by which they might head the waters of a creek which ran across their path, he gained greatly upon the Pawnees. They came upon them suddenly and unexpectedly, but the Pawnees were warriors too good to suffer total surprise. They had put out their sentries, and, though not dreaming of assault, were not unprepared to encounter it. They were sitting upon the ground, not in a group, but scattered here and there, at a few paces from one another. Some lay beneath a tree, others in the long matted grass of the prairies, and a few were entirely uncovered to the eye of the pursuers. The Indian maiden lay bound betwixt two of the most powerful of the marauders—her hair dishevelled, her face unmoved but anxious, and her demeanour that of the captive who felt all her misfortune, yet knew how to bear it. It was a sight that did not permit of a single moment's consideration with the young Enemoya. With a single bound and uplifted hatchet, he sprung forward from the covert in which his party had concealed themselves, and by thus exposing his person, destroyed the chances of a surprise. He beheld his error when too late to amend it. The Pawnees leapt to their arms, and the warrior, in the shelter of a tree which secured his person from their rifles, had leisure to repent of his rashness, so unlike the Indian, and so injurious to the prospect of success. But this was not his sole danger. On the first exhibition of his person, the two savages, to whom the custody of the maiden was given, seized her by her long hair, and raising their knives to her bosom, prepared on the first attack to put an end to her life. It was this that arrested the arm of Enemoya, and subdued a spirit that had never before quailed, and seldom hesitated. It was now necessary to take counsel, and he regained the shelter in which, as yet concealed, lay his white allies. In number they exceeded the force of the Pawnees, and could easily have destroyed them. This was, indeed, the first impulse; but from the fiendish cunning of the foe, they were taught to fear and feel that the signal of strife would be that of death to the fair Indian. The squatters were men of daring, but they were also men of experience; and while they held boldness and confidence as primary requisites in the character of the warrior, they felt that rashness and precipitance would undo and ruin every thing. Accordingly, having deliberated among themselves, it was determined that two of the squatters, in company with Enemoya, should appear, and tender the flag of truce, a white handkerchief attached to a willow, which the Indians had by this time learned to respect; to see upon what terms they could procure the freedom of the maiden. At their appearance the Indians emerged form their several places of repose and shelter, and advanced to meet them, with no more signs of civility, however, than were absolutely necessary to avoid the appearance of attack. The squatter undertook to be spokesman, and, in a way, accommodating his language to the understanding of the Pawnees, by a liberal sprinkling of words from theirs, he sought to make his business understood. He told them of their captive, and of the folly of keeping her for their torture, which was of no use, when they might make her a subject of speculation. He concluded by making proposals to purchase her for himself, offering arms, knives, and such other objects of use with the Indian, which, as a sometime trader among them, he knew would be in demand. The chief of the Pawnees heard him out with great gravity and the most respectful attention, but told him calmly and deliberately that there could be no trade—that the fate of the Pawnees or Omahas depended upon her life, and that he had, with his warriors, taken a long journey to get her into his power; that no price could tempt him to forego his hold, and that in a few hours the captive would undergo the fiery torture.

While speaking, the young and passionate Enemoya had approached his beloved Missouri. Her head had been cast down, but upon his approach, she looked up and fixed a long, fond, and earnest gaze upon him, with an entreating and pleading expression which almost maddened him. Yet, without violating the privilege afforded by his flag of truce, he could not approach or speak to her. Impatiently did he await the final determination of the Pawnee, lengthened out, as it was, by the figurative and glowing language which he employed; but when the final resolve fell upon the ears of Missouri, she rushed from between the two warriors, who had relaxed their hold upon her, and endeavoured to throw herself into the arms of her lover; but her captors were not idle, and before she could effect her object, a blow from the arm of one of them precipitated her to the earth. In a moment, the work of death had begun. The conference was broken off, and the hatchet of Enemoya had been driven deep into the scull of the brutal chief who had struck his betrothed. The Indians were taken by surprise, and did not offer a ready resistance. A second blow from the young warrior, and he had struck from his way the only opponent between himself and Missouri, and he was now rushing towards the maiden, when the leader of the Pawnees with whom the conference had been held, threw himself between them, and grappling Enemoya, they fell together to the earth. Their grasp was taken closely around the bodies of one another, and the chief effort of both was to get hold of, and employ the short broad knife which each wore in his belt. This task was not so easy, and in the meanwhile, the struggle was one rather of fatigue than danger. These employed, the rest were not idle. The Kentuckian made his retreat to a neighboring tree, the click of his rifle was the signal to the rest of his party, and before the Pawnees had dreamt of the presence of so numerous an enemy, several of them had bit the dust. The squatters rushed on with their knives, exhibiting too large a force for opposition, and the enemy fled; all but one, who, after the hesitation of a moment, with a look of concentrated and contested anger and triumph, leapt through the thicket which lay between himself and where their chief and Enemoya were still vainly struggling, seizing the still bound maiden with one hand, he struck his hatchet deep into her brain, then, without pausing to extricate it, and before the deed might be revenged, with a howl, betwixt a shout of victory and derision, he rejoined his party. Enemoya beheld the blow and sought to release himself, but without success; and turning his eyes, as it were, consciously, to where the bleeding and insensible form of the young maiden lay stretched out before him, he stood at the mercy of his enemy, who had drawn his knife, and with hand uplifted, was about to plunge it into his bosom; but before he could do so, the stroke of a rifle from one of the squatters prostrated him, and determined the struggle. But the hope of our warrior was blighted, and he moved along as a shadow. He returned with the squatters, and they reached with him the quiet lake and the beautiful island; yet he but came to hear of new disasters. The relaxed discipline and weakened force of the Omaha warriors, opposed to that of the Pawnees, added to the encouraging account of the success of the party, sent for the purpose of taking their captive, had emboldened them to an attack, which, conducted with skill, caution, and spirit, had terminated in the total defeat of the former, and the slaughter of the best of their warriors.

"We will build our cabins here," said the head man of the squatters, "by this quiet lake, and on these verdant meadows. Here will we make an abode."

"But this is the abode of my people, brother; here is the wigwam of Enemoya, and this is the dwelling I had built up for the hope of my heart, the gentle Missouri."

"Your people are destroyed, and have no dwelling, Enemoya; and Missouri is a fair spirit in the heavens. You are a brave and a good youth—be with us, and dwell with our people, and here will we live together."

"No," said the Omaha, "my people are indeed no more, but I can mix with no other. Be yours the fair island and the quiet lake, and when you have made it, and all the forest round, a dwelling for you and your children, and your children's children, as it is with you white men the way always to do, remember the Omaha, and call the nation you enjoy after the beautiful Missouri. For me, I shall go over the great lakes, and hunt the buffalo in the black prairies of the west, till the Great Spirit shall send for me to dwell once more among the people of the tribe."

The squatter gave the promise he required, and the country thus granted by Enemoya, is even to this day called "Missouri," after the beautiful maiden of Omaha.

THE SOFT-TONED, MILDLY IRONIC humor of "Logoochie" lifts this ingenious comic portrayal of an Indian wood spirit into an effective rendering of one of Simms's recurring themes, the deprivation of Native Americans of their lands and their cultures by the advance of white settlers. Despite a conventional love plot with shallow characters, the story—well written throughout—displays in the imaginative characterization of Logoochie a lightness of tone and a deftness of touch that mark only the best of Simms's humorous writings.

ᐳ *Logoochie; or, the Branch of Sweet Water. A Legend of Georgia*

I.

With the approach of the white settlers, along the wild but pleasant banks of the St. Mary's river, in the state of Georgia, the startled deities of Indian mythology began to meditate their departure to forests more secure. Tribe after tribe of the aborigines had already gone, and the uncouth gods of their idolatry presided, in numberless instances, only over their deserted habitations. The savages had carried with them no guardian divinities—no hallowed household altars—cheering them in their new places of abode, by the acceptance of their sacrifice, and with the promise of a moderate winter, or a successful hunt. In depriving them of the lands descended to them in trust from their fathers, the whites seem also to have exiled them from the sweet and mystic influences, so aptly associated with the vague loveliness of forest life, of their many twilight superstitions. Their new groves, as yet, had no spells for the huntsman; and the Manneyto of their ancient sires, failed to appreciate their tribute offerings, intended to propitiate his regards, or to disarm his anger. They were indeed outcasts; and, with a due feeling for their exiled worshippers, the forest-gods themselves determined also to depart from those long-hallowed sheltering places in the thick swamps of the Okephanokee, whence, from immemorial time, they had gone forth, to cheer or to chide the tawny hunter in his progress through life. They had served the fathers faithfully, nor were they satisfied that the sons should go forth unattended. They had consecrated his dwellings, they had stimulated his courage, they had thrown the pleasant waters along his path, when his legs failed him in the chase, and his lips were parched with the wanderings of the long day in summer; and though themselves overcome in the advent of superior gods, they had, nevertheless, prompted him to the last, in the protracted struggle which he had maintained, for so many years, and with such various successes, against his pale invaders. All that could be done for the feather-crowned and wolf-mantled warrior, had been done, by the divinities he worshipped. He was overcome, driven away from his ancient haunts, but he still bowed in spirit to the altars, holy still to him, though, haplessly, without adequate power to secure him in his possessions. They determined not to leave him unprotected in his new abodes, and gathering, at the bidding of Satilla, the Mercury of the southern Indians, the thousand gods of their worship—the wood-gods and the water-gods—crowded to the flower-island of Okephanokee, to hear the commands of the Great Manneyto.

II.

All came but Logoochie, and where was he? he, the Indian mischief-maker—the Puck, the trickiest spirit of them all,—he, whose mind, like his body, a creature of distortion, was yet gentle in its wildness, and never suffered the smallest malice to mingle in with its mischief. The assembly was dull without him—the season cheerless—the feast wanting in provocative. The Great Manneyto himself, with whom Logoochie was a favorite, looked impatiently on the approach of every new comer. In vain were all his inquiries— where is Logoochie? who has seen Logoochie? The question remained unanswered—the Great Manneyto unsatisfied. Anxious search was instituted in every direction for the discovery of the truant. They could hear nothing of him, and all scrutiny proved fruitless. They knew his vagrant spirit, and felt confident he was gone upon some mission of mischief; but they also knew how far beyond any capacity of theirs to detect, was his to conceal himself, and so, after the first attempt at search, the labor was given up in despair. They could get no tidings of Logoochie.

III.

The conference went on without him, much to the dissatisfaction of all parties. He was the spice of the entertainment, the spirit of all frolic; and though sometimes exceedingly annoying, even to the Great Manneyto, and never less so to the rival power of evil, the Opitchi-Manneyto, yet, as the recognized joker on all hands, no one found it wise to take offence at his tricks. In council, he relieved the dull discourse of some drowsy god, by the sly sarcasm, which, falling innocuously upon the ears of the victim, was yet readily comprehended and applied by all the rest. On the journey, he kept all around him from any sense of weariness,—and, by the perpetual practical application of his humor, always furnished his companions, whether above or inferior to him in dignity, with something prime, upon which to make merry. In short, there was no god like Logoochie, and he was as much beloved by the deities, as he was honored by the Indian, who implored him not to turn aside the arrow which he sent after the bounding buck, nor to spill the water out of his scooped leaf as he carried it from the running rivulet up to his mouth. All these were tricks of the playful Logoochie, and by a thousand, such as these, was he known to the Indians.

IV.

Where, then, was the absentee when his brother divinities started after the outlawed tribes? Had he not loved the Indians—had he no sympathy with his associate gods—and wherefore went he not upon the sad journey through the many swamps and the long stretches of sand and forest, that lay between the Okephanokee, and the rapidly-gushing waters of the Chatahoochie, where both the aborigines and their rude deities had now taken up their abodes. Alas! for Logoochie! He loved the wild people, it is true, and much he delighted in the association of those having kindred offices with himself; but though a mimic and a jester, fond of sportive tricks, and perpetually prac- tising them on all around him, he was not unlike the memorable buffoon of Paris, who, while ministering to the amusement of thousands, possessing them with an infinity of fun and frolic, was yet, at the very time, craving a precious mineral from the man of science to cure him of his confirmed hypochondria. Such was the condition of Logoochie. The idea of leaving the old woods and the waters to which he had been so long accustomed, and which were associated in his memory with a thousand instances of merri- ment, was too much for his most elastic spirits to sustain; and the summons to depart filled him with a nameless, and, to him, a hitherto unknown form of terror. His organ of inhabitiveness had undergone prodigious increase in the many exercises which his mind and mood had practised upon the banks of the beautiful Branch of Sweet Water, where his favorite home had been chosen by a felicitous fancy. It was indeed a spot to be loved and dwelt upon, and he who surveyed its clear and quiet waters, sweeping pleasantly onward with a gentle murmur, under the high and bending pine trees that arched over and fenced it in, would have no wonder at its effect upon a spirit so sus- ceptible, amidst all his frolic, as that of Logoochie. The order to depart made him miserable; he could not think of doing so; and, trembling all the while, he yet made the solemn determination not to obey the command; but rather to subject himself, by his refusal, to a loss of caste, and, perhaps, even severer punishment, should he be taken, from the other powers having guardianship with himself, over the wandering red men. With the determination came the execution of his will. He secreted himself from those who sought him, and in the hollow of a log lay secure, even while the hunters uttered their conjectures and surmises under the very copse in which he was hidden. His arts to escape were manifold, and, unless the parties in search of him knew intimately his practices, he could easily elude their scrutiny by the simplest contrivances. Such, too, was the susceptibility of his figure for distortion, that even Satilla, the three eyed, the messenger of the Indian divinities, the most acute and cunning among them, was not unfrequently overreached and evaded by the truant Logoochie. He too had searched for him in vain, and though having a shrewd suspicion, as he stepped over a pine knot lying across a path, just about dusk, that it was something more than it seemed to be, yet passing on without examining it, and leaving the breathless Logoochie, for it was he, to gather himself up, the moment his pursuer was out of sight, and take himself off in a more secluded direction. The back of Logoochie was, itself, little better than a stripe of the tree bark to those who remarked it casually. From his heel to his head, inclusive, it looked like so many articulated folds or scales of the pine tree, here and there bulging out into excrescences. The back of his head was a solid knot, for all the world like that of the scorched pine knot, hard and resinous. This knot ran across in front, so as to arch above and overhang his forehead, and was crowned with hair, that, though soft, was thick and woody to the eye, and even looked not unlike the plates of the pine-bur when green in season. It rose into a ridge or comb directly across the head from front to rear, like the war tuft of a Seminole warrior. His eyes, small and red, seemed, occasionally, to run into one another, and twinkled so, that you could not avoid laughing but to look upon them. His nose was flat, and the mouth was simply an incision across his face, reaching nigh to both his ears, which lapped and hung over like those of a hound. He was short in person, thick, and strangely bow-legged; and, to complete the uncouth figure, his arms, shooting out from under a high knot, that gathered like an epaulette upon each shoulder, possessed but a single though rather long bone, and terminated in a thick, squab, bur-like hand, having fingers, themselves inflexible, and but of single joints, and tipped, not with nails, but with claws, somewhat like those of the panther, and equally fearful in strife. Such was the vague general outline which, now and then, the Indian hunter, and, after him, the Georgia squatter, caught, towards evening, of the wandering Logoochie, as he stole suddenly from sight into the sheltering copse, that ran along the edges of some wide savannah.

The brother divinities of the Creek warriors had gone after their tribes, and Logoochie alone remained upon the banks of the Sweet Water Branch. He remained in spite of many reasons for departure. The white borderer came nigher and nigher, with every succeeding day. The stout log-house started up in the centre of his favorite groves, and many families, clustering within a few miles of his favorite stream, formed the nucleus of the flourishing little town of St. Mary's. Still he lingered, though with a sadness of spirit, hourly increasing, as every hour tended more and more to circumscribe the haunts of his playful wandering. Every day called upon him to deplore the overthrow, by the woodman's axe, of some well remembered tree in his neighborhood; and though he strove, by an industrious repetition of his old tricks, to prevent much of this desolation, yet the divinities which the white man brought with him were too potent for Logoochie. In vain did he gnaw by night the sharp edge of the biting steel, with which the squatter wrought so much desolation. Alas! the white man had an art given him by his God, by which he smoothed out its repeated gaps, and sharpened it readily again, or found an new one, for the destruction of the forest. Over and over again, did Logoochie think to take the trail of his people, and leave a spot in which a petty strife of this nature had become, though a familiar, a painful practice; but then, as he thought of the humiliating acknowledgment which, by so doing, he must offer to his brother gods, his pride came to his aid, and he determined to remain where he was. Then again, as he rambled along the sweet waters of the branch, and talked pleasantly with the trees, his old acquaintance, and looked down upon little groups of Indians that occasionally came to visit this or that tumulus of the buried nations, he felt a sweet pleasure in the thought, that although all were gone of the old possessors, a new people and new gods had come to sway the lands of his outlawed race, he still should linger and watch over, with a sacred regard, the few relics, and the speechless trophies, which the forgotten time had left them. He determined to remain still, as he long had been, the presiding genius of the place.

V.

From habit, at length, it came to Logoochie to serve, with kind offices, the white settlers, just as he had served the red men before him. He soon saw that, in many respects, the people dwelling in the woods, however different their color and origin, must necessarily resemble one another. They were in some particulars equally wild and equally simple. He soon discovered, too, that however much they might profess indifference to the superstitions of the barbarous race they had superseded, they were not a whit more secure from the occasional tremors which followed his own practices or presence. More than once had he marked the fright of the young woodman, as, looking towards nightfall over his left shoulder, he had beheld the funny twinkling eyes, and the long slit mouth, receding suddenly into the bush behind him. This assured Logoochie of the possession still, even with a new people, of some of that power which he had exercised upon the old; and when he saw, too, that the character of the white man was plain, gentle, and unobtrusive, he came, after a brief study, to like him also; though, certainly, in less degree, than his Indian predecessors. From one step of his acquaintance with the new comers to another, Logoochie at length began to visit, at stolen periods, and to prowl around the little cottage, of the squatter;—sometimes playing tricks upon his household, but more frequently employing himself in the analysis of pursuits, and of a character, as new almost to him as to the people whose places they had assumed. Nor will this seeming ignorance, on the part of Logoochie, subtract a single jot from his high pretension as an Indian god, since true philosophy and a deliberate reason, must, long since, have been aware, that the mythological rule of every people, has been adapted, by the superior of all, to their mental and physical condition; and the great Manneyto of the savage, in his primitive state, was, doubtless, as wise a provision for him then, as, in our time, has been the faith, which we proudly assume to be the close correlative of the highest point of moral liberty and social refinement.

VI.

In this way, making new discoveries daily, and gradually becoming known himself, though vaguely, to the simple cottagers around him, he continued to pass the time with something more of satisfaction than before; though still suffering pain at every stroke of the sharp and smiting axe, as it called up the deploring echoes of the rapidly yielding forest. Day and night he was busy, and he resumed, *in extenso,* many of the playful humors, which used to annoy the savages and compel their homage. It is true, the acknowledgment of the white man was essentially different from that commonly made by the Indians. When their camp-pots were broken, their hatchets blunted, their bows and arrows warped, or they had suffered any other mischief at his hands, they solemnly deprecated his wrath, and offered him tribute to disarm his hostility. All that Logoochie could extort from the borderer, was a sullen oath, in which the tricksy spirit was identified with no less a person than the devil, the Opitchi-Manneyto of the southern tribes. This—as Logoochie well knew the superior rank of that personage with his people—he esteemed a compliment; and its utterance was at all times sufficiently grateful in his ears to neutralize his spleen at the moment. In addition to this, the habit of smoking more frequently and freely than the Indians, so common to the white man, contributed wonderfully to commend him to the favor of Logoochie. The odor in his nostrils was savory in the extreme, and he consequently regarded the smoker as tendering, in this way, the deprecatory sacrifice, precisely as the savages had done before him. So grateful, indeed, was the oblation to his taste, that often, of the long summer evening, would he gather himself into a bunch, in the thick branches of the high tree overhanging the log-house, to inhale the reeking fumes that were sent up by the half oblivious woodman, as he lay reposing under its grateful shadow.

VII.

There was one of these little cottages, which, for this very reason, Logoochie found great delight in visiting. It was tenanted by a sturdy old farmer, named Jones, and situated on the skirts of the St. Mary's village, about three miles form the Branch of Sweet Water, the favorite haunt of Logoochie. Jones had a small family—consisting, besides himself, of his wife, his sister— a lady of certain age, and monstrous demure—and a daughter, Mary Jones, as sweet a May-flower as the eye of a good taste would ever wish to dwell upon. She was young—only sixteen, and had not yet learned a single one of the thousand arts, which, in making a fine coquette, spoil usually a fine woman. She thought purely, and freely said all that she thought. Her old father loved her—her mother loved her, and her aunt, she loved her too, and proved it, by doing her own, and the scolding of all the rest, whenever the light-hearted Mary said more in her eyes, or speech, than her aunt's conventional sense of propriety deemed absolutely necessary to be said. This family Logoochie rather loved,—whether it was because farmer Jones did more smoking than any of the neighbors, or his sister more scolding, or his wife more sleeping, or his daughter more loving, we say not, but such certainly was the fact. Mary Jones had learned this latter art, if none other. A tall and graceful lad in the settlement, named Johnson, had found favor in her sight, and she in his; and it was not long before they made the mutual discovery. He was a fine youth, and quite worthy of the maiden; but then he was of an inquiring, roving temper, and though not yet arrived at manhood, frequently indulged in rambles, rather startling, even to a people whose habit in that respect is somewhat proverbial. He had gone in his wanderings even into the heart of the Okephanokee Swamp, and strange were the wonders, and wild the stories, which he gave of that region of Indian fable—a region, about which they have as many and as beautiful traditions, as any people can furnish from the store house of its primitive romance. This disposition on the part of Ned Johnson, though productive of much disquiet to his friends and family, they hoped to overcome or restrain by the proposed union with Mary Jones—a connexion seemingly acceptable to all parties. Mary, like most other good young ladies, had no doubt, indeed, of her power to control her lover in his wanderings, when once they were man and wife; and he, like most good young gentlemen in like cases, did not scruple to swear a thousand times, that her love would be as a chain about his feet, too potent to suffer him the slightest indulgence of his rambling desires.

VIII.

So things stood, when, one day, what should appear in the Port of St. Mary's—the Pioneer of the Line—but a vessel—a schooner—a brightly painted, sharp, cunning looking craft, all the way from the eastern waters, and commanded by one of that daring tribe of Yankees, which will one day control the commercial world. Never had such a craft shown its face in those waters, and great was the excitement in consequence. The people turned out, en masse,—men, women, and children,—all gathered upon the sands at the point to which she was approaching, and while many stood dumb with mixed feelings of wonder and consternation, others, more bold and elastic, shouted with delight. Ned Johnson led this latter class, and almost rushed into the waters to meet the new comer, clapping his hands and screaming like mad. Logoochie himself, from the close hugging branches of a neighboring tree, looked down, and wondered and trembled as he beheld the fast rushing progress toward him of what might be a new and more potent God. Then, when her little cannon, ostentatiously large for the necessity, belched forth its thunders from her side, the joy and the terror was universal. The rude divinity of the red men leaped down headlong from his place of eminence, and bounded on without stopping, until removed from sight and the shouting, in the thick recesses of the neighboring wood; while the children of the squatters taking to their heels, went bawling and squalling back to the village, never thinking for a moment to reach it alive. The schooner cast her anchor, and her captain came to land. Columbus looked not more imposing, leaping first to the virgin soil of the New World, than our worthy down-easter, commencing, for the first time, a successful trade in onions, potatoes, codfish, and crab-cider, with the delighted Georgians of our little village. All parties were overjoyed, and none more so than our young lover, Master Edward Johnson. He drank in with willing ears, and a still thirsting appetite, the narrative which the Yankee captain gave the villagers of his voyage. His long yarn,

to be sure, was stuffed with wonders. The new comer soon saw from Johnson's looks how greatly he had won the respect and consideration of the
youthful wanderer, and, accordingly, addressed some of his more spirited and
romantic adventures purposely to him. Poor Mary Jones beheld, with dreadful anticipations, the voracious delight which sparkled in the eyes of Ned as
he listened to the marvellous narrative, and had the thing been at all possible
or proper, she would have insisted, for the better control of the erratic boy,
that old Parson Collins should at once do his duty, and give her legal authority to say to her lover—"obey, my dear,—stay at home, or," etc. She went back
to the village in great tribulation, and Ned—he stayed behind with Captain
Nicodemus Doolittle, of the "Smashing Nancy."

IX.

Now Nicodemus, or, as they familiarly called him "Old Nick," was a wonderfully 'cute personage; and as he was rather slack of hands—was not much
of a penman or grammarian, and felt that in his new trade he should need
greatly the assistance of one to whom the awful school mystery of fractions
and the rule of three had, by a kind fortune, been developed duly—he regarded the impression which he had obviously made upon the mind of Ned
Johnson, as promising to neutralize, if he could secure him, some few of his
own deficiencies. To this end, therefore, he particularly addressed himself,
and, as might be suspected, under the circumstances, he was eminently successful. The head of the youth was soon stuffed full of the wonders of the
sea; and after a day or two or talk, all round the subject, in which time, by the
way, the captain sold off all his "notions," he came point blank to the subject
in the little cabin of a schooner. Doolittle sat over against him with a pile of
papers before him, some of which, to the uneducated down-easter, were
grievous mysteries, calling for a degree of arithmetical knowledge which was
rather beyond his capacity. His sales and profits—his accounts with creditors
and debtors—were to be registered, and these required him to reconcile the
provoking cross currencies of the different states—the York shilling, the
Pennsylvania levy, the Georgia thrip, the pickayune of Louisiana, the Carolina
fourpence—and this matter was, alone, enough to bother him. He knew well
enough how to count the coppers on hearing them. No man was more expert
at that. But the difficulty of bringing them into one currency on paper, called
for a more experienced accountant than our worthy captain; and the youth
wondered to behold the ease with which so great a person could be bothered.

Doolittle scratched his head in vain. He crossed his right leg over his left, but still he failed to prove his sum. He reversed the movement, and the left now lay problematically of the right. The product was very hard to find. He took a sup of cider, and then he thought things began to look a little clearer; but a moment after all was cloud again, and at length the figures absolutely seemed to run into one another. He could stand it no longer, and slapped his hand down, at length, with such emphasis upon the table, as to startle the poor youth, who, all the while, had been dreaming of plunging and wriggling dolphins, seen in all their gold and glitter, three feet or less in the waters below the advancing prow of the ship. The start which Johnson made, at once showed the best mode to the captain of extrication from his difficulty.

"There—there, my dear boy,—take some cider—only a little—do you good—best thing in the world—There,—and now do run up these figures, and see how we agree."

Ned was a clever led, and used to stand head of his class. He unravelled the mystery in little time—reconciled the cross-currency of the several sovereign states, and was rewarded by his patron with a hearty slap upon the shoulder, and another cup of cider. It was not difficult after this to agree, and half fearing that all the while he was not doing right by Mary Jones, he dashed his signature, in a much worse hand than he was accustomed to write, upon a printed paper which Doolittle thrust to him across the table.

"And now, my dear boy," said the captain, "you are my secretary, and shall have best berth, and place along with myself, in the 'Smashing Nancy.'"

X.

The bargain had scarcely been struck, and the terms well adjusted with the Yankee captain, before Ned Johnson began to question the propriety of what he had done. He was not so sure that he had not been hasty, and felt that the pain his departure would inflict upon Mary Jones, would certainly be as great in degree, as the pleasure which his future adventures must bring to himself. Still, when he looked forward to those adventures, and remembered the thousand fine stories of Captain Doolittle, his dreams came back, and with them came a due forgetfulness of the hum-drum happiness of domestic life. The life in the woods, indeed—as if there was life, strictly speaking, in the eternal monotony of the pine forests, and the drowsy hum they keep up so ceaselessly. Wood-chopping, too, was his aversion, and when he reflected upon the acknowledged superiority of his own over all the minds about him, he felt that his destiny called upon him for better things, and a more elevated employment. He gradually began to think of Mary Jones, as of one of those influences which had subtracted somewhat from the nature and legitimate exercises of his own genius; and whose claims, therefore, if acknowledged by him, as she required, must only be acknowledged at the expense and sacrifice of the higher pursuits and purposes for which the discriminating Providence had designed him. The youth's head was fairly turned by his ambitious yearnings, and it was strange how sublimely metaphysical his musings now made him. He began to analyze closely the question, since made a standing one among the phrenologists, as to how far particular heads were intended for particular pursuits. General principles were soon applied to special developments in his own case, and he came to the conclusion, just as he placed his feet upon the threshold of Father Jones's cottage, that he should be contending with the aim of fate, and the original design of the Deity in his own creation, if he did not go with Captain Nicodemus Doolittle, of the "Smashing Nancy."

XI.

"Ahem! Mary—" said Ned, finding the little girl conveniently alone, half sorrowful, and turning the whizzing spinning wheel.

"Ahem, Mary—ahem—" and as he brought forth the not very intelligible introduction, his eye had in it a vague indeterminateness that looked like confusion, though, truth to speak, his head was high and confident enough.

"Well, Ned—"

"Ahem! ah, Mary, what did you think of the beautiful vessel. Wasn't she fine, eh?"

"Very—very fine, Ned, though she was so large, and, when the great gun was fired, my heart beat so—I was so frightened, Ned—that I was."

"Frightened—why what frightened you, Mary," exclaimed Ned proudly—"that was grand, and as soon as we get to sea, I shall shoot it off myself."

"Get to sea—why, Ned—get to sea. Oh, dear, why—what do you mean?" and the bewildered girl, half conscious only, yet doubting her senses, now left the wheel, and came toward the contracted secretary of Captain Doolittle.

"Yes, get to sea, Mary. What! don't you know I'm going with the captain clear away to New York?"

Now, how should she know, poor girl? He knew that she was ignorant;

but as he did not feel satisfied of the propriety of what he had done, his phraseology had assumed a somewhat indirect and distorted complexion.

"You going with the Yankee, Ned—you don't say."

"Yes, but I do—and what if he is a Yankee, and sells notions—I'm sure there's no harm in that; he's a main smart fellow, Mary, and such wonderful things as he has seen, it would make your hair stand on end to hear him. I'll see them too, Mary, and then tell you."

"Oh, Ned,—you're only joking now—you don't mean it, Ned—you only say so to tease me—Isn't it so, Ned—say it is—say yes, dear Ned, only say yes."

And the poor girl caught his arm, with all the confiding warmth of an innocent heart, and as the tears gathered slowly, into big drops, in her eyes, and they were turned appealingly up to his, the heart of the wanderer smote him for the pain it had inflicted upon one so gentle. In that moment, he felt that he would have given the world to get off from his bargain with the captain; but this mood lasted not long. His active imagination, provoking a curious thirst after the unknown; and his pride, which suggested the weakness of a vacillating purpose, all turned and stimulated him to resist and refuse the prayer of the conciliating affection, then beginning to act within him in rebuke. Speaking through his teeth, as if he dreaded that he should want firmness, he resolutely reiterated what he had said; and, while the sad girl listened, silently, as one thunder struck, he went on to give a glowing description of the wonderful discoveries in store for him during the proposed voyage. Mary sunk back upon her stool, and the spinning wheel went faster than ever; but never in her life had she broken so many tissues. He did his best at consolation, but the true hearted girl, though she did not the less suffer as he pleaded, at least forbore all complaint. The thing seemed irrevocable, and so she resigned herself, like a true woman, to the imperious necessity. Ned, after a while, adjusted his plaited straw to his cranium, and sallied forth with a due importance in his strut, but with a swelling something at his heart, which he tried in vain to quiet.

XII.

And what of poor Mary—the disconsolate, the deserted and denied of love. She said nothing, ate her dinner in silence, and then putting on her bonnet, prepared to sally forth in a solitary ramble.

"What ails it, child," said old Jones, with a rough tenderness of manner.

"Where going, baby?" asked her mother, half asleep.

"Out again, Mary Jones—out again," vociferously shouted the antique aunt, who did all the family scolding.

The little girl answered them all meekly, without the slightest show of impatience, and proceeded on her walk.

The "Branch of Sweet Water," now known by this name to all the villagers of St. Mary's, was then, as it was supposed to be his favorite place of abode, commonly styled, "The Branch of Logoochie." The Indians—such stragglers as either lingered behind their tribes, or occasionally visited the old scenes of their home,—had made the white settlers somewhat acquainted with the character, and the supposed presence of that playful God, in the region thus assigned him; and though not altogether assured of the idleness of the super- stition, the young and innocent Mary Jones had no apprehensions of his power. She, indeed, had no reason for fear, for Logoochie had set her down, long before, as one of his favorites. He had done her many little services, of which she was unaware, nor was she the only member of her family indebted to his ministering good will. He loved them all—all but the scold, and many of the annoyances to which the old maid was subject, arose from this antipa- thy of Logoochie. But to return.

It was in great tribulation that Mary set out for her usual ramble along the banks of the "Sweet Water." Heretofore most of her walks in that quarter had been made in company with her lover. Here, perched in some sheltering oak, or safely doubled up behind some swollen pine, the playful Logoochie, himself unseen, a thousand times looked upon the two lovers, as, with linked arms, and spirits maintaining, as it appeared, a perfect unison, they walked in the shade during the summer afternoon. Though sportive and mischievous, such sights were pleasant to one who dwelt alone; and there were many occa- sions, when, their love first ripening into expression, he would divert from their path, by some little adroit art or management of his own, the obtrusive and unsympathising woodman, who might otherwise have spoiled the sport which he could not be permitted to share. Under his unknown sanction and service, therefore, the youthful pair had found love a rapture, until, at length, poor Mary had learned to regard it as a necessary too. She knew the necessity from the privation, as she now rambled alone; her wandering lover mean- while improving his knowledge by some additional chit-chat, on matters and things in general, with the captain, with whom he had that day dined heartily on codfish and potatoes, a new dish to young Johnson, which gave him an additional idea of the vast resources of the sea.

XIII.

Mary Jones at length trod the banks of the Sweet Water, and footing it along the old pathway to where the rivulet narrowed, she stood under the gigantic tree which threw its sheltering and concealing arms completely across the stream. With an old habit, rather than a desire for its refreshment, she took the gourd from the limb whence it depended, *pro bono publico,* over the water, and scooping up a draught of the innocent beverage, she proceeded to drink, when, just as she carried the vessel to her lips, a deep moan assailed her ears, as from one in pain, and at a little distance. She looked up, and the moan was repeated, and with increased fervency. She saw nothing, however, and somewhat startled, was about to turn quickly on her way homeward, when a third and more distinct repetition of the moan appealed so strongly to her natural sense of duty, that she could stand it no longer; and with the noblest of all kinds of courage, for such is the courage of humanity, she hastily tripped over the log which ran across the stream, and proceeded in the direction from whence the sounds had issued. A few paces brought her in sight of the sufferer, who was no other than our solitary acquaintance, Logoochie. He lay upon the grass, doubled now into a knot, and now stretching and writhing himself about in agony. His whole appearance indicated suffering, and there was nothing equivocal in the expression of his moanings. The astonishment, not to say fright, of the little cottage maiden, may readily be conjectured. She saw, for the first time, the hideous and uncouth outline of his person—the ludicrous combination of feature in his face. She had heard of Logoochie, vaguely; and without giving much, if any credence, to the mysterious tales related by the credulous woodman, returning home at evening, of his encounter in the forest with its pine-bodied divinity;—and now, as she herself looked down upon the suffering and moaning monster, it would be difficult to say, whether curiosity or fear was the most active principle in her bosom. He saw her approach, and he half moved to rise and fly; but a sudden pang, as it seemed, brought him back to a due sense of the evil from which he was suffering, and, looking towards the maiden with a mingled expression of good humor and pain in his countenance, he seemed to implore her assistance. The poor girl did not exactly know what to do, or what to conjecture. What sort of monster was it before her. What queer, distorted, uncouth limbs—what eyes, that twinkled and danced into one another—and what a mouth. She was stupified for a moment, until he spoke, and, stranger still, in a language that she understood. And what a musical voice,—how sweetly did the words roll forth, and how soothingly, yet earnestly, did they strike upon her ear. Language is indeed a god, and power-ful before all the rest. His words told her all his misfortunes, and the tones were all-sufficient to inspire confidence in one even more suspicious than our innocent cottager. Besides, humanity was a principle in her heart, while fear was only an emotion, and she did not scruple, where the two conflicted, after the pause for reflection of a moment, to determine in favor of the for-mer. She approached Logoochie—she approached him, firmly determined in her purpose, but trembling all the while. As she drew nigh, the gentle mon-ster stretched himself out at length, patiently extending one foot towards her, and raising it in such a manner as to indicate the place which afflicted him. She could scarce forbear laughing, when she looked closely upon the strange feet. They seemed covered with bark, like that of the small leafed pine tree; but as she stooped, to her great surprise, the coating of his sole flew wide as if upon a hinge, showing below it a skin as soft, and white, and tender, seemingly, as her own. There, in the centre of the hollow, lay the cause of his suffering. A poisonous thorn had penetrated, almost to the head, as he had suddenly leaped from the tree, the day before, upon the gun being fired from the "Smashing Nancy." The spot around it was greatly inflamed, and Logoochie, since the accident, had vainly striven, in every possible way, to rid himself of the intruder. His short, inflexible arms, had failed so to reach it as to make his finger available; and then, having claws rather than nails, he could scarce have done any thing for his own relief, even could they have reached it. He now felt the evil of his isolation, and the danger of his seclusion from his brother divinities. His case was one, indeed, of severe bachelorism; and, doubtless, had his condition been less than that of a deity, the approach of Mary Jones to his aid, at such a moment, would have produced a decided revolution in his domestic economy. Still trembling, the maiden bent herself down to the task, and with a fine courage, that did not allow his uncouth limbs to scare, or his wild and monstrous features to deter, she applied her own small fingers to the foot, and carefully grappling the head of the wound-ing thorn with her nails, with a successful effort, she drew it forth, and rid him of his encumbrance. The wood-god leaped to his feet, threw a dozen antics in the air, to the great terror of Mary, then running a little way into the forest, soon returned with a handful of fresh leaves, which he bruised between his fingers, and applied to the irritated and wounded foot. He was well in a moment after, and pointing the astonished Mary to the bush from which he had taken the anointing leaves, thus made her acquainted with one item in the history of Indian pharmacy.

XIV.

"The daughter of the white clay—she has come to Logoochie,—to Logoochie when he was suffering.

"She is a good daughter to Logoochie, and the green spirits who dwell in the forest, they love, and will honor her.

"They will throw down the leaves before her, they will spread the branches above her, they will hum a sweet song in the tree top, when she walks underneath it.

"They will watch beside her, as she sleeps in the shade, in the warm sun of the noon-day,—they will keep the flat viper, and the war rattle, away from her ear.

"They will do this in honor to Logoochie, for they know Logoochie, and he loves the pale daughter. She came to him in his suffering.

"She drew the poison thorn from his foot—she fled not away when she saw him.

"Speak,—let Logoochie hear—there is sorrow in the face of the pale daughter. Logoochie would know it and serve her, for she is sweet in the eye of Logoochie."

XV.

Thus said, or rather sung, the uncouth god to Mary, as, after the first emotions of his own joy were over, he beheld the expression of melancholy in her countenance. Somehow, there was something so fatherly, so gentle, and withal, so melodious, in his language, that she soon unbosomed herself to him, telling him freely and in the utmost confidence, though without any hope of relief at his hands, the history of her lover, and the new project for departure which he had now got in his head. She was surprised, and pleased, when she saw that Logoochie smiled at the narrative. She was not certain, yet she had a vague hope, that he could do something for her relief; and her conjecture was not in vain. He spoke—"Why should the grief be in the heart and the cloud on the face of the maiden? Is not Logoochie to help her? He stands beside her to help. Look, daughter of the pale clay—look! There is power in the leaf that shall serve thee at the bidding of Logoochie;—the bough and the branch have a power for thy good, when Logoochie commands; and the little red-berry which I now pluck from the vine hanging over thee, it is strong with a spirit which is good in thy work, when Logoochie has said in thy service. Lo, I speak to the leaf, and to the bough, and to the berry. They shall speak to the water, and one draught from the branch of Logoochie, shall put chains on the heart of the youth who would go forth with the stranger."

As he spoke, he gathered the leaf, broke a bough from an overhanging tree, and, with a red berry, pulled from a neighboring vine, approached the Branch of Sweet Water, and turning to the west, muttered a wild spell of Indian power, then threw the tributes into the rivulet. The smooth surface of the stream was in an instant ruffled—the offerings were whirled suddenly around—the waters broke, boiled, bubbled, and parted, and in another moment, the bough, the berry, and the leaf, had disappeared from their sight.

XVI.

Mary Jones was not a little frightened by these exhibitions, but she was a girl of courage, and having once got over the dread and the novelty of contact with a form so monstrous as that of Logoochie, the after effort was not so great. She witnessed the incantations of the demon without a word, and when they were over, she simply listened to his farther directions, half stupified with what she had seen, and not knowing how much of it to believe. He bade her bring her lover, as had been the custom with them hitherto, to the branch, and persuade him to drink of its waters. When she inquired into its effect, which, at length, with much effort, she ventured to do, he bade her be satisfied, and all would go right. Then, with a word, which was like so much music—a word she did not understand, but which sounded like a parting acknowledgment,—he bounded away into the woods, and, a moment after, was completely hidden from her sight.

XVII.

Poor Mary, not yet relieved from her surprise, was still sufficiently aroused and excited to believe there was something in it; and as she moved off on her way home, how full of anticipation was her thoughts—pleasant anticipation, in which her heart took active interest, and warmed, at length, into a strong and earnest hope. She scarcely gave herself time to get home, and never did the distance between Sweet Water Branch and the cottage of her father appear so extravagantly great. She reached it, however, at last; and there, to her great joy sat her lover, alongside the old man, and giving him a glowing account, such as he had received from the Yankee captain, of the wonders to be met with in his coming voyage. Old Jones listened patiently, puffing his pipe all the while, and saying little, but now and then, by way of commentary, uttering an ejaculatory grunt, most commonly, of sneering disapproval.

"Better stay at home, a d——d sight, Ned Johnson, and follow the plough."

Ned Johnson, however, thought differently, and it was not the farmer's grunts or growlings that was now to change his mind. Fortunately for the course of true love, there were other influences at work, and the impatience of Mary Jones to try them was evident, in the clumsiness which she exhibited while passing the knife under the thin crust of the corn hoe-cake that night for supper, and laying the thick masses of fresh butter between the smoking and savory-smelling sides, as she turned them apart. The evening wore, at length, and, according to an old familiar habit, the lovers walked forth to the haunted and fairy-like branch of Logoochie, or the Sweet Water. It was the last night in which they were to be together, prior to his departure in the Smashing Nancy. That bouncing vessel and her dexterous captain were to depart with early morning; and it was as little as Ned Johnson could do, to spend that night with his sweetheart. They were both melancholy enough, depend upon it. She, poor girl, hoping much, yet still fearing—for when was true love without fear—she took his arm, hung fondly upon it, and, without a word between them for a long while, inclined him, as it were naturally, in the required direction. Ned really loved her, and was sorry enough when the thought came to him, that this might be the last night of their association; but he plucked up courage, with the momentary weakness, and though he spoke kindly, yet he spoke fearlessly, and with a sanguine temper, upon the prospect of sea-adventure before him. Mary said little—her heart was too full for speech, but she looked up now and then into his eyes, and he saw, by the moonlight, that her own glistened with tears. He turned away his glance as he saw it, for his heart smote him with the reproach of her desertion.

XVIII.

They came at length to the charmed streamlet, the Branch of the Sweet Water, to this day known for its fascinations. The moon rose sweetly above it, the trees coming out in her soft light, and the scatterings of her thousand beams glancing from the green polish of their crowding leaves. The breeze that rose along with her was soft and wooing as herself; while the besprinkling fleece of the small white clouds, clustering along the sky, and flying from her splendors, made the scene, if possible, far more fairy-like and imposing. It was a scene for love, and the heart of Ned Johnson grew more softened than ever. His desire for adventure grew modified; and when Mary bent to the brooklet, and scooped up the water for him to drink, with the water-gourd that hung from the bough, wantoning in the breeze that loved to play over the pleasant stream, Ned could not help thinking she never looked more beautiful. The water trickled from the gourd as she handed it to him, falling like droppings of the moonshine again into its parent stream. You should have seen her eye—so full of hope—so full of doubt—so beautiful—so earnest,—as he took the vessel from her hands. For a moment he hesitated, and then how her heart beat and her limbs trembled. But he drank off the contents at a draught, and gave no sign of emotion. Yet his emotions were strange and novel. It seemed as if so much ice had gone through his veins in that moment. He said nothing, however, and dipping up a gourd full for Mary, he hung the vessel again upon the pendant bough, and the two moved away from the water—not, however, before the maiden caught a glimpse, through the intervening foliage, of those two queer, bright, little eyes of Logoochie, with a more delightful activity than ever, dancing gayly into one.

XIX.

But the spell had been effectual, and a new nature filled the heart of him, who had heretofore sighed vaguely for the unknown. The roving mood had entirely departed; he was no longer a wanderer in spirit, vexed to be denied. A soft languor overspread his form—a weakness gathered and grew about his heart, and he now sighed unconsciously. How soft, yet how full of emphasis, was the pressure of Mary's hand upon his arm as she heard that sigh; and how forcibly did it remind the youth that she who walked beside him was his own—his own forever. With the thought came a sweet perspective—a long vista rose up before his eyes, crowded with images of repose and plenty, such as the domestic nature likes to dream of.

"Oh, Mary, I will not go with this captain—I will not. I will stay at home with you, and we shall be married."

Thus he spoke, as the crowding thoughts, such as we have described, came up before his fancy.

"Will you—shall we? Oh, dear Edward, I am so happy."

And the maiden blessed Logoochie, as she uttered her response of happy feeling.

"I will, dear—but I must hide from Doolittle. I have signed papers to go with him, and he will be so disappointed—I must hide from him."

"Why must you hide, Edward—he cannot compel you to go, unless you please; and you just to be married."

Edward thought she insisted somewhat unnecessarily upon the latter point, but he replied to the first.

"I am afraid he can. I signed papers—I don't know what they were, for I was rash and foolish—but they bound me to go with him, and unless I keep out of the way, I shall have to go."

"Oh, dear—why, Ned, where will you go—you must hide close,—I would not have him find you for the world."

"I reckon not. As to the hiding, I can go where all St. Mary's can't find me; and that's in Okephanokee."

"Oh, don't go so far—it is so dangerous, for some of the Seminoles are there!"

"And what if they are?—I don't care *that* for the Seminoles. They never did me any harm, and never will. But, I shan't go quite so far. Bull swamp is close enough for me, and there I can watch the 'Smashing Nancy' 'till she gets out to sea."

XX.

Having thus determined, it was not long before Ned Johnson made himself secure in his place of retreat, while Captain Doolittle, of the "Smashing Nancy," in great tribulation, ransacked the village of St. Mary's in every direction for his articled seaman, for such Ned Johnson had indeed become. Doolittle deserved to lose him for the trick which, in this respect, he had played upon the boy. His search proved fruitless, and he was compelled to sail at last. Ned, from the top of a high tree of the edge of Bull swamp, watched his departure, until the last gleam of the white sail flitted away from the horizon; then descending, he made his way back to St. Mary's, and it was not long before he claimed and received the hand of his pretty cottager in marriage. Logoochie was never seen in the neighborhood after this event. His accident had shown him the necessity of keeping with his brethren, for, reasoning from all analogy, gods must be social animals not less than men. But, in departing, he forgot to take the spell away which he had put upon the Sweet Water Branch; and to this day, the stranger, visiting St. Mary's, is warned not to drink from the stream, unless he proposes to remain; for still, as in the case of Ned Johnson, it binds the feet and enfeebles the enterprise of him who partakes of its pleasant waters.

"THE CHEROKEE EMBASSAGE" is a good example of Simms's fictional history, in which he transforms a historical incident into a readable story replete with satire, irony, and humor. The guile and duplicity of aristocratic Europeans in contrast with the natural dignity and integrity of Chief Tonestoi reinforces the reader's understanding that the "bright gold chain" symbolizes the trickery by which white civilization gains dominion over the Cherokees.

～ The Cherokee Embassage

————"Where go these messengers—
These untamed lords of the forest,—whither speed
Their barks o'er unknown waters—to survey
What land of blue delight, what better shore,
More grateful to the hunter than the last?"

It was deemed prudent, soon after the close of a trying war with the savages, to conciliate the Cherokee nation, then one of the largest in the colony; and Sir Alexander Cumming, himself an ostentatious person, was fitly chosen for this purpose. Charged with proposals of alliance, and amply provided with gifts more imposing than valuable, to the several leading chiefs and sages, this gentleman, in the beginning of the year 1730, set forth for the Apalachian mountains, in the neighborhood of which the principal towns of the Cherokees were situated. He was attended on this occasion, as well by several voluntary travellers, as by a numerous military retinue; and no circumstance was omitted, of display or pomp, which could impress upon the aborigines an idea of the vast power of that foreign potentate, whose representative was then to appear before them. Every expense called for by the deputation was cheerfully conceded on the part of the Royal Government, as the king well knew the great military strength of the people, whom it was the object to conciliate. The Cherokees inhabiting South-Carolina at this time, were as numerous as they were brave. The inhabitants of thirty-seven regular towns, were computed to amount to twenty thousand. Of these, six thousand were bowmen, ready, on any emergency, to take the field. In addition to this force, which may be considered the regular force of the nation, the roving tribes were supposed to reach several thousand more; not so easy to be brought together, but, if possible, far more dangerous to an enemy when once collected; as, from their continual habit of wandering, they grew even fiercer than the wild beasts, in whose pursuit only they seemed to live.

It was some time before Sir Alexander reached Keowee, a distance of three hundred miles or more from Charlestown. His way, for the most part, lay through a wilderness, seldom, if ever before, trodden by European footsteps. It was a dreary pilgrimage, and it was no small satisfaction to the English, when, as they attained the outskirts of the Cherokee territory, the chiefs of the lower town, hearing of their approach, came forth to receive and to guide them still further on their way. *Ee-fistoe*, the chief of the Green Birds or Little Estatoes, Chulochkolla, the Sachem of the Occonies, and Moytoy, the Black Warrior of Telliquo, the most renowned of all their braves, thus joined the jaded cavalcade.

Sir Alexander Cumming hailed them with a flourish; and, having disposed of his retinue, before their approach, in such a manner as to show them to the best possible advantage, he was pleased to think that he had made a favorable impression. He was not deceived. The wondering savages—themselves ostentatiously decorated, according to their sylvan fashion, in all the rich plumage of their native birds, contrasted strangely with the hideous paint, and rugged skins which formed so large a part of their ceremonial equipment—were nevertheless overcome by the more imposing splendors of the deputation. The glittering armour—the gorgeous uniform of the English, shining in gold and scarlet—the lofty plumes,—the plunging and richly caparisoned horses,—together with the thrilling military music of an English band—all combined to overpower their imaginations, and to impress the deeply excited senses of the Cherokees; and, though like the Roman Fabricius, they were not to be surprised, and suffered neither awe nor irreverent curiosity to appear upon their faces, or in their gesticulation, they were all nevertheless strongly wrought upon by both these emotions.

Sir Alexander lost no time in securing the friendship of the chiefs, as they severally came forth to meet him. He received them in great state, and to each gave some particular present, so carefully chosen as to avoid all chance of showing a preference to any one, thus giving offence to the rest. This caution had its due results. The chiefs were all well satisfied, and Moytoy, the Black Warrior of Telliquo, not to be outdone in these respects, brought from Tenassee, the principal town of the nation, the crown of the Great Keowee, the old chief and reigning sovereign—a monarch too potent according to his own, and his people's estimation, to be even looked upon by strangers. The policy of the suspicious savage had much to do with this strange seclusion. His person, like that of Montezuma, was considered sacred, and a proper watch was maintained over it accordingly. Thus, though able to have annihilated the entire force under Cumming in a single effort, it was yet thought advisable to risk nothing, by the exposure of a commodity so susceptible to injury as a reigning sovereign; and with the first annunciation, therefore, of the approach of the English, Keowee, a decrepid and almost blind old man, was hurried bodily away from the contiguous country, more deeply than before into the thick forests, and among the impassable barriers of rock, which girdled in and covered their extended territory. To Moytoy and the other chiefs or kings, was entrusted the task of receiving and providing for the strangers; and, to do them all justice, the reception was such as became a brave and honorable people. The fruits and flesh, the maize and provisions, to which they were themselves accustomed, were all freely provided; and five eagle tails and four scalps from slaughtered enemies, were also among the presents brought by Moytoy. These had a signification which, through the interpreter, the dusky warriors explained to the satisfaction of their European visitors. The feathers of the eagle marked the strength and the glory alike of Cherokee, and the scalp of their enemies announced the unerring certainty of Cherokee victory and vengeance. These were presented to the English in token that henceforward their course should be trodden on the same war path, in close affinity, and against the same enemies.

Thirty-two chiefs, each paramount with his own tribe and section, appeared at the solemn council which followed. A great deal of pompous talk was uttered, and Moytoy of Telliquo, the Black Warrior, found such high favor with Sir Alexander, that he nominated him as the Commander-in-Chief of the Cherokee armies, and presented him with a rich robe as a badge of his new office. The chiefs present agreed to recognize him as such, provided that there should be a like accountability to him, (Sir Alexander) on the part of Moytoy. Every thing went on amicably, and, emboldened by the friendly disposition which the savages evinced, the English Ambassador proposed that some of them should accompany him to England, in order, with their own eyes, to behold that great king of whom he had given them a most flaming description.

"Your brother, King George," said he, in a speech which was well remembered by the attentive chiefs, "will be glad to see you. He will load you with presents, with hatchets and knives, with rich clothes and beautiful feathers. He will bind you to his heart with a bright gold chain, which will last unbroken for a thousand years."

"He is our brother," replied the chiefs with one voice, dazzled by the glorious promise—"he is our brother—we will go to our brother George."

There was no difficulty in getting the proposed deputation; the only difficulty, indeed, was in making a selection from the number of those offering. Unconscious of the length of the voyage, of its dangers, and the new and unaccustomed scenes and circumstances through which they would have to go before realizing the prospects set before them, the simple savages, each a king in his own country, were readily persuaded to undertake the embassage which promised them so much enjoyment. The gold and the glitter—the fine armor like that which Sir Alexander wore—the pomp and the display, which, through the interpreter, the Englishman dwelt upon in the most glowing language,—were irresistible; and, full of the splendors of their brother George, they threw the bear skins about their shoulders, filled their quivers with fresh arrows from the canebrake, and kissing the sunny side, one after the other, of the broad tree that covered them during the progress of the council, they bade their farewell to the green forests, and the wild free country, their eyes might never again behold.

Six of them accompanied Sir Alexander to Charlestown, and thence, having been there joined by another chief who followed them after a brief delay, they embarked with him for Europe. The eldest of these chiefs, or kings, was Tonestoi, Prince of Nequassee, a once formidable, but now decayed warrior, and a good old man. He was renowned among the Cherokees, for his wisdom. The next in order was the famous orator, Skiajagustha—a man whose eloquence performed wonders in the councils of his people, and of whose speeches, some occur upon our own historical records, not unworthy to appear in any collection. Next came Chulockholla, another orator, neither so old nor so well renowned as Skiajagustha. The chief of Occonies, or Brown Vipers, Cenestee, was the fourth of this delegation—a chief only remarkable for the reckless audacity of his valor. The fifth was a gallant young warrior of the Little Estatoes, or Green Birds, Ee-fistoe—a warrior intelligent as valiant, and not any thing less amiable because of his acknowledged bravery. Occonostota made the sixth. He was the king of Echotee, and could himself bring three hundred warriors into the field; but he was something of a tyrant, and was deposed the very year after his return from Europe. The seventh who joined the deputation in Charlestown, was a chief also, but his name does not appear in our history. He was probably of no great renown.

These were the Cherokee kings, who, consenting to the invitation of Sir Alexander Cumming, sailed with him in the Swallow Packet, for London, some time in the month of May, 1730. Seduced by the glowing pictures spread before their minds by the English agent, full of expectation and flushed with the promise of so many novelties, the wild men of the woods, wrapped in their hunter garbs, gorgeously covered with fresh paint, and armed to the teeth, after the fashion of their people, fearlessly went on board the little vessel that awaited them, and, with favoring breezes, were soon lost to the sight of land, and plunging steadily over the bosom of the Atlantic.

The sea—a new element to the Cherokees—exacted its dues, and it was not many hours before the warriors grew heartily sick of their unusual undertaking. Much would they have given to be once more in their native forests, but they were too brave, and too well taught in the stoical morality of the savage, to confess to any such weakness. They had long before learned, that, to conquer, it is first necessary that we should bear with, our fate, and they withstood, accordingly, as well as they could, the storms and the tossings of the waters, in a manner by no means discrediting their creed or nation. They grew, in a little time, familiar with their new abiding place, and, as the initial sickness passed away, soon began to contemplate, with comparative steadiness and a growing appreciation, all the various objects and aspects of their new domain.

All was strange—all was wonderful around them. Their own complete isolation—the absence of the woods and wilds to which only they had been accustomed—their initiation into a world so new and strange, as to them was that of ocean—the singular buoyancy of their ship—the astonishing agility of the seamen, moving about with ease and dexterity, where they could scarcely maintain the most uncertain foot-hold—these were all matters of profound astonishment and curiosity. But these were all as nothing, after the first blush of novelty had passed away in comparison with the queer tricks and uncouth antics of one of the ship's company. This was no less than a monkey, belonging to one of the sailors, named Jacko,—a creature of habitual trick and mimickry, continually provoked to its exercise by some one or other of the seamen. He ran along the ropes and rigging in pursuit of them. He mounted the spars, and sat in uncouth shapes in the most dangerous places. He carried off the caps of the sailors, then pelted them down upon those who walked the deck. In short, nothing in the semblance of mischief was omitted by Jacko. Tonestoi, the venerable elder of the Indian chiefs, was absolutely ravished by the tricks of the sportive monkey. He had no thought for any other object than Jacko. He watched his movements by the hour, provoked their exercise by continual stimulating affronts, and laughed, in despite of the grave looks of his brother chiefs, as immoderately as if such had been his continual practice. Tonestoi was an ancient chief, renowned as much for wisdom as for valor, and he presumed upon his reputation. He therefore gave vent to his merriment without any fear of losing either his own or the general respect of his people. The other chiefs, who were all younger, were either differently situated in rank, or were not altogether so secure in the estimation of their people; and, though equally delighted with Tonestoi, were yet prudent enough to preserve a greater degree of gravity. They looked on with composure; and, while watching closely all the sports of Jacko, they yet forebore to take any part in the merriment. But the old chief had no such scruples, and his laughter was without reserve. He played with Jacko like a child—rolled with him about the decks—hallooed him on to all manner of mischief—clapped his hands and cheered him in his performance, and then, in his own language, pronounced a high eulogy upon his achievements. He called him 'Hickisiwackinaw,' or 'the warrior with a tail;' and at length, when he saw Jacko swing by his hind legs from a rope, and, with his paws, grapple and take fast hold upon the bushy poll of one of the sailors as he walked beneath, he called him 'Toostenugga,' after the celebrated leader of the Cherokee hobgoblins—this being one of the favorite modes by with Toostenugga, suspending himself from a tree, laid hold of, and punished, those who offended him as they walked beneath. Nothing could divert the attention of Tonestoi from the monkey. Sir Alexander Cumming, whose sense of dignity was greatly outraged by such unbecoming levity, tried his best to attract the mind of the Cherokee to more dignified amusements; and, in his vexation, was with difficulty restrained from tumbling Jacko overboard, hopeless of any other means of obtaining his object. He made a show of anger towards the monkey, but, upon beholding the sudden gravity of Tonestoi as he comprehended this design, he thought it only wise to forbear, as it was his policy, as well as his orders, to avoid all manner of offence. His dernier resort then was in his liquors, and once made acquainted with their potency, the old chief, Tonestoi,

was soon taught to prefer the intoxicating cup to the antics of his more innocent companion. Jacko, or, as he called him to the last, Toostenugga, ceased to
attract so much of his attention, and, to the shame of all parties be it said, the
good old warrior, after this, had scarcely a sober hour until they reached the
haven of their destination.

Their arrival in London was the signal for much bustle and exhibition.
Apart from the desire to impose greatly on their senses by shows and splendors, to which, in their wild abodes, they had never been accustomed, the
better to acquire dominion over them, they received a thousand attentions
as the last new lions in the metropolis. Lords and ladies thronged the hotel at
which the Cherokee kings were lodged, and the beautiful squaws of London,
as was more recently the case in our own country, submitted joyfully to the
salute of the Indian warriors for the sake of its novelty. Feasts were given
them in profusion—frolics connived on purpose to make them actors, and
from the day of their arrival to that of their departure, all was uproar and
exultation. In all these junkettings, it need scarcely be said that our Cherokees
preserved happily their usual equanimity of character. They were grave and
composed, and behaved, for all the world, as if they had been accustomed all
their lives to such honors and indulgences. Tonestoi, alone, of all the deputation, gave way to the garrulous good humor of the aged man. He laughed and
joked freely with his visitors, and nothing gave him such profound pleasure
as when his great cheek bones and painted lips came in contact with the vel-
vety skin of his lady visitors. Never had Cherokee warrior so given way before
to all the practices, and so many of the evidences, of *la belle passion.* So much
was this the case that his more youthful companions began to have doubts as
to the tenacity of that superior wisdom in the ancient chief which had been
a proverb in his own country.

But if the general acquaintance with the Indians, and their usual deportment, prevailed with and gave satisfaction to the English nobility, their conduct in the interview with the King completed the merriment, and furnished
a fitting climax to the whole proceeding. Seized somewhat with the spirit of
the fashion in reference to them, and desirous of securing, by a proper policy, the affections of these people, the British monarch desired, and determined, to do them particular honor. An especial drawing room was appointed
them, and, in the presence of a most brilliant and imposing assemblage, he
prepared to receive his distinguished visitors. Sir Alexander Cumming, who
had the chiefs in charge, attempted, before going to court, to give them

certain instructions as to their behavior in the presence of majesty; but they either did not, or would not, understand him. They comprehended sufficiently his object, however, and the native pride of an aboriginal chief rose in arms at his suggestion. Skiajagustha, the orator, was the first to take fire at what seemed an indignity. Wrapping his bear skin around him with a majesty which George himself, in all his career, and with the best teachers, never could have emulated, he looked scornfully upon his would-be tutor, while he replied:

"Skiajagustha is the great mouth of Cherokee,—he has stood before his nation when Keowee, the red arrow, was there. His words are good."

The interpreter explained; but, as similar sentiments were uttered by nearly all the party, Sir Alexander saw that it would not only be idle, but most probably offensive, were he to endeavor to teach them farther. As they approached the Chair of State, in which sat the Monarch, the aged Tonestoi took the advance. The King rose as he drew nigh, and came forward, extending his hand for the usual salute, as he did so, to the approaching Indian. But Tonestoi, remembering his own dignity, and what had been said to him on the score of the relationship between them, prior to his leaving his own country, to the great horror of the courtiers, and of Sir Alexander Cumming in particular, grasped the extended hand of the English Monarch with his own, and, giving it a squeeze that none but a bear could well have equalled, shook it heartily and long, exclaiming, in the few words of courtesy which he had committed in broken English,

"Huddye-do, Broder George—huddye-do—glad to see you"—and, continuing with a smile as he looked round upon the women—"You got plenty squaws."

The court was convulsed and shocked beyond measure. All were astounded except the King himself, and the savages. George, with his usual good nature, withdrawing his hand, though with some difficulty, from the powerful gripe of his brother monarch, smiled pleasantly, and amused with the familiarity, responded in similar style, giving the cue to those around him. Nothing then could exceed the hilarity with which the business of the conference was carried on and finished. The kings made long speeches through the interpreters, satisfactory on all sides, and a treaty of alliance was then and there agreed upon between them, to be valid and binding upon the Cherokees and English in America, as they were avowed to be so by both parties present then in England.

We quote portions of this treaty, as it not only presents us with much of the eloquence employed by the several contracting parties, but also gives us some idea of the various topics of trade and communion rendering such a treaty between people so dissimilar essential to the mutual good. It will be found, however, that the performance of duties devolves much more frequently upon the Indian than upon the white man, and that his rewards, estimated by our standards of use and value, are quite inadequate to the services required at their hands. Doubtless, however, they were such as were best calculated for the uninstructed savage.

The preamble to this treaty recites,

"That whereas the six chiefs, [without naming them, and without any reference to the chief who unquestionably joined the embassy at Charlestown, when about to sail] with the consent of the whole nation of Cherokees, at a general meeting of their nation at Nequassee, were deputed by Moytoy, their chief warrior, to attend Sir Alexander Cumming to Great Britain, where they had seen the great king George, and where, Sir Alexander, by authority from Moytoy and all the Cherokees, had laid the crown of their nation, with the scalps of their enemies and feathers of glory at his majesty's feet, as a pledge of their loyalty—and, whereas, the great king has instructed the lords commissioners of trade and plantations, to inform the Indians that the English on all sides of the mountains and lakes, were his people, their friends his friends, their enemies his enemies—that he took it kindly the great nation of Cherokee had sent them so far to brighten the chain of friendship between him and the Cherokee, is now like the sun which shines both in Britain and upon the great mountains where they live, and equally warms the hearts of Indians and Englishmen—that, as there is no spot or blackness in the sun, so neither is there any rust or foulness on this chain—and, as the king has fastened one end to his breast, [suiting the action to the word in George's best and bluffest style] he desired them to carry the other end of the chain and fasten it to the breast of Moytoy, of Telliquo, and to the breasts of all their wise old men, their captains and people, never more to be made loose or broken.

"The great king and the Cherokees being thus fastened together, by a chain of friendship, he has ordered, and it is agreed, that his children in Carolina do trade with the Indians, and furnish them with all manner of goods they want, and to make haste to build houses and plant corn from

Charlestown towards the towns of the Cherokees behind the great mountains. [Vague enough, and, like most treaties with the Indians, carried on through dishonest or imperfect interpreters, not understood by one of the parties, and a frequent source of mischief afterwards.] That he desires the English and Indians may live together as children of one family—that the Cherokees be always ready to fight against any nation, whether white men or Indians, who shall molest or hurt the English—that the nation of the Cherokee, shall, on its part, take care to keep the trading path clean—that there be no blood on the path which the English tread, *even though they should be accompanied with other people with whom the Cherokees may be at war* [what an exaction—how is it possible that the Cherokees should have understood this charge, or understanding, that they should have complied with it?]—*that the Cherokees shall not suffer their people to trade with white men of any other nation but the English*—[here is monopoly with a vengeance!]—nor permit [mark this] *nor permit white men of any other nation to build any forts or cabins, or plant any corn among them* upon lands which belong the great king."

Such was the morality of these selfish traders. They actually excluded the savages from the exercise of these wonted rites of hospitality to white men, and to Christians like themselves, (for the French and Spaniards were contemplated by the clause) which the Cherokees had freely accorded to the British, and which they must otherwise have extended freely to all others. The treaty goes on to provide that if any such attempt shall be made by the white men of any other than the British nation, the Cherokees must not only acquaint the British government of the fact, but must do whatever he directs, in order to maintain and defend the "great king's right to the country of Carolina." The treaty further provides, "that if any negroes shall run away into the woods from their English masters, the Cherokees shall endeavor to apprehend them, and bring them to the plantation from whence they ran, or to the governor."

Hitherto the contract has been all on one side, and the English king has never said "Turkey" once to his Cherokee brother; but, at this stage of the treaty, he seems to have recollected himself, and, accordingly, we find him promising, that "for every slave so apprehended and brought back, the Indian that brings him shall receive a gun and a watch-coat, and *if, by any accident,* it shall happen that an Englishman shall kill a Cherokee, [an event only possible it seems] the king of chief of the nation shall first complain to the English governor, and the man who did the harm shall be punished by the *English laws* as if he had killed an Englishman; and, in like manner, if any Indian happens to kill [by any accident is entirely wanting here] an English-man, the Indian shall be delivered up to the governor to be punished by the same English laws as if he were an Englishman."

This was the substance of the first treaty between the British and the Cherokee nation; and a precious specimen it is, of Cunning beguiling Sim-plicity, and of unfair relationship between parties originally contracting on an equal footing of advantage. The Cherokee chiefs heard it first from the lips of George, who paused at every sentence, and, as the interpreter explained it, clause by clause, a nobleman presented to the expecting chiefs, a rich present of cloths or ornaments. When the king had got through his task, he suddenly withdrew through a private door, glad to escape any farther embrace from his Cherokee brethren. The further business of the treaty was then concluded by Alured Popple, Secretary to the Lords Commissioners of Trade and Plan-tations on the one side, and by the marks of the Indian chiefs on the other. The secretary, at the same time, addressed them in a speech confirming the words of the great king whom they had just seen; and, as a token that his heart was true and open to the Cherokees, a belt was given the warriors, which the king desired them to show their children and children's children, to confirm what was now spoken, and to bind this agreement of peace and friendship between the English and the Cherokees, "as long as the rivers shall run, the mountains shall stand, or the sun shall shine."

Such was the glowing termination of the secretary's speech. When he had concluded, the old chief, Tonestoi, gave way to Skiajagustha, the famous ora-tor, who seemed to know his own claims to reply for the rest. Gathering his robe over his left shoulder, so as entirely to free the right arm, he began his reply, the greater portion of which it preserved as follows. It will be found to contain quite as much good sense, dignity and beauty, as was called for by the occasion:

"We are come hither from the mountains where there is nothing but dark-ness. But we are now in a place of light. We see the great king in you—we love you as you stand here for him. We shall die in this thought. The crown of the Cherokee is not like that in the tower; but, to us, they are the same—the chain shall be carried to our people. The great king George is the sun—he is our father—the Cherokees are his children. Though we are red and you are white—yet our hearts and hands are tied together. We shall say to our people what we have seen, and our children shall remember it. In war we will be one with you—your enemies shall be ours—we shall live together as one people— we shall die together. We are naked and poor as the worms that crawl— but you have all things. We that have nothing must love you. We will never break the chain that is between us. This small rope we show you is all that we have to bind our slaves—You have chains of iron for yours. We will catch your slave that flies—we will bind him as strongly as we can, and we shall take no pay when we bring him back to you. Your people shall build near ours in safety. The Cherokee shall hurt them not—he shall hurt nothing that belongs to them. Are we not children of one father—shall we not live and die together?"

Here he paused, and one of the other chiefs coming forward at a signal from the speaker, presented him with a bunch of eagle feather. Taking them in his hand, Skiajagustha presented them to the secretary with these words:

"This is our way of talking, which is the same thing to us as your letters in the book to you. These feathers, from the strong bird of Cherokee—these shall be witnesses for the truth of what I have said."

Thus discoursing eloquently together, the parties contracted to their mutual satisfaction, and however unequal were the general advantages obtained, there was certainly no dissatisfaction expressed among them. The terms were agreed upon without discontent or difficulty, and it will not be premature or anticipative, in this stage of our narration, to say, in the language of the historian, Ramsay, that, in consequence of this treaty, the Cherokees, for many years after, remained in "a state of perfect friendship and peace with the Colonists, who followed their various employments in the neighborhood of these Indians, without the least terror or molestation."

But the nine days' wonder was now over in the British metropolis. The Indian chiefs began to lose their importance in the sight of their European brethren. Some new monster soon occupied their place, and Sir Alexander Cumming being now prepared to return to Carolina, and the vessel ready to depart, they had little reluctance at leaving a land, where, though every kindness and courtesy had been shown them, they had found so few objects and features at all like, or kindred with their own. They set sail from England on the 23d September, 1730, and, under favoring aspects of wind and weather, were soon out upon the comprehensive world and void of ocean.

But the second voyage was more tedious to the chiefs than the first. That had novelty to recommend it—the strange mass of all objects at sea, relieved, in the first instance, its general monotony. But the second brought all this home to them; and, what added to their dullness still more, was the absence of Jacko—the monkey was no longer one of their fellow passengers. The sailor who owned, had sold him, while in London, and nothing could exceed the dissatisfaction of old Tonestoi, on hearing of the circumstance. The first thing he did on coming aboard the vessel, was to call aloud for Toostenugga. But he called in vain, and was, with difficulty, made to understand that his goblin acquaintance was left behind them. He refused consolation, and chafed and almost quarrelled with those who offered it. He drank with Sir Alexander Cumming, but that was all, in the way of relief or amusement, that he could be persuaded to do. In a state of moody absence, as soon as his fit of sea sickness was well over, he roamed about the ship, tumbling from side to side, and, in his own language, muttering continually of Toostenugga. Dreadfully, indeed, did he suffer from blue devils, and, in this mood, shooting with his arrows wantonly at little spots in the sails, he soon exhausted all his quiver, as the flying shafts would generally, after a few discharges, find their way into the bosom of the ocean. The other, and younger, chiefs bore the voyage with far more philosophy than their ancient comrade; and with that aptness which belongs to man in all situations, and which we have erringly denied to the Aborigines, they, at length, began to accommodate themselves to the novel employments of the sea. Skiajagustha, the great orator himself, was the first to set an example of this discipline. He seized upon the ropes on one occasion, and began to tug away lustily along with the sailors. His companions followed him, all but old Tonestoi, and, from a sport at first, it grew to be a common resort for exercise among them. Sir Alexander Cumming, however, thought such practices unbecoming in those who had royal blood in their veins; but, as there were no alternatives, he could suggest no objection. To Tonestoi, alone, he could address himself; and, as the old chief took no part in the amusements of his companion, he was the more ready to sit gloomily and gravely over the lengthened glass with the Englishman. But his ennui continued to increase, and, at length, to the great consternation of Sir Alexander, the poor savage grew sick, and his free habit of drinking only made him worse. The liquor was then withdrawn from him; and this seemed to increase his malady. The attack was a very severe one, and, unhappily, but few precautions had been taken against such an occasion.

There was scarcely any medicines on board; and even these the old chief, with all the fretful obstinacy of a spoiled child, could not be persuaded to take. Day by day he grew worse, and it now became evident to all that the danger was alarming. The younger chiefs assembled about him, and Sir Alexander, with deep concern, strove, through them, to persuade him to the adoption of those remedies which he proposed. He resolutely rejected all their suggestions, and, tossing about, in his fever, from side to side, he exhibited a feeble peevishness to all around him—his own people not excepted. Several days passed over in this manner, and it was evident to all that he had sunk amazingly. At this stage of his illness, and while he was chafing querulously with all of them, Skiajagustha approached him where he lay. The brow of the orator was stern and full of rebuke, and the first words which he uttered, in his own sweet but solemn and emphatic language, rivetted the attention of the dying warrior. He ceased to tumble upon his couch—he ceased to chafe and chide those about him. The appeal of Skiajagustha had been made to his manhood—to his sense of the dignity and the courage of a brave of Cherokee:

"Shall Tonestoi go to the Manneyto with the word of a child on his tongue? Shall he say to the Master of Life, wherefore has thou called me? The brave man has another spirit when the dark spirit wraps him.

"Tonestoi—it is the word of the Cherokee—is a brave among the braves. He has taken scalps from the light-heeled Catawba—he has taken scalps from the cunning Shawanese—he has taken scalps from the Creek warrior that rages —he has taken scalps from all the enemies of the Cherokees. He should have a song for his victories, that the Great Manneyto shall be glad to receive him."

"Achichai-me!" cried Tonestoi in reply—and, in his own language, proceeded as follows:

"It is good, Skiajagustha—it is good what thou hast spoken. But I heard not before the words of the Great Manneyto. I hear them through thee. He has called me—I hear him speaking in the heart of Tonestoi—I am going to the land of spirits—to the plum groves where my fathers journey on the long hunt. I am not afraid to go. The Master of Life knows I am ready."

"Ha! Ha!" he sang a moment after—

"Ha! Ha! I laugh at my enemies. The Catawba could not take the scalp— he could not drink blood from Tonestoi. Ha! Ha! *That* for the Shawanee— *that* for the Creek that rages—*that* for all the enemies of Cherokee. The Master of Life only can kill, and Tonestoi is ready for him.

"Bring my arrows, Skiajagustha—bring me arrows, young Ee-fistoe of the Green Birds—bring me arrows, young braves of Cherokee—the arrows shall speak for my victories."

They brought him arrows at his request, and he separated the bundles, laying each shaft by itself. The younger chiefs curiously gathered around him, as they well knew they were now to hear a chronicle of his own and his country's achievements; and for every arrow, he had the story of some brave adventure—some daring deed. One of them stood for his first battle with the Chickasaw, when, yet a mere boy, he went forth with his old father, Canonjahee, on the war path against that subtle nation. Another arrow was made to signify his escape from a band of roving Shawanese who had made him a prisoner while hunting; a third told the affair with the Creeks, for his bravery in which his countrymen had made him a chief—feather chief and arrow chief—a fourth recounted his long personal combat with Sarratahay of Santee, the big boned chief from that river who had come up on purpose to contend with him, at the lower town of Chinebee. Tonestoi was the victor after a long struggle, and this he dwelt upon the most emphatically of all his victories. And so, with a dozen other events, he associated the arrows. For an hour his strain proceeded, and the Indians listened with unrelaxing attention. Sir Alexander Cumming, apprised of the nature of the scene, hung over the dying chief with the deepest interest; and even the sailors, several of them came as nigh to listen as they well might without manifest impropriety. The old man lay silent for some time after his song was ended. But his chosen arrows had all been carefully gathered up by Skiajagustha, who tied them closely together with the sinews of the deer. Towards evening the chief grew much weaker, and he muttered fitfully, and started every now and then like one from sleep. When the sun was about to set, its faint delicate light streamed through the little aperture in the cabin just where the dying man lay. He started and strove to raise himself up to behold the orb now sinking like himself. But failing to do this, he only raised his right hand and waved it towards the bright object which he could not see. Skiajagustha bent towards him, and uttered two or three words in his own language, at which all the other chiefs rose and bent over him. Tonestoi gave each of them a look of recognition, and, while muttering a brief sentence, probably one of parting, his lower jaw suddenly dropped, then caught up as in a spasm, then as suddenly again relaxed and fell, never again to move. The light grew dim in the eyes which yet opened upon the spectators.

Skiajagustha laid the bunch of arrows upon the breast of Tonestoi, where they remained until the next day, when his body was committed to the deep. They were then carefully preserved by the survivors, as witnesses of the whole transaction, and received as such by the people. They form one of the tokens of Cherokee valor, and are preserved, to this very hour, among the trophies of the nation.

IN TONE, TECHNIQUE, AND SUBSTANCE "Jocassée. A Cherokee Legend" is one of the best of Simms's Indian tales. The story of the naming of the Jocassée River, told by a first-person narrator as it was originally related to him by Col. G——, captures the nuances of a venerable and gifted oral storyteller who is enamored with the setting and fascinated by the marvelous nature of the folkloric tale. That this "Cherokee legend" of human love, hatred, violence, and spirituality is largely the product of imagination matters little to the reader. Rather, a major strength of "Jocassée" is that it treats with reverence and dignity what is portrayed as the moral and spiritual core of the Cherokee culture.

ᕀ *Jocassée. A Cherokee Legend.*

CHAPTER I.

"Keowee Old Fort," as the people in that quarter style it, is a fine antique ruin and relic of the revolution, in the district of Pendleton, South Carolina. The region of country in which we find it is, of itself, highly picturesque and interesting. The broad river of Keowee, which runs through it, though comparatively small as a stream in America, would put to shame, by its size not less than its beauty, one half of the far-famed and boasted rivers of Europe;—and then the mountains, through and among which it winds its way, embody more of beautiful situation and romantic prospect, than art can well figure to the eye, or language convey to the imagination. To understand, you must see it. Words are of little avail when the ideas overcrowd utterance; and even vanity itself is content to be dumb in the awe inspired by a thousand prospects, like Niagara, the ideals of a god, and altogether beyond the standards common to humanity.

It is not long since I wandered through this interesting region, under the guidance of my friend, Col. G——, who does the honours of society, in that quarter, with a degree of ease and unostentatious simplicity, which readily makes the visiter at home. My friend was one of those citizens to whom one's own country is always of paramount interest, and whose mind and memory, accordingly, have been always most happily employed when storing away and digesting into pleasing narrative those thousand little traditions of the local genius, which give life to rocks and valleys, and people earth with the beautiful colours and creatures of the imagination. These, for the gratification of the spiritual seeker, he had forever in readiness; and, with him to illustrate them, it is not surprising if the grove had a moral existence in my thoughts, and all the waters around breathed and were instinct with poetry. To all his narratives I listened with a satisfaction which book-stories do not often afford me. The more he told, the more he had to tell; for nothing staled

"His infinite variety."

There may have been something in the style of telling his stories; there was much, certainly, that was highly attractive in his manner of doing every thing, and this may have contributed not a little to the success of his narratives. Perhaps, too, my presence, upon the very scene of each legend, may have given them a life and a *vraisemblance* they had wanted otherwise.

In this manner, rambling about from spot to spot, I passed five weeks, without being, at any moment, conscious of time's progress. Day after day, we wandered forth in some new direction, contriving always to secure, and without effort, that pleasurable excitement of novelty, for which the great city labours in vain, spite of her varying fashions, and crowding, and not always innocent indulgences. From forest to river, from hill to valley, still on horseback,—for the mountainous character of the country forbade any more luxurious form of travel,—we kept on our way, always changing our ground with the night, and our prospect with the morning. In this manner we travelled over or round the Six Mile, and the Glassy, and a dozen other mountains; and sometimes, with a yet greater scope of adventure, pushed off on a much longer ramble,—such as took us to the falls of the White Water, and gave us a glimpse of the beautiful river of Jocassée, named sweetly after the Cherokee maiden, who threw herself into its bosom on beholding the scalp of her lover dangling from the neck of his conqueror. The story is almost a parallel to that of the sister of Horatius, with this difference, that the Cherokee girl did not wait for the vengeance of her brother, and altogether spared her reproaches. I tell the story, which is pleasant and curious, in the language of my friend, from whom I first heard it.

"The Occonies and the Little Estatoees, or, rather, the Brown Vipers and the Green Birds, were both minor tribes of the Cherokee nation, between whom, as was not unfrequently the case, there sprung up a deadly enmity. The Estatoees had their town on each side of the two creeks, which, to this day, keep their name, and on the eastern side of the Keowee river. The Occonies occupied a much larger extent of territory, but it lay on the opposite, or west side of the same stream. Their differences were supposed to have arisen from the defeat of Chatuga, a favourite leader of the Occonies, who aimed to be made a chief of the nation at large. The Estatoee warrior, Toxaway, was successful; and as the influence of Chatuga was considerable with his tribe, he laboured successfully to engender in their bosoms a bitter dislike of the Estatoees. This feeling was made to exhibit itself on every possible occasion. The Occonies had no word too foul by which to describe the Estatoees. They likened them, in familiar speech, to every thing which, in the Indian imagination, is accounted low and contemptible. In reference to war, they were reputed women,—in all other respects, they were compared to dogs and vermin; and, with something of a Christian taste and temper, they did not scruple, now and then, to invoke the devil of their more barbarous creed, for the eternal disquiet of their successful neighbours, the Little Estatoees, and their great chief, Toxaway.

"In this condition of things there could not be much harmony; and, accordingly, as if by mutual consent, there was but little intercourse between the two people. When they met, it was either to regard one another with a cold, repulsive distance, or else, as enemies, actively to foment quarrel and engage in strife. But seldom, save on national concerns, did the Estatoees cross the Keowee to the side held by the Occonies; and the latter, more numerous, and therefore less reluctant for strife than their rivals, were yet not often found on the opposite bank of the same river. Sometimes, however, small parties of hunters from both tribes, rambling in one direction or another, would pass into the enemy's territory; but this was not frequent, and when they met, quarrel and bloodshed were sure to mark the adventure.

"But there was one young warrior of the Estatoees, who did not give much heed to this condition of parties, and who, moved by an errant spirit, and wholly insensible to fear, would not hesitate, when the humour seized him, to cross the river, making quite as free, when he did so, with the hunting-grounds of the Occonies as they did themselves. This sort of conduct did not please the latter very greatly, but Nagoochie was always so gentle, and at the same time so brave, that the young warriors of Occony either liked or feared him too much to throw themselves often in his path, or labour, at any time, to arrest his progress.

"In one of these excursions, Nagoochie made the acquaintance of Jocassée, one of the sweetest of the dusky daughters of Occony. He was rambling, with bow and quiver, in pursuit of game, as was his custom, along that beautiful enclosure which the whites have named after her, the Jocassée valley. The circumstances under which they met were all strange and exciting, and well calculated to give her a power over the young hunter, to which the pride of the Indian does not often suffer him to submit. It was towards evening when Nagoochie sprung a fine buck from a hollow of the wood beside him, and just before you reach the ridge of rocks which hem in and form this beautiful valley. With the first glimpse of his prey flew the keen shaft of Nagoochie; but, strange to say, though renowned as a hunter, not less than as a warrior, the arrow failed entirely and flew wide of the victim. Off he bounded headlong after the fortunate buck; but though, every now and then getting him within range,—for the buck took the pursuit coolly,—the hunter still most unaccountably failed to strike him. Shaft after shaft had fallen seemingly hurtless from his sides; and though, at frequent intervals, suffered to approach so nigh to the animal that he could not but hope still for better fortune, to his great surprise, the wary buck would dash off when he least expected it, bounding away in some new direction, with as much life and vigour as ever. What to think of this, the hunter knew not; but such repeated disappointments at length impressed it strongly upon his mind, that the object he pursued was neither more nor less than an Occony wizard, seeking to entrap him; so, with a due feeling of superstition, and a small touch of sectional venom aroused into action within his heart, Nagoochie, after the manner of his people promised a green bird—the emblem of his tribe—in sacrifice to the tutelar divinity of Estato, if he could only be permitted to overcome the potent enchanter, who had thus dazzled his aim and blunted his arrows. He had hardly uttered this vow, when he beheld the insolent deer mincingly grazing upon a beautiful tuft of long grass in the valley, just below the ledge of rock upon which he stood. Without more ado, he pressed onward to bring him within fair range of his arrows, little doubting at the moment that the Good Spirit had heard his prayer, and had granted his desire. But, in his hurry, leaping too hastily forward, and with eyes fixed only upon his proposed victim, his foot was caught by the smallest stump in the world, and the very next moment found him precipitated directly over the rock and into the valley, within a few paces of the deer, who made off with the utmost composure, gazing back, as he did so, in the eyes of the wounded hunter, for all the world, as if he enjoyed the sport mightily. Nagoochie, as he saw this, gravely concluded that he had fallen a victim to the wiles of the Occony wizard, and looked confidently to see half a score of Occonies upon him, taking him at a vantage. Like a brave warrior, however, he did not despond, but determining to gather up his loins for battle and the torture, he sought to rise and put himself in a state of preparation. What, however, was his horror, to find himself utterly unable to move;—his leg had been broken in the fall, and he was covered with bruises from head to foot.

"Nagoochie gave himself up for lost; but he had scarcely done so, when he heard a voice,—the sweetest, he thought, he had ever heard in his life,— singing a wild, pleasant song, such as the Occonies love, which, ingeniously enough, summed up the sundry reasons why the mouth, and not the eyes, had been endowed with the faculty of eating. These reasons were many, but the last is quite enough for us. According to the song, had the eyes, and not the mouth, been employed for this purpose, there would soon be a famine in the land, for of all gluttons, the eyes are the greatest. Nagoochie groaned aloud as he heard the song, the latter portion of which completely indicated the cause of his present misfortune. It was, indeed, the gluttony of the eyes which had broken his leg. This sort of allegory the Indians are fond of, and Jocassée knew all their legends. Certainly, thought Nagoochie, though his leg pained him wofully at the time, 'certainly I never heard such sweet music, and such a voice.' The singer advanced as she sung, and almost stumbled over him.

"'Who are you?' she asked timidly, neither retreating nor advancing; and, as the wounded man looked into her face, he blessed the Occony wizard, by whose management he deemed his leg to have been broken.

"'Look!' was the reply of the young warrior, throwing aside the bearskin which covered his bosom,—'look, girl of Occony! 'tis the *totem* of a chief;' and the green bird stamped upon his left breast, as the badge of his tribe, showed him a warrior of Estato, and something of an enemy. But his eyes had no enmity, and then the broken leg! Jocassée was a gentle maiden and her heart melted with the condition of the warrior. She made him a sweet promise, in very pretty language, and with the very same voice the music of which was so delicious; and then, with the fleetness of a young doe, she went off to bring him succour.

CHAPTER II.

"Night, in the meanwhile, came on; and the long howl of the wolf, as he looked down from the crag, and waited for the thick darkness in which to descend the valley, came freezingly to the ear of Nagoochie. 'Surely,' he said to himself, 'the girl of Occony will come back. She has too sweet a voice not to keep her word. She will certainly come back.' While he doubted, he believed. Indeed, though still a very young maiden, the eyes of Jocassée had in them a great deal that was good for little beside, than to persuade and force conviction; and the belief in them was pretty extensive in the circle of her rustic acquaintance. All people love to believe in fine eyes, and nothing is more natural than for lovers to swear by them. Nagoochie did not swear by those of Jocassée, but he did most religiously believe in them; and though the night gathered fast, and the long howl of the wolf came close from his crag, down into the valley, the young hunter of the green bird did not despair of the return of the maiden.

"She did return, and the warrior was insensible. But the motion stirred him; the lights gleamed upon him from many torches; he opened his eyes, and when they rested upon Jocassée, they forgot to close again. She had brought aid enough, for her voice was powerful as well as musical; and, taking due care that the totem of the green bird should be carefully concealed by the bearskin, with which her own hands covered his bosom, she had him lifted upon a litter, constructed of several young saplings, which, interlaced with withes, binding it closely together, and strewn thickly with leaves, made a couch as soft as the wounded man could desire. In a few hours, and the form of Nagoochie rested beneath the roof of Attakulla, the sire of Jocassée. She sat beside the young hunter, and it was her hand that placed the fever balm upon his lips and poured into his wounds and bruises the strong and efficacious balsams of Indian pharmacy.

"Never was nurse more careful of her charge. Day and night she watched by him, and few were the hours which she then required for her own pleasure or repose. Yet why was Jocassée so devoted to the stranger? She never asked herself so unnecessary a question; but as she was never so well satisfied, seemingly, as when near him, the probability is she found pleasure in her tendance. It was fortunate for him and for her, that her father was not rancorous towards the people of the Green Bird, like the rest of the Occonies. It might have fared hard with Nagoochie otherwise. But Attakulla was a wise old man, and a good; and when they brought the wounded stranger to his lodge, he freely yielded him shelter, and went forth himself to Chinabee, the wise medicine of the Occonies. The eyes of Nagoochie were turned upon the old chief, and when he heard his name, and began to consider where he was, he was unwilling to task the hospitality of one who might be disposed to regard him, when known, in an unfavourable or hostile light. Throwing aside, therefore, the habit of circumspection, which usually distinguishes the Indian warrior, he uncovered his bosom, and bade the old man look upon the totem of his people, precisely as he had done when his eye first met that of Jocassée.

"'Thy name? What do the people of the Green Bird call the young hunter?' asked Attakulla.

"'They name Nagoochie among the braves of the Estato: they will call him a chief of the Cherokee, like Toxaway,' was the proud reply.

"This reference was to a sore subject with the Occonies, and perhaps it was quite as imprudent as it certainly was in improper taste for him to make it. But, knowing where he was, excited by fever, and having—to say much in little—but an unfavourable opinion of Occony magnanimity, he was more rash than reasonable. At that moment, too, Jocassée had made her appearance, and the spirit of the young warrior, desiring to look big in her eyes, had prompted him to a fierce speech not altogether necessary. He knew not the generous nature of Attakulla; and when the old man took him by the hand, spoke well of the Green Bird, and called him his 'son,' the pride of Nagoochie was something humbled, while his heart grew gentler than ever. His 'son!'— that was the pleasant part; and as the thoughts grew more and more active in his fevered brain, he looked to Jocassée with such a passionate admiration that she sunk back with a happy smile from the flame-glance which he set upon her. And, day after day she tended him until the fever passed off, and the broken limb was set and had reknitted, and the bruises were all healed upon him. Yet he lingered. He did not think himself quite well, and she always agreed with him in opinion. Once and again did he set off, determined not to return, but his limb pained him, and he felt the fever come back whenever he thought of Jocassée; and so the evening found him again at the lodge, while the fever-balm, carefully bruised in milk, was in as great demand as ever for the invalid. But the spirit of the warrior at length grew ashamed of these weaknesses; and, with a desperate effort, for which he gave himself no little credit, he completed his determination to depart with the coming of the new moon. But even this decision was only effected by compromise. Love settled the affair with conscience, after his own fashion; and, under his direction, following the dusky maiden into the little grove that stood beside the cottage, Nagoochie claimed her to fill the lodge of a young warrior of the Green Bird. She broke the wand which he presented her, and seizing upon the torch which she carried, he buried it in the bosom of a neighbouring brook; and thus, after their simple forest ceremonial, Jocassée became the betrothed of Nagoochie.

CHAPTER III.

"But we must keep this secret to ourselves, for as yet it remained unknown to Attakulla, and the time could not come for its revealment until the young warrior had gone home to his people. Jocassée was not so sure that all parties would be so ready as herself to sanction her proceeding. Of her father's willingness, she had no question, for she knew his good nature and good sense; but she had a brother of whom she had many fears and misgivings. He was away, on a great hunt of the young men, up at Charashilactay, or the falls of the White Water, as we call it to this day—a beautiful cascade of nearly forty feet, the water of which is of a milky complexion. How she longed, yet how she dreaded, to see that brother! He was a fierce, impetuous, sanguinary youth, who, to these characteristics, added another still more distasteful to Jocassée;—there was not a man among all the Occonies who so hated the people of the Green Bird as Cheochee. What hopes, or rather what fears, were in the bosom of that maiden!

"But he came not. Day after day they looked for his return, and yet he came not; but in his place a runner, with a bearded stick, a stick covered with slips of skin, torn from the body of a wolf. The runner passed by the lodge of Attakulla, and all its inmates were aroused by the intelligence he brought. A wolf-hunt was commanded by Moitoy, the great war-chief or generalissimo of the Cherokee nation, to take place, instantly, at Charashilactay, where an immense body of wolves had herded together, and had become troublesome neighbours. Old and young, who had either taste for the adventure, or curisity to behold it, at once set off upon the summons; and Attakulla, old as he was, and Nagoochie, whose own great prowess in hunting had made it a passion, determined readily upon the journey. Jocassée, too, joined the company,—for the maidens of Cherokee were bold spirits, as well as beautiful, and loved to ramble, particularly when, as in the present instance, they went forth in company with their lovers. Lodge after lodge, as they pursued their way, poured forth its inmates, who joined them in their progress, until the company had swollen into a goodly caravan, full of life, anxious for sport, and carrying, as is the fashion among the Indians, provisions of smoked venison and parched grain, in plenty, for many days.

"They came at length to the swelling hills, the long narrow valleys of the Keochee and its tribute river of Toxaway, named after that great chief of the Little Estatoees, of whom we have already heard something. At one and the same moment they beheld the white waters of Charashilactay, plunging over the precipice, and the hundred lodges of the Cherokee hunters. There they had gathered—the warriors and their women—twenty different tribes of the same great nation being represented on the ground; each tribe having its own cluster of cabins, and rising up, in the midst of each, the long pole on which hung the peculiar emblem of the clan. It was not long before Nagoochie marshalled himself along with his brother Estatoees—who had counted him lost—under the beautiful green bird of his tribe, which waved about in the wind, over the heads of their small community.

"The number of warriors representing the Estato in that great hunt was inconsiderable—but fourteen—and the accession, therefore, of so promising a brave as Nagoochie, was no small matter. They shouted with joy at his coming, and danced gladly in the ring between the lodges—the young women in proper taste, and with due spirit, hailing, with a sweet song, the return of so handsome a youth, and one who was yet unmarried.

"Over against the lodges of the Estatoees, lay the more imposing encampment of the rival Occonies, who turned out strongly, as it happened, on this occasion. They were more numerous than any other of the assembled tribes, as the hunt was to take place on a portion of their own territory. Conscious of their superiority, they had not, you may be sure, forborne any of the thousand sneers and sarcasms which they were never at a loss to find when they spoke of the Green Bird warriors; and of all their clan, none was so bitter, so uncompromising, generally, in look, speech, and action, as Cheochee, the fierce brother of the beautiful Jocassée. Scorn was in his eye, and sarcasm on his lips, when he heard the rejoicings made by the Estatoees on the return of the long-lost hunter.

"'Now wherefore screams the painted bird to-day? why makes he a loud cry in the ears of the brown viper that can strike?' he exclaimed contemptuously yet fiercely.

"It was Jocassée that spoke in reply to her brother, with the quickness of wo-man's feeling, which they wrong greatly who hold it subservient to the strength of woman's cunning. In her reply, Cheochee saw the weakness of her heart.

"'They scream for Nagoochie,' said the girl; 'it is joy that the young hunter comes back that makes the green bird to sing to-day.'

"'Has Jocassée taken a tongue from the green bird, that she screams in the ears of the brown viper? What has the girl to do with the thoughts of the warrior? Let her go—go, bring drink to Cheochee.'

"Abashed and silent, she did as he commanded, and brought meekly to the fierce brother, a gourd filled with the bitter beverage which the Cherokees love. She had nothing further to say on the subject of the Green Bird warrior, for whom she had already so unwarily spoken. But her words had not fallen unregarded upon the ears of Cheochee, nor had the look of the fond heart which spoke out in her glance, passed unseen by the keen eye of that jealous brother. He had long before this heard of the great fame of Nagoochie as a hunter, and in his ire he was bent to surpass him. Envy had grown into hate, when he heard that this great reputation was that of one of the accursed Estatoees; and, not satisfied with the desire to emulate, he also aimed to destroy. This feeling worked like so much gall in his bosom; and when his eyes looked upon the fine form of Nagoochie, and beheld its symmetry, grace, and manhood, his desire grew into a furious passion which made him sleepless. The old chief, Attakulla, his father, told him all the story of Nagoochie's accident—how Jocassée had found him; and how, in his own lodge, he had been nursed and tended. The old man spoke approvingly of Nagoochie; and, the better to bring about a good feeling for her lover, Jocassée humbled herself greatly to her brother,—anticipated his desires, and studiously sought to serve him. But all this failed to effect a favourable emotion in the breast of the malignant young savage towards the young hunter of the Green Bird. He said nothing, however, of his feelings; but they looked out and were alive to the sight, in every aspect, whenever any reference, however small, was made to the subject of his ire. The Indian passion is subtlety, and Cheochee was a warrior already famous among the old chiefs of Cherokee.

Chapter IV.

"The next day came the commencement of the great hunt, and the warriors were up betimes and active. Stations were chosen, the keepers of which, converging to a centre, were to hem in the wild animal on whose tracks they were going. The wolves were known to be in a hollow of the hills, near Cha-rashilactay, which had but one outlet; and points of close approximation across this outlet were the stations of honour; for, goaded by the hunters to this passage, and failing of egress in any other, the wolf, it was well known, would be then dangerous in the extreme. Well calculated to provoke into greater activity the jealousies between the Occonies and the Green Birds, was the assignment made by Moitoy, the chief, of the more dangerous of these stations to these two clans. They now stood alongside of one another, and the action of the two promised to be joint and corresponsive. Such an appoint-ment, in the close encounter with the wolf, necessarily promised to bring the two parties into immediate contact; and such was the event. As the day advanced, and the hunters, contracting their circles, brought the different bands of wolves into one, and pressed upon them to the more obvious and indeed the only outlet, the badges of the Green Bird and the Brown Viper—the one consisting of the stuffed skin and plumage of the Carolina parrot, and the other the attenuated viper, filled out with moss, and winding, with erect head, around the pole, to the top of which it was stuck—were, at one moment, in the indiscriminate hunt, almost mingled over the heads of the two parties. Such a sight was pleasant to neither, and would, at another time, of a certainty, have brought about a squabble. As it was, the Occonies drove their badge-carrier from one to the other end of their ranks, thus studiously avoiding the chance of another collision between the viper so adored, and the green bird so detested. The pride of the Estatoees was exceedingly aroused at this exhibition of impertinence, and though a quiet people enough, they began to think that forbearance had been misplaced in their relations with their presuming and hostile neighbours. Had it not been for Nagoochie, who had his own reasons for suffering yet more, the Green Birds would certainly have plucked out the eyes of the Brown Vipers, or tried very hard to do it; but the exhortations to peace of the young warrior, and the near neighbourhood of the wolf, quelled any open show of the violence they meditated; but, Indian-like, they determined to wait for the moment of greatest quiet, as that most fitted for taking away a few scalps from the Occony. With a muttered curse, and a contemptuous slap of the hand upon their thighs, the more furi-ous among the Estatoees satisfied their present anger, and then addressed themselves more directly to the business before them.

"The wolves, goaded to desperation by the sight and sound of hunters strewn all over the hills around them, were now, snapping and snarling, and with eyes that flashed with a terrible anger, descending the narrow gully towards the outlet held by the two rival tribes. United action was therefore demanded of those who, for a long time past, had been conscious of no feeling or movement in common. But here they had no choice—no time, indeed, to think. The fierce wolves were upon them, doubly furious at finding the only passage stuck full of enemies. Well and manfully did the hunters stand and seek the encounter with the infuriated beasts. The knife and the hatchet, that day, in the hand of Occony and Estato, did fearful execution. The Brown Vipers fought nobly, and with their ancient reputation. But the Green Birds were the hunters, after all; and they were now stimulated into double adventure and effort, by an honourable ambition to make up for all deficiencies of number by extra valour, and the careful exercise of all that skill in the arts of hunting for which they have always been the most renowned of the tribes of Cherokee. As, one by one, a fearful train, the wolves wound into sight along this or that crag of the gully, arrow after arrow told fearfully upon them, for there were no marksmen like the Estatoees. Nor did they stop at this weapon. The young Nagoochie, more than ever prompted to such audacity, led the way; and dashing into the very path of the teeth-gnashing and claw-rending enemy, he grappled in desperate fight the first that offered himself, and as the wide jaws of his hairy foe opened upon him, with a fearful plunge at his side, adroitly leaping to the right, he thrust a pointed stick down, deep, as far as he could send it, into the monster's throat, then pressing back upon him, with the rapidity of an arrow, in spite of all his fearful writhings he pinned him to the ground, while his knife, in a moment after, played fatally in his heart. Another came, and, in a second, his hatchet cleft and crunched deep into the skull of the angry brute, leaving him senseless, without need of a second stroke. There was no rivalling deed of valour so desperate as this; and with increased bitterness of soul did Cheochee and his followers hate in proportion as they admired. They saw the day close, and heard the signal calling them to the presence of the great chief Moitoy, conscious, though superior in numbers, they could not at all compare in skill and success with the long-despised, but now thoroughly-hated Estatoees.

"And still more great the vexation, still more deadly the hate, when the prize was bestowed by the hand of Moitoy, the great military chief of Cherokee—when, calling around him the tribes, and carefully counting the number of their several spoils, consisting of the skins of the wolves that had been slain, it was found that of these the greater number, in proportion to their force, had fallen victims to the superior skill or superior daring of the people of the Green Bird. And who had been their leader? The rambling Nagoochie— the young hunter who had broken his leg among the crags of Occony, and, in the same adventure, no longer considered luckless, had won the young heart of the beautiful Jocassée.

"They bore the young and successful warrior into the centre of the ring, and before the great Moitoy. He stood up in the presence of the assembled multitude, a brave and fearless, and fine looking Cherokee. At the signal of the chief, the young maidens gathered into a group, and sung around him a song of compliment and approval, which was just as much as to say,—'Ask, and you shall have.' He did ask; and before the people of the Brown Viper could so far recover from their surprise as to interfere, or well comprehend the transaction, the bold Nagoochie had led the then happy Jocassée into the presence of Moitoy and the multitude, and had claimed the girl of Occony to fill the green lodge of the Estato hunter.

"That was the signal for uproar and commotion. The Occonies were desperately angered, and the fierce Cheochee, whom nothing, not even the presence of the great war-chief, could restrain, rushed forward, and dragging the maiden violently from the hold of Nagoochie, hurled her backward into the ranks of his people; then, breathing nothing but blood and vengeance, he confronted him with ready knife and uplifted hatchet, defying the young hunter in that moment to the fight.

"'*E-cha-e-cha, e-herro—echa-herro-echa-herro*,' was the warwhoop of the Occonies; and it gathered them to a man around the sanguinary young chief who uttered it. '*Echa-herro, echa-herro*,' he continued, leaping wildly in air with the paroxysm of rage which had seized him,—'the brown viper has a tooth for the green bird. The Occony is athirst—he would drink blood from the dog-heart of the Estato. '*E-cha-e-cha-herro, Occony*.' And again he concluded his fierce speech with that thrilling roll of sound, which, as the so much dreaded warwhoop, brought a death feeling to the heart of the early pioneer, and made the mother clasp closely, in the deep hours of the night, the young and unconscious infant to her bosom. But it had no such influence upon the fearless spirit of Nagoochie. The Estato heard him with cool composure, but, though evidently unafraid, it was yet equally evident that he was unwilling to meet the challenger in strife. Nor was his decision called for on the subject. The great chief interposed, and all chance of conflict was prevented by his intervention. In that presence they were compelled to keep the peace, though both the Occonies and Little Estatoees retired to their several lodges with fever in their veins, and a restless desire for that collision which Moitoy had denied them. All but Nagoochie were vexed at this denial; and all of them wondered much that a warrior, so brave and daring as he had always shown himself, should be so backward on such an occasion. It was true, they knew of his love for the girl of Occony; but they never dreamed of such a feeling acquiring an influence over the hunter, of so paralyzing and unmanly a character. Even Nagoochie himself, as he listened to some of the speeches uttered around him, and reflected upon the insolence of Cheochee—even he began to wish that the affair might happen again, that he might take the hissing viper by the neck. And poor Jocassée—what of her when they took her back to the lodges? She did nothing but dream all night of Brown Vipers and Green Birds in the thick of battle.

CHAPTER V.

"The next day came the movement of the hunters, still under the conduct of Moitoy, from the one to the other side of the upper branch of the Keowee river, now called the Jocassée, but which, at that time, went by the name of Sarratay. The various bands prepared to move with the daylight; and, still near, and still in sight of one another, the Occonies and Estatoees took up their line of march with the rest. The long poles of the two, bearing the green bird of the one, and the brown viper of the other, in the hands of their respective bearers—stout warriors chosen for this purpose with reference to strength and valour—waved in parallel courses, though the space between them was made as great as possible by the common policy of both parties. Following the route of the caravan, which had been formed of the ancient men, the women and children, to whom had been entrusted the skins taken in the hunt, the provisions, utensils for cooking, &c., the great body of hunters were soon in motion for other and better hunting-grounds, several miles distant, beyond the river.

"The Indian warriors have their own mode of doing business, and do not often travel with the stiff precision which marks European civilization. Though having all one point of destination, each hunter took his own route to gain it, and in this manner asserted his independence. This had been the education of the Indian boy, and this self-reliance is one source of that spirit and character which will not suffer him to feel surprise in any situation. Their way, generally, wound along a pleasant valley, unbroken for several miles, until you came to Big-knob, a huge crag which completely divides it, rising formidably up in the midst, and narrowing the valley on either hand to a fissure, necessarily compelling a closer march for all parties than had heretofore been pursued. Straggling about as they had been, of course but little order was perceptible when they came together, in little groups, where the mountain forced their junction. One of the Bear tribe found himself alongside a handful of the Foxes, and a chief of the Alligators plunged promiscuously into the centre of a cluster of the Turkey tribe, whose own chief was probably doing the proper courtesies among the Alligators. These little crossings, however, were amusing rather than annoying, and were, generally, productive of little inconvenience and no strife. But it so happened that there was one exception to the accustomed harmony. The Occonies and Estatoees, like the rest, had broken up in small parties, and, as might have been foreseen, when they came individually to where the crag divided the valley into two, some took the one and some the other hand, and it was not until one of the paths they had taken opened into a little plain in which the woods were bald—a sort of prairie—that a party of seven Occonies discovered that they had among them two of their detested rivals, the Little Estatoees. What made the matter worse, one of these stragglers was the ill-fated warrior who had been chosen to carry the badge of his tribe; and there, high above their heads—the heads of the Brown Vipers—floated that detestable symbol, the green bird itself.

"There was no standing that. The Brown Vipers, as if with a common instinct, were immediately up in arms. They grappled the offending stragglers without gloves. They tore the green bird from the pole, stamped it under foot, smothered it in the mud, and pulling out the cone-tuft of its head, utterly degraded it in their own as well as in the estimation of the Estatoees. Not content with this, they hung the desecrated emblem about the neck of the bearer of it, and, spite of all their struggles, binding the arms of the two stragglers behind their backs, the relentless Vipers thrust the long pole which had borne the bird, in such a manner between their alternate arms as effectually to fasten them together. In this manner, amidst taunts, blows and revilings, they were left in the valley to get on as they might, while their enemies, insolent enough with exultation, proceeded to join the rest of their party.

CHAPTER VI.

"An hundred canoes were ready on the banks of the river Sarratay, for the conveyance to the opposite shore of the assembled Cherokees. And down they came, warrior after warrior, tribe after tribe, emblem after emblem, descending from the crags around, in various order, and hurrying all with shouts, and whoops and songs, grotesquely leaping to the river's bank, like so many boys just let out of school. Hilarity is, indeed, the life of nature! Civilization refines the one at the expense of the other, and then it is that no human luxury or sport, as known in society, stimulates appetite for any length of time. We can only laugh in the woods—society suffers but a smile, and desperate sanctity, with the countenance of a crow, frowns even at that.

"But, down, around, and gathering from every side, they came—the tens and the twenties of the several tribes of Cherokee. Grouped along the banks of the river, were the boats assigned to each. Some, already filled, were sporting in every direction over the clear bosom of that beautiful water. Moitoy himself, at the head of the tribe of Nequassée, from which he came, had already embarked; while the venerable Attakulla, with Jocassée, the gentle, sat upon a little bank in the neighbourhood of the Occony boats, awaiting the arrival of Cheochee and his party. And why came they not? One after another of the several tribes had filled their boats, and were either on the river or across it. But two clusters of canoes yet remained, and they were those of the rival tribes—a green bird flaunted over the one, and a brown viper, in many folds, was twined about the pole of the other.

"There was sufficient reason why they came not. The strife had begun;— for, when, gathering his thirteen warriors in a little hollow at the termination of the valley through which they came, Nagoochie beheld the slow and painful approach of the two stragglers upon whom the Occonies had so practised —when he saw the green bird, the beautiful emblem of his tribe, disfigured and defiled—there was no longer any measure or method in his madness. There was no longer a thought of Jocassée to keep him back; and the feeling of ferocious indignation which filled his bosom was the common feeling with his brother warriors. They lay in wait for the coming of the Occonies, down at the foot of the Yellow Hill, where the woods gathered green and thick. They were few—but half in number of their enemies—but they were strong in ardour, strong in justice, and even death was preferable to a longer endurance of that dishonour to which they had already been too long subjected. They beheld the approach of the Brown Vipers, as, one by one, they wound out from the gap of the mountain, with a fierce satisfaction. The two parties were now in sight of each other, and could not mistake the terms of their encounter. No word was spoken between them, but each began the scalp-song of his tribe, preparing at the same time his weapon, and advancing to the struggle.

"'The green bird has a bill,' sang the Estatoees; 'and he flies like an arrow to his prey.'

"'The brown viper has poison and a fang,' responded the Occonies; 'and he lies under the bush for his enemy.'

"'Give me to clutch the war-tuft,' cried the leaders of each party, almost in the same breath.

"'To taste the blood,' cried another.

"'And make my knife laugh in the heart that shrinks,' sung another and another.

"'I will put my foot on the heart,' cried an Occony.

"'I tear away the scalp,' shouted an Estato, in reply; while a joint chorus from the two parties, promised—

"'A dog that runs, to the black spirit that keeps in the dark.'

"'*Echa-herro, echa-herro, echa-herro*,' was the grand cry, or fearful war-whoop, which announced the moment of onset and the beginning of the strife.

"The Occonies were not backward, though the affair was commenced by the Estatoees. Cheochee, their leader, was quite as brave as malignant, and now exulted in the near prospect of that sweet revenge, for all the supposed wrongs and more certain rivalries which his tribe had suffered from the Green Birds. Nor was this more the feeling with him than with his tribe. Disposing themselves, therefore, in readiness to receive the assault, they rejoiced in the coming of a strife, in which, having many injuries to redress, they had the advantages, at the same time, of position and numbers.

"But their fighting at disadvantage was not now a thought with the Little Estatoees. Their blood was up, and like all usually patient people, once aroused, they were not so readily quieted. Nagoochie, the warrior now, and no longer the lover, led on the attack. You should have seen how that brave young chief went into battle—how he leapt up in air, slapped his hands upon his thighs in token of contempt for his foe, and throwing himself open before his enemies, dashed down his bow and arrows, and waving his hatchet, signified to them his desire for the conflict, *à l'outrance,* and, which would certainly make it so, hand to hand. The Occonies took him at his word, and throwing aside the long bow, they bounded out from their cover to meet their adversaries. Then should you have seen that meeting—that first rush—how they threw the tomahawk—how they flourished the knife—how the brave man rushed to the fierce embrace of his strong enemy—and how the two rolled along the hill in the teeth-binding struggle of death.

"The tomahawk of Nagoochie had wings and a tooth. It flew and bit in every direction. One after another, the Occonies went down before it, and still his fierce war cry of '*Echa-mal-Occony,*' preceding every stroke, announced another and another victim. They sank away from him like sheep before the wolf that is hungry, and the disparity of force was not so great in favour of the Occonies, when we recollect that Nagoochie was against them. The parties, under his fierce valour, were soon almost equal in number, and something more was necessary to be done by the Occonies before they could hope for that favourable result from the struggle which they had before looked upon as certain. It was for Cheochee now to seek out and to encounter the gallant young chief of Estato. Nagoochie, hitherto, for reasons best known to himself, had studiously avoided the leader of the Vipers; but he could no longer do so. He was contending, in close strife, with Okonettee, or the One-Eyed—a stout warrior of the Vipers—as Cheochee approached him. In the next moment, the hatchet of Nagoochie entered the skull of Okonettee. The One-Eyed sunk to the ground, as if in supplication, and, seizing the legs of his conqueror, in spite of the repeated blows which descended from the deadly instrument, each of which was a death, while his head swam, and the blood filled his eyes, and his senses were fast fleeting, he held on with a death-grasp which nothing could compel him to forego. In this predicament, Cheochee confronted the young brave of Estato. The strife was short, for though Nagoochie fought as bravely as ever, yet he struck in vain, while the dying wretch, grappling his legs, disordered, by his convulsions, not less than by his efforts, every blow which the strong hand of Nagoochie sought to give. One arm was already disabled, and still the dying wretch held on to his legs. In another moment, the One-Eyed was seized by the last spasms of death, and in his struggles, he dragged the Estato chief to his knees. This was the fatal disadvantage. Before any of the Green Bird warriors could come to his succour, the blow was given, and Nagoochie lay under the knee of the Brown

Viper. The knife was in his heart, and the life not yet gone, when the same instrument encircled his head, and his swimming vision could behold his own scalp waving in the grasp of his conqueror. The gallant spirit of Nagoochie passed away in a vain effort to utter his song of death—the song of a brave warrior conscious of many victories.

"Jocassée looked up to the hills when she heard the fierce cry of the descending Vipers. Their joy was madness, for they had fought with—they had slain, the bravest of their enemies. The intoxication of tone which Cheochee exhibited, when he told the story of the strife, and announced his victory, went like a deathstroke to the heart of the maiden. But she said not a word—she uttered no complaint—she shed no tear. Gliding quietly into the boat in which they were about to cross the river, she sat silent, gazing, with the fixedness of a marble statue, upon the still dripping scalp of her lover, as it dangled about the neck of his conqueror. On a sudden, just as they had reached the middle of the stream, she started, and her gaze was turned once more backward upon the banks they had left, as if, on a sudden, some object of interest had met her sight,—then, whether by accident or design, with look still intent in the same direction, she fell over the side, before they could save or prevent her, and was buried in the deep waters of Sarratay for ever. She rose not once to the surface. The stream, from that moment, lost the name of Sarratay, and both whites and Indians, to this day, know it only as the river of Jocassée. The girls of Cherokee, however, contend that she did not sink, but walking 'the waters like a thing of life,' that she rejoined Nagoochie, whom she saw beckoning to her from the shore. Nor is this the only tradition. The story goes on to describe a beautiful lodge, one of the most select in the valleys of Manneyto, the hunter of which is Nagoochie of the Green Bird, while the maiden who dresses his venison is certainly known as Jocassée."

"THE ARM-CHAIR OF TUSTENUGGEE" illustrates Simms's uncommon ability to transform ancient strains of European folklore into a delightfully comic story that reflects his strong interest in Native Americans. Simms writes as an artist, not an ethnohistorian; each Catawba character is a unique individual— yet with a touch of irony and wit, Simms reveals them collectively as possessing a full range of human qualities.

ᕇ *The Arm-Chair of Tustenuggee. A Tradition of the Catawba.*

CHAPTER I.

The windy month had set in, the leaves were falling, and the light-footed hunters of Catawba, set forth upon the chase. Little groups went off in every direction, and before two weeks had elapsed from the beginning of the campaign, the whole nation was broken up into parties, each under the guidance of an individual warrior. The course of the several hunting bands was taken according to the tastes or habits of these leaders. Some of the Indians were famous for their skill in hunting the otter, could swim as long with head under water as himself, and be not far from his haunches, when he emerged to breathe. These followed the course of shallow waters and swamps, and thick, dense bays, in which it was known that he found his favourite haunts. The bear hunter pushed for the cane brakes and the bee trees; and woe to the black bear whom he encountered with his paws full of honeycomb, which he was unwilling to leave behind him. The active warrior took his way towards the hills, seeking for the brown wolf and the deer; and, if the truth were known, smiled with wholesale contempt at the more timorous who desired less adventurous triumphs. Many set forth in couples only, avoiding with care all the clamorous of the tribe; and some few, the more surly or successful— the inveterate bachelors of the nation—were content to make their forward progress alone. The old men prepared their traps and nets, the boys their blow guns, and followed with the squaws slowly, according to the division made by the hunters among themselves. They carried the blankets and bread stuffs, and camped nightly in noted places, to which, according to previous arrangement, the hunters might repair at evening and bring their game. In this way, some of the tribes followed the course of the Catawba, even to its source. Others darted off towards the Pacolet and Broad rivers, and there were some, the most daring and swift of foot, who made nothing of a journey to the Tiger river, and the rolling mountains of Spartanburg.

There were two warriors who pursued this course. One of them was named Conattee, and a braver man and more fortunate hunter never lived. But he had a wife who was a greater scold than Xantippe. She was the wonder and the terror of the tribe, and quite as ugly as the one-eyed squaw of Tustenuggee, the grey demon of Enoree. Her tongue was the signal for "slinking," among the bold hunters of Turkey-town; and when they heard it, "now," said the young women, who sympathised, as all proper young women will do, with the handsome husband of an ugly wife, "now," said they, "we know that poor Conattee has come home." The return of the husband, particularly if he brought no game, was sure to be followed by a storm of that "dry thunder," so well known, which never failed to be heard at the farthest end of the village.

The companion of Conattee on the present expedition was named Selonee—one of the handsomest lads in the whole nation. He was tall and straight like a pine tree; had proved his skill and courage in several expeditions against the Chowannee red sticks, and had found no young warriors of the Cherokee, though he had been on the war path against them and had stricken all their posts, who could circumvent him in stratagem or conquer him in actual blows. His renown as a hunter was not less great. He had put to shame the best wolf-takers of the tribe, and the lodge of his venerable father, Chifonti, was never without meat. There was no good reason why Conattee, the married man, should be so intimate with Selonee, the single—there was no particular sympathy between the two; but, thrown together in sundry expeditions, they had formed an intimacy, which, strange to say, was neither denounced nor discouraged by the virago wife of the former. She who approved of but few of her husband's movements, and still fewer of his friends and fellowships, forbore all her reproaches when Selonee was his companion. She was the meekest, gentlest, sweetest tempered of all wives whenever the young hunter came home with her husband; and he, poor man, was consequently, never so well satisfied as when he brought Selonee with him. It was on such occasions, only, that the poor Conattee could persuade himself to regard Macourah as a tolerable personage. How he came to marry such a creature—such a termagant, and so monstrous ugly—was a mystery which none of the damsels of Catawba could elucidate, though the subject was one on which, when mending the young hunter's mocasins, they expended no small quantity of conjecture. Conattee, we may be permitted to say, was still quite popular among them, in spite of his bad taste, and manifest unavailableness; possibly, for the very reason that his wife was universally detested; and it will, perhaps, speak something for their charity, if we pry no deeper into their motives, to say that the wish was universal among them that the Opitchi Manneyto, or Black Devil of their belief, would take the virago to himself, and leave to the poor Conattee some reasonable hope of being made happy by a more indulgent spouse.

CHAPTER II.

Well, Conattee and Selonee were out of sight of the smoke of "Turkey-town," and, conscious of his freedom as he no longer heard the accents of domestic authority, the henpecked husband gave a loose to his spirits, and made ample amends to himself, by the indulgence of joke and humour, for the sober constraints which fettered him at home. Selonee joined with him in his merriment, and the resolve was mutual that they should give the squaws the slip and not linger in their progress till they had thrown the Tiger river behind them. To trace their course till they came to the famous hunting ground which bordered upon the Pacolet, will scarcely be necessary, since, as they did not stop to hunt by the way, there were necessarily but few incidents to give interest to their movements. When they had reached the river, however, they made for a cove, well known to them on previous seasons, which lay between the parallel waters of the Pacolet, and a little stream called the Thicketty—a feeder of the Eswawpuddenah, in which they had confident hopes of finding the game which they desired. In former years the spot had been famous as a sheltering place for herds of wolves; and, with something like the impatience of a warrior waiting for his foe, the hunters prepared their strongest shafts and sharpest flints, and set their keen eyes upon the closest places of the thicket, into which they plunged fearlessly. They had not proceeded far, before a single boar-wolf, of amazing size, started up in their path; and, being slightly wounded by the arrow of Selonee, which glanced first upon some twigs beneath which he lay, he darted off with a fearful howl in the direction of Conattee, whose unobstructed shaft, penetrating the side beneath the fore shoulders, inflicted a fearful, if not a fatal wound, upon the now thoroughly enraged beast. He rushed upon Conattee in his desperation, but the savage was too quick for him; leaping behind a tree, he avoided the rashing stroke with which the white tusks threatened him, and by this time was enabled to fit a second arrow to his bow. His aim was true, and the stone blade of the shaft went quivering into the shaggy monster's heart; who, under the pang of the last convulsion, bounded into the muddy waters of the Thicketty Creek, to the edge of which the chase had now brought all the parties. Conattee beheld him plunge furiously forward—twice—thrice—then rest with his nostrils in the water, as the current bore him from sight around a little elbow of the creek. But it was not often that the Indian hunter of those days lost the game which he had stricken. Conattee stripped to it, threw his fringed hunting shirt of buckskin on the bank, with his bow and arrows, his mocasins and leggins beside it, and reserving only his knife, he called to Selonee, who was approaching him, to keep them in sight, and plunged into the water in pursuit of his victim. Selonee gave little heed to the movements of his companion, after the first two or three vigorous strokes which he beheld him make. Such a pursuit, as it promised no peril, called for little consideration from this hardy and fearless race, and Selonee amused himself by striking into a thick copse which they had not yet traversed, in search of other sport. There he started the she-wolf, and found sufficient employment on his own hands to call for all his attention to himself. When Selonee first came in sight of her, she was lying on a bed of rushes and leaves, which she had prepared under the roots of a gigantic Spanish oak. Her cubs, to the number of five, lay around her, keeping a perfect silence, which she had no doubt enforced upon them after her own fashion, and which was rigidly maintained until they saw him. It was then that the instincts of the fierce beasts could no longer be suppressed, and they joined at once in a short chopping bark, or cry, at the stranger, while their little eyes flashed fire, and their red jaws, thinly sprinkled with the first teeth, were gnashed together with a show of that ferocious hatred of man, which marks their nature, but which, fortunately for Selonee, was too feeble at that time to make his approach to them dangerous. But the dam demanded greater consideration. With one sweep of her fore-paw she drew all the young ones behind her, and showing every preparedness for flight, she began to move backward slowly beneath the overhanging limbs of the tree, still keeping her keen, fiery eye fixed upon the hunter. But Selonee was not disposed to suffer her to get off so easily. The success of Conattee had just given him sufficient provocation to make him silently resolve that the she-wolf—who is always more to be dreaded than the male, as, with nearly all his strength, she has twice his swiftness, and, with her young about her, more than twice his ferocity—should testify more completely to his prowess than the victory just obtained by his companion could possibly speak for his. His eye was fixed upon hers, and hers, never for a moment, taken from him. It was his object to divert it, since he well knew, that with his first movement, she would most probably spring upon him. Without lifting his bow, which he nevertheless had in readiness, he whistled shrilly as if to his dog; and answered himself by a correct imitation of the bark of the Indian cur, the known enemy of the wolf, and commonly his victim. The keen eye of the angry beast looked suddenly around as if fearing an assault upon her young ones from behind. In that moment, the arrow of Selonee was driven through her neck, and when she leaped forward to the place where he stood, he was no longer to be seen.

From a tree which he had thrown between them, he watched her movements and prepared a second shaft. Meanwhile she made her way back slowly to her young, and before she could again turn towards him a second arrow had given her another and severer wound. Still, as Selonee well knew the singular tenacity of life possessed by these fierce animals, he prudently changed his position with every shaft, and took especial care to place himself in the rear of some moderately sized tree, sufficiently large to shelter him from her claws, yet small enough to enable him to take free aim around it. Still he did not, at any time, withdraw more than twenty steps from his enemy. Divided in her energies by the necessity of keeping near her young, he was conscious of her inability to pursue him far. Carrying on the war in this manner he had buried no less than five arrows in her body, and it was not until his sixth had penetrated her eye, that he deemed himself safe in the nearer approach which he now meditated. She had left her cubs, on receiving his last shot, and was writhing and leaping, blinded, no less than maddened, by the wound, in a vain endeavour to approach her assailant. It was now that Selonee determined on a closer conflict. It was the great boast of the Catawba warriors to grapple with the wolf, and while he yet struggled, to tear the quick quivering heart from his bosom. He placed his bow and arrows behind the tree, and taking in his left hand a chunk or fragment of a bough, while he grasped his unsheathed knife in his right, he leapt in among the cubs, and struck one of them a severe blow upon the head with the chunk. Its scream, and the confusion among the rest, brought back the angry dam, and though she could see only imperfectly, yet, guided by their clamour, she rushed with open jaws upon the hunter. With keen, quick eyes, and steady resolute nerves, he waited for her approach, and when she turned her head aside, to strike him with her sharp teeth, he thrust the pine fragment which he carried in his left hand, into her extended jaws, and pressing fast upon her, bore back her haunches to the earth. All this while the young ones were impotently gnawing at the heels of the warrior, which had been fearlessly planted in the very midst of them. But these he did not heed. The larger and fiercer combatant called for all his attention, and her exertions, quickened by the spasms of her wounds, rendered necessary all his address and strength to preserve the advantage he had gained. The fierce beast had sunk her teeth by this into the wood, and, leaving it in her jaws, he seized her with the hand, now freed, by the throat, and, bearing her upward, so as to yield him a plain and easy stroke at her belly, he drove the deep knife into it, and drew the blade upwards, until resisted by the bone of the breast. It was then, while she lay writhing and rolling upon the ground in the agonies of death, that he tore the heart from the opening he had made, and hurled it down to the cubs, who seized on it with avidity. This done, he patted and caressed them, and while they struggled about him for the meat, he cut a fork in the ears of each, and putting the slips in his pouch, left the young ones without further hurt, for the future sport of the hunter. The dam he scalped, and with this trophy in possession, he pushed back to the place where he had left the accoutrements of Conattee, which he found undisturbed in the place where he had laid them.

CHAPTER III.

But where was Conattee himself during all this period? Some hours had elapsed since he had taken the river after the tiger that he had slain, and it was something surprising to Selonee that he should have remained absent and without his clothes so long. The weather was cold and unpleasant, and it could scarce be a matter of choice with the hunter, however hardy, to suffer all its biting bleaknesses when his garments were within his reach. This reflection made Selonee apprehensive that some harm had happened to his companion. He shouted to him, but received no answer. Could he have been seized with the cramp while in the stream, and drowned before he could extricate himself. This was a danger to which the very best of swimmers is liable at certain seasons of the year, and in certain conditions of the body. Selonee reproached himself that he had not waited beside the stream until the result of Conattee's experiment was known. The mind of the young hunter was troubled with many fears and doubts. He went down the bank of the river, and called aloud with all his lungs, until the woods and waters re-echoed, again and again, the name of Conattee. He received no other response. With a mind filled with increasing fears, each more unpleasant than the last, Selonee plunged into the creek, and struck off for the opposite shore, at the very point at which the tiger had been about to turn, under the influence of the current, when Conattee went in after him. He was soon across, and soon found the tracks of the hunter in the gray sands upon its margin. He found, too, to his great delight, the traces made by the carcass of the tiger—the track was distinct enough from the blood which dropped from the reeking skin of the beast, and Selonee rejoiced in the certainty that the traces which he followed would soon lead him to his friend. But not so. He had scarcely gone fifty yards into the wood when his tracks failed him at the foot of a crooked, fallen tree, one of the most gnarled and complicated of all the crooked trees of the forest; here all signs disappeared. Conattee was not only not there, but had left no sort of clue by which to follow him further. This was the strangest thing of all. The footprints were distinct enough till he came to the spot where lay the crooked tree, but there he lost them. He searched the forest around him, in every direction. Not a copse escaped his search—not a bay—not a thicket— not an island—and he came back to the spot where the tiger had been skinned, faint and weary, and more sorrowful than can well be spoken. At one time he fancied his friend was drowned, at another, that he was taken prisoner by the Cherokees. But there were his tracks from the river, and there were no other tracks than his own. Besides, so far as the latter supposition was concerned, it was scarcely possible that so brave and cunning a warrior would suffer himself to be so completely entrapped and carried off by an enemy, without so much as being able to give the alarm; and, even had that been the case, would it be likely that the enemy would have suffered him to pass without notice. "But," here the suggestion naturally arose in the mind of Selonee, "may they not even now be on the track!" With the suggestion the gallant youth bounded to his feet. "It is no fat turkey that they seek!" he exclaimed, drawing out an arrow from the leash that hung upon his shoulders, and fitting it to his bow, while his busy, glancing eye watched every shadow in the wood, and his keen, quick ear noted every sound. But there were no signs of an enemy, and a singular and mournful stillness hung over the woods. Never was creature more miserable than Selonee. He called aloud, until his voice grew hoarse, and his throat sore, upon the name of Conattee. There was no answer, but the gibing echoes of his own hoarse accents. Once more he went back to the river, once more he plunged into its bosom, and with lusty sinews struck out for a thick green island that lay some quarter of a mile below, to which he thought it not improbable that the hunter might have wandered in pursuit of other game. It was a thickly wooded but small island, which he traversed in an hour. Finding nothing, he made his weary way back to the spot from which his friend had started on leaving him. Here he found his clothes where he had hidden them. The neighbourhood of this region he traversed in like manner with the opposite—going over ground, and into places, which it was scarcely in the verge of physical possibility that his friend's person could have gone.

The day waned and night came on, and still the persevering hunter gave not up his search. The midnight found him at the foot of the tree, where they had parted, exhausted but sleepless, and suffering bitterly in mind from those apprehensions which every moment of hopeless search had necessarily helped to accumulate and strengthen. Day dawned, and his labour was renewed. The unhappy warrior went resolutely over all the ground which he had traversed the night before. Once more he crossed the river, and followed, step by step, the still legible foot tracks of Conattee. These, he again noted, were all in the opposite direction to the stream, to which it was evident he had not returned. But, after reaching the place where lay the fallen tree, all signs failed. Selonee looked round the crooked tree, crawled under its sprawling and twisted limbs, broke into the hollow which was left by its uptorn roots, and again shouted, until all the echoes gave back his voice, the name of Conattee, imploring him for an answer if he could hear him and reply. But the echoes died away, leaving him in a silence that spoke more loudly to his heart than before, that his quest was hopeless. Yet he gave it not up until the day had again failed him. That night, as before, he slept upon the ground. With the dawn, he again went over it, and with equally bad success. This done, he determined to return to the camp. He no longer had any spirit to pursue the sports for which alone he had set forth. His heart was full of sorrow, his limbs were weary, and he felt none of that vigorous elasticity which had given him such great renown as a brave and a hunter, among his own and the neighbouring nations. He tied the clothes of Conattee upon his shoulders, took his bow and arrows, now sacred in his sight, along with him, and turned his eyes homeward. The next day, at noon, he reached the encampment.

CHAPTER IV.

The hunters were all in the woods, and none but the squaws and the papooses left in the encampment. Selonee came within sight of their back settlements, and seated himself upon a log at the edge of the forest with his back carefully turned towards the smoke of the camp. Nobody ventured to approach him while in this situation; but, at night, when the hunters came dropping in, one by one, Selonee drew nigh to them. He called them apart from the women, and then told them his story.

"This is a strange tale which the wolf-chief tells us," said one of the old men, with a smile of incredulity.

"It is a true tale, father," was the reply.

"Conattee was a brave chief!"

"Very brave, father," said Selonee.

"Had he not eyes to see?"

"The great bird, that rises to the sun, had not better," was the reply.

"What painted jay was it that said Conattee was a fool?"

"The painted bird lied, that said so, my father," was the response of Selonee.

"And comes Selonee, the wolf-chief, to us, with a tale that Conattee was blind, and could not see; a coward that could not strike the she-wolf; a fool that knew not where to set down his foot; and shall we not say Selonee lies upon his brother, even as the painted bird that makes a noise in my ears. Selonee has slain Conattee with his knife. See, it is the blood of Conattee upon the war-shirt of Selonee."

"It is the blood of the she-wolf," cried the young warrior, with a natural indignation.

"Let Selonee go to the woods behind the lodges, till the chiefs say what shall be done to Selonee, because of Conattee, whom he slew."

"Selonee will go, as Emathla the wise chief, has commanded," replied the young warrior. "He will wait behind the lodges, till the chiefs have said what is good to be done to him, and if they say that he must die because of Conattee, it is well. Selonee laughs at death. But the blood of Conattee is not upon the war-shirt of Selonee. He has said it is the blood of the wolf's mother." With these words the young chief drew forth the skin of the wolf which he had slain, together with the tips of the ears taken from the cubs, and leaving them in the place where he had sat, withdrew, without further speech, from the assembly which was about to sit in judgment upon his life.

CHAPTER V.

The consultation that followed was close and earnest. There was scarcely any doubt in the minds of the chiefs that Conattee was slain by his companion. He had brought back with him the arms and all the clothes of the hunter. He was covered with his blood, as they thought; and the chief which filled his heart and depressed his countenance, looked, in their eyes, rather like the expression of guilt than suffering. For a long while did they consult together. Selonee had friends who were disposed to save him; but he had enemies also, as merit must have always, and these were glad of the chance afforded them to put out of their reach, a rival of whom they were jealous, and a warrior whom they feared. Unfortunately for Selonee, the laws of the nation but too well helped the malice of his foes. These laws, as peremptory as those of the Medes and Persians, held him liable in his own life for that of the missing hunter; and the only indulgence that could be accorded to Selonee, and which was obtained for him, was, that he might be allowed a single moon in which to find Conattee, and bring him home to his people.

"Will Selonee go seek Conattee—the windy moon is for Selonee—let him bring Conattee home to his people." Thus said the chiefs, when the young warrior was again brought before them.

"Selonee would die to find Conattee," was the reply.

"He will die if he finds him not!" answered the chief Emathla.

"It is well!" calmly spoke the young warrior. "Is Selonee free to go?"

"The windy moon is for Selonee. Will he return to the lodges if he finds not Conattee?" was the inquiry of Emathla.

"Is Selonee a dog, to fly!" indignantly demanded the warrior. Let Emathla send a young warrior on the right and or the left of Selonee, if he trusts not what is spoken by Selonee."

"Selonee will go alone, and bring back Conattee."

CHAPTER VI.

The confidence thus reposed in one generally esteemed a murderer, and actually under sentence as such, is customary among the Indians; nor is it often abused. The loss of caste which would follow their flight from justice, is much more terrible among them than any fear of death—which an Indian may avoid, but not through fear. Their loss of caste among themselves, apart from the outlawry which follows it, is, in fact, a loss of the soul. The heaven of the great Manneyto is denied to one under outlawry of the nation, and such a person is then the known and chosen slave of the demon, Opitchi-Manneyto. It was held an unnecessary insult on the part of Emathla, to ask Selonee if he would return to meet his fate. But Emathla was supposed to favour the enemies of Selonee.

With such a gloomy alternative before him in the event of his proving unsuccessful, the young hunter retraced his steps to the fatal waters where Conattee had disappeared. With a spirit no less warmly devoted to his friend, than anxious to avoid the disgraceful doom to which he was destined, the youth spared no pains, withheld no exertion, overlooked no single spot, and omitted no art known to the hunter, to trace out the mystery which covered the fate of Conattee. But days passed of fruitless labour, and the last faint slender outlines of the moon which had been allotted him for the search, gleamed forth a sorrowful light upon his path, as he wearily traced it onward to the temporary lodges of the tribe.

Once more he resumed his seat before the council and listened to the doom which was in reserve for him. When the sentence was pronounced, he untied his arrows, loosened the belt at his waist, put a fillet around his head, made of the green bark of a little sapling which he cut in the neighbouring woods, then rising to his feet, he spoke thus, in language, and with a spirit, becoming so great a warrior. "It is well. The chiefs have spoken, and the wolf-chief does not tremble. He loves the chase, but he does not weep like a woman, because it is forbidden that he go after the deer—he loves to fright the young hares of the Cherokee, but he laments not that ye say ye can conquer the Cherokee without his help. Fathers, I have slain the deer and the wolf—my lodge is full of their ears. I have slain the Cherokee, till the scalps are about my knees when I walk in the cabin. I go not to the dark valley without glory—I have had the victories of grey hairs, but there is no grey hair in my own. I have no more to say—there is a deed for every arrow that is here. Bid the young men get their bows ready, let them put a broad stone upon their arrows that may go soon into the life—I will show my people how to die."

They led him forth as he commanded, to the place of execution—a little space behind the encampment, where a hole had been already dug for his burial. While he went, he recited his victories to the youths who attended him. To each he gave an arrow which he was required to keep, and with this arrow, he related some incident in which he had proved his valour, either in conflict with some other warrior, or with the wild beasts of the woods. These deeds, each of them was required to remember and relate, and show the arrow which was given with the narrative on occasion of this great state solemnity. In this way, their traditions are preserved. When he reached the grave, he took his station before it, the executioners, with their arrows, being already placed in readiness. The whole tribe had assembled to witness the execution, the warriors and boys in the foreground, the squaws behind them. A solemn silence prevailed over the scene, and a few moments only remained to the victim; when the wife of Conattee darted forward from the crowd bearing in her hands a peeled wand, with which, with every appearance of anger, she struck Selonee over the shoulders, exclaiming as she did so:

"Come, thou dog, thou shalt not die—thou shalt lie in the doorway of Conattee, and bring venison for his wife. Shall there be no one to bring meat to my lodge? Thou shalt do this, Selonee—thou shalt not die."

A murmur arose from the crowd at these words.

"She hath claimed Selonee for her husband, in place of Conattee—well, she hath the right."

The enemies of Selonee could not object. The widow had, in fact, exercised a privilege which is recognized by the Indian laws almost universally; and the policy by which she was governed in the present instance, was sufficiently apparent to all the village. It was evident, now that Conattee was gone, that nobody could provide for the woman who had no sons, and no male relations, and who was too execrably ugly, and too notorious as a scold, to leave it possible that she could ever procure another husband so inexperienced or so flexible as the one she had lost. Smartly striking Selonee on his shoulders, she repeated her command that he should rise and follow her.

"Thou wilt take this dog to thy lodge, that he may hunt thee venison?" demanded the old chief, Emathla.

"Have I not said?" shouted the scold—"hear you not? The dog is mine—I bid him follow me."

"Is there no friendly arrow to seek my heart?" murmured the young warrior, as, rising slowly from the grave into which he had previously descended, he prepared to obey the laws of his nation, in the commands of the woman who claimed him to replace the husband who was supposed to have died by his hands. Even the foes of Selonee looked on him with lessened hostility, and the pity of his friends was greater now than when he stood on the precipice of death. The young women of the tribe wept bitterly as they beheld so monstrous a sacrifice. Meanwhile, the exulting hag, as if conscious of her complete control over the victim, goaded him forward with repeated strokes of her wand. She knew that she was hated by all the young women, and she was delighted to show them a conquest which would have been a subject of pride to any among them. With this view she led the captive through their ranks. As they parted mournfully, on either hand, to suffer the two to pass, Selonee stopped short and motioned one of the young women who stood at the greatest distance behind the rest, looking on with eyes which, if they had no tears, yet gave forth an expression of desolateness more woeful than any tears could have done. With clasped hands, and trembling as she came, the gentle maiden drew nigh. "Was it a dream," said Selonee sorrowfully, "that told me of the love of a singing bird, and a green cabin by the trickling waters? Did I hear a voice that said to me sweetly, wait but a little, till the green corn breaks the hill, and Medoree will come to thy cabin and lie by thy side? Tell me, is this thing true, Medoree?"

"Thou sayest, Selonee—the thing is true," was the reply of the maiden, uttered in broken accents that denoted a breaking heart.

"But they will make Selonee go to the lodge of another woman—they will put Macourah into the arms of Selonee."

"Alas! Alas!"

"Wilt thou see this thing, Medoree? Can'st thou look upon it, then turn away, and going back to thy own lodge, can'st thou sing a gay song of forgetfulness as thou goest?"

"Forgetfulness!—Ah, Selonee."

"Thou art the beloved of Selonee, Medoree—thou shalt not lose him. It would vex thy heart that another should take him to her lodge!"—

The tears of the damsel flowed freely down her cheeks, and she sobbed bitterly, but said nothing.

"Take the knife from my belt, Medoree, and put its sharp tooth into my heart, ere thou sufferest this thing! Wilt thou not?"

The girl shrunk back with an expression of undisguised horror in her face.

"I will bless thee, Medoree," was the continued speech of the warrior. She turned from him, covering her face with her hands.

"I cannot do this thing, Selonee—I cannot strike thy heart with the knife. Go—let the woman have thee. Medoree cannot kill thee—she will herself die."

"It is well," cried the youth, in a voice of mournful self-abandonment, as he resumed his progress towards the lodge of Macourah.

Chapter VII.

It is now time to return to Conattee, and trace his progress from the moment when, plunging into the waters, he left the side of Selonee in pursuit of the wolf, whose dying struggles in the stream he had beheld. We are already acquainted with his success in extricating the animal from the water, and possessing himself of its hide. He had not well done this when he heard a rushing noise in the woods above him, and fancying that there was a prospect of other game at hand, and inflated with the hope of adding to his trophies, though without any weapon but his knife, Conattee hastened to the spot.

When he reached it, however, he beheld nothing. A gigantic and singularly deformed pine tree, crooked and most irregular in shape, lay prostrate along the ground, and formed such an intricate covering above it, that Conattee deemed it possible that some beast of prey might have made its den among the recesses of its roots. With this thought he crawled under the spreading limbs, and searched all their intricacies. Emerging from the search, which had been fruitless, he took a seat upon the trunk of the tree, and spreading out the wolf's hide before him, proceeded to pare away the particles of flesh which, in the haste with which he had performed the task of flaying him, had been suffered to adhere to the skin. But he had scarcely commenced the oper- ation, when two gigantic limbs of the fallen tree upon which he sat, curled over his thighs and bound him to the spot. Other limbs, to his great horror, while he strove to move, clasped his arms and covered his shoulders. He strove to cry aloud, but his jaws were grasped before he could well open them, by other branches; and, with his eyes, which were suffered to peer through little openings in the bark, he could see his legs encrusted by like coverings with his other members. Still seeing, his own person yet escaped his sight. Not a part of it now remained visible to himself. A bed of green velvet- like moss rested on his lap. His knees shot out a thorny excrescence; and his hands, flattened to his thighs, were enveloped in as complete a casing of bark as covered the remainder of the tree around him. Even his knife and wolf skin, to his great surprise, suffered in like manner, the bark having contracted them into one of those huge bulging knobs that so numerously deformed the tree. With all his thoughts and consciousness remaining, Conattee had yet lost every faculty of action. When he tried to scream aloud, his jaws felt the contraction of a pressure upon them, which resisted all their efforts, while an oppressive thorn growing upon a wild vine that hung before his face, was brought by every movement of himself or of the tree into his very mouth. The poor hunter immediately conceived his situation—he was in the power of Tustenuggee, the Grey Demon of Enoree. The tree upon which he sat was one of those magic trees which the tradition of his people entitled the "Arm-Chair of Tustenuggee." In these traps for the unwary the wicked demon caught his victim, and exulted in his miseries. Here he sometimes remained until death released him; for it was not often that the power into whose clutches he had fallen, suffered his prey to escape through a sudden feeling of lenity and good humour. The only hope of Conattee was that Selonee might suspect his condition; in which event his rescue was simple and easy enough. It was only to hew off the limbs, or pare away the bark, and the victim was uncovered in his primitive integrity. But how improbable that this discovery should be made. He had no voice to declare his bondage. He had no capacity for movement by which he might reveal the truth to his comrade's eyes; and unless some divine instinct should counsel his friend to an experiment which he would scarcely think upon, of himself, the poor prisoner felt that he must die in the miserable bondage into which he had fallen. While these painful convictions were passing through his mind, he heard the distant shoutings of Selonee. In a little while he beheld the youth anxiously seeking him in every quarter, following his trail at length to the very tree in which he was bound, crawling like himself beneath its branches, but not sitting like himself to be caught upon its trunk. Vainly did the poor fellow strive to utter but a few words, however faintly, apprising the youth of his condition. The effort died away in the most imperfect breathing sounding in his own ears like the faint sigh of some budding flower. With equal ill success did he aim to struggle with his limbs. He was too tightly grasped, in every part, to stir in the slightest degree a single member. He saw the fond search, meanwhile, which his comrade maintained, and his heart yearned the more in fondness for the youth. But it was with consummate horror that he saw him depart as night came on. Miserable, indeed, were his feelings that night. The voice of the Grey Demon alone kept him company, and he and his one-eyed wife made merry with his condition, goading him the livelong night with speeches of cruel gibe and mischievous reflection, such as the following

"There is no hope for you, Conattee, till some one takes your place. Some one must sit in your lap, whom you are willing to leave behind you, before you can get out of mine," was the speech of the Grey Demon, who, perched upon Conattee's shoulders, bent his huge knotty head over him, while his red eyes looked into the half-hidden ones of the environed hunter, and glared upon him with the exultation of the tyrant at last secure of his prey. Night passed away at length, and, with the dawn, how was the hopeless heart of Conattee refreshed as he again saw Selonee appear. He then remembered the words of Tustenuggee, which told him that he could not escape until some one sat in his lap whom he was willing to leave behind him. The fancy rose in his mind that Selonee would do this; but could it be that he would consent to leave his friend behind him. Life was sweet, and great was the temptation. At one moment he almost wished that Selonee would draw nigh and seat himself after his fatigue. As if the young hunter knew his wish, he drew nigh at that instant; but the better feelings in Conattee's heart grew strong as he approached, and, striving to twist and writhe in his bondage, and labouring at the same time to call out in warning to his friend, he manifested the noble resolution not to avail himself of his friend's position to relieve his own; and, as if the warning of Conattee had really reached the understanding of Selonee, the youth retraced his steps, and once more hurried away from the place of danger. With his final departure the fond hopes of the prisoner sunk within him; and when hour after hour had gone by without the appearance of any of his people, and without any sort of change in his condition, he gave himself up utterly for lost. The mocks and jeers of the Grey Demon and his one-eyed squaw filled his ears all night, and the morning brought him nothing but flat despair. He resigned himself to his fate with the resolution of one who, however unwilling he might be to perish in such a manner, had yet faced death too frequently not to yield him a ready defiance now.

Chapter VIII.

But hope had not utterly departed from the bosom of Selonee. Perhaps the destiny which had befallen himself had made him resolve the more earnestly to seek farther into the mystery of that which hung above the fate of his friend. The day which saw him enter the cabin of Macourah saw him the most miserable man alive. The hateful hag, hateful enough as the wife of his friend, whose ill treatment was notorious, was now doubly hateful to him as his own wife; and now, when, alone together, she threw aside the harsh and termagant features which had before distinguished her deportment, and, assuming others of a more amorous complexion, threw her arms about the neck of the youth and solicited his endearments, a loathing sensation of disgust was coupled with the hate which had previously possessed his mind. Flinging away from her embrace, he rushed out of the lodge with feelings of the most unspeakable bitterness and grief, and bending his way towards the forest, soon lost sight of the encampment of his people. Selonee was resolved on making another effort for the recovery of his friend. His resolve went even farther than this. He was bent never to return to the doom which had been fastened upon him, and to pursue his way into more distant and unknown forests—a self-doomed exile—unless he could restore Conattee to the nation. Steeled against all those ties of love or of country, which at one time had prevailed in his bosom over all, he now surrendered himself to friendship or despair. In Catawba, unless he restored Conattee, he could have no hope; and without Catawba he had neither hope nor love. On either hand he saw nothing but misery; but the worst form of misery lay behind him in the lodge of Macourah. But Macourah was not the person to submit to such a determination. She was too well satisfied with the exchange with which fortune had provided her, to suffer its gift to be lost so easily; and when Selonee darted from the cabin in such fearful haste, she readily conjectured his determination. She hurried after him with all possible speed, little doubting that those thunders—could she overtake him—with which she had so frequently overawed the pliant Conattee, would possess an effect not less influential upon his more youthful successor. Macourah was gaunt as a greyhound, and scarcely less fleet of foot. Besides, she was as tough as a grey-squirrel in his thirteenth year. She did not despair of overtaking Selonee, provided she suffered him not to know that she was upon his trail. Her first movements therefore were marked with caution. Having watched his first direction, she divined his aim to return to the hunting grounds where he had lost or slain his companion; and these hunting grounds were almost as well known to herself as to him. With a rapidity of movement, and a tenacity of purpose, which could only be accounted for by a reference to that wild passion which Selonee had unconsciously inspired in her bosom for himself, she followed his departing footsteps; and when, the next day, he heard her shouts behind him, he was absolutely confounded. But it was with a feeling of surprise and not of dissatisfaction that he heard her voice. He—good youth—regarding Conattee as one of the very worthiest of the Catawba warriors, seemed to have been impressed with an idea that such also was the opinion of his wife. He little dreamed that she had any real design upon himself; and believed that, to show her the evidences which were to be seen, which led to the fate of her husband, might serve to convince her that not only he was not the murderer, but that Conattee might not, indeed, be murdered at all. He coolly waited her approach, therefore, and proceeded to renew his statements, accompanying his narrative with the expression of the hope which he entertained of again restoring her husband to herself and the nation. But she answered his speech only with upbraidings and entreaties; and when she failed, she proceeded to thump him lustily with the wand by which she had compelled him to follow her to the lodge the day before. But Selonee was in no humour to obey the laws of the nation now. The feeling of degradation which had followed in his mind, from the moment when he left the spot where he had stood up for death, having neither fear nor shame, was too fresh in his consciousness to suffer him to yield a like acknowledgment to it now; and though sorely tempted to pummel the Jezabel in return for the lusty thwacks which she had already inflicted upon his shoulders, he forbore, in consideration of his friend, and contented himself with simply setting forward on his progress, determined to elude her pursuit by an exercise of all his vigour and elasticity. Selonee was hardy as the grisly bear, and fleeter than the wild turkey; and Macourah, virago as she was, soon discovered the difference in the chase when Selonee put forth his strength and spirit. She followed with all her pertinacity, quickened as it was by an increase of fury at that presumption which had ventured to disobey her commands; but Selonee fled faster than she pursued, and every additional moment served to increase the space between them. The hunter lost her from his heels at length, and deemed himself fortunate that she was no longer in sight and hearing, when he again approached the spot where his friend had so mysteriously disappeared. Here he renewed his search with a painful care and minuteness, which the imprisoned Conattee all the while beheld. Once more Selonee crawled beneath those sprawling limbs and spreading arms that wrapped up in their solid and coarse rinds the person of the warrior. Once more he emerged from the spot disappointed and hopeless. This he had hardly done when, to the great horror of the captive, and the annoyance of Selonee, the shrill shrieks and screams of the too well-known voice of Macourah rang through the forests. Selonee dashed forward as he heard the sounds, and when Macourah reached the spot, which she did unerringly in following his trail, the youth was already out of sight.

"I can go no further," cried the woman—"a curse on him and a curse on Conattee, since in losing one I have lost both. I am too faint to follow. As for Selonee, may the one-eyed witch of Tustenuggee take him for her dog."

With this delicate imprecation, the virago seated herself in a state of exhaustion upon the inviting bed of moss which formed the lap of Conattee. This she had no sooner done, than the branches relaxed their hold upon the limbs of her husband. The moment was too precious for delay, and sliding from under her with an adroitness and strength which were beyond her powers of prevention, and indeed, quite too sudden for any effort at resistance, she had the consternation to behold her husband starting up in full life before her, and, with the instinct of his former condition, preparing to take to flight. She cried to him, but he fled the faster—she strove to follow him, but the branches which had relaxed their hold upon her husband had resumed their contracted grasp upon her limbs. The brown bark was already forming above her on every hand, and her tongue, allotted a brief term of liberty, was alone free to assail him. But she had spoken but few words when the bark encased her jaws, and the ugly thorn of the vine which had so distressed Conattee, had taken its place at their portals.

CHAPTER IX.

The husband looked back but once, when the voice ceased—then, with a shivering sort of joy that his own doom had undergone a termination, which he now felt to be doubly fortunate—he made a wide circuit that he might avoid the fatal neighbourhood, and pushed on in pursuit of his friend, whom his eyes, even when he was surrounded in the tree, had followed in his flight. It was no easy task, however, to overtake Selonee, flying, as he did, from the supposed pursuit of the termagant. Great however was the joy of the young warriors when they did encounter, and long and fervent was their mutual embrace. Conattee described his misfortunes, and related the manner in which he was taken; showed how the bark had encased his limbs, and how the intricate magic had even engrossed his knife and the wolf skin which had been the trophy of his victory. But Conattee said not a word of his wife and her entrapment, and Selonee was left in the conviction that his companion owed his escape from the toils to some hidden change in the tyrannical mood of Tustenuggee, or the one-eyed woman, his wife.

"But the skin and the knife, Conattee, let us not leave them," said Selonee, "let us go back and extricate them from the tree."

Conattee showed some reluctance. He soon said, in the words of Macbeth, which he did not use however as a quotation, "I'll go no more." But Selonee, who ascribed this reluctance to very natural apprehensions of the demon from whose clutches he had just made his escape, declared his readiness to undertake the adventure if Conattee would only point out to his eyes the particular excrescence in which the articles were enclosed. When the husband perceived that his friend was resolute, he made a merit of necessity.

"If the thing is to be done," said he, "why should you have the risk, I myself will do it. It would be a woman-fear were I to shrink from the danger. Let us go."

The process of reasoning by which Conattee came to this determination was a very sudden one, and one, too, that will not be hard to comprehend by every husband in his situation. It was his fear that if Selonee undertook the business, an unlucky or misdirected stroke of his knife might sever a limb, or remove some portions of the bark which did not merit or need removal. Conattee trembled at the very idea of the revelations which might follow such an unhappy result. Strengthening himself, therefore, with all his energies, he went forward with Selonee to the spot and while the latter looked on and witnessed the operation, he proceeded with a nicety and care which amused and surprised Selonee, to the excision of the swollen scab upon the tree in which he had seen his wolf skin encompassed. While he performed the operation, which he did as cautiously as if it had been the extraction of a mote from the eye of a virgin; the beldam in the tree, conscious of all his movements, and at first flattered with the hope that he was working for her extrication, maintained the most ceaseless efforts of her tongue and limbs, but without avail. Her slight breathing, which Conattee knew where to look for, more like the sighs of an infant zephyr than the efforts of a human bosom, denoted to his ears an overpowering but fortunately suppressed volcano within; and his heart leaped with a new joy, which had been unknown to it for many years before, when he thought that he was now safe, and, he trusted, for ever, from any of the tortures which he had been fain to endure patiently so long. When he had finished the operation by which he had re-obtained his treasures, he ventured upon an impertinence which spoke surprisingly for his sudden acquisition of confidence; and looking up through the little aperture in the bark, from whence he had seen every thing while in the same situation, and from whence he concluded she was also suffered to see, he took a peep— a quick, quizzical and taunting peep, at those eyes which he had not so dared to offend before. He drew back suddenly from the contact—so suddenly, indeed, that Selonee, who saw the proceeding, but had no idea of the truth, thought he had been stung by some insect, and questioned him accordingly.

"Let us be off, Selonee," was the hurried answer, "we have nothing to wait for now."

"Yes," replied Selonee, "and I had forgotten to say to you that your wife, Macourah, is on her way in search of you. I left her but a little ways behind, and thought to find her here. I suppose she is tired, however, and is resting by the way."

"Let her rest," said Conattee, "which is an indulgence much greater than any she ever accorded me. She will find me out soon enough, without making it needful that I should go in search of her. Come."

Selonee kindly suppressed the history of the transactions which had taken place in the village during the time when the hunter was supposed to be dead; but Conattee heard the facts from other quarters, and loved Selonee the better for the sympathy he had shown, not only in coming again to seek for him, but in not loving his wife better than he did himself. They returned to the village, and every body was rejoiced to behold the return of the hunters. As for the termagant Macourah, nobody but Conattee knew her fate; and he, like a wise man, kept his secret until there was no danger of its being made use of to rescue her from her predicament. Years had passed, and Conattee had found among the young squaws one that pleased him much better than the old. He had several children by her, and years and honours had alike fallen numerously upon his head, when, one day, one of his own sons, while hunting in the same woods, knocked off one of the limbs of the Chair of Tustenuggee, and to his great horror discovered the human arm which they enveloped. This led him to search farther, and limb after limb became detached under the unscrupulous action of his hatchet, until the entire but unconnected members of the old squaw became visible. The lad knocked about the fragments with little scruple, never dreaming how near was his relation to the form which he treated with so little veneration. When he came home to the lodge and told his story, Selonee looked at Conattee, but said nothing. The whole truth was at once apparent to his mind. Conattee, though he still kept his secret, was seized with a sudden fit of piety, and taking his sons with him, he proceeded to the spot which he well remembered, and, gathering up the bleached remains, had them carefully buried in the trenches of the tribe.

It may properly end this story, to say that Selonee wedded the sweet girl who, though willing to die herself to prevent him from marrying Macourah, yet positively refused to take his life to defeat the same event. It may be well to state, in addition, that the only reason Conattee ever had for believing that Selonee had not kept his secret from every body, was that Medoree, the young wife of the latter, looked on him with a very decided coolness. "But, we will see," muttered Conattee as he felt this conviction. "Selonee will repent of this confidence, since now it will never be possible for him to persuade her to take a seat in the Arm-chair of Tustenuggee. Had he been a wise man he would have kept his secret, and then there would have been no difficulty in getting rid of a wicked wife."

OF GROWING INTEREST to readers of today is the implicit comparison of black and red culture that evolves in "Caloya; or, the Loves of the Driver," Simms's most controversial short story.* As the first line of the story reveals, Simms is drawing largely on personal observation in making an assessment of the idiosyncrasies of Catawba customs and habits—an appraisal noteworthy in its intensity, depth, and fidelity. The gradual disintegration of Catawba culture—a phenomenon made inevitable by the encroachment of white civilization—is symbolized by the decline in the art of pottery making, once a cherished calling among Catawbas, as well as by the laziness, lack of nobility, and lack of ambition in Richard Knuckles, the once-proud warrior who is now the mordant husband of the beautiful and intelligent Caloya. The debate between Knuckles (Enefisto) and Mingo—arguably the most fully developed African American character in pre–Civil War American fiction— raises important questions about the comparative levels of oppression experienced by the two subjugated races and their differing awarenesses of the meaning of freedom and slavery.

ᆗ *Caloya; or, the Loves of the Driver.*

CHAPTER I.

When I was a boy, it was the custom of the Catawba Indians—then reduced to a pitiful remnant of some four hundred persons, all told—to come down, at certain seasons, from their far homes in the interior, to the seaboard, bringing to Charleston a little stock of earthen pots and pans, skins and other small matters, which they bartered in the city for such commodities as were craved by their tastes, or needed by their condition. They did not, however, bring their pots and pans from the nation, but descending to the low country empty-handed, in groups or families, they squatted down on the rich clay lands along the Edisto, raised their poles, erected their sylvan tents, and there established themselves in a temporary abiding place, until their simple potteries had yielded them a sufficient supply of wares with which to throw themselves into the market. Their productions had their value to the citizens,

---

* For a discussion of the controversy provoked by the story's original publication in 1841, see John Caldwell Guilds, *Simms: A Literary Life* (Fayetteville: University of Arkansas Press, 1988), 102–3.

and, for many purposes, were considered by most of the worthy housewives of the past generation, to be far superior to any other. I remember, for example, that it was a confident faith among the old ladies, that okra soup was always inferior if cooked in any but an Indian pot; and my own impressions make me not unwilling to take sides with the old ladies on this particular tenet. Certainly, an iron vessel is one of the last which should be employed in the preparation of this truly southern dish. But this aside. The wares of the Indians were not ill made, nor unseemly to the eye. They wrought with much cleaner hands than they usually carried; and if their vases were sometimes unequal in their proportions, and uncouth in their forms, these defects were more than compensated by their freedom from flaws and their general capaciousness and strength. Wanting, perhaps, in the loveliness and perfect symmetry of Etruscan art, still they were not entirely without pretensions of their own. The ornamental enters largely into an Indian's idea of the useful, and his taste pours itself out lavishly in the peculiar decorations which he bestows upon his wares. Among his first purchases when he goes to the great city, are vermilion, umber, and other ochres, together with sealing wax of all colours, green, red, blue and yellow. With these he stains his pots and pans until the eye becomes sated with a liberal distribution of flowers, leaves, vines and stars, which skirt their edges, traverse their sides, and completely illuminate their externals. He gives them the same ornament which he so judiciously distributes over his own face, and the price of the article is necessarily enhanced to the citizen, by the employment of materials which the latter would much rather not have at all upon his purchases. This truth, however, an Indian never will learn, and so long as I can remember, he has still continued to paint his vessels, though he cannot but see that the least decorated are those which are always the first disposed of. Still, as his stock is usually much smaller than the demand for it, and as he soon gets rid of it, there is no good reason which he can perceive why he should change the tastes which preside over his potteries.

Things are greatly altered now-a-days, in these as in a thousand other particulars. The Catawbas seldom now descend to the seaboard. They have lost the remarkable elasticity of character which peculiarly distinguished them among the aboriginal nations, and, in declining years and numbers, not to speak of the changing circumstances of the neighbouring country, the ancient potteries are almost entirely abandoned. A change has taken place among the whites, scarcely less melancholy than that which has befallen the savages. Our grandmothers of the present day no longer fancy the simple and rude vessels in which the old dames took delight. We are for Sèvre's Porcelain, and foreign goods wholly, and I am saddened by the reflection that I have seen the last of the Indian pots. I am afraid, henceforward, that my okra soup will only be made in vessels from Brummagem; nay, even now, as it comes upon the table, dark, dingy, and discoloured to my eye, I think I see unequivocal tokens of metallic influence upon the mucilaginous compound, and remember with a sigh, the glorious days of Catawba pottery. New fashions, as usual, and conceited refinements, have deprived us of old pleasures and solid friends. A generation hence, and the fragment of an Indian pot will be a relic, a treasure, which the lover of the antique will place carefully away upon the upper shelf of the *sanctum,* secure from the assaults of noisy children and very tidy housekeepers, and honoured in the eyes of all worthy-minded persons, as the sole remaining trophy of a time when there was perfection in one, at least, of the achievements of the culinary art. I am afraid that I have seen the last of the Indian pots!

But let me avoid this melancholy reflection. Fortunately, my narrative enables me to do so. It relates to a period when this valuable manufacture was in full exercise, and, if not encouraged by the interference of government, nor sought after by a foreign people, was yet in possession of a patronage quite as large as it desired. To arrive at this important period we have only to go back twenty years—a lapse made with little difficulty by most persons, and yet one which involves many and more trying changes and vicissitudes than any of us can contemplate with equanimity. The spring season had set in with the sweetest of countenances, and the Catawbas, in little squads and detachments, were soon under way with all their simple equipments on their backs for the lower country. They came down, scattering themselves along the Edisto, in small bodies which pursued their operations independently of each other. In this distribution they were probably governed by the well known policy of the European Gipseys, who find it much easier, in this way, to assess the several neighbourhoods which they honour, and obtain their supplies without provoking apprehension and suspicion, than if they were, *en masse,* to concentrate themselves on any one plantation. Their camps might be found in famed loam-spots, from the Eutaws down to Parker's Ferry, on the Edisto, and among the numerous swamps that lie at the head of Ashley River, and skirt the Wassamasaw country. Harmless usually, and perfectly inoffensive, they were seldom repelled or resisted, even when they made their camp contiguously to a planter's settlements; though, at such periods, the proprietor had his misgivings that his poultry yard suffered from other enemies than the Wild-cat, and his hogs from an assailant as unsparing as the Alligator. The overseer, in such cases, simply kept a sharper lookout than ever, though it was not often that any decisive consequences followed his increased vigilance. If the Indians were at any time guilty of appropriation, it was not often that they suffered themselves to be brought to conviction. Of all people, they, probably, are the most solicitous to obey the scripture injunction, and keep the right hand from any unnecessary knowledge of the doings of the left.

Chapter II.

One morning, early in this pleasant season, the youthful proprietor of a handsome plantation in the neighbourhood of the Ashley River, might have been seen taking his solitary breakfast, at a moderately late hour, in the great hall of his family mansion. He was a tall, fine-looking young man, with quick, keen, lively gray eyes, that twinkled with good humour and a spirit of playful indulgence. A similar expression marked his features in general, and lessened the military effect of a pair of whiskers, of which the display was too lavish to be quite becoming. He had but recently come into possession of his property, which had been under the guardianship of an uncle. His parents had been cut off by country fever while he was yet a child, and, as an only son, he found, at coming of age, that his estates were equally ample and well managed. He was one of those unfortunate young bachelors, whose melancholy loneliness of condition is so apt to arrest the attention, and awaken the sympathies of disinterested damsels, and all considerate mothers of unappropriated daughters, who are sufficiently well-informed in scripture authority, to know that "it is not meet for man to be alone." But young Col. Gillison was alone, and continued, in spite of good doctrine, to be alone for several long years after. Into the causes which led to this strange and wilful eccentricity, it forms no part of our object to inquire. Our story does not so much concern the master of the plantation as one of his retainers, whom the reader will please to imagine that he has seen, more than once, glancing his eye impatiently from the piazza through the window, into the apartment, awaiting the protracted moment when his young master should descend to his breakfast. This was a stout negro fellow, of portly figure and not uncomely countenance. He was well made and tall, and was sufficiently conscious of his personal attractions, to take all pains to exhibit them in the most appropriate costume and attitude. His pantaloons were of very excellent nankin, and his coat, made of seersucker, was one of the most picturesque known to the southern country. It was fashioned after the Indian hunting shirt, and formed a very neat and well-fitting frock, which displayed the broad shoulders and easy movements of Mingo—for that was the negro's name—to the happiest advantage.

Mingo was the driver of the estate. The driver is a sort of drill-sergeant to the overseer, who may be supposed to be the Captain. He gets the troops in line, divides them into squads, sees to their equipments, and prepares them for the management and command of the superiors. On the plantation of Col. Gillison, there was at this time no overseer; and, in consequence, the importance of Mingo was not a little increased, as he found himself acting in the highest executive capacity known to his experience. Few persons of any race, colour, or condition, could have had a more elevated idea of their own pretensions than our present subject. He trod the earth very much as its Lord—the sovereign shone out in every look and movement, and the voice of supreme authority spoke in every tone. This feeling of superiority imparted no small degree of grace to his action, which, accordingly, would have put to shame the awkward louting movements of one half of those numbed and cramped figures which serve at the emasculating counters of the trading city. Mingo was a Hercules to the great majority of these; and, with his arms akimbo, his head thrown back, one foot advanced, and his hands, at intervals, giving life to his bold, and full-toned utterance, he would startle with a feeling not unlike that of awe, many of those bent, bowed and mean-looking personages who call themselves freemen, and yet have never known the use, either of mind or muscle, in one twentieth part the degree which had been familiar to this slave.

At length, after a delay which evidently did not diminish the impatience of Mingo, his young master descended to the breakfast room. His appearance was the signal for the driver to enter the same apartment, which he accordingly did without pause or preparation.

"Well, Mingo," said the young man, with lively tones—"what's the word this morning? Your face seems full of news! and now that I consider you closely, it seems to have smitten your body also. You look fuller than I have ever seen you before. Out with your burden, man, before you burst. What sow's littered—what cow's cast her calf—how many panels in the fence are burnt—how many chickens has the hawk carried off this morning? What! none of these?" he demanded, as the shake of the head, on the part of his hearer, which followed every distinct suggestion of the speaker, disavowed any subject of complaint from those current evils which are the usual subject of a planter's apprehension. "What's the matter, then, Mingo?"

"Matter 'nough, Mossa, ef we don't see to it in time," responded Mingo, with a becoming gravity. "It's a needcessity," a driver's English is sometimes terribly emphatic, "it's a needcessity, Sir, to see to other cattle, besides hogs and cows. The chickens too, is intended to, as much as they wants; and *I* ha'nt lost a panel by fire, eber sence Col. Parker's hands let the fire get 'way by Murray's Thick. There, we did lose a smart chance, and put us back mightily, I reckon; but that was in old mossa's time, and we had Mr. Groning, den, as the obershar—so, you see, Sir, I couldn't be considered bound 'sponsible for that; sence I've had the management, there ha'nt been any loss on my plantation of any kind. My fences ha'nt been burn, my cattle's on the rise, and as for my hogs and chickens, I reckon there's not a plantation on the river that kin make so good a count at Christmas. But——"

"Well, well, Mingo," said the youthful proprietor, who knew the particular virtue of the driver, and dreaded that his tongue should get such headway as to make it unmanageable—"if there's no loss, and no danger of loss—if the hogs and chickens are right, and the cattle and the fences—we can readily defer the business until after breakfast. Here, boy, hand up the coffee."

"Stop a bit, Mossa—it aint right—all aint right—" said the impressive Mingo—"it's a business of more transaction and deportance than the cattle and the fences—it's——"

"Well, out with it then, Mingo—there's no need for a long preamble. What is the trouble?"

"Why, Sir, you mus' know," began the driver, in no degree pleased to be compelled to give his testimony in any but his own fashion, and drawling out his accents accordingly, so as to increase the impatience of his master, and greatly to elongate the sounds of his own voice—sounds which he certainly esteemed to be among the most musical in nature.——"You mus' know den, Sir, that Limping Jake came to me a while ago, tells me as how, late last night, when he was a-hunting 'possum, he came across an Indian camp, down by the 'Red Gulley.' They had a fire, and was a-putting up the poles, and stripping the bark to cover them. Jake only seed two of them; but it's onpossible that they'll stick at that. Before we know anything, they'll be spreading like varmints all about us, and putting hands and teeth on every thing, without so much as axing who mout be the owner."

"Well, Mingo, what of all this?" demanded the master, as the driver came to a pause, and looked volumes of increased dignity, while he concluded the intelligence which he meant to be astounding.

"Wha' of all this, Mossa!—Why, Sir, de'rs 'nough of it. Ef the hogs and the chickens did'nt go before, they'll be very apt to go now, with these red varmints about us."

"Surely, if you don't look after them; but that's your business, Mingo. You must see to the poultry houses yourself, at night, and keep a close watch over these squatters so long as they are pleased to stay."

"But, Mossa, I aint gwine to let 'em stay! To my idee, that's not the wisdom of the thing. Now, John Groning, the obershar of old mossa—though I don't much reprove of his onderstanding in other expects, yet he tuk the right reason, when he druv them off, bag and baggage, and wouldn't let hoof nor hide of 'em stretch off upon the land. I ha'nt seen these red varmints, myself, but I come to let you know, that I was gwine out to asperse, and send 'em off, under the shake of a cowhide, and then there's no farther needcessity to keep a look out upon them. I'm not willing to let such critters hang about *my* plantation."

The reader has already observed, that an established driver speaks always of his charge as if it were a possession of his own. With Mingo, as with most such, it was *my* horse, *my* land, *my* ox, and *my* ass, and all that is *mine*. His tone was much subdued, as he listened to the reply of his master, uttered in accents something sterner than he had been wont to hear.

"I'm obliged to you, Mingo, for coming to inform me of your intentions. Now, I command you to do nothing of this sort. Let these poor devils remain where they are, and do you attend to your duty, which is to see that they do no mischief. If I mistake not, the 'Red Gulley' is the place where they have been getting their clay ever since my grandfather settled this plantation."

"That's a truth, Sir, but———"

"Let them get it there still. I prefer that they should do so, even though I may lose a hog now and then, and suffer some decrease in the fowl yard. I am pleased that they should come to the accustomed place for their clay———"

"But, Sir, only last year, John Groning druv 'em off."

"I am the better pleased then, at the confidence they repose in me. Probably they know that John Groning can no longer drive them off. I am glad that they give me an opportunity to treat them more justly. They can do me little harm, and as their fathers worked in the same holes, I am pleased that they, too, should work there. I will not consent to their expulsion for such small evils as you mention. But I do not mean, Mingo, that they shall be suffered to infest the plantation, or to do any mischief. You will report to me, if you see any thing going wrong, and to do this while they stay; you will look very closely into their proceedings. I, myself, will have an eye upon them, and if there be but two of them, and they seem sober, I will give them an allowance of corn while they stay."

"Well, but Mossa, there's no needcessity for that, and considering that the Corn-House aint oberfull—"

"No more at present, Mingo. I will see into the matter during the day. Meanwhile, you can ride out to the 'Red Gulley,' see these people, and say to them, from me, that, so long as they behave themselves civilly, they may remain. I am not satisfied that these poor wretches should be denied camping ground and a little clay, on a spot which their people once possessed exclusively. I shall probably see them after you, and will then be better able to determine upon their deserts."

Chapter III.

Mingo retired from the conference rather chap-fallen. He was not so well satisfied with the result of his communication. He had some hope to commend himself more than ever to his youthful master by the zeal and vigilance which he had striven to display. Disappointed in this hope, he was still further mortified to perceive how little deference was shown him by one, whose youthful judgment he hoped to direct, and of whose inexperience he had possibly some hope to take advantage. He loved to display his authority, and sometimes seemed absolutely to fancy himself the proprietor whose language of command he had habituated himself to employ; on the present occasion, he made his way from the presence of his master with no complacent feelings, and his displeasure vented itself very unequivocally upon a favourite hound who lay at the foot of the outer steps, and whom he kicked off with a savage satisfaction, and sent howling to his kennel. A boy coming to him with a message from the kitchen, was received with a smart application of his wagon whip, and made to follow the example, if he did not exactly imitate the peculiar music of the hound. Mingo certainly made his exit in a rage. Half an hour after, he might have been seen, mounted on his marsh tacky, making tracks for the "Red Gulley," determined, if he was not suffered to expel the intruders, at least, to show them that it was in his power, during their stay, to diminish very considerably the measure of their satisfaction. His wrath—like that of all consequential persons who feel themselves in the wrong, yet lack courage to be right—was duly warmed by nursing; and, pregnant with terrible looks and accents, he burst upon the little encampment at "Red Gulley," in a way that "was a caution" to all evil doers!

The squatters had only raised one simple habitation of poles, and begun a second which adjoined it. The first was covered in with bushes, bark and saplings; the second was slightly advanced, and the hatchet lay before it, in waiting for the hand by which it was to be completed. The embers of a recent fire were strewed in front of the former, and a lean cur—one of those gaunt, far sighted, keen nosed animals which the Indians employed; dock tailed, short haired, bushy eyed—lay among the ashes, and did not offer to stir at the appearance of the terror-breathing Mingo. Still, though he moved not, his keen eyes followed the movements of the Driver with as jealous a glance as those of his owner would have done; while the former alighted from his horse, peered around the wigwam, and finally penetrated it. Here he saw nobody, and nothing to reward his scrutiny. Reappearing from the hut, he hallooed with the hope of obtaining some better satisfaction, but his call was unanswered. The dog alone raised his head, looked up at the impatient visitor, and, as if satisfied with a single glance, at once resumed his former luxurious position. Such stolidity, bad enough in an Indian, was still more impertinent in an Indian dog; and, forgetting every thing but his consequence, and the rage with which he had set out from home, Mingo, without more ado, laid his lash over the animal with no measured violence of stroke. It was then that he found an answer to his challenge. A clump of myrtles opened at a little distance behind him, and the swarthy red cheeks of an Indian man appeared through the aperture, to which his voice summoned the eyes of the assailant.

"You lick dog," said the owner, with accents which were rather soft and musical than stern, "dog is good, what for you lick dog?"

Such a salutation, at the moment, rather startled the imperious driver; not that he was a timid fellow, or that his wrath had in the least degree abated; but that he was surprised completely. Had the voice reached him from the woods in front, he would have been better prepared for it; but, coming from the rear, his imagination made it startling, and increased its solemnity. He turned at the summons, and, at the same moment, the Indian, making his way through the myrtles, advanced toward the negro. There was nothing in his appearance to awaken the apprehensions of the latter. The stranger was small and slight of person, and evidently beyond the middle period of life. Intemperance, too, the great curse of the Indian who has long been a dweller in contact with the Anglo-Saxon settler—(the French, *par parenthèse,* seem to have always civilized the Indian without making him a drunkard)—had made its ravages upon his form, and betrayed itself in every lineament of his face. His step, even while he approached the negro, was unsteady from the influence of liquor; and as all these signs of feebleness became obvious to the eye of Mingo, his courage, and with it his domineering insolence of character, speedily returned to him.

"Lick dog!" he exclaimed, as he made a movement to the Catawba, and waved his whip threateningly, "lick dog, and lick Indian too."

"Lick Indian—get knife!" was the quiet answer of the savage, whose hand, at the same instant, rested upon the horn handle of his *couteau de chasse,* where it stuck in the deerskin belt that girdled his waist.

"Who's afeard?" said Mingo, as he clubbed his whip and threw the heavy loaded butt of it upon his shoulder. The slight frame of the Indian moved his contempt only; and the only circumstance that prevented him from instantly putting his threat into execution, was the recollection of that strange interest which his master had taken in the squatters, and his positive command that they should not be ill treated or expelled. While he hesitated, however, the Catawba gave him a sufficient excuse, as he fancied, for putting his original intention into execution. The threatening attitude, partial advance of the foe, together with the sight of the heavy handled whip reversed and hanging over him, had, upon the mind of the savage, all the effect of an absolute assault. He drew his knife in an instant, and flinging himself forward to the feet of the negro, struck an upright blow with his weapon, which would have laid the entrails of his enemy open to the light, but for the promptitude of the latter, who, receding at the same instant, avoided and escaped the blow. In the next moment, levelling his whip at the head of the stooping Indian, he would most probably have retorted it with fatal effect, but for an unlooked for interruption. His arms were both grappled by some one from behind, and, for the perilous moment, effectually prevented from doing any harm. With some difficulty, he shook off the last comer, who, passing in front, between the hostile parties, proved to be an Indian woman.

CHAPTER IV.

Before this discovery was fairly made, the wrath of Mingo had been such as to render him utterly forgetful of the commands of his master. He was now ready for the combat to the knife; and had scarcely shaken himself free from his second assailant, before he advanced with redoubled resolution upon the first. He, by the way, equally aroused, stood ready, with closed lips, keen eye and lifted knife, prepared for the encounter. All the peculiarities of the Indian shone out in the imperturbable aspect, composed muscles, and fiery gleaming eyes of the now half-sobered savage; who, as if conscious of the great disparity of strength between himself and foe, was mustering all his arts of war, all his stratagems and subtleties, to reduce those inequalities from which he had every thing to apprehend. But they were not permitted to fight. The woman now threw herself between them; and, at her appearance, the whip of Mingo fell from his shoulder, and his mood became instantly pacific. She was the wife of the savage, but certainly young enough to have been his daughter. She was decidedly one of the comeliest squaws that had ever enchanted the eyes of the Driver, and her life-darting eyes, the emotion so visible in her face, and the boldness of her action, as she passed between their weapons, with a hand extended toward each, was such as to inspire him with any other feelings than those which possessed him towards the squatters. Mingo was susceptible of the tender influences of love. As brave as Julius Caesar, in his angry mood, he was yet quite as pliant as Mark Antony in the hour of indulgence; and the smile of one of the ebon damsels of his race, at the proper moment, has frequently saved her and others from the penalties incurred by disobedience of orders, or unfinished tasks. Nor were his sentiments towards the sex confined to those of his master's plantation only. He penetrated the neighbouring estates with the excursive and reckless nature of the Prince of Troy, and, more than once, in consequence of this habit, had the several plantations rung with wars, scarcely less fierce, though less protracted than those of Ilium. His success with the favoured sex was such as to fill him with a singular degree of confidence in his own prowess and personal attractions. Mingo knew that he was a handsome fellow, and fancied a great deal more. He was presumptuous enough—surely there are no white men so!—to imagine that it was scarcely possible for any of the other sex, in their sober senses, to withstand him. This impression grew singularly strong, as he gazed upon the Indian woman. So bright an apparition had not met his eyes for many days.

His local associations were all staling—the women he was accustomed to behold, had long since lost the charm of novelty in his sight—and, with all his possessions, Mingo, like Alexander of Macedon, was still yearning for newer conquests. The first glance at the Indian woman, assured his roving fancies that they had not yearned in vain. He saw in her a person whom he thought destined to provoke his jaded tastes anew, and restore his passions to their primitive ascendancy. The expression of his eye softened as he surveyed her. War fled from it like a discomfited lion; and if love, squatting quietly down in his place, did not look altogether so innocent as the lamb, he certainly promised not to roar so terribly. He now looked nothing but complacence on both the strangers; on the woman because of her own charms; on the man because of the charms which he possessed in her. But such was not the expression in the countenance of the Indian. He was not to be moved by the changes which he beheld in his enemy, but still kept upon him a wary watch, as if preparing for the renewal of the combat. There was also a savage side-glance which his keen fiery eyes threw upon the woman, which seemed to denote some little anger towards herself. This did not escape the watchful glance of our gay Lothario, who founded upon it some additional hope of success in his schemes. Meanwhile, the woman was not idle nor silent. She did not content herself with simply going between the combatants, but her tongue was active in expostulation with her sovereign, in a dialect not the less musical to the ears of Mingo because he did not understand a word of it. The tones were sweet, and he felt that they counselled peace and good will to the warrior. But the latter, so far as he could comprehend the expression of his face, and the mere sounds of his brief, guttural replies, had, like Sempronius, a voice for war only. Something, too, of a particular harshness in his manner, seemed addressed to the woman alone. Her answers were evidently those of deprecation and renewed entreaty; but they did not seem very much to influence her Lord and master, or to soften his mood. Mingo grew tired of a controversy in which he had no share, and fancied, with a natural self-complacency, that he could smooth down some of its difficulties.

"Look yer, my friend," he exclaimed, advancing, with extended hand, while a volume of condescension was written upon his now benignant features—"Look yer, my friend, it's no use to be at knife-draw any longer. I didn't mean to hurt you when I raised the whip, and as for the little touch I gin the dog, why that's neither here nor there. The dog's more easy to squeal than most dogs I know. Ef I had killed him down to the brush at his tail eend, he could'nt ha' holla'd more. What's the sense to fight for dogs? Here—here's my hand—we won't quarrel any longer, and, as for fighting, I somehow never could fight when there was a woman standing by. It's onbecoming, I may say, and so here's for peace between us. Will you shake?"

The proffered hand was not taken. The Indian still kept aloof with the natural caution of his race; but he seemed to relax something of his watchfulness, and betrayed less of that still and deliberate anxiety which necessarily impresses itself upon the most courageous countenance in the moment of expected conflict. Again the voice of the woman spoke in tones of reconciliation, and, this time, words of broken English were audible, in what she said, to the ears of the Driver. Mingo fancied that he had never heard better English—of which language he considered himself no humble proficient—nor more sweetly spoken by any lips. The savage darted an angry scowl at the speaker in return, uttered but a single stern word in the Catawba, and pointed his finger to the wigwam as he spoke. Slowly, the woman turned away and disappeared within its shelter. Mingo began to be impatient of the delay, probably because of her departure, and proceeded, with more earnestness than before, to renew his proposition for peace. The reply of the Indian, betrayed all the tenacity of his race in remembering threats and injuries.

"Lick dog, lick Indian; lick Indian, get knife—hah!"

"Who's afeard!" said the Driver. "Look yer, my friend: 'taint your knife, let me tell you, that's gwine to make me turn tail on any chicken of your breed. You tried it, and what did you git? Why, look you, if it hadn't been for the gripe of the gal—maybe she's your daughter, mout-be your sister?—but it's all one—ef it hadn't been her gripe which fastened my arm, the butt of my whip would have flattened you, until your best friend couldn't ha' said where to look for your nose. You'd ha' been all face after that, smooth as bottom land, without e'er a snag or a stump; and you'd have passed among old acquaintance for any body sooner than yourself. But I'm no brag dog—nor I don't want to be a biting dog, nother; when there's nothing to fight for. Let's be easy. P'rhaps you don't feel certain whose plantation you're on here. Mout be if you know'd, you'd find out it wa'nt altogether the best sense to draw knife on Mingo Gillison.—Why, look you, my old boy, I'm able to say what I please here—I makes the law for this plantation—all round about, so far as you can see from the top of the tallest of them 'ere pine trees, I'm the master! I look 'pon the pine land field, and I say, 'Tom, Peter, Ned, Dick, Jack, Ben,

Toney, Sam—boys—you must 'tack that field to-morrow.' I look 'pon the swamp field, and I say to 'nother ten, 'boys, go there!'—high land and low land, upland and swamp, corn and cotton, rice and rye, all 'pen 'pon me for order; and jis' as Mingo say, jis' so they do. Well, wha' after dat! It stands clear to the leetlest eye, that 'taint the best sense to draw knife on Mingo Gillison; here, on he own ground. 'Spose my whip can't do the mischief, it's a need-cessity only to draw a blast out of this 'ere horn, and there'll be twenty nig-gers 'pon you at once, and ebery one of dem would go off wid 'he limb. But I ain't a hard man, my fren', ef you treat me softly. You come here to make your clay pots and pans. Your people bin use for make 'em here for sebenty nine—mout-be forty seben year—who knows? Well, you can make 'em here, same as you been usen to make 'em, so long as you 'habe you'self like a gem-plemans. But none of your knife-work, le' me tell you. I'll come ebery day and look 'pon you. 'Mout-be, I'll trade with you for some of your pots. Clay-pot is always best for bile hom'ny."

We have put in one paragraph the sum and substance of a much longer discourse which Mingo addressed to his Indian guest. The condescensions of the negro had a visible effect upon the squatter, the moment that he was made to comprehend the important station which the former enjoyed; and when the Indian woman was fairly out of sight, Richard Knuckles, for such was the English name of the Catawba, gradually restored his knife to his belt, and the hand which had been withheld so long, was finally given in a gripe of amity to the negro, who shook it as heartily as if he had never meditated towards the stranger any but the most hospitable intentions. He was now as affectionate and indulgent, as he had before shown himself hostile; and the Indian, after a brief space, relaxed much of the *hauteur* which distinguishes the deportment of the Aborigines. But Mingo was pained to observe that Richard never once asked him into his wigwam, and, while he remained, that the squaw never once came out of it. This reserve betokened some latent apprehension of mischief; and the whole thoughts of our enamoured Driver were bent upon ways and means for overcoming this austerity, and removing the doubts of the strangers. He contrived to find out that Caloya—such was the woman's name—was the wife of the man; and he immediately jumped to a conclusion which promised favourably for his schemes. "An ole man wid young wife!" said he, with a complacent chuckle, "Ah, ha! he's afeard!—well, he hab' good 'casion for fear'd, when Mingo Gillison is 'pon de ground."

Chapter V.

But though warmed with these encouraging fancies, our conceited hero found the difficulties to be much more numerous and formidable than he had anticipated. The woman was as shy as the most modest wife could have shown herself, and no Desdemona could have been more certainly true to her liege lord. Mingo paid no less than three visits that day to the wigwam, and all without seeing her, except at his first coming, when she was busied with, but retired instantly from, her potteries, in which Richard Knuckles took no part, and seemingly no interest. Lazy, like all his race, he lay in the sun, on the edge of the encampment, with an eye but half open, but that half set directly upon the particular movements of his young wife. Indians are generally assumed to be cold and insensible, and some doubts have been expressed, whether their sensibilities could ever have been such as to make them open to the influence of jealousy. These notions are ridiculous enough; and prove nothing half so decidedly as the gross ignorance of those who entertain them. Something, of course, is to be allowed for the natural differences between a civilized and savage people. Civilization is prolific, barbarism sterile. The dweller in the city has more various appetites and more active passions than the dweller in the camp; and the habits of the hunter, lead, above all things, to an intense gathering up of all things in self; a practice which tends, necessarily, to that sort of independence which is, perhaps, neither more nor less than one aspect of barrenness. But, while the citizen is allowed to have more various appetites and intenser passions in general, the Indian is not without those which, indeed, are essential to constitute his humanity. That he can love, is undeniable—that he loves with the ardour of the white, may be more questionable. That he can love, however, with much intensity, may fairly be inferred from the fact that his hate is subtle and is nourished with traditional tenacity and reverence. But the argument against the sensibility of the savage, in his savage state, even if true, would not apply to the same animal in his degraded condition, as a borderer of the white settlements. Degraded by beastly habits, and deprived by them of the fiercer and warlike qualities of his ancestors, he is a dependent, (and jealousy is a creature of dependence)— a most wretched dependent, and that, too, upon his women—she who, an hundred years ago, was little other than his slave, and frequently his victim. In his own feebleness, he learns to esteem her strength; and, in due degree with his own degradation, is her rise into importance in his sight. But it does not matter materially to our present narrative, whether men should, or should not agree, as to the sensibilities of the savage to the tender passion. It is probable, that few warlike nations are very susceptible of love; and as for the middle ages, which might be urged as an exception to the justice of this remark, Sismondi is good authority to show that Burke had but little reason to deplore their loss: *"Helas! cet heroisme universel nous avons nomme la chevalerie, n'exista jamais comme fictions brillantes!"* There were no greater brutes than the warriors of the middle ages.

Richard Knuckles, whether he loved his young wife or not, was certainly quite as jealous of her as Othello was of his. Not, perhaps, so much of her affections as of her deference; and this, by the way, was also something of the particular form of jealousy under which the noble Moor suffered. The proud spirit chafes that another object should stand for a moment between his particular sunlight and himself. His jealousy had been awakened long before, and this led to his temporary separation from his tribe. Caloya, it may be added, yielded, without a murmur, to the caprices of her lord, to whom she had been given by her father. She was as dutiful as if she loved him; and, if conduct alone could be suffered to test the quality of virtue, her affection for him was quite as earnest, pure and eager, as that of the most devoted woman. That she could not love him, is a conclusion only to be drawn from the manifest inequalities between them. He was old and brutal—a truly worthless, sottish savage—while she, if not a beauty, was yet comely to the eye, very youthful, and, in comparison with Indian squaws in general, remarkably tidy in person, and good humoured in disposition.

Our hero, Mingo, was not only persuaded that she could not love Knuckles, but he equally soon became convinced that she could be made to love himself. He left no opportunity untried to effect this desirable result; and, after a most fatiguing trial, he succeeded so far in a part of his scheme as to beguile the husband into good humour if not blindness. Returning towards nightfall to the camp, Mingo brought with him a "chunk-bottle" of whiskey, the potency of which, over the understanding of an Indian, he well knew; and displaying his treasure to Knuckles, was invited by him, for the first time, with a grunt of cordiality, to enter the wigwam of the squatters. The whiskey while it lasted convinced Knuckles, that he had no better friend in the world than Mingo Gillison, and he soon became sufficiently blinded by its effects, to suffer the frequent and friendly glances of the Driver towards his wife, without discovering that they were charged with any especial signs of intelligence. Yet never was a more ardent expression of wilful devotion thrown into human eyes before. Mingo was something of an actor, and many an actor might have taken a goodly lesson of his art from the experienced Driver. He was playing Romeo, an original part always, to his own satisfaction. Tenderness, almost to tears, softened the fiery ardour of his glance, and his thick lips grew doubly thick, in the effort to throw into them an expression of devoted languor. But all his labour seemed to go for nothing—nay, for something worse than nothing—in the eyes of the faithful wife. If her husband *could* not see the arts of the amorous negro, she *would* not see them; and when, at supper, it sometimes became necessary that her eyes should look where the lover sat, the look which she gave him was stony and inexpressive—cold to the last degree; and, having looked, it would be averted instantly with a haste, which, to a less confident person would have been vastly discouraging and doubtful. As it was, even the self-assured Mingo was compelled to acknowledge, in his mental soliloquy that night as he made his way homeward, that, so far his progress was not a subject of brag, and scarcely of satisfaction. The woman, he felt, had resisted his glances, or, which was much worse, had failed to see them. But this was owing, so he fancied, entirely to her caution and the natural dread which she had of her fiercely minded sovereign. Mingo retired to his couch that night to plan, and to dream of plans, for overcoming the difficulties in the way of his own, and, as he persisted in believing, the natural desires of Caloya. It may be stated in this place, that, under the new aspects which the squatters had assumed in his eyes, he did not think it necessary to make any very copious statement of his proceedings to his master; but, after the fashion of certain public committees, when in difficulty among themselves, he wisely concluded to report progress and beg permission to sit again.

Chapter VI.

"Dem 'ere Indians," he said the next morning to his master—"dem 'ere Indians—der's only two ob 'em come yet, sir—I aint altogether sure about 'em— I has'n't any exspecial 'spicion, sir, from what I seed yesterday, that they's very honest in particklar, and then agen, I see no reasons that they aint honest. It mout be, they might steal a hen, sir, if she was reasonable to come at—it mout be, they mout eben go deeper into a hog;—but then agen, it mout'n't be after all, and it wouldn't be right justice to say, tell a body knows for certain. There's no telling yet, sir. An Indian, as I may say, naterally, is honest or he aint honest;—and there's no telling which, sir, 'tell he steals something, or tell he goes off without stealing;—and so all that kin be done, sir, is to find out if he's a thief, or if he's not a thief; and I think, sir, I'm in a good way to git at the rights of the matter before worse comes to worser. As you say, Mossa, it's my business to see that you ain't worsened by 'em."

Without insisting that Col. Gillison entirely understood the ingenious speech of his driver, we can at least assert, with some confidence, that he was satisfied with it. Of an indolent disposition, the young master was not unwilling to be relieved from the trouble of seeing himself after the intruders; and though he dismissed the amorous Mingo with an assurance, that he would take an early opportunity to look into their camp, the cunning driver, who perhaps guessed very correctly on the subject of his master's temperament, was fully persuaded that his own movements would suffer no interruption from the command or supervision of the other. Accordingly, sallying forth immediately after breakfast, he took his way to the encampment, where he arrived in time to perceive some fragments of a Catawba *dejeûné*, which, while it awakened his suspicions, did not in any measure provoke his appetite. There were numerous small well-picked bones, which might have been those of a squirrel, as Richard Knuckles somewhat gratuitously alleged, or which might have been those of one of his master's brood-hens, as Mingo Gillison half suspected. But, though he set forth with a declared resolve not to suffer his master's interests to be "worsened," our driver did not seem to think it essential to this resolution to utter his suspicions, or to search more narrowly into the matter. He seemed to take for granted that Richard Knuckles had spoken nothing but the truth, and he himself showed nothing but civility. He had not made his visit without bringing with him a goodly portion of whiskey in his flask, well knowing that no better medium could be found for procuring the confidence and blinding the jealous eyes of the Indian. But he soon discovered that this was not his true policy, however much he had fancied in the first instance that it might subserve it. He soothed the incivilities of the Catawba, and warmed his indifference by the liquor, but he, at the same time, and from the same cause, made him stationary in the camp. So long as the whiskey lasted, the Indian would cling to the spot, and when it was exhausted he was unable to depart. The prospect was a bad one for the Driver that day in the camp of the squatters, since, though the woman went to *her* tasks without delay, and clung to them with the perseverance of the most devoted industry, the Hunter was neither able nor willing to set forth upon his. The bow was unbent and unslung, lying across his lap, and he, himself, leaning back against his tree, seemed to have no wish beyond the continued possession of the genial sunshine in which he basked. In vain did Mingo, sitting beside him, cast his wistful eyes towards the woman who worked at a little distance, and whom, while her husband was wakeful, he did not venture to approach. Something, he thought, might be done by signs, but the inflexible wife never once looked up from the clay vessel which her hands were employed to round—an inflexibility which the conceited negro ascribed not so much to her indifference to his claims, as to her fears of her savage husband. We must not forget to say that the tongue of the Driver was seldom silent, however much his thoughts might be confused and his objects baffled. He had a faith in his own eloquence, not unlike that of the greater number of our young and promising statesmen; and did not doubt, though he could not speak to the woman directly, that much that he did say would still reach her senses, and make the desired impression. With this idea, it may be readily supposed that he said a great many things which were much better calculated to please her, than to meet the assent of her husband.

"Now," for example, continuing a long dissertation on the physiological and psychological differences between his own and the Indian race, in which he strove to prove to the satisfaction of the Catawba, the infinite natural and acquired superiorities of the former,—"Now," said he, stretching his hand forth towards the toiling woman, and establishing his case, as he thought conclusively, by a resort to the *argumentum ad hominem*—"now, you see, if that 'ere gal was my wife instead of your'n, Knuckles, de you think I'd let her extricate herself here in a br'iling sun, working her fingers off, and I lying down here in the grass a-doing nothing and only looking on? No! I'd turn in and give her good resistance; 'cause why, Knuckles? 'Cause, you see, it's not, I may say, a 'spectable sight to see the woman doing all the work what's a need-cessity, and the man a-doing nothing. The woman warn't made for hard work at all. My women I redulges—I never pushes 'em—I favours them all that I kin, and it goes agin me mightily, I tell you, when it's a needcessity to give 'em the lash. But I scores the men like old Harry. I gives them their desarbings; and if so be the task ain't done, let them look out for thick jackets. 'Twont be a common homespun that'll keep off my cuts. I do not say that I overwork my people. That's not the idee. My tasks is a'most too easy, and there's not a nigger among 'em that can't get through, if he's exposed that way, by tree o'clock in de day. The women has their task, but they're twice as easy, and then I don't open both eyes when I'm looking to see if they've got through 'em. 'Tain't often you hear my women in trivilation; and, I know, it stands to reason what I'm telling you, that a black Gentlemen is always more 'spectable to a woman than an Indian. Dere's your wife now, and dere's you. She ain't leff her business since I bin here, and you haint gone to your'n, nor you ain't gin her a drop of the whiskey. Not to say that a gal so young as that ought to drink whiskey and chaw tobacco—but for the sake of compliment now, 'twas only right that you should ha' ax her to try a sup. But then for the working. You ain't offered to resist her; you ain't done a stroke since breakfast. Ef you was under me, Knuckles, I'd a laid this green twig over your red jacket in a way that would ha' made a 'possum laugh."

"Eh!" was the only exclamation of the half drunken Indian, at this characteristic conclusion of the negro's speech; but, though Knuckles said nothing that could denote his indignation at the irreverent threat, which, though contingent only, was excessively annoying to the *amour propre* of the Catawba, there was a gleam of angry intelligence which flashed out for a moment from his eyes and his thin lips parted to a grin that showed his white teeth with an expression not unlike that of a wolf hard pressed by one more daring cur than the rest. Either Mingo did not see this, or he thought too lightly of the prowess of his companion to heed it. He continued in the same strain and with increasing boldness.

"Now I say, Knuckles, all that's onbecoming. A woman's a woman, and a man's a man. A woman has her sort of work, and it's easy. And a man has his sort of work, and that's hard. Now, here you make this poor gal do your work and her own too. That's not fair, it's a despisable principle, and I may say, no man's a gempleman that believes it. Ha'n't I seed, time upon time, Indian men going along, stiff and straight as a pine tree, carrying nothing but a bow and arrow, and mout be, a gun; and, same time, the squaws walking amost double under the load. That's a common ex-servation. Iv'e seed it a hundred times. Is that 'spectful or decent to the fair seck? I say no, and I'll stand by, and leave it to any tree gentlemen of any complexion, ef I ain't right."

It was well, perhaps, for the maintenance of peace between the parties, that Knuckles was too drunk and too ignorant to comprehend all that was spoken by the Driver. The leading idea, however, was sufficiently clear for his comprehension, and to this he answered with sufficient brevity and phlegm.

"Indian woman is good for work—Indian man for hunt; woman is good for hab children; man for shoot—man for fight. The Catawba man is very good for fight;" and as the poor, miserable creature spoke, the fire of a former and a better day, seemed to kindle his cheeks and give lustre to his eye. Probably, the memory of that traditional valour which distinguished the people to which he belonged in a remarkable degree, in comparison with the neighbouring nations, came over his thoughts, and warned him with something like a kindred sentiment with those which had been so long forgotten by his race.

"Oh, go 'long!" said the negro. "How you talk, Knuckles! wha make you better for fight more dan me? Ki, man! Once you stan' afore Mingo, you tumble. Ef I was to take you in my arms and give you one good hug, Lor' ha' massy 'pon you! You'd neber feel yourself after that, and nothing would be lef' of you for you wife to see, but a long greasy mark, most like a little old man, yer, 'pon my breast and thighs. I never seed the Indian yet that I couldn't lick, fair up and down, hitch cross, or big cross, hand over, hand under, arm lock and leg lock, in seventeen and nine minutes, by the sun. You don't know, Knuckles, else you would'nt talk so foolish. Neber Indian kin stan' agen black man, whedder for fight or work. That's the thing I'm talking 'bout. You can't fight fair and you can't work. You aint got strengt' for it. All your fighting is bush fighting and behind tree, and you' woman does the work. Now, wha' make you lie down here, and not go 'fore you' hunting? That's 'cause you're lazy. You come look at my hands, see 'em plough, see 'em hoe, see 'em mak' ditch, cut tree, split rail, buil' house—when you see dem, you'll see wha' I call man. I would'nt give tree snap of a finger for any pusson that's so redolent as an Indian. They're good for nothing but eat."

"Catawba man is good for fight!" sullenly responded the Indian to a speech which the negro soon found to have been imprudently concerted and rashly spoken, in more respects than one. "Nigger man and squaw is good for work!" continued the other disdainfully, his thin lips curling into an expression of scorn which did not escape the eyes of Mingo, obtuse as his vanity necessarily made him. "Catawba man is a free man, he can sleep or he can hunt," pursued the savage, retorting decidedly upon the condition of the slave, but without annoying the sleek, well fed and self-complacent driver. "Nigger man ain't free man—he must work, same like Indian squaw."

"Oh, skion! Oh! skion! wha's all dat, Knuckles? You don't know wha' you say. Who make you free? wha' make you free? How you show you got freedom, when here you expen' 'pon poor woman for work your pot, and half de time you got not'ing to put in 'em. Now, I is free man! Cause, you see my pot is always full, and when I does my work like a gempleman,—who cares? I laughs at mossa jist the same as I laughs at you. You free eh?—you! Whay you hab coat like mine? Whay, you hab breeches? Why, Knuckles, you aint decent for stan' 'fore you wife. Dat's trut' I'm telling you. How you can be free when you aint decent? How you can be free when you no work? How you can be free when you half-starving all de time? When you aint got blanket to you' back—when you aint got fat 'pon you rib. When here, you expen' 'pon my land to get the mud-stuff for you' pots and pans! Psho, psho, Knuckles, you don't know wha' you talk 'bout. You aint hab sensible notion of dem tings wha make free pusson. Nebber man is freeman, ef he own arm can't fill he stomach. Nebber man is freeman if he own work can't put clothes 'pon he back. Nebber man is freeman—no, nor gempleman neider, when he make he purty young wife do all de work, him lying same time, wid he leg cross and he eye half shut, in de long grass smelling ob de sunshine. No, no, Knuckles, you must go to you' work, same as I goes to mine, ef you wants people to desider you a freeman. Now you' work is hunting—my work is for obersee my plantation. It's a trut', your work aint obermuch—'taint wha' gempleman kin call work altogedder, but nebber mind, it's someting. Now, wha for you no go to you' work? Come, I gwine to mine. You strike off now 'pon your business. I reckon you' wife can make he pots, same as ef we bin' stan' look 'pon 'em. Woman don't like to be obershee, and when I tink 'pon de seck, I don't see any needcessity for it."

The Indian darted a fierce glance at the authoritative negro, and simply exclaiming, "Eh! Eh!" rose from his position, and tottering towards the spot where the woman was at work, uttered a few brief words in her ear which had the immediate effect of sending her out of sight, and into the hovel. He then returned quietly to his nest beneath the tree. Mingo was somewhat annoyed by the conviction that he had overshot his object, and had provoked the always eager suspicions of the savage. Knuckles betrayed no sort of intention to go on the hunt that day; and his fierce glances, even if he had no words to declare his feelings, sufficiently betrayed to the negro the jealousies that were awakened in his mind. The latter felt troubled. He fancied that, in the pursuit of his desires, were the woman alone concerned, he should have no difficulty, but he knew not what to do with the man. To scare him off was impossible— to beguile him from his treasure seemed equally difficult, and, in his impatience, the dogmatical driver, accustomed to have his will instantly obeyed, could scarcely restrain himself from a second resort to the whip. A moment's reflection brought a more prudent resolution to his mind, and seeing that the squatters were likely to go without food that day, he determined to try the effect which the presentation of a flitch of his master's bacon would have, upon the jealousy of the husband, and the affections of the wife. With this resolution, he retired from the ground, though without declaring his new and gracious purpose to either of the parties whom it was intended especially to benefit.

CHAPTER VII.

The flitch was brought, boiled, and laid before the squatters. It was accompanied by a wholesome supply of corn bread; and this liberality, which had, for its sanction, in part, the expressed determination of the master, had for its effect, the restoration of Mingo to that favour in the mind of the savage, which his imprudent opinions had forfeited. Even a jealous Indian, when so very hungry as our Catawba, and so utterly wanting in resources of his own, cannot remain insensible to that generosity, however suspicious, which fills his larder with good cheer in the happy moment. He relaxed accordingly, Mingo was invited into the hovel, and made to partake of the viands which he had provided. A moderate supply of whiskey accompanied the gift, enough to give a flavour to the meal, yet not enough to produce intoxication. Mingo was resolved henceforth, to do nothing which would keep himself and Knuckles from an uninterrupted pursuit of their several game. But while the meal lasted, he saw but few results beyond the thawing of Knuckles, which promised him success in his object. Caloya was, if possible, more freezing than ever. She never deigned him the slightest acknowledgment for his numerous civilities, which were not merely profitless, but which had the additional disadvantage of attracting the eyes, and finally re-awakening the jealous apprehensions of Knuckles; still, the good cheer was so good, and the facility with which it had been procured, so very agreeable to a lazy Indian, that he swallowed his dissatisfaction with his pottage, and the meal passed over without any special outbreak. Mingo, so near the object of his desire, was by no means disposed to disputation with her husband, and contented himself with only an occasional burst of declamation, which was intended rather for her ears than for those of her lord. But he strove to make amends for their forbearance, by addressing the most excruciating glances across the table to the fair—glances which she did not requite with favour, and which she did not often seem to see.

Mingo was in hopes, when dinner was over, that Knuckles would take up his bow and arrows, and set forth on the hunt. To this he endeavoured, in an indirect manner, to urge the savage. He told him that game was plenty in the neighbouring woods and swamps—that deer might be found at all hours, and even proceeded to relate several marvellous stories of his own success, which failed as well to persuade as to deceive the hunter. The whiskey being exhausted by this time, and his hunger being pacified, the jealous fit of the latter returned upon him with all the vigour of an ague. "Why," he asked himself, "should this negro steal his master's bacon to provide Richard Knuckles with a dinner? Because Richard Knuckles has a young wife, the youngest and handsomest of the whole tribe. Why should he urge me to go hunting, and take such pains to show me where the buck stalks, and the doe sleeps, but that he knows I must leave my doe behind me? Why should he come and sit with me half a dozen times a day, but that he may see and sit with my young wife also?" An Indian reasons very much like every body else, and jumps very rationally to like conclusions. The reserve of Knuckles grew with his reflections, and Mingo had sense enough to perceive that he could hope for no successful operations that day. The woman was sent from the presence, and her husband began to exhibit very decided symptoms of returning sulks. He barely answered the civilities of the driver, and a savage grin displayed his white teeth, closely clenched, whenever his thin lips parted to reply. The parting speech of the negro was not precisely the D.I.O. of the rattle-dandy of fashionable life, but was very much like it. If he did not swear like a trooper at bidding adieu, he marked every step on his way homewards with a most bitter oath.

But success is no ripe fruit to drop at the first opening of the mouth of the solicitous. Mingo was not the person to forego his efforts, and he well knew from old experience, that a woman is never so near won, as when she seems least willing. He was not easily given to despair, however he might droop, and the next day, and the next, and the next found him still a frequent visitor at the camp of Knuckles; and still he provided the corn, the bacon, and the whiskey, and still he found the Catawba a patient recipient of his favours. The latter saw no reason to leave home to hunt venison when his larder was so easily provided, and the former could not, but at some discredit, discontinue the liberal practices which he had so improvidently begun.

But if Knuckles was not unwilling to be fed after this fashion, he was not altogether insensible to some of the conditions which it implied. He could not but perceive that the negro had his objects, and those objects his jealous blood had led him long before to conjecture with sufficient exactness. He raged inwardly with the conviction that the gallant, good looking, and always well dressed Driver sought to compass his dishonour; and he was not without the natural fears of age and brutality that, but for his own eminent watchfulness, he might be successful. As there was no equality in the conditions of himself and wife, there was but little confidence between them—certainly none on his part;—and his suspicions—schooled into silence in the presence of Mingo, as well because of the food which he brought, as of the caution which the great physical superiority of the latter was calculated to inspire— broke out with unqualified violence when the two were alone together. The night of the first day when Mingo provided the table of the squatters so bountifully, was distinguished by a concussion of jealousy, on the part of Knuckles, which almost led the poor woman to apprehend for her life. The effects of the good cheer and the whiskey had subsided and the departure of Mingo was the signal for the domestic storm.

"Hah! hah! nigger is come for see Ingin wife. Ingin wife is look 'pon nigger—hah?"

It was thus that he begun the warfare. We have endeavoured to put into the Indian-English, as more suitable to the subject, and more accessible to the reader, that dialogue which was spoken in the most musical Catawba. The reply of the woman, though meekly expressed, was not without its sting.

"Ingin man eats from nigger hand, drinks from nigger bottle, and sits down by nigger side in the sunshine. Is Caloya to say, nigger go to the cornfield—Ingin man go look for meat?"

The husband glared at the speaker with fiery eyes, while his teeth gleamed maliciously upon her, and were suddenly gnashed in violence, as he replied:

"Hah! Ingin man must not look pon his wife! Hah! Ingin woman says— 'go hunt, man, go—that no eyes may follow nigger when he crawls through the bush. Hah!'"

"Caloya is blind when the nigger comes to the camp. Caloya looks not where he lies in the sunshine with the husband of Caloya. Is Enefisto (the Indian name for Knuckles) afraid of nigger?—is he afraid of Caloya?—let us go: Caloya would go to her people where they camp by the Edisto."

"Hah! What said Chickawa, to Caloya? Did he say, come to our people where they camp by the Edisto? Wherefore should Caloya go beside the Edisto—Hah?"

This question declared another object of the husband's jealousy. The woman's reply was as wild as it was immediate.

"Caloya sees not Chickawa—she sees not the nigger—she sees the clay and she sees the pans—and she sees Enefisto—Enefisto has said, and her eyes are shut to other men."

"Caloya lies!"

"Ah!"

"Caloya lies!"

The woman turned away without another word, and re-entering the miserable wigwam, slunk out of sight in the darkest corner of it. Thither she was pursued by the inveterate old man, and there, for some weary hours, she suffered like language of distrust and abuse without uttering a sentence either of denial or deprecation. She shed no tears, she uttered no complaints, nor did her tormentor hear a single sigh escape from her bosom; yet, without question, her poor heart suffered quite as much from his cruelty and injustice, as if her lips had betrayed all the extravagant manifestations known to the sorrows of the civilized.

Chapter VIII.

It is at least one retributive quality of jealousy, to torment the mind of the tormentor quite as much, if not more, than it does that of the victim. The anger of Richard Knuckles kept him awake the better part of the night; and, in his wakefulness, he meditated little else than the subject of his present fears. The indirect reproaches of his wife stung him, and suggested, at the same time, certain additional reasons for his suspicions. He reflected that, while he remained a close sentinel at home, it was impossible that he should obtain sufficient evidence to convict the parties whom he suspected, of the crime which he feared; for, by so doing, he must deprive the sooty Paris, who sought his hovel, of every opportunity for the prosecution of his design. With that morbid wilfulness of temper which marks the passions of man aroused beyond the restraints of right reason, he determined that the negro should have his opportunity; and, changing his plans, he set forth the next morning before day-peep, obviously for the purpose of hunting. But he did not remain long absent. He was fortunate enough just after leaving his cabin to shoot a fat wild turkey from his roost, on the edge of a little *bay* that stood about a mile from his camp; and with this on his shoulder, he returned stealthily to its neighbourhood, and, hiding himself in the covert, took such a position as enabled him to keep a keen watch over his premises and all the movements of Caloya. Until ten o'clock in the day he saw nothing to produce dissatisfaction or to alarm his fears. He saw the patient woman come forth according to custom, and proceed instantly to the "Red Gulley," where she resumed her tasks, which she pursued with quite as much industry, and, seemingly, much more cheerfulness than when she knew that he was watching. Her lips even broke forth into song while she pursued her tasks, though the strain was monotonous and the sentiment grave and melancholy. At ten o'clock, however, Knuckles's ague returned as he saw the negro make his appearance with wonted punctuality. The Indian laid his heaviest shaft upon the string of his bow, and awaited the progress of events. The movements of Mingo were made with due circumspection. He did not flatter himself, at first, that the field was clear, and looked round him with grave anxiety in momentary expectation of seeing the husband. His salutation of the wife was sufficiently distant and deferential. He began by asking after the chief, and received an answer equally cold and unsatisfactory. He gathered from this answer, however, that Knuckles was absent; but whether at a distance or at hand, or for how long a period, were important items of intelligence, which, as yet, he failed to compass; and it was only by a close cross-examination of the witness that he arrived at the conclusion, that Knuckles had at length resumed the duties of the hunter. Even this conclusion reached him in a negative and imperfect form.

"Shall Ingin woman say to Ingin man, when he shall hunt and where, and how long he shall be gone?" demanded the woman in reply to the eager questioning of the negro.

"Certainly not, most angelical!" was the elevated response of the black, as his lips parted into smiles, and his eyes shot forth the glances of warmer admiration than ever. The arrow of Knuckles trembled meanwhile upon the string.

"Certainly not, most angelical!—but Ingin man, ef he lob and respects Indian woman, will tell her all about his consarns without her axing. I'm sure, most lubly Caloya, ef you was wife of mine, you should know all my outgivings and incomings, my journeyings and *backslidings*, to and fro,—my ways and my wishes;—there shouldn't be nothing that I wouldn't let you know. But there's a mighty difference, you see, twixt an old husband and a young one. Now, an old man like Knuckles, he's mighty close—he don't talk out his mind like a young fellow that's full of infections—a young fellow like me, that knows how to look 'pon a handsome young wife, and treat her with proper respectableness. Do you think now, ef you was wife of mine, that I'd let you do all that work by yourself? No! not for all the pots and jars twixt this and Edisto forks! Ef I did ask you to do the pans, and round 'em, and smooth 'em, and put the red stain 'pon 'em why that wouldn't be onreasonable, you see, 'cause sich delical and slim fingers as woman's has, kin always manage them despects better than man's—but then, I'd dig the clay for you, my gal—I'd work it, ef I hadn't horse, I'd work it with my own legs—I'd pile it up 'pon the board, and cut the wood to make the fire, and help you to burn it; and when all was done, I'd bend my own shoulders to the load, and you should follow me to Charleston, like a Lady, as you is. That's the way, my gal, that I'd treat wife of mine. But Ingin don't know much 'bout woman, and old Ingin don't care;—now, black Gempleman always has strong infections for the seck—he heart is tender—he eye is lub for look 'pon beauty—he hab soul for consider 'em in de right way, and when he sees 'em bright eye, and smood, shiny skin, and white teet', and long arm, and slender wais', and glossy black hair, same like you's, ah, Caloya, he strengt' is melt away widin 'em, and he feels like not'ing only so much honey, lub and infections. He's all over infections, as I may say. Wha' you tink?"

Here the Driver paused, not so much from having nothing more to say, as from a lack of the necessary breath with which to say it. Knuckles heard every word, though it would be an error to assume that he understood one half. Still, the liquorish expression in the face of the negro sufficiently illustrated his meaning to satisfy the husband that the whole speech was pregnant with the most audacious kind of impertinence. The reflection upon his weight of years, and the exulting reference to his own youth and manhood, which Mingo so adroitly introduced, was, however, sufficiently intelligible and insulting to the Catawba, and he hesitated whether to draw the arrow to its head at once and requite this second Paris for his affront, even in the midst of it, or to await until farther wrong should yield him a more perfect justification for the deed. He reflected upon the danger of the attempt, and his resolution was already taken as to the mode and direction of his flight. But a morbid wish to involve Caloya in the same fate—a lingering desire to find a sanction in her weakness and guilt for all his own frequent injustice and brutality, determined him to await her answer, and see to what extremities the negro would be permitted to carry his presumption. Strange to say, the answer of the wife, which was such as must have satisfied a husband that loved truly, gave him no gratification.

"Black man is too foolish!" said the woman with equal brevity and scorn in reply to the long speech of the Driver.

"Don't say so, most lubly of all the Catawba gals—you don't mean what you say for sartain. Look you—yer is as nice a pullet as ever was roasted, and yer is some hard biled eggs, and hoecake. I reckon that old fellow, your husband, aint brung in your breckkus yet; so you must be mighty hungry by this time, and there's no better stay-stomach in the worl than hard biled eggs. It's a mighty hard thing to work tell the sun stands atop of your head, afore getting any thing to go 'pon: I guessed how 'twould be, and so I *brung* you these few eatables."

He set down a small basket as he spoke, but the woman did not seem to perceive it, and manifested no sort of disposition to avail herself of his gift and invitation.

"What! you wont take a bite?"

"Enefisto will thank you when he come," was the answer, coldly spoken, and the woman toiled more assiduously, while she spoke, at her potteries.

"Enefisto!—oh, that's only an Ingin name for Knuckles, I s'pose. But who care for him, Caloya? Sure, you don't care 'bout an old fellow like that— fellow that makes you work and gives you not eben dry hominey? Prehaps, you're feard he'll beat you; but don't you feard—neber he kin lay heaby hand 'pon you, so long as Mingo is yer."

Could Mingo have seen the grin which appeared upon the mouth of the Indian as he heard these words, and have seen the deliberateness with which he thrice lifted the shaft and thrust its point between the leaves so as to bear upon his heart, he might have distrusted his own securities and strength, and have learned to be more respectful in estimating the powers of his foe. But the Indian seemed to content himself with being in a state of preparedness and in having possession of the entire field. He did not shoot; his worse feelings remained unsatisfied—he saw nothing in the deportment of Caloya which could feed the morbid passion which prevailed over all others in his breast, and he probably forbore wreaking his malice upon the one victim, in hopes that by a little delay he might yet secure another.

"Black man is too foolish. Why he no go to his work? Catawba woman is do her work."

"And I will help you, my gal. It's mighty hard to do all by you self, so here goes. Lor', if I was your husband, Caloya, instead of that old fellow, Knuckles, you should be a lady—I'd neber let you touch a pot or a pan, and you should hab a frock all ob seersuck jist like this."

As the negro spoke, he threw off his hunting shirt, which he cast over a bush behind him, rolled up his shirt sleeves, displaying his brawny and well made arms to the woman—perhaps the chief motive for this present gallant proceeding—and, advancing to the pile of clay in which Caloya was working, thrust his hands into the mass and began to knead with all the energy of a baker, striving with his dough. The woman shrank back from her place, as she received this new accession of labour, and much to the annoyance of Mingo, retired to a little distance, where she seemed to contemplate his movements in equal surprise and dissatisfaction. Meanwhile, a change had taken place in the mood and movements of Knuckles. The sight of the gaudy garment which Mingo had hung upon the myrtle bushes behind him, awakened the cupidity of the Catawba. For a time, a stronger passion than jealousy seized his mind, and he yearned to be the possessor of a shirt which he felt assured would be the envy of the tribe. It hung in his eyes like a fascination— he no longer saw Caloya—he no longer heeded the movements of the negro who had been meditating so great an injury to his honour and peace of mind; and, so long as the bright stripes of the seersucker kept waving before him, he forgot all his own deeply meditated purposes of vengeance. The temptation at last became irresistible. With the stealthy movement of his race, he rose quietly from the spot where he had been lurking, sank back in the depths of the woods behind him, and, utterly unheard, unobserved and unsuspected by either of the two in front, he succeeded in making a compass, still under cover, which brought him in the rear of the myrtles on which the coat was suspended. Meanwhile, Mingo, with his face to the kneading trough, and his back upon the endangered garment, was in the full stream of a new flood of eloquence, and the favourite Seersucker disappeared in the rapid grasp of the husband, while he was most earnest, though at a respectful distance, in an endeavour to deprive the Indian of a yet dearer possession. In this aim his arguments and entreaties were equally fond and impudent; and with his arms buried to the elbows in the clay, and working the rigid mass as if life itself depended upon it, he was pouring forth a more unctuous harangue than ever, when, suddenly looking up to the spot where Caloya had retreated, his eye rested only upon the woods. The woman had disappeared from sight. He had been "wasting his sweetness on the desert air"—

he had been talking to the wind only. Of this, at first, he was not so perfectly assured.

"Hello!" he exclaimed, "Whare you gone, Caloya? Hello—hello! Whoo—whoo—whoop!"

He waited in silence until he became convinced that his responses were those only of the echo.

"Can't be!" he exclaimed, "can't be, he gone and lef' me in de middle of my talking! Caloya, Caloya,—Hello, gal! hello—whay you day? Whoo! whoop!"

Utter silence followed the renewal of his summons. He stuck his fingers, coated as they were with clay, into his wiry shock of wool—a not unfrequent habit with the negro when in a quandary,—and, could the blushes of one of his colour have been seen, those of Mingo would have been found of a scarlet beyond all comparison as the conviction forced itself upon him, that he was laughed at and deserted.

"Cuss de woman!" he exclaimed, "wha make me lub 'em so. But he mus'nt tink for git 'way from me wid dis sort of acceedint. 'Speck he can't be too fur; ef he day in dese woods wha' for keep me from fin' 'em. As for he husband, better he no meet me now. Ef he stan' in my way tree minutes, I'll tumble em sure as a stone."

Thus soliloquizing, he darted into the woods, traversing every opening and peeping behind every bush and tree for a goodly hour, but without success. Man and wife had disappeared with a success and secrecy equally inscrutable. Breathless and angry he emerged once more, and stood within the camp. His anger put on the aspect of fury, and disappointment became desperation. He looked round for the dog, intending to renew the flogging which he had administered on the first day of his acquaintance, and in bestowing which he had been so seasonably interrupted by the owner; but the cur had departed also; and no signs remained of any intention on the part of the squatters to resume their temporary lodging place, but the rude specimens of clay manufacture, some two dozen pots and pans, which stood under a rude shelter of twigs and bushes, immediately adjoining the wigwam. These, with foot and fist, Mingo demolished, trampling, with the ingenious pains-taking of a wilful boy, the yet unhardened vases out of all shape and character into the earth on which they rested. Having thus vented his spleen and displayed a less noble nature than he usually pretended to, the driver proceeded to resume his coat, in mood of mind as little satisfied with what he had done in his anger as with the disappointment that had provoked it.

But here a new wonder and vexation awaited him. His fingers again recurred to his head, but no scratching of which they were capable, could now keep him from the conviction that there was "magic in the web of it." He looked and lingered, but he was equally unsuccessful in the search after his hunting shirt, as for his good humour. He retired from the ground in some doubt whether it was altogether safe for him to return to a spot in which proceedings of so mysterious a character had taken place. All the events in connection with his new acquaintance began to assume a startling and marvellous character in his eyes;—the lazy dog;—the old husband of a wife so young and lovely! What could be more strange or unnatural! But her flight—her sudden disappearance, and that too at a time when he was employing those charms of speech which heretofore had never proved ineffectual! Mingo jumped to the conclusion that Knuckles was a Catawba wizard, and he determined to have nothing more to do with him:—a determination which he maintained only until the recollection of Caloya's charms made him resolve, at all hazards, to screen her from so ugly an enchanter.

Chapter IX.

But a little time had passed after Mingo had left the camp when Knuckles returned to it. He approached with stealthy pace, keeping himself under cover until he found that the enemy had departed. During the search which the Driver had made after himself and wife, he had been a quiet observer of all his movements. He fancied that the search was instituted for the recovery of the hunting shirt, and did not dream that his wife had left the ground as well as himself to the single possession of the visitor. When he returned and found her gone, his first impression was that she had departed with the negro. But a brief examination of their several footsteps, soon removed his suspicions and enabled him to pursue the route which the woman had taken on leaving the camp. He found her without difficulty, as she came forward, at his approach, from the copse in which she had concealed herself. He encountered her with the bitterest language of suspicion and denunciation. His jealousy had suffered no decrease in consequence of his failure to find cause for it; but fattening from what it fed on—his own consciousness of unworthiness—the conviction that he did not deserve and could not please one, so far superior and so much younger than himself—vented itself in coarse charges and vindictive threats. With the patience of Griselda, the Catawba woman followed him in silence to the camp, where they soon found cause for new affliction in the discovery which they there made, of the manner in which the disappointed Driver had vented his fury upon their wares. The wrath of Knuckles increased at this discovery, though it did not, as it should have done, lead to any abatement of his jealous feeling towards his wife. Perhaps, on the contrary, it led to the farther proceeding of extremity, which he now meditated, and which he began to unfold to her ears. We forbear the unnecessary preliminaries in the conversation which followed between them, and which were given simply to a re-assertion, on his part, of old and groundless charges, and on hers of a simple and effortless denial of them. Her final reply, spoken of course in her own language, to the reiterated accusation, was such as to show that even the exemplary patience which she had hitherto manifested was beginning to waver. There was something in it to sting the worthless old sinner, not with a feeling of remorse, but of shame and vexation.

"If Enefisto loves not the black man, wherefore does he take the meat which he brings, and the poison drink from his bottle? If he loves not the black man, wherefore takes he the garment, which wrapt his limbs? Caloya loves not the black man, and has eaten none of his meat, has drank none of his poison water, and has stolen none of his garments. Let Enefisto cast the shirt over the myrtles, and now, now, let the woman go back to seek her people that camp on the waters of the Edisto. Caloya looks not where the black man sits; Caloya sees not where he stands, and hears not when he speaks. Caloya hears only a snake's hissing in her ears. Enefisto believes not the woman, and she cares not much to speak;—but let him take up the hatchet and the bow, and she will follow where he leads. Let her go to her people, where there is no black man. She would not stay at the 'Red Gulley,' where the black man comes."

"But she would go to the Edisto where is Chickawa? Hah! Caloya shall stay by the 'Red Gulley,' where is Enefisto—she shall not go to the Edisto where is Chickawa. Enefisto sees; Enefisto knows."

"Ah, and Caloya knows! Caloya knows! Enefisto sees Chickawa and the nigger Mingo every where. But let Enefisto take up his hatchet and go from this place. See," pointing to the broken pottery, "there is nothing to stay for. The nigger will break the pans when she makes them."

"Enefisto will take up the hatchet,—he will drive it into the head of the nigger. He will not go where Caloya may see Chickawa. She shall stay by the 'Red Gulley,' and when Mingo, the nigger comes, she shall smile upon him. She shall go into the wigwam. Then will he go to her in the wigwam—Hah?"

"What would Enefisto?" demanded the squaw in some consternation at this seeming and very sudden change in the disposition of her spouse.

"Mingo will say to Caloya, 'come, old man is gone hunting, come. Am I not here for Caloya, come. I love Caloya, let Caloya love Mingo, come!'"

"But Caloya hates Mingo, Caloya will spit upon the nigger!" was the indignant exclamation.

"Oh, no, no!," was the almost musical and certainly wild reply of the husband, while a savage smile of scorn and suspicion covered his features. "Caloya knows not what she says—she means not what she says. Nigger is young man—Enefisto is old man. Nigger hab good meat—Enefisto is old hunter, he cannot see where the deer sleep, he cannot follow the deer in a long chase, for his legs grow weary. Caloya loves young man who can bring her 'nough venison and fine clothes, hah? Let Caloya go into the wigwam, and nigger will say 'come,' and Caloya will come."

"Never!" was the indignant answer. "Caloya will never come to the nigger —Caloya will never come to Chickawa. Let Enefisto strike the hatchet into the head of Caloya, for his words make her very wretched. It is better she should die."

"Caloya shall live to do the will of Enefisto. She shall go where Mingo comes into the wigwam, and when he shall follow her, she shall stay and look upon him face to face. Mingo is young,—Caloya loves to look upon young man. When he shall put his hand upon the shoulder of Caloya then shall Caloya put her hand upon his. So shall it be—thus says Enefisto."

"Wherefore shall it be so?"

"Thus says Enefisto. Will Caloya say no?"

"Let Enefisto kill Caloya ere her hand rests upon the shoulder of Mingo. The hatchet of Enefisto——"

"Shall sink into the head of the nigger, when his hand is upon the shoulder of Caloya."

"Ha!"

"It is done. Does Caloya hear?"

"She hears."

"Will she go into the wigwam when Mingo comes?"

"She will go."

"And when he follows her,—when he puts his hand upon her shoulder, and looks, Ha! ha! ha!—looks thus, thus, into her eyes"—his own assumed an expression, or he strove at that moment to make them assume an expression of the most wilful love,—an attempt in which he signally failed, for hate, scorn and jealousy predominating still, gave him a most ghastly aspect, from which the woman shrunk with horror—"when he looks thus into her eyes, then will Caloya put her hand upon the shoulder of Mingo and hold him fast till the hatchet of Enefisto goes deep into his head. Will Caloya do this,—Ha? Will Caloya look on him thus, and grasp him thus, until Enefisto shall strike him thus, thus, thus, till there shall be no more life in his forehead?"

A moment's pause ensued, ere the woman spoke.

"Let Enefisto give the hatchet to Caloya. Caloya will herself strike him in the head if he goes after her into the wigwam."

"No! Caloya shall not. Enefisto will strike. Caloya shall grasp him on the shoulder. Enefisto will see by this if Caloya loves not that the black man should seek her always in the wigwam of the chief. Is Caloya ready—will she do this thing?"

"Caloya is ready—she will do it."

"Ha! ha!—black man is foolish to come to the camp of Enefisto, and look on the woman of Enefisto. He shall die."

CHAPTER X.

Mingo Gillison almost stumbled over his young master that morning, as he was returning home from his visit so full of strange and unwonted incidents. The latter was about to visit the camp of the squatters in compliance with his promise to that effect, when diverted from his intention by the intelligence which the negro gave him, that the Indians were gone from home. Somehow, it seemed to Mingo Gillison, that it was no part of his present policy that his master should see the intruders. A consciousness of guilt—a conviction that he had not been the faithful custodian of the interests given to his charge, and that, in some respects, they had suffered detriment at his hands, made him jealously apprehensive that the mere visit of his owner to the Red Gulley, would bring his defection to light.

"But where's your coat, Mingo?" was the natural question of Colonel Gillison, the moment after meeting him. Mingo was as ready as any other lover at a lie, and taking for granted that Jove would laugh at this, quite as generously as at a more dangerous perjury, he told a long cock-and-a-bull story about his having had it torn to such a degree in hunting cattle the evening before, as to put it beyond the power of recovery by the seamstress.

"A handsome coat, too, Mingo: I must give you another."

Mingo was gratified and expressed his acknowledgments quite as warmly as it was in his power to do under the feeling of shame and undesert which at that moment oppressed him. His master did not fail to see that something had occurred to lessen the assurance of his driver, and diminish the emphasis and abridge the eloquence of his usual speech, but being of an inert disposition of mind, he was not curious enough to seek the solution of a circumstance which, though strange, was unimportant. They separated after a few inquiries on the part of the latter, touching various plantation topics, to all of which the answers of Mingo were uttered with a sufficient degree of readiness and boldness to make them satisfactory. The master returned to the residence, while Mingo went off to the negro quarter to meditate how to circumvent Richard Knuckles, and win the smiles of his handsome but haughty wife.

It was probably two hours after the supper things had been removed, that the youthful proprietor of the estate of which Mingo held the highly important office in the duties of which we have seen him busy, was startled by the easy opening of the door of the apartment in which he sat, groping through the newspapers of the day, and, immediately after, by the soft tread of a female footstep, heedfully set down upon the floor. He turned at the unusual interruption, for it may as well be stated passingly, that young Gillison had set out in life with notions of such inveterate bachelorship that his domestic establishment was not suffered to be invaded by any of the opposite sex in any capacity. It is not improbable, that, later in life, his rigour in this respect, may have undergone some little relaxation, but as we are concerned with present events only, it will be no object with us either to speculate upon or to inquire into the future. Sufficient for the day is the evil thereof. Enough for us that his present regulations were such as we have here declared them, and had been laid down with so much emphasis in his household, on coming to his estate, that he turned upon the servant,—for such he assumed the intruder to be—with the determination to pour forth no stinted measure of anger upon the rash person who had shown herself so heedless of his commands.

The reader will be pleased to express no surprise, when we tell him that the nocturnal visitant of our young bachelor was no other than the Indian woman, Caloya. She had threaded her way, after nightfall, through all the mazes of the plantation, and, undiscovered and unnoticed, even by the watch dog who lay beneath the porch, had penetrated into the mansion and into the presence of its master. She had probably never been in the same neighbourhood before, but with that sagacity,—we might almost deem it an instinct—which distinguishes the North American Indian, probably, beyond all other people,—she had contrived to elude every habitation which lay between the "Red Gulley" and the dwelling-house—to avoid contact with the negro houses of fifty slaves, and keep herself concealed from all observation, until that moment when she pleased to discover herself. The surprise of Gillison was natural enough. He rose, however, as soon as he was conscious that the intruder was a stranger, and perceiving her to be an Indian, he readily concluded that she must be one of the squatters at the "Red Gulley," of whom the eloquent Mingo had given him such emphatic warning. With that due regard for the sex which always distinguishes the true gentleman, even when the particular object which calls for it may be debased and inferior, Gillison motioned her to a chair, and, with a countenance expressing no other feelings than those of kindness and consideration, inquired into her wants and wishes. His language, to one of a tribe whom it is customary to regard as thieves and beggars, would have proved him to be something less hostile to the sex, than his household regulations would altogether seem to indicate.

Caloya advanced with firmness, and even dignity, into the apartment. Her deportment was equally respectful and unconstrained. Her face was full of sadness, however, and when she spoke, it might have been observed that her tones were rather more tremulous than usual. She declined the proffered seat, and proceeded to her business with the straightforward simplicity of one having a single purpose. She began by unfolding a small bundle which she carried beneath her arm, and in which, when unrolled and laid upon the table, Col. Gillison fancied he discovered a strong family likeness to that hunting shirt of his driver, of the fate of which he had received such melancholy intelligence a few hours before. But for the particularity of Mingo, in describing the rents and rips, the slits and slashes of his favourite garment, the youthful proprietor would have rashly jumped to the conclusion that this had been the same. His large confidence in the veracity of Mingo, left him rather unprepared for the narrative which followed. In this narrative, Caloya did not exhibit the greatest degree of tenderness towards the amorous driver. She freely and fully declared all the particulars of his forced intimacy with herself and husband from the beginning; and though, with instinctive feminine delicacy, she suppressed every decided overture which the impudent Mingo had made to herself *par amours,* still there was enough shown, to enable his master to see the daring game which his driver, had been playing. Nor, in this narrative, did the woman omit to inform him of the hams and eggs, the chickens and the corn, which had been brought by the devoted negro in tribute to her charms. Up to this point, the story had assumed none but a ludicrous aspect in the sight of the young planter. The petty appropriations of his property of which Mingo had been guilty, did not awaken any very great degree of indignation, and, with the levity of youth, he did not seem to regard in the serious light which it merited, the wanton pursuit and lascivious purposes of the driver. But as the woman quietly proceeded in her narrative, and described the violence which had destroyed her pottery, the countenance of the master darkened. This act seemed one of such determined malignity, that he inly determined to punish it severely. The next statement of Caloya led him to do more justice to virtue, and make a darker estimate yet of the doings of his driver. She did not tell him that her husband was jealous, but she unfolded the solemn requisition which he had last made of her to secure the arms of Mingo in her embrace, while he revenged himself for the insults to which he had been subjected with the sharp edge of the hatchet. The young planter started as he heard the statement. His eye was fixed intently and inquiringly upon the calm, resolute, and seemingly frozen features of the speaker. She ceased to speak, and the pause of a few seconds followed ere Gillison replied:

"But you and your husband surely mean not to murder the fellow, my good woman? He has done wrong and I will have him punished; but you must not think to use knife and hatchet upon him."

"When Enefisto says 'strike' to Caloya—Caloya will strike! Caloya is the woman of Enefisto. Let not Mingo come into the wigwam of the Indian."

Gillison could not doubt her resolution as he heard the deliberate and subdued accents of her voice, and surveyed the composed features of her countenance. The determination to do the bidding of her husband was there expressed in language the least equivocal. His own countenance was troubled; he had not resolved what course to pursue, and the woman, having fulfilled her mission, was about to depart. She had brought back the stolen coat, though, with the proper tenderness of a wife, she omitted to say that it had been stolen. According to her story Mingo had left it behind him on the myrtles. Her second object had been to save the driver from his fate, and no more effectual mode suggested itself to her mind than by revealing the whole truth to the master. This had been done and she had no further cause to stay.

The young planter, after he had instituted a series of inquiries from which he ascertained what were the usual periods when Mingo visited the encampment, how he made his approaches, and in what manner the hovel was built, and where it lay, did not seek to delay her longer. His own knowledge of the "Red Gulley"—a knowledge obtained in boyhood—enabled him to form a very correct notion of all the circumstances of the place; and to determine upon the particulars of a plan which had risen in his mind, by which to save his driver from the danger which threatened him. This done, he begged her to await for a few moments his return, while he ascended to an upper chamber, from whence he brought and offered her a piece of bright calico, such as he well knew would be apt to provoke the admiration of an Indian woman; but she declined it, shaking her head mournfully as she did so, and moving off hurriedly as if to lose the temptation from her sight as quickly as possible. Gillison fancied there was quite as much of despondency as pride in her manner of refusing the gift. It seemed to say that she had no heart for such attractions now. Such indeed was the true exposition of her feelings. What pride could she have in gorgeous apparel, allied to one so brutal, so cruel, so worthless as her husband; and why should she care for such display, when, by his jealous policy, she was withdrawn from all connection with her people, in whose eyes alone she might desire to appear attractive. But the young planter was not to be refused. He would have forced the gift upon her, and when she suffered it to drop at her feet, he expressed himself in words of remonstrance, the tones of which were, perhaps, of more influence than the sense.

"Why not take the stuff, my good woman? You have well deserved it, and much more at my hands. If you do not take it, I will think you believe me to be as bad as Mingo."

She looked at him with some earnestness for a few seconds, then stooping, picked up the bundle, and immediately placed it beneath her arm.

"No, no!" she said, "white man is good. Black man is bad. Does the master remember? Let not Mingo come into the wigwam of Enefisto."

Colonel Gillison promised that he would endeavour to prevent any further mischief, and, with a sad smile of gratitude upon her countenance, the woman retired from his presence as stealthily as she came. He had enjoined her, if possible, to avoid being seen on leaving the settlement, and it was not hard for one of Catawba birth to obey so easy an injunction. She succeeded in gaining the "Red Gulley" undiscovered, but there, to her consternation, who should she encounter, at the very first glance, but the impudent and formidable Mingo, sitting, cheek-by-jowl, with her jealous husband, each, seemingly, in a perfect mood of equal and christian amity. It was a sight to gratify the credulous, but Caloya was not one of these.

CHAPTER XI.

Meanwhile, the youthful master of the veteran Mingo, meditated in the silence of his hall, the mode by which to save that amorous personage from the threatened consequences of his impertinence. Not that he felt any desire to screen the fellow from chastisement. Had he been told that husband and wife had simply resolved to scourge him with many stripes, he would have struck hands and cried "cheer" as loudly as any more indifferent spectator. But the vengeance of the Catawba Othello, promised to be of a character far too extreme, and, the inferior moral sense and sensibility of both Indian and negro considered, too greatly disproportioned to the offence. It was therefore necessary that what he proposed to do should be done quickly; and, taking his hat, Colonel Gillison sallied forth to the negro quarter, in the centre of which stood the superior habitation of the Driver. His object was simply to declare to the unfaithful servant that his evil designs and deeds were discovered, as well by himself as by the Catawba—to promise him the due consequences of his falsehood to himself, and to warn him of what he had to fear, in the event of his again obtruding upon the privacy of the squatters. To those who insist that the working classes in the South should enjoy the good things of this world in as bountiful a measure as the wealthy proprietors of the soil, it would be very shocking to see that they lived poorly, in dwellings which, though rather better than those of the Russian boor, are yet very mean in comparison with those built by Stephen Girard, John Jacob Astor, and persons of that calibre. Nay, it would be monstrous painful to perceive that the poor negroes are constantly subjected to the danger of ophthalmic and other diseases, from the continued smokes in which they live, the fruit of those liberal fires which they keep up at all seasons, and which the more fortunate condition of the poor in the free States, does not often compel them to endure at any. It would not greatly lessen the evil of this cruel destiny, to know that each had his house to himself, exclusively; that he had his little garden plat around it, and that his cabbages, turnips, corn and potatoes, not to speak of his celery, his salad, &c., are, in half the number of cases, quite as fine as those which appear on his master's table. Then, his poultry-yard, and pig-pen—are they not there also?—but then, it must be confessed that his stock is not quite so large as his owner's, and there, of course, the parallel must fail. He has one immunity, however, which is denied to the owner. The hawk, (to whose unhappy door most disasters of the poultry yard are referred,) seldom troubles his chickens—his hens lay more numerously than his master's, and the dogs always prefer to suck the eggs of a white rather than those of a black proprietor. These, it is confessed, are very curious facts, inscrutable, of course, to the uninitiated; and, in which the irreverent and sceptical alone refuse to perceive any legitimate cause of wonder. You may see in his hovel and about it, many little additaments which, among the poor of the South, are vulgarly considered comforts; with the poor of other countries, however, as they are seldom known to possess them, they are no doubt regarded as burthens, which it might be annoying to take care of and oppressive to endure. A negro slave not only has his own dwelling, but he keeps a plentiful fire within it for which he pays no taxes. That he lives upon the fat of the land you may readily believe, since he is proverbially much fatter himself than the people of any other class. He has his own grounds for cultivation, and, having a taste for field sports, he keeps his own dog for the chase—an animal always of very peculiar characteristics, some of which we shall endeavour one day to analyse and develope. He is as hardy and cheerful as he is fat, and, but for one thing, it might be concluded safely that his condition was very far before that of the North American Indian—his race is more prolific, and, by increasing rather than diminishing, multiply necessarily, and unhappily the great sinfulness of mankind. This, it is true, is sometimes urged as a proof of improving civilization, but then, every justly-minded person must agree with Miss Martineau, that it is dreadfully immoral. We suspect we have been digressing.

Col. Gillison soon reached the negro quarter, and tapping at the door of the Driver's wigwam, was admitted, after a brief parley, by the legitimate spouse of that gallant. Mingo had been married to Diana, by the Reverend Jonathan Buckthorn, a preacher of the Methodist persuasion, who rode a large circuit, and had travelled, with praiseworthy charity, all the way from Savannah River, in all weathers, and on a hard going nag, simply to unite this worthy couple in the holy bonds of wedlock. At that time, both the parties were devout members of the Church, but they suffered from frequent lapses; and Mingo, having been engaged in sundry *liaisons*—which, however creditable to, and frequent among the French, Italian and English nobility, are highly censurable in a slave population, and a decisive proof of the demoralizing tendency of such an institution—was, at the formal complaint of the wife, "suspended" from the enjoyment of the Communion Table, and finally, on a continuance of this foreign and fashionable practice, fully expelled from all the privileges of the brotherhood. Diana had been something of a termagant, but Mingo had succeeded in outstorming her. For the first six months after marriage, the issue was considered very doubtful; but a decisive battle took place at the close of that period, in which the vigorous woman was compelled to give in and Mingo remained undisputed master of the field. But though overthrown and conquered, she was not quiescent; and her dissatisfaction at the result, showed itself in repeated struggles, which, however, were too convulsive and transient, to render necessary any very decided exercise of the husband's energies. She growled and grumbled still, without cessation, and though she did not dare to resent his frequent infidelities, she nevertheless pursued them with an avidity, and followed the movements of her treacherous lord with a jealous watchfulness, which proved that she did not the less keenly feel them. Absolute fear alone made her restrain the fury which was yet boiling and burning in her soul. When her master declared his desire to see Mingo, what was her answer? Not, certainly, that of a very dutiful or well satisfied spouse.

"Mingo, mossa? Whay him dey? Ha! mossa, you bes' ax ebbry woman on de plantation 'fore you come to he own wife. I bin marry to Mingo by Parson Buckthorn, and de Parson bin make Mingo promis' for lub and 'bey me, but he forget all he promise tree day after we bin man and wife. He nebber bin lub 't all and as for 'bey,—lor' ha' massy 'pon me, mossa, I speak noting but de trute when I tell you,—he 'bey ebbry woman from yer to town 'fore he 'bey he own dear wife. Der's not a woman, mossa, 'pon de tree plantation, he aint lub more dan Di. Sometime he gone to Misser Jack's place—he hab wife dere! Sometime he gone to Misser Gabeau—he hab wife dere! Nex' time, he gone to Squir' Collins,—he hab wife dere! Whay he no hab wife, mossa? Who call tell? He hab wife ebbry which whay, and now, he no *sacrify*, he gone—you aint gwine to bleeb me, mossa, I know you aint—he gone and look for wife at Indian camp, whay down by de 'Red Gulley.' De trute is, mossa, Mingo is a mos' powerful black rascal of a nigger as ebber lib on gentleman plantation."

It was fortunate for young Gillison that he knew something of the nature of a termagant wife, and could make allowances for the injustice of a jealous one. He would otherwise have been persuaded by what he heard that his driver was one of the most uncomely of all the crow family. Though yielding no very credulous faith to the complaints of Diana, he still found it impossible to refuse to hear them; and all that he could do by dint of perseverance, was to diminish the long narratives upon which she was prepared to enter to prove her liege lord to be no better than he should be. Having exhausted all his efforts and his patience in the attempt to arrive at some certain intelligence of the husband's "whereabouts," without being able to divert the stream of her volubility from the accustomed channels, he concluded by exclaiming—

"Well, d—n the fellow, let him take the consequences. He stands a chance of having his throat cut before twenty-four hours are over, and you will then be at liberty, Di., to get a husband who will be more faithful. Should Mingo not see me by ten o'clock to-morrow, he's a dead man. So, you had better stir your stumps, my good woman, and see after him, unless you are willing to be a widow before you have found out a better man for your husband. Find Mingo and send him to me to-night, or he's a dead man to-morrow."

"Le' 'em dead—who care? He d'zarb for dead. I sure he no care if Di bin dead twenty tousand time. Le' 'em dead!"

Gillison left the hut and proceeded to other parts of the settlement where he thought it not improbable that the driver might be found; but a general ignorance was professed by all the negroes with respect to the particular movements of that worthy; and he soon discovered that his search was fruitless. He gave it up in despair, trusting that he should be able to succeed better at an hour seasonably early in the morning, yet half disposed, from his full conviction of his roguery, to leave the fellow to his fate.

Strange to say, such was not the determination of the dissatisfied Diana. Wronged and neglected as she had been, and was, there was still a portion of the old liking left, which had first persuaded her to yield her youthful affections to the keeping of this reckless wooer; and though she had avowed her willingness to her young master, that the "powerful black rascal of a nigger" should go to the dogs, and be dog's meat in twenty-four hours, still, better feelings came back to her, after due reflection, to soften her resolves. Though not often blessed with his kind words and pleasant looks, now-a-days, still, "she could not but remember such things were, and were most precious to her."

Left to herself, she first began to repeat the numberless conjugal offences of which he had been guilty; but the memory of these offences did not return alone. She remembered that these offences brought with them an equal number of efforts at atonement on the part of the offender; and when she thought of his vigorous frame, manly, dashing and graceful carriage, his gorgeous coat, his jauntily worn cap, his white teeth, and the insinuating smile of his voluminous lips, she could not endure the idea of such a man being devoted to a fate so short and sudden as that which her young master had predicted. She had not been told, it is true, from what quarter this terrible fate was to approach. She knew not under what aspect it would come, but the sincerity of her master was evident in his looks, words, and general air of anxiety, and she was convinced that there was truth in his assurance. Perhaps, her own attachment for the faithless husband—disguised as it was by her continual grumbling and discontent—was sufficiently strong to bring about this conviction easily. Diana determined to save her husband, worthless and wicked as he was,—and possibly, some vague fancy may have filled her mind as she came to this resolution, that, gratitude alone, for so great a service, might effect a return of the false one to that allegiance which love had hitherto failed to secure. She left her dwelling to seek him within half an hour after the departure of her master. But the worst difficulty in her way was the first. She trembled with the passion of returning jealousy when she reflected that the most likely place to find him would be at the "Red Gulley" in instant communion with a hateful rival—a red Indian—a dingy squaw,— whose colour, neither white nor black, was of that sort, which, according to Diana in her jealous mood, neither gods nor men ought to endure. Her husband's admiration she naturally ascribed to Catawba witchcraft. She doubted—she hesitated—she almost re-resolved against the endeavour. Fortunately, however, her better feelings prevailed. She resolved to go forward— to save her husband—but, raising her extended hands and parted fingers, as she came to this determination, and gnashing her teeth with vindictive resolution as she spoke, she declared her equal resolve to compensate herself for so great a charity, by sinking her ten claws into the cheeks of any copper coloured damsel whom she should discover at the Red Gulley in suspicious propinquity with that gay deceiver whom she called her lord. Having thus, with due solemnity, registered her oath in Heaven—and she was not one under such circumstances to "lay perjury upon her soul"—she hurried away under the equal impulse of a desire to save Mingo, and to "capper-claw"

Caloya. It was not long after, that young Gillison, who was more troubled about the fate of his driver than he was willing to acknowledge even to himself, came to a determination also to visit the "Red Gulley." A little quiet reflection, after he had reached home, led him to fear that he might not be in season to prevent mischief if he waited till the morning for Mingo's appearance; and a sudden conjecture that, at that very moment, the audacious negro might be urging his objects, in the wigwam of the squatters, made him fearful that even his instant interference would prove too late. As soon as this conjecture filled his mind, he seized his cap, and grasping his rifle, and calling his favourite dog, set forth with all possible speed towards the spot, destined to be memorable forever after in all local chronicles, in consequence of these events.

CHAPTER XII.

The horror and vexation of Caloya may be imagined, when, on returning from her visit to the master of the impudent Mingo, she discovered him, cheek-by-jowl, with her husband. The poor woman was miserable in the extreme from various causes. Resolved steadfastly and without scruple to do the will of her jealous spouse, she yet shrank from the idea of perpetrating the bloody deed which the latter contemplated, and which was so suitable to the fierce character of Indian vindictiveness. She was, in fact, a gentle, though a firm, simple, and unaffected woman, and had not this been the prevailing nature of her heart, the kindness with which Gillison had received, and the liberality with which he had treated her, would have been sufficient to make her reluctant to do any thing which might be injurious to his interests.

But, taught in the severe school of the barbarian those lessons which insist always upon the entire subordination of the woman, she had no idea of avoiding, still less of rebelling against, the authority which prescribed her laws. "To hear was to obey," and with a deep sigh she advanced to the wigwam, with a firm resolution to do as she had been commanded, though, with a prayer in her mind, not the less fervent because it remained unspoken by her lips, that the fearful necessity might pass away, and her husband be prevented, and she be spared, the commission of the threatened deed.

It was deemed fortunate by Caloya, that, observing the habitual caution of the Indian, she had kept within the cover of the woods until the moment when she came within sight of the wigwam. This caution enabled her still to keep from discovery, and "fetching a compass" in the covert so as to pass into the rear of the hut, she succeeded by pulling away some fragments of the bark which covered it, in entering its narrow precincts without having been perceived. With a stealthy footstep and a noiseless motion, she deposited her bundle of calicoes in a corner of the hut, and sinking down beside it, strove to still even those heavings of her anxious bosom, which she fancied, in her fears, might become audible to the persons without.

To account for the return of Mingo Gillison to the spot where he had been guilty of so much impertinence, and had done so much mischief, is not a difficult matter. It will here be seen that he was a fellow whom too much authority had helped to madden—that he was afflicted with the disease of intense self-consequence, and that his passions, accordingly, were not always to be restrained by prudence or right reason. These qualities necessarily led to frequent errors of policy and constant repentings. He had not many moral misgivings, however, and his regrets were solely yielded to the evil results, in a merely human and temporary point of view, which followed his excesses of passion and frequent outbreaks of temper. He had not well gone from the "Red Gulley" after annihilating the pottery thereof, without feeling what a fool he had been. He readily conceived that his rashness would operate greatly, not only against his success with the woman, but against his future familiarity with the man. It was necessary that he should heal the breach with the latter if he hoped to win any favours from the former; and, with this conviction, the rest of the day was devoted to a calm consideration of the *modus operandi* by which he might best succeed in this desire. A rough investigation of the moral nature of an Indian chief, led Mingo to the conclusion that the best defence of his conduct, and the happiest atonement which he could offer, would be one which was addressed to his appetites rather than to his understanding. Accordingly, towards nightfall, having secured an adequate supply of whiskey—that bane equally of negro and Indian—he prepared with some confidence, to re-appear before the parties whom he had so grievously offended. He had his doubts, it is true, of the sort of reception which he should meet;—he was not altogether sure of the magical effect of the whiskey, in promoting christian charity, and leading the savage to forgiveness; but none of the apprehensions of Mingo were of personal danger. He would have laughed to scorn a suggestion of harm at the hands of so infirm and insignificant a person as Richard Knuckles; and looking upon his own stout limbs and manly frame, he would have found in the survey, a sufficient assurance that Mingo Gillison was equally irresistible to man and wife.

It was with a boldness of carriage, therefore, that corresponded adequately with the degree of confidence which he felt in his equal powers of persuasion, and the whiskey, rather than his personal prowess, that he appeared that night before the hovel of the squatters. He found Knuckles alone, and seated a little in advance of his habitation. The Indian was sober from the necessity of the case. The policy of the negro had not lately allowed him liquor, and he had not himself any means for procuring it. He watched the approach of the enemy without arising from the turf, and without betraying in his look any of that hostility which was active in his bosom. His face, indeed, seemed even less grave than usual, and a slight smile upon his lips, in which it would have tasked a far more suspicious eye than that of Mingo to have discovered anything sinister, betrayed, seemingly, a greater portion of good humour than usually softened his rigid and coarse features. Mingo approached with a conciliating grin upon his visage, and with hands extended in amity. As the Indian did not rise to receive him, he squatted down upon his haunches on the turf opposite, and setting down the little jug which he brought between them, clapped the Indian on his shoulders with a hearty salutation, which was meant to convey to the other a pleasant assurance of his own singular condescension.

"Knuckles, my boy, how you does? You's bex with me, I reckons, but there's no needcessity for that. Say I did kick over the pots and mash the pans?—well! I can pay for 'em, can't I? When a man has got the coppers he's a right to kick; there's no use to stand in composition with a fellow that's got the coppers. He kin throw down and he kin pick up—he kin buy and he kin sell; he kin break and he kin men'; he kin gib and he kin tak'; he kin kill and he kin eat—dere's no'ting he can't do ef he hab money—he's mossa to all dem d——d despisable rackrobates, what's got no coppers. I once bin' ye'r a sarmint from Parson Buckthorn, and he tink on dis object jis' as you ye'r me tell you. He tex' is take from de forty-seben chapter—I 'speck it's de forty-seben—which say, 'what he gwine to profit a gempleman what's mak' de best crop in de world, if he loss he soul,'—which is de same t'ing, Knuckles, you know, as ef I was to ax you, wha's de difference ef Mingo Gillison kick over you' pans and pots, and bre'k 'em all to smash, and ef he pick 'em, like he pick up eggs, widout bre'k any, so long as he pay you wha' you ax for 'em. You sell 'em, you git you money, wha' matter wha' I do wid 'em arter dat? I bre'k 'em or I men' 'em, jis' de same t'ing to you. 'Spose I eat 'em, wha's de difference? He stick in Mingo stomach, he no stick in your'n; and all de time de coppers is making purty jingle in you' pocket. Well, my boy, I come to do de t'ing now. I bre'k you' pots, I 'tan ye'r to pay you for 'em. But you mus' be t'irsty, my old fellow, wid so much talking—tak' a drink 'fore we exceed to business."

The Catawba needed no second invitation. The flavour of the potent beverage while the negro had been so unprofitably declaiming, ascended to his nostrils with irresistible influence, in spite of the stopper of corn cob which imperfectly secured it, and which among the negroes of the Southern plantations, makes a more common than seemly apology for a velvet cork. The aroma of the beverage soon reconciled Knuckles to the voice of his enemy, and rendered those arguments irresistible, which no explanations of Mingo could ever have rendered clear. As he drank, he became more and more reconciled to the philosophy of his comrade, and, strengthened by his draughts, his own became equally explicit and emphatic.

"Ha! Ha! Biskey good too much!" was the long drawn and fervent exclamation which followed the withdrawal of the reluctant vessel from his lips.

"You may say dat wid you' own ugly mout,' Dick, and tell no lie nother," was the cool response. Any biskey is good 'nough, but dat's what I calls powerful fine. Dat' fourt' proof, gennywine, and 'trong like Sampson, de Philistian. Der's no better in all Jim Hollon's 'stablishment. *We* gin a mighty great price for it, so it ought to be good, ef ther's any justice done. But don't stan', Knuckles—ef you likes it, sup at it again. It's not like some women's I know—it gives you smack for smack, and holds on as long as you let it."

"Huh!—woman is fool!" responded the savage with an air of resentment which his protracted draught of the potent beverage did not altogether dissipate. The reference to the sex reminded him of his wife, and when he looked upon the speaker he was also reminded of his presumptuous passions, and of the forward steps which he had taken for their gratification. But his anger did not move him to any imprudence so long as the power of reflection was left him. It was only as his familiarity with the bottle advanced that his jealous rage began to get the better of his reason and lead him into ebullitions, which, to a more acute or less conceited person than Mingo, would have certainly betrayed the proximity of that precipice in the near neighbourhood of which he stood. The savage grew gradually eloquent on the subject of woman's worthlessness, weakness, folly, &c.; and as the vocabulary of broken and imperfect English which he possessed was any thing but copious, his resort to the Catawba was natural and ready to give due expression to his resentment and suspicions.

"Huh! woman is fool—Ingin man spit 'pon woman—ehketee—boozamo-gettee!—d—n, —d—n,—damn! tree d—n for woman!—he make for cuss. Caloya Ganchacha!—he dog,—he wuss dan dog—romonda!—tree time dog! anaporee, toos-wa-ne-dah! Ingin man say to woman, go! fill you mout' wid grass,—woman is dog for cuss!"

The English portion of this blackguardism is amply sufficient to show the spirit of the speaker, without making necessary any translation of that part of the speech, which, in his own dialect, conceals matter far more atrocious. Enough was understood by Mingo, as well from the action and look of the Catawba, as from the vulgar English oath which he employed in connection with his wife's sex and name, to convince the negro that Caloya was an object rather of hate than of suspicion to her worthless husband. As this notion filled his sagacious cranium, new hopes and fancies followed it, and it was with some difficulty that he could suppress that eager and precipitate utterance of a scheme, which grew out of this very grateful conjecture.

"You no lub woman, Knuckles,—eh?"

"Huh! woman is dog. Ingin man say to dog—go! and he go!—say to dog, come, and he come! Dog hunt for meat, woman's put meat in de pot! Woman is dog and dog is woman. Nomonda-yaw-ee—d—n tree time—wassiree—woman is tree time d—n!"

"Well, Knuckles, old boy! take a drink! You don't seem to defections womans no how!"

"Heh?"—inquiringly.

"Prehaps you don't altogether know what I mean by defections? Well, I'll tell you. Defections means a sort of chicken-lub; as if you only had it now and then, and something leetler than common. It aint a pow'rful attack,—it don't take a body about de middle as I may say, and gib 'em an up and down h'ist. It's a sort of lub that lets you go off when you chooses, and come back when you wants to, and don't keep you berry long about it. That's to say, it's a sort of defections."

A monosyllable from the Indian, like the last, attested any thing but his mental illumination in consequence of the very elaborate metaphysical distinctions which Mingo had undertaken. But the latter was satisfied that Knuckles should have become wiser if he had not; and he proceeded, making short stages toward the point which he desired to attain.

"Well, now, Knuckles, if so be you don't affections womans, what makes you keeps her 'bout you? Ef she's only a dog in your sight, why don't you sen' her a-packing? Ingin man kin find somebody, I 'speck, to take care ob he dog for 'em."

"Heh? Dog—wha' dog?"

"Dat is to say—but take a drink, old fellow! Take a long pull—dat jug's got a long body, an' you may turn it upside down heap o' times 'fore you'll git all the life out of it. It gin my arm a smart tire, I kin tell you, to tote it all the way here! Dat is to say—but sup at it agin, Knuckles,—please de pigs, you don't know much about what's good, or you would'nt put it down, tell the red water begins to come into you' eyes."

"Aw—yaw—yaw! Biskey good too much!"

Was the exclamation, accompanied with a long drawn, hissing sound, of equal delight and difficulty, which issued spontaneously from the Indian's mouth, as he withdrew the jug from his lips. The negro looked at him with manifest satisfaction. His eyes were suffused with water, and exhibited a hideous stare of excitement and imbecility. A fixed glaze was overspreading them fast, revealing some of those fearful aspects which distinguish the last fleeting gleams of consciousness in the glassy gaze of the dying. Portions of the liquor which, in his feebleness he had failed to swallow, ran from the corners of his mouth; and his fingers, which still clutched the handle of the jug, were contracted about it like the claws of a vulture in the spasms of a mortal agony. His head, as if the neck were utterly unsinewed, swung from side to side in his repeated efforts to raise it to the usual Indian erectness, and, failing in this attempt, his chin sunk at last and settled down heavily upon his breast. He was evidently in prime condition for making a bargain, and, apprehensive that he might have overdone the matter, and that the fellow might be too stupid even for the purposes of deception, Mingo hastened with due rapidity to make the proposition which he had conceived, and which was of a character with the audacity of his previous designs.

"Well, Knuckles, my frien', what's to hender us from a trade? Ef so be you hates woman's and loves Biskey—ef woman's is a d—n dog, and biskey is de only ting dat you most defections in dis life,—den gib me you d—n dog, and I'll gib you 'nough and plenty of de ting you lub. You yerry me?"

"Aw, yaw, yaw, yaw! Biskey berry good!" A torrent of hiccoughs concluded the reply of the Indian, and for a brief space rendered the farther accents of the negro inaudible even to himself.

"To be sure,—da's trute! Biskey is berry good, and da's wha' I'm sayin' to you, ef you'd only pay some detention. I'm a offering you, Knuckles—I'm offering to buy you dog from you. I'll gib you plenty biskey for you dog. Wha' you say, man? eh?"

"Aw, yaw! Black man want Ingin dog!" The question was concluded by a faint attempt to whistle. Drunkenness had made the Catawba more literal than usual, and Mingo's apprehensions increased as he began to apprehend that he should fail entirely in reaching the understanding of his companion.

"Psho! git out, Knuckles, I no want you' four-legged dog—it's you' two-legged dog I day arter. Enty you bin call you woman a dog? Enty you bin say, dat you wife, Caloya, is d—n dog?"

"Ya-ou! ramonda yau-ee, Caloya! woman is tree time d—n dog!"

"To be sure he is. Da's wha we bin say. Now, I want dog, Knuckles; and you hab dog wha's jis suit me. You call him Caloya—you dog! You sell me Caloya, I gie you one whole barrel biskey for da same dog, Caloya."

"Hah!" was the sudden exclamation of the Indian, as this impudent but liberal offer reached his senses; but, whether in approbation or in anger, it was impossible, in the idiot inexpressiveness of his drunken glance, for the negro to determine. He renewed his offer with certain additional inducements in the shape of pipes and tobacco, and concluded with a glowing eulogy upon the quality of his "powerful, fine, gennywine, fourt' proof," the best in Holland's establishment, and a disparaging reference to the small value of the dog that he was prepared to buy with it. When he finished, the Indian evidently comprehended him better, and laboured under considerable excitement. He strove to speak, but his words were swallowed up in hiccoughs, which had been increasing all the while. What were his sentiments, or in what mind he received the offer, the negro vainly strove, by the most solicitous watchfulness, to ascertain; but he had too completely overdosed his victim, and the power of speech seemed entirely departed. This paralysis did not, however, extend entirely to his limbs. He struggled to rise, and, by the aid of a hickory twig which grew beside him, he succeeded in obtaining a doubtful equilibrium, which he did not, however, very long preserve. His hand clutched at the knife within his belt, but whether the movement was designed to vindicate his insulted honour, or was simply spasmodic, and the result of his condition, could not be said. Muttering incoherently at those intervals which his continual hiccoughing allowed, he wheeled about and rushed incontinently towards the hovel, as if moved by some desperate design. He probably knew nothing definitely at that moment, and had no precise object. A vague and flickering memory of the instructions he had given to his wife, may have mingled in with his thoughts in his drunken mood, and probably prompted him to the call which he thrice loudly made upon her name. She did not answer, but, having heard in her place of concealment the offensive proposition which the negro had made her husband, she now crouched doubly closely and cautious, lest the latter, under this novel form of provocation, might be moved to vent his wrath upon her head. Perhaps, too, she fancied, that by remaining quiet, she might escape the necessity of contributing in any wise to the execution of the bloody plot in which his commands had engaged her. Whatever may have been her fear, or the purposes of the husband, Caloya remained silent. She moved not from the corner in which she lay, apprehensively waiting events, and resolved not to move or show herself unless her duty obviously compelled her.

Mingo, meanwhile, utterly blinded by his prodigious self-esteem, construed all the movements of the Catawba into favourable appearances in behalf of his desires; and when Knuckles entered the hovel calling upon his wife, he took it for granted that the summons had no other object than to deliver the precious commodity into his own hands. This conviction warmed his imagination to so great a degree, that he forgot all his prudence, and following Knuckles into the wigwam, he prepared to take possession of his prize, with that unctuous delight and devotedness which should convince her that she too had made an excellent bargain by the trade. But when he entered the hovel, he was encountered by the savage with uplifted hatchet.

"Hello, Knuckles, wha' you gwine to do wid you' hatchet? You wouldn't knock you bes' frien' 'pon de head, eh?"

"Nigger is d——n dog!" cried the savage, his hiccoughs sufficiently overcome by his rage to allow him a tolerable clear utterance at last. As he spoke the blow was given full at the head of the driver. Mingo threw up his left hand to ward off the stroke, but was only partially successful in doing so. The keen steel smote the hand, divided the tendon between the fore-finger and thumb, and fell with considerable force upon the forehead.

"Oh you d——n black red-skin, you kill mossa best nigger!" shrieked the driver, who fancied, in the first moment of his pain, that his accounts were finally closed with the world. The blood, streaming freely from the wound, though it lessened the stunning effects of the blow, yet blinded his eyes and increased his terrors. He felt persuaded that no surgeon could do him service now, and bitterly did he reproach himself for those amorous tendencies which had brought him to a fate so unexpected and sudden. It was the very moment when the exhortations of the Rev. Jonathan Buckthorn would have found him in a blessed state of susceptibility and saving grace. The evil one had not suffered so severe a rebuke in his present habitation for a very long season. But as the Reverend Jonathan was not nigh to take advantage of the circumstance, and as the hapless Mingo felt the continued though impotent struggle of his enemy at his feet, his earthly passions resumed their sway, and, still believing that he had not many hours to live, he determined to die game and have his revenge in his last moments. The Catawba had thrown his whole remaining strength into the blow, and the impetus had carried him forward. He fell upon his face, and vainly striving and striking at the legs of his opponent, lay entirely at his mercy; his efforts betraying his equal feebleness and fury. At first Mingo doubted his ability to do anything. Though still standing, he was for some time incapable of perceiving in that circumstance any strong reason for believing that he had any considerable portion of vitality left, and most certainly doubted his possession of a sufficient degree of strength to take his enemy by the throat. But with his rage came back his resolution, and with his resolution his vigour.

"Ef I don't stop your kicking arter dis, you red sarpent, my name's Blind Buzzard. Ef Mingo mus' dead, you shall dead too, you d—n crooked, little, old, red rascal. I'll squeeze you t'roat, tell you aint got breat' 'nough in you body to scar' 'way mosquito from peeping down your gullet. Lor' ha' massey!—to 'tink Mingo mus' dead 'cause he git knock on de head by a poor, little, shrinkle up Injun, dat he could eat up wid he eyes and no make tree bite ob he carcass."

This reflection increased the wrath of the negro, who prepared with the most solemn deliberation to take the Indian's life by strangling him. With this design he let his knee drop upon the body of the prostrate Knuckles, while his hand was extended in order to secure an efficient grasp upon his throat. But his movements had been closely watched by the keen-eyed Caloya from the corner where she crouched, who, springing forward at the perilous moment, drew the hatchet from the hand of the sprawling and unconscious savage and took an attitude of threatening which effectually diverted the anger of the negro. Surprised at her appearance, rather than alarmed at her hostility, he began to conjecture, in consequence of the returning passion which he felt, that his danger was not so great as he had at first fancied. The sight of those charms which had led him into the danger, seemed to induce a pleasant forgetfulness of the hurts which had been the result of his rashness;

and with that tenacity of purpose which distinguishes a veteran among the sex, the only thought of Mingo was the renewal of his practices of evil. He thought no more of dying, and of the Reverend Jonathan Buckthorn, but with a voice duly softened to the gentler ears which he was preparing to address, he prefaced his overtures by a denunciation of the "dead-drunk dog what was a-lying at his foot." A wretch, as he loudly declared, who was no more worthy of such a woman than he was worthy of life.

"But der's a man wha's ready to tak' you, my lubly one, and tak' care ob you, and treat you as you d'zarb. He's a gempleman—he's no slouch, nor no sneak. He's always dress in de bes'—he's always hab plenty for eat and plenty for drink—der's no scarcity where he hab de mismanagement; and nebber you'll hab needcessity for work, making mud pot and pan, ef he tak' you into his defections. I reckon, Caloya, you's want for know who is dat pusson I tell you 'bout. Who is dat gempleman wha's ready for do you so much benefactions? Well! look a' yer, Caloya, and I reckon you'll set eye on de very pusson in perticklar."

The woman gave him no answer, but still, with weapon uplifted, kept her place, and maintained a watch of the utmost steadfastness upon all his movements.

"Wha'! you won't say not'ing? Can't be you care someting for dis bag of feaders, wha's lie at my foot!"

With these words the irreverent negro stirred the body of Knuckles with his foot, and Caloya sprang upon him in the same instant, with as determined a hand as ever her husband's had been, struck as truly, though less successfully, at the forehead of her wooer. This time, Mingo was rather too quick to suffer harm from a feebler arm than his own. His eye detected her design the moment she moved, and he darted aside in season to avoid the blow. With equal swiftness he attempted to seize her in his arms the instant after, but, eluding his grasp, she backed towards the entrance of the wigwam, keeping her weapon uplifted, and evidently resolved to use it to the best advantage as soon as an opportunity offered. Mingo was not to be baffled in this fashion— the difficulties in the way of his pursuit seemed now reduced to a single issue—the husband was *hors de combat,* and the wife—she certainly held out only because she was still in his presence. To this moment, Mingo never doubted that his personal prowess and pretensions had long since impressed Caloya with the most indulgent and accessible emotions. He advanced, talking all the while in the most persuasive accents, but without inducing any relaxation of watchfulness or resolution on the part of the woman. He was prepared to rush upon, and wrest the hatchet from her hand—and farther ideas of brutality were gathering in his mind—when he was arrested by the presence of a new and annoying object which suddenly showed itself at the entrance and over the shoulder of the Indian woman. This was no other than his lawful spouse, Diana.

"Hello, Di! what de dibble you come for, eh?"

"I come for you, to be sure. Wha' de dibble you is doing yer, wid Injun woman?"

Surprised at the strange voice, and feeling herself somewhat secure in the presence of a third person, Caloya ventured to look round upon the new comer. The sight of her comely features was a signal of battle to the jealous wife, who, instantly, with a fearful shriek, struck her talons into the cheeks of her innocent rival, and followed up the assault by dashing her head into her face. The hatchet fell involuntary upon the assailant, but the latter had too successfully closed in, to receive much injury from the blow, which, however, descended upon her back, between the shoulders, and made itself moderately felt. Diana, more vigorous than the Indian woman, bore her to the earth, and, doubtlessly, under her ideas of provocation, would have torn her eyes from their sockets, but for the prompt interposition of her husband, who, familiar with the marital rights sanctioned by the old English law, prostrated her to the earth with a single blow of his fist. He might have followed up this violence to a far less justifiable extent, for the audacity which his wife had shown had shocked all his ideas of domestic propriety, but that he was interrupted before he could proceed further by a hand which grasped tightly his neckcloth from behind, and giving it a sudden twist, curtailed his powers of respiration to a most annoying degree. He turned furiously though with difficulty upon the new assailant, to encounter the severe eyes of his young master.

Here was an explosion! Never was an unfaithful steward more thoroughly confounded. But the native impudence of Mingo did not desert him. He had one of the fairest stories in the world to tell. He accounted for every thing in the most rational and innocent manner—but in vain. Young Gillison had the eye of a hawk when his suspicions were awakened, and he had already heard the testimony of the Indian woman, whom he could not doubt. Mingo was degraded from his trust, and a younger negro put over him. To compensate the Indian woman for the injuries which she received, was the first care of the planter as he came upon the ground. He felt for her with increased interest as she did not complain. He himself assisted her from the ground and conducted her into the wigwam. There, they found Knuckles almost entirely insensible. The liquor with which the negro had saturated him, was productive of effects far more powerful than he had contemplated. Fit had succeeded to fit, and paralysis was the consequence. When Gillison looked upon him, he saw that he was a dying man. By his orders, he was conveyed that night to the settlement, where he died the next day.

Caloya exhibited but little emotion, but she omitted no attention. She observed the decorum and performed all the duties of a wife. The young planter had already learned to esteem her, and when, the day after the funeral, she prepared to return to her people, who were upon the Edisto, he gave her many presents which she received thankfully, though with reluctance.

A year after, at the same season, the "Red Gulley" was occupied by the whole tribe, and the evening following their arrival, Col. Gillison, sitting within the hall of his family mansion, was surprised by the unexpected appearance of Caloya. She looked younger than before, comelier, and far more happy. She was followed by a tall and manly looking hunter, whom she introduced as her husband, and who proved to be the famous Chickawa, of whom poor old Knuckles had been so jealous. The grateful Caloya came to bring to the young planter a pair of moccasins and leggins, neatly made and fancifully decorated with beads, which, with her own hands, she had wrought for him. He received them with a sentiment of pleasure, more purely and more enduringly sweet than young men are often apt to feel; and, esteeming her justly, there were few articles of ordinary value in his possession with which he would not sooner have parted, than the simple present of that Catawba woman.

WHEN SIMMS EXPANDED "Indian Sketch," his first story about Indians, into "Oakatibbé, or the Choctaw Sampson," most of the transformation was accounted for by the debate between the first-person narrator, S., and the owner of the Mississippi plantation he is visiting, Colonel Harris. Simms called "Oakatibbé" one of his "best labors—not as a story perhaps, but as ... a very bold, original philosophical argument" on the subject "most vital to the interests ... of the South." Using the opposing philosophies of S. and Colonel Harris as the catalyst to raise "grave questions with regard to the

Indian & negro races," Simms sought to make the discourse "equally fanciful & philosophic" (Simms to Sarah Drew Griffin, June 1841; *Letters* 6:29). Simms scholars are divided on the merits of "Oakatibbé," some lamenting the loss of the sharp focus of "Indian Sketch" and others maintaining that the timeliness and urgency of the "bold, original" debate outweighs any diminution of narrative excellence.

ᕙ *Oakatibbe, or, the Choctaw Sampson*

CHAPTER I.

It was in the year 182—, that I first travelled in the vallies of the great southwest. Circumstances, influenced in no slight degree by an "errant disposition," beguiled me to the Choctaw nation, which, at that time, occupied the greater part of the space below the Tennessee line, lying between the rivers Tombeckbe and Mississippi, as low, nearly, as the town of Jackson, then, as now, the capital of the State of Mississippi. I loitered for several weeks in and about this region, without feeling the loss or the weight of time. Yet, the reader is not to suppose that travelling at that day was so simple a matter, or possessed many, if any of the pleasant facilities of the present. *Au contraire:* It was then a serious business. It meant *travail* rather than *travel.* The roads were few and very hard to find. Indian foot-paths—with the single exception of the great military traces laid out by General Jackson, and extending from Tennessee to Lake Ponchartrain—formed almost the only arteries known to the "Nation"; and the portions of settled country in the neighbourhood, nominally civilized only, were nearly in the same condition. Some of the Indian paths, as I experienced, seemed only to be made for the perplexity of the stranger. Like Gray's passages which "led to nothing," they constantly brought me to a stand. Sometimes they were swallowed up in swamps, and, in such cases, your future route upon the earth was to be discovered only by a deliberate and careful survey of the skies above. The openings in the trees over head alone instructed you in the course you were to pursue. You may readily imagine that this sort of progress was as little pleasant as edifying, yet, in some respects, it was not wanting in its attractions, also. To the young and ardent mind, obstacles of this nature tend rather to excite than to depress. They contain the picturesque in themselves, at times, and always bring out the moral in the man. "To learn to rough it," is an educational phrase, in the dialect of the new countries, which would be of great service, adopted as a rule of government for the young in all. To "coon a log"—a mysterious process to the uninitiated—swim a river—experiment, at a guess, upon the properties of one, and the proprieties of another route—parley with an Indian after his own fashion—not to speak of a hundred other incidents which the civilized world does not often present—will reconcile a lad of sanguine temperament to a number of annoyances much more serious than will attend him on an expedition through our frontier countries.

It was at the close of a cloudy day in November, that I came within hail of the new but rude plantation settlements of Colonel Harris. He had but lately transferred his interests to Mississippi, from one of the "maternal thirteen"— had bought largely in the immediate neighbourhood of the Choctaw nation, and had also acquired, by purchase from the natives, certain reserves within it, to which he chiefly owes that large wealth, which, at this day, he has the reputation of possessing. In place of the stately residence which now adorns his homestead, there was then but a miserable log-house, one of the most ordinary of the country, in which, unaccompanied by his family, he held his temporary abiding place. His plantation was barely rescued from the dominions of nature. The trees were girdled only the previous winter, for his first crop, which was then upon the ground, and an excellent crop it was for that immature condition of his fields. There is no describing the melancholy aspect of such a settlement, seen in winter, on a cloudy day, and in the heart of an immense forest, through which you have travelled for miles, without glimpse of human form or habitation. The worm-fence is itself a gloomy spectacle, and the girdled trees, erect but dead, the perishing skeletons of recent life, impress you with sensations not entirely unlike those which you would experience in going over some battle-field, from which the decaying forms of man and horse have not yet been removed. The fences of Col. Harris were low in height, though of great extent. They were simply sufficient to protect the fields from the random assaults of cattle. Of his out-houses, the most respectable in size, solidity and security, was the corn crib. His negro-houses, like the log-house in which he himself dwelt, were only so many temporary shanties, covered with poles and thatched with bark and pine-straw. In short, every thing that met my eye only tended the more to frown upon my anticipations of a cheerful fireside and a pleasant arrangement of the creature-comforts. But my doubts and apprehensions all vanished at the moment of my reception. I was met by the proprietor with that ease and warmth of manner which does not seem to be conscious of any deficiencies of preparation, and is resolved that there shall be none which sincere hospitality can remedy. I was soon prepared to forget that there were deficiencies. I felt myself very soon at home. I had letters to Col. Harris, which made me particularly welcome, and in ten minutes we were both in full sail amongst all the shallows and deeps of ordinary conversation.

Not that we confined ourselves to these. Our discourse, after a little while, turned upon a circumstance which I had witnessed on riding through his fields and while approaching his dwelling, which struck me with considerable surprise, and disturbed, in some degree, certain pre-conceived opinions in my mind. I had seen, interspersed with his negro labourers, a goodly number of Indians of both sexes, but chiefly young persons, all equally and busily employed in cotton picking. The season had been a protracted one, and favourable, accordingly, to the maturing of great numbers of the bolls which an early and severe winter must have otherwise destroyed. The crop, in consequence, had been so great as to be beyond the ability, to gather in and harvest, of the "force" by which it was made. This, in the new and fertile vallies of the south-west, is an usual event. In ordinary cases, when this happens, it is the custom to buy other negroes from less productive regions, to consummate and secure the avails of labour of the original "force." The whole of these, united, are then addressed to the task of opening additional lands, which, should they yield as before, necessarily demand a second purchase of an extra number to secure and harvest, in season, the surplus fruits of their industry. The planter is very readily persuaded to make this purchase so long as the seeming necessity shall re-occur; and in this manner has he continued expanding his interests, increasing the volume of his lands, and incurring debt for these and for his slaves, at exorbitant prices, in order to the production of a commodity, every additional bag of which, disparages its own value, and depreciates the productive power, in an estimate of profit, of the industry by which it is produced. It will not be difficult, keeping this fact in mind as a sample of the profligacy of western adventure—to account, in part, for the insolvency and desperate condition of a people in possession of a country naturally the most fertile of any in the world.

The crop of Col. Harris was one of this description. It far exceeded the ability of his "force" to pick it in; but instead of buying additional slaves for the purpose, he conceived the idea of turning to account the lazy Choctaws by whom he was surrounded. He proposed to hire them at a moderate compensation, which was to be paid them weekly. The temptation of gain was greedily caught at by these hungering outcasts, and, for a few dollars, or an equivalent in goods, groceries, and so forth, some forty-five of them were soon to be seen, as busy as might be, in the prosecution of their unusual labours. The work was light and easy—none could be more so—and though not such adepts as the negro, the Indian women soon contrived to fill their bags and baskets, in the course of the day. At dark, you might behold them trudging forward under their burdens to the log-house, where the proprietor stood ready to receive them. Here he weighed their burdens, and gave them credit, nightly, for the number of pounds which they each brought in. The night of my arrival was Saturday, and the value of the whole week's labour was then to be summed up and accounted for. This necessarily made them all punctual in attendance, and nothing could be more amusing than the interest which they severally displayed as Col. Harris took out his memorandum book, and proceeded to make his entries. Every eye was fixed upon him, and an old Indian, who, though he did not work himself, represented the interests of a wife and two able-bodied daughters, planted himself directly behind this gentleman, and watched, with looks of growing sagacity, every stroke that was made in this—to him—volume of more than Egyptian mystery and hieroglyphics. Meanwhile, the squaws stood about their baskets with looks expressive of similar interest, but at the same time of laudable patience. The negroes in the rear, were scarcely less moved by curiosity, though a contemptuous grin might be seen on nearly all their countenances, as they felt their superiority in nearly every physical and intellectual respect, over the untutored savages. Many Indians were present who neither had nor sought employment. Of those employed, few or none were of middle age. But these were not wanting to the assemblage. They might be seen prowling about the rest—watchful of the concerns of their wives, sons and daughters, with just that sort and degree of interest, which the eagle may be supposed to feel, who, from his perch on the treetop or the rock, beholds the fish-hawk dart into the water in pursuit of that prey which he meditates to rend from his jaws as soon as he shall re-ascend into the air. Their interest was decidedly greater than that of the poor labourer. It was in this manner that these vultures appropriated the fruits of his industry, and there was no remedy. They commonly interfered, the moment it was declared what was due to the *employee,* to resolve the pay into a certain number of gallons of whiskey; so many pounds of tobacco; so much gunpowder and lead. If the employer, as was the case with Col. Harris, refused to furnish them with whiskey, they required him to pay in money. With this, they soon made their way to one of those moral sinks, called a grog-shop, which English civilization is always ready to plant, as its first, most familiar, and most imposing standard, among the hills and forests of the savage.

It may be supposed that this experiment upon the inflexibility of Indian character and habit—for it was an experiment which had been in trial only a single week—was a subject of no little curiosity to me, as it would most probably be to almost every person at all impressed with the humiliating moral and social deterioration which has marked this fast decaying people. Could it possibly be successful? Could a race, proud, sullen, incommunicative, wandering, be persuaded, even by gradual steps, and with the hope of certain compensation, to renounce the wild satisfaction afforded by their desultory and unconstrained modes of life? Could they be beguiled for a season into employments which, though they did not demand any severe labours, at least required pains-taking, regular industry, and that habitual attention to daily recurring tasks, which, to their roving nature, would make life a most monotonous and unattractive possession? How far the lightness of the labour and the simplicity of the employment, with the corresponding recompense, would reconcile them to its tasks, was the natural subject of my inquiry. On this head, my friend, Col. Harris, could only conjecture and speculate like myself. His experiment had been in progress but a few days. But our speculations led us to very different conclusions. He was a person of very ardent character, and sanguine, to the last degree, of the success of his project. He had no question but that the Indian, even at his present stage, might be brought under the influence of a judicious civilization. We both agreed that the first process was in procuring their labour—that this was the preliminary step, without taking which, no other could be made; but how to bring them to this was the question.

"They can be persuaded to this," was his conclusion. "Money, the popular god, is as potent with them as with our own people. They will do any thing for money. You see these now in the field. They have been there, and just as busy, and in the same number, from Monday last."

"How long will they continue?"

"As long as I can employ and pay them."

"Impossible! They will soon be dissatisfied. The men will consume and squander all the earnings of the females and the feeble. The very motive of their industry, money, to which you refer, will be lost to them after the first payment. I am convinced that a savage people, not as yet familiar with the elements of moral prudence, can only be brought to habitual labour, by the one process of coercion."

"We shall see. There is no coercion upon them now, yet they work with wonderful regularity."

"This week will end it. Savages are children in all but physical respects. To do any thing with them, you must place them in that position of responsibility, and teach them that law, without the due employment of which, any attempt to educate a child, must be an absurdity—you must teach them obedience. They must be made to know, at the outset, that they know nothing—that they must implicitly defer to the superior. This lesson they will never learn, so long as they possess the power, at any moment, to withdraw from his control."

"Yet, even were this to be allowed, there must be a limit. There must come a time when you will be required to emancipate them. In what circumstances will you find that time? You cannot keep them under this coercion always; when will you set them free?"

"When they are fit for freedom."

"How is that to be determined? Who shall decide their fitness?"

"Themselves; as in the case of the children of Israel. The children of Israel went out from bondage as soon as their own intellectual advancement had been such as to enable them to produce from their own ranks a leader like Moses:—one whose genius was equal to that of the people by whom they had been educated, and sufficient for their own proper government thereafter."

"But has not an experiment of this sort already been tried in our country?"

"Nay, I think not—I know of none."

"Yes: an Indian boy was taken in infancy from his parents, carried to one of the Northern States, trained in all the learning and habits of a Northern college and society, associated only with whites, beheld no manners, and heard no morals, but those which are known to Christian communities. His progress was satisfactory—he learned rapidly—was considered something of a prodigy, and graduated with eclât. He was then left, with the same option as the rest enjoyed, to the choice of a profession. And what was his choice? Do you not remember the beautiful little poem of Freneau on this subject? He chose the buck-skin leggins, the moccasins, bow and arrows, and the wide, wild forests, where his people dwelt."

"Freneau's poem tells the story somewhat differently. The facts upon which it is founded, however, are, I believe, very much, as you tell them. But what an experiment it was! How very silly! They take a copper-coloured boy from his people, and carry him, while yet an infant, to a remote region. Suppose, in order that the experiment may be fairly tried, that they withhold from him all knowledge of his origin. He is brought up precisely as the other lads around him. But what is the first discovery which he makes? That he is a copper-coloured boy—that he is, alone, the only copper-coloured boy—that wherever he turns he sees no likeness to himself. This begets his wonder, then his curiosity, and finally his suspicion. He soon understands—for his suspicion sharpens every faculty of observation—that he is an object of experiment. Nay, the most cautious policy in the world could never entirely keep this from a keen-thoughted urchin. His fellow pupils teach him this. He sees that, to them, he is an object of curiosity and study. They regard him, and he soon regards himself, as a creature set apart, and separated, for some peculiar purposes, from all the rest. A stern and singular sense of individuality and isolation is thus forced upon him. He asks—Am I, indeed, alone?—Who am I?—What am I?—These inquiries naturally occasion others. Does he read? Books give him the history of his race. Nay, his own story probably meets his eye in the newspapers. He learns that he is descended from a nation dwelling among the secret sources of the Susquehannah. He pries in all corners for information. The more secret his search, the more keenly does he pursue it. It becomes the great passion of his mind. He learns that his people are fierce warriors and famous hunters. He hears of their strifes with the white man—their successful strifes, when the nation could send forth its thousand bow-men, and the whites were few and feeble. Perhaps, the young pale faces around him, speak of his people, even now, as enemies; at least, as objects of suspicion, and perhaps antipathy. All these things tend to elevate and idealize, in his mind, the history of his people. He cherishes a sympathy, even beyond the natural desires of the heart, for the perishing race from which he feels himself, "like a limb, cast bleeding and torn." The curiosity to see his ancestry—the people of his tribe and country—would be the most natural feeling of the white boy, under similar circumstances—shall we wonder that it is the predominant passion in the bosom of the Indian, whose very complexion forces him away from any connection with the rest! My idea of the experiment—if such a proceeding may be called an experiment—is soon spoken. As a statement of facts, I see nothing to provoke wonder. The result was the most natural thing in the world, and a man of ordinary powers of reflection might easily have predicted it, precisely as it happened. The only wonder is, that there should be found, among persons of common education and sagacity, men who should have undertaken such an experiment, and fancied that they were busy in a moral and philosophical problem."

"Why, how would you have the experiment tried?"

"As it was tried upon the Hebrews, upon the Saxons—upon every savage people who ever became civilized. It cannot be tried upon an individual: it must be tried upon a nation—at least upon a community, sustained by no succour from without—having no forests or foreign shores upon which to turn their eyes for sympathy—having no mode or hope of escape—under the full control of an already civilized people—and sufficiently numerous among themselves, to find sympathy, against those necessary rigours which at first will seem oppressive, but which will be the only hopeful process by which to enforce the work of improvement. They must find this sympathy from beholding others, like themselves in aspect, form, feature and condition, subject to the same unusual restraints. In this contemplation they will be content to pursue their labours under a restraint which they cannot displace. But the natural law must be satisfied. There must be opportunities yielded for the indulgence of the legitimate passions. The young of both sexes among the subjected people, must commune and form ties in obedience to the requisitions of nature and according to their national customs. What, if the Indian student, on whom the "experiment" was tried, had paid his addresses to a white maiden! What a revulsion of the moral and social sense would have followed his proposition in the mind of the Saxon damsel;—and, were she to consent, what a commotion in the community in which she lived. And this revulsion and commotion would have been perfectly natural, and, accordingly, perfectly proper. God has made an obvious distinction between certain races of men, setting them apart, and requiring them to be kept so, by subjecting them to the resistance and rebuke of one of the most jealous sentinels of sense which we possess—the eye. The prejudices of this sense, require that the natural barriers should be maintained, and hence it becomes necessary that the race in subjection, should be sufficiently numerous to enable it to carry out the great object of every distinct community, though, perchance, it may happen to be an inferior one. In process of time, the beneficial and blessing effects of labour would be felt and understood by the most ignorant and savage of the race. Perhaps, not in one generation, or in two, but after the fifth and seventh, as it is written, "of those who keep my commandments." They would soon discover that, though compelled to toil, their toils neither enfeebled their strength nor impaired their happiness—that, on the contrary, they still resulted in their increasing strength, health, and comfort;—that their food, which before was precarious, depending on the caprices of the seasons, or the uncertainties of the chase, was now equally plentiful, wholesome and certain. They would also perceive that, instead of the sterility which is usually the destiny of all wandering tribes, and one of the processes by which they perish—the fecundity of their people was wonderfully increased. These discoveries—if time be allowed to make them—would tacitly reconcile them to that inferior position of their race, which is proper and inevitable, so long as their intellectual inferiority shall continue. And what would have been the effect upon our Indians—decidedly the noblest race of aborigines that the world has ever known—if, instead of buying their scalps at prices varying from five to fifty pounds each, we had conquered and subjected them? Will any one pretend to say that they would not have increased with the restraints and enforced toils of our superior genius?—that they would not, by this time, have formed a highly valuable and noble integral in the formation of our national strength and character? Perhaps their civilization would have been comparatively easy—the Hebrews required four hundred years—the Britons and Saxons, possibly, half that time after the Norman Conquest. Differing in colour from their conquerors, though I suspect, with a natural genius superior to that of the ancient Britons, at the time of the Roman invasion under Julius Caesar, the struggle between the two races must have continued for some longer time, but the union would have been finally effected, and then, as in the case of the Englishman, we should have possessed a race, in their progeny, which, in moral and physical structure, might have challenged competition with the world."

"Ay, but the difficulty would have been in the conquest."

"True, that would have been the difficulty. The American colonists were few in number and feeble in resource. The nations from which they emerged put forth none of their strength in sending them forth. Never were colonies so inadequately provided—so completely left to themselves; and hence the peculiar injustice and insolence of the subsequent exactions of the British, by which they required their colonies to support their schemes of aggrandizement and expenditure by submitting to extreme taxation. Do you suppose, if the early colonists had been powerful, that they would have ever deigned to treat for lands with the roving hordes of savages whom they found on the continent? Never! Their purchases and treaties were not for lands, but tolerance. They bought permission to remain without molestation. The amount professedly given for land, was simply a tribute paid to the superior strength of the Indian, precisely as we paid it to Algiers and the Musselmens, until we grew strong enough to whip them into respect. If, instead of a few ships and a few hundred men, timidly making their approaches along the shores of Manhattan, Penobscot and Ocracocke, some famous leader, like Æneas, had brought his entire people—suppose them to be the persecuted Irish—what a wondrous difference would have taken place. The Indians would have been subjected—would have sunk into their proper position of humility and dependence; and, by this time, might have united with their conquerors, producing, perhaps, along the great ridge of the Alleghany, the very noblest specimens of humanity, in mental and bodily stature, that the world has ever witnessed. The Indians were taught to be insolent by the fears and feebleness of the whites. They were flattered by fine words, by rich presents, and abundance of deference, until the ignorant savage, but a single degree above the brute—who, until then, had never been sure of his porridge for more than a day ahead—took airs upon himself, and became one of the most conceited and arrogant lords in creation. The colonists grew wiser as they grew stronger; but the evil was already done, and we are reaping some of the bitter fruits, at this day, of seed unwisely sown in that. It may be that we shall yet see the experiment tried fairly."

"Ah, indeed—where?"

"In Mexico—by the Texians. Let the vain, capricious, ignorant, and dastardly wretches who now occupy and spoil the face and fortunes of the former country, persevere in pressing war upon those sturdy adventurers, and their doom is written. I *fear* it may be the sword—I *hope* it may be the milder fate of bondage and subjection. Such a fate would save, and raise them finally to a far higher condition than they have ever before enjoyed. Thirty thousand Texians, each with his horse and rifle, would soon make themselves masters of the city of Montezuma, and then may you see the experiment tried upon a scale sufficiently extensive to make it a fair one. But your Indian student drawn from

"Susquehannah's farthest springs,"

and sent to Cambridge, would present you with some such moral picture as that of the prisoner described by Sterne. His chief employment, day by day, would consist in notching upon his stick, the undeviating record of his daily suffering. It would be to him an experiment almost as full of torture, as that of the Scottish Boot, the Spanish Thumb-screw—or any of those happy devices of ancient days, for impressing pleasant principles upon the mind, by impressing unpleasant feelings upon the thews, joints and sinews. I wish that some one of our writers, familiar with mental analysis, would make this poem of Freneau, the subject of a story. I think it would yield admirable material. To develope the thoughts and feelings of an Indian boy, taken from his people, ere yet he has formed such a knowledge of them, or of others, as to have begun to discuss or to compare their differences—follow him to a college such as that of Princeton or Cambridge—watch him within its walls—amid the crowd, but not of it—looking only within himself, while all others are looking into him, or trying to do so—surrounded by active, sharp-witted lads of the Anglo-Norman race; undergoing an hourly repeated series of moral spasms, as he hears them wantonly or thoughtlessly dwell upon the wild and ignorant people from whom he is chosen;—listening, though without seeming to listen, to their crude speculations upon the great problem which is to be solved only by seeing how well he can endure his spasms, and what use he will make of his philosophy if he survives it—then, when the toils of study and the tedious restraints and troubles of prayer and recitation are got over, to behold and describe the joy with which the happy wretch flings by his fetters, when he is dismissed from those walls which have witnessed his tortures—even supposing him to remain (which is very unlikely,) until his course of study is pronounced to be complete. With what curious pleasure will he stop in the shadow of the first deep forest, to tear from his limbs those garments which make him seem unlike his people! How quick will be the beating at his heart as he endeavours to dispose about his shoulders the blanket robe in the manner in which it is worn by the chief warrior of his tribe! With what keen effort—should he have had any previous knowledge of his kindred—will he seek to compel his memory to restore every, the slightest, custom or peculiarity which distinguished them when his eyes were first withdrawn from the parental tribe; and how closely will he imitate their indomitable pride and lofty, cold, superiority of look and gesture, as, at evening, he enters the native hamlet, and takes his seat in silence at the door of the Council House, waiting, without a word, for the summons of the Elders!"

"Quite a picture. I think with you, that, in good hands, such a subject would prove a very noble one."

"But the story would not finish here. Supposing all this to have taken place, just as we are told it did—supposing the boy to have graduated at college, and to have flung away the distinction—to have returned, as has been described, to his savage costume—to the homes and habits of his people;—it is not so clear that he will fling away all the lessons of wisdom, all the knowledge of facts, which he will have acquired from the tuition of the superior race. A natural instinct, which is above all lessons, must be complied with; but this done—and when the first tumults of his blood have subsided, which led him to defeat the more immediate object of his social training—there will be a gradual resumption of the educational influence in his mind, and his intellectual habits will begin to exercise themselves anew. They will be provoked necessarily to this exercise by what he beholds around him. He will begin to perceive, in its true aspects, the wretchedness of that hunter-state, which, surveyed at a distance, appeared only the embodiment of stoical heroism and the most elevated pride. He will see and lament the squalid poverty of his people; which, his first lessons in civilization must have shown him, is due only to the mode of life and pursuits in which they are engaged. Their beastly intoxication will offend his tastes—their superstition and ignorance —the circumscribed limits of their capacity for judging of things and relations beyond the life of the bird or beast of prey—will awaken in him a sense of shame when he feels that they are his kindred. The insecurity of their liberties will awaken his fears, for he will instantly see that the great body of the people in every aboriginal nation are the veriest slaves in the world; and the degrading exhibitions which they make in their filth and drunkenness, which reduce the man to a loathesomeness of aspect which is never reached by the vilest beast which he hunts or scourges, will be beheld by the Indian student in very lively contrast with all that has met his eyes during that novitiate among the white sages, the processes of which have been to him so humiliating and painful. His memory reverts to that period with feelings of reconciliation. The torture is over, and the remembrance of former pain, endured with manly fortitude, is comparatively a pleasure. A necessary reaction in his mind takes place; and, agreeably to the laws of nature, what will, and what should follow, but that he will seek to become the tutor and the reformer of his people? They themselves will tacitly raise him to this position, for the man of the forest will defer even to the negro who has been educated by the white man. He will try to teach them habits of greater method and industry—he will overthrow the altars of their false gods—he will seek to bind the wandering tribes together under one head and in one nation—he will prescribe uniform laws of government. He will succeed in some things—he will fail in others; he will offend the pride of the self-conceited and the mulish—the priesthood will be the first to declare against him—and he will be murdered most probably, as was Romulus, and afterwards deified. If he escapes this fate, he will yet, most likely, perish from mortification under failure, or, in consequence of those mental strifes which spring from that divided allegiance between the feelings belonging to his savage, and those which have had their origin in his Christian schools—those natural strifes between the acquisitions of civilization on the one hand, and those instinct tendencies of the blood which distinguish his connection with the inferior race. In this conflict, he will, at length, when the enthusiasm of his youthful zeal has become chilled by frequent and unexpected defeat, falter, and finally fail. But will there be nothing done for his people? Who can say? I believe that no seed falls without profit by the wayside. Even if the truth produces no immediate fruits, it forms a moral manure which fertilizes the otherwise barren heart, in preparation for the more favourable season. The Indian student may fail, as his teachers did, in realizing the object for which he has striven; and this sort of failure, is, by the way, one of the most ordinary of human allotment. The desires of man's heart, by an especial Providence, that always wills him to act for the future, generally aim at something far beyond his own powers of performance. But the labour has not been taken in vain, in the progress of successive ages, which has achieved even a small part of its legitimate purposes. The Indian student has done for his people much more than the white man achieves ordinarily for his generation, if he has only secured to their use a single truth which they knew not before—if he has overthrown only one of their false gods—if he has smitten off the snaky head of only one of their superstitious prejudices. If he has added to their fields of corn a field of millet, he has induced one farther physical step towards moral improvement. Nay, if there be no other result, the very deference which they will have paid him, as the *elève* of the white man, will be a something gained of no little importance, towards inducing their more ready, though still tardy, adoption of the laws and guidance of the superior race."

Chapter II.

I am afraid that my reader will suffer quite as much under this long discussion, as did my excellent companion, Col. Harris. But he is not to suppose that all the views here expressed, were uttered consecutively, as they are above set down. I have simply condensed, for more easy comprehension, the amount of a conversation which lasted some two hours. I may add, that, at the close, we discovered, as is very often the case among disputants, there was very little substantial difference between us. Our dispute, if any, was rather verbal than philosophical. On the subject of his experiment, however, Col. Harris fancied, that, in employing some forty or fifty of the Indians, of both sexes, he had brought together a community sufficiently large for the purposes of a fair experiment. Still, I thought that the argument remained untouched. They were not subordinate; they were not subdued; they could still exercise a free and absolute will, in despite of authority and reason. He could resort to no method for compelling their obedience; and we know pretty well what will result—even among white men—from the option of vagrancy.

"But," I urged, "even if the objections which I have stated, fail of defeating your scheme, there is yet another agent of defeat working against it, in the presence of these elderly Indians, who do not join in the labour, and yet, according to your own showing, still prowl in waiting to snatch from the hands of the industrious all the fruits of their toil. The natural effect of this will be to discourage the industry of those who work; for, unless the labourer is permitted to enjoy a fair proportion of the fruits of his labour, it is morally impossible that he should long continue it."

Our conference was interrupted by the appearance of the labourers, Indians and Negroes, who now began to come in, bringing with them the cotton which they had severally gathered during the day. This was accumulated in the court-yard, before the dwelling; each Indian, man or woman, standing beside the bag or basket which contained the proofs of his industry. You may readily suppose, that, after the dialogue and discussion which is partially reported above, I felt no little interest in observing the proceedings. The parties present were quite numerous. I put the negroes out of the question, though they were still to be seen, lingering in the background, grinning spectators of the scene. The number of Indians, men and women, who had *that day* been engaged in picking, was thirty-nine. Of these, twenty-six were females; three, only, might be accounted men, and ten were boys—none over sixteen. Of the females the number of elderly and young women was nearly equal. Of the men, one was very old and infirm; a second of middle age, who appeared to be something of an idiot; while the third, whom I regarded for this reason with more consideration and interest than all the party beside, was one of the most noble specimens of physical manhood that my eyes had ever beheld. He was fully six feet three inches in height, slender but muscular in the extreme. He possessed a clear, upright, open, generous cast of countenance, as utterly unlike that sullen, suspicious expression of the ordinary Indian face, as you can possibly imagine. Good nature and good sense were the predominant characteristics of his features, and—which is quite as unusual with Indians when in the presence of strangers—he laughed and jested with all the merry, unrestrainable vivacity of a youth of Anglo-Saxon breed. How was it that so noble a specimen of manhood consented to herd with the women and the weak of his tribe, in descending to the mean labours which the warriors were accustomed to despise?

"He must either be a fellow of great sense, or he must be a coward. He is degraded."

Such was my conclusion. The answer of Col. Harris was immediate.

"He is a fellow of good sense, and very far from being a coward. He is one of the best Choctaws that I know."

"A man, then, to be a leader of his people. It is a singular proof of good sense and great mental flexibility, to find an Indian, who is courageous, voluntarily assuming tasks which are held to be degrading among the hunters. I should like to talk with this fellow when you are done. What is his name?"

"His proper name is Oakatibbé; but that by which he is generally known among us—his English name is Slim Sampson, a name which he gets on the score of his superior strength and great slenderness. The latter name, in ordinary use, has completely superseded the former, even among his own people. It may be remarked, by the way, as another proof of the tacit deference of the inferior to the superior people, that most Indians prefer to use the names given by the whites to those of their own language. There are very few among them who will not contrive, after a short intimacy with white men, to get some epithet—which is not always a complimentary one—but which they cling to as tenaciously as they would to some far more valuable possession."

This little dialogue was whispered during the stir which followed the first arrival of the labourers. We had no opportunity for more.

The rest of the Indians were in no respect remarkable. There were some eight or ten women, and perhaps as many men, who did not engage in the toils of their companions, though they did not seem the less interested in the result. These, I noted, were all, in greater or less degree, elderly persons. One was full eighty years old, and a strange fact for one so venerable, was the most confirmed drunkard of the tribe. When the cotton pickers advanced with their baskets, the hangers-on drew nigh also, deeply engrossed with the prospect of reaping the gains from that industry which they had no mood to emulate. These, however, were very moderate, in most cases. Where a negro woman picked from one to two hundred weight of cotton, *per diem,* the Indian woman, at the utmost, gathered sixty-five; and the general average among them, did not much exceed forty-five. Slim Sampson's basket weighed eighty-six pounds—an amount considerably greater than any of the rest— and Col. Harris assured me, that his average during the week had been, at no time, much below this quantity.

The proceedings had gone on without interruption or annoyance for the space of half an hour. Col. Harris had himself weighed every basket, with scrupulous nicety, and recorded the several weights opposite to the name of the picker, in a little memorandum book which he kept exclusively for this purpose; and it was amusing to see with what pleasurable curiosity, the Indians, men and women, watched the record which stated their several accounts. The whole labour of the week was to be settled for that night (Saturday), and hence the unusual gathering of those whose only purpose in being present, was to grasp at the spoils.

Among these hawks was one middle-aged Indian—a stern, sulky fellow, of considerable size and strength—whose skin was even then full of liquor, which contributing to the usual insolence of his character, made him at times very troublesome. He had more than once, during the proceedings, interfered between Col. Harris and his *employées,* in such a manner as to provoke, in the mind of that gentleman, no small degree of irritation. The English name of this Indian, was Loblolly Jack. Loblolly Jack had a treble motive for being present and conspicuous. He had among the labourers, a wife and two daughters. When the baskets of these were brought forward to be weighed, he could no longer be kept in the background, but, resolutely thrusting himself before the rest, he handled basket, book and steelyards in turn, uttered his suspicions of foul play, and insisted upon a close examination of every movement which was made by the proprietor. In this manner, he made it very difficult for him to proceed in his duties; and his conduct, to do the Indians justice, seemed quite as annoying to them as to Col. Harris. The wife frequently expostulated with him, in rather bolder language than an Indian squaw is apt to use to her liege lord; while Slim Sampson, after a few words of reproach, expressed in Choctaw, concluded by telling him in plain English, that he was, "a rascal dog." He seemed the only one among them who had no fear of the intruder. Loblolly Jack answered in similar terms, and Slim Sampson clearing the baskets at a single bound, confronted him with a show of fight, and a direct challenge to it, on the spot where they stood. The other seemed no ways loth. He recoiled a pace, drew his knife—a sufficient signal for Slim Sampson to get his own in readiness—and, thus opposed, they stood, glaring upon each other with eyes of the most determined expression of malignity. A moment more—an additional word of provocation from either—and blows must have taken place. But Col. Harris, a man of great firmness, put himself between them, and calling to one of his negroes, bade him bring out from the house his double-barreled gun.

"Now," said he, "my good fellows, the first man of you that lifts his hand to strike, I'll shoot him down; so look to it. Slim Sampson, go back to your basket, and don't meddle in this business. Don't you suppose that I'm man enough to keep Loblolly Jack in order? You shall see."

It is not difficult for a determined white man to keep an Indian in subordination, so long as both of them are sober. A few words more convinced Loblolly Jack, who had not yet reached the reckless stage in drunkenness, that his wiser course was to give back and keep quiet, which he did. The storm subsided almost as suddenly as it had been raised, and Col. Harris resumed his occupation. Still, the Indian who had proved so troublesome before, continued his annoyances, though in a manner somewhat less audacious. His last proceeding was to get as nigh as he could to the basket which was about to be weighed—his wife's basket—and, with the end of a stick, adroitly introduced into some little hole, he contrived to press the basket downwards, and thus to add so much to the weight of the cotton, that his squaw promised to bear off the palm of victory in that day's picking. Nobody saw the use to which the stick was put, and for a few moments no one suspected it. Had the cunning fellow been more moderate, he might have succeeded in his attempt upon the steelyards; but his pressure increased with every approach which was made to a determination of the weight, and while all were wondering that so small a basket should be so heavy, Slim Sampson discovered and pointed out the trick to Col. Harris, who suddenly snatching the stick from the grasp of the Indian, was about to lay it over his head. But this my expostulation prevented; and, after some delay, the proceedings were finally ended; but in such a manner as to make my friend somewhat more doubtful than he had been before, on the subject of his experiment. He paid off their accounts, some in cloths and calicoes, of which he had provided a small supply for this purpose; but the greater number, under the evil influence of the idle and the elder, demanded and received their pay in money.

CHAPTER III.

It was probably about ten o'clock that evening. We had finished supper, and Col. H. and myself had resumed the subject upon which we had been previously engaged. But the discussion was languid, and both of us were unquestionably lapsing into that state, when each readily receives an apology for retiring for the night, when we were startled from our drowsy tendencies by a wild and terrible cry, such as made me thrill instinctively with the conviction that something terrible had taken place. We started instantly to our feet, and threw open the door. The cry was more distinct and piercing, and its painful character could not be mistaken. It was a cry of death—of sudden terror, and great and angry excitement. Many voices were mingled together— some expressive of fury, some of fear, and many of lamentation. The tones which finally prevailed over, and continued long after all others had subsided, were those of women.

"These sounds come from the shop of that trader. Those rascally Choctaws are drunk and fighting, and ten to one but somebody is killed among them!" was the exclamation of Col. H. "These sounds are familiar to me. I have heard them once before. They signify murder. It is a peculiar whoop which the Indians have, to denote the shedding of blood—to show that a crime has been committed."

The words had scarcely been uttered, before Slim Sampson came suddenly out into the road, and joined us at the door. Col. H. instantly asked him to enter, which he did. When he came fully into the light, we discovered that he had been drinking. His eyes bore sufficient testimony to the fact, though his drunkenness seemed to have subsided into something like stupor. His looks were heavy, rather than calm. He said nothing, but drew nigh to the fireplace, and seated himself upon one corner of the hearth. I now discovered that his hands and hunting shirt were stained with blood. His eyes beheld the bloody tokens at the same time, and he turned his hand curiously over, and examined it by the fire-light.

"Kurnel," said he, in broken English, "me is one dog fool!"

"How, Sampson?"

"Me drunk—me fight—me kill Loblolly Jack! Look ya! Dis blood 'fore my hands. 'Tis Loblolly Jack blood! He dead! I stick him wid de knife!"

"Impossible! What made you do it?"

"Me drunk! Me dog fool!—Drink whiskey at liquor shop—hab money— buy whiskey—drunk come, and Loblolly Jack dead!"

This was the substance of the story, which was confirmed a few moments after, by the appearance of several other Indians, the friends of the two parties. From these it appeared that all of them had been drinking, at the shop of Ligon, the white man; that, when heated with liquor, both Loblolly Jack and Slim Sampson had, as with one accord, resumed the strife which had been arrested by the prompt interference of Col. H.; that, from words they had got to blows, and the former had fallen, fatally hurt, by a single stroke from the other's hand and knife.

The Indian law, like that of the Hebrews, is eye for eye, tooth for tooth, life for life. The fate of Slim Sampson was ordained. He was to die on the morrow. This was well understood by himself as by all the rest. The wound of Loblolly Jack had proved mortal. He was already dead; and it was arranged among the parties that Slim Sampson was to remain that night, if permitted, at the house of Col. H., and to come forth at early sunrise to execution. Col. H. declared his willingness that the criminal should remain in his house; but, at the same time, disclaimed all responsibility in the business; and assured the old chief, whose name was "Rising Smoke," that he would not be answerable for his appearance.

"He won't run," said the other, indifferently.

"But you will not put a watch over him—I will not suffer more than the one to sleep in my house."

The old chief repeated his assurance that Slim Sampson would not seek to fly. No guard was to be placed over him. He was expected to remain quiet, and come forth to execution at the hour appointed.

"He got for dead," continued Rising Smoke—"he know the law. He will come and dead like a man. Oakatibbé got big heart." Every word which the old fellow uttered went to mine.

What an eulogy was this upon Indian inflexibility! What confidence in the passive obedience of the warrior! After a little farther dialogue, they departed,—friends and enemies—and the unfortunate criminal was left with us alone. He still maintained his seat upon the hearth. His muscles were composed and calm—not rigid. His thoughts, however, were evidently busy; and, once or twice, I could see that his head was moved slowly from side to side, with an expression of mournful self-abandonment. I watched every movement and look with the deepest interest, while Col. H. with a concern necessarily deeper than my own, spoke with him freely, on the subject of his crime. It was, in fact, because of the affair of Col. H. that the unlucky deed was committed. It was true, that, for this, the latter gentleman was in no wise responsible; but that did not lessen, materially, the pain which he felt at having, however unwittingly, occasioned it. He spoke with the Indian in such terms of condolence as conventional usage among us has determined to be the most proper. He proffered to buy off the friends and relatives of the deceased, if the offence could be commuted for money. The poor fellow was very grateful, but, at the same time, told him that the attempt was useless.—The tribe had never been known to permit such a thing, and the friends of Loblolly Jack were too much his enemies, to consent to any commutation of the penalty.

Col. H., however, was unsatisfied, and determined to try the experiment. The notion had only suggested itself to him after the departure of the Indians. He readily conjectured where he should find them, and we immediately set off for the grogshop of Ligon. This was little more than a quarter of a mile from the plantation. When we reached it, we found the Indians, generally, in the worst possible condition to be treated with. They were, most of them, in the last stages of intoxication. The dead body of the murdered man was stretched out in the piazza, or gallery, half covered with a bear-skin. The breast was bare—a broad, bold, manly bosom—and the wound, a deep narrow gash, around which the blood stood, clotted, in thick, frothy masses. The nearer relations of the deceased, were perhaps the most drunk of the assembly. Their grief necessarily entitled them to the greatest share of consolation, and this took the form of whiskey. Their love of excess, and the means of indulgence, encouraged us with the hope that their vengeance might be bought off without much difficulty, but we soon found ourselves very much deceived. Every effort, every offer, proved fruitless; and after vainly exhausting every art and argument, old Rising Smoke drew us aside to tell us that the thing was impossible.

"Oakatibbé hab for die, and no use for talk. De law is make for Oakatibbé, and Loblolly Jack, and me, Rising Smoke, and all, just the same. Oakatibbé will dead to-morrow."

With sad hearts, we left the maudlin and miserable assembly. When we returned, we found Slim Sampson employed in carving with his knife upon the handle of his tomahawk. In the space thus made, he introduced a small bit of flattened silver, which seemed to have been used for a like purpose on some previous occasion. It was rudely shaped like a bird, and was probably one of those trifling ornaments which usually decorate the stocks of rifle and shot-gun. I looked with increasing concern upon his countenance. What could a spectator—one unacquainted with the circumstances—have met with there? Nothing, surely, of that awful event which had just taken place, and of that doom which now seemed so certainly to await him. He betrayed no sort of interest in our mission. His look and manner denoted his own perfect conviction of its inutility; and when we told him what had taken place, he neither answered nor looked up.

It would be difficult to describe my feelings and those of my companion. The more we reflected upon the affair, the more painful and oppressive did our thoughts become. A pain, little short of horror, coupled itself with every emotion. We left the Indian still beside the fire. He had begun a low chanting song just before we retired, in his own language, which was meant as a narrative of the chief events of his life. The death song—for such it was—is neither more nor less than a recital of those deeds which it will be creditable to a son or a relative to remember. In this way the valor of their great men, and the leading events in their history, are transmitted through successive ages. He was evidently refreshing his own memory in preparation for the morrow. He was arranging the narrative of the past, in proper form for the acceptance of the future.

We did not choose to disturb him in this vocation, and retired. When we had got to our chamber, H. who already had one boot off, exclaimed suddenly—"Look you, S., this fellow ought not to perish in this manner. We should make an effort to save him. We must save him!"

"What will you do?"

"Come—let us go back and try and urge him to flight. He can escape easily while all these fellows are drunk. He shall have my best horse for the purpose."

We returned to the apartment.

"Slim Sampson."

"Kurnel!" was the calm reply.

"There's no sense in your staying here to be shot."

"Ugh!" was the only answer, but in an assenting tone.

"You're not a bad fellow—you didn't mean to kill Loblolly Jack—it's very hard that you should die for what you didn't wish to do. You're too young to die. You've got a great many years to live. You ought to live to be an old man and have sons like yourself; and there's a great deal of happiness in this world, if a man only knows where to look for it. But a man that's dead is of no use to himself, or to his friends, or his enemies. Why should you die—why should you be shot?"

"Eh?"

"Hear me; your people are all drunk at Ligon's—blind drunk—deaf drunk—they can neither see nor hear. They won't get sober till morning—perhaps not then. You've been across the Mississippi, haven't you? You know the way?"

The reply was affirmative.

"Many Choctaws live over the Mississippi now—on the Red River, and far beyond, to the Red Hills. Go to them—they will take you by the hand—they will give you one of their daughters to wife—they will love you—they will make you a chief. Fly, Sampson, fly to them—you shall have one of my horses, and before daylight you will be down the country, among the white people, and far from your enemies—Go, my good fellow, it would be a great pity that so brave a man should die."

This was the substance of my friend's exhortation. It was put into every shape, and addressed to every fear, hope, or passion which might possibly have influence over the human bosom. A strong conflict took place in the mind of the Indian, the outward signs of which were not wholly suppressible. He started to his feet, trod the floor hurriedly, and there was a tremulous quickness in the movement of his eyes, and a dilation of their orbs, which amply denoted the extent of his emotion. He turned suddenly upon us, when H. had finished speaking, and replied in language very nearly like the following.

"I love the whites—I was always a friend to the whites. I believe I love their laws better than my own. Loblolly Jack laughed at me because I loved the whites, and wanted our people to live like them. But I am of no use now. I can love them no more. My people say that I must die. How can I live?"

Such was the purport of his answer. The meaning of it was simple. He was not unwilling to avail himself of the suggestions of my friend—to fly—to live—but he could not divest himself of that habitual deference to those laws to which he had given implicit reverence from the beginning. Custom is the superior tyrant of all savage nations.

To embolden him on this subject, was now the joint object of Col. H. and myself. We spared no argument to convince him that he ought to fly. It was something in favour of our object, that the Indian regards the white man as so infinitely his superior; and, in the case of Slim Sampson, we were assisted by his own inclinations in favour of those customs of the whites, which he had already in part begun to adopt. We discussed for his benefit that which may be considered one of the leading elements in civilization—the duty of saving and keeping life as long as we can—insisted upon the morality of flying from any punishment which would deprive us of it; and at length had the satisfaction of seeing him convinced. He yielded to our arguments and solicitations, accepted the horse, which he promised voluntarily to find some early means to return, and, with a sigh—perhaps one of the first proofs of that change of feeling and of principle which he had just shown, he declared his intention to take the road instantly.

"Go to bed, Kurnel. Your horse will come back." We retired, and a few moments after heard him leave the house. I am sure that both of us felt a degree of light-heartedness which scarcely any other event could have produced. We could not sleep, however. For myself I answer—it was almost dawn before I fell into an uncertain slumber, filled with visions of scuffling Indians—the stark corpse of Loblolly Jack, being the conspicuous object, and Slim Sampson standing up for execution.

CHAPTER IV.

Neither Col. H. nor myself arose at a very early hour. Our first thoughts and feelings at waking were those of exultation. We rejoiced that we had been instrumental in saving from an ignominious death, a fellow creature, and one who seemed so worthy, in so many respects. Our exultation was not a little increased, as we reflected on the disappointment of his enemies; and we enjoyed a hearty laugh together, as we talked over the matter while putting on our clothes. When we looked from the window the area in front of the house was covered with Indians. They sat, or stood, or walked, all around the dwelling. The hour appointed for the delivery of Slim Sampson had passed, yet they betrayed no emotion. We fancied, however, that we could discern in the countenances of most among them, the sentiment of friendship or hostility for the criminal, by which they were severally governed. A dark, fiery look of exultation—a grim anticipation of delight—was evident in the faces of his enemies; while, among his friends, men and women, a subdued concern and humbling sadness, were the prevailing traits of expression.

But when we went below to meet them—when it became known that the murderer had fled, taking with him the best horse of the proprietor, the outbreak was tremendous. A terrible yell went up from the party devoted to Loblolly Jack; while the friends and relatives of Slim Sampson at once sprang to their weapons, and put themselves in an attitude of defence. We had not foreseen the effects of our interposition and advice. We did not know, or recollect, that the nearest connection of the criminal, among the Indian tribes, in the event of his escape, would be required to suffer in his place; and this, by the way, is the grand source of that security which they felt the night before, that flight would not be attempted by the destined victim. The aspect of affairs looked squally. Already was the bow bent and the tomahawk lifted. Already had the parties separated, each going to his own side, and ranging himself in front of some one opponent. The women sunk rapidly into the rear, and provided themselves with billets or fence-rails, as they occurred to their hands; while little brats of boys, ten and twelve years old, kept up a continual shrill clamour, brandishing aloft their tiny bows and *blow-guns,* which were only powerful against the lapwing and the sparrow. In political phrase, "a great crisis was at hand." The stealthier chiefs and leaders of both sides, had sunk from sight, behind the trees or houses, in order to avail themselves of all the arts of Indian strategy. Every thing promised a sudden and stern conflict. At the first show of commotion, Col. H. had armed himself. I had been well provided with pistols and bowie knife, before leaving home; and, apprehending the worst, we yet took our places as peace-makers, between the contending parties.

It is highly probable that all our interposition would have been fruitless to prevent their collision; and, though our position certainly delayed the progress of the quarrel, yet all we could have hoped to effect by our interference would have been the removal of the combatants to a more remote battle ground. But a circumstance that surprised and disappointed us all, took place, to settle the strife forever, and to reconcile the parties without any resort to blows. While the turmoil was at the highest, and we had despaired of doing any thing to prevent bloodshed, the tramp of a fast galloping horse was heard in the woods, and the next moment the steed of Col. H. made his appearance, covered with foam, Slim Sampson on his back, and still driven by the lash of his rider at the top of his speed. He leaped the enclosure, and was drawn up still quivering in every limb, in the area between the opposing Indians. The countenance of the noble fellow told his story. His heart had smitten him by continual reproaches, at the adoption of a conduct unknown in his nation; and which all its hereditary opinions had made cowardly and infamous. Besides, he remembered the penalties which, in consequence of his flight, must fall heavily upon his people. Life was sweet to him—very sweet! He had the promise of many bright years before him. His mind was full of honourable and—speaking in comparative phrase—lofty purposes, for the improvement of himself and nation. We have already sought to show that, by his conduct, he had taken one large step in resistance to the tyrannous usages of customs in order to introduce the elements of civilization among his people. But he could not withstand the reproaches of a conscience formed upon principles which his own genius was not equal to overthrow. His thoughts, during his flight, must have been of a very humbling character; but his features now denoted only pride, exultation and a spirit strengthened by resignation against the worst. By his flight and subsequent return, he had, in fact, exhibited a more lively spectacle of moral firmness, than would have been displayed by his simple submission in remaining. He seemed to feel this. It looked out from his soul in every movement of his body. He leaped from his horse, exclaiming, while he slapped his breast with his open palm:

"Oakatibbé heard the voice of a chief, that said he must die. Let the chief look here—Oakatibbé is come!"

A shout went up from both parties. The signs of strife disappeared. The language of the crowd was no longer that of threatening and violence. It was understood that there would be no resistance in behalf of the condemned. Col. H. and myself, were both mortified and disappointed. Though the return of Slim Sampson, had obviously prevented a combat *à outrance,* in which a dozen or more might have been slain, still we could not but regret the event. The life of such a fellow seemed to both of us, to be worth the lives of any hundred of his people.

Never did man carry with himself more simple nobleness. He was at once surrounded by his friends and relatives. The hostile party, from whom the executioners were to be drawn, stood looking on at some little distance, the very pictures of patience. There was no sort of disposition manifested among them, to hurry the proceedings. Though exulting in the prospect of soon shedding the blood of one whom they esteemed an enemy, yet all was dignified composure and forbearance. The signs of exultation were no where to be seen. Meanwhile, a conversation was carried on in low, soft accents, unmarked by physical action of any kind, between the condemned and two other Indians. One of these was the unhappy mother of the criminal—the other was his uncle. They rather listened to his remarks, than made any of their own. The dialogue was conducted in their own language. After a while this ceased, and he made a signal which seemed to be felt rather than understood, by all the Indians, friends and enemies. All of them started into instant intelligence. It was a sign that he was ready for the final proceedings. He rose to his feet and they surrounded him. The groans of the old woman, his mother, were now distinctly audible, and she was led away by the uncle, who, placing her among the other women, returned to the condemned, beside whom he now took his place. Col. H. and myself, also drew nigh. Seeing us, Oakatibbé simply said, with a smile:

"Ah, kurnel, you see, Injun man ain't strong like white man!"

Col. H. answered with emotion.

"I would have saved you, Sampson."

"Oakatibbé hab for dead!" said the worthy fellow, with another, but a very wretched smile.

His firmness was unabated. A procession was formed, which was headed by three sturdy fellows, carrying their rifles conspicuously upon their shoulders. These were the appointed executioners, and were all near relatives of the man who had been slain. There was no mercy in their looks. Oakatibbé followed immediately after these. He seemed pleased that we should accompany him to the place of execution. Our way lay through a long avenue of stunted pines, which conducted us to a spot where an elevated ridge on either hand produced a broad and very prettily defined valley. My eyes, in all this progress, were scarcely ever drawn off from the person of him who was to be the principal actor in the approaching scene. Never, on any occasion, did I behold a man with a step more firm—a head so unbent—a countenance so sweetly calm, though grave—and of such quiet unconcern, at the obvious fate in view. Yet there was nothing in his deportment of that effort which would be the case with most white men on a similar occasion, who seek to wear the aspect of heroism. He walked as to a victory, but he walked with a staid, even dignity, calmly, and without the flush of any excitement on his cheek. In his eye there was none of that feverish curiosity, which seeks for the presence of his executioner, and cannot be averted from the contemplation of the mournful paraphernalia of death. His look was like that of the strong man, conscious of his inevitable doom, and prepared, as it is inevitable, to meet it with corresponding indifference.

The grave was now before us. It must have been prepared at the first dawn of the morning. The executioners paused, when they had reached a spot within thirty steps of it. But the condemned passed on, and stopped only on the edge of its open jaws. The last trial was at hand with all its terrors. The curtain was about to drop, and the scene of life, with all its hopes and promises and golden joys—even to an Indian golden—was to be shut forever. I felt a painful and numbing chill pass through my frame, but I could behold no sign of change in him. He now beckoned his friends around him. His enemies drew nigh also, but in a remoter circle. He was about to commence his song of death—the narrative of his performances, his purposes, all his living experience. He began a low chant, slow, measured and composed, the words seeming to consist of monosyllables only. As he proceeded, his eyes kindled, and his arms were extended. His action became impassioned, his utterance more rapid, and the tones were distinguished by increasing warmth. I could not understand a single word which he uttered, but the cadences were true and full of significance. The rise and fall of his voice, truly proportioned to the links of sound by which they were connected, would have yielded a fine lesson to the European teacher of school eloquence. His action was as graceful as that of a mighty tree yielding to and gradually rising from the pressure of a sudden gust. I felt the eloquence which I could not understand. I fancied, from his tones and gestures, the play of the muscles of his mouth, and the dilation of his eyes, that I could detect the instances of daring valour, or good conduct, which his narrative comprised. One portion of it, as he approached the close, I certainly could not fail to comprehend. He evidently spoke of his last unhappy affray with the man whom he had slain. His head was bowed— the light passed from his eyes, his hands were folded upon his heart, and his voice grew thick and husky. Then came the narrative of his flight. His glance was turned upon Col. H. and myself, and, at the close, he extended his hand to us both. We grasped it earnestly, and with a degree of emotion which I would not now seek to describe. He paused. The catastrophe was at hand. I saw him step back, so as to place himself at the very verge of the grave—he then threw open his breast—a broad, manly, muscular bosom, that would have sufficed for a Hercules—one hand he struck upon the spot above the heart, where it remained—the other was raised above his head. This was the signal. I turned away with a strange sickness. I could look no longer. In the next instant I heard the simultaneous report, as one, of the three rifles, and when I again looked, they were shoveling in the fresh mould, upon the noble form of one, who, under other more favouring circumstances, might have been a father to his nation.

"LUCAS DE AYLLON" is an important work of fiction for several reasons. First, it clearly demonstrates Simms's "strong sympathy" with the American Indian: as much as any other of his works, it presents its Indian characters as not only equal to, but—in terms of their honesty and spirituality—superior to its European characters. Second, its setting in time, the early sixteenth century, is among the earliest of Simms's many works designed to recount in fiction the development of what would become the United States. The story demonstrates that the values, the suffering, and the eventual triumph of the Indians are, to Simms, essential parts of the larger saga of early America. Third, as a stellar example of Simms's *fictional histories*, "Lucas de Ayllon" proceeds from the scant details available from the historic Ayllon expedition and enlivens these "dry bones of history" with a purely imaginative flesh-and-blood subplot intended to whet American readers' appetites for the important story of their land and their nation.

ᆺ *Lucas de Ayllon. A Historical Nouvellette**

* [SIMMS'S NOTE] *The three chapters which constitute this narrative, originally formed part of a plan which I meditated of dealing with the early histories of the South, somewhat after the manner of Henry Neele, in his romance of English History. Of course I did not mean to follow slavishly in the track pointed out by him, nor, indeed, would the peculiar and large difference between our respective materials, admit of much similarity of treatment. The reader must understand that the essential facts, as given in these sketches, are all historical, and that he is in fact engaged in the perusal of the real adventures of the Spanish voyager, enlivened only by the introduction of persons of whom history says nothing in detail—speaking vaguely, as is but too much of her wont, of those whose deficient stature fails to inform or to influence her sympathies. It is the true purpose of fiction to supply her deficiencies, and to correct her judgments. It will be difficult for any chronicler to say, of what I have written, more than that he himself knows nothing about it. But his ignorance suggests no good reason why better information should not exist in my possession.*

CHAPTER I. THE SNARE OF THE PIRATE.

Sebastian Cabot is supposed to have been the first European voyager who ever laid eyes upon the low shores of Carolina. He sailed along the coast and looked at it, but did not attempt to land,—nor was such a proceeding necessary to his objects. His single look, according to the laws and morals of that day, in civilized Europe, conferred a sufficient right upon the nation by which he was employed, to all countries which he might discover, and to all people, worshipping at other than Christian altars, by whom they might be occupied. The supposed right, however, thus acquired by Cabot, was not then asserted by the English whom he served. It was reserved for another voyager, who, with greater condescension, surveyed the coast and actually set foot upon it. This was Lucas Velasquez de Ayllon, whose adventures in Carolina we propose briefly to relate. Better for him that he had never seen it!—or, seeing it, if he had posted away from its shores for ever. They were the shores of destiny for him. But he was a bad man, and we may reasonably assume that the Just Providence had ordained that his crimes should there meet with that retribution which they were not likely to encounter any where else. Here, if he found paganism, he, at the same time, found hospitality; and here, if he brought cunning, he encountered courage! Fierce valour and generous hospitality were the natural virtues of the Southern Indians.

But we must retrace our steps for a brief period. Some preliminaries, drawn from the history of the times, are first necessary to be understood.—The feebleness of the natives of Hayti, as is well known, so far from making them objects of pity and indulgence in the sight of other Spanish conquerors, had the contrary effect of converting an otherwise brave soldiery into a reckless band of despots, as brutal in their performances as they were unwise in their tyrannies. The miserable Indians sunk under their domination. The blandness of their climate, its delicious fruits, the spontaneous gifts of nature, had rendered them too effeminate for labour and too spiritless for war. Their extermination was threatened; and, as a remedial measure, the benevolent father, Las Casas,—whose humanity stands out conspicuously in contrast with the proverbial cruelty and ferocity of his countrymen,—suggested the policy of making captures of slaves, to take the places of the perishing Haytians, from the Caribbean Islands and from the coasts of Florida. The hardy savages of these regions, inured to war, and loving it for its very dangers and exercises, were better able to endure the severe tasks which were prescribed by the conquerors. This opened a new branch of business for these bold and reckless adventurers. Predatory incursions were made along the shores of the Gulf, and seldom without profit. In this way one race was made to supersede another, in the delicious country which seems destined never to rear a population suited to its characteristics. The stubborn and sullen Caribbean was made to bend his shoulders to the burden, but did not the less save the feeble Haytian from his doom. The fierce tribes of Apalachia took the place of the delicate limbed native of the Ozama; and, in process of years, the whole southern coasts of North America became tributary, in some degree, to the novel and tyrannical policy which was yet suggested by a spirit of the most genuine benevolence.

The business of slave capture became somewhat more profitable than the fatiguing and protracted search after gold—a search much more full of delusions than of any thing substantial. It agreed better with the hardy valour of those wild adventurers. Many bold knights adopted this new vocation. Among these was one Lucas Velasquez de Ayllon, already mentioned as succeeding Cabot in his discovery of Carolina. He was a stern, cold man, brave enough for the uses to which valour was put in those days; but having the narrow contracted soul of a miser, he was incapable of noble thoughts or generous feelings. The love of gold was the settled passion of his heart, as it was too much the passion of his countrymen. He soon distinguished himself by his forays, and was among the first to introduce his people to a knowledge of Carolina, where they subsequently made themselves notorious by their atrocities. Some time in the year 1520, he set forth, in two ships, on an expedition of this nature. He seems to have been already acquainted with the region. Wending north, he soon found himself in smooth water, and gliding along by numberless pleasant islands, that broke the billows of the sea, and formed frequent and safe harborages along the coasts of the country. Attracted by a spacious opening in the shores, he stood in for a prominent headland, to which he gave the name of Cape St. Helena; a name which is now borne by the contiguous sound. The smoothness of the waters; the placid and serene security of this lovely basin; the rich green of the verdure which encountered the eyes of the adventurers on all sides, beguiled them onward; and they were at length rejoiced at the sight,—more grateful to their desire than any other, as it promised them the spoils which they sought—of numerous groups of natives that thronged the lands-ends at their approach. They cast anchor near the mouth of a river, which, deriving its name from the Queen of the country, is called, to this day, the Combahee.

The natives were a race as unconscious of guile as they were fearless of danger. They are represented to have been of very noble stature; graceful and strong of limb; of bright, dark flashing eyes, and of singularly advanced civilization, since they wore cotton clothes of their own manufacture, and had even made considerable progress in the arts of knitting, spinning and weaving. They had draperies to their places of repose; and some of the more distinguished among their women and warriors, wore thin and flowing fringes, by way of ornament, upon which a free and tasteful disposition of pearls might occasionally be seen. Like many other of the native tribes, they were governed by a queen whose name has already been given. The name of the country they called Chicora, or, more properly, Chiquola.

Unsuspecting as they were brave, the savages surrounded the vessels in their boats, and many of them even swam off from shore to meet them, being quite as expert in the water as upon the land. The wily Spaniard spared no arts to encourage and increase this confidence. Toys and implements of a kind likely to attract the eyes, and catch the affections, of an ignorant people, were studiously held up in sight; and, by little and little, they grew bold enough, at length, to clamber up the sides of the ships, and make their appearance upon the decks. Still, with all their arts, the number of those who came on board was small, compared with those who remained aloof. It was observed by the Spaniards that the persons who forbore to visit them were evidently the persons of highest consequence. Those who came, as constantly withdrew to make their report to others, who either stayed on the land, or hovered in sight, but at a safe distance, in their light canoes. De Ayllon shrewdly conjectured that if he could tempt these more important persons to visit his vessels, the great body of the savages would follow. His object was numbers; and his grasping and calculating soul scanned the crowds which were in sight, and thought of the immense space in his hold, which it was his policy and wish to fill. To bring about his object, he spared none of the customary modes of temptation. Beads and bells were sparingly distributed to those who came and they were instructed by signs and sounds to depart, and return with their companions. To a certain extent, this policy had its effect, but the appetite of the Spaniard was not easily glutted.

He noted, among the hundred canoes that darted about the bay, one that was not only of larger size and better construction than the rest, but which was fitted up with cotton stuffs and fringes like some barge of state. He rightly conjectured that this canoe contained the Cassique or sovereign of the country. The canoe was dug from a single tree, and was more than forty feet in length. It had a sort of canopy of cotton stuff near the stern, beneath which sat several females, one of whom was of majestic demeanour, and seemed to be an object of deference with all the rest. It did not escape the eyes of the

Spaniards that her neck was hung with pearls, others were twined about her brows, and gleamed out from the folds of her long glossy black hair, which, streaming down her neck, was seen almost to mingle with the chafing billows of the sound. The men in this vessel were also most evidently of the better order. All of them were clad in fringed cotton stuffs of a superior description to those worn by the gathering multitude. Some of these stuffs were dyed of a bright red and yellow, and plumes, similarly stained, were fastened in many instances to their brows, by narrow strips of coloured fringe, not unfrequently sprinkles artfully with seed pearl.

The eyes of De Ayllon gloated as he beheld this barge, from which he did not once withdraw his glance. But, if he saw the importance of securing this particular prize, he, at the same time, felt the difficulty of such a performance. The Indians seemed not unaware of the special value of this canoe. It was kept aloof, while all the rest ventured boldly alongside the Spanish vessels. A proper jealousy of strangers,—though it does not seem that they had any suspicion of their particular object—restrained the savages. To this natural jealousy, that curiosity which is equally natural to ignorance, was opposed. De Ayllon was too sagacious to despair of the final success of this superior passion. He redoubled his arts. His hawk's bells were made to jingle from the ship's side; tinsel, but bright crosses—the holiest sign in the exercise of his religious faith—were hung in view, abused as lures for the purposes of fraud and violence. No toy, which had ever yet been found potent in Indian traffic, was withheld from sight; and, by little and little, the unconscious arms of the Indian rowers impelled the destined bark nearer and nearer to the artful Spaniards. Still, the approach was slow. The strokes of the rowers were frequently suspended, as if in obedience to orders from their chiefs. A consultation was evidently going on among the inmates of the Indian vessels. Other canoes approached it from the shore. The barge of state was surrounded. It was obvious that the counsellors were averse to the unnecessary exposure of their sovereigns.

It was a moment of anxiety with De Ayllon. There were not twenty Indians remaining on his decks; at one time there had been an hundred. He beheld the hesitation, amounting to seeming apprehension among the people in the canoes; and he now began to reproach himself with that cupidity, which, grasping at too much, had probably lost all. But so long as curiosity hesitates there is hope for cupidity. De Ayllon brought forth other lures: he preferred fraud to fighting.

"Look!" said a princely damsel in the canoe of state, as a cluster of bright mirrors shone burningly in the sunlight. "Look!"—and every eye followed her finger, and every feminine tongue in the vessel grew clamorous for an instant, in its own language, expressing the wonder which was felt at this surpassing display. Still, the canoe hung, suspended on its centre, motionless. The contest was undecided: a long, low discussion was carried on between a small and select number in the little vessel. De Ayllon saw that but from four to five persons engaged in this discussion. One of these, only, was a woman— the majestic but youthful woman, of whom we have already given a brief description. Three others were grave middle-aged men; but the fourth was a tall, bright-eyed savage, who had scarcely reached the term of manhood, with a proud eager aspect, and a form equally combining strength and symmetry. He wore a coronet of eagle feathers, and from his place in the canoe, imme- diately next that of the queen, it was inferred correctly by the Spanish captain that he was her husband. He spoke earnestly, almost angrily; pointed several times to the ships, whenever the objects of attraction were displayed; and, from his impatient manner, it was very clear that the counsel to which he listened did not correspond with the desires which he felt. But the discussion was soon ended. De Ayllon waved a bright scimitar above his head, and the young chief in the canoe of state started to his feet, with an unrestrainable impulse, and extended his hand for the gift. The brave soul of the young war- rior spoke out without control when he beheld the true object of attraction. De Ayllon waved the weapon encouragingly, and bowed his head, as if in compliance with his demand. The young savage uttered a few words to his people, and the paddles were again dipped in water; the bark went forward, and, from the Spanish vessel, a rope was let down to assist the visitors as soon as they were alongside.

The hand of the young chief had already grasped the rope, when the fingers of Combahee, the queen, with an equal mixture of majesty and grace, were laid upon his arm.

"Go not, Chiquola," she said, with a persuasive, entreating glance of her deep, dark eyes. He shook off her hand impatiently, and, running up the sides of the vessel, was already safely on the deck, before he perceived that she was preparing to follow him. He turned upon her, and a brief expostulation seemed to follow from his lips. It appeared as if the young savage was only made conscious of his imprudence, by beholding hers. She answered him with a firmness of manner, a dignity and sweetness so happily blended, that the Spanish officers, who had, by this time, gathered round them, looked on and listened with surprise. The young chief, whom they learned to call by the name of Chiquola—which they soon understood was that of the country, also—appeared dissatisfied, and renewed his expostulations, but with the same effect. At length he waved his hand to the canoe, and, speaking a few words, moved once more to the side of the ship at which she had entered. The woman's eye brightened; she answered with a single word, and hurried in the same direction. De Ayllon, fearing the loss of his victims, now thought it time to interfere. The sword, which had won the eyes of the young warrior at first, was again waved in his sight, while a mirror of the largest size was held before the noble features of the Indian princess. The youth grasped the weapon, and laughed with a delighted but brief chuckle as he looked on the glittering steel, and shook it hurriedly in the air. He seemed to know the use of such an instrument by instinct. In its contemplation, he forgot his own suspicions and that of his people; and no more renewing his suggestions to depart, he spoke to Combahee only of the beauties and the use of the new weapon which had been given to his hands.

The woman seemed altogether a superior person. There was a stern mournfulness about her, which, while it commanded respect, did not impair the symmetry and sweetness of her very intelligent and pleasing features. She had the high forehead of our race, without that accompanying protuberance of the cheek bones, which distinguished hers. Her mouth was very small and sweet, like that which is common to her people. Her eyes were large, deeply set, and dark in the extreme, wearing that pensive earnestness of expression which seems to denote presentiment of many pangs and sorrows. Her form, we have already said, was large and majestical; yet the thick masses of her glossy black hair streamed even to her heels. Superior to her companions, male as well as female, the mirror which had been put into her hands— a glance at which had awakened the most boisterous clamours of delight among her female attendants, all of whom had followed her into the Spanish vessel—was laid down, after a brief examination, with perfect indifference. Her countenance, though not uninformed with curiosity, was full of a most expressive anxiety. She certainly felt the wonder which the others showed, at the manifold strange objects which met their eyes; but this feeling was entertained in a more subdued degree, and did not display itself in the usual language of surprise. She simply seemed to follow the footsteps of Chiquola, without participating in his pleasures, or in that curiosity which made him traverse the ship in every accessible quarter, from stem to stern, seeking all objects of novelty, and passing from one to the other with an appetite which nothing seemed likely soon to satiate.

Meanwhile, the example set by their Queen, the Cassiques, the Iawas, or Priests, and other headmen of the Nation, was soon followed by the common people; and De Ayllon had the satisfaction, on exchanging signals with his consort, to find that both ships were crowded with quite as many persons as they could possibly carry. The vessel under his immediate command was scarcely manageable from the multitudes which thronged her decks, and impeded, in a great measure, all the operations of the crew. He devised a remedy for this evil, and, at the same time, a measure very well calculated to give complete effect to his plans. Refreshments were provided in the hold; wines in abundance; and the trooping savages were invited into that gloomy region, which a timely precaution had rendered more cheerful in appearance by the introduction of numerous lights. A similar arrangement conducted the more honourable guests into the cabin, and a free use of the intoxicating beverages, on the part of the great body of the Indians, soon rendered easy all the remaining labours of the wily Spaniard. The hatches were suddenly closed when the hold was most crowded, and two hundred of the unconscious and half stupid savages were thus entrapped for the slave market of the City of Columbus.

In the cabin the same transaction was marked by some distinguishing differences. The wily De Ayllon paid every attention to his guests. A natural homage was felt to be the due of royalty and rank, even among a race of savages; and this sentiment was enforced by the obvious necessity of pursuing that course of conduct which would induce the confidence of persons who had already shown themselves so suspicious. De Ayllon, with his officers, himself attended Chiquola and the Queen. The former needed no persuasion. He freely seated himself on the cushions of the cabin, and drank of the proffered wines, till his eyes danced with delight, his blood tingled, and his speech, always free, became garrulity, to the great annoyance of Combahee. She had followed him with evident reluctance into the interior of the vessel; and now, seated with the rest, within the cabin, she watched the proceedings with a painful degree of interest and dissatisfaction, increasing momently as she beheld the increasing effect upon him of the wine which he had taken. She herself utterly declined the proffered liquor; holding herself aloof with as much natural dignity as could have been displayed by the most polished princess of Europe. Her disquiet had made itself understood by her impatience of manner, and by frequent observations in her own language, to Chiquola. These, of course, could be understood only by themselves and their attendants. But the Spaniards were at no loss to divine the purport of her speech from her tones, the expression of her face, and the quick significant movements of her hands.

At length she succeeded in impressing her desires upon Chiquola, and he rose to depart. But the Spaniards had no intention to suffer this. The plot was now ready for execution. The signal had been made. The entrance to the cabin was closed, and a single bold and decisive movement was alone necessary to end the game. De Ayllon had taken care silently to introduce several stout soldiers into the cabin, and these, when Chiquola took a step forward, sprang upon him and his few male companions and bore them to the floor. Chiquola struggled with a manful courage, which, equally with their forests, was the inheritance of the American Indians; but the conflict was too unequal, and it did not remain doubtful very long. De Ayllon saw that he was secure, and turned, with an air of courteous constraint, to the spot where Combahee stood. He approached her with a smile upon his countenance and with extended arms; but she bestowed upon him a single glance; and, in a mute survey, took in the entire extent of her misfortune. The whole proceeding had been the work of an instant only. That she was taken by surprise, as well as Chiquola, was sufficiently clear; but her suspicions had never been wholly quieted, and the degree of surprise which she felt did not long deprive her of her energies. If her eye betrayed the startled apprehension of the fawn of her native forests, it equally expressed the fierce indignation which flames in that of their tameless eagle. She did not speak as De Ayllon approached; and when, smiling, he pointed to the condition of Chiquola, and with extended arms seemed to indicate to her the hopelessness of any effort at escape, she hissed at him, in reply, with the keen defiance of the angry coppersnake. He advanced—his hand was stretched forth towards her person—when she drew up her queenly form to its fullest height; and, with a single word hurriedly spoken to the still struggling Chiquola, she turned, and when De Ayllon looked only to receive her submission, plunged suddenly through the stern windows of the cabin, and buried herself in the deep waters of the sea.

CHAPTER II.

CHIQUOLA, THE CAPTIVE.

> "Now mounts he the ocean wave, banished, forlorn,
> Like a limb from his country cast bleeding and torn."
>
> CAMPBELL.

The flight of Combahee, and her descent into the waters of the bay, were ominous of uproar. Instantly, the cry of rage arose from a thousand voices. The whole body of the people, as with a common instinct, seemed at once to comprehend the national calamity. A dozen canoes shot forth from every quarter, with the rapidity of arrows in their flight, to the rescue of the Queen. Like a bright mermaid, swimming at evening for her own green island, she now appeared, beating with familiar skill the swelling waters, and, with practiced hands, throwing behind her their impelling billows. Her long, glossy, black hair was spread out upon the surface of the deep, like some veil of network meant to conceal from immodest glances the feminine form below. From the window of the cabin whence she disappeared, De Ayllon beheld her progress, and looked upon the scene with such admiration as was within the nature of a soul so mercenary. He saw the fearless courage of the man in all her movements, and never did Spaniard behold such exquisite artifice in swimming on the part of any of his race. She was already in safety. She had ascended, and taken her seat in one of the canoes, a dozen contending, in loyal rivalry, for the privilege of receiving her person.

Then rose the cry of war! Then sounded that fearful whoop of hate, and rage, and defiance, the very echoes of which have made many a faint heart tremble since that day. It was probably, on this occasion, that the European, for the first time, listened to this terrible cry of war and vengeance. At the signal, the canoes upon the bay scattered themselves to surround the ships; the warriors along the shore loosened the fasts of the boats, and pushed off to join the conflict; while the hunter in the forests, stopped sudden in the eager chase, sped onward, with all the feeling of coercive duty, in the direction of those summoning sounds.

The fearless Combahee, with soul on fire, led the van. She stood erect in her canoe. Her form might be seen from ever part of the bay. The hair still streamed, unbound and dripping, from her shoulders. In her left hand she grasped a bow such as would task the ability of the strong man in our day. Her right hand was extended, as if in denunciation towards that

"—fatal bark
Built in the eclipse and rigged with curses dark,"

in which her husband and her people were held captive. Truly, hers was the form and the attitude for a high souled painter;—one, the master of the dramatic branches of his art. The flashing of her eye was a voice to her warriors;—the waving of her hand was a summons that the loyal and the brave heart sprang eager to obey! A shrill signal issued from her half parted lips, and the now numerous canoes scattered themselves on every side as if to surround the European enemy, or, at least, to make the assault on both vessels simultaneous.

The Spaniard beheld, as if by magic, the whole bay covered with boats. The light canoes were soon launched from the shore, and they shot forth from its thousand indentations as fast as the warriors poured down from the interior. Each of these warriors came armed with the bow, and a well filled quiver of arrows. These were formed from the long canes of the adjacent swamps; shafts equally tenacious and elastic, feathered with plumes from the eagle or the stork, and headed with triangular barbs of flint, broad but sharp, of which each Indian had always a plentiful supply. The vigour with which these arrows were impelled from the string was such, that, without the escaupil or cotton armour which the Spaniards generally wore, the shaft has been known to pass clean through the body of the victim. Thus armed and arranged, with numbers constantly increasing, the people of Combahee, gathering at her summons, darted boldly from shore, and, taking up positions favourable to the attack, awaited only the signal to begin.

Meanwhile, the Spanish ships began to spread forth their broad wings for flight. Anticipating some such condition of things as the present, the wily De Ayllon had made his preparations for departure at the same time that he had planned the scheme for his successful treachery. The one movement was devised to follow immediately upon the footsteps of the other. His sails were loosened and flapping in the wind. To trim them for the breeze, which, though light, was yet favourable to his departure, was the work of a moment only; and ere the word was given for the attack, on the part of the Indians, the hue fabrics of the Spaniards began to move slowly through the subject waters. Then followed the signal. First came a shaft from Combahee herself; well aimed and launched with no mean vigour; that, striking full on the bosom of De Ayllon, would have proved fatal but for the plate mail which was hidden beneath his coat of buff. A wild whoop succeeded, and the air was instantly clouded by the close flight of the Indian arrows. Nothing could have been more decided, more prompt and rapid, than this assault. The shaft had scarcely been dismissed from the string before another supplied its place; and however superior might have been the armament of the Spanish captain, however unequal the conflict from the greater size of his vessels, and the bulwarks which necessarily gave a certain degree of protection, it was a moment of no inconsiderable anxiety to the kidnappers! De Ayllon, though a base, was not a bloody-minded man. His object was spoil, not slaughter. Though his men had their firelocks in readiness, and a few pieces of cannon were already prepared and pointed, yet he hesitated to give the word, which should hurry into eternity so many ignorant fellow beings upon whom he had just inflicted so shameful an injury. He commanded his men to cover themselves behind the bulwarks, unless where the management of the ships required their unavoidable exposure, and, in such cases, the persons employed were provided with the cotton armour which had been usually found an adequate protection against arrows shot by the feebly hands of the Indians of the Lucayos.

But the vigorous savages of Combahee were a very different race. They belonged to the great family of the Muscoghees; the parent stock, without question, of those indomitable tribes which under the names of Yemassee, Stono, Muscoghee, Mickasukee, and Seminole, have made themselves remembered and feared through successive years of European experience, without having been entirely quelled or quieted to the present hour. It was soon found by De Ayllon that the escaupil was no protection against injury. It baffled the force of the shaft but could not blunt it, and one of the inferior officers, standing by the side of the commander, was pierced through his cotton gorget. The arrow penetrated his throat, and he fell, to all appearance, mortally wounded. The Indians beheld his fall. They saw the confusion that the event seemed to inspire, and their delight was manifested in a renewed shout of hostility, mingled with screams, which denoted, as clearly as language, the delight of savage triumph. Still, De Ayllon forbore to use the destructive weapons which he had in readiness. His soldiers murmured; but he answered them by pointing to the hold, and asking:

"Shall we cut our own throats in cutting theirs? I see not present enemies but future slaves in all these assailants."

It was not mercy but policy that dictated his forbearance. But it was necessary that something should be done in order to baffle and throw off the

Indians. The breeze was too light and baffling, and the movements of the vessels too slow to avoid them. The light barks of the assailants, impelled by vigorous arms, in such smooth water, easily kept pace with the progress of the ships. Their cries of insult and hostility increased. Their arrows were shot, without cessation, at every point at which an enemy was supposed to harbour himself; and, under the circumstances, it was not possible always to take advantage of a cover in performing the necessary duties which accrued to the seamen of the ships. The Indians had not yet heard the sound of European cannon. De Ayllon resolved to intimidate them. A small piece such as in that day was employed for the defence of castles, called a falconet, was elevated above the canoes, so that the shot, passing over the heads of their inmates, might take effect upon the woods along the shore. As the sudden and sullen roar of this unexpected thunder was heard, every Indian sunk upon his knees; every paddle was dropped motionless in the water; while the uplifted bow fell from the half-paralyzed hands of the warrior, and he paused, uncertain of safety, but incapable of flight. The effect was great, but momentary only. To a truly brave people, there is nothing more transient than the influence of panic. When the Indian warriors looked up, they beheld one of their people still erect—unalarmed by the strange thunder—still looking the language,—still acting the part of defiance,—and, oh! shame to their manhood, this person was their Queen. Instead of fear, the expression upon her countenance was that of scorn. They took fire at the expression. Every heart gathered new warmth at the blaze shining from her eyes. Besides, they discovered that they were unharmed. The thunder was a mere sound. They had not seen the bolt. This discovery not only relieved their fears but heightened their audacity. Again they moved forward. Again the dart was clapt upon the string. Singing one chorus, the burden of which, in our language, would be equivalent to a summons to a feast of vultures, they again set their canoes in motion; and now, not as before, simply content to get within arrow distance, they boldly pressed forward upon the very course of the ships; behind, before, and on every side, sending their arrows through every opening, and distinguishing, by their formidable aim, every living object which came in sight. Their skill in the management of their canoes; in swimming; their great strength and agility, prompted them to a thousand acts of daring; and some were found bold enough to attempt, while leaping from their boats, beneath the very prow of the slowly advancing vessels, to grasp the swinging ropes and thus elevate themselves to individual conflict with their enemies. These failed, it is true, and sank into the waters; but such an event implied no sort of risk to these fearless warriors. They were soon picked up by their comrades, only to renew, in this or in other forms, their gallant but unsuccessful efforts.

But these efforts might yet be successful. Ships in those days were not the monstrous places which they are in ours. An agile form, under favouring circumstances, might easily clamber up their sides; and such was the equal activity and daring of the savages, as to make it apparent to De Ayllon that it would need something more decisive than had yet been done, on his part, to shake himself free from their inveterate hostility. At a moment when their fury was redoubled and increased by the impunity which had attended their previous assaults—when every bow was uplifted and every arrow pointed under the eye of their Queen, as if for a full application of all their strength, and skill and courage;—her voice, now loud in frequent speech, inciting them to a last and crowning effort; and she herself, erect in her bark as before, and within less than thirty yards of the Spanish vessel;—at this moment, and to avert the storm of arrows which threatened his seamen who were then, perforce, busy with the rigging in consequence of a sudden change of wind;—De Ayllon gave a signal to bring Chiquola from below. Struggling between two Spanish officers, his arms pinioned at the elbows, the young Cassique was dragged forward to the side of the vessel and presented to the eyes of his Queen and people, threatened with the edge of the very weapon which had beguiled him to the perfidious bark.

A hollow groan arose on every hand. The points of the uplifted arrows were dropped; and, for the first time, the proud spirit passed out of the eyes of Combahee, and her head sunk forward, with an air of hopeless self-abandonment, upon her breast! A deep silence followed, broken only by the voice of Chiquola. What he said, was, of course, not understood by his captors; but they could not mistake the import of his action. Thrice, while he spoke to his people, did his hand, wresting to the utmost the cords upon his arms, smite his heart, imploring, as it were, the united arrows of his people to this conspicuous mark. But the Amazon had not courage for this. She was speechless! Every eye was turned upon her, but there was no answering response in hers; and the ships of the Spaniard proceeded on their way to the sea with a momently increasing rapidity. Still, though no longer assailing, the canoes followed close, and kept up the same relative distance between themselves and enemies, which had been observed before. Combahee now felt all her feebleness, and as the winds increased, and the waves of the bay feeling the more immediate influence of the ocean, rose into long heavy swells, the complete conviction of her whole calamity seemed to rush upon her soul. Chiquola had now been withdrawn from sight. His eager adjurations to his Queen and people, might, it was feared, prompt them to that Roman sort of sacrifice which the captive himself seemed to implore; and perceiving that the savages had suspended the assault, De Ayllon commanded his removal. But, with his disappearance, the courage of his Queen revived. Once more she gave the signal for attack in a discharge of arrows; and once more the captive was set before their eyes, with the naked sword above his head, in terrorem, as before. The same effect ensued. The arm of hostility hung suspended and paralyzed. The cry of anguish which the cruel spectacle extorted from the bosom of Combahee, was echoed by that of the multitude; and without a purpose or a hope, the canoes hovered around the course of the retreating ships, till the broad Atlantic, with all its mighty billows, received them.— The vigorous breath of the increasing wind, soon enabled them to shake off their hopeless pursuers. Yet still the devoted savages plied their unremitting pad-dles; the poor Queen straining her eyes along the waste, until, in the grey of twilight and of distance the vessels of the robbers were completely hidden from her sight.

Meanwhile, Chiquola was hurried back to the cabin, with his arms still pinioned. His feet were also fastened and a close watch was put upon him. It was a courtesy which the Spaniards considered due to his legitimacy that the cabin was made his place of imprisonment. With his withdrawal from the presence of his people, his voice, his eagerness and animation, all at once ceased. He sunk down on the cushion with the sullen, stolid indifference which distinguishes his people in all embarrassing situations. A rigid immo-bility settled upon his features; yet De Ayllon did not fail to perceive that when he or any of his officers approached the captive, his eyes gleamed upon them with the fury of his native panther;—gleamed bright, with irregular flashes, beneath his thick black eye-brows, which gloomed heavily over their arches with the collected energies of a wild and stubborn soul.

"He is dangerous," said De Ayllon, "be careful how you approach him."

But though avoided he was not neglected. De Ayllon himself proffered him food; not forgetting to tender him a draught of that potent beverage by which he had been partly overcome before. But the sense of wrong was uppermost, and completely subdued the feeling of appetite. He regarded the proffer of the Spaniard with a keen, but composed look of ineffable disdain; never lifted his hand to receive the draught, and beheld it set down within his reach without indicating, by word or look, his consciousness of what had been done. Some hours had elapsed and the wine and food remained untouched. His captor still consoled himself with the idea that hunger would subdue his stubbornness;—but when the morning came, and the noon of the next day, and the young savage still refused to eat or drink, the case became serious; and the mercenary Spaniard began to apprehend that he should lose one of the most valuable of his captives. He approached the youth and by signs expostulated with him upon his rejection of the food; but he received no satisfaction. The Indian remained inflexible, and but a single glance of his large, bright eye, requited De Ayllon for his selfish consideration. That look expressed the hunger and thirst which in no other way did Chiquola deign to acknowledge; but that hunger and thirst were not for food but for blood;— revenge, the atonement for his wrongs and shame. Never had the free limbs of Indian warrior known such an indignity—never could indignity have been conceived less endurable. No words can describe, as no mind can imagine, the volume of tumultuous strife, and fiercer, maddening thoughts and feelings, boiling and burning in the brain and bosom of the gallant but inconsiderate youth;—thoughts and feelings so strangely subdued, so completely hidden in those composed muscles,—only speaking through that dilating, but fixed, keen, inveterate eye!

De Ayllon was perplexed. The remaining captives gave him little or no trouble. Plied with the liquors which had seduced them at first, they were very generally in that state of drunkenness, when a certainty of continued supply reconciles the degraded mind very readily to any condition. But with Chiquola the case was very different. Here, at least, was character—the pride of self-dependence; the feeling of moral responsibility; the ineradicable consciousness of that shame which prefers to feel itself and not to be blinded. De Ayllon had known the savage nature only under its feebler and meaner aspects. The timid islanders of the Lucayos—the spiritless and simple natives of Hayti—were of quite another class. The Indian of the North American continent, whatever his vices or his weaknesses, was yet a man. He was more. He was a conqueror—accustomed to conquer! It was his boast that where he came he stood; where he stood he remained; and where he remained, he was the only man! The people whom he found were women. He made them and kept them so.—

"Severe the school that made them bear
The ills of life without a tear;
And stern the doctrine that denied
The sachem fame, the warrior pride,
Who, urged by nature's wants, confess'd
The need that hunger'd in his breast:—
Or, when beneath his foeman's knife,
Who utter'd recreant prayer for life;—
Or, in the chase, whose strength was spent,
Or, in the fight, whose knee was bent;
Or, when with tale of coming fight,
Who sought his allies' camp by night,
And, ere the missives well were told,
Complain'd of hunger, wet and cold!—
A woman, if in strife, his foe,
Could give, yet not receive, a blow;—
Or if, undextrously and dull,
His hand and knife should fail to win
The dripping warm scalp from the skull
To trim his yellow mocasin!"

Such was the character of his race, and Chiquola was no recreant. Such was his character. He had no complaint. He looked no emotions. The marble could not have seemed less corrigible; and, but for that occasional flashing from his dark eye, whenever any of his captors drew near to the spot where he sat, none would have fancied that in his bosom lurked a single feeling of hostility or discontent. Still he ate not and drank not. It was obvious to the Spaniard that he had adopted the stern resolution to forbear all sustenance, and thus defeat the malice of his enemies. He had no fear of death, and he could not endure bonds. That he would maintain that resolution to the last, none could doubt who watched his sullen immobility—who noted the fact that he spoke nothing, neither in the language of entreaty nor complaint. He was resolved on suicide! It is an error to suppose, as has been asserted, that the Indians never commit suicide. The crime is a very common one among them in periods of great national calamity. The Cherokee warrior frequently destroyed himself when the small pox had disfigured his visage: for, it must be remembered, that an Indian warrior is, of all human beings, one of the vainest, on the score of his personal appearance. He unites, as they are usually found united even in the highest states of civilization, the strange extremes of ferocity and frivolity.

De Ayllon counselled with his officers as to what should be done with their captive. He would certainly die on their hands. Balthazar de Morla, his lieutenant—a stern fierce savage himself—proposed that they should kill him, as a way of shortening their trouble, and dismissing all farther cares upon the project.

"He is but one," said he, "and though you may call him King or Cassique, he will sell for no more than any one of his own tribe in the markets of Isabella. At worst, it will only be a loss to him, for the fellow is resolved to die. He will bring you nothing unless for the skin of his carcase, and that is not a large one."

A young officer of more humanity, Jaques Carazon, offered different counsel. He recommended that the poor Indian be taken on deck. The confinement in the cabin he thought had sickened him. The fresh air, and the sight of the sky and sea, might work a change and provoke in him a love of life. Reasoning from the European nature, such advice would most probably have realized the desired effect; and De Ayllon was struck with it.

"Let it be done," he said; and Chiquola was accordingly brought up from below, and placed on the quarter deck in a pleasant and elevated situation. At first, the effect promised to be such as the young officer had suggested. There was a sudden looking up, in all the features of the captive. His eyes were no longer cast down; and a smile seemed to pass over the lips which, of late, had been so rigidly compressed. He looked long, and with a keen expression of interest at the sky above, and the long stretch of water before and around him. But there was one object of most interest, upon which his eyes fastened with a seeming satisfaction. This was the land. The low sandy shores and island slips that skirt the Georgia coast, then known under the general name of Florida, lay on the right. The gentleness of the breeze, and smoothness of the water, enabled the ships, which were of light burthen, to pursue a course along with the land, at a small distance, varying from five to ten miles. Long and earnestly did the captive gaze upon this, to him, Elysian tract. There dwelt tribes, he well knew, which were kindred to his people. From any one of the thousand specks of shore which caught his eye, he could easily find his way back to his queen and country! What thoughts of bliss and wo, at the same moment, did these two images suggest to his struggling and agonized spirit. Suddenly, he caught the eyes of the Spanish Captain gazing upon him, with a fixed, inquiring glance; and his own eyes were instantly averted from those objects which he alone desired to see. It would seem as if he fancied that the Spaniard was able to look into his soul. His form grew more erect beneath the scrutiny of his captor, and his countenance once more put on its former expression of immobility.

De Ayllon approached, followed by a boy bringing fresh food and wine, which were once more placed within his reach. By signs, the Spaniard encouraged him to eat. The Indian returned him not the slightest glance of recognition. His eye alone spoke, and its language was still that of hate and defiance. De Ayllon left him, and commanded that none should approach or seem to observe him. He conjectured that his stubbornness derived something of its stimulus from the consciousness that eyes of strange curiosity were fixed upon him, and that Nature would assert her claims if this artificial feeling were suffered to subside without farther provocation.

But when three hours more had elapsed, and the food still remained untouched, De Ayllon was in despair. He approached Chiquola, attended by the fierce Balthazar de Morla.

"Why do you not eat, savage!" exclaimed this person, shaking his hand threateningly at the Indian, and glancing upon him with the eyes of one, only waiting and anxious for the signal to strike and slay. If the captive failed to understand the language of the Spaniard, that of his looks and action was in no wise unequivocal. Chiquola gave him glance for glance. His eye lighted up with those angry fires which it shed when going into battle; and it was sufficiently clear to both observers, that nothing more was needed than the freedom of hand and foot to have brought the unarmed but unbending savage, into the death grapple with his insulting enemy. The unsubdued tiger-like expression of the warrior, was rather increased than subdued by famine; and even De Ayllon recoiled from a look which made him momentarily forgetful of the cords which fastened the limbs and rendered impotent the anger of his captive. He reproved Balthazar for his violence, and commanded him to retire. Then, speaking gently, he endeavoured to soothe the irritated Indian, by kind tones and persuasive action. He pointed to the food, and, by signs, endeavoured to convey to his mind the idea of the painful death which must follow his wilful abstinence much longer. For a few moments Chiquola gave no heed to these suggestions, but looking round once more to the strip of shore which lay upon his right, a sudden change passed over his features. He turned to De Ayllon, and muttering a few words in his own language, nodded his head, while his fingers pointed to the ligatures around his elbows and ancles. The action clearly denoted a willingness to take his food, provided his limbs were set free. De Ayllon proceeded to consult with his officers upon this suggestion. The elder, Balthazar de Morla, opposed the indulgence.

"He will attack you the moment he is free."

"But," replied the younger officer, by whose counsel he had already been brought upon the deck—"but of what avail would be his attack? We are armed, and he is weaponless. We are many, and he is but one. It only needs that we should be watchful, and keep in readiness."

"Well!" said Balthazar, with a sneer, "I trust that you will be permitted the privilege of undoing his bonds; for if ever savage had the devil in his eye, this savage has."

"I will do it," replied the young man, calmly, without seeming to heed the sneer. "I do not fear the savage, even if he should grapple with me. But I scarcely think it possible that he would attempt such a measure. He has evidently too much sense for that."

"Desperate men have no sense!" said the other; but the counsels of the younger officer prevailed with De Ayllon, and he was commissioned to undo the bonds of the captive. At the same time every precaution was taken, that the prisoner, when set free, should do the young man no hurt. Several soldiers were stationed at hand, to interpose in the event of danger, and De Ayllon and Balthazar, both with drawn swords, stood beside Jaques Carazon as he bent down on one knee to perform the duty of supposed danger which had been assigned him. But their apprehensions of assault proved groundless. Whether it was that Chiquola really entertained no design of mischief, or that he was restrained by prudence, on seeing the formidable preparations which had been made to baffle and punish any such attempt, he remained perfectly quiescent, and, even after his limbs had been freed, showed no disposition to use them.

"Eat!" said De Ayllon, pointing to the food. The captive looked at him in silence, but the food remained untouched.

"His pride keeps him from it," said De Ayllon. "He will not eat so long as we are looking on him. Let us withdraw to some little distance and watch him."

His orders were obeyed. The soldiers were despatched to another quarter of the vessel, though still commanded to remain under arms. De Ayllon with his two officers then withdrew, concealing themselves in different situations where they might observe all the movements of the captive. For a time, this arrangement promised to be as little productive of fruits as the previous ones. Chiquola remained immovable, and the food untouched. But, after a while, when he perceived that none was immediately near, his crouching form might be seen in motion, but so slightly, so slily, that it was scarcely perceptible to those who watched him. His head revolved slowly, and his neck turned, without any corresponding movement of his limbs, until he was able to take in all objects, which he might possibly see, on almost every part of the deck. The man at the helm, the sailor on the yard, while beholding him, scarcely saw the cat-like movement of his eyes. These, when he had concluded his unobtrusive examination of the vessel, were turned upon the shore, with the expression of an eager joy. His heart spoke out its feelings in the flashing of his dilating and kindled eyes. He was free. That was the feeling of his soul! That was the feeling which found utterance in his glance. The degrading cords were no longer on the limbs of the warrior, and was not his home almost beneath his eyes? He started to his feet erect. He looked around him; spurned the food and the wine cup from his path, and shrieking the war whoop of his tribe, with a single rush and bound, he plunged over the sides of the vessel into those blue waters which dye, with the complexion of the Gulf, the less beautiful waves of the Atlantic.

This movement, so unexpected by the captors, was quite too sudden for them to prevent. De Ayllon hurried to the side of his vessel as soon as he distinguished the proceeding. He beheld, with mingled feelings of admiration and disappointment, where the bold savage was buffeting the billows in the vain hope of reaching the distant shores. A boat was instantly let down into the sea, manned with the ablest seamen of the ship. It was very clear that Chiquola could neither make the land, nor contend very long with the powerful waters of the deep. This would have been a task beyond the powers of the strongest man, and the most skilful swimmer, and the brave captive had been without food more than twenty-four hours. Still he could be seen, striving vigorously in a course straight as an arrow for the shore; rising from billow to billow; now submerged, still ascending, and apparently without any diminution of the vigour with which he began his toils.

The rowers, meanwhile, plied their oars, with becoming energy. The Indian, though a practiced swimmer, began, at length, to show signs of exhaustion. He was seen from the ship, and with the aid of a glass, was observed to be struggling feebly. The boat was gaining rapidly upon him. He might be saved. It needed only that he should will it so. Would he but turn and employ his remaining strength in striving for the boat, instead of wasting it in an idle effort for those shores which he could never more hope to see!

"He turns!" cried De Ayllon. "He will yet be saved. The boat will reach him soon. A few strokes more, and they are up with him!"

"He turns, indeed," said Carazon, "but it is to wave his hand in defiance."

"They reach him—they are up with him!" exclaimed the former.

"Ay!" answered the latter, "but he sinks—he has gone down."

"No! they have taken him into the boat!"

"You mistake, sir, do you not see where he rises? almost a ship's length on the right of the boat. There spoke the savage soul. He will not be saved!"

This was true. Chiquola preferred death to bondage. The boat changed its course with that of the swimmer. Once more it neared him. Once more the hope of De Ayllon was excited as he beheld the scene from the ship; and once more the voice of his lieutenant cried discouragingly—

"He has gone down, and for ever. He will not suffer us to save him."

This time he spoke truly. The captive had disappeared. The boat, returning now, alone appeared above the waters, and De Ayllon turned away from the scene, wondering much at the indomitable spirit and fearless courage of the savage, but thinking much more seriously of the large number of pesos which this transaction had cost him. It was destined to cost him more, but of this hereafter.

CHAPTER III.

COMBAHEE; OR, THE LAST VOYAGE OF LUCAS DE AYLLON.

> "—Bind him, I say;
> Make every artery and sinew crack;
> The slave that makes him give the loudest shriek,
> Shall have ten thousand drachmas! Wretch! I'll force thee
> To curse the Pow'r thou worship'st."
>
> MASSINGER.—THE VIRGIN MARTYR.

But the losses of De Ayllon were not to end with the death of his noble captive, the unfortunate Chiquola. We are told by the historian, that "one of his vessels foundered before he reached his port, and captors and captives were swallowed up in the sea together. His own vessel survived, but many of his captives sickened and died; and he himself was reserved for the time, only to suffer a more terrible form of punishment. Though he had lost more than half of the ill-gotten fruits of his expedition, the profits which remained were still such as to encourage him to a renewal of his enterprise. To this he devoted his whole fortune, and, with three large vessels and many hundred men, he once more descended upon the coast of Carolina."*

Meanwhile, the dreary destiny of Combahee was to live alone. We have heard so much of the inflexibility of the Indian character, that we are apt to forget that these people are human; having, though perhaps in a small degree, and in less activity, the same vital passions, the same susceptibilities—the hopes, the fears, the loves and the hates, which establish the humanity of the whites. They are colder and more sterile,—more characterized by individuality and self-esteem than any more social people; and these characteristics are the natural and inevitable results of their habits of wandering. But to suppose that the Indian is "a man without a tear," is to indulge in a notion equally removed from poetry and truth. At all events, such an opinion is, to say the least of it, a gross exaggeration of the fact.

Combahee, the Queen of Chiquola, had many tears. She was a young wife;—the crime of De Ayllon had made her a young widow. Of the particular fate of her husband she knew nothing; and, in the absence of any certain knowledge, she naturally feared the worst. The imagination, once excited by fear, is the darkest painter of the terrible that nature has ever known. Still, the desolate woman did not feel herself utterly hopeless. Daily she manned her little bark, and was paddled along the shores of the sea, in a vain search after that which could never more be found. At other times she sat upon, or wandered along, the headlands, in a lonely and silent watch over those vast, dark, dashing waters of the Atlantic, little dreaming that they had already long since swallowed up her chief. Wan and wretched, the sustenance which she took was simply adequate to the purposes of life. Never did city maiden more stubbornly deplore the lost object of her affections than did this single-hearted woman. But her prayers and watch were equally unavailing. Vainly did she skirt the shores in her canoe by day;—vainly did she build her fires, as a beacon, to guide him on his home return by night. His people had

· * [SIMMS'S NOTE] History of South Carolina, page 11.

already given him up for ever; but love is more hopeful of the object which it loves. She did not yet despair. Still she wept, but still she watched; and when she ceased to weep, it was only at moments when the diligence of her watch made her forgetful of her tears.

The season was becoming late. The fresh and invigorating breezes of September began to warn the tribes of the necessity of seeking the shelter of the woods. The maize was already gathered and bruised for the stocks of winter. The fruits of summer had been dried, and the roots were packed away. The chiefs regarded the condition of mind under which their Queen laboured with increasing anxiety. She sat apart upon the highest hill that loomed out from the shore, along the deep. She sat beneath the loftiest palmetto. A streamer of fringed cotton was hung from its top as a signal to the wanderer, should he once more be permitted to behold the land, apprizing him where the disconsolate widow kept her watch. The tribes looked on from a distance unwilling to disturb those sorrows, which, under ordinary circumstances, they consider sacred. The veneration which they felt for their Queen increased this feeling. Yet so unremitting had been her self-abandonment—so devoted and unchangeable her daily employments, that some partial fears began to be entertained lest her reason might suffer. She had few words now for her best counsellors. These few words, it is true, were always to the purpose, yet they were spoken with impatience, amounting to severity. The once gentle and benignant woman had grown stern. There was a stony inflexibility about her glance which distressed the observer, and her cheeks had become lean and thin, and her frame feeble and languid, in singular contrast with that intense spiritual light which flashed, whenever she was addressed, from her large black eyes.

Something must be done! such was the unanimous opinion of the chiefs. Nay, two things were to be done. She was to be cured of this affection; and it was necessary that she should choose one, from among her "beloved men,"— one, who should take the place of Chiquola. They came to her, at length, with this object. Combahee was even then sitting upon the headland of St. Helena. She looked out with straining eyes upon the sea. She had seen a speck. They spoke to her, but she motioned them to be silent, while she pointed to the object. It disappeared, like a thousand others. It was some porpoise, or possible some wandering grampus, sending up his *jets d'eau* in an unfamiliar ocean. Long she looked, but profitlessly. The object of her sudden hope had already disappeared. She turned to the chiefs. They prostrated themselves before her. Then, the venerable father, Kiawah,—an old man who had witnessed the departure of an hundred and twenty summers,—rose, and seating himself before her, addressed her after the following fashion:

"Does the daughter of the great Ocketee, look into the grave of the warrior that he may come forth because she looks?"

"He sleeps, father, for Combahee. He has gone forth to hunt the deer in the blue land of Maneyto."

"Good! he has gone. Is the sea a hunting land for the brave Chiquola? Is he not also gone to the blue land of spirits?"

"Know'st thou? Who has told Kiawah, the old father? Has it come to him in a dream?"

"Chiquola has come to him."

"Ah!"

"He is a hunter for Maneyto. He stands first among the hunters in the blue forests of Maneyto. The smile of the Great Spirit beckons him to the chase. He eats of honey in the golden tents of the Great Spirit."

"He has said? Thou hast seen?"

"Even so! Shall Kiawah say to Combahee the thing which is not? Chiquola is dead!"

The woman put her hand upon her heart with an expression of sudden pain. But she recovered herself with a little effort.

"It is true what Kiawah has said. I feel it here. But Chiquola will come to Combahee?"

"Yea! He will come. Let my daughter go to the fountain and bathe thrice before night in its waters. She will bid them prepare the feast of flesh. A young deer shall be slain by the hunters. Its meat shall be dressed, of that shall she eat, while the maidens sing the song of victory, and dance the dance of rejoicing around her. For there shall be victory and rejoicing. Three days shall my daughter do this; and the night of the third day shall Chiquola come to her when she sleeps. She shall hear his voice, she shall do his bidding, and there shall be blessings. Once more shall Combahee smile among her people."

He was obeyed religiously. Indeed, his was a religious authority. Kiawah was a famous priest and prophet among the tribes of the sea coast of Carolina—in their language an Iawa,—a man renowned for his supernatural powers. A human policy may be seen in the counsels of the old man; but by the Indians it was regarded as coming from a superior source. For three days did Combahee perform her lustrations, as required, and partake plentifully of the feast which had been prepared. The third night, a canopy of green bushes was reared for her by the sea side around the palmetto where she had been accustomed to watch, and from which her cotton streamer was still flying. Thither she repaired as the yellow moon was rising above the sea. It rose, bright and round, and hung above her tent, looking down with eyes of sad, sweet brilliance, like some hueless diamond, about to weep, through the green leaves, and into the yet unclosed eyes of the disconsolate widow. The great ocean all the while kept up a mournful chiding and lament along the shores. It was long before Combahee could sleep. She vainly strove to shut her eyes. She could not well do so, because of her expectation, and because of that chiding sea, and those sad eyes of the moon, big, wide, down staring upon her. At length she ceased to behold the moon and to hear the ocean; but, in place of these, towards the rising of the morning star, she heard the voice of Chiquola, and beheld the young warrior to whom her virgin heart had been given. He was habited in loose flowing robes of blue, a bunch of feathers, most like a golden sunbeam, was on his brow, bound there by a circle of little stars. He carried a bow of bended silver, and his arrows looked like darts of summer lightning. Truly, in the eyes of the young widow, Chiquola looked like a very god himself. He spoke to her in a language that was most like a song. It was a music such as the heart hears when it first loves and when hope is the companion of its affections. Never was music in the ears of Combahee so sweet.

"Why sits the woman that I love beside the cold ocean? Why does she watch the black waters for Chiquola? Chiquola is not there."

The breathing of the woman was suspended with delight. She could not speak. She could only hear.

"Arise, my beloved, and look up at Chiquola."

"Chiquola is with the Great Spirit. Chiquola is happy in the blue forests of Maneyto;" at length she found strength for utterance.

"No! Chiquola is cold. There must be fire to warm Chiquola, for he perished beneath the sea. His limbs are full of water. He would dry himself. Maneyto smiles, around him are the blue forests, he chases the brown deer, till the setting of the sun; but his limbs are cold. Combahee will build him a fire of the bones of his enemies, that the limbs of Chiquola may be made warm against the winter."

The voice ceased, the bright image was gone. In vain was it that the woman, gathering courage in his absence, implored him to return. She saw him no more, and in his place the red eye of the warrior star of morning was looking steadfastly upon her.

But where were the enemies of Chiquola? The tribes were all at peace. The war-paths upon which Chiquola had gone had been very few, and the calumet had been smoked in token of peace and amity among them all. Of whose bones then should the fire be made which was to warm the limbs of the departed warrior? This was a question to afflict the wisest heads of the nation, and upon this difficulty they met, in daily council, from the moment that the revelation of Chiquola was made known by his widow. She, meanwhile, turned not once from her watch along the waters where he had disappeared! For what did she now gaze? Chiquola was no longer there! Ah! the fierce spirit of the Indian woman had another thought. It was from that quarter that the pale warriors came by when he was borne into captivity. Perhaps, she had no fancy that they would again return. It was an instinct rather than a thought, which made her look out upon the waters and dream at moments that she had glimpses of their large white-winged canoes.

Meanwhile, the Iawas and chief men sat in council, and the difficulty about the bones of which the fire was to be made, continued as great as ever. As a respite from this difficulty they debated at intervals another and scarcely less serious question:

"Is it good for Combahee to be alone?"

This question was decided in the negative by an unanimous vote. It was observed, though no argument seemed necessary, that all the younger and more handsome chiefs made long speeches in advocacy of the marriage of their Queen. It was also observed that, immediately after the breaking up of the council, each darted off to his separate wigwam, and put on his newest mocasins, brightest leggins, his yellowest hunting shirt, and his most gorgeous belt of shells. Each disposed his plumes after the fashion of his own taste, and adjusted, with newer care, the quiver at his back; and each strove, when the opportunity offered, to leap, dance, run, climb, and shoot, in the presence of the lovely and potent woman.

Once more the venerable Iawa presented himself before the Queen.

"The cabin of my daughter has but one voice. There must be another. What sings the Coonee Latee? (mocking bird.) He says, 'though the nest be withered and broken, are there not sticks and leaves; shall I not build another? Though the mate-wing be gone to other woods, shall no other voice take up the strain which I am singing, and barter with me in the music which is love?' Daughter, the beloved men have been in council; and they say, the nest must be repaired with newer leaves; and the sad bird must sing lonely no longer. Are there not other birds? Lo! behold them, my daughter, where they run and bound, and sing and dance. Choose from these, my daughter,— choose the noblest, that the noble blood of Ocketee may not perish for ever."

"Ah!"—she said impatiently—"but have the beloved men found the enemies of Chiquola? Do they say, here are the bones?"

"The Great Spirit has sent no light to the cabin of council."

"Enough! when the beloved men shall find the bones which were the enemies of Chiquola, then will the Coonee Latee take a mate-wing to her cabin. It is not meet that Combahee should build the fire for another hunter before she has dried the water from the limbs of Chiquola!"

"The Great Spirit will smile on their search. Meanwhile, let Combahee choose one from among our youth, that he may be honoured by the tribe."

"Does my father say this to the poor heart of Combahee?"

"It is good."

"Take this," she said, "to Edelano, the tall brother of Chiquola. He is most like the chief. Bid him wear it on his breast. Make him a chief among our people. He is the choice of Combahee."

She took from her neck as she spoke, a small plate of rudely beaten native gold, upon which the hands of some native artist, had, with a pointed flint or shell, scratched uncouth presentments of the native deer, the eagle, and other objects of their frequent observation.

"Give it him—to Edelano!"—she added; "but let him not come to Combahee till the beloved men shall have said—these are the bones of the enemies of Chiquola. Make of these the fires which shall warm him."

There was something so reasonable in what was said by the mourning Queen, that the patriarch was silenced. To a certain extent he had failed of his object. That was to direct her mind from the contemplation of her loss by the substitution of another in his place—the philosophy of those days and people, not unlike that of our own, leading people to imagine that the most judicious and successful method for consoling a widow is by making her a wife again as soon as possible. Combahee had yielded as far as could be required of her; yet still they were scarcely nearer to the object of their desire: for where were the bones of Chiquola's enemies to be found?—He who had no enemies! He, with whom all the tribes were at peace? And those whom he had slain,—where were their bodies to be found? They had long been hidden by their friends in the forests where no enemy might trace out their places of repose. As for the Spaniards—the white men—of these the Indian sages did not think. They had come from the clouds, perhaps,—but certainly, they were not supposed to have belonged to any portion of the solid world to which they were accustomed. As they knew not where to seek for the "pale faces," these were not the subjects of their expectation.

The only person to whom the proceedings, so far, had produced any results, was the young warrior, Edelano. He became a chief in compliance with the wish of Combahee, and, regarded as her betrothed, was at once admitted into the hall of council, and took his place as one of the heads and fathers of the tribe. His pleasant duty was to minister to the wants and wishes of his spouse, to provide the deer, to protect her cabin, to watch her steps— subject to the single and annoying qualification, that he was not to present himself conspicuously to her eyes. But how could youthful lover—one so brave and ardent as Edelano—submit to such interdict? It would have been a hard task to one far less brave, and young, and ardent, than Edelano. With him it was next to impossible. For a time he bore his exclusion manfully. Set apart by betrothal, he no longer found converse or association with the young women of the tribe; and his soul was accordingly taken up with the one image of his Queen and future spouse. He hung about her steps like a shadow, but she beheld him not. He darted along the beach when she was gazing forth upon the big, black ocean, but he failed to win her glance. He sang, while hidden in the forest, as she wandered through its glooms, the wildest and sweetest songs of Indian love and fancy; but her ear did not seem to note any interruption of that sacred silence which she sought. Never was sweeter or tenderer venison placed by the young maidens before her, than that which Edelano furnished; the Queen ate little and did not seem to note its obvious superiority. The devoted young chief was in despair. He knew not what to do. Unnoticed, if not utterly unseen by day, he hung around her tent by night. Here, gliding by like a midnight spectre, or crouching beneath some neighbouring oak or myrtle, he mused for hours, catching with delighted spirit every sound, however slight, which might come to his ears from within; and occasionally renewing his fond song of devoted attachment, in the hope that, amidst the silence of every other voice, his own might be better heard. But the soughing of the sad winds and the chafing of the waters against the sandy shores, as they reminded the mourner of her loss, were enough to satisfy her vacant senses, and still no token reached the unwearied lover that his devotion had awakened the attention of the object to whom it was paid.

Every day added to his sadness and his toils; until the effect began to be as clearly visible on his person as on hers; and the gravity of the sages became increased, and they renewed the inquiry, more and more frequently together, "Where can the bones of Chiquola's enemies be found?"

The answer to this question was about to be received from an unexpected quarter. The sun was revolving slowly and certainly while the affairs of the tribe seemed at a stand. The period when he should cross the line was approaching, and the usual storms of the equinox were soon to be apprehended. Of these annual periods of storm and terror, the aborigines, through long experience, were quite as well aware as a more book-wise people. To fly to the shelter of the forests was the policy of the Indians at such periods. We have already seen that they had been for some time ready for departure. But Combahee gave no heed to their suggestions. A superstitious instinct made them willing to believe that the Great Spirit would interfere in his own good time; and, at the proper juncture, bestow the necessary light for their guidance. Though anxious, therefore, they did not press their meditations upon those of their princess. They deferred, with religious veneration, to her griefs. But their anxiety was not lessened as the month of September advanced—as the days became capricious,—as the winds murmured more and more mournfully along the sandy shores, and as the waters of the sea grew more blue, and put on their whiter crests of foam. The clouds grew banked in solid columns, like the gathering wings of an invading army, on the edges of the southern and southeastern horizon. Sharp, shrill, whistling gusts, raised a warning anthem through the forests, which sounded like the wild hymn of the advancing storm. The green leaves had suddenly become yellow as in the progress of the night, and the earth was already strewn with their fallen honours. The sun himself was growing dim as with sudden age. All around, in sky, sea and land, the presentments were obvious of a natural but startling change. If the anxieties of the people were increased, what were those of Edelano? Heedless of the threatening aspects around her, the sad-hearted Combahee, whose heaviest storm was in her own bosom, still wilfully maintained her precarious lodge beneath the palmetto, on the bleak head-land which looked out most loftily upon the sea. The wind strewed the leaves of her forest tent upon her as she slept, but she was conscious of no disturbance; and its melancholy voice, along with that of the ocean, seemed to her to increase in interest and sweetness as they increased in vigour. She heeded not that the moon was absent from the night. She saw not that black clouds had risen in her place, and looked down with visage full of terror and of frowning. It did not move her fears that the palmetto under which she lay, groaned within its tough coat of bark, as it bent to and fro beneath the increasing pressure of the winds. She was still thinking of the wet, cold form of the brave Chiquola.

The gloom thickened. It was the eve of the 23d of September. All day the winds had been rising. The ocean poured in upon the shores. There was little light that day. All was fog, dense fog, and driving vapour, that only was not rain. The watchful Edelano added to the boughs around the lodge of the Queen. The chief men approached her with counsel to persuade her to withdraw to the cover of the stunted thickets, so that she might be secure. But her resolution seemed to have grown more firm, and duly to increase in proportion to their entreaties. She had an answer, which, as it appealed to their superstitions, was conclusive to silence them.

"I have seen him. But last night he came to me. His brow was bound about with a cloud, such as goes round the moon. From his eye shot arrows of burning fire, like those of the storm. He smiled upon me, and bade me smile. 'Soon shalt thou warm me, Combahee, with the blazing bones of mine enemies. Be of good cheer—watch well that ye behold them where they lie. Thou shalt see them soon.' Thus spoke the chief. He whispers to my heart even now. Dost thou not hear him, Kiawah? He says soon—it will be soon!"

Such an assurance was reason good why she should continue her desolate and dangerous watch. The generous determination of the tribe induced them to share it with her. But this they did not suffer her to see. Each reared his temporary lodge in the most sheltered contiguous places, under his favourite clump of trees. Where the growth was stunted, and the thicket dense, little groups of women and children were made to harbour in situations of comparative security. But the warriors and brave men of the tribe advanced along the shores to positions of such shelter as they could find, but sufficiently nigh to their Queen to give her the necessary assistance in moments of sudden peril. The more devoted Edelano, presuming upon the prospective tie which was to give him future privileges, quietly laid himself down behind the isolated lodge of the princess, with a delight at being so near to her, that made him almost forgetful of the dangers of her exposed situation.

He was not allowed to forget them, however! The storm increased with the progress of the night. Never had such an equinoctial gale been witnessed, since the memory of Kiawah. The billows roared as if with the agony of so many wild monsters under the scourge of some imperious demon. The big trees of the forest groaned, and bent, and bowed, and were snapped off, or torn up by the roots; while the seas, surcharged with the waters of the Gulf, rushed in upon the land and threatened to overwhelm and swallow it. The waves rose to the brow of the headland, and small streams came flashing around the lodge of Combahee. Her root-tree bent and cracked, but, secure in its lowliness, it still stood; but the boughs were separated and whirled away, and, at the perilous moment, the gallant Edelano, who had forborne, through a natural timidity, to come forward until the last instant, now darted in, and with a big but fast beating heart, clasped the woman of his worship to his arms and bore her, as if she had been a child, to the stunted thickets which gave a shelter to the rest. But, even while they fled—amidst all the storm—a sudden sound reached the ears of the Queen, which seemed to awaken in her a new soul of energy. A dull, booming noise, sullen, slow rolling, sluggish,—something like that of thunder, rolled to their ears, as if it came from off the seas. No thunder had fallen from the skies in the whole of the previous tempest. No lightning had illuminated to increase the gloom. "What is that sound," said the heart of Combahee, filled with its superstitious instincts, "but the thunder of the pale-faces—the sudden thunder which bellows from the sides of their big-winged canoes?"

With this conviction in her mind, it was no longer possible for Edelano to detain her. Again and again did that thunder reach their ears, slowly booming along the black precipices of the ocean. The warriors and chiefs peered along the shores, with straining eyes, seeking to discover the hidden objects; and among these, with dishevelled hair, quivering lips, eyes which dilated with the wildest fires of an excited, an inspired soul, the form of Combahee was conspicuous. Now they saw the sudden flash—now they heard the mournful roar of the minute gun—and then all was silent.

"Look closely, Kiawah—look closely, Edelano; for what said the ghost of Chiquola?—'watch well! Soon shall ye see where the bones of my enemies lie.'—And who were the enemies of Chiquola? Who but the pale-faces? It is their thunder that we hear—the thunder of their big canoes. Hark, ye hear it now,—and hear ye no cries as of men that drown and struggle? Hark! Hark! There shall be bones for the fire ere the day opens upon us."

And thus they watched for two hours, which seemed ages, running along the shores, waving their torches, straining the impatient sight, and calling to one another through the gloom. The spirit of the bravest warrior quailed when he beheld the fearless movements of Combahee, down to the very edges of the ocean gulf, defying the mounting waves, that dashed their feathery jets of foam, twenty feet above them in the air. The daylight came at last, but with it no relaxation of the storm. With its light what a picture of terror presented itself to the eyes of the warriors—what a picture of terror—what a prospect of retribution! There came, head on shore, a noble vessel, still struggling, still striving, but predestined to destruction. Her sails were flying in shreds, her principal masts were gone, her movement was like that of a drunken man—reeling to and fro—the very mockery of those winds and waters, which, at other periods, seem only to have toiled to bear her and to do her bidding. Two hundred screaming wretches clung to her sides, and clamoured for mercy to the waves and shores. Heaven flung back the accents, and their screams now were those of defiance and desperation. Combahee heard their cries, detected their despair, distinguished their pale faces. Her eyes gleamed with the intelligence of the furies. Still beautiful, her wan, thin face,—wan and thin through long and weary watching, exposure and want of food—looked like the loveliness of some fallen angel. A spirit of beauty in the highest degree—a morning star in brightness and brilliance,—but marked by the passions of demoniac desolation, and the livid light of some avenging hate. Her meagre arms were extended, and waved, as if in doom to the onward rushing vessel.

"Said I not," she cried to her people,—"Said I not that there should be bones for the fire, which should warm the limbs of Chiquola?—See! these are they. They come. The warrior shall be no longer cold in the blue forests of the good Maneyto."

While one ship rushed headlong among the breakers, another was seen, bearing away, at a distance, under bare poles. These were the only surviving vessels of the armament of Lucas de Ayllon. All but these had gone down in the storm, and that which was now rushing to its doom bore the ill-fated De Ayllon himself. The historian remarks—(see History of South Carolina, p. 11) —"As if the retributive Providence had been watchful of the place, no less than of the hour of justice, it so happened that, at the mouth of the very river where his crime had been committed, he was destined to meet his doom." The Indian traditions go farther. They say, that the form of Chiquola was beheld by Combahee, standing upon the prow of the vessel, guiding it to the place set apart by the fates for the final consummation of that destiny which they had allotted to the perfidious Spaniards. We will not contend for the tradition; but the coincidence between the place of crime and that of retribution, was surely singular enough to impress, not merely upon the savage, but also upon the civilized mind, the idea of an overruling and watchful justice. The breakers seized upon the doomed ship, as the blood-hounds seize upon and rend the expiring carcass of the stricken deer. The voice of Combahee was heard above the cries of the drowning men. She bade her people hasten with their arrows, their clubs, their weapons of whatever kind, and follow her to the beach. She herself bore a bow in her hand, with a well filled quiver at her back; and as the vessel stranded, as the winds and waves rent its planks and timbers asunder, and billows bore the struggling and drowning wretches to the shore, the arrows of Combahee were despatched, in rapid execution. Victim after victim sunk, stricken, among the waters, with a death of which he had had no fear. The warriors strode, waist deep, into the sea, and dealt with their stone hatchets upon their victims. These when despatched, were drawn ashore, and the less daring were employed to heap them up, in a vast and bloody mound, for the sacrifice of fire.

The keen eyes of Combahee distinguished the face of the perfidious De Ayllon among the struggling Spaniards. His richer dress had already drawn upon him the eyes of an hundred warriors, who only waited with their arrows until the inevitable billows should bear him within their reach.

"Spare *him!*" cried the widow of Chiquola. They understood her meaning at a glance, and a simultaneous shout attested their approbation of her resolve.

"The arrows of fire!" was the cry. The arrows of reed and flint were expended upon the humble wretches from the wreck. The miserable De Ayllon little fancied the secret of this forbearance. He grasped a spar which assisted his progress, and encouraged in the hope of life, as he found himself spared by the shafts which were slaying all around him, he was whirled onward by the breakers to the shore. The knife touched him not—the arrow forbore his bosom, but all beside perished. Two hundred spirits were dismissed to eternal judgment, in that bloody hour of storm and retribution, by the hand of violence. Senseless amidst the dash of the breakers,—unconscious of present or future danger, Lucas De Ayllon came within the grasp of the fierce warriors, who rushed impatient for their prisoner neck deep into the sea. They bore him to the land. They used all the most obvious means for his restoration, and had the satisfaction to perceive that he at length opened his eyes. When sufficiently recovered to become aware of what had been done for him, and rushing to the natural conclusion that it had all been done in kindness, he smiled upon his captors, and, addressing them in his own language, endeavoured still further, by signs and sounds, to conciliate their favour.

"Enough!" said the inflexible Combahee, turning away from the criminal with an expression of strong disgust—

"Enough! wherefore should we linger? Are not the limbs of Chiquola still cold and wet? The bones of his enemies are here—let the young men build the sacrifice. The hand of Combahee will light the fire arrow!"

A dozen warriors now seized upon the form of De Ayllon. Even had he not been enfeebled by exhaustion, his struggles would have been unavailing. Equally unavailing were his prayers and promises. The Indians turned with loathing from his base supplications, and requited his entreaties and tears with taunts, and buffetings, and scorn! They bore him, under the instructions of Combahee, to that palmetto, looking out upon the sea, beneath which, for so many weary months, she had maintained her lonely watch. The storm had torn her lodge to atoms, but the tree was unhurt. They bound him to the shaft with withes of grape vines, of which the neighbouring woods had their abundance. Parcels of light-wood were heaped about him, while, interspersed with other bundles of the resinous pine, were piled the bodies of his slain companions. The only living man, he was the centre of a pile composed of two hundred, whose fate he was now prepared to envy. A dreadful mound, it rose conspicuous, like a beacon, upon the head-land of St. Helena; he, the centre, with his head alone free, and his eyes compelled to survey all the terrible preparations which were making for his doom. Layers of human carcasses, followed by layers of the most inflammable wood and brush, environed him with a wall from which, even had he not been bound to the tree, he could never have effected his own extrication. He saw them pile the successive layers, sparing the while no moment which he could give to expostulation, entreaty, tears, prayers, and promises. But the workmen with steady industry pursued their task. The pile rose,—the human pyramid was at last complete!

Combahee drew nigh with a blazing torch in her hand. She looked the image of some avenging angel. She gave but a single glance upon the face of the criminal. That face was one of an agony which no art could hope to picture. Hers was inflexible as stone, though it bore the aspect of hate, and loathing, and revenge! She applied the torch amid the increased cries of the victim, and as the flame shot up, with a dense black smoke to heaven, she turned away to the sea, and prostrated herself beside its billows. The shouts of the warriors who surrounded the blazing pile attested their delight; but, though an hundred throats set up their united clamours, the one piercing shriek of the burning man was superior, and rose above all other sounds. At length it ceased! all ceased! The sacrifice was ended. The perfidy of the Spaniard was avenged.

The sudden hush declared the truth to the Queen. She started to her feet. She exclaimed:—

"Thou art now blessed, Chiquola! Thou art no longer cold in the blue forests of Maneyto. The bones of thy enemies have warmed thee. I see thee spring gladly upon the chase;—thine eye is bright above the hills;—thy voice rings cheerfully along the woods of heaven. The heart of Combahee is very glad that thou art warm and happy."

A voice at her side addressed her. The venerable Kiawah, and the young Edelano were there.

"Now, thou hast done well, my daughter!" said the patriarch. "Chiquola is warm and happy in heaven. Let the lodge of Combahee be also warm in the coming winter."

"Ah! but there is nothing to make it warm here!" she replied, putting her hand upon her heart.

"The bird will have its mate, and build its nest, and sing a new song over its young."

"Combahee has no more song."

"The young chief will bring song into her lodge. Edelano will build a bright fire upon the hearth of Combahee. Daughter! the chief ask, 'Is the race of Ocketee to perish?'"

"Combahee is ready," answered the Queen, patiently, giving her hand to Edelano. But, even as she spoke, the muscles of her mouth began to quiver. A sudden groan escaped her, and, staggering forward, she would have fallen but for the supporting arms of the young chief. They bore her to the shade beneath a tree. They poured some of their primitive specifics into her mouth, and she revived sufficiently to bid the Patriarch unite her with Edelano in compliance with the will of the nation. But the ceremony was scarcely over, before a second and third attack shook her frame with death-like spasms. They were, indeed, the spasms of death—of a complete paralysis of mind and body. Both had been too severely tried, and the day of bridal was also that of death. Edelano was now the beloved chief of the nation, but the nation was without its Queen. The last exciting scene, following hard upon that long and lonely widow-watch which she had kept, had suddenly stopped the currents of life within her heart, as its currents of hope and happiness had been cut off before. True to Chiquola while *he* lived, to the last moment of *her* life she was true. The voice of Edelano had called her his wife, but her ears had not heard his speech, and her voice had not replied. Her hand had been put within his, but no other lips had left a kiss where those of Chiquola had been. They buried her in a lovely but lonely grove beside the Ashepoo. There, the Coonee-Latee first repairs to sing in the opening of spring, and the small blue violet peeps out from her grave as if in homage to her courage and devotion. There the dove flies for safety when the fowler pursues, and the doe finds a quiet shelter when the beagles pant on the opposite side of the stream. The partridge hides her young under the long grass which waves luxuriantly above the spot, and the eagle and hawk look down watching from the tree-tops in vain. The spirit of the beautiful Princess presides over the place as some protecting Divinity, and even the white man, though confident in a loftier and nobler faith, still finds something in the spot which renders it mysterious, and makes him an involuntary worshipper! Ah! there are deities which are common to all human kind, whatever be the faith which they maintain. Love is of this sort, and truth, and devotion; and of these the desolate Combahee had a Christian share, though the last deed of her life be not justified by the doctrine of Christian retribution. Yet, look not, traveller, as in thy bark thou sailest beside the lovely headlands of Saint Helena, at the pile of human sacrifice which thou seest consuming there. Look at the frail lodge beneath the Palmetto, or wander off to the dark groves beside the Ashepoo and think of the fidelity of that widowed heart.

> "She died for him she loved—her greatest pride,
> That, as for him she lived, for him she died:
> Make her young grave,
> Sweet fancies, where the pleasant branches lave
> Their drooping tassels in some murmuring wave!"

"**The Legend of Guernache**" illustrates Simms's effective use of history in creating a compelling narrative, well-written and well-constructed. Though its sympathies lie with the Indians, the story is remarkably even-handed in its treatment of hostilities between Frenchmen and aborigines in sixteenth-century Florida. The protagonists—Guernache, the sensitive, fair-minded, weak, sensuous French musician; and Monaletta, the beautiful, intelligent, vain, and passionate niece of Chief Audusta—both come alive in Simms's adept characterization of them. The description of the spectacular, ritualistic festival of Toya, which erupts into violence, is memorable in its discerning use of graphic details.

In this story and in other portions of *The Lily and the Totem* Simms discusses and seems to quote the ideas and writings of French colonist and historian René Laudonnière, one of the principal officers in the French Huguenot colonization of the coast of South Carolina and Florida in 1562–65.

ॐ *The Legend of Guernache*

CHAPTER I.

SHOWING HOW GUERNACHE, THE MUSICIAN, A GREAT FAVORITE WITH OUR FRENCHMEN, LOST THE FAVOR OF CAPTAIN ALBERT, AND HOW CRUELLY HE WAS PUNISHED BY THE LATTER.

Guernache, the drummer, was one of the finest fellows, and the handsomest of our little colony of Frenchmen. Though sprung of very humble origin, Guernache, with a little better education, might have been deemed to have had his training among the highest circles of the Court. He was of tall and erect figure, and of a carriage so noble and graceful that, even among his associates, he continued to be an object of admiration. Besides, he was a fellow of the happiest humor. His kindness of heart was proverbial. His merriment was contagious. His eye flashed out in gayety, and his spirit was ever on the alert to seize upon the passing pleasure, and subject it to the enjoyment of his companions. Never was fellow so fortunate in finding occasion for merriment; and happy, indeed, was the Frenchman who could procure Guernache as a comrade in the performance of his daily tasks. The toil was unfelt in which he shared—the weight of the task was dissipated, and, where it wore heavily, he came to the succor of his drooping companion, and his superior expertness soon succeeded in doing that which his pleasantry had failed to effect. He was the best fisherman and hunter—was as brave as he was light-hearted—was, altogether, so perfect a character, in the estimation of the little band of Albert, that he found no enemy among his equals, and could always choose his companion for himself. His successes were not confined to his own countrymen. He found equal favor in the sight of the Indians. Among his other accomplishments, he possessed the most wonderful agility—had belonged, at one time, to a company of strolling players, and his skill on tight and slack rope—if we are to credit old stories—would put to the blush the modern performances of the Ravels and Herr Cline. It was through his means, and partly by his ingenuity, that the Indian hunter was entrapped and brought into the fort,—through whose agency the intimacy had been effected with the people of Audusta and the other chiefs; and, during this intimacy, Guernache had proved, in various ways, one of the principal instruments for confirming the favorable impressions which the Indian had received in his intercourse with the Frenchmen. He was everywhere popular with the red men. Nothing, indeed, could be done without him. Ignorant of his inferior social position among the whites, the simple savages sent for him to their feasts and frolics, without caring for the claims of any other person. He had but to carry his violin—for, among his other accomplishments, that of fiddling was not the smallest—to secure the smiles of the men and the favors of the women; and it was not long before he had formed, among the savages, a class for dancing, after the European fashion, upon the banks of the Edisto. Think of the red men of Apalachia, figuring under a Parisian teacher, by night, by torch-light, beneath the great oaks of the original forest! Such uncouth antics might well offend, with never-lessening wonder, the courtly nymphs of the Seine and the Loire. But the Indians suffered from no conventional apprehensions. They were not made to feel their deficiencies under the indulgent training of Guernache, and footed it away as merrily, as if each of their damsels sported on a toe as light and exquisite as that of Ellsler or Taglioni. King Audusta, himself, though well stricken in years, was yet seduced into the capricious mazes which he beheld with so much pleasure, and, for a season, the triumph of Guernache among the palms and pines of *Grande Riviere,* was sufficiently complete, to make him wonder at times how his countrymen ever suffered his departure for the shores of La Belle France!

At first, and when it was doubtful to what extent the favor of the red-men might be secured for the colony, Captain Albert readily countenanced the growing popularity of his fiddler among them. His permission was frequently given to Guernache, when king Audusta solicited his presence. His policy prompted him to regard it as highly fortunate that so excellent an agent for his purposes was to be found among his followers; and, for some months, it needed only a suggestion of Guernache, himself, to procure for him leave of absence. The worthy fellow never abused his privileges—never was unfaithful to his trust—never grew insolent upon indulgence. But Captain Albert, though claiming to be the cadet of a noble house, was yet a person of a mean and ignoble nature. Small and unimposing of person, effeminate of habit, and accustomed to low indulgences, he was not only deficient in the higher resources of intellect, but he was exceedingly querulous and tyrannical of temper. His aristocratical connexions alone had secured him the charge of the colony, for which nature and education had equally unfitted him. His mind was contracted and full of bitter prejudices; and, as is the case commonly with very small persons, he was always tenacious, to the very letter, of the nicest observances of etiquette. After a little while, and when he no longer had reason to question the fidelity of the red men, he began to exhibit some share of dislike towards Guernache; and to withhold the privileges which he had hitherto permitted him to enjoy. He had become jealous of the degree of favor in which his musician was held among the savages, and betrayed this change in his temper, by instances of occasional severity and denial, the secret of which the companions of Guernache divined much sooner than himself. Though not prepared, absolutely, to withhold his consent, when king Audusta entreated that the fiddler might be spared him, he yet accorded it ungraciously; and Guernache was made to suffer, in some way, for these concessions, as if they had been so many favors granted to himself.

They were, indeed, favors to the musician, though, to what extent, Albert entertained no suspicion. It so happened that among his other conquests, Guernache had made that of a very lovely dark-eyed damsel, a niece of Audusta, and a resident of the king's own village. After the informal fashion of the country, into which our Frenchmen were apt readily to fall, he had made the damsel his wife. She was a beautiful creature, scarcely more than sixteen; tall and slender, and so naturally agile and graceful, that it needed but a moderate degree of instruction to make her a dancer whose airy movements would not greatly have misbeseemed the courtly theatres of Paris. Monaletta,—for such was the sweet name of the Indian damsel,—was an apt pupil, because she was a loving one. She heartily responded to that sentiment of wonder—common among the savages—that the Frenchmen should place themselves under the command of a chief, so mean of person as Albert, and so inferior in gifts, when they had among them a fellow of such noble presence as Guernache, whose qualities were so irresistible. The opinions of her head were but echoes from the feelings in her heart. Her preference for our musician was soon apparent and avowed; but, in taking her to wife, Guernache kept his secret from his best friend. No one in Fort Charles ever suspected that he had been wived in the depth of the great forests, through

pagan ceremonies, by an Indian Iawa,* to the lovely Monaletta. Whatever may
have been his motive for keeping the secret, whether he feared the ridicule of
his comrades, or the hostility of his superior, or apprehended a difficulty
with rivals among the red men, by a discovery of the fact, it is yet very certain
that he succeeded in persuading Monaletta, herself, and those who were present at his wild betrothal, to keep the secret also. It did not lessen, perhaps, the
pleasure of his visits to the settlements of Audusta, that the peculiar joys
which he desired had all the relish of a stolen fruit. It was now, only in this
manner that Monaletta could be seen. Captain Albert, with a rigid austerity,
which contributed also to his evil odor among his people, had interdicted the
visits of all Indian women at the fort. This interdict was one, however, which
gave little annoyance to Guernache. A peculiar, but not unnatural jealousy,
had already prompted him repeatedly to deny this privilege to Monaletta.
The simple savage had frequently expressed her desire to see the fortress of the
white man, to behold his foreign curiosities, and, in particular, to hearken to
the roar of that mimic thunder which he had always at command, and which,
when heard, had so frequently shaken the very hearts of the men of her people.

In this relation stood the several parties, when, one day, a messenger came
to Fort Charles from King Audusta, bearing a special invitation to Captain
Albert to attend, with the savage tribes, the celebration of the great religious
"feast of Toya." He was invited to bring as many of his men as he thought
proper, but, in particular, not to forget their favorite Guernache. The feast of
Toya, seems to have constituted the great religious ceremonial of the nation.
It took place about the middle, or the close of summer, and seems to have
been a sort of annual thanksgiving, after the laws of a natural religion, for the
maturing of their little crops. Much of the solemnities were obvious and
ostentatious in their character. Much more, however, was involved and mysterious, and held particularly sacred by the priesthood. The occasion was one,
at all events, to which the Indians attached the greatest importance; and, naturally anxious to acquire as great a knowledge as possible of their laws, customs and sentiments, Captain Albert very readily acceded to the invitation,—
preparing, with some state, to attend the rustic revels of Audusta. He took
with him a fair proportion of his little garrison, and did not omit the in-
imitable Guernache. Ascending the river in his pinnace, he soon reached

* [SIMMS'S NOTE] Iawa was the title of the priest of prophet of The Floridian. The word
was thus written by Laudonniére in Hakluyt. It is probably a misprint only which, in
Charlevoix, writes it "Iona."

the territories of the Indian monarch. Audusta, with equal hospitality and dignity, anticipated his approach, and met him, with his followers, at the river landing. With a hearty welcome, he conducted him to his habitations, and gave him, at entrance, a draught of the cassina beverage, the famous tea of the country. Then came damsels who washed their hands in vessels of water over which floated the leaves of the odorous bay, and flowers of rare perfume; drying them after with branches of plumes, scarlet and white, which were made of the feathers of native birds of the most glorious variety of hue. Mats of reed, woven ingeniously together by delicate wythes of all colors, orange and green, and vermillion, dyed with roots of the forest, were then spread upon the rush-strewn floor of the royal wigwam; and, with a grace not unbecoming a sovereign born in the purple, Audusta invited our Frenchmen to place themselves at ease, each according to his rank and station. The king took his place among them, neither above the first, nor below the last, but like a friend within a favorite circle, in which some might stand more nearly than others to his affections. They were then attended with the profoundest deference, and served with the rarest of delicacies of the Indian *cuisine*. As night came on, fresh rushes were strewed upon the floor, and they slept with the cheerful music of songs and laughter, which reached them at intervals, through the night, from the merry makers in the contiguous forests. With the dawning of the next day, preparations for the great festival were begun.

CHAPTER II. THE FESTIVAL OF TOYA.
BEING A CONTINUATION OF THE LEGEND OF GUERNACHE; SHOWING THE SUPERSTITIONS OF THE RED-MEN; HOW GUERNACHE OFFENDED CAPTAIN ALBERT, AND WHAT FOLLOWED FROM THE SECRET EFFORTS OF THE FRENCHMEN TO PENETRATE THE MYSTERIES OF TOYA!

It would be difficult to say, from the imperfect narratives afforded us by the chroniclers, what were the precise objects of the present ceremonials;—what gods were to be invoked;—what evil beings implored;—what wrath and anger to be deprecated and diverted from the devoted tribes. As the Frenchmen received no explanation of their mystic preparations, so are we left unenlightened by their revelations. They do not even amuse us by their conjectures, and Laudonniére stops short in his narrative of what did happen, apologizing for having said so much on so trifling a matter. We certainly owe him no gratitude for his forbearance. What he tells us affords but little clue to the motive of their fantastic proceedings. The difficulty, which is at present ours, was not less that of Albert and his Frenchmen. They were compelled to behold the outlines of a foreign ritual whose mysteries they were not permitted to explore, and had their curiosity provoked by shows of a most exciting character, which only mocked their desires, and tantalized their appetites. On the first arrival of Albert, and after he had been rested and refreshed, Audusta himself had conducted him, with his followers, to the spot which had been selected for the ceremonies of the morrow. "This was a great circuit of ground with open prospect and round in figure." Here they saw "many women roundabout, which labored by all means to make the place cleane and neate." The ceremonies began early on the morning of the ensuing day. Hither they repaired in season, and found "all they which were chosen to celebrate the feast," already "painted and trimmed with rich feathers of divers colours." These led the way in a procession from the dwelling of Audusta to the "place of Toya." Here, when they had come, they set themselves in new order under the guidance of three Indians, who were distinguished by plumes, paint, and a costume entirely superior to the rest. Each of them carried a tabret, to the plaintive and lamenting music of which they sang in wild, strange, melancholy accents; and, in slow measures, dancing the while, they passed gradually into the very centre of the sacred circle. They were followed by successive groups, which answered to their strains, and to whose songs they, in turn, responded with like echoes. This continued for awhile, the music gradually rising and swelling from the slow to the swift, from the sad to the passionate, while the moods of the actors and the spectators, also varying, the character of the scene changed to one of the wildest excitement. Suddenly, the characters—those who were chief officiators in this apparent hymn of fate—broke from the enchanted circle—darted through the ranks of the spectators, and dashed, headlong, with frantic cries, into the depths of the neighboring thickets. Then followed another class of actors. As if a sudden terrible doom overhung the nation, the Indian women set up cries of grief and lamentation. Their passion grew to madness. In their rage, the mothers seized upon the young virgins of the tribe, and, with the sharp edges of mussel shells, they lanced their arms, till the blood gushed forth in free streams, which they eagerly flung into the air, crying aloud at every moment, "He-to-yah! He-to-yah! He-to-yah!"*

---

* [SIMMS'S NOTE] Adair likens the cry of the Southern Indians to the sacred name among the Jews—"Je-ho-vah." He writes the Indian syllables thus—"Yo-he-wah," and it constitutes one of his arguments for deducing the origin of the North American redmen from the ancient Hebrews.

These ceremonies, though not more meaningless, perhaps, in the eyes of the Christian, than would be our most solemn religious proceedings in those of the Indian, provoked the laughter of Albert and some of his Frenchmen. This circumstance awakened the indignation of their excellent friend, Audusta. His displeasure was now still farther increased by a proceeding of Captain Albert. It was an attempt upon their mysteries. That portion of the officiating priesthood—their Iawas—who fled from the sacred enclosure to deep recesses of the woods, sought there for the prosecution, in secret, of rites too holy for the vulgar eye. Here they maintained their *sanctum sanctorum*. This was the place consecrated to the communion of the god with his immediate servants—the holy of holies, which it was death to penetrate or pass. Albert suffered his curiosity to get the better of his discretion. Offended by the laughter of the Frenchmen, at what they had already beheld, and fearing lest their audacity should lead them farther, the king, Audusta, had gathered them again within the royal wigwam, where he sought, by marked kindness and distinction, to make them forgetful of what had been denied. They had seen, as he told them, the more impressive portions of the ceremonial. There were others, but not of a kind to interest them. But the fact that there was something to conceal, stimulated the curiosity of Albert. In due degree with the king's anxiety to keep his secret, was that of the French captain's to fathom it. Holding a brief consultation with his men, accordingly, he declared his desire to this effect; and proposed, that one of their number should contrive to steal forth, and, finding his way to the forbidden spot, should place himself in such a position as would enable him to survey all the mysterious proceedings. To this course, Guernache frankly opposed his opinions. His greater intimacy with the red-men led him properly to conceive the danger which might ensue, from their discovery of the intrusion. He had been well taught by Monaletta, the degree of importance which they attached to the security of their mystic rites. Arguing with the honesty of his character, he warned his captain of the risk which such unbecoming curiosity would incur—the peril to the offender, himself, if detected; and the hazards to the colony from the loss of that friendship to which they had been already so largely indebted. But the counsels of Guernache were rejected with indignity. Prepared, already, to regard him with dislike and suspicion, Albert heard his suggestions only as so much impertinence; and rudely commanded him not to forget himself and place, nor to thrust his undesired opinions upon the consideration of gentlemen. The poor fellow was effectually silenced by this rebuke. He sank out of sight, and presumed no farther to advise. But the counsel was not wholly thrown away. Disregarded by Albert, it was caught up, and insisted on, by others, who had better conventional claims to be heard, and the proposition might have been defeated but for the ready interposition of one Pierre Renaud, a young fellow, who, perceiving the captain's strong desire to seek out the mystery, and anxious to ingratiate himself with that person, boldly laughed at the fears of the objectors, and volunteered, himself, to defy the danger, in his own person, in order to gratify his chief. This silenced the controversy. Albert readily availed himself of the offer, and Pierre Renaud was commanded to try his fortune. This he did, and, notwithstanding the surveillance maintained over them by Audusta and his attendants, "he made such shift, that, by subtle meanes, he gotte out of the house of Audusta, and secretly went and hid himselfe behinde a very thick bush, where, at his pleasure, he might easily descry the ceremonies of the feaste."

We will leave Renaud thus busy in his espionage, while we rehearse the manner in which the venerable Audusta proceeded to treat his company. A substantial feast was provided for them, consisting of venison, wild fowl, and fruits. Their breadstuffs were maize, batatas, and certain roots sodden first in water, and then prepared in the sun. A drink was prepared from certain other roots, which, though bitter, was refreshing and slightly stimulant. Our Frenchman, in the absence of the beverages of Italy and France, did not find it unpalatable. They ate and drank with a hearty relish, which gratified the red-men, who lavished on them a thousand caresses. The feast was followed by the dance. In a spacious area, surrounded by great ranks of oaks, cedars, pines, and other trees, they assembled, men and women, in their gayest caparison. The men were tattooed and painted, from head to foot, and not inartistically, in the most glowing colors. Birds and beasts were figured upon their breasts, and huge, strange reptiles were made to coil up and around their legs and arms. From their waists depended light garments of white cotton, the skirts being trimmed with a thick fringe of red or scarlet. Some of them wore head-dresses consisting of the skins of snakes, or eagles, the panther or the wild cat, which, stuffed ingeniously, were made to sit erect above the forehead, and to look abroad, from their novel place of perch, in a manner equally natural and frightful. The women were habited in a similarly wild but less offensive manner. The taste which presided in their decorations, was of a purer and a gentler fashion. Their cheeks were painted red, their arms, occasionally but slightly tattooed, and sometimes the figure of a bird, a flower or a star, might be seen engrained upon the breast. A rather scanty robe of white cotton concealed, in some degree, the bosom, and extended somewhat below the knees. Around the necks of several, were hung thick strands of native pearls, partially discolored by the action of fire which had been employed to extricate them from the shells. Pearls were also mingled ingeniously with the long tresses of their straight, black hair; trailing with it, in not unfrequent instances, even to the ground. Others, in place of this more valuable ornament, wore necklaces, anklets and tiaras, formed wholly of one or other of the numerous varieties of little sea shells, by which, after heavy storms, the low and sandy shores of the country were literally covered. Strings of the same shell encircled the legs, which were sometimes of a shape to gratify the nicest exactions of the civilized standard. The forms of our Indian damsels were generally symmetrical and erect, their movements at once agile and graceful—their foreheads high, their lips thin, and, with a soft, persuasive expression, inclining to melancholy; while their eyes, black and bright, always shone with a peculiar forest fire that seemed happily to consort with their dark, but not unpleasing complexions. Well, indeed, with a pardonable vanity, might their people call them the "Daughters of the Sun." He had made them his, by his warmest and fondest glances. These were the women, whose descendants, in after days, as Yemassees and Muscoghees and Seminoles, became the scourge of so large a portion of the Anglo-American race.

When the Frenchmen beheld this rude, but really brilliant assemblage, and saw what an attractive show the young damsels made, they were delighted beyond measure. Visions of the rout and revel, as enjoyed in *La Belle France,* glanced before their fancies; and the lively capering that followed among the young Huguenots, informed Captain Albert of the desire which was felt by all. In stern, compelling accents, he bade Guernache take his violin, and provide the music, while the rest prepared to dance. But Guernache excused himself, alleging the want of strings for his instrument. These were shown, in a broken state, to his commander. He had broken them, we may state *en passant,* for the occasion. His pride had been hurt by the treatment of his captain. He felt that the purpose of the latter was to degrade him. Such a performance as that required at his hands, was properly no part of his duty; and his proud spirit revolted at the idea of contributing, in any way, to the wishes of his superior, when the object of the latter was evidently his own degradation. Albert spoke to him testily, and with brows that did not seek to subdue or conceal their frowns. But Guernache was firm, and though he studiously forebore, by word or look, to increase the provocation which he had already given, he yet made no effort to pacify the imperious nature which he had offended. The excuse was such as could not but be taken. There was the violin, indeed, but there, also, were the broken strings. Albert turned from the musician with undisguised loathing; and the poor fellow sunk back with a secret presentiment of evil. He but too well knew the character of his superior.

Meanwhile, the red men had resort to their own primitive music. Their instruments consisted of simple reeds, which, bound together, were passed, to and fro, beneath the lips and discoursed very tolerable harmonies;—and a rude drum formed by stretching a raw deer skin over the mouth of a monstrous calabash, enabled them, when the skin had been contracted in the sun, to extort from it a very tolerable substitute for the music of the tambourine. There were other instruments, susceptible of sound if not of sweetness. Numerous damsels, none over fifteen, lithe and graceful, carried in their hands little gourds, which were filled with shells and pebbles, and tied over with skins, dried also in the sun. With these, as they danced, they kept time so admirably as might have charmed the most practised European master. Thus, all provided, some with the drum, and others with flute-like reeds and hollow, tinkling gourds, they only awaited the summons of their partners to the area. Shaking their tinkling gourds, as if in pretty impatience at the delay, the girls each waited, with anxious looks, the signal from her favorite.

The Frenchmen were not slow in seeking out their partners. At the word and signal of their captain, they dashed in among the laughing group of dusky maidens, each seeking for the girl whose beauties had been most grateful to his tastes. Nor was Captain Albert, himself, with all his pride and asceticism, unwilling to forget his dignity for a season, and partake of the rude festivities of the occasion. When, indeed, did mirth and music fail to usurp dominion in the Frenchman's heart? Albert greedily cast his eyes about, seeking a partner, upon whom he might bestow his smiles. He was not slow in the selection. It so happened, that Monaletta, the spouse of Guernache, was not only one of the loveliest damsels present, but she was well known as the niece of King Audusta. Her beauty and royal blood, equally commended her to the favor of our captain. She stood apart from all the rest, stately and graceful as the cedar, not seeming to care for the merriment in which all were now engaged. There was a dash of sadness in her countenance. Her thoughts were elsewhere—her eyes scarcely with the assembly, when the approach of Albert startled her from her reverie. He came as Cæsar did, to certain conquest; and was about to take her hand, as a matter of course, when he was equally astounded and enraged to find her draw it away from his grasp.

"You will not dance with *me*, Monaletta?"

"No," she answered him in broken French—"No dance with you—dance with *him*!" pointing to Guernache.

Speaking these words, she crossed the floor, with all the bold imprudence of a truly loving heart, to the place where stood our sorrowful and unhappy violinist. He had followed the movements of Albert, with looks of most serious apprehension, and his heart had sunk, with a sudden terror, when he saw that he approached Monaletta. The scene which followed, however grateful to his affections, was seriously calculated to arouse his fears. He feared for Monaletta, as he feared for himself. Nothing escaped him in the brief interview, and he saw, in the vindictive glances of Albert, the most evil auguries for the future. Yet how precious was her fondness to his heart! He half forgot his apprehensions as he felt her hand upon his shoulder, and beheld her eyes looking with appealing fondness up into his own. That glance was full of the sweetest consolation,—and said everything that was grateful to his terrified affections. She, too, had seen the look of hate and anger in the face of Albert, and she joyed in the opportunity of rebuking the one with her disdain, and of consoling the other with her sympathies. It was an unhappy error. Bitter, indeed, was the look with which the aroused and mortified Albert regarded the couple as they stood apart from all the rest. Guernache beheld this look. He knew the meaning of that answering glance of his superior which encountered his own. His looks were those of entreaty, of deprecation. They seemed to say, "I feel that you are offended, but I had no purpose or part in the offence." His glance of humility met with no answering indulgence. It seemed, indeed, still farther to provoke his tyrant, who, advancing midway across the room, addressed him in stern, hissing accents, through his closed and almost gnashing teeth.

"Away, sirrah, to the pinnace! See that you remain in her until I summon you! Away!"

The poor fellow turned off from Monaletta. He shook himself free from the grasp which she had taken of his hand. He prepared to obey the wanton and cruel order, but he could not forbear saying reproachfully as he retired—

"You push me too hard, Captain Albert."

"No words, sir! Away!" was the stern response. The submissive fellow instantly disappeared. With his disappearance, Albert again approached Monaletta, and renewed his application. But this time he met with a rejection even more decided than before. He looked to King Audusta; but an Indian princess, while she remains unmarried, enjoys a degree of social liberty which the same class of persons in Europe would sigh for and supplicate in vain. There were no answering sympathies in the king's face, to encourage Albert in the prosecution of his suit. Nay, he had the mortification to perceive, from the expression of his countenance, that his proceedings toward Guernache— who was a general favorite—had afforded not more satisfaction to him, than they had done to Monaletta. It was, therefore, in no very pleasant mood with himself and those around him, that our captain consoled himself in the dance with the hand of an inferior beauty. Jealous of temper and frivolous of mind—characteristics which are frequently found together—Albert was very fond of dancing, and enjoyed the sport quite as greatly as any of his companions. But, even while he capered, his soul, stung and dissatisfied, was brooding vexatiously over its petty hurts. His thoughts were busied in devising ways to revenge himself upon the humble offender by whom his mortification originally grew. Upon this sweet and bitter cud did he chew while the merry music sounded in his ears, and the gaily twinkling feet of the dusky maidens were whirling in promiscuous mazes beneath his eye. But these festivities, and his own evil meditations, were destined to have interruption as startling as unexpected.

While the mirth was at its highest, and the merriment most contagious, the ears of the assembly were startled by screams, the most terrible, of fright and anguish. The Frenchmen felt a nameless terror seizing upon them. The cries and shrieks were from an European throat. Wild was the discord which accompanied them,—whoops of wrath and vengeance, which, as evidently issued only from the throats of most infuriated savages. The music ceased in an instant. The dance was arrested. The Frenchmen rushed to their arms, fully believing that they were surrounded by treachery—that they had been beguiled to the feast only to become its victims. With desperate decision, they prepared themselves for the worst. While their suspense and fear were at their highest, the cause of the alarm and uproar soon became apparent to their eyes. Bursting, like a wounded deer, suddenly, from the woods by which the dwelling of Audusta was surrounded, a bloody figure, ghastly and spotted, appeared before the crowd. In another moment the Frenchmen recognized the spy, Pierre Renaud, who had volunteered to get at the heart of the Indian mysteries—to follow the priesthood to their sacred haunts, and gather all the secrets of their ceremonials.

We have already seen that he reached his place of watch in safety. But here his good fortune failed him: his place of espionage was not one of concealment. In the wild orgies of their religion,—for they seem to have practised rites not dissimilar to, and not less violent and terrible than those of the British Druids,—the priests darted over the crouching spy. Detected in the very act, where he lay, "squat like a toad," the Iawas fell upon him with the sharp instruments of flint with which they had been lancing and lacerating their own bodies. With these they contrived, in spite of all his struggles and entreaties, to inflict upon him some very severe wounds. Their rage was unmeasured, and the will to slay him was not wanting. But Renaud was a fellow equally vigorous and active. He baffled their blows as well as he could, and at length breaking from their folds, he took fairly to his heels. Howling with rage and fury, they darted upon his track, their wild shrieks ringing through the wood like those of so many demons suffering in mortal agony. They cried to all whom they saw, to stay and slay the offender. Others joined in the chase, as they heard the summons. But fortune favored the fugitive. His terror added wings to his flight. He was not, it seems, destined to such a death as they designed him. He outran his pursuers, and, dodging those whom he accidentally encountered, he made his way into the thick of the area, where his comrades, half bewildered by the uproar, were breaking up the dance. He sank down in the midst of them, exhausted by loss of blood and fatigue, only a moment before the appearance of his pursuers.

The French instantly closed around their companion. They had not put aside their weapons, and they now prepared themselves to encounter the worst. The aspect of the danger was threatening in the last degree. The Iawas were boiling with sacred fury. They were the true rulers of their people. Their will was sovereign over the popular moods. They demanded, with violent outcry, the blood of the individual by whom their sacred retreats had been violated, and their shekinah polluted by vulgar and profane presence. They demanded the blood of *all* the Frenchmen, as participating in the crime. They called upon Audusta to assert his own privileges and theirs. They appealed to the people in a style of phrenzied eloquence, the effects of which were soon visible in the inflamed features and wild action of the more youthful warriors. Already were these to be seen slapping their sides, tossing their hands in air, and, with loud shrieks, lashing themselves into a fury like that which enflamed their prophets. King Audusta looked confounded. The Frenchmen were his guests. He had invited them to partake of his hospitality, and to enjoy the rites of his religion. He was in some sort pledged for their safety, though one of them had violated the conditions of their coming. His own feelings revolted at giving any sanction for the assault, yet he appeared unable or unwilling to resist the clamors of the priesthood. But *he* also demanded, though with evident reluctance, the blood of the offender. He was not violent, though urgent, in this demand. He showed indignation rather than hostility; and he gave Albert to understand that in no way could the people or the priesthood be appeased, unless by the sacrifice of the guilty person.

But Albert could not yield the victim. The French were prepared to perish to a man before complying with any such demand. They were firm. They fenced him in with their weapons, and declared their readiness to brave every peril ere they would abandon their comrade. This resolution was the more honorable, as Pierre Renaud was no favorite among them. Though seriously disquieted by the event, and apprehensive of the issue, Albert was man enough to second their spirit. Besides, Renaud had been his own emissary in the adventure which threatened to terminate so fatally. His denial was inferred from his deportment; and the clamor of the Indians was increased. The rage of the Iawas was renewed with the conviction that no redress was to be given them. Already had the young warriors of Audusta procured their weapons. More than an hundred of them surrounded our little band of Frenchmen, who were only thirteen in number. Bows were bent, lances were set in rest, javelins were seen lifted, and ready to be thrown; and the drum which had been just made to sound, in lively tones, for the dance, now gave forth the most dismal din, significant of massacre and war. Already were to be seen, in the hands of some more daring Indian than the rest, the heavy war-club, or the many-teethed macana, waving aloft and threatening momently to descend upon the victim; and nothing was wanting but a first blow to bring on a general massacre. Suddenly, at this perilous moment, the fiddle of Guernache was heard without; followed, in a moment after, by the appearance of the brave fellow himself. Darting in between the opposing ranks, attended by the faithful Monaletta, with a grand crash upon his instrument, now newly-strung, followed by a rapid gush of the merriest music, he took both parties by the happiest surprise, and instantly produced a revulsion of feeling among the savages as complete as it was sudden.

"Ami! ami! ami!" was the only cry from an hundred voices, at the reappearance of Guernache among them. They had acquired this friendly epithet among the first words which they had learned at their coming, from the French; and their affection for our fiddler had made its application to himself, in particular, a thing of general usage. He *was* their friend. He had shown himself their friend, and they had a faith in *him* which they accorded to no other of his people. The people were with him, and the priesthood not unfriendly. Time was gained by this diversion; and, in such an outbreak as that which has been described, time is all that is needful, perhaps, to stay the arm of slaughter. Guernache played out his tune, and cut a few pleasant antics, in which the now happy Monaletta, though of the blood royal, readily joined him. The musician had probably saved the party from massacre. The subsequent work of treaty and pacification was comparatively easy. Pierre Renaud was permitted to depart for the pinnace, under the immediate care of Guernache and Monaletta. The Iawas received some presents of gaudy costume, bells, and other gew-gaws, while a liberal gift of knives and beads gratified their warriors and their women. The old ties of friendship were happily reunited, and the calumet went round, from mouth to mouth, in token of restored confidence and renewed faith. Before nightfall, happily relieved from his apprehensions, Albert, with his detachment, was rapidly making his way with his pinnace, down the waters of the swiftly-rolling Edisto.

CHAPTER III.
THE LEGEND OF GUERNACHE IS CONTINUED, SHOWING HOW THE FORTRESS OF THE HUGUENOTS WAS DESTROYED, AND WHAT HAPPENED THEREAFTER TO GUERNACHE THE MUSICIAN.

The fidelity which Guernache had shown in the recent difficulty with the Indians, did not appear to lessen in any degree the unfavorable impressions which Capt. Albert had received of that worthy fellow. Indeed, the recent and remarkable service which he had rendered, by which, in all probability, the whole party had been preserved from massacre, rather increased, if any thing, the hostile temper of his superior. The evil spirit still raged within the bosom of Capt. Albert, utterly baffling a judgment at no period of particular excellence, and blinding every honorable sentiment which might have distinguished him under other influences. He was now doubly mortified, that he should be supposed to owe his present safety to the person he had wronged— a mortification which found due increase as he remembered how much greater had been the respect and deference of the savages for his drummer than for himself. This recollection was a perpetual goad to that working malice in his heart, which was already busied in devising schemes of revenge, which were to salve his hurts of pride and vanity, by the sufferings as well as humiliation of his subordinate. It will scarcely be believed that, when fairly out of sight of the village of Audusta, he rebuked Guernache sharply, for leaving the pinnace against his orders, and even spoke of punishing him for this disobedience.* But the murmurs of some of his officers, and, perhaps, a little lurking sentiment of shame in his own bosom, prevented him from attempting any such disgraceful proceeding. But the felling of hostility only rankled the more because of its suppression, and he soon contrived to show Guernache and, indeed, everybody besides, that from that hour he was his most bitter and unforgiving enemy, with a little and malignant spirit, he employed various petty arts, which a superior of a base nature may readily command on all occasions, by which to make the poor fellow feel how completely he was at his mercy; and each day exposed him to some little snare, or some stem caprice, by which Guernache became involuntarily an offender. His tyrant subjected him to duties the most troublesome and humiliating, while denying, or stinting him of all those privileges which were yet commonly accorded to his comrades. But all this would have been as nothing to Guernache, if he had not been denied permission to visit, as before, the hamlet of Audusta, where his princess dwelt. On the miserable pretext that the priesthood might revenge upon him the misconduct of Renaud, Albert insisted upon his abstaining wholly from the Indian territories. But this pretence deceived nobody, and nobody less than Guernache. Little did the petty tyrant of Fort Charles imagine that the object of his malice enjoyed a peculiar source of consolation for all these privations. His comrades were his friends. They treated him with a warmth and kindness, studiously proportioned to the ill-treatment of his superior. They assisted him in the severer tasks which were allotted him to fulfil—gave him their company whenever this was possible, while he was engaged in the execution of his most cheerless duties, and soothed his sorrows by the expression of their almost unanimous

* [SIMMS's NOTE] Charlevoix thus describes Captain Albert: "Le Commandant de Charles-Fort étoit un homme de main, et qui ne manquoit pas absolument de conduite, mais il etoit brutal jusqu' à la férocité,' et ne sçavoit pas meme garder les bienséances. . . . . Il punissoit les moindres fautes, and toujours avec excès, & c.—N. France, Liv. 1 p. 51.

sympathies. Nor did they always withhold their bitter denunciations of the miserable despotism under which he suffered, and which they feared. Dark hints of remedy were spoken, brows frowned at the mention of the wrongs of their companion, and the head shaken ominously, when words of threatening significance were uttered—appealed gratefully to certain bitter desires which had taken root in the mind of the victim. But these sympathies, though grateful, were of small amount in comparison with another source of consolation, which contributed to sustain Guernache in his tribulation. This was found in the secret companionship of his young and beautiful Indian wife. Denied to see him at the village of Audusta, the fond and fearless woman determined to seek him at all hazards in his own domain. She stole away secretly to the fortress of the Huguenots. Long and earnest was the watch which she maintained upon its portals, from the thickets of the neighboring wood. Here, vigilant as the sentinel that momently expects his foe, she harbored close, in waiting for the beloved one. Her quick instincts had already taught her the true cause of his denial, and of her disappointment; and her Indian lessons had made that concealment, which she now believed to be necessary to her purpose, a part of the habitual policy of her people. She showed herself to none of the people of the fortress. She suspected them all; she had no faith but in the single one. And he, at length, came forth, unaccompanied, in the prosecution of an occasional labor—that of cutting and procuring wood. She suffered him to make his way into the forests— to lose sight of the fortress, and, with a weary spirit and a wounded soul, to begin his lonely labors with the axe. Then did she steal behind him, and beside him; and when he moaned aloud—supposing that he had no auditor— how startling fell upon his ear the sweet, soft whisper of that precious voice which he had so lovingly learned to distinguish from all others. He turned with a gush of rapturous delight, and, weeping, she rushed into his arms, pouring forth, in a wild cry, upon his breast, the whole full volume of her warm, devoted heart!

That moment, in spite of all his fears, was amply compensative to Guernache for all his troubles. He forgot them all in the intensity of his new delights. And when Monaletta led him off from his tasks to the umbrageous retreat in the deeper woods where her nights had been recently passed,— when she conducted him to the spot where her own hands had built a mystic bower for her own shelter—when she declared her purpose still to occupy this retreat, in the solitude alone,—that she might be ever near him, to behold him at a distance, herself unseen, when he came forth accompanied by others—to join him, to feel his embrace, hear his words of love, and assist him in his labors when he came forth unattended—when, speaking and promising thus, she lay upon the poor fellow's bosom, looking up with tearful and bright eyes in his wan and apprehensive countenance—then it was that he could forget his tyrant—could lose his fears and sorrows in his love, and in the enjoyment of moments the most precious to his heart, forget all the accompanying influences which might endanger his safety.

But necessity arose sternly between the two, and pointed to the exactions of duty. The tasks of Guernache were to be completed. His axe was required to sound among the trees of the forest, and a certain number of pieces of timber were required by sunset at his hands. It was surprising as it was sweet to behold the Indian woman as she assisted him in his tasks. Her strength did not suffice for the severer toils of the wood-cutter, but she contrived a thousand modes for contributing to his performances. Love lightens every labor, and invents a thousand arts by which to do so. Monaletta anticipated the wants of Guernache. She removed the branches as he smote them, she threw the impediments from his way,—helped him to lift and turn the logs as each successive side was to be hewn. She brought him water, when he thirsted, from the spring. She spoke and sung to him in the most encouraging voice when he was weary. He was never weary when with her.

Guernache combatted her determination to remain in the neighborhood of the fortress; but his objections were feebly urged, and she soon overcame them. He had not the courage to insist upon his argument, as he had not the strength to resist the consolations which her presence brought him. She soon succeeded in assuring him that there was little or no danger of detection by their enemy. She laughed at the idea of the Frenchmen discovering her place of concealment, surprising her in her progress through the woods, or overtaking her in flight; and Guernache knew enough of Indian subtlety readily to believe that the white was no match for the dusky race in the exercise of all those arts which are taught by forest life. "But her loneliness and privation, exposed to the season's changes, and growing melancholy in the absence from old associates?" But how could she be lonely, was her argument, when near the spot where he dwelt—when she could see and hear and speak with him occasionally? She wished no other communion. As for the exposure of her present abode, was it greater than that to which the wandering life of the redman subjects his people at all seasons? The Indian woman is quite as much at home in the forest as the Indian warrior. She acquires her resources of strength and dexterity in his company, and by the endurance of similar necessities and the employment of like exercises. She learns even in childhood to build her own green bower at night, to gather her own fuel, light her own fire, dress her own meat—nay, provide it; and, weaponed with bow, and javelin and arrow, bring down buck or doe bounding at full speed through the wildest forests. Her skill and spirit are only not equal to those of the master by whom she is taught, but she acquires his arts to a degree which makes her sometimes worthy to be lifted by the tribe from her own rank into his. Monaletta reminded Guernache of all these things. She had the most conclusive and convincing methods of argument. She reassured him on all his doubts, and, in truth, it was but too easy to do so. It was unhappy for them both, as we shall see hereafter, that the selfish passion of the poor musician too readily reconciled him to a self-devotion on the part of his wife, which subjected her to his own perils, and greatly tended to their increase. With the evil eye of Albert upon him, he should have known that safety was impossible for him in the event of error. And error was inevitable now, with the pleasant tempter so near his place of coventry. We must not wonder to discover now that Guernache seldom sleeps within the limits of the fortress. At midnight, when all is dark and quiet, he leaps over the walls, those nights excepted when it is his turn of duty to watch within. His secret is known to some of his comrades; but they are too entirely his friends to betray him to a despot who had, by this time, outraged the feelings of most of those who remained under his command. Guernache was now enabled to bear up more firmly than ever against the tyranny of Albert. His, indeed, were nights of happiness. How sweetly sped the weeks, in which, despite his persecutions, he felt that he enjoyed a life of luxurious pleasures, such as few enjoy in any situation. His were the honest excitements of a genuine passion, which, nourished by privation and solitude, and indulged in secresy, was of an intensity corresponding with the apparent denial, and the real embarrassments of such a condition. His pleasures were at once stolen and legitimate; the apprehension which attends their pursuit giving a wild zest to their enjoyment; though, in the case of Guernache, unlike that of most of those who indulge in stolen joys, they were honest, and left no cruel memories behind them.

It was the subject of a curious study and surprise to Captain Albert, that our musician was enabled to bear up against his tyranny with so much equal firmness and forbearance. He watched the countenance of Guernache,

whenever they met, with a curious interest. By what secret resource of fortitude and hope was it that he could command so much elasticity, exhibit so
much cheerfulness, bear with so much meekness, and utter no complaint. He
wondered that the irksome duties which he studiously thrust upon him, and
the frequently brutal language with which his performances were acknowledged, seemed to produce none of the cruel effects which he desired. His victim grew neither sad nor sullen. His violin still was heard resounding merrily
at the instance of his comrades; and still his hearty, whole-souled laughter
rang over the encampment, smiting ungraciously upon the senses of his
basely-minded chief. In vain did this despot study how to increase and frame
new annoyances for his subordinate. His tyranny contrived daily some new
method to make the poor fellow unhappy. But, consoled by the peculiar
secret which he possessed, of sympathy and comfort, the worthy drummer
bore up cheerfully under his afflictions. He was resolved to wait patiently the
return of Ribault with the promised supplies for the colony, and meanwhile
to submit to his evil destiny without a murmur. It was always with a secret
sense of triumph that he reminded himself of the near neighborhood of his
joys, and he exulted in the success with which he could baffle nightly the malice of his superior. But, however docile, the patience and forbearance of
Guernache availed him little. They did not tend to mitigate the annoyances
which he was constantly compelled to endure. We are now to recall a portion
of the preceding narrative, and to remind our reader of the visit which Captain Albert paid to the territories of Ouade, and the generous hospitalities of
the King thereof. Guernache had been one of the party, and the absence of
several days had been a serious loss to him in the delightful intercourse with
his dusky bride. He might naturally hope, after his return from a journey so
fatiguing, to be permitted a brief respite from his regular duties. But this was
not according to the policy of his malignant superior. Some hours were consumed after arriving at the fort, in disposing of the provisions which had
been obtained. In his labor Guernache had been compelled to partake with
others of his companions. Whether it was that he betrayed an unusual degree
of eagerness in getting through his task—showing an impatience to escape
which his enemy detected and resolved to baffle, cannot now be said; but to
his great annoyance and indignation, he was burdened with a portion of the
watch for the night—a duty which was clearly incumbent only upon those
who had not shared in the fatigues of the expedition. But to expostulate or
repine was alike useless, and Guernache submitted to his destiny with the best

possible grace. The provisions were stored, the gates closed, the watches set, and the garrison sunk to sleep, leaving our unhappy musician to pace, for several hours, the weary watch along the ramparts. How he looked forth into the dense forests which harbored his Monaletta! How he thought of the weary watch she kept! What were her fears, her anxieties? Did she know of his return? Did she look for his coming? The garrison slept—the woods were mysteriously silent! How delightful it would be to surprise her in the midst of her dreams, and answer to her murmurs of reproach—uttered in the sweet-est fragmentary Gallic—"Monaletta! I am here! Here is your own Guernache!"

The temptation was perilously sweet! The suggestion was irresistible; and, in a moment of excited fancy and passion, Guernache laid down his piece, and leaped the walls of the fortress. He committed an unhappy error to enjoy a great happiness, for which the penalties were not slow to come. In the dead of midnight, the garrison, still in a deep sleep, they were suddenly aroused in terror by the appalling cry of "fire!" The fort, the tenements in which they slept, the granary, which had been stored with their provisions, were all ablaze, and our Frenchmen woke in confusion and terror, unknowing where to turn, how to work, or what to apprehend. Their military stores were saved—their powder and munitions of war—but the "mils and beanes," so recently acquired from the granaries of King Ouade, with the building that contained them, were swept in ashes to the ground.

This disaster, full of evil in itself, was productive of others, as it led to the partial discovery of the secret of our drummer. Guernache was not within the fort when the alarm was given. It is not improbable that, had he not left his post, the conflagration would have been arrested in time to save the fort and its provisions. His absence was noted, and he was discovered, approaching from the forests, by those who bore forth the goods as they were rescued from the flames. These were mostly friends of Guernache, who would have main-tained a generous silence; but, unhappily, Pierre Renaud was also one of the discoverers. This person not only bore him no good will,—though gratitude for the service rendered him at the feast of Toya should have bound him for-ever to the cause of Guernache,—but he was one who had become a gross sycophant and the mere creature of the governor. He knew the hatred which the latter bore to Guernache, and a sympathizing nature led him promptly to divine the cause. Overjoyed with the discovery which he had made, the base fellow immediately carried the secret to his master, and when the first confusion was over, which followed the disaster, Guernache was taken into custody, and a day assigned for his trial as a criminal. To him was ascribed the fire as well as desertion from his post. The latter fact was unquestionable— the former was inferred. It might naturally be assumed, indeed, that, if the watch had not been abandoned, the flames could not have made such fearful headway. It was fortunate for our Frenchmen that the intercourse maintained with the Indians had been of such friendly character. With the first intima- tion of their misfortune, the kings, Audusta and Maccou, bringing with them a numerous train of followers, came to assist them in the labor of restoration and repair. "They uttered unto their subjects the speedy diligence which they were to use in building another house, showing unto them that the French- men were their loving friends and that they had made it evident unto them by the gifts and presents which they had received;—protesting that he whoso- ever put not his helping hand to the worke with all his might, should be esteemed as unprofitable." The entreaties and commands of the two kings were irresistible. But for this, our Huguenots, "being farre from all succours, and in such extremitie," would have been, in the language of their own chron- icler, "quite and cleane out of all hope." The Indians went with such hearty good will to the work, and in such numbers, that, in less than twelve hours, the losses of the colonists were nearly all repaired. New houses were built; new granaries erected; and, among the fabrics of this busy period, it was not forgotten to construct a keep—a close, dark, heavy den of logs, designed as a prison, into which, as soon as his Indian friends had departed, our poor fiddler, Guernache, was thrust, neck and heels! The former were rewarded and went away well satisfied with what they had seen and done. They little conjectured the troubles which awaited their favorite. He was soon brought to trial under a number of charges—disobedience of orders, neglect of duty, desertion of his post, and treason! To all of these, the poor fellow pleaded "*not guilty;*" and, with one exception, with a good conscience. But he had not the courage to confess the truth, and to declare where he had been, and on what mission, when he left the fort, on the night of the fire. He had committed a great fault, the consequences of which were serious, and might have been still more so; and the pleas of invariable good conduct, in his behalf, and the assertion of his innocence of all evil intention, did not avail. His judges were not his friends; he was found guilty and remanded to his dungeon, to await the farther caprices and the judgment of his enemy.

CHAPTER IV.

THE DUNGEON AND THE SCOURGE.

BEING THE CONTINUATION OF THE MELANCHOLY LEGEND OF GUERNACHE.

The absence of Guernache from his usual place of meeting with Monaletta, brought the most impatient apprehension to the heart of the devoted woman. As the time wore away—as night after night passed without his coming, she found the suspense unendurable, and gradually drew nigh to the fortress of the Huguenots. More than once had he cautioned her against incurring a peril equally great to them both. But her heart was already too full of fears to be restrained by such dangers as he alone could have foreseen; and she now lurked about the fort at nightfall, and continued to hover around long after dawn, keeping watch upon its walls and portal. So close and careful, however, was this watch, that she herself remained undetected. One day, however, to her great satisfaction, one of the inmates came forth whom she knew to be a friend and associate of Guernache. This was one Lachane, affectionately called *La Chere** by the soldiery, by whom he was very much beloved. Lachane was a sergeant, a good soldier, brave as a lion, but with as tender a heart, when the case required it, as ever beat in human bosom. He had long since learned to sympathize with the fate of Guernache, and had made frequent attempts to mollify the hostile feelings of his captain, in behalf of his friend. To the latter he had given much good counsel; and, but for *his* earnest entreaties and injunctions, he would have revealed to Albert the true reason for the absence of Guernache from his post. But Guernache dreaded, as well he might, that the revelation would only increase the hate and rage of his superior, and, perhaps, draw down a portion of his vengeance upon the head of the unoffending woman. Lachane acquiesced in his reasoning, and was silent. But he was not the less active in bringing consolation, whenever he could, to the respective parties. He afforded to Monaletta, whose approach to the fort he suspected, an opportunity of meeting with him; and their interviews, once begun, were regularly continued. Day by day he contrived to convey to her the messages, and to inform her of the condition of the prisoner; to whom, in turn, he bore all necessary intelligence, and every fond avowal which was sent by Monaletta. But the loving and devoted wife was not

---

* [SIMMS's NOTE] The names are thus written by Laudonniere in Hakluyt. But in Charlevoix there is only one given to this personage, and that is "Lachau."

satisfied with so frigid a mode of intercourse; and, in an evil hour, Lachane, whose own heart was too tender to resist the entreaties of one so fond, was persuaded to admit her within the fort, and into the dungeon of Guernache. We may censure his prudence and hers, but who shall venture to condemn either? The first visit led to a second, the second to a third, and, at length, the meetings between the lovers took place nightly. Lachane, often entreating, often exhorting, was yet always complying. Monaletta was admitted at midnight, and conducted forth by the dawn in safety; and thus meeting, Guernache soon forgot his own danger, and was readily persuaded by Monaletta to believe that she stood in none. The hours passed with them as with any other children, who, sitting on the shores of the sea, in the bright sunset, see not the rising of the waters, and feel not the falling of the night, until they are wholly overwhelmed. They were happy, and in their happiness but too easily forgot that there was such a person as Captain Albert in their little paradise.

But the pitcher which goes too often to the well, is at last broken. They were soon destined to realize the proverb in their own experience. Something in the movements of Lachane, awakened the suspicions of Pierre Renaud, whose active hostility to Guernache has been shown already. This man now bore within the fortress the unenviable reputation of being the captain's spy upon the people. This miserable creature, his suspicions once awakened, soon addressed all his abilities to the task of detecting the connection of Lachane with his prisoner; and it was not long before he had the malignant satisfaction of seeing him accompany another into the dungeon of Guernache. Though it was after midnight when the discovery was made, it was of a kind too precious to suffer delay in revealing it, and he hurried at once to the captain's quarters, well aware that, with such intelligence as he brought, he might safely venture to disturb him at any hour. But his eagerness did not lessen his caution, and every step was taken with the greatest deliberation and care. Albert was immediately aroused; but, unwilling, by a premature alarm, to afford the offenders an opportunity to escape, or to place themselves in any situation to defy scrutiny, some time was lost in making arrangements. The progress of Albert, and his satellites, going the rounds, was circuitous. The sentries were doubled with singular secrecy and skill. Such soldiers as were conceived to be most particularly bound to him, were awakened, and placed in positions most convenient for action and observation; —for Albert and Renaud, alike, conscious as it would seem of their own demerits, had come to suspect many of the soldiers of treachery and insurrection. These, perhaps, are always the fears most natural to a tyranny. Accordingly, with everything prepared for an explosion of the worst description, Captain Albert, in complete armor, made his appearance upon the scene.

Meantime, however, the proceedings of Renaud had not been carried on without, at length, commanding the attention and awakening the fears of so good a soldier as Lachane. Having discovered, on his rounds, that the guards were doubled, and that the sentinel at the sally-port had not only received a companion, but that the individual by whom Monaletta had been admitted was now removed to make way for another, he hurried away to the dungeon of Guernache. Here, whispering hurriedly his apprehensions, he endeavored to hasten the departure of the Indian woman. But his efforts were made too late. He was arrested, even while thus busied, by the Commandant himself, who, followed by Renaud and two other soldiers, suddenly came upon him from the rear of the building, where they had been harboring in ambush. Lachane was taken into immediate custody. An uproar followed, the alarm was given to the garrison, torches were brought, and Guernache, with the devoted Monaletta, were dragged forth together from the dungeon. She was wrapped up closely in the cloak of Lachane, but when Renaud waved a torch before her eyes, in order to discover who she was, she boldly threw aside the disguise, and stood revealed to the malignant scrutiny of the astonished but delighted despot. Upon beholding her, the fury of Albert knew no bounds. The secret of Guernache was now apparent; and the man whose vanity she had outraged, by preferring another in the dance, was now in full possession of the power to revenge himself upon both offenders. In that very moment, remembering his mortification, he formed a resolution of vengeance, which declared all the venom of a mean and malignant nature. He needed no art beyond his own to devise an ingenious torture for his victim. A few words sufficed to instruct the willing Renaud in the duty of the executioner. He commanded that the Indian woman should be scourged from the fort in the presence of the garrison. Then it was that the sullen soul of Guernache shuddered and succumbed beneath his tortures. With husky and trembling accents, he appealed to his tyrant in behalf of the woman of his heart.

"Oh! Captain Albert, as you are a man, do not do this cruel thing. Monaletta is innocent of any crime but that of loving one so worthless as Guernache. She is my wife! Do with me as you will, but spare her—have mercy on the innocent woman!"

"Ah! you can humble yourself now, insolent. I have found the way, at last, to make you feel. You shall feel yet more. I will crush you to the dust. What, ho! there, Pierre Renaud! Have I not said? the lash! the lash! Wherefore do ye linger?"

"Do not, Captain Albert! I implore you, for your own sake, do not lay the accursed lash upon this young and innocent creature. Remember! She is a woman—a princess—a blood relation of our good friend, King Audusta. Upon me—upon my back bestow the punishment, but spare her—spare her, in mercy!"

But the prayers and supplications of the wretched man were met only by denunciation and scorn. The base nature of Albert felt only his own mortification. His appetite for revenge darkened his vision wholly. He saw neither his policy nor humanity; and the creatures of his will were not permitted to hesitate in carrying out his brutal resolution. Armed with little hickories from the neighboring woods, they awaited but his command, and with his repeated utterance, the lash descended heavily upon the uncovered shoulders of the unhappy woman. With the first stroke, she bounded from the earth with a piercing shriek, at once of entreaty, of agony, and horror. Up to this moment, neither she, nor, indeed, any of the spectators, except Renaud, and possibly Guernache himself, had imagined that Albert would put in execution a purpose so equally impolitic and cruel. But when the blow fell upon the almost fair and naked shoulders of the woman—when her wild, girlish, almost childlike shriek rent the air, then the long suppressed agonies of Guernache broke forth in a passion of fury that looked more like the excess of the madman than the mere ebullition, however intense, of a simply desperate man. He had struggled long at endurance. He had borne, hitherto, without flinching, everything in the shape of penalty which his petty tyrant could fasten upon him—much more, indeed, than the ordinary nature, vexed with frequent injustice, is willing to endure. But, in the fury and agony of that humiliating moment, all restraints of prudence or fear were forgotten, or trampled under foot. He flung himself loose from the men who held him, and darting upon the individual by whom the merciless blow had been struck, he felled him to the earth with a single blow of his Herculean fist. But he was permitted to do no more. In another instant, grappled by a dozen powerful arms, he was borne to the earth, and secured with cords which not only bound his limbs but were drawn so tightly as to cut remorselessly into the flesh. Here he lay, and his agony may be far more easily conceived than described, thus compelled to behold the further tortures of the woman of his heart, without being able to struggle and to die in her defence. His own tortures were forgotten, as he witnessed hers. In vain would his ears have rejected the terrible sound, stroke upon stroke, which testified the continuance of this brutal outrage upon humanity. Without mercy was the punishment bestowed; and, bleeding at every blow from the biting scourge, the wretched innocent was at length tortured out of the garrison. But with that first shriek to which she gave utterance, and which declared rather the mental horror than the bodily pain which she suffered from such a cruel degradation, she ceased any longer to acknowledge her suffering. Oh! very powerful for endurance is the strength of a loving heart! The rest of the punishment she bore with the silence of one who suffers martyrdom in the approving eye of heaven; as if, beholding the insane agonies of Guernache, she had steeled herself to bear with any degree of torture rather than increase his sufferings by her complaints. In this manner, and thus silent under her own pains, she was expelled from the fortress. She was driven to the margin of the cleared space by which it was surrounded. She heard the shouts which drove her thence, and heard nothing farther. She had barely strength to totter forward, like the deer with a mortal hurt, to the secret cover of the forest, when she sank down in exhaustion;—nature kindly interposing with insensibility, to save her from those physical sufferings which she could no longer feel and live!

With the morning of the next day, Guernache was brought before the judgment-seat of Albert. The charges were sufficiently serious under which he was arraigned. He had neglected his duty—had permitted, if not caused, the destruction of the fort by fire—had violated the laws, resisted their execution, and used violence against the officer of justice! In this last proven offence all of these which had been alleged were assumed against him. He was convicted by the rapid action of his superior, as a traitor and a mutineer; and, to the horror of his friends, and the surprise of all his comrades, was condemned to expiate his faults by death upon the gallows. Few of the garrison had anticipated so sharp a judgment. They knew that Guernache had been faulty, but they also knew what had been his provocations. They felt that his faults had been the fruit of the injustice under which he suffered. But they dared not interpose. The prompt severity with which Captain Albert carried out his decisions—the merciless character of his vindictiveness—discouraged even remonstrance. Guernache, as we have shown, was greatly beloved, and had many true friends among his people; but they were taken by surprise; and, so much stunned and confounded by the rapidity with which events had taken place, that they could only look on the terrible proceedings with a mute and self-reproachful horror. The transition from the seat of judgment to the place of execution was instantaneous. Guernache appealed in vain to the justice of Ribault, whose coming from France was momently expected. This denied, he implored the less ignoble doom of the sword or the shot, in place of that upon the scaffold. But it did not suit the mean malice of Albert to omit any of his tortures. Short was the shrift allowed the victim;—ten minutes for prayer—and sure the cord which stifled it forever. In deep horror, in a hushed terror, which itself was full of horror, his gloomy comrades gathered at the place of execution, by the commands of their petty despot. There was no concert among them, by which the incipient indignation and fury in their bosoms might have declared itself in rescue and commotion. One groan, the involuntary expression of a terror that had almost ceased to breathe, answered the convulsive motion which indicated the last struggle of their beloved comrade.* Then it was that they began to feel that they could have died for him, and might have saved him. But it was now too late; and prudence timely interposed to prevent a rash explosion. The armed myrmidons of Albert were about them. He, himself, in complete armor, with his satellite, Pierre Renaud, also fully armed, standing beside him; and it was evident that every preparation had been made to quell insubordination, and punish the refractory with as sharp and sudden a judgment as that which had just descended upon their comrade.

The poor Monaletta, crouching in the cover of the woods, recovered from her stupor in the cool air of the morning, but it was sunset before she could regain the necessary strength to move. Then it was, that, with the natural tendency of a loving heart, curious only about the fate of him for whom alone her heart desired life, she bent her steps towards that cruel fortress which had been the source of so much misery to both. Very feeble and slow was her progress, but it was still too rapid; it brought her too soon to a knowledge of that final blow which fell, with worse terrors than the scourge, upon the soul. She arrived in season to behold the form of the unfortunate Guernache, abandoned by all, and totally lifeless, waving in the wind from the branches

---

* [SIMMS'S NOTE] Says Charlevoix:—"Il pendit lui-même un soldat, qui n'avoit point merité la mort, il en dégrada un autre des arms avec aussi peu de justice, puis il l'exila, et l'on crut que son dessein étoit de le laisser mourir de faim et de misere, etc." But we must not anticipate the revelations of the text.

of a perished oak, directly in front of the fortress. The deepest sorrows of the heart are those which are born dumb. There are some woes which the lip can never speak, nor the pen describe. There are some agonies over which we draw the veil without daring to look upon them, lest we freeze to stone in the terrible inspection. There is no record of that grief which seized upon the heart of the poor Indian woman, Monaletta, as she gazed upon the beloved but unconscious form of her husband. She approached it not, though watching it from sunset till the gray twilight lapsed away into the denser shadows of the night. But, with the dawn of day, when the Frenchmen looked forth from the fortress for the body of their comrade, it had disappeared. They searched for it in vain. From that day Monaletta disappeared also. She was neither to be found in the neighboring woods, nor among the people of her kindred. But, long afterwards they told, with shuddering and apprehension, of a voice upon the midnight air, which resembled that of their murdered comrade, followed always by the piercing shriek of a woman, which reminded them of the dreadful utterance of the Indian woman, when first smitten upon the shoulders by the lash of the ruffian. Thus endeth the legend of Guernache, and the Princess Monaletta.

THE GRADUAL REVELATION of the character of Daniel Nelson as he tells, in the vernacular of the backwoodsman, the story of his adventures on the frontier of western North Carolina is the key to the charm of "The Two Camps." The story he tells is replete with themes that recur in Simms: the white man's prejudice against, and exploitation of, the Indian; the inevitability of the land's conquest by European Americans and the near genocide of the Native Americans. It is also significant that the old frontiersman—who, through knowledge of nature, respect for humanity, and a strong spiritual sense, has learned tolerance and compassion—comes closest to understanding and accepting the Indian and his culture.

John Pendleton Kennedy (1795–1870), the Maryland novelist and author of *Horseshoe Robinson* (1835; see below, 369), was admired by Simms, who dedicated one of his books to him.

ᔕ *The Two Camps. A Legend of the Old North State*

> "These, the forest born
> And forest nurtured—a bold, hardy race,
> Fearless and frank, unfettered, with big souls
> In hour of danger."

Chapter I.

It is frequently the case, in the experience of the professional novelist or tale-writer, that his neighbour comes in to his assistance when he least seeks, and, perhaps, least desires any succour. The worthy person, man or woman, however,—probably some excellent octogenarian whose claims to be heard are based chiefly upon the fact that he himself no longer possesses the faculty of hearing,—has some famous incident, some wonderful fact, of which he has been the eyewitness, or of which he has heard from his great-grandmother, which he fancies is the very thing to be woven into song or story. Such is the strong possession which the matter takes of his brain, that, if the novelist whom he seeks to benefit does not live within trumpet-distance, he gives him the narrative by means of post, some three sheets of stiff foolscap, for which the hapless tale-writer, whose works are selling in cheap editions at twelve or twenty cents, pays a sum of one dollar sixty-two postage. Now, it so happens, to increase the evil, that, in ninety-nine cases in the hundred, the fact thus laboriously stated is not worth a straw—consisting of some simple deed of violence, some mere murder, a downright blow with gun butt or cudgel over the skull, or a hidden thrust, three inches deep, with dirk or bowie knife, into the abdomen, or at random among the lower ribs. The man dies and the murderer gets off to Texas, or is prematurely caught and stops by the way— and still stops by the way! The thing is fact, no doubt. The narrator saw it himself, or his brother saw it, or—more solemn, if not more certain testimony still—his grandmother saw it, long before he had eyes to see at all. The circumstance is attested by a cloud of witnesses—a truth solemnly sworn to—and yet, for the purposes of the tale-writer, of no manner of value. This assertion may somewhat conflict with the received opinions of many, who, accustomed to find deeds of violence recorded in almost every work of fiction, from the time of Homer to the present day, have rushed to the conclusion that this is all, and overlook that labour of the artist, by which an ordinary event is made to assume the character of novelty; in other words, to become an extraordinary event. The least difficult thing in the world, on the part of the writer of fiction, is to find the assassin and the bludgeon; the art is to make them appear in the right place, strike at the right time, and so adapt one fact to another, as to create mystery, awaken curiosity, inspire doubt as to the result, and bring about the catastrophe, by processes which shall be equally natural and unexpected. All that class of sagacious persons, therefore, who fancy they have found a mare's nest, when, in fact, they are only gazing at a goose's, are respectfully counselled that no fact—no tradition—is of any importance to the artist, unless it embodies certain peculiar characteristics of its own, or unless it illustrates some history about which curiosity has already been awakened. A mere brutality, in which John beats and bruises Ben, and Ben in turn shoots John, putting eleven slugs, or thereabouts, between his collar-bone and vertebrae—or, maybe, stabs him under his left pap, or any where you please, is just as easily conceived by the novelist, without the help of history. Nay, for that matter, he would perhaps rather not have any precise facts in his way, in such cases, as then he will be able to regard the picturesque in the choice of his weapon, and to put the wounds in such parts of the body, as will better bear the examination of all persons. I deem it right to throw out this hint, just at this moment, as well for the benefit of my order as for my own protection. The times are hard, and the post-office requires all its dues in hard money. Literary men are not proverbially prepared at all seasons for any unnecessary outlay—and to be required to make advances for commodities of which they have on hand, at all times, the greatest abundance, is an injustice which, it is to be hoped, that this little intimation will somewhat lessen. We take for granted, therefore, that our professional brethren will concur with us in saying to the public, that we are all sufficiently provided with "disastrous chances" for some time to come—that our "moving accidents by flood and field" are particularly numerous, and of "hair-breadth 'scapes" we have enough to last a century. Murders, and such matters, as they are among the most ordinary events of the day, are decidedly vulgar; and, for mere cudgelling and bruises, the taste of the belles-lettres reader, rendered delicate by the monthly magazines, has voted them equally gross and unnatural.

But, if the character of the materials usually tendered to the novelist by the incident-mongers, is thus ordinarily worthless as we describe it, we sometimes are fortunate in finding an individual, here and there, in the deep forests,—a sort of recluse, hale and lusty, but white-headed,—who unfolds from his own budget of experience a rare chronicle, on which we delight to linger. Such an one breathes life into his deeds. We see them as we listen to his words. In lieu of the dead body of the fact, we have its living spirit— subtle, active, breathing and burning, and fresh in all the provocations and associations of life. Of this sort was the admirable characteristic narrative of Horse-Shoe Robinson, which we owe to Kennedy, and for which he was indebted to the venerable hero of the story. When we say that the subject of the sketch which follows was drawn from not dissimilar sources, we must beg our readers not to understand us as inviting any reference to that able and national story—with which it is by no means our policy or wish to invite or provoke comparison.

Chapter II.

There are probably some old persons still living upon the upper dividing line between North and South Carolina, who still remember the form and features of the venerable Daniel Nelson. The old man was still living so late as 1817. At that period he removed to Mississippi, where, we believe, he died in less than three months after his change of residence. An old tree does not bear transplanting easily, and does not long survive it. Daniel Nelson came from Virginia when a youth. He was one of the first who settled on the southern borders of North Carolina, or, at least in that neighbourhood where he afterwards passed the greatest portion of his days.

At that time the country was not only a forest, but one thickly settled with Indians. It constituted the favourite hunting-grounds for several of their tribes. But this circumstance did not discourage young Nelson. He was then a stalwart youth, broad-chested, tall, with a fiery eye, and an almost equally fiery soul—certainly with a very fearless one. His companions, who were few in number, were like himself. The spirit of old Daniel Boone was a more common one than is supposed. Adventure gladdened and excited their hearts,— danger only seemed to provoke their determination,—and mere hardship was something which their frames appeared to covet. It was as refreshing to them as drink. Having seen the country, and struck down some of its game,—tasted of its bear-meat and buffalo, its deer and turkey,—all, at that time, in the greatest abundance,—they returned for the one thing most needful to a brave forester in a new country,—a good, brisk, fearless wife, who, like the damsel in Scripture, would go whithersoever went the husband to whom her affections were surrendered. They had no fear, these bold young hunters, to make a home and rear an infant family in regions so remote from the secure walks of civilization. They had met and made an acquaintance and a sort of friendship with the Indians, and, in the superior vigour of their own frames, their greater courage, and better weapons, they perhaps had come to form a too contemptuous estimate of the savage. But they were not beguiled by him into too much confidence. Their log houses were so constructed as to be fortresses upon occasion, and they lived not so far removed from one another, but that the leaguer of one would be sure, in twenty-four hours, to bring the others to his assistance. Besides, with a stock of bear-meat and venison always on hand, sufficient for a winter, either of these fortresses might, upon common calculations, be maintained for several weeks against any single band of the Indians, in the small numbers in which they were wont to range together in those neighbourhoods. In this way these bold pioneers took possession of the soil, and paved the way for still mightier generations. Though wandering, and somewhat averse to the tedious labours of the farm, they were still not wholly unmindful of its duties; and their open lands grew larger every season, and increasing comforts annually spoke for the increasing civilization of the settlers. Corn was in plenty in proportion to the bear-meat, and the squatters almost grew indifferent to those first apprehensions, which had made them watch the approaches of the most friendly Indian as if he had been an enemy. At the end of five years, in which they had suffered no hurt and but little annoyance of any sort from their wild neighbours, it would seem as if this confidence in the security of their situation was not without sufficient justification.

But, just then, circumstances seemed to threaten an interruption of this goodly state of things. The Indians were becoming discontented. Other tribes, more frequently in contact with the larger settlements of the whites,— wronged by them in trade, or demoralized by drink,—complained of their sufferings and injuries, or, as is more probable, were greedy to obtain their treasures, in bulk, which they were permitted to see, but denied to enjoy, or only in limited quantity. Their appetites and complaints were transmitted, by inevitable sympathies, to their brethren of the interior, and our worthy settlers upon the Haw, were rendered anxious at signs which warned them of a change in the peaceful relations which had hitherto existed in all the intercourse between the differing races. We need not dwell upon or describe these signs, with which, from frequent narratives of like character, our people are already sufficiently familiar. They were easily understood by our little colony, and by none more quickly than Daniel Nelson. They rendered him anxious, it is true, but not apprehensive; and, like a good husband, while he strove not to frighten his wife by what he said, he deemed it necessary to prepare her mind for the worst that might occur. This task over, he felt somewhat relieved, though, when he took his little girl, now five years old, upon his knee that evening, and looked upon his infant boy in the lap of his mother, he felt his anxieties very much increase; and that very night he resumed a practice which he had latterly abandoned, but which had been adopted as a measure of strict precaution, from the very first establishment of their little settlement. As soon as supper was over, he resumed his rifle, thrust his *couteau de chasse* into his belt, and, taking his horn about his neck, and calling up his trusty dog, Clinch, he proceeded to scour the woods immediately around his habitation. This task, performed with the stealthy caution of the hunter, occupied some time, and, as the night was clear, a bright starlight, the weather moderate, and his own mood restless, he determined to strike through the forest to the settlement of Jacob Ransom, about four miles off, in order to prompt him, and, through him, others of the neighbourhood, to the continued exercise of a caution which he now thought necessary. The rest of this night's adventure we propose to let him tell in his own words, as he has been heard to relate it a thousand times in his old age, at a period of life when, with one foot in his grave, to suppose him guilty of falsehood, or of telling that which he did not himself fervently believe, would be, among all those who knew him, to suppose the most impossible and extravagant thing in the world.

Chapter III.

"Well, my friends," said the veteran, then seventy, drawing his figure up to its fullest height, and extending his right arm while his left still grasped the muzzle of his ancient rifle, which he swayed from side to side, the butt resting on the floor—"Well, my friends, seeing that the night was cl'ar, and there was no wind, and feeling as how I didn't want for sleep, I called to Clinch and took the path for Jake Ransom's. I knew that Jake was a sleepy sort of chap, and if the redskins caught any body napping, he'd, most likely, be the man. But I confess, 'twarn't so much for his sake, as for the sake of all,—of my own as well as the rest;—for, when I thought how soon, if we warn't all together in the business, I might see, without being able to put in, the long yellow hair of Betsy and the babies twirling on the thumbs of some painted devil of the tribe,—I can't tell you how I felt, but it warn't like a human, though I shivered mightily like one,—'twas wolfish, as if the hair was turned in and rubbing agin the very heart within me. I said my prayers, where I stood, looking up at the stars, and thinking that, after all, all was in the hands and the marcy of God. This sort o' thinking quieted me, and I went ahead pretty free, for I knew the track jest as well by night as by day, though I didn't go so quick, for I was all the time on the look-out for the enemy. Now, after we reached a place in the woods where there was a gully and a mighty bad crossing, there were two roads to get to Jake's—one by the hollows, and one jest across the hills. I don't know why, but I didn't give myself time to think, and struck right across the hill, though that was rather the longest way.

"Howsomedever, on I went, and Clinch pretty close behind me. The dog was a good dog, with a mighty keen nose to hunt, but jest then he didn't seem to have the notion for it. The hill was a sizeable one, a good stretch to foot, and I began to remember, after awhile, that I had been in the woods from blessed dawn; and that made me see how it was with poor Clinch, and why he didn't go for'ad; but I was more than half way, and wasn't guine to turn back till I had said my say to Jake. Well, when I got to the top of the hill, I stopped, and rubbed my eyes. I had cause to rub 'em, for what should I see at a distance but a great fire. At first I was afeard lest it was Jake's house, but I considered, the next moment, that he lived to the left, and this fire was cl'ar to the right, and it did seem to me as if 'twas more near to my own. Here was something to scare a body. But I couldn't stay there looking, and it warn't now a time to go to Jake's; so I turned off, and, though Clinch was mighty onwilling, I bolted on the road to the fire. I say road, but there was no road; but the trees warn't over-thick, and the land was too poor for undergrowth; so we got on pretty well, considering. But, what with the tire I had had, and the scare I felt, it seemed as if I didn't get for'ad a bit. There was the fire still burning as bright and almost as far off as ever. When I saw this I stopt and looked at Clinch, and he stopped and looked at me, but neither of us had any thing to say. Well, after a moment's thinking, it seemed as if I shouldn't be much of a man to give up when I had got so far, so I pushed on. We crossed more than one little hill, then down and through the hollow, and then up the hill again. At last we got upon a small mountain the Indians called Nolleehatchie, and then it seemed as if the fire had come to a stop, for it was now burning bright, on a little hill below me, and not two hundred yards in front. It was a regular camp fire, pretty big, and there was more than a dozen Indians sitting round it. 'Well,' says I to myself, 'it's come upon us mighty sudden, and what's to be done? Not a soul in the settlement knows it but myself, and nobody's on the watch. They'll be sculped, every human of them, in their very beds, or, moutbe, waken up in the blaze, to be shot with arrows as they run.' I was in a cold sweat to think of it. I didn't know what to think and what to do. I looked round to Clinch, and the strangest thing of all was to see him sitting quiet on his haunches, looking at me, and at the stars, and not at the fire jest before him. Now, Clinch was a famous fine hunting dog, and jest as good on an Indian trail as any other. He know'd my ways, and what I wanted, and would give tongue, or keep it still, jest as I axed him. It was sensible enough, jest then, that he shouldn't bark, but, dang it!—he didn't even seem to see. Now, there warn't a dog in all the settlement so quick and keen to show sense as Clinch, even when he didn't say a word;—and to see him looking as if he didn't know and didn't care what was a-going on, with his eyes sot in his head and glazed over with sleep, was, as I may say, very onnatural, jest at that time, in a dog of any onderstanding. So I looked at him, half angry, and when he saw me looking at him, he jest stretched himself off, put his nose on his legs, and went to sleep in 'arnest. I had half a mind to lay my knife-handle over his head, but I considered better of it, and though it did seem the strangest thing in the world that he shouldn't even try to get to the fire, for warm sake, yet I recollected that dog natur,' like human natur,' can't stand every thing, and he hadn't such good reason as I had, to know that the Indians were no longer friendly to us. Well, there I stood, a pretty considerable chance, looking, and wondering, and onbeknowing what to do. I was mighty beflustered. But at last I felt ashamed to be so oncertain, and then again it was a needcessity that we should know the worst one time or another, so I determined to push for'ad. I was no slouch of a hunter, as you may suppose; so, as I was nearing the camp, I begun sneaking; and, taking it sometimes on hands and knees, and sometimes flat to the ground, where there was neither tree nor bush to cover me, I went ahead, Clinch keeping close behind me, and not showing any notion of what I was after. It was a slow business, because it was a ticklish business; but I was a leetle too anxious to be altogether so careful as a good sneak ought to be, and I went on rather faster than I would advise any young man to go in a time of war, when the inimy is in the neighbourhood. Well, as I went, there was the fire, getting larger and larger every minute, and there were the Indians round it, getting plainer and plainer. There was so much smoke that there was no making out, at any distance, any but their figures, and these, every now and then, would be so wrapt in the smoke that not more than half of them could be seen at the same moment. At last I stopped, jest at a place where I thought I could make out all that I wanted. There was a sizeable rock before me, and I leaned my elbows on it to look. I reckon I warn't more than thirty yards from the fire. There were some bushes betwixt us, and what with the bushes and the smoke, it was several minutes before I could separate man from man, and see what they were all adoing, and when I did, it was only for a moment at a time, when a puff of smoke would wrap them all, and make it as difficult as ever. But when I did contrive to see clearly, the sight was one to worry me to the core, for, in the midst of the redskins, I could see a white one, and that white one a woman. There was no mistake. There were the Indians, some with their backs, and some with their faces to me; and there, a little a-one side, but still among them, was a woman. When the smoke blowed off, I could see her white face, bright like any star, shining out of the clouds, and looking so pale and ghastly that my blood cruddled in my veins to think lest she might be dead from fright. But it couldn't be so, for she was sitting up and looking about her. But the Indians were motionless. They jest sat or lay as when I first saw them—doing nothing—saying nothing, but jest as motionless as the stone under my elbow. I couldn't stand looking where I was, so I began creeping again, getting nigher and nigher, until it seemed to me as if I ought to be able to read every face. But what with the paint and smoke, I couldn't make out a single Indian. Their figures seemed plain enough in their buffalo-skins and blankets, but their faces seemed always in the dark. But it wasn't so with the woman. I could make her out clearly. She was very young; I reckon not more than fifteen, and it seemed to me as if I knew her looks very well. She was very handsome, and her hair was loosed upon her back. My heart felt strange to see her. I was weak as any child. It seemed as if I could die for the gal, and yet I hadn't strength enough to raise my rifle to my shoulder. The weakness kept on me the more I looked; for every moment seemed to make the poor child more and more dear to me. But the strangest thing of all was to see how motionless was every Indian in the camp. Not a word was spoken—not a limb or finger stirred. There they sat, or lay, round about the fire, like so many effigies, looking at the gal, and she looking at them. I never was in such a fix of fear and weakness in my life. What was I to do? I had got so nigh that I could have stuck my knife, with a jerk, into the heart of any one of the party, yet I hadn't the soul to lift it; and before I knew where I was,

I cried like a child. But my crying didn't make 'em look about 'em. It only brought my poor dog Clinch leaping upon me, and whining, as if he wanted to give me consolation. Hardly knowing what I did, I tried to set him upon the camp, but the poor fellow didn't seem to understand me; and in my desperation, for it was a sort of madness growing out of my scare, I jumped headlong for'ad, jest where I saw the party sitting, willing to lose my life rather than suffer from such a strange sort of misery.

CHAPTER IV.

"Will you believe me! there were no Indians, no young woman, no fire! I stood up in the very place where I had seen the blaze and the smoke, and there was nothing! I looked for'ad and about me—there was no sign of fire any where. Where I stood was covered with dry leaves, the same as the rest of the forest. I was stupefied. I was like a man roused out of sleep by a strange dream, and seeing nothing. All was dark and silent. The stars were overhead, but that was all the light I had. I was more scared than ever, and, as it's a good rule when a man feels that he can do nothing himself, to look to the great God who can do every thing, I kneeled down and said my prayers—the second time that night that I had done the same thing, and the second time, I reckon, that I had ever done so in the woods. After that I felt stronger. I felt sure that this sign hadn't been shown to me for nothing; and while I was turning about, looking and thinking to turn on the back track for home, Clinch began to prick up his ears and waken up. I clapped him on his back, and got my knife ready. It might be a *painter* that stirred him, for he could scent that beast a great distance. But, as he showed no fright, only a sort of quickening, I knew there was nothing to fear. In a moment he started off, and went boldly ahead. I followed him, but hadn't gone twenty steps down the hill and into the hollow, when I heard something like a groan. This quickened me, and keeping up with the dog, he led me to the foot of the hollow, where was a sort of pond. Clinch ran right for it, and another groan set me in the same direction. When I got up to the dog, he was on the butt-end of an old tree that had fallen, I reckon, before my time, and was half buried in the water. I jumped on it, and walked a few steps for'ad, when, what should I see but a human, half across the log, with his legs hanging in the water, and his head down. I called Clinch back out of my way, and went to the spot. The groans were pretty constant. I stooped down and laid my hands upon the person, and, as I felt the hair, I knew it was an Indian. The head was clammy with blood, so that my fingers stuck, and when I attempted to turn it, to look at the face, the groan was deeper than ever; but 'twarn't a time to suck one's fingers. I took him up, clapped my shoulders to it, and, fixing my feet firmly on the old tree, which was rather slippery, I brought the poor fellow out without much trouble. Though tall, he was not heavy, and was only a boy of fourteen or fifteen. The wonder was how a lad like that should get into such a fix. Well, I brought him out and laid him on the dry leaves. His groans stopped, and I thought he was dead, but I felt his heart, and it was still warm, and I thought, though I couldn't be sure, there was a beat under my fingers. What to do was the next question. It was now pretty late in the night. I had been all day a-foot, and, though still willing to go, yet the thought of such a weight on my shoulders made me stagger. But 'twouldn't do to leave him where he was to perish. I thought, if so be I had a son in such a fix, what would I think of the stranger who should go home and wait till daylight to give him help! No, darn my splinters, said I,—though I had just done my prayers,—if I leave the lad—and, tightening my girth, I give my whole soul to it, and hoisted him on my shoulders. My cabin, I reckoned, was good three miles off. You can guess what trouble I had, and what a tire under my load, before I got home and laid the poor fellow down by the fire. I then called up Betsy, and we both set to work to see if we could stir up the life that was in him. She cut away his hair, and I washed the blood from his head, which was chopped to the bone, either with a knife or hatchet. It was a God's blessing it hadn't gone into his brain, for it was fairly enough aimed for it, jest above the ear. When we come to open his clothes, we found another wound in his side. This was done with a knife, and, I suppose, was pretty deep. He had lost blood enough, for all his clothes were stiff with it. We knew nothing much of doctoring, but we had some rum in the cabin, and after washing his wounds clean with it, and pouring some down his throat, he began to groan more freely, and by that we knew he was coming to a nateral feeling. We rubbed his body down with warm cloths, and after a little while, seeing that he made some signs, I give him water as much as he could drink. This seemed to do him good, and having done every thing that we thought could help him, we wrapped him up warmly before the fire, and I stretched myself off beside him. 'Twould be a long story to tell, step by step, how he got on. It's enough to say that he didn't die that bout. We got him on his legs in a short time, doing little or nothing for him more than we did at first. The lad was a good lad, though, at first, when he first came to his senses, he was mighty shy, wouldn't look steadily in our faces, and, I do believe, if he could have got out of the cabin, would have done so as soon as he could stagger. But he was too weak to try that, and, meanwhile, when he saw our kindness, he was softened. By little and little, he got to play with my little Lucy, who was not quite six years old; and, after a while, he seemed to be never better pleased than when they played together. The child, too, after her first fright, leaned to the lad, and was jest as willing to play with him as if he had been a cl'ar white like herself. He could say a few words of English from the beginning, and learnt quickly; but, though he talked tolerable free for an Indian, yet I could never get him to tell me how he was wounded, or by whom. His brow blackened when I spoke of it, and his lips would be shut together, as if he was ready to fight sooner than to speak. Well, I didn't push him to know, for I was pretty sure the head of the truth will be sure to come some time or other, if you once have it by the tail, provided you don't jerk it off by straining too hard upon it.

Chapter V.

"I suppose the lad had been with us a matter of six weeks, getting better every day, but so slowly that he had not, at the end of that time, been able to leave the picket. Meanwhile, our troubles with the Indians were increasing. As yet, there had been no bloodshed in our quarter, but we heard of murders and sculpings on every side, and we took for granted that we must have our turn. We made our preparations, repaired the pickets, laid in ammunition, and took turns for scouting nightly. At length, the signs of Indians got to be thick in our parts, though we could see none. Jake Ransom had come upon one of their camps after they had left it; and we had reason to apprehend every thing, inasmuch as the outlyers didn't show themselves, as they used to do, but prowled about the cabins and went from place to place, only by night, or by close skulking in the thickets. One evening after this, I went out as usual to go the rounds, taking Clinch with me, but I hadn't got far from the gate, when the dog stopped and gave a low bark;—then I knew there was mischief, so I turned round quietly, without making any show of scare, and got back safely, though not a minute too soon. They trailed me to the gate the moment after I had got it fastened, and were pretty mad, I reckon, when they found their plan had failed for surprising me. But for the keen nose of poor Clinch, with all my skill in scouting,—and it was not small even in that early day,— they'd 'a had me, and all that was mine, before the sun could open his eyes to see what they were after. Finding they had failed in their ambush, they made the woods ring with the war-whoop, which was a sign that they were guine to give us a regular siege. At the sound of the whoop, we could see the eyes of the Indian boy brighten, and his ears prick up, jest like a hound's when he first gets scent of the deer, or hears the horn of the hunter. I looked closely at the lad, and was dub'ous what to do. He moutbe only an enemy in the camp, and while I was fighting in front, he might be cutting the throats of my wife and children within. I did not tell you that I had picked up his bow and arrows near the little lake where I had found him, and his hunting-knife was sticking in his belt when I brought him home. Whether to take these away from him, was the question. Suppose I did, a billet of wood would answer pretty near as well. I thought the matter over while I watched him. Thought runs mighty quick in time of danger! Well, after turning it over on every side, I concluded 'twas better to trust him jest as if he had been a sure friend. I couldn't think, after all we had done for him, that he'd be false, so I said to him—'Lenatewá!'—'twas so he called himself—'those are your people!' 'Yes!' he answered slowly, and lifting himself up as if he had been a lord—he was a stately-looking lad, and carried himself like the son of a Micco,* as he was—'Yes, they are the people of Lenatewá—must he go to them?' and he made the motion of going out. But I stopped him. I was not willing to lose the security which I had from his being a sort of prisoner. 'No,' said I; 'no, Lenatewá, not to-night. To-morrow will do. To-morrow you can tell them I am a friend, not an enemy, and they should not come to burn my wigwam.' 'Brother—friend!' said the lad, advancing with a sort of freedom and taking my hand. He then went to my wife, and did the same thing,— not regarding she was a woman,—'Brother—friend!' I watched him closely, watched his eye and his motions, and I said to Betsy, 'The lad is true; don't be afeard!' But we passed a weary night. Every now and then we could hear the whoop of the Indians. From the loop-holes we could see the light of three fires on different sides, by which we knew that they were prepared to cut off any help that might come to us from the rest of the settlement. But I didn't give in or despair. I worked at one thing or another all night, and though Lenatewá gave me no help, yet he sat quietly, or laid himself down before the fire, as if he had nothing in the world to do in the business. Next morning by daylight, I found him already dressed in the same bloody clothes which he had on when I found him. He had thrown aside all that I gave him, and

---

* [SIMMS'S NOTE] A prince or a chief.

though the hunting-shirt and leggins which he now wore, were very much stained with blood and dirt, he had fixed them about him with a good deal of care and neatness, as if preparing to see company. I must tell you that an Indian of good family always has a nateral sort of grace and dignity which I never saw in a white man. He was busily engaged looking through one of the loop-holes, and though I could distinguish nothing, yet it was cl'ar that he saw something to interest him mightily. I soon found out that, in spite all my watchfulness, he had contrived to have some sort of correspondence and communication with those outside. This was a wonder to me then, for I did not recollect his bow and arrows. It seems that he had shot an arrow through one of the loop-holes, to the end of which he had fastened a tuft of his own hair. The effect of this was considerable, and to this it was owing that, for a few hours afterwards, we saw not an Indian. The arrow was shot at the very peep of day. What they were about, in the meantime, I can only guess, and the guess was only easy, after I had known all that was to happen. That they were in council what to do was cl'ar enough. I was not to know that the council was like to end in cutting some of their own throats instead of ours. But when we did see the enemy fairly, they came out of the woods in two parties, not actually separated, but not moving together. It seemed as if there was some strife among them. Their whole number could not be less than forty, and some eight or ten of these walked apart under the lead of a chief, a stout, dark-looking fellow, one-half of whose face was painted black as midnight, with a red circle round both his eyes. The other party was headed by an old white-headed chief, who couldn't ha' been less than sixty years—a pretty fellow, you may be sure, at his time of life, to be looking after sculps of women and children. While I was kneeling at my loop-hole looking at them, Lenatewá came to me, and touching me on the arm, pointed to the old chief, saying—'Micco Lenatewá Glucco,' by which I guessed he was the father or grandfather of the lad. 'Well,' I said, seeing that the best plan was to get their confidence and friendship if possible,—'Well, lad, go to your father and tell him what Daniel Nelson has done for you, and let's have peace. We can fight, boy, as you see; we have plenty of arms and provisions; and with this rifle, though you may not believe it, I could pick off your father, the king, and that other chief, who has so devilled himself up with paint.' 'Shoot!' said the lad quickly, pointing to the chief of whom I had last spoken. 'Ah! he is your enemy then?' The lad nodded his head, and pointed to the wound on his temple, and that in his side. I now began to see the true state of the case. 'No,' said

I; 'no, Lenatewá, I will shoot none. I am for peace. I would do good to the Indians, and be their friend. Go to your father and tell him so. Go, and make him be my friend.' The youth caught my hand, placed it on the top of his head, and exclaimed, 'Good!' I then attended him down to the gate, but, before he left the cabin, he stopped and put his hand on the head of little Lucy,—and I felt glad, for it seemed to say, 'you shan't be hurt—not a hair of your head!' I let him out, fastened up, and then hastened to the loop-hole.

Chapter VI.

"And now came a sight to tarrify. As soon as the Indians saw the young prince, they set up a general cry. I couldn't tell whether it was of joy, or what. He went for'ad boldly, though he was still quite weak, and the king at the head of his party advanced to meet him. The other and smaller party, headed by the black chief, whom young Lenatewá had told me to shoot, came forward also, but very slowly, and it seemed as if they were doubtful whether to come or go. Their leader looked pretty much beflustered. But they hadn't time for much study, for, after the young prince had met his father, and a few words had passed between them, I saw the finger of Lenatewá point to the black chief. At this, he lifted up his clenched fists, and worked his body as if he was talking angrily. Then, sudden, the war-whoop sounded from the king's party, and the other troop of Indians began to run, the black chief at their head; but he had not got twenty steps when a dozen arrows went into him, and he tumbled for'a'ds, and grappled with the earth. It was all over with him. His party was scattered on all sides, but were not pursued. It seemed that all the arrows had been aimed at the one person, and when he sprawled, there was an end to it: the whole affair was over in five minutes.

Chapter VII.

"It was a fortunate affair for us. Lenatewá soon brought the old Micco to terms of peace. For that matter, he had only consented to take up the red stick because it was reported by the black chief—who was the uncle of the young Micco, and had good reasons for getting him out of the way—that he had been murdered by the whites. This driv' the old man to desperation, and brought him down upon us. When he knew the whole truth, and saw what friends we had been to his son, there was no end to his thanks and promises. He swore to be my friend while the sun shone, while the waters run, and while the mountains stood, and I believe, if the good old man had been spared so long, he would have been true to his oath. But, while he lived, he kept it, and so did his son when he succeeded him as Micco Glucco. Year after year went by, and though there was frequent war between the Indians and the whites, yet Lenatewá kept it from our doors. He himself was at war several times with our people, but never with our settlement. He put his *totem* on our trees, and the Indians knew that they were sacred. But, after a space of eleven years, there was a change. The young prince seemed to have forgotten our friendship. We now never saw him among us, and, unfortunately, some of your young men—the young men of our own settlement— murdered three young warriors of the Ripparee tribe, who were found on horses stolen from us. I was very sorry when I heard it, and began to fear the consequences; and they came upon us when we least looked for it. I had every reason to think that Lenatewá would still keep the warfare from my little family, but I did not remember that he was the prince of a tribe only, and not of the nation. This was a national warfare, in which the whole Cherokee people were in arms. Many persons, living still, remember that terrible war, and how the Carolinians humbled them at last; but there's no telling how much blood was shed in that war, how many sculps taken, how much misery suffered by young and old, men, women, and children. Our settlement had become so large and scattered that we had to build a sizeable blockhouse, which we stored, and to which we could retreat whenever it was necessary. We took possession of it on hearing from our scouts that Indian trails had been seen, and there we put the women and children, under a strong guard. By day we tended our farms, and only went to our families at night. We had kept them in this fix for five weeks or thereabouts, and there was no attack. The Indian signs disappeared, and we all thought the storm had blown over, and began to hope and to believe that the old friendship of Lenatewá had saved us. With this thinking, we began to be less watchful. The men would stay all night at the farms, and sometimes, in the day, would carry with them the women, and sometimes some even the children. I cautioned them agin this, but they mocked me, and said I was gitting old and scary. I told them, 'Wait and see who'll scare first.' But, I confess, not seeing any Indians in all my scouting, I began to feel and think like the rest, and to grow careless. I let Betsy go now and then with me to the farm, though she kept it from me that she had gone there more than once with Lucy, without any man protector. Still, as it was only a short mile and a half from the block, and we could hear of no Indians, it did not seem so venturesome a thing. One day we heard of some very large b'ars among the thickets—a famous range for them, about four miles from the settlement; and a party of us, Simon Lorris, Hugh Darling, Jake Ransom, William Harkless, and myself, taking our dogs, set off on the hunt. We started the b'ar with a rush, and I got the first shot at a mighty big she b'ar, the largest I had ever seen—lamed the critter slightly, and dashed into the thickets after her! The others pushed, in another direction, after the rest, leaving me to finish my work as I could.

"I had two dogs with me, Clap and Claw, but they were young things, and couldn't be trusted much in a close brush with a b'ar. Old Clinch was dead, or he'd ha' made other guess-work with the varmint. But, hot after the b'ar, I didn't think of the quality of the dogs till I found myself in a fair wrestle with the brute. I don't brag, my friends, but that *was* a fight. I tell you my breath was clean gone, for the b'ar had me about the thin of my body, and I thought I was doubled up enough to be laid down without more handling. But my heart was strong when I thought of Betsy and the children, and I got my knife, with hard *jugging*—though I couldn't use my arm above my elbow—through the old critter's hide, and in among her ribs. That only seemed to make her hug closer, and I reckon I was clean gone, if it hadn't been that she blowed out before me. I had worked a pretty deep window in her waist, and then life run out plentiful. Her nose dropped agin my breast, and then her paws; and when the strain was gone, I fell down like a sick child, and she fell on top of me. But she warn't in a humour to do more mischief. She roughed me once or twice more with her paws, but that was only because she was at her last kick. There I lay a matter of half an hour, with the dead b'ar alongside o' me. I was almost as little able to move as she, and I vomited as if I had taken physic. When I come to myself and got up, there was no sound of the hunters. There I was with the two dogs and the b'ar, all alone, and the sun already long past the turn. My horse, which I had fastened outside of the thicket, had slipped his bridle, and, I reckoned, had either strayed off grazing, or had pushed back directly for the block. These things didn't make me feel much better. But, though my stomach didn't feel altogether right, and my ribs were as sore as if I had been sweating under a coating of hickory, I felt that there was no use and no time to stand there grunting. But I made out to skin and to cut up the b'ar, and a noble mountain of fat she made. I took the skin with me, and, covering the flesh with bark, I whistled off the dogs, after they had eat to fill, and pushed after my horse. I followed his track for some time, till I grew fairly tired. He had gone off in a scare and at a full gallop, and, instead of going home, had dashed down the lower side of the thicket, then gone aside, to round some of the hills, and thrown himself out of the track, it moutbe seven miles or more. When I found this, I saw there was no use to hunt him that day and afoot, and I had no more to do but turn about, and push as fast as I could for the block. But this was work enough. By this time the sun was pretty low, and there was now a good seven miles, work it how I could, before me. But I was getting over my b'ar-sickness, and though my legs felt weary enough, my stomach was better, and my heart braver; and, as I was in no hurry, having the whole night before me, and knowing the way by night as well as by light, I began to feel cheerful enough, all things considering. I pushed on slowly, stopping every now and then for rest, and recovering my strength this way. I had some parched meal and sugar in my pouch which I ate, and it helped me mightily. It was my only dinner that day. The evening got to be very still. I wondered I had seen and heard nothing of Jake Ransom and the rest, but I didn't feel at all oneasy about them, thinking that, like all other hunters, they would naterally follow the game to any distance. But, jest when I was thinking about them, I heard a gun, then another, and after that all got to be as quiet as ever. I looked to my own rifle and felt for my knife, and put forward a little more briskly. I suppose I had walked an hour after this, when it came on close dark, and I was still four good miles from the block. The night was cloudy, there were no stars, and the feeling in the air was damp and oncomfortable. I began to wish I was safe home, and felt queerish, almost as bad as I did when the b'ar was 'bracing me; but it warn't so much the body-sickness as the heartsickness. I felt as if something was going wrong. Jest as this feeling was most worrisome, I stumbled over a human. My blood cruddled, when, feeling about, I put my hand on his head, and found the sculp was gone. Then I knew there was mischief. I couldn't make out who 'twas that was under me, but I reckoned 'twas one of the hunters. There was nothing to be done but to push for'ad. I didn't feel any more tire. I felt ready for fight, and when I thought of our wives and children in the block, and what might become of them, I got wolfish, though the Lord only knows what I was minded to do. I can't say I had any raal sensible thoughts of what was to be done in the business. I didn't trust myself to think whether the Indians had been to the block yet or no; though ugly notions came across me when I remembered how we let the women and children go about to the farms. I was in a complete fever and agy. I scorched one time and shivered another, but I pushed on, for there was now no more feeling of tire in my limbs than if they were made of steel. By this time I had reached that long range of hills where I first saw that strange campfire, now eleven years gone, that turned out to be a deception, and it was nateral enough that the thing should come fresh into my mind, jest at that moment. While I was thinking over the wonder, and asking myself, as I had done over and often before, what it possibly could mean, I reached the top of one of the hills, from which I could see, in daylight, the whole country for a matter of ten miles or more on every side. What was my surprise, do you reckon, when there, jest on the very same hill opposite where I had seen that apparition of a camp, I saw another, and this time it was a raal one. There was a rousing blaze, and though the woods and undergrowth were thicker on this than on the other side, from which I had seen it before, yet I could make out that there were several figures, and them Indians. It sort o' made me easier to see the enemy before, and then I could better tell what I had to do. I was to spy out the camp, see what the red-devils were thinking to do, and what they had already done. I was a little better scout and hunter this time than when I made the same sort o' search before, and I reckoned that I could get nigh enough to see all that was going on, without stirring up any dust among 'em. But I had to keep the dogs back. I couldn't tie 'em up, for they'd howl; so I stripped my hunting-shirt and put it down for one to guard, and I gave my cap and horn to another. I knew they'd never leave 'em, for I had l'arned 'em all that sort of business—to watch as well as to fetch and carry. I then said a sort of short running prayer, and took the trail. I had to work for'ad slowly. If I had gone on this time as I did in that first camp transaction, I'd ha' lost my sculp to a sartainty. Well, to shorten a long business, I tell you that I got nigh enough, without scare or surprise, to see all that I cared to see, and a great deal more than I wished to see; and now, for the first time, I saw the meaning of that sight which I had, eleven years before, of the camp that come to nothing. I saw that first sight over again, the Indians round the fire, a young woman in the middle, and that young woman my own daughter, my child, my poor, dear Lucy!

Chapter VIII.

"That was a sight for a father. I can't tell you—and I won't try—how I felt. But I lay there, resting upon my hands and knees, jest as if I had been turned into stone with looking. I lay so for a good half hour, I reckon, without stirring a limb; and you could only tell that life was in me, by seeing the big drops that squeezed out of my eyes now and then, and by a sort of shivering that shook me as you sometimes see the canebrake shaking with the gust of the pond inside. I tried to pray to God for help, but I couldn't pray, and as for thinking, that was jest as impossible. But I could do nothing by looking, and, for that matter, it was pretty cla'r to me, as I stood, with no help—by myself—one rifle only and knife—I couldn't do much by moving. I could have lifted the gun, and in a twinkle, tumbled the best fellow in the gang, but what good was that guine to do me? I was never fond of blood-spilling, and if I could have been made sure of my daughter, I'd ha' been willing that the red devils should have had leave to live for ever. What was I to do? Go to the block? Who know'd if it warn't taken, with every soul in it? And where else was I to look for help? Nowhere, nowhere but to God! I groaned—I groaned so loud that I was dreadful 'feared that they'd hear me; but they were too busy among themselves, eating supper, and poor Lucy in the midst, not eating, but so pale, and looking so miserable—jest as I had seen her, when she was only a child—in the same fix, though 'twas only an appearance—eleven years ago! Well, at last, I turned off. As I couldn't say what to do, I was too miserable to look, and I went down to the bottom of the hill and rolled about on the ground, pulling the hair out of my head and groaning, as if that was to do me any good. Before I knew where I was, there was a hand on my shoulder. I jumped up to my feet, and flung my rifle over my head, meaning to bring the butt down upon the stranger—but his voice stopped me.

"'Brother,' said he, 'me Lenatewá!'

"The way he talked, his soft tones, made me know that the young prince meant to be friendly, and I gave him my hand; but the tears gushed out as I did so, and I cried out like a man struck in the very heart, while I pointed to the hill—'My child, my child!'

"'Be man!' said he, 'come!' pulling me away.

"'But, will you save her, Lenatewá?'

"He did not answer instantly, but led me to the little lake, and pointed to the old tree over which I had borne his lifeless body so many years ago. By that I knew he meant to tell me, he had not forgotten what I had done for him; and would do for me all he could. But this did not satisfy me. I must know how and when it was to be done, and what was his hope; for I could see from his caution, and leading me away from the camp, that he did not command the party, and had no power over them. He then asked me, if I had not seen the paint of the warriors in the camp. But I had seen nothing but the fix of my child. He then described the paint to me, which was his way of show-ing me that the party on the hill were his deadly enemies. The paint about their eyes was that of the great chief, his uncle, who had tried to murder him years ago, and who had been shot, in my sight, by the party of his father. The young chief, now in command of the band on the hill was the son of his uncle, and sworn to revenge the death of his father upon him, Lenatewá. This he made me onderstand in a few minutes. And he gave me farther to onder-stand, that there was no way of getting my child from them onless by cun-ning. He had but two followers with him, and they were even then busy in making preparations. But of these preparations he either would not or could not give me any account; and I had to wait on him with all the patience I could muster; and no easy trial it was, for an Indian is the most cool and slow-moving creature in the world, unless he's actually fighting, and then he's about the quickest. After awhile, Lenatewá led me round the hill. We fetched a pretty smart reach, and before I knew where I was, he led me into a hollow that I had never seen before. Here, to my surprise, there were no less than twelve or fourteen horses fastened, that these red devils had stolen from the settlement that very day, and mine was among them. I did not know it till the young prince told me.

"'Him soon move,' said he, pointing to one on the outside, which a close examination showed me to be my own—'Him soon move,'—and these words gave me a notion of his plan. But he did not allow me to have any hand in it—not jest then, at least. Bidding me keep a watch on the fire above, for the hollow in which we stood was at the foot of the very hill the Indians had made their camp on—though the stretch was a long one between—he pushed for'ad like a shadow, and so slily, so silently, that, though I thought myself a good deal of a scout before, I saw then that I warn't fit to hold a splinter to him. In a little time he had unhitched my horse, and quietly led him farther down the hollow, half round the hill, and then up the opposite hill. There was very little noise, the wind was from the camp, and, though they didn't show any alarm, I was never more scary in my life. I followed Lenatewá, and found where he had fastened my nag. He had placed him sev-eral hundred yards from the Indians, on his way to the block; and, where we now stood, owing to the bend of the hollow, the camp of the Indians was between us and where they had hitched the stolen horses. When I saw this, I began to guess something of his plan. Meantime, one after the other, his two followers came up, and made a long report to him in their own language.

This done, he told me that three of my hunting companions had been sculped, the other, who was Hugh Darling, had got off cl'ar, though fired upon twice, and had alarmed the block, and that my daughter had been made prisoner at the farm to which she had gone without any company. This made me a little easier, and Lenatewá then told me what he meant to do. In course, I had to do something myself towards it. Off he went, with his two men, leaving me to myself. When I thought they had got pretty fairly round the hill, I started back for the camp, trying my best, you may be sure, to move as slily as Lenatewá. I got within twenty-five yards, I reckon, when I thought it better to lie by quietly and wait. I could see every head in the huddle, and my poor child among them, looking whiter than a sheet, beside their ugly painted skins. Well, I hadn't long to wait, when there was such an uproar among the stolen horses in the hollow on the opposite side of the hill—such a trampling, such a whinnying and whickering, you never heard the like. Now, you must know, that a stolen horse, to an Indian, is jest as precious as a sweetheart to a white man; and when the rumpus reached the camp, there was a rush of every man among them, for his critter. Every redskin, but one, went over the hill after the horses, and he jumped up with the rest, but didn't move off. He stood over poor Lucy with his tomahawk, shaking it above her head, as if guine to strike every minute. She, poor child—I could see her as plain as the fire-light, for she sat jest on one side of it—her hands were clasped together. She was praying, for she must have looked every minute to be knocked on the head. You may depend, I found it very hard to keep in. I was a'most biling over, the more when I saw the red devil making his flourishes, every now and then, close to the child's ears, with his bloody we'pon. But it was a needcessity to keep in till the sounds died off pretty much, so as not to give them any scare this side, till they had dashed ahead pretty far 'fore the other. I don't know that I waited quite as long as I ought to, but I waited as long as my feelings would let me, and then I dropped the sight of my rifle as close as I could fix it on the breast of the Indian that had the keeping of my child. I took aim, but I felt I was a little tremorsome, and I stopped. I know'd I had but one shoot, and if I didn't onbutton him in that one, it would be a bad shoot for poor Lucy. I didn't fear to hit *her,* and I was pretty sure I'd hit him. But it must be a dead shot to do good, for I know'd if I only hurt him, that he'd sink the tomahawk in her head with what strength he had left him. I brought myself to it again, and this time I felt strong. I could jest hear a little of the hubbub of men and horses afar off. I knew it was the time, and, resting the side of the muzzle against a tree, I give him the whole bless-ing of the bullet. I didn't stop to ask what luck, but run in, with a sort o' cry, to do the finishing with the knife. But the thing was done a'ready. The beast was on his back, and I only had to use the knife in cutting the vines that fas-tened the child to the sapling behind her. The brave gal didn't scream or faint. She could only say, 'Oh, my father!' and I could only say, 'Oh! my child!' And what a precious hug followed; but it was only for a minute. We had no time to waste in hugging. We pushed at once for the place where I had left the crit-ter, and if the good old nag ever used his four shanks to any purpose, he did that night. I reckon it was a joyful surprise to poor Betsy when we broke into the block. She had given it out for sartin that she'd never see me or the child again, with a nateral sculp on our heads.

CHAPTER IX.

"There's no need to tell you the whole story of this war between our people and the redskins. It's enough that I tell you of what happened to us, and our share in it. Of the great affair, and all the fights and burnings, you'll find enough in the printed books and newspapers. What I tell you, though you can't find it in any books, is jest as true, for all that. Of our share in it, the worst has already been told you. The young chief, Oloschottee—for that was his name—the cousin and the enemy of Lenatewá, had command of the Indi-ans that were to surprise our settlements; and though he didn't altogether do what he expected and intended, he worked us quite enough of mischief as it was. He soon put fire to all our farms to draw us out of the block, but find-ing that wouldn't do, he left us; for an Indian gets pretty soon tired of a long siege where there is neither rum nor blood to git drunk on. His force was too small to trouble us in the block, and so he drawed off his warriors, and we saw no more of him until the peace. That followed pretty soon after General Middleton gave the nation that licking at Echotee,—a licking, I reckon, that they'll remember long after my day. At that affair Lenatewá got an ugly bul-let in his throat, and if it hadn't been for one of his men, he'd ha' got a bag'net in his breast. They made a narrow run with him, head foremost down the hill, with a whole swad of the mounted men from the low country at their heels. It was some time after the peace before he got better of his hurt, though the Indians are naterally more skilful in cures than white men. By this time we had all gone home to our farms, and had planted and rebuilt, and begun to forget our troubles, when who should pop into our cabin one day, but

Lenatewá. He had got quite well of his hurts. He was a monstrous fine-looking fellow, tall and handsome, and he was dressed in his very best. He wore pantaloons, like one of us, and his hunting shirt was a raally fine blue, with a white fringe. He wore no paint, and was quite nice and neat with his person. We all received him as an old friend, and he stayed with us three days. Then he went, and was gone for a matter of two weeks, when he came back and stayed with us another three days. And so, off and on, he came to visit us, until Betsy said to me one day, 'Daniel, that Indian, Lenatewá, comes here after Lucy. Leave a woman to guess these things.' After she told me, I recollected that the young prince was quite watchful of Lucy, and would follow her out into the garden, and leave us, to walk with her. But then, again, I thought—'What if he is favourable to my daughter? The fellow's a good fellow; and a raal, noble-hearted Indian, that's sober, is jest as good, to my thinking, as any white man in the land.' But Betsy wouldn't hear to it. 'Her daughter never should marry a savage, and a heathen, and a redskin, while her head was hot':—and while her head was so hot, what was I to do? All I could say was this only, 'Don't kick, Betsy, till you're spurred. 'Twill be time enough to give the young Chief his answer when he asks the question; and it won't do for us to treat him rudely, when we consider how much we owe him.' But she was of the mind that the boot was on the other leg,—that it was he and not us that owed the debt; and all that I could do couldn't keep her from showing the lad a sour face of it whenever he came. But he didn't seem much to mind this, since I was civil and kind to him. Lucy too, though her mother warned her against him, always treated him civilly as I told her; though she naterally would do so, for she couldn't so easily forget that dreadful night when she was a prisoner in the camp of the enimy, not knowing what to expect, with an Indian tomahawk over her head, and saved, in great part, by the cunning and courage of this same Lenatewá. The girl treated him kindly, and I was not sorry she did so. She walked and talked with him jest as if they had been brother and sister, and he was jest as polite to her as if he had been a born Frenchman.

"You may be sure, it was no pleasant sight to my wife to see them two go out to walk. 'Daniel Nelson,' said she, 'do you see and keep an eye on those people. There's no knowing what may happen. I do believe that Lucy has a liking for that redskin, and should they run!'—'Psho!' said I,—but that wouldn't do for her, and so she made me watch the young people sure enough. 'Twarn't a business that I was overfond of, you may reckon, but I was a rough man and didn't know much of woman natur.' I left the judgment of such things to my wife, and did pretty much what she told me. Whenever they went out to walk, I followed them, rifle in hand, but it was only to please Betsy, for if I had seen the lad running off with the girl, I'm pretty sure, I'd never ha' been the man to draw trigger upon him. As I said before, Lenatewá was jest as good a husband as she could have had. But, poor fellow, the affair was never to come to that. One day, after he had been with us almost a week, he spoke softly to Lucy, and she got up, got her bonnet and went out with him. I didn't see them when they started, for I happened to be in the upper story,—a place where we didn't so much live, but where we used to go for shelter and defence whenever any Indians came about us. 'Daniel,' said my wife, and I knew by the quickness and sharpness of her voice what 'twas she had to tell me. But jest then I was busy, and, moreover, I didn't altogether like the sort of business upon which she wanted me to go. The sneaking after an enimy, in raal warfare, is an onpleasant sort of thing enough; but this sneaking after one that you think your friend is worse than running in a fair fight, and always gave me a sheepish feeling after it. Besides, I didn't fear Lenatewá, and I didn't fear my daughter. It's true, the girl treated him kindly and sweetly, but that was owing to the nateral sweetness of her temper, and because she felt how much sarvice he had been to her and all of us. So, instead of going out after them, I thought I'd give them a look through one of the loop-holes. Well, there they went, walking among the trees, not far from the picket, and no time out of sight. As I looked at them, I thought to myself 'Wouldn't they make a handsome couple!' Both of them were tall and well made. As for Lucy, there wasn't, for figure, a finer set girl in all the settlement, and her face was a match for her figure. And then she was so easy in her motion, so graceful, and walked, or sate, or danced,—jest, for all the world, as if she was born only to do the particular thing she was doing. As for Lenatewá, he was a lad among a thousand. Now, a young Indian warrior, when he don't drink, is about the noblest-looking creature, as he carries himself in the woods, that God ever did make. So straight, so proud, so stately, always as if he was doing a great action—as if he knew the whole world was looking at him. Lenatewá was pretty much the handsomest and noblest Indian I had ever seen; and then, I know'd him to be raally so noble. As they walked together, their heads a little bent downwards, and Lucy's pretty low, the thought flashed across me that, jest then, he was telling her all about his feelings; and perhaps, said I to myself, the girl thinks about it pretty much as I do. Moutbe now, she likes him better than any body she has ever seen, and what more nateral? Then I thought, if there is any picture in this life more sweet and beautiful than two young people jest beginning to feel love for one another, and walking together in the innocence of their hearts, under the shady trees,—I've never seen it! I laid the rifle on my lap, and sat down on the floor and watched 'em through the loop until I felt the water in my eyes. They walked backwards and for'ads, not a hundred yards off, and I could see all their motions, though I couldn't hear their words. An Indian don't use his hands much generally, but I could see that Lenatewá was using his,—not a great deal, but as if he felt every word he was saying. Then I began to think, what was I to do, if so be he was raally offering to marry Lucy, and she willing! How was I to do? what was I to say?—how could I refuse him when I was willing? how could I say 'yes,' when Betsy said 'no!'

"Well, in the midst of this thinking, what should I hear but a loud cry from the child, then a loud yell,—a regular war-whoop,—sounded right in front, as if it came from Lenatewá himself. I looked up quickly, for, in thinking, I had lost sight of them, and was only looking at my rifle; I looked out, and there, in the twinkle of an eye, there was another sight. I saw my daughter flat upon the ground, lying like one dead, and Lenatewá staggering back as if he was mortally hurt; while, pressing fast upon him, was an Indian warrior, with his tomahawk uplifted, and striking—once, twice, three times—hard and heavy, right upon the face and forehead of the young prince. From the black paint on his face, and the red ring about his eyes, and from his figure and the eagle feathers in his head, I soon guessed it was Oloschottee and I then knew it was the old revenge for the killing of his father; for an Indian never forgets that sort of obligation. Of course, I didn't stand quiet to see an old friend, like Lenatewá, tumbled in that way, without warning, like a bullock; and there was my own daughter lying flat, and I wasn't to know that he hadn't struck her too. It was only one motion for me to draw sight upon the savage, and another to pull trigger; and I reckon he dropped jest as soon as the young Chief. I gave one whoop for all the world as if I was an Indian myself, and run out to the spot; but Lenatewá had got his discharge from further service. He warn't exactly dead, but his sense was swimming. He couldn't say much, and that warn't at all to the purpose. I could hear him, now and then, making a sort of singing noise, but that was soon swallowed up in a gurgle and a gasp, and it was all over. My bullet was quicker in its working than Oloschottee's hatchet; he was stone dead before I got to him.

As for poor Lucy, she was not hurt, either by bullet or hatchet; but she had a hurt in the heart, whether from the scare she had, or because she had more feeling for the young prince than we reckoned, there's no telling. She warn't much given to smiling after that. But, whether she loved Lenatewá, we couldn't know, and I never was the man to ask her. It's sartain she never married, and she had about as many chances, and good ones, too, as any girl in our settlement. You've seen her—some among you—and warn't she a beauty—though I say it myself—the very flower of the forest!"

"THE NARRATIVE OF LE BARBU" has greater literary than ethnohistorical value in its revelation of the details of Indian life, including the ceremony of human sacrifice in which the heart of the still-alive victim is torn from his body. Simms gains verisimilitude by electing to have Barbu, the bearded white-man-turned-Indian, tell his own tale of rescue and capture, as related by the omniscient narrator. Barbu, with emotional ties to both the race of his birth and the race of his adoption, has a biracial, multicultural point of view that makes him perhaps unique among Simms's characters.

"The Martyrs" (396) is the early Spanish name for the Florida Keys, islands which posed notable hazards for early navigation.

∿ The Narrative of Le Barbu: The Bearded Man of Calos

Now when Barbu, the bearded man, who had been dwelling among the people of Calos, had been shorn of the long and matted hair and beard, which had made him much more fearful to the eye than any among the savages themselves,—and when our right worthy captain had commanded that we should bathe and cleanse him, and had given him shirts of fine linen and clothes from his own wardrobe, so that he should once more appear like a Christian man among his kindred,—albeit he seemed to be greatly disquieted, and exceedingly awkward therein,—then did he conduct himself into the *corps de garde*, where our people were all bidden to assemble. There, being seated all, Barbu, the Spaniard, being entreated thereto by our right worthy captain, proceeded to unfold the full relation of the grievous strait and peril by which he had fallen into the power of King Calos, and what happened to him thereafter. And it was curious to see how that he, a Spaniard born, and not ill-educated in one of the goodly towns of old Spain, in all gentle learning, should, in the space of fifteen years sojourn among the savages, have so greatly suffered the loss of his native tongue. Slow was he of speech, and greatly minded to piece out with the Indian language the many words in which the memory of his own had failed him. Well was it for our understanding of what he delivered, that so many of us had been dwelling among the red-men at other times,—to speak nothing of Monsieur D'Erlach, Monsieur Ottigny, both lieutenants in the garrison, and Monsieur La Roche Ferriere, who, with another, by special commandment of our captain, had dwelt for a matter of several months among the people of King Olata Utina. By means of the help brought by these, we were enabled to find the meaning of those words in which Barbu failed in his Spanish. So it was that we followed the fortunes of the bearded man, according to the narrative as here set down.

ᦔ

Then, at the repeated entreaty of Monsieur Laudonniere, Barbu arose and spoke:

"First, Señor Captain, I have to declare how much I thank you for the protection you have given me, the kindness which has clad me once more in Christian garments, and the cost and travail with which you have recovered me from my bonds among the heathen. Albeit, that I feel strangely in these new habits, and that my native tongue comes back to me slowly when I would speak from a full and overflowing heart, yet will I strive to make you sensible of all the facts in my sad history, and of the great gratitude which I feel for those by whose benevolence I may fondly hope that my troubles are about to end. I know not now the day or season when we left the port of Nombre de Dios, in an excellent ship, well filled with treasures of the mine, and a goodly company, on our return to the land of our fathers beyond the sea. My own share in the wealth of this vessel was considerable, and I had other treasures in the person of a dear brother, and a sister who accompanied us. Our sister was married to one who was with us also, and the united wealth of the three, such was our fond expectations, would enable us to retire to our native town of Burgos, and commend us to the favor of our people. But it was written that we should not realize these blessed expectations, and that I alone, of the four, should be again permitted to dwell among a Christian people. Yet I give not up the hope that I shall yet see my brother, who was carried away among the Indians of the far west, when we were scattered among the tribes, in the grand division of our captives. But this part of my story comes properly hereafter.

"We put to sea from the port of Nombre de Dios with very favoring winds; and these lasted us not long, ere they came out from all quarters of the heavens, and we ran before the storm under a rag of sail, without knowing in what course we sped. Thus, for three days, we were driven before the baffling winds; and when the storm lulled, the clouds still hung about us, and our pilot wot nothing of that part of the sea in which we went. Two days more followed, and still we were saddened by the clouds that kept evermore coming down from heaven, and brooding upon the deep like great fogs that gather in the morn among the mountains. Thus we sped, weary and desponding as we were, without any certainty as to the course we kept, or the region of space or country round about us. Meanwhile, the seams of our vessel began to yawn, and great was the labor which followed, to all hands, to keep her clear of water. This we did not wholly; and it was in vain that our carpenter sought for, in order to stop, the leak. Thus, weary and sad, we continued still sweeping forward slowly, looking anxiously, with many prayers, for the sun by day and the moon and stars by night. But the Blessed Virgin was implored in vain. We had offended. There was treasure aboard the vessel, but it was stained with blood. You have not heard in your histories of the bloody Juan de Mores y Silva, who tortured the unhappy Mexicans by fire, even in the caverns where they resided, seeking the gold, which they gained not sufficiently soon, or in sufficient quantity, to satisfy his cruel lust for wealth. He was one of our companions on this voyage, bound homewards with an immense subsidy of ingots—huge chests of gold and silver—with which he aimed to swell into grandeur with new titles, when he arrived in Spain. But the just Providence willed it otherwise. He was, doubtless, the Jonah in our vessel, who fought against the prayers for mercy and protection which the true believers addressed to the Holy Virgin in our behalf."

Here our captain, Laudonniere, interrupted Barbu, and said—

"Verily, Señor Spaniard, had thy prayer been addressed to God himself, the Father, through the intervention and mediation of the Blessed Saviour, his Son, whose blood was shed for sinners, it might have better profited thy case. Thy prayers to the Virgin were an unseemly elevation of a mortal woman over the divinity of the Godhead. But I will not vex thee with disputation. Thou art a Christian, though it is after a fashion which, to me seems scarcely more becoming than that of these poor savages of Calos, who yield faith, as thou tellest me, to the spells and enchantments of their bloody sovereign. But, proceed with thy story, which I shall be slow to break in upon again until thou art well ended."

With the permission thus vouchsafed him, the bearded man, thus resumed his discourse:

"We plead for the interposition of the Virgin, Monsieur le Capitaine, not as we deem her the source of power and of mercy, but as we hold it irreverent to rush even with our prayers to the feet of the awful Father himself; and rejoice to believe that she who was specially chosen, as one who should bear the burden of the Saviour-child, was of spirit properly sanctified and pure for such purposes of interposition. But, as thou sayest, we will leave this matter. If we offend in our rites and offices, it is because we err in judgement, and not that our hearts wish to afflict the feelings or the thoughts of those who see with other eyes the truth. Besides, my long and outlandish abode among the red-men, might well excuse me many errors."

"And so, indeed, it might, Señor Spaniard," said Laudonniere graciously; then, as the latter remained silent, Barbu continued:

"Doubtless, Señor, as I said before, the bloody Juan de Mores y Silva, was the Jonah of our vessel, on whose account the Blessed Providence turned a deaf ear to our prayers and entreaties. It was not decreed that he should escape to rejoice in his ill-gotten treasure; and his fortunes were so mixed up with ours, that the overthrow of one was necessarily at the grievous loss and peril of us all. How many days we lay tossing on the tumultuous waves, or swept to and fro, beaten and sore distressed by the violent and changeful winds, I do not remember, but it was in very sickness and hopelessness of heart, that we lay down at night as one lies down and submits to a power with which he feels wholly powerless to contend. Thus did we cast ourselves down—as the dreary shades of night came over us, with a deeper and drearier cloud than ever,—not seeking sleep, but seized upon by it, as it were, to save us from the suffering, akin to madness, which must haply follow upon our fearful waking thoughts. While we slept, our vessel struck upon the low flats of the Martyrs—those shoals which have laid bare the ribs of so many goodly and gold-laden ships of my countrymen, sucking down their brave hearts and all their treasures in the deep. We were lifted high by the surges, and rested, beyond recovery, upon the shoals, from which the remorseless seas refused again to lift us off. Our vessel lay upon one side, and the greedy waves rushed into her hold. We were stunned rather than awakened by the shock. We strove not for safety or repair. How many perished in the moment when the ship fell over I know not, but one of these was the husband of my sister. He was drowned in the first rush of the billows into the ship, though, as it was night, we knew it not. My sister had thrown herself beside my brother, and was sleeping upon his arm. She was the first to learn her misfortune, awaking, as she averred, to hear the faint cries of her lord for succor, though she knew not whence the sounds arose. When our eyes opened upon the scene, strange to say, the clouds had disappeared. The dark waves of the tempest had sped away to other regions. A gentle breeze from the land had arisen, full of sweet fragrance and a healing freshness, and, bright over head, in the blessed heavens, blossomed fresh the eternal host of the stars. Oh! the life and soothing in that smile of God. But we were not strong for the blessing, not sufficiently grateful that life was still vouchsafed us. The day dawned upon us to increase our wretchedness. It left us without hope. Our food was ruined by the waves that filled the vessel, and though the land was spread before us in a lengthened stripe, bearing forests which were surely full of fragrance, we beheld not the means by which we should gain its pleasant shores with safety. Our boats had perished in the surf; one of them stove to pieces, and the other swept away. In our despondency and our sleep we had yielded our courage and our providence, and we lay now in the sight of heaven, amidst the equal realm of sea and sky, and with the land spreading lovelily before us, yet we could do nothing for ourselves. We lay without food or drink all day, seeing nothing but the bare skies, the sea, and the shore, which only mocked our eyes. My sister sorrowed and sickened in my arms. She cried for water as one cries in the delirious agonies of fever. She would drink of the water of the deep, but this we denied her; and the day sunk again, and with it her hope and strength. With the increase of the winds that night, she grew delirious; and, when we knew not—and this was strange, for I cannot believe that I closed mine eyes that night—she disappeared. Once, it seemed that I heard her voice, in a wild scream, calling me by name, and I started forward to feel that she was gone. She left my arms while I lay insensible. It was not sleep. It was stupor. My consciousness was drowned in my great grief, and in the exhaustion of all my strength for lack of food.

"My brother and myself alone survived of all our family. With the knowledge that our sister was really gone—swallowed up, doubtless, in the remorseless deep, into which she had darted in her delirium—we came to a full consciousness. Then, when it was only misery to know, we were permitted to know all, and to feel the whole terrible truth pressing upon us, that we were alone in that dreary world of sea. Not alone of our company; only of our people. Many there were who still kept in life, watchful but hopeless. We could see their dusky forms by the faint light of the stars, crouching along the slanting plane of the vessel, upon which, by cord, and sail, and spar, we still contrived to maintain foothold; and, anon, our company would lessen. The solemn silence of all things, except the dash of the waves against us, rolling up with murmurs, and breaking away in wrath, was interrupted only by a sudden plunge, ever and anon, into the engulphing deep, as the hope went out utterly in the heart of the victim, and he yielded to death, rather than prolong the wretched endurance of a life so full of misery.

"Thus the night passed; not without other signs to cheer as well as startle us. Through the darkness we could see lights in the direction of the shore, as if borne by human hands. With the dawn of day, our eyes were turned eagerly in that direction. Nor did we look in vain. The shore swarmed with human forms. A hundred canoes were already darting along the margin of the great deep, and evident were the preparations of the people of this wild region, to visit our stranded vessel. In a little time they came. Their canoes were some of them large enough to carry forty warriors, though made from a single tree. They came to us in order of battle; a hundred boats, holding each from ten to fifty warriors. These carried spear and shield, huge lances, and well-carved bows, drawn with powerful sinews of the deer. Their arrows were long shafts of the feathery reed, such as flourish in all these forests. The feather from the eagle's wing gave it buoyancy, and the end of the shaft was barbed with a keen flint, wrought by art to an edge such as our best workmen give to steel. Many were the chief men among these warriors, who approached us in full panoply of barbaric pomp. Turbans of white and crimson-stained cotton, such as the Turk is shown to wear, though folded in a still nobler fashion, were wrapped about their heads, over which shook bunches of plumes taken from the paroquet, the crane, and the eagle. Robes of cotton, white, or crimson, or scarlet, covered with native dyes of the forest, clothed their loins, and fell flowing from their shoulders; and, ever and anon, as they came, they shook a thousand gourds which they had made to rattle with little pebbles, which, with their huge drum, wrought of the mammoth gourd, and covered with raw deer skin, made a clamor most astounding to our hapless ears. Thus they hailed our vessel, making it appear as if they intended to have fought us; but when they beheld how famishing we lay before them, with scarcely strength and courage enough to plead for mercy—speaking only through our dry and scalded eyes, and by clasping our hard and weary hands together—then it seemed as if they at once understood and felt for us; and they drew nigh with their canoes, and lowered their weapons, and darting with lithe sinews upon the sides of our leaning vessel, they held gourds of water to our lips, which cheered us while we swallowed, as with the sense of a fresh existence.

"Thus were we rescued from the yawning deep. The savages took us, with a rough kindness, from the wreck. They carried us in their canoes to the shore; and several were the survivors, as well women as men. They gave us food and nourishment, and when we were refreshed and strengthened, they separated us from our comrades, sharing us among our captors, each according to his rank, his power, or his favor with his sovereign. Seventeen of our poor Christians were thus scattered among the tribes and over the territories of the king of Calos. Some were kept in his household; but my hapless brother was not among them. He was given to a chief of the far tribes of the West, who made instant preparation to depart with him. When they would have borne us apart, with a swift bound and a common instinct, we buried ourselves in a mutual embrace. The chiefs looked on with a laughter that made us shudder; while he to whom my brother was given, with a savage growl, thrust his hands into the flowing locks of my brother, and hurled him away to the grasp of those who stood in waiting for the captive. He struggled once more to embrace me, and long after I could hear his cry—'Brother, brother, shall we see each other never more!' They heeded not his cries or struggles, or mine. They threw him to the ground with violence, bound him hand and foot, with gyves of the forest, and placing him in one of their great canoes, they sped away with him along the shores, as they treaded to the mighty West, where roll the great waters of the Mechachebe.

"Thus I was separated from my only surviving kinsman; and neither of us could tell the fate which was in waiting for the other. Verily, then did I look to find the worst. I no longer had a hope. It is my shame, as a Christian, that, in that desolate moment, I ceased to have a fear. I not only expected death, but I longed for it. I could have kissed the friendly hand that had driven the heavy stone hatchet of the savage into my brain. But, the Blessed Mother of God be praised, I thought not, in my despair, to do violence to my own self. That sin was spared me among my many sins, in that hour of despondency and woe; and all my crime consisted in the criminal indifference which made me too little heedful to preserve life. But this indifference lasted not long. I was captive to the king of Calos himself. Nine others were kept by him including me, and among these was the cruel tyrant upon whose head lay the blood of so many of the wretched people of Mexico, Don Juan de Mores y Silva. He was the tyrant no longer. All his strength and courage had departed in his afflictions; and in the hour of our despair and terror, he was feebler than the meanest among us; feebler of soul than the girl whose heart beats with the dread she cannot name, fearfully, as that of the little bird which you cover with your hand. We loathed him the worse for his miserable fear; and it made us all more resolute in courage to see one so cast down with his terrors, whom we had seen of late so insolent in his triumphs.

"When the lots were determined, the king of Calos drew nigh to examine us more heedfully. He had not before regarded us with any consideration. Verily, he was a noble savage to the eye. His person was tall, like one of the sons of Anak, and his carriage was that of a great warrior, born a prince, to whom it was natural equally to conquer and to rule. Rich were the garments of flowing cotton which he wore loosely, like a robe, mostly white, but with broad stains of crimson about the skirts and shoulders.

"A great baldrick hung suspended at his back, which bore a quiver, made of the skins of a rattle-snake, filled with arrows, each shaft better than a cloth-yard's length. The macana which he carried in his grasp, was a mighty club of hard wood, close in grain, and weighty as stone, which, save at the grasp or handle, was studded with sharp blades of flint, which resembled it to the mighty blade of the sword-fish. With this weapon mine eyes have seen him smite down two powerful enemies at a single stroke. Great was his forehead and high, and his cheek bones stood forth like knots upon his face, as if the cheeks were guarded by a shield. Black was his piercing eye, which grew red and fiery when he was angered; and, at such seasons, it was easier for him to smite than to speak. Unlike his people, he wore a natural growth of his hair, long and flowing straight adown his back, glossy with its original black-ness, and with the oil of the bear, of which, like all his people, the lord of Calos made plentiful use. This king might be full forty years of age. Yet he looked neither young nor old—neither so young that you might hold him the gravest and best counsellor of wisdom in the land, nor so old, but that he might better and more ingeniously lead in battle than any of his warriors. Certes, he was the most ready first to march when the invasion of the distant tribes had been resolved on; and, of a truth, never was statesman in the great courts of Europe—not the counsellors of the great Carlos himself—so cool in speculation, so just in judgment, so heedful to consider all the advan-tages and all the risks of an enterprise, before the first step was set down in the adoption of a policy. For seven years had I sufficient means, in the imme-diate service of his household, to watch the courses of his thoughts and character, and to know the virtues and strength thereof. I saw him devise among his chiefs, and inform them with his own devices. I have seen him lead in battle, when all the plans were his own, and it was his equal teaching and valiancy by which the field was won. Verily, I say that this lord of Calos were a prince to mate with the best in Europe; and, but that we have in European warfare such engines of mischief that come not within the use or knowledge of his race, it were difficult to circumvent him in stratagem, or overcome his braves in battle. With an hundred shot—no less—and employing at the same time all the red-men as allies, who are hostile to this king of Calos—and there are many—and I doubt not Monsieur Laudonniere, but that you could penetrate his dominions and make the conquest thereof. But of him could you make no conquest. He is a warrior of the proudest stomach, who would rather perish than lose the victory; and who, most surely, would never survive the overthrow of his dominion.

"Me, did this great king examine with more curious eyes than he bestowed upon the other captives. I know not for what reason, unless because of the superior size and strength which I possess, and the extreme length and thickness of my beard and hair, of which, as a Christian man, I have always made too much account. All of us did he assign to labor; to the gathering of wood, and work in the maize fields, with the women. By-and-by, there came a preference for me beyond the others. I was brought into the king's household, and barbed his arrows, and wrought upon his great macanas, and strove, among the Indians, in hewing out his canoes from the cypress, first burning out the greater core with fire. But when harvest time came, a great festivity was held among the savages. Bitter roots were gathered in the woods, and great vessels of the beverage which was made thereof, was placed within the council or round-house of the nation. Thither did the chiefs resort and drink; and ever as they drank they danced, though the liquor wrought upon the like *aguardiente* with the European, and moved them even as the most violent of emetic medicines. Still they danced, and still they danced for the space of three whole days.—But the lord of Calos seemed not to mingle at this strange festival. He purposed rites still more strange—rites, which even now, I think upon with horror only. He had a dwelling to himself in the deep woods, whither he retired the night before the day when the great feast of the nation was to begin. Here he waited all night, watching with reverence and patience the burning of a strange fire which had been wrought of many curious and fragrant herbs and roots. Three of the ancient people, the priests or Iawas, as they style themselves, retired with him to build his fire, which, when it began to burn, placing in store a sufficient supply of aromatic fuel that he might feed it still, they left him, with strange exorcising, to himself. And there he kept watch throughout the night. But early with the next morning he came forth, and he sprinkled the ashes of the fire upon the maize field, and he cried thrice, with a loud voice, of Yo-he-wah, which, I believe to mean the sacred name as known among the red-men. With each cry, as our poor Spaniards, myself among them, were gathering the green ears from the maize stalks, the priests who followed the king of Calos, seized bodily upon three of our brethren, taking us by surprise, and putting us all in a quaking fear. These three were all brought before the lord of Calos, who, not looking upon them as they lay bound at his feet, threw yet another vessel of sacred ashes into the air, and as these three Spaniard lay separate, with their faces looking up, I beheld the ashes sink immediately upon the breast of him whom I have already named to you—the Jonas by whom our vessel was doomed to wreck— the cruel Don Juan de Mores y Silva. Now, though the king surely looked not as he threw the ashes into the air, yet did it descend upon the breast of this said Spaniard, as certainly as if the eye and arm of this lord had been upon this particular person at the moment when he threw. Verily, though I know not well how it should be—being counselled by Holy Church against such belief—yet, verily, had the lord of Calos certain powers which did seem to justify the saying among his people, that he was a master of magic and of arts superior to those of common men.

"Now, when the Iawas, or priests, beheld where the ashes fell, they seized incontinently upon the Spaniard aforesaid. They bore him away from us, wondering and fearing all the while. But those who remained loosed the other two who had been bound, and they were set free with the rest, to pursue their labors in the corn-field. But we were not let to know the awful fate which befel the Spaniard who was taken. Verily, he saw his danger in the moment when the ashes lighted on his breast. His face was whiter than the blossom of the dogwood when it first opens to the spring. His eye glared, and his lip quivered like a leaf in the gusts of March, though nothing he spake at anything they did to him. But when they bore him away from our eyes, then a terrible fear and agony caused him to cry aloud—'Oh! my countrymen, will you not save me from the bloody savage!' I cannot soon forget that cry, which was clearly that of a person who beholds his doom. But of what avail? We had not the people, nor the strength, nor the weapons! A thousand savages danced wildly around the council-house, and the fields were full of those who came to drink and dance. Besides, we thought not of any danger but our own. We knew not how soon the fate was to befal us; for had it not seized upon Don Juan without a warning or a sign?

"They bore him to the secret tabernacle in the woods, where the lord of Calos watched alone. We saw not then, but afterwards we knew, what had been his fate. There they laid him upon a great mound of earth, with the sacred fire burning at his head in a large vessel of baked clay, formed with a nice art by the savages, and painted with the mystic figure of a bloody hand. The garments which he wore were taken off, and his limbs were fastened separately to great stakes driven in places about the mound. Thus were his hands and legs, his body and his very neck made fast, so that whatever might be the deed done upon him, he could not oppose it even in the smallest measure. But it was permitted him to cry aloud—and those of us who stole into the woods seeking to hear,—with a terrible curiosity which our very apprehensions fed,—we heard,—we heard,—and even as the awful scream of our late companion came piercing through the woods upon our ears,—we fled afar from the sound, which was that of a mortal agony and anguish. And, verily, the torture to which he was doomed was that which might well compel the poor outraged heart of humanity to cry aloud. With a keen knife, and the hand of one who had practised long at the cruel rite, the lord of Calos laid bare the breast of the victim, he was not able to struggle even,—only to shriek,—he laid it bare as one peels the ripe fruit, and exposes the precious heart thereof! Even this did the lord of Calos. He stripped the skin from the breast of his victim, then, with sharp strokes, he smote away the flesh, until the quaking ribs lay bare to his point. With a sharp stone chisel, he smote the breast-bone asunder, lifted the ribs, and tore away the smoking heart, which he cast, reeking red, into the burning fire of odorous woods and herbs, which then flamed up and brightened in the dark chamber, as if fed by some ichorous fuel. In that terrible agony, when the soul and the human life were thus mutually torn apart from the mutual embrace, it was told me by my lord of Calos, himself, that the victim burst one of the wythes that bound him, and freed his right hand, which he waved violently thrice, even while his murderer was plucking his heart away from its quivering fastenings! Oh! the horror, though for a moment only, of that awful consciousness! Verily, my friends, if the lord of Calos did possess a power of magic such as his people affirm, verily, I say, he paid a terrible price to the eternal hater of human souls, when he gat from him his perditious privilege!

"But the sufferings of that wretched victim, who then and thus perished, were they greater than those which followed our footsteps,—we, the survivors,—haunting us by night and day, with the mortal terrors of a fear that such must be our doom also? Every rustle of an approaching footstep among the maize-stalks where we toiled, breaking the stems and gathering the ripened ears, seemed to our woe-stricken souls, as the step of one who came as an executioner; while we labored in the gloomy thicket, gathering fuel for the winter fires, the same fear was hanging over us with a threat of the impending doom. We lived and slept in a continual dread of death, which made the hair whiten on every brow, even of the youngest, before that terrible winter was gone over.

"To us it was assigned to put away the body of our murdered comrade. But this was only after the three days of the feast was elapsed, and when the duty was tenfold distressing. Still, though all our senses revolted at the task, a fearful curiosity compelled a close examination of the victim. Then it was that we saw how the execution had been done, though we knew not then, nor until some time after, that the cell which enshrined and kept the heart had been torn open, and the sacred possession wrenched away with violent hands, even while the wretched victim had eyes to see, as well as sensibilities to feel, the sacrilegious and bloody theft. We bore the body far into the woods, wrapping it with leaves so as to hide it from our eyes, while we carried it in the bottom of an old canoe which we found for this purpose. Our burial was conducted after the fashion of the red-men. We laid the corse of our comrade upon a bed of leaves on the naked earth, and laid heavy fragments of pine and other combustible wood about him. With this we made a great pile, which we set on fire, and let to burn until everything was consumed. We then, with sad, sorrowing, and trembling hearts, returned, each one of us, in a mournful silence that wist not what to say, to our separate tasks, and the places which had been assigned to us.

"Now, many months had passed in this manner, and still I was employed about the king's household. The lord of Calos distinguished me, as I have said, beyond my comrades. I had a great vigor of limb which was not common among this people, except in so much as it moves them to great agility. They are rather light, swift and expert, than powerful in war; and trust rather to great cunning than superior strength, in meeting with their enemies. The king of Calos greatly admired to see me lift heavy logs of timber, such as would have borne down any of his people if laid upon his shoulders. But he himself had a strength superior to his people, and he wondered even more when, striving to lift the logs, he found it beyond his mastery. Then, he put his bow into my hand, and giving me a yard-cloth shaft of reed, well tipped with a flinty barb, and dressed with an eagle's feather, he bade me to draw it to the head, and send it as I would. Upon which, doing so, he greatly wondered to see how rapid and distant was the flight, for well he knew that the ability to shoot the arrow far comes rather from sleight than from strength, and is an art that grows only from practice. But this, perhaps, had not fully given me to the confidence of the king, had it not been for a service which I rendered on one occasion to his favorite son, a boy of but twelve years of age, whom I plucked from beneath the feet of a great stag, which the hunters had wounded in the forest. The red-men greatly delight to see their sons take part in the chase, even while their gristle is yet soft and their limbs feeble; for by this early practice they desired to make them strong and skillful. The son of the lord of Calos was a youth, tall and strong beyond his years; and because of the fondness of his father, exceedingly audacious in all manner of sports and strifes. Thus it was that, having seen a great stag wounded by the shaft of his sire, he had run in upon him with his slender spear. The staff of the spear broke, even as the barb penetrated the breast of the beast, and the boy fell forward at the mercy of his mighty antlers. Then was it that, seeing the lad's danger,—for I was at hand, bearing the victuals for the hunters—I threw down the basket, and rushing in, took the stag by his horns, in season for the lad to recover himself. The lord of Calos drew nigh and saw, but he offered no help, leaving it to his son to draw the keen knife which he carried, over the throat of the struggling beast. And, excepting what the boy said to me of thanks, nothing did I hear of the thing which I had done. But, three weeks after, the king made his preparations for a war party against the mountain Indians. Then he spoke to me, saying, in his own language,—which, by this time, I could understand,—Barbu,—this was the name which had been given me because of my beard—Barbu, it is not fit that one with such limbs and skills as thou hast, should labor in the occupation of the women. Get thee a spear, such as will suit thy grasp, and there are bows and arrows for thy choice,—make thee satisfied with sufficient provision, and get thee ready to go against mine enemies. Thou shalt have to tear the flesh of a strong man!

"Verily, my friends, though it shames me to confess, that I, a Christian man, could lift a weapon on behalf of one against another savage in the wilderness, yet such had been my sorrow, and so wretched did I feel at the base tasks to which I had been given,—so very unlike the valiant duties which had distinguished mine ancient service in the armies of Castile,—that I even rejoiced at the chance of putting on the armor of war,—and the meaner weapon of the red-men satisfied me then, who of old had carried, with great favor, the matchlock and the sword. But the weapon of the savage, as perchance thou knowest, is not greatly inferior according to their usage, in their country, to the superior implements with which the Christian warrior takes the field. If the arquebuse is more fatal than the barbed arrow of the Indian, it is yet less frequently ready for the danger. While you should have put your pieces in readiness for a second fire, the savage will deliver thirty javelins, each of which, if within bullet reach, shall inflict such an injury, short of death, as may disarm the wounded person. Their reeds are always ready at hand. To them every bay and river bank affords an armory, and the loss of their weapons, which were fatal to the Frenchman or Spaniard, causes them but little mischief, since a single night will repair all their losses. Neither much time nor much cost is it to them to supply their munitions, of which they can always carry a more abundant supply than we. The great superiority of the European, in his encounter with the red-man, is in his wisdom, the fruit of many ages of civilization, and not in the weapons which he wields in conflict. Let him exchange weapons with the savage, and he will still obtain the victory.

"It was because of this showing of superiority, together with the service which I had thus rendered to his son, that made the lord of Calos take me with him, armed as a warrior, on his expedition against the mountain Indians of Apalachy. I hastened to provide myself with weapons, as I was commanded, and I made for myself a great mace, such as that which the strongest warriors carried, which was a billet of hard wood, not more than four feet in length, with a handle easy to grasp, while at each side ran down a great row of flinty teeth, each broad and sharpened like a spear-head. It is a fatal weapon, with a well-delivered blow. In a like manner did I imitate the practice of the red-men in dressing the head and breast for war. I put on the paints, red and black, which I beheld them use; but, instead of the unmeaning and rude figures which they scored upon the breast, I drew there the figure of a large cross, by which, though none but myself might know, I made anew my assurance to Holy Mother, of a faith unperishing, in Him who bore its burthen; and implored His protection against the perils which might lurk along the path. In the same manner, with a bloody cross, did I inscribe my forehead and each cheek, while I dipped my hands above my wrists in the black dyes which they also used as paints, and which they took from the walnut and other woods of the forest. Greatly did my Christian comrades wonder to behold me, painted after this fashion, with a bunch of turkey feathers tied about my head like the savage, and the strange weapons of the red-men in my grasp. These rejoiced exceedingly as they beheld me, and laughed and chatted among themselves, saying—'Yah-hee-wee! Yah-hee-wee!' with other words, by which they testified their satisfaction. But our Spaniards were in the same degree sorry, as if it seemed to them that, in spite of the holy emblem upon my breast, I had delivered myself up to the enemy, and had put on, with the habit, all the superstitions of the Heathen. They had sorrow on other grounds, since I was about to leave them, and, from the favor I had found with the lord of Calos, I had grown to become one to whom they began to look as to a mediator and protector.

"We set out thus for the country of the enemy, the lord of Calos leading the way upon the march, as is the custom with the Indians, while the foe is yet at a distance from the spot. But, as we drew nigh to the hills of the Apalachian, the young men were scattered on every hand, as so many light troops. They covered all the paths, they harbored in all places where they could maintain watch and find security, and nightly they sent in runners to the camp, reporting their discoveries. I entreated with the lord of Calos to be sent with these young men; but, whether he feared that I would seek an opportunity to fly and escape to the enemy, I know not. He refused, saying that it required scouts of experience,—men who knew the ways of the country, and that I could be of no use in such adventures. He was pleased to add that he wished me near him, as one of his own warriors—that is, the warriors of his family or tribe—that I might do battle at his side, and in his sight!

"We were not long in finding the enemy, who had received tidings of our approach. Several battles were fought, in which I did myself credit in the eyes of our warriors. The lord of Calos was greatly pleased. He took me with him into counsel, and it was fortunate that the advice which I gave, as to the conduct of the war, was adopted, and was greatly successful. Many were the warriors of the mountain whom we slew. Many scalps were taken, and more than a hundred captive boys and damsels. These, if young, are always spared, and taken into the conquering tribe. The former are newly marked with the totem of the people who take them, while the latter become the wives of the chiefs, who greatly value them. I confess to you, my brethren, that I was guilty of the sin of taking one of these same women into my cabin, who was to me as a wife, though no holy priest, with appointed ceremonials of the church, gave his sanction to our communion. She was a lovely and loving creature, scarcely sixteen, but very fair, almost like a Spaniard, and of hair so long that she hath thrice wrapt it around her own neck and mine."

"Why didst thou not tell me of that woman?" said Laudonniere, interrupting the narrator. Had we known, she should have been procured with thee. But, even now, it is not too late. We will bid the chief, Onathaqua, send her after thee, so that thou may'st wed her according to the rites of the church."

"Alas!" replied Barbu, "thou compellst me, Señor Laudonniere, to unravel sin after sin before thee. I have greatly erred and wandered from the paths of virtue, and from the laws of the Holy Church, in my grievous sojourn among the savages. That woman filled no longer the place which she first had in my affections. With increase of power and security, I grew wanton. I grew weary of her, and sold her to one of the chiefs for a damsel of his own house, which mine eyes coveted."

The Spaniard hung his head as he made this confession, while Laudonniere with severe aspect rated him for his lecheries. When the captain had ceased his rebuke, Le Barbu continued his story thus:

"We gained many battles in this war with the mountain Indians, who are neither so fierce, nor so subtle as those who dwell along the regions of the sea. Verily, the people of the lord of Calos are great dissemblers, treacherous beyond the serpent, valiant of their persons, and fight with excellent address. Great was the favor I found with them because of my conduct in the war; and, in each succeeding war, for a space of six years, I became, in like manner, distinguished, until I became a most favorite chief with the lord of Calos, and a bosom friend and companion of his son—he whom I had rescued from the stag, and who had now grown up to manhood. Greatly did this lad favor his father. He was of a light olive complexion, scarcely more dark than the people of the Spanish race, but superior in stature, well-limbed, and of admirable dexterity. With him I hunted from the fall of the leaf in autumn, to the budding of the leaf again in spring; and, when the summer time came, we sped away in our canoes, up the vast rivers of the country, through great lakes, many of which lie embedded in forests of mangrove and palm, where the forest swims upon the water. If it were possible for a Christian man—for one who has heard the sound of a great bell in the cities of the old world, and who has communed with the various good and wondrous things of civilization—to be content with a loss of these, and their utter exclusion from sight for ever, then might I have passed pleasantly the years of my captivity among the people of Calos. I had become a chief and was greatly honored. I had power and I was much feared. I had wealth—such wealth as the savage estimates—and I was loved; and the lord of Calos and his noble son, put me in a faith which never betrayed a doubt or a denial. But I had not power to shield my brother Christians, save in one case. Each year witnessed the sacrifice of a comrade. They were the victims to the Iawas. The priesthood was a power under which the kings themselves were made to tremble. With them was it to determine upon peace or war, life or death, bonds or freedom; the strength of the king lay greatly in his alliance with the priesthood. But for this, the rule among the savage nations would be wholly with the people. Season after season, when came the harvest, one of our luckless Spaniards was taken away from the rest and doomed to the sacrifice. In this way the savages propitiate the unknown God, to whom they looked for victory over their enemies. Do not suppose that I beheld this cruelty without toiling against it. But I spoke in vain. I made angry the Iawas, until the lord of Calos himself addressed me, after this fashion—'Son of the stranger, art thou not well thyself? Why wouldst thou be sick, being well? Art thou not thyself safe? Why, being so, put thy head under the macana? It is not wise in thee to *see* the things over which the power is denied thee. Go then, with Mico Wa-ha-la,'—such was the name of his son—'go then with him into the great lake of the forest, and come not back for a season. Depart thou thus, always, when the maize is ready for the harvest.'

"I obeyed him; but not until I found that I was endangering my own safety to attempt further expostulation; and then it was that my companions perished, all save the one who now sits before thee with myself, and whom I saved because of a service which I rendered to the Iawa, and whom I persuaded to take my white brother into his wigwam. He went, even before myself, but through my means, into the service of Onathaqua."

Here Captain Laudonniere interrupted the speaker.

"For what reason," said he, "being such a favorite with the king of Calos and his son, didst thou have to leave his service for that of the King Onathaqua?"

"Alas, Señor Laudonniere, thy question shames me again, since it requires me to lay bare another of the vices of my evil heart, and to confess how the bad passions thereof could lead me into the follies which proved fatal to my better fortune. I had gained great honor among the savages by my prudence and my skill in war, my strength in battle, and the excellence of my counsel in the country of the enemy. I had gained the good will and protection of the great king of Calos, and the affection of his son, the noble young Mico Wa-ha-la! But these contented me nothing, though they brought plenty and security to my wigwam, and such delights as might satisfy the man, a dweller in the wilderness. I have said that I was greatly trusted by the king, the prince, and the head men of the country. These then, after I had been eight years in their service, confided to my charge a great and sacred commission. The time had come when it became proper that this Mico Wa-ha-la should take to himself a wife. Now, tidings had reached Calos of a creature, lovely as a daughter of the sun, who was the youngest child of King Onathaqua. A treaty was agreed upon between the two kings for the marriage of their children; and I was dispatched, with a select body of warriors, to bring the maiden home to her new sovereign. It was not the custom for a chief desiring a wife, that he should seek her in person. Accordingly I was dispatched, and I reached the territories of Onathaqua in safety. Here I beheld the maiden in pursuit of whom I came, and my froward heart instantly conceived the wildest affection for her beauty. Beautiful she was as any of our Castilian maidens, and as delicate and modestly proper in her bearing, as one may see in the gentlest damsel of a Christian country. Deeply was I smitten with this new flame, and deeply did I strive to please the maiden who had fired me with these fresh fancies. I spake with her in the Indian language, with charms of thought which had been taken from the Castilian, such as were vastly superior to those which belonged to Indian courtship. I sang to her many a glorious ballad of the sweet romance of my country, discoursing of the tender loves between the Castilian cavaliers and the dark-eyed and dark-tressed maidens of Grenada. Verily, the beauty of the delicate daughter of Onathaqua, the precious Istakalina—by which the people of Onathaqua understand the white lily of the lake before it opens—was no unbecoming representative of that choice dark beauty which made the charm of the Moorish damsel of my land, ere Boabdil gave up his sceptre into the hands of the holy Ferdinand. For Istakalina, I rendered the language of the Castilian romance into the dialect of her people; and with a sad fondness in her eyes, that drooped ever while looking upwards at the passionate gaze of mine, did she listen to the story of feelings and affections to which her own young and innocent nature did now tenderly incline. Thus it was that she was delivered into my keeping by her sire, that I should conduct her to the young Mico Wa-ha-la, my friend. And thus, with fond discourse of song and story, which grew more fond with every passing hour—with me to speak and she to listen—did we commence our journey homewards to the dominions of the lord of Calos. Alas! for me, and alas! for the hapless maiden, that, in the fondness of my passion, I forgot my trust; forgot preciously to guard and protect the precious treasure in my keeping; and, in the increase of my blind love, forgot all the lessons of war and wisdom, and all the necessary providence which these equally demand. Thus it was that I was dispossessed of my charge, at the very moment when it was most dear to my delight. Didst thou ask me for the hope which grew with this blind passion, verily, señor, I should have to say to thee that I had none. I thought not of the morrow; I dared not think of the time when Istakalina should fill the cabin of Wa-ha-la. I knew nothing but that she was with me, her dark eyes ever glistening beneath their darker lids, as she met the burning speech of mine; that we thridded the sinuous paths of silent and shady forests, with none to reproach our speech or glances; our attendants, some of them going on before, and some following; and that, when she ascended the litter, which was borne by four stout savages, or sat in the canoe as we sped across lake or river—for both of these modes of travel did we at times pursue—I was still the nearest to her side, drunk with her sweet beauty, and the sad tenderness which dwelt in all her looks and actions. Nor was it less my madness that I fondly set to the account of her fondness for me, the very sadness with which she answered my looks, and the sweet sigh which rose so often to her softly parted lips. Verily, was never man and Christian so false and foolish as was I, in those bitter blessed moments. Thus was I blinded to all caution—thus was I heedless of all danger—thus was I caught in the snare, to the loss of all that was precious as well to my captor as myself."

"How was this? How happened it?" demanded Laudonniere as Le Barbu paused, and covered his face with his hands in silence, as if overcome with a great misery.

"Thou shalt hear, Señor. I will keep nothing from thee of this sad confession; for, verily, I have long since repented of the sin and folly which brought after them so much evil. Thou shalt know that, distant from the territories of the lord of Calos, a journey of some three days, and nearly that far distant also from the dwelling of Onathaqua, there lieth a great lake of fresh water, in the midst of which is an island named Sarropee. This island and the country which surrounds the lake, is kept by a very powerful nation, a fierce people, not so numerous as strong, because they have places of retreat and refuge, whither no enemy dare pursue them. On the firm land, and in open conflict, the lord of Calos had long before conquered this strange people; but in their secure harborage and vast water thickets, they mocked at the power of all the surrounding kings. These, accordingly, kept with them a general peace, which was seldom broken, except under circumstances such as those which I shall now unfold. The people of this lake and island are rich in the precious root called the *Coonti*, of which they have an abundance, of a quality far superior to that of all the neighboring country. Their dates, which give forth a delicious honey, are in great abundance also, and of these their traffic is large with all other nations. But that they are a most valiant people, and occupy a territory so troublesome to penetrate, they had been destroyed by other nations, all of whom are greedy for the rich productions which their watery realm bestows. Now, it was, that, in our journey homewards, we drew nigh to the great lake of the people of the isle of Sarropee. Here it was that my discretion failed me in my passion. Here it was that my footstep faltered, and the vision of mine eyes was completely shut. I knew that our people were at peace with the people of Sarropee, and I thought not of them. But had I not been counselled to vigilance in bringing home the daughter of Onathaqua, even as if the woods were thick with enemies? But I had forgotten this caution. I sent forth no spies; I sought for no wisdom from my young warriors; and, like an ignorant child that knows not the deep gulf beneath, I stepped confidently into the little canoe which was to take Istakalina and myself across an arm of the lake which set inwards, while our warriors fetched a long compass around it. Alas! señor, I was beguiled to this folly by the fond desire that I might have the lovely maiden wholly to myself in the little canoe, for already did I begin to grieve with the thought that in a few days, the journey would be at an end, and I should then yield her unto the embraces of another. And thus we entered the canoe. I made for her a couch, in the bottom of the little boat, of leaves gathered from the scented myrtle. With the paddle in my hand, I began to urge the vessel, but very slowly, lest that we should too soon reach the shore, and find the warriors waiting for us. Sweetly did I strive to discourse in her listening ears; and with what dear delight did I behold her as she answered me only with her tears. But these were as the cherished drops of hope about mine heart, which gave it a life which it never knew before. While thus we sped, dreaming nothing of any danger, over the placid waters, with the dark green mangrove about us, and a soft breeze playing on the surface of the great lake, suddenly, from out the palm bushes, darted a cloud of boats, filled with painted warriors, that bore down upon us with shows of fury and a mighty shout of war. I answered them with a shout, not unlike their own, for already had I imbibed something of the Indian nature. I shouted the war-whoop of the lord of Calos, and tried to make myself heard by the distant warriors who formed my escort. And they did hear my clamors; for already, they had rounded the bayou or arm of the lake which I had sought to cross, and were pressing down towards us upon the opposite banks. Then did I bestir the paddle in my grasp, making rapid progress for the shore, while the canoes of the Sarropee strove to dart between us and the place for which I bent. But what could my single paddle avail against their better equipment? Theirs were canoes of war, carrying each more than a score of powerful warriors armed for action, and prepared to peril their lives in the prosecution of their object. I, too, was armed as an Indian warrior, and with their approach, I betook me to my weapon. I had learned to throw the short lance, or the javelin of the savage, with a dexterity like his own; and, ere they could approach me, I had fatally struck with these darts two of their most valiant warriors. They strove not to return the arrows lest they should hurt the maiden, Istakalina, who had raised herself at the first danger, and now strove with the paddle which I had thrown down. As one of the canoes which threatened us drew nigh, I seized the great macana which I carried, and prepared myself to use it upon the most forward warriors; but when I expected that they would assail me with the war-club and spear, the cunning savages thrust their great prow against our little boat, amidships, and even as my macana lighted on the head of one of the assailants, smiting him fatally, I fell over into the lake with the upsetting of our vessel. In a moment had they grasped Istakalina from the lake, and taken her to themselves in their own canoe, and as I raised my head from the water, beholding this mishap, a heavy stroke upon my shoulder, which narrowly missed my head, warned me of my danger. Then, seeing that I could no longer save the captive maiden, I dived deeply under, making my way like an otter, beneath the water, for the shore. A flight of arrows followed my rising to take the air, but they were hurriedly delivered, with little aim, and only one of them grazed my cheek. The mark is still here as thou seest. Again I dived beneath the water, still swimming shoreward, and when I next rose into the light and air, I was among the people of the lord of Calos. They were now assembled along the banks of the lake, as near as they could go to the enemy, some of them, indeed, having waded waist deep in their wild fury and desperate defiance. But of what avail were their weapons or their rage? The maiden, Istakalina, the princess and the betrothed of Wa-ha-la, was gone. The people of the Sarropee had borne her off, heeding me little even as they had taken her. She was already far off, moving towards the centre of the lake, and faint were the cries which now came from her, though it delighted my poor vain heart, in that desperate hour, to perceive that, in her last cries, it was my unhappy name that she uttered. They bore her away to the secret island where they dwelt, in secure fastnesses; and long and fruitless, though full of desperation, was the war that followed for her recovery. But, though I myself fought in this war, as I never have fought before, yet did I not dare to do battle under the eye, or among the warriors of the lord of Calos. I fled from his sight and from the reproaches of my friend, the Mico Wa-ha-la, for, in my soul, I felt how deep had been my guilt, and my conscience did not dare the encounter with their eyes. I took refuge with Onathaqua, the father of Istakalina; and when he knew of the valor with which I strove against the captivity of the maiden, he forgave me that I lost her through my own imprudence. Of the blind and selfish passion which prompted that imprudence, he did not dream, and he so forgave me. Under his lead, I took up arms against the tribes of Sarropee, and for two years did the war continue, with great slaughter and distress among the several nations. But, in all our battles, I kept ever to the northern side of the great lake, and never allowed myself to join with the warriors of Calos. They but too well conceived my guilt. The keen eyes of mine escort distinguished my passion, and saw that it was not ungracious in the sight of Istakalina. Too truly did they report us to the lord of Calos, and to my friend, the young Mico Wa-ha-la. Bitter was the reproach which he made me in a last gift which he sent me, while I dwelt with Onathaqua. It consisted of a single arrow, from which depended a snake skin, with the warning rattles still hanging thereto. 'Say to the bearded man,' said the Mico, 'when you give him this, that it comes from Wa-ha-la. Tell him that his friend sends him this, in token that he knows how much he hath been wronged. Say to the bearded man, that Wa-ha-la had but one flower of the forest, and that his friend hath gathered it. Let his friend beware the arrow of the warrior, and the deadly fang of the war-rattle, for the path between us is everywhere sown with the darts of death.'

"Thus he spake, and I was silent. I was guilty. I could not excuse myself, and did not entreat. I felt the truth of his complaint and the justice of his anger. I felt how great had been my folly and my crime. Istakalina was lost to us both. Thus then, a fugitive, and an outlaw from Calos, dreading every moment the vengeance of Wa-ha-la and his warriors, I dwelt for seven years with Onathaqua, who hath ever treated me as a son. I have fought among his warriors, and shared the fortunes of his people, of which nothing more need be said. Tidings at last came to me, of a people in the country bearded like myself. Then came your messengers to Onathaqua, and you behold me here. I looked not for Frenchmen but for Spaniards. I thank and praise the Blessed Mother of God, that I have found friends if not countrymen, and that I see, once more, the faces of a Christian people."

Thus ended the narrative of Le Barbu, or the Bearded Man of Calos.

PERHAPS THE MOST ROMANTICIZED of Simms's stories about Indians, "Iracana" paints a sentimental picture of the beautiful and sensuous Queen Iracana and her namesake village on the Satilla River—the "Eden of the Floridian" in the eyes of battle-weary Frenchmen, who are almost overwhelmed by its commitment to love and pleasure. The simple, unsophisticated story with its subdued tone has an easy grace.

Paracoussi is a Timucuan word for "chief."

ᴄᴡ *Iracana, or, the Eden of the Floridian*

The disasters which befel his detachment, brought Laudonniere to his knees. He had now been humbled severely by the dispensations of Providence— punished for that disregard of the things most important to the colonization of a new country, which, in his insane pursuit of the precious metals, had marred his administration. His misfortunes reminded him of his religion.

"Seeing, therefore, mine hope frustrate on that side, I made my prayer unto God, and thanked him of his grace which he had shown unto my poore souldiers which were escaped."

But his prayers did not detain him long. The necessities of the colony continued as pressing as ever. "Afterward, I thought upon new meanes to obtaine victuals, as well for our returne into France, as to drive out the time untill our embarking." These were meditations of considerable difficulty. The petty fields of the natives, never contemplated with reference to more than a temporary supply of food;—never planted with reference to providing for a whole year, were really inadequate to the wants of such a body of men, unless by grievously distressing their proprietors. The people of Olata Utina had been moved to rage in all probability, quite as much because of their grain crops, about to be torn from them, as with any feeling of indignation in consequence of the detention of their Paracoussi. In the sacks of corn which the Frenchmen bore away upon their shoulders, they beheld the sole provision upon which, for several months, their women and children had relied to feed; and their quick imagination were goaded to desperation, as they depicted vivid horrors of a summer in vain search after crude roots and indigestible berries, through the forest. No wonder the wild wretches fought to avert such a danger; as little may we wonder that they fought successfully. The Frenchmen, compelled to cast down their sacks of grain, to use their weapons, the red-men soon repossessed themselves of all their treasure. When Laudonniere reviewed his harrassed soldiers on return from this expedition, "all the mill that he found among his company came but to two men's burdens." To attempt to recover the provisions thus wrested from them, or to revenge themselves from the indignity and injury they had undergone, were equally out of the question. The people of the Paracoussi could number their thousands; and, buried in their deep fortresses of forest, they could defy pursuit. Laudonniere was compelled to look elsewhere for the resources which should keep his company from want.

Two leagues distant from La Caroline, on the opposite side of May River, stood the Indian village of Saravahi. Not far from this might be seen the smokes of another village, named Emoloa. The Frenchmen, wandering through the woods in search of game, had alighted suddenly upon these primitive communities. Here they had been received with gentleness and love. The natives were lively and benevolent. They had never felt the wrath of the white man, nor been made to suffer because of his improvidence and necessities. His thunderbolts had never hurled among their columns, and mown them down as with a fiery scythe from heaven. The Frenchmen did not fail to remark that they were provident tribes, with corn-fields much more ample than were common among the Indians. These, they now concluded, must be covered with golden grain, in the season of harvest, and thither, accordingly, Laudonniere dispatched his boats. A judicious officer conducted the detachment, and stores of European merchandise were confided to him for the purposes of traffic. He was not disappointed in his expectations. His soldiers were received with open arms; and a "good store of mil," speaking comparatively, was readily procured from the abundance of the Indians.

But in preparation for the return to France, other and larger supplies were necessary. The boats were again made ready, and confided to La Vasseur and D'Erlach. They proceeded to the river to which the French had given their name of Somme, now known as the Satilla, but which was then called among the Indians, the Iracana, after their own beautiful queen. Of this queen our Frenchmen had frequently been told. She had been described to them as the fairest creature, in the shape of a woman, that the country had beheld: nor was the region over which she swayed, regarded with less admiration. This was spoken as a sort of terrestrial paradise. Here, the vales were more lovely; the waters more cool and pellucid than in any other of the territories of earth. Here, the earth produced more abundantly than elsewhere; the trees were more stately and magnificent, the flowers more beautiful and gay, and the vines more heavily laden with grapes of the most delicious flavor. Sweetest islets rose along the shore over which the moon seemed to linger with a greater fondness, and soft breezes played over in the capacious forests, always kindling to emotions of pleasure, the soft beatings of the delighted heart. The influences of scene and climate were felt for good amongst the people who were represented at once as the most generous and gentle of all the Florida natives. They had no wild passions, and coveted no fierce delights. Under the sway of a woman, at once young and beautiful, the daughter of their most favorite monarch, their souls had become attuned to sympathies which greatly tended to subdue and to soothe the savage nature. Their lives were spent in sports and dances. No rebukes or restraints of duty, no sordid cares or purposes, impaired the dream of youth and rapture which prevailed everywhere in the hearts of the people. Gay assemblages were ever to be found among villages in the forests; singing their own delights and imploring the stranger to be happy also. They had a thousand songs and sports of youth and pleasure, which made life a perpetual round of ever freshening felicity. Innocent as wild, no eye of the ascetic could rebuke enjoyments which violated no cherished laws of experience and thought, and their glad and sprightly dances, in the deep shadows of the woods, to the lively clatter of Indian gourds and tambourines, were quite as significant of harmless fancies as of thoughtless lives. Happy was the lonely voyager, speeding along the coast, in his frail canoe, when, suddenly darting out from the forests of Iracana, a slight but lovely creature, with flowing tunic of white cotton, stood upon the head land, waving her branch of palm or myrtle, entreating his approach, and imploring him to delay his journey, while he shared in the sweet festivities of love and youth, for a season, upon the shore,—crying with a sweet chant,—

"Love you me not, oh, lonely voyager—love you me not? Lo! am I not lovely; I who serve the beautiful queen of Iracana? Will you not come to me, for a while!—come, hide the canoe among the reeds, along the shore, and make merry with the damsels of Iracana. I give to thee the palm and the myrtle, in token of a welcome of peace and love. Come hither, oh! lonely voyager, and be happy for a season!"

And seldom were these persuasions unavailing. The lonely voyager was commonly won, as was he who, sailing by Scylla and Charybdis, refused to seal his ears with wax against the song of the Syren. But our charmers, along the banks of the Satilla, entreated to no evil, laid no snares for the unwary, meditating their destruction. They sought only to share the pleasures which they themselves enjoyed. The benevolence of that love which holds its treasure as of little value, unless its delights may be bestowed on others, was the distinguishing moral in the Indian Eden of Iracana; and he who came with love, never departed without a sorrow, such as made him linger as he went, and soon return, when this were possible, to a region, which, among our Floridians, realized that period of the Classic Fable, which has always been designated, par excellence, as the "age of gold."

Our Frenchmen, under the conduct of La Vasseur and D'Erlach, reached the frontiers of Iracana, at an auspicious period. The season of harvest, among all primitive and simple nations, is commonly a season of great rejoicing. Among a people like those of Iracana, habitually accustomed to rejoice, it is one in which delight becomes exultation, and when in the supreme felicity of good fortune, the happy heart surpasses itself in the extraordinary expression of its joy. Here were assembled to the harvest, all the great lords of the surrounding country. Here was Athoree, the gigantic son of Satouriova, a very Anak, among the Floridians. Here were Apalou, a famous chieftain,— Tacadocorou, and many others, whom our Frenchmen had met and known before;—some of whom indeed, they had known in fierce conflict, and a strife which had never been healed by any of the gentle offices of peace.

But Iracana was the special territory of peace. It was not permitted, among the Floridians, to approach this realm with angry purpose. Here war and strife were tabooed things,—shut out, denied and banished, and peace and love, and rapture, were alone permitted exercise in abodes which were too grateful to all parties, to be desecrated by hostile passions. When, therefore, our Frenchmen, beholding those only with whom they had so lately fought, were fain to betake themselves to their weapons, the chiefs themselves, with whom they had done battle, came forward to embrace them, with open arms.

"Brothers, all—brothers here, in Iracana;" was the common speech. "Be happy here, brothers, no fight, no scalp, nothing but love in Iracana,— nothing but dance and be happy."

Even had not this assurance sufficed with our Frenchmen, the charms of the lovely Queen herself, her grace and sweetness, not unmixed with a dignity which declared her habitual rule, must have stifled every feeling of distrust in their bosoms, and effectually exorcised that of war. She came to meet the strangers with a mingled ease and state, a sweetness and a majesty, which were inexpressibly attractive. She took a hand of La Vasseur and of D'Erlach, with each of her own. A bright, happy smile lightened in her eye, and warmed her slightly dusky features with a glow. Rich in hue, yet delicately thin, her lips parted with a pleasure, as she spoke to them, which no art could simulate. She bade them welcome, joined their hands with those of the great warriors by whom she was attended, and led them away among her damsels, of whom a numerous array were assembled, all habited in the richest garments of their scanty wardrobes.

The robes of the Queen herself were ample. The skirts of her dress fell below her knees, a thing very uncommon with the women of Florida. Over this, she wore a tunic of crimson, which descended below her hips. A slight cincture embraced, without confining, her waist. Long strings of sea-shell, of the smallest size, but of colors and tints the most various and delicate, drooped across her shoulders, and were strung, in loops and droplets, to the skirts of her dress and her symar. Similar strings encircled her head, from which the hair hung free behind, almost to the ground, a raven-like stream, of the deepest and most glossy sable. Her form was equally stately and graceful— her carriage betrayed a freedom, which was at once native and the fruit of habitual exercise. Nothing could have been more gracious than the sweetness of her welcome; nothing more utterly unshadowed than the sunshine which beamed in her countenance. She led her guests among the crowd, and soon released La Vasseur to one of the loveliest girls who came about her. Alphonse D'Erlach she kept to herself. She was evidently struck with the singular union of delicacy and youth with sagacity and character, which declared itself in his features and deportment.

Very soon were all the parties engaged in the mazes of the Indian dance of Iracana,—a movement which, unlike the waltz of the Spaniards, less stately perhaps, and less imposing—yet requires all its flexibility and freedom, and possesses all its seductive and voluptuous attractions. Half the night was consumed with dancing; then gay parties could be seen gliding into canoes, and darting across the stream to other villages and places of abode. Anon, might be perceived a silent couple gliding away to sacred thickets; and with the sound of a mighty conch, which strangely broke the silence of the forest, the Queen herself retired with her attendants, having first assigned to certain of her chiefs the task of providing for the Frenchmen. Of these she had already shown herself sufficiently heedful and solicitous. Not sparing of her regards to La Vasseur, she had particularly devoted herself to D'Erlach, and, while they danced together, if the truth could be spoken of her simple heart, great had been its pleasure at those moments, when the spirit of the dance required that she should yield herself to his grasp, and die away languidly in his embrace.

"Ah! Handsome Frenchman," she said to her companion,—"You please me so much."

His companions were similarly entertained. Captain La Vasseur was soon satisfied that he was too greatly pleasing to the fair and lovely savage who had been assigned to him; and not one of the Frenchmen, but had his share of the delights and endearments which made the business of life in Iracana. The soldiers had each a fair creature, with whom he waltzed and wandered; and fond discourse, everywhere in the great shadows of the wood, between sympathizing spirits, opened a new idea of existence to the poor Huguenots who, hitherto, had only known the land of Florida by its privations and its gold. The dusky damsels, alike sweet and artless, brought back to our poor adventurers precious recollections of youthful fancies along the banks of the Garonne and the Loire, and it is not improbable, that, under the excitement of new emotions, had Laudonniere proposed to transfer La Caroline to the Satilla, or Somme, instead of May River, they might have been ready to waive, for a season at least, their impatient desire to return to France.

Night was at length subdued to silence on the banks of the Satilla. The sounds of revelry had ceased. All slept, and the transition from night to day passed, sweetly and insensibly, almost without the consciousness of the parties. But, with the sunrise, the great conch sounded in the forest. The Eden of the Floridian did not imply a life of mere repose. The people were gathered to their harvesting, and the labors of the day, under the auspices of a gracious rule, were made to seem a pleasure. Hand in hand, the Queen Iracana, with her maidens, and her guests, followed to the maize fields. Already had she found D'Erlach, and her slender fingers, without any sense of shame, had taken possession of his hand, which she pressed at moments very tenderly. He had already informed her of the wants and the sufferings of his garrison, and she smiled with a new feeling of happiness, as she eagerly assured him that his people should receive abundance. She bent with her own hands the towering stalks; and, detaching the ears, flung to the ground a few in all these places, on which it was meant that the heaps should be accumulated. "Give these to our friends, the Frenchmen," she said, indicating with a sweep of the hand, a large tract of the field, through which they went. D'Erlach felt this liberality. He squeezed her fingers fondly in return,—Saying words of compliment which, possibly, in her ear, meant something more than compliment.

Then followed the morning feast; then walks in the woods; then sports upon the river in their canoes; and snaring the fish in weirs, in which the Indians were very expert. Evening brought with it a renewal of the dance, which again continued late in the night. Again did Alphonse D'Erlach dance with Iracana; but it was now seen that her eyes saddened with overfulness of her heart. Love is not so much a joy as a care. It is so vast a treasure, that the heart, possessed of the fullest consciousness of its value, is for ever dreading its loss. The happiness of the Floridian Eden had been of a sort which never absorbed the soul. It lacked the intensity of a fervent passion. It was the life of childhood—a thing of sport and play, of dance and dream—not that eager and avaricious passion which knows never content, and is never sure, even when most happy, from the anxieties and doubts which beset all mortal felicity. Already did our Queen begin to calculate the hours between the present, and that which should witness the departure of the pleasant Frenchmen.

"You will go from me," said she to D'Erlach, as they went apart from the rest, wandering along the banks of the river and looking out upon the sea. "You will go from me, and I shall never see you any more."

"I will come again, noble Queen, believe me," was the assurance.

"Ah! come soon," she said, "come soon, for you please me very much, *Aphon.*"

Such was the soft Indian corruption of his christened name. No doubt, she too gave pleasure to 'Aphon.' How could it be otherwise? How could he prove insensible to the tender and fervid interest which she so innocently betrayed in him? He did not. He was not insensible; and vague fancies were quickening in his mind as respects the future. He was opposed to the plan of returning to France. He was for carrying out the purposes of Coligny, and fulfilling the destinies of the colony. He had warned Laudonniere against the policy he pursued, had foreseen all the evils resulting from his unwise counsels, and there was that in his bosom that urged the glorious results to France, of a vigorous and just administration of a settlement in the western hemisphere, in which he was to participate, with his energy and forethought, without having these perpetually baffled by the imbecility and folly of an incapable superior. In such an event, how sweetly did his fancy mingle with his own fortunes those of the gentle and loving creature who stood beside him. He told her not his thoughts—they were indeed, fancies, rather than thoughts—but his arm gently encircled her waist, and while her head drooped down upon her bosom, he pressed her hand with a tender earnestness, which spoke much more loudly than any language to the heart.

The hour of separation came at length. Three days had elapsed in the delights of the Floridian Eden. Our Frenchmen were compelled to tear themselves away. The objects for which they came had been gratified. The bounty of the lovely Iracana had filled with grain their boats. Her subjects had gladly borne the burdens from the fields to the vessels, while strangers revelled with the noble and the lovely. But their revels were now to end. The garrison at La Caroline, it was felt, waited with hunger, as well as hope and anxiety for their return, and they dared to delay no longer. The parting was more difficult than they themselves had fancied. All had been well entertained, and all made happy by their entertainment. If Alphonse D'Erlach had been favored with the sweet attentions of a queen, Captain La Vasseur had been rendered no less happy by the smiles of the loveliest among her subjects. He had touched her heart also, quite as sensibly as had the former that of Iracana. Similarly fortunate had been their followers. Authority had ceased to restrain in a region where there was no danger of insubordination, and our Frenchmen, each in turn, from the sergeant to the sentinel, had been honored by regards of beauty, such as made him forgetful, for the time, of precious memories in France. Nor had these favors, bestowed upon the Frenchmen, provoked the jealousy of the numerous Indian chieftains who were present, and who shared in these festivities. It joyed them rather to see how frankly the white men could unbend themselves to unwonted pleasures, throwing aside that jealous state, that suspicious vigilance, which, hitherto, had distinguished their bearing in all their intercourse with the Indians.

"Women of Iracana too sweet," said the gigantic son of Satouriova, Athoree, to Captain La Vasseur, as the parties, each with a light and laughing damsel in his grasp, whirled beside each other in the mystic maze of the dance.

"I love much these women of Iracana," said Apalou, as fierce a warrior in battle, as ever swore by the altars of the Indian Moloch. "I glad you love them too, like me. Iracana women good for too much love! They make great warrior forget his enemies."

"Ha!" said one addressing D'Erlach, "You have beautiful women in your country, like Iracana, the Queen?"

But, we need not pursue these details. The hour of separation had arrived. Our Frenchmen had brought with them a variety of commodities grateful to the Indian eye, with which they designed to traffic; but the bounty of Iracana, which had anticipated all their wants, had asked for nothing in return. The treasures of the Frenchmen were accordingly distributed in gifts among the noble men and women of the place. Some of these Iracana condescended to take from the hands of Aphon. Her tears fell upon his offering. She gave him in return two small mats, woven of the finer straws of the country, with her own hands—wrought, indeed, while D'Erlach sat beside her in the shade of a great oak by the river bank—and "so artificially wrought," in the language of the chronicle, "as it was impossible to make it better." The poor Queen had few words—

"You will come to me, *Aphon*—you will? you will? I too much want you! Come soon, *Aphon*. Iracana will dance never no more till *Aphon* be come."

"*Aphon*" felt, at that moment, that he could come without sorrow. He promised that he would. Perhaps he meant to keep his promise; but we shall see. The word was given to be aboard, and the trumpet rang, recalling the soldier who still lingered in the forest shadows, with some dusky damsel for companion. All were at length assembled, and with a last squeeze of her hand, D'Erlach took leave of his sorrowful queen. She turned away into the woods, but soon came forth again, unable to deny herself another last look.

But the Frenchmen were delayed. One of their men was missing. Where was Louis Bourdon? There was no answer to his name. The boats were searched, the banks of the river, the neighboring woods, the fields, the Indian village, and all in vain. The Frenchmen observed that the natives exhibited no eagerness in the search. They saw that many faces were clothed with smiles, and their efforts resulted fruitlessly. They could not suppose that any harm had befallen the absent soldier. They could not doubt the innocence of the hospitality, which had shown itself so fond. They conjectured rightly when they supposed that Louis Bourdon, a mere youth of twenty, had gone off with one of the damsels of Iracana, whose seductions he had found it impossible to withstand. D'Erlach spoke to the Queen upon the subject. She gave him no encouragement. She professed to know nothing, and probably did not, and she would promise nothing. She unhesitatingly declared her belief that he was in the forest, with some one that "he so much loved:" but she assured D'Erlach that to hunt them up would be an impossibility.

"Why not stay with me, Aphon, as your soldier stay with the woman he so much love? It is good to stay. Iracana will love you too much more than other woman. Ah! you love not much the poor Iracana."

"Nay, Iracana, I love you greatly. I will come to you again. I find it hard to tear myself away. But my people—"

"Ah! you stay with Iracana, and much love Iracana, and you have all these people. They will plant for you many fields of corn; you shall no more want; and we will dance when the evening comes, and we shall be so happy, Aphon and Iracana, to live together; Aphon the great Paracoussi, and Iracana to be Queen no more."

It was not easy to resist these pleadings. But time pressed. Captain La Vasseur was growing impatient. The search after Louis Bourdon was abandoned, and the soldiers were again ordered on board. The anxieties of La Vasseur being now awakened, lest others of his people should be spirited away. Of this the danger was considerable. The Frenchman was a more flexible being than either the Englishman or the Spaniard. It was much easier for him to assimilate with the simple Indian; and our Huguenot soldiers, who had very much forgotten their religion in their diseased thirst after gold, now, in the disappointment of the one appetite were not indifferent to the consolations afforded by a life of ease and sport, and the charms which addressed them in forms so persuasive as those of the damsels of Iracana. La Vasseur began to tremble for his command, as he beheld the reluctance of his soldiers to depart. He gave the signal hurriedly to Alphonse D'Erlach, and with another sweet single pressure of the hand, he left the lovely Queen to her own melancholy musings. She followed with her eyes the departing boats till they were clean gone from sight, then buried herself in the deepest thickets where she might weep in security.

Other eyes than hers pursued the retiring barks of the Frenchmen, with quite as much anxiety; and long after she had ceased to see them. On a little headland jutting out upon the river below, in the shade of innumerable vines and flowers, crouching in suspense, was the renegade, Louis Bourdon. By his side sat the dusky damsel who had beguiled him from his duties. While his comrades danced, he was flying through the thickets. The nation were, many of them, conscious of his flight; but they held his offence to be venial, and they encouraged him to proceed. They lent him help in crossing the river, at a point below; the father of the woman with whom he fled providing the canoe with which to transport him beyond the danger of pursuit. Little did our Frenchmen, as the boats descended, dream who watched them from the headland beneath which they passed. Many were the doubts, frequent the changes, in the feelings of the capricious renegade, as he saw his countrymen approaching him, and felt that he might soon be separated from them and home forever, by the ocean walls of the Atlantic. Whether it was that his Indian beauty detected in his face the fluctuations of his thoughts, and feared that, on the near approach of the boats, he would change his purpose and abandon her for his people, cannot be said; but just then she wound herself about within his arms, and looked up in his face, while her falling hair enmeshed his hands, and contributed, perhaps, still more firmly to ensnare his affections. His heart had been in his mouth; he could scarcely have kept from crying out to his comrades as the boats drew nigh to the cliff; but the dusky beauty beneath his gaze, the soft and delicate form within his embrace, silenced all the rising sympathies of brotherhood in more ravishing emotions. In a moment their boats had gone by; in a little while they had disappeared from sight, and the arms of the Indian woman, wrapped about her captive, declared her delight and rapture in the triumph which she now regarded as secure. Louis Bourdon knew little how much he had escaped, in thus becoming a dweller in the Floridian Eden.

IN "THE SPECTRE CHIEF OF ACCABEE" Simms blends his love of the supernatural with his interest in Indian affairs. First of all, it is an excellent ghost story—well-written and well-developed, with interesting characters and sparkling dialogue. Like "Ephraim Bartlett," another suspenseful and humorous ghost story by Simms, "The Spectre Chief" is made plausible by its use of heavy drinking as a possible explanation for the witnessing of strange events. But under the façade of humor is a serious theme: white men's injustice to red men, illustrated specifically in this case by the former's usurpation of the latter's favorite old haunts. The double-edged satire without didactic tone enhances rather than diminishes the raucous humor.

ᏜᎧ *The Spectre Chief of Accabee*

They tell of a wagoner, descending the Dorebreier road, whose wagon broke down about a mile above this place, and probably the greater distance from the dwelling-house at Accabee. He had heard of the settlement, and proceeded to Accabee for assistance. The place, at that time, happened to be in the occupation of a poor fellow, a sort of tolerated squatter, who was suffered, though known to be useless, to live upon the estate rent free, in order that the house should enjoy some degree of protection. The tenant thus tolerated, was an idle, worthless dog: a harmless rapscallion; not vicious; not evil of purpose in any way; but simply worthless; an indolent, lazy, lounging tyke, one of that tribe, almost gipsy in its habits, which we call "Sandlappers," a name given to them, as is supposed, on account of the vicious custom prevailing among them, of eating clay. This tribe is now almost extinct in this region. At all events, they have pretty generally abandoned this vile practice. But their lounging, lazy, listless, lifeless nature is still sufficient to individualize the race. They do nothing if they can help it, and help nothing, no matter what they do. To lie in the sunshine, in the full enjoyment of the *dolce far niente* of another and corresponding, but foreign race—to wallow in strong drink when they can get it—and open their eyes to no care more serious than that of seeking to shut them again as soon as possible—are the strongest, if not the only passions of this class of people. Fortunately, there are few of them now to be found, and the number lessens every day. Our squatter at Accabee was a fair sample of this tribe, one of the best of them, in fact. He loved the sunshine only as he could sleep in it, and the shade only as he could enjoy his slumbers coolly. He drank like a Dutch dragoon, was drunk as long as his liquor lasted, and sober only in spite of himself. His exertions, in search of a living, were continued only so long as to enable him to earn the means to procure fresh supplies of whiskey. These exertions were almost wholly confined to hunting—*birding*, rather, for he had not energy enough for the pursuit of deer and turkey—and fishing, for which the neighboring expanse of Accabee bay, in the Ashley, afforded him the most ample province. This is enough, by way of general description.

Our squatter, at the time of the visit of the wagoner seeking assistance, was in a condition of unusual affluence. Recent sales of wild ducks, doves, partridges, and fish, had enabled him to visit the city and to lay in his supplies of the creature comforts—such creature comforts as sufficed for his wants—a jug of whiskey being the most conspicuous item. He was engaged in testing its qualities at the very moment when the wagoner made his appearance. The squatter was by no means selfish, and his own love of the liquor was not superior to his hospitality and love of company. He received his visitor with a rude civility, rinsed his best tin cup, and invited him to partake of the beverage.

The wagoner was not averse, and the two sat down, awhile, to this agreeable employment. A couple of draughts having been swallowed, the wagoner made known the object of his visit, and the promise of assistance was readily given by his Host. Tom Waters, for that was the name of our drowsy runagate who then had charge of Accabee, was a good-natured fellow in the main, and though by no means fond of toil, was yet not unwilling to lend a hand in small offices like those required of him;—he was not unwilling to engage in any labor but that which was unvaried and continuous. He had no horse, but shouldering his long, single-barrelled, bird gun, he trotted away on foot, keeping up with the mounted wagoner. When they reached the place in the road where the wagon had foundered, the two went to work manfully. Every wagoner travels with his axe, a bucket of tar, a few spikes or nails, a sufficient quantity of rope, as well as camp-kettles and frying pan. The axe was quickly at work, a tree was thrown down, the old axle was replaced by a new one, and between the pair the hurts of the vehicle were all stoutly repaired by sunset. But there was no sunset to be seen; darkness was rapidly approaching, the prospect of a seven miles drive to the city was discouraging, and an encampment in the woods, with the certainty of a storm of sleet or rain, was calculated to make one shiver in anticipation. The wagoner, accordingly, acceded promptly to the invitation of Tom Waters, to drive down to Accabee, and roost with him that night. The equal prospect of whiskey and bad weather left no room for hesitation. The evening was growing momently colder and colder. A north-easter had set in, one of the vilest of winds, accompanied by a raw and driving drizzle. The drizzle was promising to become a torrent, and the torrent, as Tom Waters phrased it, "a screamer." Everything conspired to make both parties anxious for a rousing fire and a dry bed, to say nothing of a good supper and a good stoup of liquor at the close of it. The class of idle, runagate hunters and fishermen, who pursue this manner of life in preference to all others, and who are always poor and wretched, are yet, no matter what their poverty, most liberal in bestowing what they have. Though Tom Waters was too indolent to hunt regularly, and invariably gave himself a long rest after he had earned enough to lay in temporary supplies, he was yet as lavish in sharing his good things as if his storehouse were supplied by fairy service. He had precious little meal, and less bacon, but the wagoner had both. But Tom had some well-parched and well-ground coffee, and sugar to match, and we have already indicated his recent supply of whiskey.

To stable the horses, house the wagon, build a rousing fire in the great chimney-place of the hall at Accabee, and get the supper things in readiness, occupied comparatively little time, where both the parties were so honestly disposed to the duty. Scarcely had they housed themselves, and the wagon and horses, when the storm began; but our boon companions snapt their fingers in defiance. The winds rattled the old shutters, and howled bitterly at being denied to enter. At every blast, Tom and the wagoner piled the fire with fresh fuel. They made a famous blaze, and forgot the tempest. The good things soon began to appear. They baked a couple of monstrous hoe-cakes, and fried great slices of bacon. A couple of huge tin cups held capacious draughts of coffee, and every moment, as they ate and drank, found the happiness of the parties increase. Tam O'Shanter and Souter Johnnie never passed an evening more merrily. Though they had never before met, they were sworn friends and mutually satisfied with each other. While the wagoner's eyes dilated to the dimensions of young moons, Tom's, joyous in equal pleasures, seemed to diminish into little pointed specks of light that showed ludicrously modest in comparison with those of the wagoner. The latter roared his happiness aloud, while Tom, too lazy for such an effort, was content with a modest cackle and snigger, which were still extraordinary performances for him. The wagoner was a brave, hardy, swaggering, dashing blade, insolent in his pleasures, and anxious that the whole world should see and hear. Tom, on the contrary, enjoyed himself after a sneaking fashion, very much as the boy devours his stolen fruit in a corner, constantly looking around to assure himself that he is unseen. For a time, their talk was naturally about themselves. Each was curious about the other, his affairs and associations, and each had something to recount and something to hear. The story which Tom had to tell of himself was not remarkable for its interest. His life had little of event and little to excite; that he lived, after a fashion of his own, was pretty much all that he could say. How he lived the other saw. His meal tub was sometimes empty, and never *quite* full. Occasionally, he bought a shoulder of bacon with the money obtained by the game he sold; but his whiskey jug was never without a sufficient flavor for his nostrils, and it was a rule of duty with him, never to suffer it to sink so low as to deprive him of the capacity to feast a friend. His idea of feasting a friend, however, was pretty much confined to the one commodity. His philosophy taught him that meal and bacon could be dispensed with, perhaps, but whiskey never; and that no care could possibly be fatal, while there was liquor enough in which to drown it!

Thus discoursing, they fed and were satisfied. The supper things having been cleared away, and the coffee dismissed, the tin cups were carefully rinsed, and the whiskey jug took the place upon the table which the coffee-pot had occupied. Fresh brands were thrown upon the fire, and the two friends, thus newly brought together, evidently prepared to make a night of it. Meanwhile, the storm increased without, and the two rubbed their hands together, and their eyes sparkled, and their voices were raised, as they congratulated themselves on the condition of pleasant security in which they found themselves within.

"Better be here, I reckon," said the wagoner, "than camping out at 'the Forks' to-night. I swow, Waters, but I'm glad I struck upon your trail. You're a raal good fellow—the true grit; I'm blasted if you a'int! Here's your health, now, and a thousand years to run!"

The pledge was quickly swallowed. The storm increased, and Tom Waters shivered as he listened to the mournful soughing of the wind without, and the heavy peltings of the rain.

"Let's fill," said he to the wagoner, who had just emptied his flagon.

"Agreed; have you got any cards, any pictures, Tom Waters?"

"Yes—an old deck here. What do you play?"

"Old Sledge, I reckon."

"Well, I'm good for it. We must be doing something to keep bright such an ugly night."

"Oh! we're in the dry! I feel prime for anything. Shall we liquor before we deal?"

"Agreed;" answered Tom, filling the cans as he answered. Thus they played and drank; the hour grew late; the storm seemed to increase rather than diminish. The rain fell heavier and faster every moment; the wind now rather screamed than sighed around the shutters, and whistled occasionally down the chimneys, filling the room with smoke.

"It's a most fearsome night," said Tom—"I feel it mightily, sich weather, in this lonesome place when I have no company. It's just on sich a night as this that the Old Chief walks about the place."

"What!" cried the wagoner—"The Old Chief—and who's he?"

"Ah! he's a sperrit—the sperrit of a great old Indian Chief that owned all this part of the country. His wigwam stood jest where this house was built, and they say his sperrit doesn't like it. So he walks. I've seen him, more than once, on the edge of the woods, at dark, going into them; and sometimes, when in spring-time, and it was warm, I've left the shutter open, I've hearn something, and looked up, and seen him jest walking away from the window. This was always in rainy weather. Many's the night I've hearn the war-whoop, in spite of all the beating of the rain and the whistling of the wind."

"The war-whoop!" cried the wagoner, feeling in his belt for his knife, and looking to the corner where he had leaned his rifle;—"but," he continued— "you say he's a sperrit."

"Yes!—that's what they says."

"Well, I aint afeard of sperrits! I never seed one yit, and with such good sperrit before me, I reckon I could meet the devil, and snap my fingers in his face. Thar, Tom, play to that. Thar's the king of trumps! and thar's the queen—Jack or ten-spot must come now! I know'd it! That's game enough! High, low, jack, and four before—seven's up! What say you, shall we liquor before we deal?"

"Es you say, Bill," was the response of Tom, never slow at so grateful a suggestion. They filled, and as they were about to drink, the wagoner exclaimed—

"Well, Tom, here's to your Injin sperrit. Ef he was here he should drink with us, for he must find it bitter bad to have to walk in sich weather; and I'd like to have a look at him, and see what sort of a comb he carries!"

Scarcely had he spoken, when the door was dashed open wide, apparently by the blast, and a rush of wind and rain shook the apartment, whirling the smoke and ashes about the room until all was in a cloud. The wagoner laid down his cup and rushed forward to close the entrance, when, suddenly, he found a huge figure of a man, who passed him slowly, moving forward to the table. An exclamation from Tom Waters, at the same moment, prompted the wagoner to turn about immediately; and, as by this time, the door was shut again, seemingly by itself, and the smoke had somewhat subsided, he was now confounded to see that the stranger was a stalwart Indian, in the old-fashioned hunting shirt of stained buckskin, with heavy cape, and a massive yellow fringe about the skirt and shoulders. Before he could recover from his surprise, he beheld the Indian take up the can of liquor which he had laid down, and, looking to him civilly, with a grave nod, toss off the beverage in a twinkling. Nothing daunted, the wagoner addressed the intruder, with—

"Well, now, Squire Red Paint, I say, you seem to make yourself quite at home."

"And who has a better right?" was the answer, in very tolerable English. The Indian chief took the seat which the wagoner had left, and the latter had some difficulty in constructing another by turning his meal-tub upon end, and raising an old box upon it. The difficulty he encountered in this performance, and the uneasiness of the seat, did not diminish the annoyance which he felt at the cool manner of the intruder. He was pottle-valiant by this time, and Tom Waters pottle-stagnant, in other words, quite as stupid as the wagoner was fiery. The latter, having fixed his seat with tolerable steadiness, cried out to Waters—

"Look you, Tom, we haint had that drink together yit," and, rising as he spoke, he bent over the table and possessed himself of the cup which stood immediately before the Indian. The latter offered no objection, and sat moodily, without seeming to observe either of the parties. The half insolent, half apologetic address of the wagoner—"By your leave, stranger," went entirely unnoticed. The can was filled, and set upon the table, while the wagoner resumed his seat.

"Fill, Tom," said he; then, seeing that the other was rather slow about it, being exceedingly reluctant to diminish the distance between himself and the Indian, he himself bravely undertook the office, and poured from the jug into his friend's beaker. Meanwhile, the Indian very deliberately stretched out his hand and emptied, at a gulp, that which the wagoner had filled for himself. The latter, not seeing what had been done, took up his cup, and was now doubtful whether he had left it empty or full. For a moment he was bewildered, and looked alternately at Tom and the Indian. But recovering himself, he muttered, "Mighty strange!—I don't ricollect drinking that cup!"—and refilled the vessel. Then, seizing the well-thumbed pack of cards, he began shuffling.

"Shall we have a new deal, Waters?"

"Yes, I reckon."

"Deal me a hand," said the Indian, still in a very intelligible English.

"You!"

"Yes, to be sure! Why not?"

"Well! I can't 'zactly say! There's no objection, in course; none at all. But, you see, Squire Red Paint, there's no telling how such a strange sort of fellow, as you seems to be, may like to play. Are you a betting man, stranger?"

"To be sure, I am! I do no other business."

"Eh! indeed."

"But I only bet moderately. You have quite a clever nag in the stable— a short, coal-black. So have I—at the door. You may look at him. One against the other—short game—*three* up."

"See you d——d first," cried the wagoner, irreverently.

"As you please! But, it's your challenge! What will you bet?"

"Ef it's a pound of North Carolina tobacco, now, old Red Paint.—But let's see this horse of yourn, that you keep out in this etarnal weather."

He opened the door—a coal-black and splendid looking Indian pony was truly fastened at the entrance; but the wagoner had scarcely time to see him, when a perfect torrent of wind and rain drove him back for shelter to the hall.

"Well," said the Indian, "how do you like him?"

"Famous! He's real grit."

"What say you, then? Three up—horse against horse."

"N—o! thank you for nothing!"

"Head then against head;" answered the Indian, taking his own off from his shoulders, with the most singular indifference, and clapping it down upon the table, to the consternation of the two mortal sinners who beheld it. There was no mistake—no doubt. There it stood—a human head fairly removed from, and independent of, the shoulders, resting quietly between them, look- ing all the while intelligent with life. The eyes glared in those of the wagoner with a fierce and significant expression—the lips were parted, and the teeth grinned upon him with the appetite of a tiger. The wagoner, discomfited at first, became furious as he gazed, and recovered in a few seconds all his audacity. He had only a moment before tossed off his can of liquor. He had taken too many draughts to feel much fear of anything. For a moment, how- ever, starting to his feet, he stood aghast. Where was Tom Waters? It appeared that he had slunk from sight, somewhere—was possibly under the table. The wagoner felt himself alone—unsustained, unsupported, except by honest John Barleycorn. The reflection brought back all his courage; with despera- tion in his eye, wildly shrieking defiance, he grapples with the long hair of the heathen's head, as it sat upon the table, with its great glassy eyes and grinning teeth confronting him. With a single, furious effort, he thought to whirl the offensive head into the fire-place, and desperate, indeed, was the energy with which he addressed himself to this object. But, to his consternation, as he wound his fingers in with the long hair, the shoulders once more rose beneath the head, and, with the shoulders, the full grown man. The wagoner was grappled with in turn, and fell was the contest that ensued between the parties. Over went the benches and tables, and, at length, after a furious and prolonged struggle, the two came down upon the floor together, just before the fire-place. The combatants, still in each other's gripe, lay for a moment gasping, face to face. At this juncture, the fire, which had been smouldering, now blazed up brightly, and our wagoner recoiled as he discovered, that, instead of the heathen Indian, his opponent was no other than his host, Tom Waters, himself. Tom was equally confounded apparently, as he recognized his good-humoured guest, the wagoner.

"One stupid moment, motionless they stood," or rather lay, and the wagoner cried out—

"Great Gimini! Tom! Can that be you?"

"Yes, I reckon! what you've left of me!"

"And whar's the etarnal Injin—the War Paint!"

"Ah, Lord! I was jubious what was to happen, when you said you'd like to see him! A sperrit, they say, always wants to be axed in."

"But where's he gone; and when did he go; and how did he git off, and nobody see him?"

To this, there was no answer. Tom rose slowly and stiffly, following the example of the wagoner, who was pretty soon upon his feet. Then they proceeded on the search for their enemy, staggering about the room, looking under the table, into the closets, and even up the chimney, but without satisfaction. No Indian was to be found. Seizing a torch, the wagoner rushed to the door. The storm had subsided. He looked down, and sure enough, there were hoof-tracks all about the entrance, just as if a steed had been stamping there for an hour. The event was of a sort to sober the two sinners. They mused with wonder and awe at the wild sort of *diablerie* to which they had so nearly fallen victims, and discussed it over their whiskey for the rest of the night—for neither of them dared to go to sleep—without being any nigher to a conclusion. The mysterious thing to the wagoner was how the Indian could have slipped his head from his grasp, at the very moment when he had fairly grappled with the hair, and how that of Tom Water's could be found so directly in his way, and within his reach, though, up to that moment, Tom had been crouching at the opposite end of the table. One of the curious facts, in this history, which contributed most, in the mind of Tom, to the confirmation of the whole horrible affair, was the discovery, which he made in the morning, that fully one third of his three gallons of whiskey, bought only the day before in the city, had disappeared. Tom never for a moment ventured so monstrous a conjecture, as that such a quantity could be consumed, in such a space of time, by only two customers, even though these should happen to be persons as capable of good performance, as his friend the wagoner and himself. The only, and most natural conclusion, was that they must have been greatly assisted by some third person, and that the Indian chief had certainly carried away under his belt much more than his allowance. At all events, Tom and the wagoner were taught, by this lesson, the value of the old proverb, that he who would sup with the devil should always be sure to provide himself with a long handle to his spoon.

This is only one of the many legends which you may pick up in a visit to Accabee. I recommend you, when next you happen to be at Charleston, to run up there. You will find a hearty welcome from Brown, the proprietor. Give him notice of your coming, a day before, and notify him that you want a purely fish dinner. Signify a sheep's head, as among your wants;—you may indicate as accompaniments, a fry of whiting, and wind up with a dish of devilled oysters. He has fifty acres (more or less) of oysters on the tract. He has a boat, and you may fish for yourself. He is full of anecdote, and talks like a Trojan. He will supply you with other legends; but don't you believe a word he says, if he undertakes to persuade you that all my stories are obtained from him. The vanity of the *raconteur*, as you know, is too frequently exercised at the expense of his veracity; and I not unfrequently listen to the stories of my own manufacture, repeated as real occurrences in their own experience, by sad, uninventive dogs, who know nothing of fiction but its vices—who lie, but never invent.

POEMS

SIMMS'S FIRST POEM dealing with Indians, "The Broken Arrow," based on the author's experience "while travelling through the nation" during "my 19th year," was written in May 1825. The assassination of General William McIntosh had occurred on 1 May 1825, a few weeks before Simms's visit to the Creek nation, and according to Simms, he "picked up, as well from Indian as from white authorities, sundry small particulars relating to the event."

ᕳ *The Broken Arrow**

Ye warriors! who gather the brave to deplore,
   And repine for the Chief who shall conquer no more,
Let the hatchet of fight, still unburied remain,
   Whilst we joy in the glory of him that is slain.

Unbounded in soul, as unfearing in fight;
   Yet mild as the dove, when, untempted to smite;
His arm was resistless, his tomahawk true,
   And his eye, like the eagle's, was lightning to view.

Far down in the valley, when evening was still,
   I heard the deep voice of the Wolf† on the hill:
And "hark!" said the Chief, as it echoed below,
   "'Tis the voice of Menawe!‡ the cry of my foe!

"He comes not, the coward, to mingle in fight,
   "When the Day-God can offer one streak of his light;
"But in darkness, that emblems his bosom's own hue,
   "He seeks to perform, what he trembles to do!"

---

* [SIMMS'S NOTE] The followers of the Indian chief Mackintosh, are called the "People of the Broken Arrow."
† [SIMMS'S NOTE] Mad Wolf was the Indian who shot Gen. William Mackintosh.
‡ [SIMMS'S NOTE] Menawe was commander of the party, about 200 in number, who went in pursuit of the chief. He, as well as Mad Wolf, are signers to the late Georgia Treaty.

The Chief took his rifle, unerring as fate,
　His eye glow'd as proud, as his bosom was great;
I heard the flint strike on the steel, but in vain,
　For I heard not the rifle re-echo again.

Go, sigh not away, as the coward has done,
　The remnant of life, o'er the fields we have won;
But a mournful farewell, to our fruit trees* we'll leave,
　They o'ershadow our fathers, and honor their grave.

Farther West! farther West! where the buffalo roves
　And the red deer is found in the valley he loves;
Our hearts shall be glad, in the hunt once again,
　'Till the white man shall seek for the lands that remain.†

Farther West! farther West! where the Sun as he dies,
　Still leaves a deep lustre abroad in the skies;
Where the hunter may roam, and his woman may rove,
　And the white man not blight, what he cannot improve!

One song of regret to the wilds that we leave,
　To the Chief, o'er whose grave still his warriors must grieve;
He died as a hero—and equall'd by few—
　Himself his worst foe, to the white man too true!

Farther West! farther West, it is meet that we fly,
　Where the red deer will bound at the glance of an eye:—
And lonely and sad be the strain that is sung,
　For the arrow is broken, the bow is unstrung!

                                          1825 (published 1826)

---

* [SIMMS's NOTE] The idea of fruit trees being an object of regret to the Indian in leaving his home, may appear to us absurd, particularly, when we consider how many other causes there were for grief, more influential in our own view than this. It is, however, less extravagant, when we discover their propensity to fruits of all kinds, particularly plumbs. Their orchards, probably the site of old towns, are continued even for miles on the road, without order or inclosure.

† [SIMMS's NOTE] This is literal. I observed to an Indian that was one of those who came under that class in the late treaty, who were to fly farther West, that there were good hunting grounds near the setting sun, and his response was nearly similar—"Yes," said he, with mournful expression of countenance, "Yes, but when the white man sees us living comfortably there, he will want more land, and we will be sent farther yet." They seem to apprehend to its fullest extent, the miseries of leaving the home of childhood, associated so firmly by the ligament of a past eternity.

LIKE "THE BROKEN ARROW," "The Love of Mackintosh" is a product of Simms's visits to Mississippi territory in 1825–26. First published untitled, it came off the press in September 1826, although the title page of *Lyrical and Other Poems* is dated 1827.

The Love of Mackintosh

I saw the love of Mackintosh, she lay
    Upon the warrior's tumuli, and breath'd
Sad music, such as may be heard to stray
    From mermaid, as her string of shells she wreath'd;
She lay upon the tumuli reclined,
And breath'd her song upon the list'ning wind.
Its tones were low and beautiful, they stole,
    Like the low ripple of the O-co-ne wave,
When winds are sighing over it—the soul
    Of feeling, mingled with the strain, and gave
A rich, and melancholy note, which told,
How all that love had sigh'd for, now was cold.

'Twas in that language, which the Indian deems
    The sole-one in his fabled heaven, behind
The western hills, where rivulets nor streams,
    Shall intercept the chase, or cloud the mind:
Where life shall be all morning, where fatigue
Shall never clog the form, tho' wand'ring many a league.

"And" sung the maiden, "shall the white man pale,
    O'erspread our homes, and from the river's bank,
Pluck the red strawberry, and on hill and vale
    Build the great house from whence the swift-foot* shrank,
And from thy grave the cedar tree remove,
And each memorial of thy latest love!

"Yet, 'tis not this," she sung in wilder mood,
    Tho' nought of feeling stole upon her look,
"Not, that the cedar tree has not withstood

* [SIMMS'S NOTE] The Deer. I have never heard it termed "Swift-Foot," but have endeavored to conceive in this, as in other instances, the originality and boldness of their figures of epithet.

The ploughshare man, or that the silver brook
Must make the mill-dam, and the red-deer shrink,
No longer in its crystal wave to drink;

"But, that the Indian with the sun must glide,
    To the big waters of the western sea,
And leave the vales and mountains, once our pride,
    And thee, O, desert Arrow, fly from thee;
Where none shall know the story of the brave,
And strangers heedless, trample on thy grave.

Here shall thy spirit seek in vain to find,
    When the pale white man has our land o'erspread,
Aught in the wilderness that may remind,
    And tell thee of the glories of the dead;
The tall pine shall be torn away from earth,
As if it never had, in this wide valley, birth.

It is morning's dawn, I know it well,
    By the faint ripple on the silver stream,
And op'ning of the red flower's early bell,
    And through the distant woods the faint light gleam;
Another day—Oh! Mackintosh will see
Thy woman wand'ring, from thy grave and thee."*

                                            1826 (published 1827)

∾ The Last of the Yemassees

[SIMMS'S NOTE] *The Yemassees were a powerful nation of savages, occupying, in the lower parts of the State of South Carolina, a tract of country extending from Beaufort on the sea coast. Incited to insurrection by Spanish persuasion, they had laid a deep plan for the destruction of the Carolinians, in which, with the cunning of Philip, they had contrived to involve many of the independent neighbouring tribes. Fortunately for the whites, the design was discovered, and in the contest which ensued, the Yemassees were completely exterminated as a nation. The following lines refer to this event, and the last survivor is here made to furnish the record of their overthrow. . . .*

* [SIMMS'S NOTE] The party of Mackintosh in the Creek nation are those destined to vacate their homes for others farther west.

He fought his nation's foes 'til night
   Had cast her mantle round,
Nor, in the stern, unequal fight,
Where freemen battled for their right,
   Gave undisputed ground.
His followers fell before his face—
He stood—the last of all his race.

His brother—him that pride had named
   The eagle of his land—
In hunt, as well as battled, famed,
Who once, the furious wolf had tamed,
   And with unweaponed hand—
Himself the panther in the fight,
Who sought it with a fierce delight—

Before him fast expiring lay:—
   And he—whose name had been
The signal, many a bloody day,
For long and well contested fray—
   Known by his uncurb'd mien;
Were then a trophy, worth the toil,
Of young ambition, mad for spoil.

Yet who shall tread the thicket's brake,
   And with undaunted heart,
Arouse the coil'd and glittering snake
With fearful fang, and eye awake,
   Nor backward shuddering start?
There, coil'd as fate, the serpent lies,
And he, who first approaches, dies.

Thus, o'er his dying brother's brow,
   The brave Sanute bends—
He wails his prostrate nation low,
Lamenting for his kindred now—
   His people and his friends—
But, with a fearful burst of grief,
He mourns o'er all, that bleeding chief.

"And thou," he sung in earnest train,
   "Shalt seek the hunt no more—

Nor whet the battle knife again,
Nor strike the living, scalp the slain—
   Thy battle fields are o'er.
Yet 'mong the western hills alone,
Thou hast not, all-untended, gone.

"Slain by thy self, full many a ghost
   Thy journey must partake—
To waft thee to the happy coast,
The spoilers of our land, a host,
   O'erspread the ocean lake—
And many a maiden there, for thee,
Shall make the sweet sagamite.

"And I have seen thee bend the bow,
   And I have watch'd thee spring,
With gleaming knife upon the foe,
And far and fell the hatchet throw,—
   As swallow, swift on wing,
Pursue the triumph with a flight,
Unbroken by the long day's fight.

"And, as becomes the Indian brave,
   When, in the battle's strife,
O'erpower'd, he finds a bloody grave,
Thou didst not vainly seek to save
   The last remains of life—
Content, if fortune could not give
Thy country freedom, not to live!

1827

❧ The Green Corn Dance

[SIMMS'S NOTE] *This is one of the primitive and pleasing festivals common to many of the Indian tribes of North America; and presents a pleasing portrait of the naturally devotional temperament of this savage people. On the first appearance of the green corn from the earth, old and young, male and female, assemble together in their several classes, and, rejoicing in the promise of a good harvest, unite in offering their acknowledgment to the Great Spirit for his beneficence.*

This is the poetry of truth—of religion; and is one of those fine traits in the habits of every people, however savage, by which they still seem to indicate a consciousness, not merely of a superior being, but of a higher hope and destiny for themselves—a consciousness, which must always, to a certain extent, work out its own fulfillment.

Come hither, hither, old and young—the gentle and the strong,
And gather in the green corn dance, and mingle with the song—
The summer comes, the summer cheers, and with a spirit gay,
We bless the smiling boon she bears, and thus her gifts repay.
    Eagle from the mountain,
        Proudly descend!
    Young dove from the fountain,
        Hitherward bend—
    Bright eye of the bower—
    Bird, and bud, and flower,—
Come—while beneath the summer's sunny glance,
The green leaf peeps from earth, and mingle in the dance.

Not now reluctant do we come to gladden in the boon,
The gentle summer brings us now, so lavishly and soon—
From every distant village, and from deep secluded glen,
They gather to the green corn dance, bright maids and warrior men.
    Of the grave, the gravest,
        Smiling, now come—
    Of the brave, the bravest—
        Give the brave room.
    Loftiest in station,
    Sweetest of the nation,
Come—while beneath the summer's sunny glance,
The green blade peeps from earth, and mingle in the dance.

Now give the choral song and shout, and let the green woods ring,
And we will make a merry rout to usher in the spring—
Sing high, and while the happy mass in many a ring goes round,
The birds shall cheer, the woods shall hear, and all the hills resound.
    Fathers, who have taught us
        Ably our toil,
    For the blessing brought us,
        Share with us the spoil.
    Spirit-God above us,

Deign thou still to love us,
While long beneath the summer's sunny glance,
We see the green corn spring from earth, and gather in the dance.

1827

ENTITLED "GREAT IS THE YEMASSEE" when first published anonymously in *Southern Literary Gazette* in 1829, the poem was inserted in the text of Simms's *The Yemassee* six years later.

Mighty is the Yemassee

"Mighty is the Yemassee,
Strong in the trial,
Fearless in the strife,
Terrible in wrath—
Look, Opitchi-Manneyto—
He is like the rush of clouds,
He is like the storm by night,
When the tree-top bends and shivers,
When the lodge goes down.
The Westo and the Edisto,
What are they to him?—
Like the brown leaves to the cold,
Look, they shrink before his touch,
Shrink and shiver as he comes—
Mighty is the Yemassee."

1829

WITHOUT A TITLE, this poem appears in "The Choctaw Criminal" (1833), an expanded version of "Indian Sketch" (1828), which contains a similar poem—yet different enough to be considered a separate entity. To compare this poem with its earlier version, see above, 131–33.

[I was a wanderer long . . .]

I was a wanderer long, and loved the wild,
Even as a child his mother. I grew fond
Of the sweet keeping of the wilderness,—
The solemn warmth, the wooing solitude,

And the deep winding and the silent glooms,
Where, troubled not by hungry pioneer,
Nature still keeps her place, even as at birth.
To me, such home is sacred, and when there,
The bonds of social life I straight forget,
And grow a part of that which I survey.
Nor is this solitude as men may deem,
But a wide glance, even in her palace home,
Where still she keeps her mighty sovereignty,
At all existing Nature. There she sits,
Supreme in tangled bow'r, and toppling hill,
And deep umbrageous forest. At her feet,
Lake, wood and rivulet, bird and bud and beast,
Tree, flow'r and leaf, in matchless quietude,
Consorting with her mood. I bend before
Her solemn temple, and I lay me down,
Even at her turfy footstool, while around,
Her mantle, redolent of flow'rs and fruits,
Hangs o'er, and shields me from the noonday beam.

Have I not on that gentle couch reposed,
The lowly plat of green?—a tufted bed
Of leaves and delicate flow'rs beneath my head,
While, sweeter than the soft recorder's voice,
Or lute of ravishing syren, in my ear,
The gentle diapason of the woods,
Soft airs and bending pines and murmuring birds,
Won me to slumber with their strange discourse.
Thus, by that awe-attuning sympathy,—
That spirit language, which, upon mine ear,
Came like the wayward whispers of the sea,
To the coy wind-harp in the hands of Night,—
O'ercome, in that most wild society,—
Far from my home, and human home, I slept,
In a deep Indian forest, where still dwell
The lingering Choctaw—melancholy men,
Who love the woods, their ancient fathers gave,
And in their shelter half forget their shame.
    Who speaks?—the dream is sooth—around me stand
The gathering nation; each with solemn brow,
As to a sacrifice—a deed of dread!
They bring the guilty, the proud, self-arraigned,

To judgment and to death. There, he stands forth,
Alone, unaw'd, unbound—and in his eye,
As on his tongue, and in his lofty soul,
No fond, appealing thought—no fear of death!
He speaks, while all is silence, where had been
Howling, and many a horrible voice before.

"I come to die—no vain delay,
   I ask for none, to vex my soul—
Prepare, ye fellow chiefs, the way,
   And let the storms about me roll—
By me, Mewanto's blood was spilt,
Behold! my hands are red with guilt.

"The tribe has lost its bravest steel—
   The arrow from the bow is gone;
I saw the brave Mewanto reel,
   And I, the fatal deed have done.
Madly I struck him with my knife,
And tore away the slumbering life.

"He cross'd me in my hour of wrath,
   When hell was in my heart and mood;
Spirits of ill were on my path,
   And he and they, alike, pursued,—
They look'd the same before mine eye,
   And dreadful forms were shouting by.

"My fingers grasped my ready knife—
   A struggle—that alone I knew—
I grappled, as it were, for life,
   With that dread, dark, infernal crew—
And 'till I struck the fearful blow,
I knew not that my friend was low.

"The thought that would have spared him then,
   Too late appear'd for his relief—
He stood no more with living men—
   And I grew mad with grief.
Yet what is sorrow—can it bring
The spirit to that silent thing?

"Am I not ready—do ye sleep,
    Why strike ye not, why pause so long?
Your sorrow like mine own is deep,
    Is not your vengeance strong?
His form is by, whom late I slew,
I hear him call for vengeance too.

"Far wandering on the distant hills,
    Yet watching for the morning's dawn,
He lingers o'er the western rills,
    All anxious to be gone:—
And only waits my kindred shade
To guide him from the grave I made.

"His hatchet ready for the fight,
    When first the war-whoop's cry is heard,
I've placed to meet his waking sight,
    When carols forth the bird;
Nor, did my bosom's care forget,
The rifle, knife, and calumet.

"Oh, brother, whom I madly slew,
    Then shall our kindred spirits join—
The red-deer's path by day pursue,
    The tented camp by night entwine,
Close, at one time, the mutual eye,
And on one blanket's bosom lie."

No longer spoke the warrior chief,
    But sullen sternness clothed his brow—
Whilst fate and anguish, fixed and brief,
    Proclaimed him—ready now!
No council spoke—no pray'r was made,
No pomp, no mockery, no parade.

He walk'd erect, unaw'd, unbound,
    He stood upon the grave's dread brink,
And look'd with fearless eye around,
    Nor did his spirit shrink
In terror from that final test,—
The fearful rifle at his breast.

A moment's pause—no voice is heard—
He only, with unchanging look,
Himself, gave forth the signal word,
With which the valley shook—
And when the smoke had clear'd away,
The dark brow'd chief before me lay.

1833

ESPECIALLY WRITTEN FOR *The Yemassee,* "The 'Coonee-Latee,' or, 'Trick-Tongue'" was integrated into the text by Simms with the following commentary: "[S]he carolled forth in an exquisite ballad voice, one of those little fancies of the Indians, which may be found among nearly all the tribes from Carolina to Mexico. It recorded the achievements of that Puck of the American forests, the mocking-bird; and detailed the manner in which he procured his imitative powers. The strain, playfully simple in the sweet language of the original, must necessarily lose in the more frigid verse of the translator."

The "Coonee-Latee," or, "Trick-Tongue."

I.

"As the Coonee-latee looked forth from his leaf,
He saw below him a Yemassee chief,
    In his war-paint, all so grim—
Sung boldly, then, the Coonee-latee,
I, too, will seek for mine enemy;
    And when the young moon grows dim,
I'll slip through the leaves, nor shake them,—
I'll come on my foes, nor wake them,—
    And I'll take off their scalps like him.

II.

"In the forest grove, where the young birds slept,
Slyly by night, through the leaves he crept,
    With a footstep free and bold—
From bush to bush, from tree to tree,
They lay wherever his eye could see,
    The bright, the dull, the young, and the old;
I'll cry my war-whoop, said he, at breaking

The sleep, that shall never know awaking,
    And their hearts shall soon grow cold.
                    III.
"But, as nigher and nigher the spot he crept,
And saw that with open mouth they slept,
    The thought grew strong in his brain—
And from bird to bird, with a cautious tread,
He unhook'd the tongue, out of every head,
    Then flew to his perch again;—
And thus it is, whenever he chooses,
The tongues of all the birds he uses,
    And none of them dare complain."*

                                    1835

॰ *Selected Untitled Poems from* The Yemassee

IN THE PREFACE to the 1853 edition of *The Yemassee,* Simms staunchly testified to the truthfulness of his portrayal of the character of the Yemassee people, but he candidly admitted that their "mythology" was "pure invention."
This admission is in keeping with his theory that the artist must fill the gaps
in history with imaginative details to make his narrative alive and convincing.
Contributing nothing to our knowledge of authentic Indian culture, the
songs and poems that follow, put into the mouths of Yemassee priests and
warriors, add credence to the tense, hostile atmosphere that, as an artist,
Simms is trying to depict.

॰ *[The arrows—]*

            "The arrows—
            The feathers—
            The dried scalps, and the teeth,
            The teeth from slaughtered enemies—
            Where are they—where are they?
        We burn them for thee,—black spirit—
        We burn them for thee, Opitchi-Manneyto—
            Leave us, leave us, black spirit."

                                    1835

* [SIMMS'S NOTE] The grove is generally silent when the mocking-bird sings.

[*Let the Yemassee have ears*]

"Let the Yemassee have ears,
For Opitchi-Manneyto—
'Tis Opitchi-Manneyto,
Not the prophet, now that speaks,
Hear Opitchi-Manneyto.

"In my agony, he came,
And he hurl'd me to the ground;
Dragged me through the twisted bush,
Put his hand upon my throat,
Breathed his fire into my mouth—
That Opitchi-Manneyto.

"And he said to me in wrath,—
Listen, what he said to me;
Hear the prophet, Yemassees—
For he spoke to me in wrath;
He was angry with my sons,
For he saw them bent to slay,
Bent to strike the council-chiefs,
And he would not have them slain,
That Opitchi-Manneyto."

1835

[*What is the Seratee?*]

"What is the Seratee?—
He is but a dog
Sneaking in the long grass—
I have stood before him,
And he did not look—
By his hair I took him,—
By the single tuft—
From his head I tore it,
With it came the scalp,—
On my thigh I wore it—
With the chiefs I stood,
And they gave me honour,
Made of me a chief,
To the sun they held me,

And aloud the prophet
Bade me be a chief—
Chief of all the Yemassee—
Feather chief and arrow chief—
Chief of all the Yemassee...."

1835

୬ *[Hear, Opitchi-Manneyto]*

"Hear, Opitchi-Manneyto,
Hear Occonestoga speak—
Who of the Savannah stood
In the council, in the fight—
With the gallant Suwannee?—
Bravest he, of all the brave,
Like an arrow path in flight—
When he came, his tomahawk—
(Hear, Opitchi-Manneyto,
Not a forked tongue is mine—)
Frighted the brave Yemassee—
Till Occonestoga came—
Till Occonestoga stood
Face to face with Suwannee,
By the old Satilla swamp.
Then his eyes were in the mud—
With these hands I tore away
The war ringlet from his head—
With it came the bleeding scalp—
Suwannee is in the mud;
Frighted back, his warriors run,
Left him buried in the mud—
Ho! the gray-wolf speaks aloud,
Hear, Opitchi-Manneyto;
He had plenty food that night,
And for me he speaks aloud—
Suwannee is in his jaw—
Look, Opitchi-Manneyto—
See him tear Suwannee's side,
See him drink Suwannee's blood—
With his paw upon his breast,
Look, he pulls the heart away,
And his nose is searching deep,

Clammy, thick with bloody drink,
In the hollow where it lay.
Look, Opitchi-Manneyto,
Look, the gray-wolf speaks for me."

1835

ᔑ *[I take from thee the earth of Yemassee—]*

"I take from thee the earth of Yemassee—
I take from thee the water of Yemassee—
I take from thee the arrow of Yemassee—
Thou art no longer a Yemassee—
The Yemassee knows thee no more."

1835

ᔑ *[Sangarrah-me, Yemassee]*

"Sangarrah-me, Yemassee,
Sangarrah-me—Sangarrah-me—
Battle-god Manneyto,
Here's a scalp, here's a scull,
This is blood, 'tis a heart,
Scalp, scull, blood, heart,
'Tis for thee, battle-god,
'Tis to make the feast for thee,
Battle-god of Yemassee!"

1835

"The Widow of the Chief" is one of Simms's moving poems on the destruction of the Indian and his culture when "the pale white man shall our land o'erspread."

ᔑ *The Widow of the Chief*

I.

'Twas in the hidden depth of Indian vales,
A wall of woods and waters swelling round,
Where seldom came the strong and stormy gales,

Or with maimed force and mitigated sound,
The tumulus of many an age arose,
Where long forgotten nations found repose.

II.

The broken earth, the freshly gathered clay,
  Told of a recent burial, while above,
Moaning in accents wild, a woman lay,
  With look that spoke of a dissever'd love!
And singing mournfully a lingering strain,
Of mingling shame and glory—pride and pain.

III.

'Twas in that language which the Indian deems
  Sole in his fabled heaven, that soars behind
The western waters—there where swamps and streams
  Shall neither stay the chase, nor taint the wind—
Where life shall be all morning—where fatigue
Shall never clog the form, tho' wandering many a league.

IV.

Its tones were soft and delicate—they stole
  Like the faint murmur on the Oconé* wave
When first the morning meets it—the warm soul
  Of a strong feeling mingling with it, gave
A deep and melancholy strain, which told
How all that love once lived for had grown cold.

V.

The chief she wail'd had led the tribe to war,
  And won his hundred battles. He had stood,
Unvanquish'd, bleeding at full many a scar,
  Marking his path through the dread field in blood,
Nor, though the bravest at his side lay slain,
Until the foe was vanquish'd left the plain.

VI.

Yet he who to his foe had never shown
  His back in battle, in his highest pride,
By traitor weapons, in the dark struck down,
  May well bring lamentations to his bride—

---

* [SIMMS'S NOTE] Oconé, or Occonyee, a small river in the State of Georgia.

And mingle with the memory of a chief
So well beloved and worthy, many a grief.

VII.

A deeper sorrow yet—a sterner fate
   Hangs o'er the mourner: she who lov'd the brave,
Whose death had left her lone and desolate,
   Must, with her people, fly the warrior's grave—
Must yield the mournful solace, to behold,
And deck the mound where sleeps the bravest bold.

VIII.

And sung she mournfully—"The invader pale
   Shall seize our homes, and by the swelling brink
Of broad waters, and on hill and vale,
   Build up his dwellings, till the deer shall shrink
Stealthily back, into his forests deep,
Nor from the cover of the thick swamp sleep.

IX.

"And they shall rob the woods of all that make
   Them lovely to the Indian. They shall bring
Forbidden sounds into the silent brake,
   And banish thence the birds, and blight the spring,
Nor spare the warrior's bones, nor leave the bloom
And beauty of the flow'rs that hang above his tomb.

X.

"Yet 'tis not this," in wilder mood she sung,
   "Not that they take the silence from the woods,
And chase the bird away and chide his tongue,
   And turn to other paths the gentle floods,
Making the mill course; while the red deer shrink,
And tremble, in the troubled waves to drink—

XI.

"But that the Indian with the sun must glide,
   No more a chief of the woods, no longer free,
And leave the vales and waters, once his pride,
   The home endeared by a long infancy,
The woods he roved for ages, and the graves
Where lie the sacred bones of all his braves.

XII.

"In vain their troubled shades would seek to find,
    When the pale white man shall our land o'erspread,
The scenes—the fields—the homes that may remind
    And tell them of the glories of the dead.
The tall pine shall be torn away from the earth
As if it never had in the deep valley birth.

XIII.

"A people shall succeed who shall not know
    The race they robb'd of home and heritage—
And they shall boast, perchance, when we are low,
    Of homes descended through full many an age,
To them unbroken:—Who shall ask the lot
Of the great nation vanish'd and forgot?"

1835

SIMMS'S INNATE REALISM comes to the fore in "The Indian Village," which portrays the degeneration of the Indian after the arrival of the white man. Far from being an idealistic representation of the noble savage, "The Indian Village" depicts besotted Native Americans whose cruelty, selfishness, and laziness make inevitable the demise of their village and its replacement by "a city of the paler race." After the Civil War Simms wrote a much longer, more rhetorical poem, "Chilhowee, the Indian Village," that retains the theme of the original.

∾ The Indian Village

Nature and Freedom! These are glorious words
That make the world mad. Take a glimpse at both,
Such as you readily find, when, at your ease,
You plough the ancient military trace,
From Georgia to the "Burnt Corn" settlements—
Or, higher up, if, happily, you speed,
Where the gaunt Choctaw lingers by the swamps
That fence the Yazoo, or the Chickasaw
Steals his hog nightly from the woodman's close,
And gets a furlough from all service thence,

In a keen bullet from an hundred yards.—
—Uplift thy glass, and tell me what thou seest.

A screaming brat that lash'd upon his board
Hangs rocking in the tree—the dam beneath,
A surly drudge that never once looks up,
But hills and hoes her corn, as if her soul
Lay clamoring there for sudden and strong help,
And perish'd in her pause—an ugly cur,
Mangy and mostly unclean, that, yelping, runs
For shelter at our coming—two green skins
That clothed the brown deer of the woods last night,
Wrapped now about the oak, beneath whose boughs,
Their owners browsed at evening, ere the tribe
Sent the young hunters forth—and lo! a group,
Women and children, in that happy state,
Ere Adam wore his fig leaves, and became
A tailor for the nonce—that round one hole
Bend down, clay digging for their pots and pans,
The baking fire at hand—and then the huts,
They fill the background—linger not to look,
Or, in rebellion, justified of man,
Our nostrils will rise up and nullify.
A more legitimate picture for good taste,
And the heroic, basking in the sun,
Behold the chiefs—five warriors of the wild,
That may be sung in story—vigorous men,
Ready for strife and trial, scalp and stroke,
But monstrous lazy. There is "Turkey-Foot"—
Not slow to run;—Achilles-like, his heel
Is sadly mortal. There's "Fat Terrapin,"
No runner he, I ween. A braver man
Than the "Gray Weasel" never sought the fight,
But then he loves fire water, and even now,
Not scrupulous to meet the stranger's eye,
See, his head dangles on the unsinew'd neck,
And bobs from side to side. "The Crooked Path,"
A double-dealing rogue as ever lived,
Looks like a cutpurse, and among the tribe
Such is his high renown. No counsellor
Can deal with him in subtle argument,
No fox-like politician double so,
In getting round the wild "Cape Positive,"

To channel "non-committal;"—happy he,
To steer between those breakers "yes" and "no,"
Yet leave no furrow on his sinuous path
As guide point to a troublous enemy.
Last of this group, behold old "Blazing Pine,"
Though but a pine knot now. His seventy years
Have all been tasted, yet his limbs are strong,
And bear him still in the chase. His keen eye
Not often fails to mark—his steady hand,
Still sends the bolt, with most unerring stroke,
Into the brown deer's flank.

                    These warriors brave
Will all be drunk by night. The sober now,
Drunk with the drunkest. The already drunk,
Mad—looking for their weapons in the dark,
Beating the winds, the walls, striving with trees,
And one another—impotent but fierce,
And foaming with the fury unappeased—
Till, in their madness, with their emptied bottles
They'll break the old squaw's head, and she will fly
Howling for vengeance. She will swim yon stream,
Her blood still streaking, as she scuds along,
The wave that washes gainst her shatter'd scull.
Seeking for safety 'mong her kindred tribe
Of the "Mud Turtles," she will head a war,
And they will lose their scalps with infinite grace
To one another. War, with its long train
Of toils and injuries, will rive their fields,
Destroy their little maize crops and frail towns,
And leave them starving. Want will then produce
The peace that came not with prosperity,
And they will link their arms, and, in small groups,
Steal nightly over to the opposite shore
And rob the squatter's farm yard. Cows and calves
They'll drive across the stream. The young corn
They'll burst from its green column, and the pigs—
They barbacue as well at an Indian camp
As at a white man's muster. What comes next?
The squatter goes against the savages,
And drives them—a most sad necessity,
Much mourned by modern-mouthed philanthropy—
Into yet deeper forests. Five years hence,

And the foul settlement we gaze on now
Will be a city of the paler race,
Having its thousand souls. Churches will rise,
With taverns on each hand. To the right, see,
A gloomy house of morals, called a gaol,
And, from the town hall, on the opposite square,
You yet shall hear some uncombed orator,
Discourse of freedom, politics, and law,
In tones shall make your blood bound, and your hair
Start up in bristles. Turning, you shall see,
"Fat Terrapin," "Grey Weasel," and, perchance,
The aged "Blazing Pine,"—all christians now,
Cowering, bewildered, 'mong the heedful crowd
Which hangs delighted on the patriot's words—
Heedful, delighted, drunk as any there!

1837

IN REVIEWING *Areytos* for the *Democratic Review* (29 [July 1846]: 31–32), Edgar
Allan Poe termed Simms "beyond doubt, one of our most original writers"
and added: "Altogether I prefer . . . 'Indian Serenade' to any of Mr. Simms'
poems." In the preface to the volume, Simms commented that the "melodious"
word *Areytos* "is borrowed from the Indian language of the Island of Cuba."

ᵔ *Indian Serenade*

I.

'Mong Lucayo's isles and waters,
 Leaping to the evening light,
Dance the moonlight's silver daughters,
Tresses streaming, glances gleaming,
 Ever beautiful and bright.

II.

And their wild and mellow voices,
 Still to hear along the deep,
Every brooding star rejoices,
While the billow, on its pillow,
 Lull'd to silence, sinks to sleep.

III.

Yet they wake a song of sorrow,
    Those sweet voices of the night—
Still from grief a gift they borrow,
And hearts shiver, as they quiver,
    With a wild and sad delight.

IV.

'Tis the wail for life they waken,
    By Bonita's silver shore—
With the tempest, it is shaken;
The wide ocean, is in motion,
    And the song is heard no more.

V.

But the gallant bark comes sailing,
    At her prow the chieftain stands,
He hath heard the tender wailing;—
It delights him—it invites him
    To the joys of other lands.

VI.

Bright the moonlight round and o'er him,
    And O! see, a picture lies,
In the yielding waves before him—
Woman smiling, still beguiling,
    With her dark and wondrous eyes.

VII.

White arms toss above the waters,
    Pleading murmurs fill his ears,
And the gem of ocean's daughters,
Love assuring, still alluring,
    Wins him down with tears.

VIII.

On the good ship speeds without him,
    By Bonita's silver shore—
They have twined their arms about him,
Ocean's daughters, in the waters,
    Sadly singing as before.

1846

Cassique of Accabee, original painting in possession of Mary Simms Oliphant Furman.

JAMES KIBLER IS CORRECT in calling "The Cassique of Accabee" Simms's finest narrative poem, and it may also be his best poem on the subject of the Indian. An outgrowth of the much shorter "Accabee—A Ballad," "The Cassique of Accabee" embodies the combination of qualities that make this poetic portrayal of the Indian a literary tour de force: sustained skill in prosody and narration; firsthand knowledge of Indian character, sympathetic yet realistic; and an underlying awareness of injustice to Native Americans as the manifest destiny of white civilization unfolds.

The cassique is portrayed as a complex human being, possessed of dignity, honesty, and generosity as well as cruelty and barbarism. His loyalty and commitment stand in sharp contrast to the ingratitude, flightiness, and greed of his white ward and her white lover. He has a sense of humor, whereas they have little; his culture has taught him to honor the environment, whereas theirs has led them to exploit it. One of the poem's themes is the passing of land sacred to the Indian into white hands incapable of appreciating and nurturing it. An irony in its contrast of cultures is the beautiful white girl's repulsion and shock at seeing the scalp that the cassique has proudly and honorably taken in her defense; yet it is the cassique, not his ward, who finds infidelity reprehensible. Simms's point is clear: Indian values are often markedly different from white values, and this difference can be a source of misunderstandings on both sides; but in this poem, the cassique's ideals and values seem superior to those of his white counterparts. "The Cassique of Accabee" has fast-moving action, a strong sense of place, and a reverence for the supernatural powers that haunt and protect that place.

❧ The Cassique of Accabee; A Legend of the Ashley River

It was a night of calm—o'er Ashley's waters
    Crept the sweet billows to their own soft tune,
While she, most bright of Keawah's fair daughters,
    Whose voice might spell the footsteps of the moon,
        As slow we swept along,
        Pour'd forth her own sweet song,
A lay of rapture not forgotten soon.

Hush'd was our breathing, stay'd the lifted oar,
    Our spirits rapt, our souls no longer free,

While the boat drifting softly to the shore,
   Brought us within the shades of Accabee;—
      "Ah!" sudden cried the maid,
      In the dim light afraid;
"'Tis here the ghost still walks of the old Yemassee."

And sure the spot was haunted by a power,
   To fix the pulses in each youthful heart;
Never was moon more gracious in a bower,
   Making delicious fancy work for art;
      Weaving, so meekly bright,
      Her pictures of delight,
That, though afraid to stay, we sorrow'd to depart.

"If these old groves are haunted"—sudden then,
   Said she, our sweet companion—"it must be
By one who loved, and was beloved again,
   And joy'd all forms of loveliness to see:—
      Here, in these groves they went,
      Where love and worship, blent,
Still framed the proper God for each idolatry.

"It could not be that love should here be stern,
   Or beauty fail to sway the sov'ran might;
These, from so bless\u00e9d scenes, should something learn,
   And swell with tenderness and shape delight:
      These groves have had their power,
      And bliss, in bygone hour,
Hath charm'd, with sight and song, the passage of the night."

"It were a bliss to think so;" made reply
   Our Hubert—"yet the tale is something old,
That checks us with denial;—and our sky,
   And these brown woods that, in its glittering fold,
      Look like a fairy clime,
      Still unsubdued by time,
Have evermore the tale of wrong'd devotion told."

"Give us thy legend, Hubert;" cried the maid;—
   And, with down-drooping oars, our yielding prow
Shot to a still lagoon, whose ample shade
   Droop'd from the gray moss of an old oak's brow:
      The groves, meanwhile, lay bright,

Like the broad stream, in light,
Soft, sweet as ever yet the lunar loom display'd.

"Great was the native chief,"—'twas thus began
    The legend of our comrade—"who, in sway,
Held the sweet empire which to-night we scan,
    Stretching, on either hand, for miles away:
        A stalwart chief was he,
        Cassique of Accabee,
And lord o'er numerous tribes who did with pride obey.

"War was his passion, 'till the white-man came,
    And then his policy;—and well he knew,
How, over all, to plan the desperate game,
    And when to rise, and when to sink from view;
        To plant his ambush well,
        And how, with horrid yell,
To dart, at midnight forth, in fury arm'd with flame.

"His neighbours by the Ashley, the pale race,
    Were friends and allies 'gainst all other foes;
They dwelt too nearly to his royal place,
    To make the objects of their commerce blows;
        But no such scruple staid
        His wild and cruel raid,
When, by Heléna's Bay, the Gaelic hamlet rose.

"And moved by Spanish wile that still misled,
    Our chieftain, in one dark November night,
With all his warriors, darted from his bed,
    And drove the Gaelic chief from his, in flight:—
        Scalplocks and other spoils,
        Rewarded well his toils,
And captives graced his triumph after fight.

"But, when the strife was wildest, and the fire
    Play'd fiercest on the roofs of bough and leaf,
A fair-hair'd child, misdeeming him her sire,
    Rush'd headlong to the arms of the red chief:—
        'Twas not his hour to spare—
        His fingers in her hair,
And tomahawk, lifted high, declar'd his savage ire.

"But, in the light of her own blazing home,
　　He caught the entreaty in her soft blue eye,
Which, weeping still the while, would wildly roam,
　　From him who held, to those who hurried by;—
　　　　Strange was the emotion then,
　　　　That bade him stay his men,
And, in his muscular arms, lift that young damsel high.

"He bore her through the forest, many a mile,
　　With a rude tenderness and matchless strength;
She slept upon his arm—she saw his smile,
　　Seen seldom, and reached Accabee at length;
　　　　Here, for a term, he kept
　　　　The child, her griefs unwept,
With love, that did from her a seeming love beguile.

"Daughter of ancient Albyn, she was bright,
　　With a transparent beauty; on her cheek,
The rose and lily, struggling to unite,
　　Did the best blooms of either flow'r bespeak;
　　　　Whilst floods of silken hair,
　　　　Free flowing, did declare
The gold from western heavens when sinks the sun from sight.

"Our chief had reach'd his thirtieth summer —she
　　Was but thirteen; yet, 'till he saw this maid,
Love made no portion of his reverie:
　　Strife was his passion, and the midnight raid;
　　　　The dusky maids, in vain,
　　　　Had sought to weave their chain,
About that fierce wild heart that still from all went free.

"But, free no longer, they beheld him bound
　　By his fair captive; strife was now unsought;
The chase abandon'd; and his warriors found
　　Their chief no more where fields were to be fought;—
　　　　He better loved to brood
　　　　In his sweet solitude,
She still in sight, who thus her captor's self had caught.

"She little dream'd her conquest, for he still
　　Maintain'd her as his child, with tenderness;—

As one who seeks no farther of his will,
    Than to protect and with sweet nurture bless;
        Such love as sire might show,
        Did that dark chief bestow,
When, in a gentle clasp, he met her child-caress.

"She grew to be the blossom of his sight—
    For her he snared the fawn,—for her he brought
Gay gauds of foreign fabric;—her delight
    Being still the sweetest recompense he sought;—
        And, when her feet would rove,
        He led her through the grove,
Show'd her its devious paths and all its secrets taught.

"She grew apace in beauty as in years,
    And he the more devoted:—until now
His eye beheld her growth and had no fears,—
    But soon a shadow rose above his brow;—
        That shadow, born of doubt,
        Which finds love's secret out,
And, o'er its sunniest bower, still spans an arch of tears.

"This shadow had its birth with our dark chief,
    When to his home, one eve, returning late,
He saw, with passion still subdued by grief,
    A stranger with his beauty, in his gate;—
        One of the pale white race,
        Whose presence, in that place,
Brought to his heart a fear that troubled it like fate.

"Yet was he but a pedlar,—he who came,—
    Thus troubling waters which had slept before;
He brought his glittering wares, and did but claim
    To show them, and night's lodging to implore:
        And, o'er his pack, with eyes
        Of eager, glad surprize,
Stoop'd our young maid when stept the chief within his door.

"His stealthy footsteps stirr'd no single sound;
    They knew not of the eyes upon them set—
She, the gay thoughtless girl, in thought profound,

Deep in such wealth as had not tempted yet;
 While his—the stranger's—gaze,
 In a most pleasant maze,
Scann'd her bright cheeks, unseen, from eyes of glittering jet.

"A handsome youth, of dark and amorous glance,
 Showing a grateful consciousness of power,
Yet thoughtless, in that moment of sweet trance,
 How best to woo and win the forest flower;
  Even at that moment, stood
  The red-man from the wood,
Gazing, with instinct grief, that had its birth that hour.

"Quickly he broke the silence and came forth,
 While the fair girl, upstarting from her dream,
Hurried his search into such stores of worth,
 As did on eyes of young Aladdin gleam:—
  Clipping his neck with arms
  That spoke of dearer charms,
The maid Othello loved might she that moment seem.

"And, with a pleased, but still a sinking heart,
 He yielded to her pleading: he had stores,—
Such treasures as the red-man might impart,
 Of precious value borne to foreign shores;
  Spoils in the forest caught,
  By tribute hunter brought,
Soft furs from beaver won by snares of sylvan art.

"Sadly, the indulgent chief—but with a smile,—
 Gave up his treasure at his ward's demand;
The precious gauds which did her eyes beguile,
 Soon clasp'd her neck, or glitter'd in her hand.
  All had she won—but still
  There was a feminine will,
That led her glance astray beneath that stranger's wile.

"Their eyes commerced beside the blazing fire,
 Hers still unconscious of the erring vein;
The chief beheld, in his, the keen desire,
 And his heart swell'd with still increasing pain;
  Yet, though the sting was deep,

His passion, made to sleep,
Look'd calm through eyes that seem'd a stranger still to ire.

"His board was spread with hospitable hand,
    Crisp'd the brown bread and smoked the venison steak;
An ancient squaw, still ready at command,
    Pour'd the casina tea, their thirst to slake;
        Then, as the hour grew late,
        With calm and lofty state,
The chief himself, with care, the stranger's couch did make.

"At sunrise they partook the morning meal,
    And then the white-man went upon his way;
Not without feeling—teaching her to feel—
    How sweet to both had been his still delay:—
        The nature, long at rest,
        Rose, pleading, at her breast,
For that pale race from which, perforce, she dwelt astray.

"She long'd for their communion,—for the youth
    Had waken'd memories, not to be subdued,
Of that dear home, and friends whose tender ruth
    Possess'd her still in that sweet solitude;
        And, saddening with the thought,
        Her secret soul grew fraught
With hopes, with doubts, with dreams, o'er which she loved to brood.

"The chief beheld the trouble in her eye,
    He felt as well the trouble in his heart,
And, ere the morrow's sun was in the sky,
    He bade her make her ready to depart;—
        He had a wider home,
        Where love might safely roam,
Nor fear the stranger's foot, nor tremble at his art.

"Cassique among the Edistos, he bore
    His treasure to the river of that name;
He sought the forests on its western shore,
    Millions of acres he alone might claim;
        Where the great stream divides,
        He cross'd its double tides,
Still seeking denser empires to explore.

"At length, he paused beside a little lake,
    A clear sweet mirror for the midnight star;
'Soon, weary one, thy slumbers shalt thou take;
    In sooth, to-day, our feet have wander'd far;
        Yet look, and thou shalt see,
        The wigwam smokes for thee,—
Those fires that gleam through woods show where our people are.

"'Here shalt thou have fond service—here the clime
    Is sweet and healthful;—buskin'd, with thy bow,
Thou'lt wander forth with me, at morning's chime,
    And I to snare or slay the game, will show:
        Broad are the sheltering woods,
        Bright are the streams, the floods,
And safe the realm that hence thy youthful heart shall know.'

"Thus counselling, he led her o'er the plain,
    Down the smooth hill, beside the lakelet clear;
They tread the gloomy forest paths again,
    'Till sudden, the whole landscape opens fair;
        'Look! weary one,' he cries;
        'Our realm before us lies,
Far spread as bird can fly, or speeds by day the deer.'

"In sooth, to one whose heart is still at rest,
    With not a human care to call it thence,
It was a home that rapture might have bless'd,
    Lovely to sight and dear to innocence;
        Great trees, a welcome shade,
        Of beech and poplar made,
Fortress of peace that love might deem his best defence.

"Long groves of pine and cedar led through wastes
    Made lovely by wild flow'rs of every hue;
Through arching boughs and vines the river hastes,
    Still with the song of birds that wander too;
        A fresh green realm, unbroke
        By plow or woodman's stroke,
Rich in savannahs green, and lakes of skyey blue.

"His was the realm, and at his bidding came
    The tribes that peopled it; beneath his sway

They framed their rude society;—his blame,
   Or praise, sufficient guide to shape their way;
     Still, with the falling leaf,
     The signal of our chief
Prepared them for the chase and counsell'd their array.

"And thus, for many a moon, within that shade,
   Dwelling 'mongst vassals rude but loyal still,
Remote, but not in loneliness, our maid
   Had all that love could sigh for, but its will;
     Submissive still she found
     The gentle tribes around,
The squaws received her law, the warriors too obey'd.

"No censure check'd her walks—no evil eyes
   Darken'd upon her childish sports at eve;
If o'er the chieftain's brow a trouble lies,
   'Tis sure no fault of hers that makes him grieve;
     For her he still hath smiles,
     And, in her playful wiles,
He finds a charm that still must artlessly deceive.

"Her wild song cheers him at the twilight hour,
   As, on the sward, beside her sylvan cot,
He throws him down, meet image of a power
   Subdued by beauty to the vassal's lot;
     With half unconscious gaze,
     His eye her form surveys,
And fancies fill his heart which utterance yet have not.

"She had expanded into womanhood
   In those brief years of mild captivity,
And now, as 'neath his glance the damsel stood,
   Nothing more sweet had ever met his eye;—
     Fair, with her Saxon face,
     Her form a forest grace
Had won from woodland sports of rare agility.

"Her rich blue eyes, her streaming yellow hair,
   The soft white skin that show'd the crimson tide,
And perfect features—made her beauties rare,
   That well the charms of Indian race defied;—

Her motion, as of flight,
Tutor'd by wild delight,
Brought to her form a grace at once of love and pride.

"And, as he gazed, with rapture ill suppress'd,
Inly the chief resolved that she should be
The woman he would take unto his breast,
Ere the next moon should ride up from the sea;
His child no more,—he felt
His soul within him melt,
To hear her voice in song, her thought in fancy free.

"She felt at last her power upon his heart,
As she beheld the language in his eye;
And, with this knowledge, came a natural art,
Which bade her glances unto his reply;
Made happy by her look
His soul new poison took,
He drew her to his breast, nor seem'd she to deny.

"'I shall go hence,' quoth he, 'the Hunter's Moon—
These sticks shall tell thee of the broken days;
When all are gone, I shall return,—and soon
The beauties that I hold within my gaze,
Shall bless, if thou approve,
This heart, and the fond love
That knows thee as the star the ocean stream that sways.'

"And she was silent while he spake—her head
Sunk, not in sadness, and upon his breast;
Fondly he kiss'd her—other words he said,
And still, in dear embrace, her form caress'd;
Then parting, sped afar,
Led by the Hunter's Star,
Where the bear wallows in his summer nest.

"She had no sorrow to obey his will
That ruled a nation: true, he slew her sire,
But he had been a gentle guardian still,
Baffling each danger, soothing each desire;
The power that he possess'd
Was grateful to her breast,
And warm'd with pride the heart, that lack'd each holier fire.

"That night there rose an image in her dreams,
    Of the young trader seen at Accabee;
His fair soft face upon her memory gleams,
    His keen, dark, searching eye, still wantonly
        Pursues her with its blaze;
        And she returns the gaze,
And thus her heart communes with one she cannot see.

"It was as if the chief, by the same word
    That told his own fond purpose, had compell'd
The image of the person she preferr'd,—
    And, seeing him in dreams, her soul was spell'd
        With fancies that, in vain,
        She strove to hush again—
She saw their shapes by day, by night their voices heard.

"Saddened by this communion, she withdrew
    From those who sought her; in deep forests went,
By lonely streams and shades, from human view,
    Nursing a vague and vexing discontent;—
        For the first time, a care
        Hung on her heart like fear—
The shadows from a soul not wholly innocent.

"There is a fate beside us day and night,
    Obedient to the voice within our hearts;
Boldly we summon, and it stands in sight;
    We speak not, and in silence it departs;—
        'Twas thus with her, as still
        She roved with aimless will,
Beside the swamps through which the Edisto still darts.

"She spoke aloud, or did not speak, his name,
    Whose image was the sole one in her breast;
But, suddenly, from out the woods he came,
    And mutual glances mutual joy express'd:—
        'Ah! sought so long before,
        I fear'd that, never more,
Mine eyes should see the form that kept my soul from rest.

"'How have I search'd for you in devious path,
    Forgetful of the mercenary trade!

And now, though perill'd by the redman's wrath,
    I seek you in forbidden forest shade;
        For never, since that night,
        When first you met my sight,
Hath beauty on my heart such sweet impression made.'

"They sat beneath the shade of silent trees,
    Close guarded by a thicket dense and deep;
There, onward, stole the river at its ease,
    And, through the air, the birds made easy sweep;—
        Those bow'rs were sweetly dight
        For safety and delight;—
The stranger won the prize the chieftain still would keep.

"He came, the dark-brow'd chieftain, from the chase,
    Laden with precious spoils of forest pride;
His heart exulting as he near'd the place
    Where the fair Saxon waited as his bride:
        But who shall speak the grief
        That shook the warrior chief,
When they declared her flight with yester-eventide.

"He had no voice for anguish or regret;—
    He spake not of his purpose—but went forth,
With a keen spirit, on one progress set,
    Now on the southern stream side, now the north;
        Following, with sleuthhound's scent,
        The way the lovers went,
Tracking each footfall sure, in leaf, in grass, and earth.

"Nor did he track in vain! They little knew
    The unerring instinct of that hunter race;
A devious progress did the twain pursue,
    Through streams and woods, to baffle still the trace;
        But how should they beguile
        The master of each wile,
Each art pursued in war or needful in the chase?

"In fancy safe, and weary now with flight,
    The lovers lay at noonday in the shade;
Soft through the leaves and grateful to the sight,
    The sun in droplets o'er the valley play'd;
        But two short leagues, and they

Should leave the perilous way,
On Keawah secure, in home by squatter made.

"Thus satisfied, with seeming certainty,
   Won by the hour's sweet stillness, did the pair,
Shelter'd beneath the brows of an old tree,
    Give freedom to the love they joy'd to share;
      His arm about her press'd,
      She lay upon his breast,
Life's self forgot in bliss that left no room for care.

"They little dream'd that, lurking in the wood,
   A witness to the freedom of their bliss,
The fiery chieftain they had baffled stood,
    Fierce, with envenom'd fang and fatal hiss;
      The lord of death and life,
      He grasp'd the deadly knife,
And shook the tomahawk high but rarely known to miss.

"But, ere he sped the weapon to its mark,
   His heart grew gentle 'neath a milder sway;
True, they had left his dwelling lone and dark,
    But should he make it glad were he to slay?
      Nor, if the man he slew,
      Could he again renew
The trust he gave the maid as in his happier day.

"Nor could he strike, with stern and fatal blow,
   Her whose fair beauties were too precious still;
A noble purpose came to soothe his wo,
    And crown, with best revenge, a generous will;—
      Forth strode he from the wood,
      And ere they knew, he stood,
With weapon bared, and look still resolute to kill.

"As one who at the serpent's rattle starts,
   Sharp, sudden sounded in the covert nigh,
They heard his voice, and both their guilty hearts
    Sunk, hopeless, 'neath the expected penalty;
      But, stifling his deep grief,
      With few stern words, the chief,
Declared, though worthy death, the guilty should not die!

"O'erjoy'd at respite scarcely yet believed,
    The girl had risen and rush'd to clasp his knees,
But he whose faith had been so much deceived,
    No homage now could pacify or please;
        Calm, but with gloomy face,
        He checks the false embrace,
And still, the crouching youth, with scornful eye, he sees.

"He bade them rise and follow where he led,
    Himself conducted to the dwelling near;
Here, till the dawn, each found a separate bed;
    With morning o'er the Keawah they steer;
        Still guided he the way,
        And, ere the close of day,
Once more the three to shades of Accabee repair.

"'Here,' said he, 'is your future dwelling-place,
    This be, my gift, your heritage of right;
The holy man, of your own foreign race,
    Shall, with the coming day, your hands unite;
        And men of law shall know
        That these lands I forego,
For her who still hath been the apple of my sight.

"'See that you cherish her with proper faith;—
    If that you wrong her, look for wrong from me:
Once have I spared you, when the doom was death;
    Beware the future wrath you may not flee;
        Mine eye shall watch for hers,
        And if a breath but stirs
Her hair too rudely,—look for storms on Accabee.'

"He did as he had promised; they were wed
    By Christian rites,—and legal deeds convey'd
The heritage;—without a word then sped
    The chief into his forests, seeking shade:
        Months pass'd—a year went by,
        And none beheld his eye,
Where still his thought, with love, through these sweet places stray'd.

"He grew to be forgotten by the twain;
    Or if not wholly by the woman, she

Ne'er spoke of him,—ne'er look'd for him again,
　　Though much it might have gladden'd her to see;
　　　　For love had lost its flow'r,
　　　　And soon there came an hour,
When all her young heart's pleasure grew to pain!

"The first sweet flush of summer dalliance gone,
　　The first most precious bloom of passion o'er,
Indifference follow'd in the heart that won,
　　And scorn found place where rapture woke no more;
　　　　No kindly nurture bless'd
　　　　With love her lonely breast,
And soon even peace had fled the home so glad before.

"And scorn grew into hate, and hate to wrath,
　　And wrath found speech in violence;—his arm
Smote the unhappy woman from his path;—
　　Submission could not sooth, nor tears disarm,
　　　　The cruel mood, the will
　　　　True to past passions still,
Which Love and Beauty now, no more sufficed to charm.

"The profligate husband, reckless of her wo,
　　Her meek submission and her misery,
Prepared, in secret, still another blow,
　　And bargain'd for the sale of Accabee;
　　　　Already he had drawn
　　　　The fatal deed—had gone,
Resolved, in other lands, remote, his wife to flee.

"He little knew that eyes were on his flight,
　　That long had mark'd his deeds;—his way led through
The umbrageous groves of Eutaw:—long ere night
　　His footsteps to the white-man's clearings drew;—
　　　　Exulting in the dream,
　　　　Successful, of his scheme,
He hails the cottage-smokes of him who bought, in sight.

"But now a voice arrests him as he goes—
　　Forth starts the red chief from the covering wood;
At once he knew him for the worst of foes;

Guilt quell'd his courage, terror froze his blood;
    The horse is stay'd—in vain,
    He jerks the extended rein,
Vainly applies the spur, and show'rs his flanks with blows.

"Stern was the summons—in a single word—
    'Down!'—and he yielded to the vigorous hand;
'I gave thee all!' were then the accents heard—
    'The woman from my bosom, and my land;—
        I warn'd thee, ere I went,
        Of wrath and punishment,
If hair upon her head, in wrath was ever stirr'd.

"'I know thee, and thy deeds; and thou shalt die!'
    'Mercy!' implored the profligate in vain.
Vainly he struggles—vainly seeks to fly—
    Even as he strives, the hatchet cleaves his brain.
        Quivering, he lies beneath,
        While from his leathern sheath,
The warrior draws his knife, and coldly scalps the slain.

"Another night, and on the Accabee,
    Softly the moon was smiling through its grove;
Yet sad the woman hail'd its light, for she
    No longer warm'd with hope, or glow'd with love:
        Grief, and a wan despair,
        Reign'd in her soul of care,
Whence love, expell'd by wrath, had long been forced to flee.

"She crouch'd beside the hearth in vacant mood,
    Silence and wo close crouched on either hand,—
Life's hope all baffled,—all the innocent brood
    Of joys, that once had crowded at command,
        Dead—gone like summer flowers;
        Desolate all her hours,
Her life was now one dread, one deathlike solitude.

"With dreary gaze she watch'd the flickering fire,
    Nor mark'd around the thickening growth of gloom;
She sees, unheeding, the bright flame expire,
    Nor marks the fearful aspect in her room;
        Beside her rest the brands—

'Tis but to stretch her hands:
Alas! her desolate soul for light hath no desire.

"But lo! another form, beside her own,
    Bends to the task;—sudden, the resinous pine
Flames up;—she feels she is no more alone;
    She sees a well-known eye upon her shine,
        And hides her face, and cries—
        'The Chief!' His silent eyes
Still saddening o'er the shape too long and dearly known.

"'The man whom thou didst wed, will never more
    Lay angry hand upon thee—he had sold
Thy land, and fled thee for another shore;
    But that I wound him in the serpent's fold,
        And took from him the pow'r
        That had usurp'd thy dow'r;
In proof of what I tell thee,—lo! behold!'

"Thus speaking, he, beside her, on the floor,
    Cast down the white man's written instrument;
Sign'd, seal'd, and witness'd; framed with legal lore;
    Conveying—such the document's intent—
        All these fair groves and plains,
        The Accabee domains,
To one, of kindred race, whose name the paper bore.

"And she had sign'd it, with unwilling hand,
    Ignorant of its meaning, but in dread;
Obedient to her tyrant's fierce command,
    While his arm shook in threat'ning o'er her head;
        'Twas in that very hour,
        His blow, with brutal power,
Had stricken her to the earth, where long she lay as dead.

"He little dream'd that the avenger near,
    Beheld him, and prepared his punishment;
You ask, Why came he not to interfere,
    And stay, ere yet was wrought the foul intent;
        Enough, the red-man knows
        His time to interpose:—
Sternly his hour he takes, with resolute will unbent.

"Unerring, we have seen him in pursuit—
 Unsparing, we have seen him in his blow;—
His mission was not ended; and, though mute,
 He stood surveying her, who, cowering low,
  Crept humbly to his feet,
  As seeming to entreat,—
He had another task, which found the warrior slow.

"But he was firm:—'This paper is your own,—
 Another proof is mine, that you will be
Safe from the blows of him so lately known;
 He hath his separate lands henceforth from me;
  Ample the soil I gave,
  Beside the Eutaw's wave;
In token of my truth—this bloody scalplock see.'

"Then shriek'd the unhappy woman with affright,
 Revolting at the trophy, dripping yet,
That, down upon the paper, in her sight,
 With quiet hand, the haughty chieftain set;
  'Spare me! Oh, spare!' she cries:
  And crouching, with shut eyes,
Backward she crept, as if she safety sought in flight.

"'Fear nothing!' said the chieftain; ''twas for thee,
 I brought this bloody token of my truth,
To show thee, from this moment, thou art free
 To the possession of thy life and youth;
  Still hast thou beauty; still
  Thy heritage—thy will;
Go, seek thy kindred pale, secure of love and ruth.

"'From him, who, in thy thoughtlessness of heart,
 Thou mad'st a master over thee, I save;
I slew thy father—I have done his part,
 And give thee wealth more ample than he gave;
  Henceforth, thou wilt not see
  The Chief at Accabee;
Beware again lest passion make thee slave.

"'I leave thee now forever!' 'No!' she cried:
 Oh! take me to thy people;—let me dwell

Lone, peaceful, on the Edisto's green side,
   Which, had I left not, I had still been well:—
      Forgive me, that the child,
      With heart both weak and wild,
Err'd, in not loving, where she might have loved with pride!'

"'I had believed thee once; but now, too late!
   Henceforth I know thee, only to forget.'
'Thou canst not!'—'It may be, that thus my fate
   Hath spoken; but my resolute will is set,
      In manhood,—and I know,
      Though all of life be wo,
Thus better—than with faithlessness to mate.'

"She crouch'd beneath his feet, incapable
   Of answer to that speech; and his sad look,
As if his eyes acknowledged still a spell,
   One long, deep survey of the woman took;—
      She still unseeing aught,
      Of that sad, searching thought,
Which, speaking through his eye, her soul could never brook.

"Sudden as spectre, waving wide his hand,
   He parted from her presence:—He was gone,
Into the shadows of that forest land;
   And, desolate now, the woman lay alone,—
      Crouching beside the hearth,
      Whilst thousand fears had birth,
Haunting her thought with griefs more fearful than the known.

"Our story here is ended. Of her fate
   Nothing remains to us, but that she sold,
Of Accabee, the beautiful estate,
   And sought her shelter in the city's fold;
      The purchaser, meanwhile,
      Made the dark forest smile,
And crown'd its walks with works most lovely to behold.

"A noble dwelling rose amidst the trees,
   Fair statues crown'd the vistas—pathways broke
The umbrageous shadows,—and sweet melodies,

Among the groves, at noon and morning woke;—
   And great reserves of game,
   In which the wild grew tame—
And pleasant lakes, by art, were scoop'd for fisheries.

"Here pleasure strove to make her own abode;
   She left no mood uncherish'd which might cheer;
Through the grim forests she threw wide the road,
   And welcom'd Beauty, while expelling care:
     Wealth spared no toils to bless,
     And still, with due caress,
Honor'd the daily groups that sought for pastime there.

"But still the spot was haunted by a grief;—
   Joy ever sank in sadness:—guests depart;
A something sorrowful, beyond belief,
   Impairs the charms of music and of art;
     'Till sadly went each grace,
     And, as you see the place,
Gradual the ruin grew, a grief to eye and heart.

"The native genius, born in solitude,
   Is still a thing of sorrow; and his spell,
Whatever be the graft of foreign mood,
   Maintains its ancient, sorrowful, aspect well;—
     Still reigns its gloomy lord,
     With all his sway restored,
Lone, o'er his barren sceptre doom'd to brood."

Slow sped our skiff into the open light,—
   The billows bright before us,—but no more
Rose love's sweet ditty on our ears that night;—
   Silent the maid look'd back upon the shore,
     And thought of those dark groves,
     And that wild chieftain's loves,
As they had been a truth her heart had felt of yore.

1849

Simms had at one time hoped to publish "The Last Fields of the Biloxi" in a collection of "Tales in verse, illustrative of events in our history in the different states" under the title *Lays of Apalachia*—the plans for which did not materialize. The poem in its final form appeared among "Tales and Traditions of the South" in *Poems Descriptive, Dramatic, Legendary and Contemplative* (1853). "The Last Fields of the Biloxi" illustrates Simms's use of Native American legend for the purposes of fiction, with the unusual theme of the destruction of one Indian tribe ("rich and populous people, accomplished in the arts") by another, barbaric rather than artistic.

❧ The Last Fields of the Biloxi; A Tradition of Louisiana

[Simms's note] *The Bay of Pascagoula is a lovely and retired spot, lying at nearly equal travelling distances between the cities of Mobile and New Orleans. It has long been famous among persons of taste in those cities for its quiet beauties; but more so on account of a very singular and sweet superstition which pertains to it. A remarkable, and most spiritual kind of music, is heard above and around its waters, from which it is supposed to issue. The sound is fitful occurring by day and night, at all hours, sometimes with more or less strength and fulness, but always very sweet and touching in its strains. Some compare it to the wind-harp, which, indeed, it sometimes most wonderfully resembles. Others liken it to the humming of an insect of great and curious powers. The Indian tradition explanatory of this music,—which no philosophical explanation has yet ventured to disturb,—is one of a beauty not often surpassed. The story goes that the whole Southwest was once controlled, and in the possession of a people called the Biloxi; that these people had attained a very high, if not perfect civilization— that they were versed in various arts, profound lovers of music, and were finally enervated by the arts which they possessed. They were overrun and conquered by the fiercer tribes coming from the West. They made a last stand on the borders of the sea, by Pascagoula, when driven from all other positions. Here they erected a fortress, the ruins of which are still said to be seen; though the work so described as theirs was probably erected by some of the roving bands of Spanish and French who first brought European civilization into the country. The last struggles of the Biloxi were protracted, as became the efforts of a brave nation fighting for life and liberty. But they fought in vain. Famine came in to the assistance of their enemies, and unconditional submission or death were the only alternatives. They* chose the last; and men, women, and children proceeded to the sacrifice—which was as solemn, and perhaps more touching, than that of the citizens of Numantia under like circumstances. Throwing open the gates of their fortress, at a moment when the assailants are withdrawn, they marched down to the waters of the bay, singing their last song of death and defiance. With unshaken resolution they pressed forward until the waters finally engulfed them all. None survived. The strange spiritual music of the Bay of Pascagoula is said to be the haunting echo of that last melancholy strain. . . . The Poet is supposed to be a spectator of the scene,—one greatly ravished with the quiet and sweet beauty of the landscape, and beguiled by it into a long train of dreamy speculations, which insensibly conduct him to the state of mind when he shall be most susceptible to spiritual influences. It is then that he is suddenly made aware of the awakening murmurs of the mysterious music. The reflections which precede the revelation are designed as a natural prelude to the strain.

I.

Beautiful spread these waters 'neath mine eye,
Glassy and bright, with myrtles overhung;
Blue stretch the heavens above them—in their depths,
Far down reflected—arch more beautiful,
Seen through the mellowing medium of the wave,
Than in its native empire,—spann'd above,
Blazing, all cloudless, with the noonday star.
I wander by the islets near the sea,
That, from the Mexique bay, a tribute deep,
Rolls on in Pascagoula. There it sinks,
And sleeps with faintest murmurs; or, with strife
Brought from more turbulent regions, still bears on,
With threatening crest, and lips of whitening foam,
To battle with Biloxi. Short the strife!
Feebler at each recoil, its languid waves
Fling themselves, listless, on the yellow sands,
With a sweet chiding, as of grief that moans,
Oblivious not in slumber, of the strife,
That slumber still subdues. A dream of peace
Succeeds, and all her images arise,
To hallow the fair picture. Ocean sleeps

Lock'd in by earth's embrace. Her islets stand
Grey sentinels, that guard her waste domain,
And, from their watch-towers station'd by the deep,
Survey the midnight legions of the Gulf,
Numberless, wild, in their blue armor clad,
Forever bent on spoil. A sweet repose
Hangs o'er the groves, and on the sloping shore
And the far ocean. Not a murmur chides
The sacred silence. From the lone lagoon,
The patriarch of the ancient pelican,
Leads forth his train; though not with plashy wing
Break they the glassy stream, whose buoyant wave
Maintains each breast, and still reflects each form,
Without a ripple on its face to mar
The perfect image. Gliding thus, they steer
To islands of green rushes, where they hide
In sports most human;—in white glimpses seen,—
Or by the light tops of the reeds that stoop,
Divided in the press of struggling forms.
But rapture hath a reign as short as peace—
The wild fowls' sports are ended. They repose
By the still marge of lakes, that, in the embrace
Of groves of cane and myrtle, steal away,
And crouch in sleep secure; while through the Gulf
Rolls the black hurricane. The summer noon
Prevails. A universal hush
Absorbs the drowsy hours, and Nature droops
With sweetness; as upon the listless eyes
Of beauty, steal the images of dreams,
Made up of star-crown'd hopes and truest loves,
And joy's own purple prospects. The still air
Falters with perfume of delicious fruits;—
The orange flings its fragrance to the seas,
Wooing the zephyr thence; and lo! he comes
Fresh from the toiling conflict with the deep,
Upon whose breast, subduing and subdued,
He snatches fitful rest. The glassy wave,

Smooth and serene as heaven, is broken now
Into complaining ripples. Now, his breath
Sweeps the rush islands, while the tall reed stoops
Its feathery crest to ocean. The gray sands,
Whirl'd suddenly beneath his arrowy tread,
Pursue his flight in vain;—and now he glides
Over the sacred bay, whose clear serene
Is whimpled by his wing. Anon, he stirs
The orange blossoms,—drinks full surfeit thence,
And sleeps among their leaves.

II.

I lay me down
In the sweet keeping of the wilderness,
Listless and blest as he! Not wild to me,
Though lonely, all the silent groves and streams,
That slumber in my glance. For I have been
A wanderer, and denied all human ties:—
I made my friends among the hills and streams
Least loved or sought by man. To me, they wear
Aspects of love and kindness. Voices call,
And fair hands beckon me from alleys green,
Amidst a world of shadow;—solitudes
That woo the thoughtful footstep, and persuade
To realms of pensive silence,—beautiful groves,
Sad only, as their beauty blooms unsought.

III.

These win me from my path. I turn aside;
My heart drinks in the sweetness of the scene
I gaze on;—and how lovelier grows the spot,
To him who comes in love! I bow my head—
Where still she holds her matchless sov'reignty—
To all endowing Nature. Here she sits
Supreme, in tangled bower, and sunny mead,
And high umbrageous forest. At her feet,
Broad lakes spread forth their bosoms to the skies,
Whose beauties still they bear. Sweet fountains swell
From loneliest depths, among the hidden dells.

That, crouching 'neath the sway of sullen hills,
Yet send their crystal sorrows down the stream,
In secret channels; that the world may seek,
And free them from their darksome prison-place.
Tree, flower, and leaf, consorting with her mood,
Impress their calm on mine. I lay me down,
Within her solemn temple. Altars rise
About me, of green turf; and tufted beds,
Of grassy and blue flowers, beneath my head,
Pillow it gently. Mightiest subjects stand
Around me, grouped, and bending still, to serve—
Thick-bearded giants, that spread wide their arms,
And shield me from the burning shafts of noon.

IV.

Now, sweeter than the soft recorder's voice,
Or lute of ravishing syren, in mine ear,
This gentle diapason of the woods—
This sacred concert,—airs with bending pines,
Whose murmurs melt to one, and part again
With new accords,—with now a catch of song,
From bird that starts and sleeps. The fancy glows
In spiritual converse, as I dream
Of the old fated men of these sweet plains,—
Departed—all their dwelling-places waste,
And their wild gods grown powerless!

                      Powerless?—No!
They have a spell for fancy, and a charm
To waken echoes in the dreaming heart;
And from the prompt and sleepless sympathies,
Extort unfailing homage. For the Past,
They live, and live forever! That which speaks
For the sole moral of the faded race,
Dies not when it hath perished. Song will speak,—
Tradition, and the venerable groves,
With mounds, and fragments of old implements,
Even for the heathen;—as in temples, books,
Old columns, and the echoes of deep strains

From Phœbus-smitten minstrels, still survive
The proofs of mightier nations—godlike proofs,
That challenge human toil, the tooth of time,
And speak when he is voiceless. These connect
Races which mingle not; whose separate eyes—
By years and oceans separate—never saw
Their mutual aspects; yet, by sympathies,
Born of like trials, strifes, and mightiest deeds,
Yearn for communion,—yearn to see and love;
And when the earthquake threatens, bear, in flight,
Each glorious token of the transmitted race.

V.

Thus lives the savage god. Here, still, he roves
Among his hills made consecrate. Here, still,—
By this broad glassy lake, among these groves
Of yellow fruits and fragrance,—o'er yon isles,
The limit of his reign,—his old gray eye
Still ranges, as if watchful of the trust
His sway no more may compass.

———————Yet, no more
Gather the simple tribes that bow'd the knee,
In love, or deprecation of his wrath;—
No more from plain to hill-top glows the pile
Fired in his sacrifice;—and, to glad his ear,
Rolls the deep strain of forest worshippers,
A wild and antique song of faith and fear,
No more! no more!

VI.

———————'Tis sure a dream that stirs
These sounds within my soul; or, do I hear
A swell of song,—sweet, sad, upon mine ear,
That, like a wayward chant from out the sea,
Rises and floats along the yellow sands!
A note most like the wind-harp, hung in trees
Where the coy zephyr harbors. Still it comes,
In more elaborate windings; with a tone
Most human, and a fitfulness of sound

That speaks for various woes, as if it link'd
The deep, despairing, still defying cry,
From man in his last struggle,—with the shriek
Of passionate woman, not afraid to die,
Though pleading still for pity,—and the scream
Of childhood, conscious only of the woes
It feels not, but beholds in those who feel,
Unutterable still! A long-drawn plaint,
It swells and soars, until the difficult breath
Fails me;—I gasp;—I may not follow it
With auditory sense! It glows—it spreads—
'Till the whole living atmosphere is flush
With the strange harmony; and now it sinks,
Sudden, but not extinguished! A faint tone
Survives, in quivering murmurs, that awhile
Tremble like life within the flickering pulse
Of the consumptive. Losing it, we hush
Our breathing; and suspend the struggling sense,
Whose utterance mars its own; and still we hear
Its mellow and lone cadences, that float,
Prolong'd, and finally lost, as the deep sounds
Superior rise, of winds and waving trees!

VII.

It is a sweet tradition of these shores,
Told by the Choctaw, that, when ages gone,
His savage sire descended from the west,
A dark and desperate hunter,—all these woods,
From the rich valleys where the Missouri bounds,
To mix his turbid waters with the streams
Of him, the Sire of Waters,*—to the blue hills
Of Apalachia,—dwelt a numerous race,
Named "The Biloxi." Towns and villages,
Cities and colleges, and various arts,
Declared their vast antiquity. They were proud—
More proud than all the living tribes of men;

---

* [SIMMS'S NOTE] The Mississippi.

Wiser, and versed in many sciences;
And, from their towers of earth, that sought the skies,
In emulous mountain-stretches, watch'd the stars,
In nightly contemplation. With a skill
Wondrous, by other tribes unmatchable,
They rear'd high temples, which they fill'd with forms
Of love and beauty. In their thousand homes,
Joy was a living presence. There they danced
At evening; while the mellow song went forth,
Married to fitting strains, from instruments
Of curious form, but fill'd with strangest power,
That, when the savage hearken'd, half subdued
His bloody thirst, and made the reptile's fang
Forget his venomous office. By these arts
Were they at last betray'd. They soon forgot
The vigorous toils of manhood, and grew weak,
Incapable of arms. Voluptuous joys,
Morning and evening in their courts, surprised
The strength of their young people till they grew,
Like the rank grass upon the bearded plain,
Fit for fire and scythe.

VIII.

————The Choctaw Chief
Look'd, from his dusky hills, upon their vales,
Exulting. When he heard their songs of love,
That floated upward on the perfumed air,
And saw, below, their loose, effeminate forms
Link'd in voluptuous dance,—he shouted loud
His scornful satisfaction; while he bade
His warriors nigh, to look upon their homes,
And mark their easy victims. They, below,
By happiness made deaf and arrogant,
Heard not the mighty discord, which, above,
Mock'd their soft harmonies. Their dream went on;
The midnight dance and revel; the sweet song
Of love and gold-eyed fancy; and the prayer,
Unbroken, of true genius, in his cell,

Toiling, with pen or pencil, to prepare
His triumph for the adoring eyes of day!

IX.

But with the day came conflict. The fierce tribes,
With hellish shout, that shook the affrighted walls
Till the high temples quaked, rush'd down the vale,
Smiting with heavy mace; or, from above,
Shooting their poison'd arrows at each mark,
Unerring. Though surprised, the Biloxi fought
Fiercely, and with an ardency of soul
Superior to their strength. The savage press'd
More resolute when baffled. Day by day,
Some citadel was won—some lovelier town
Despoil'd by the barbarian. Thousands fell
In conflict; yet the thousands that remain'd
Breathed nothing but defiance. With each loss,
Rose a new spirit in their hopeless breasts,
That warm'd them with fresh courage; and they swore
A terrible oath, with link'd hands, each in each,
And all, to their old deities, to yield
Life first, and freedom never! Well they kept
Their sacramental pledges. They could die,
But could not conquer. Yielding sullenly
Each foothold, they departed from the towns
They could no more maintain; and, fighting, fled;
Till from the hills of Memphis—from the springs
Of Loosahatchie—from the golden ridge,
Where the gay streams of Noxabee arise,—
Contented captives that complain not oft
Against the rocks, that, from the western streams,
Bar their free passage—gradual still they fled—
Still turning, still at bay, and battling oft
The dread pursuer.

X.

————To this spot they came—
They pitch'd their tents where Pascagoula flows,
Through shallows of gray shells, and finds its way

To the embraces of the purple Gulf.
"Here!" said the Prince—his subjects gather'd round—
"Make the last stand! The land beneath our feet
Slips rapidly, and farther flight is none,
Save to the ocean. We must stand and die!"

XI.

Sad were their hearts, but fearless. Not a lip
Spoke for submission. Soul and arm were firm;
And here, in resolute silence, they threw up
Their earthen ramparts. On the narrow walls
Of their rude fortress, in that perilous hour,
Ranged their few champions. To the hills, their eyes
Turn'd ever, till the savage rose in sight.
Then they took up their weapons. Flight no more
Was in their choice; but, in its place, there came,
From hopelessness, resolve—and such resolve,
As makes man terrible as fate. They stood,
Silent, with lips compress'd. No answering shout
Admonish'd the invader of the strength
Thus newly found; and down his warriors rush'd,
As to an easy conquest. But they shrunk,—
And wonder'd whence should come the singular might,
So sudden, of a race so feeble late!
Days, weeks, and months, and the Biloxi fought,
Invincible. Their narrow boundary grew
More strong and powerful, in the invader's eyes,
Than had been their sole empire. Spring, at length,
Put on her flowers. Green leaves and blossoming fruits
Declared for mercy; but the barbarian tribes,
Strengthen'd by fiercer thousands from the west,
Maintain'd the leaguer. Rescue there was none;
Despair had no more strength, for famine sapp'd
The hearts of the Biloxi.

XII.

One bright noon
Beheld them met in council—women and men;
The mother newly made, with the young babe,
Unconscious, striving at her bloodless breasts;—

For all are equal in the hour of woe,
And all are heard, or none!—
                            It needed not
That they should ask what doom awaited them!
They saw it in the tottering march—the face,
Pinch'd by lean famine;—the imperfect speech,
That falter'd with the syllable prolong'd;—
The hollow eyes from which a spiritual glare
Shot out like death. They saw it in all sights,
And sounds, that fate, in that protracted term
Of struggle and endurance, still vouchsafed;—
And there was silence—a long, dreary pause
Broken by feminine sobs. Then spoke the Prince,
Last of a line of kings!—
                        ——"Shall we submit
To bonds and probable torture, or go forth,
Made free by death?"
                      Brief silence follow'd then:—
In that brief silence, memories of years,
And ages, crowded thick. Years of delight—
Ages of national fame! They thought of all
The grace of their old homes,—the charm, the song,
Pure rights and soothing offices,—and pride,
Made household, by the trophies, richly strown,
Through court and chamber, of creative art;—
All lost!—and then the probable doom of bonds,—
The only slavery,—the superior race
Bow'd to the base and barbarous!—and one voice
Proclaim'd the unanimous will of all—to die!

XIII.

That eve, while yet within the western heavens,
Linger'd the rosy sunset—while the waves
Lay calm before them in the crystal bay,
And the soft winds were sleeping—and a smile,
As of unbroken peace and happiness,
Mantled the glittering forest green, and far,
Sprinkled the yellow beach with glinting fires,
That shone like precious gems;—the destined race

Threw wide their fortress gate. Thence went they forth
In sad procession. At their head, the Prince,
Who still had led their fortunes;—then, the chiefs,
And soldiers—few, but fearless;—the old men—
Patriarchs, who still remain'd,—memorials
Of the more fortunate past—and, last of all,
The women and the children. 'Twas an hour,
When Nature craved a respite from her toils;
And, from the strife withdrawn, the savage foe
Were distant, in their woodland tents retired.
These started with strange wonder to behold
The solemn march, unwitting of its end
And glorious aim; nor strove they to disturb
The rights which they divined not. On they went,
That ancient nation. Weapons bore they none;
But with hands cross'd upon their fearless hearts,
The warriors led the way. The matron clung
To her son's arm, that yielded no support.
The infant, hush'd upon its mother's breast,
Was sleeping; but the mother's sobs were still
Audible with her song;—and, with her song,
Rose that of thousands, mingling in one strain!
The art which in their happier days had been
Most loved among them, in spontaneous voice,
Unsummon'd, pour'd itself upon the air,
As, slowly, but with steps unfaltering still,
March'd the pale band, self-destined to the deep!
Never had Ocean in his balmiest hours,
Look'd less like death—less terrible, less wild!
An infant's slumber had not been more free
From all commotion. Beautiful and bright,
In the declining sunset, lay the scene
That witness'd the sad sacrifice; and sweet,
Like the fair prospect, was the united song,—
That epicedium o'er a nation's fate,
Self-chanted, which went with them to the waves,
And still survives them—breathing, from their graves,

The story of their empire,—of its fame,—
Its fall, and their devoted faith that knew
No life unbless'd with freedom. Sweetest strain!—
Once more it rises into sounds, that grow
Human in strength; and now, it floats away,
Subdued and sinking, as in that sad hour
When its last breathings from the warrior's throat
Stopp'd suddenly; and through the desolate air
Went a more desolate hush that told the rest!

WHEN INTENSELY STUDYING William Bartram's *Travels* during the 1840s, Simms made extensive notes (see above, xix–xx)—"mostly in a metrical form," he later explained, "—in blank verse—using his imagery and amplifying his suggestions with my own, the better to perfect his pictures." James Kibler recognized the poetic quality of Simms's "Notes from Bartram" and published a selection in his definitive edition, *Selected Poems of William Gilmore Simms* (1990), 116–25; see also 356–57.

ᴄᴠ *Indians Spearing Salmon*

The red man that you see,
Reclining on the bank above the stream,
Watches the unconscious salmon as he glides,
Beneath the bluff, and with his arrowy shaft,
Transfixes his bright sides.

1858

IN HIS OWN HEADNOTE to "Thlecathcha; or the Broken Arrow," as well as in the poem itself, Simms judiciously gives both sides of William McIntosh's assassination by Menawe and thus heightens the tragedy both of the murder of the chief and of his perceived betrayal of his people to the whites. The ambiguity of McIntosh's actions Simms fully captures: good motives lead him to negotiate with the United States in the best interest of his people versus any cession of Muscoghee land displaces his people and violates his own sacred pledge.

Thlecathcha; or, the Broken Arrow

It was a voice of wail, and yet a song—
Such song as wells from soul of bitterness,
That finds no adequate voice in common speech,
And yet *must* speak; and from its agony
Draws its best music.
     Through the forest rang
That strange, sad chaunt—that might have been despair,
But that exulting memories of old days
Blent pride with agony; and lifted up
The spirit, through its sorrows, into Hope!
Look through the pines, where, droopingly, they wind,
In sad procession, gloomy as the waste,
Whose shades primeval shroud them as they go—
A thousand warriors of the wild, strong men,
Lithe and well sinew'd; but with drooping gait,
As of the falcon wounded in the wing;
Yet, with a fiery glare in each dark eye
Dilating, that looks battle to the last,
And asks for grand revenges.
     By the side
Of each stern warrior, see, a woman glides,
Slowly as sadly; yet, with foot as firm
As if the ancient plain o'er which she treads
Might yet be called her own. One hand conducts
A boy, with bended bow within his grasp,
The little shaft made ready on the string,
As if for mimic battle. On her back
She bears a muffled infant, whose black eyes
Peer o'er her shoulder—lively, full of light,
As curious of the progress, all unknown.

So journey on the melancholy group;
Long, winding trains; peoples of several tribes;
The fragments of a nation torn with strifes,
And now divided; sunder'd, cut in twain

By subtlety, and the treacherous arts of men,
Who, in the guise of Christian love and peace,
Brought poison to the camps of the wild race,
And drug'd their veins with passions born of hell.

They skirt the hill; they wind throughout the plain;
And now they crowd together, in a *cirque,*
Around a gloomy realm—a mystic haunt,
Sacred to ancient memories, and the dead
Of the lost ages of long centuries.
'Tis the performance of a sacred rite,
Ere yet they take their way from the old homes,
To seek, in exile, for a strange abode,
Unnatural, and never to persuade
The old affections of the birthplace born,
To any living exercise of Hope.

That wailing chaunt, that pauses and subsides,
To find renewal, most irregular;
Discordant, passionate, wild, yet still subdued,
As, in obedience to the moment mood,
Now rises into diapason deep,
As of the gathering eagles of the rocks,
Because of some dark destiny, that made
Their rocky realm a dread, and doomed their flight
O'er unknown tracts of ocean.

                    Never a tear
Swells in the great eyes of the warrior men;
Nor do the women weep, how e'er they wail!
Sadly, but sternly—desolate, but strong—
These stoics of the forest and the wild,
Have reached the ideals of philosophy,
Without its books or teachers—taught by nature
How little the tear may profit the strong man,
Or soften fates, he may no longer brave!

The circle opens wide; and, in the midst,
Even as the stern, monotonous, sad chaunt,
Hath reached its utmost volume, there is seen,
On a rude bier, the *Micco* of their race,
The mighty chief—colossal—he who stood,
With head and shoulders taller than the rest!

"Thlecathcha!"—ominous name, which, in our tongue,
Denotes the "Broken Arrow!"

     Stretched at length,
He, broken lies!—
     The tall and muscular form,
Reposes, as in sleep, in warrior garb,
As when he went to battle!—

    On his head
A feathery circlet, with a single quill,
Fresh plucked from out the mountain eagle's wing!
His right hand grasps the tomahawk—his left
The sheaf of *broken* arrows.
    On his breast
Hang medals, tributes from the pale white race,
To him, the red chief, whom they held a brother,
Having led his tribe to battle in their wars!

Cold and unconscious, he will lead no more
His braves to battle. He will teach no more,
With voice made sweetly subtle for all senses,
His chiefs in the Great Council; never more
Persuade to peace, or with wild eloquence
Inspire their rages for the work of war!

He had been their patriarch! In his fall they lose
Their country!
    From his death their exile flows—
And, with the moment-growing consciousness
Of what he had been, and can be no more,
Swells the deep chaunt anew.

Well may they wail,
For broken is the arrow from their bow;
Their mightiest overthrown, and—all is o'er;
And we but rescue from their parting song,
In feeble strain, of our less passionate tongue,
The fond memories of that burial rite:

Ye warriors, who gather the brave to deplore,
With a wail o'er the chief who shall lead you no more,
Let the hatchet of fight still unburied remain,
While we joy in the glory of him that is slain.

Unfettered in soul as unfearing in fight,
In council and conflict still greater in might;
In battle the tiger, in peace the young fawn,
Whose footstep scarce brushes the dew from the lawn.

Saw ye not, in the thick of the battle's affray,
While the warm blood, like rain, o'er the smoking grass lay,
How the Seminole braves from his tomahawk fled,
While the best of their warriors beneath him lay dead.

How long did their women in agony mourn,
Looking forth for their chiefs who shall never return,
For their scalps the full swell of his legs have embraced,
While their corses, unburied, still cumber the waste.

And when did the braves of the Cherokee dare
To sing their proud war-song in sight of his lair?
He had tracked them through thickets that never knew path,
Till they crouched and did homage to soften his wrath.

Not in vain were his triumphs, though now we deplore
That he leads us to triumph in battle no more;
He has fought the good fight to the last, and now goes
Where the Great Spirit crowns him with sway o'er his foes.

His death-song was grand as the storm wind that leaps
Like the torrent that sudden bursts high o'er the steeps;

Its echoes poured down the great valleys, 'mid cries
From the people who roar when the great chieftain dies.

Not for him be the wail, as we gaze on the face
Of the bravest and best that e'er died for his race;
Our right hand hath perished that gave us the might,
And the arrow lies broken that won us the fight.

Heard ye not his proud speech at the closing of day,
When he knew that the wolf was all hot for the fray;
When he dream'd how the snake from the covert would steal,
Yet sounding no rattle, to strike at his heel.

Had he given but warning, how quick were the blow
To crush with the hatchet the head of the foe,
Had they sought him by day, though with hundreds to one,
How greater than all were the deeds he had done!

Far off, through the forests, when evening grew still,
We heard the long howl of the wolf on the hill—
And, "hark!" cried the chief, at the hiss, soft and low,
"'Tis the tongue of Menawe, the snake, from below.

"They come not, the cowards, to brave me in fight,
While my people look on, with the Day-God in sight,
But sly, through the covert, as subtly as base,
The heel they would sting, always fearing the face.

"They have gathered their hosts, all with hearts full of hate,
They would gird me with fire, and o'erwhelm me with fate;
But I've lived a long triumph; if now it be o'er,
Nor I, nor my people, have cause to deplore.

"I have rear'd them grand pillars on heights that shall last,
That rise like great smokes o'er the hills of the past;
These shall lead them to valor, where the eagles make song,
Singing ever to the warrior, 'be fearless and strong!'"

Then the chief took his rifle and whetted his knife,
And went where the wolf lay in wait for the strife;
He knew, by the howl and the hiss, where they stood,
Wolf and serpent, both eagerly panting for blood.

Here his voice, like a trumpet, rang out on the air;
But the rifle-shot sped from the wolf in his lair!
There came up a clamor of death to the hill,
And a wail as of women—and all was then still!

And the chieftain lay dead in his gore! but his hand
Still clutched the long knife, buried deep in the sand.
They dared not come nigh him, though dead where he lay,
And they tore not the scalp from his forehead away!

Oh! fling not aside, though the arrow be lost,
The bow we still keep at such perilous cost;
We may find a fit shaft for the string when afar,
And go with the Sioux and Dogskin to war.

Farther west! farther west! where the buffalo roves,
And the red deer still wanders, o'er plains that he loves,
Our hearts shall be glad in the hunt once again,
'Till the white man shall seek for the lands that remain.

Farther west! farther west! where the sun, as he dies,
Still leaves his red robes o'er the couch where he lies;
There the red man shall roam, and his women shall rove,
And the white man not blight what he cannot improve.

One song for our hero—not now of regret—
The song of a sorrow for a sun that has set;
A wail o'er the hills and the valleys, and one
For the great arrow broken—the nation undone!

Farther west! farther west! it is meet that we fly,
Where the red deer still bounds at the glance of an eye;
Yet, slowly the song of our parting be sung,
For the great arrow broken—the great bow unstrung.

1825 (published 1868)

THE MOUNTAIN TRAMP

❧ History of Composition

This publication of "The Mountain Tramp. Tselica; A Legend of the French Broad" uncovers a rough-hewn yet priceless literary treasure that lay buried for more than a century and a half. The complicated history of its origin and composition sheds light on Simms's efforts to get the manuscript completed and published during the 1840s and 50s, but it fails to explain why Simms seems to have put it aside—apparently forgotten, and almost certainly neglected—for almost two decades before his death. The first mention by Simms of his work on "an Indian legend in the octo syllabic" comes in a 17 December 1849 letter to Nathaniel Beverley Tucker (*Letters* 2:573); however, it is evident that the subject had occurred to Simms at least seven or eight years earlier, for the Beinecke Library at Yale has an autograph manuscript of a poem entitled "Tselica, an Indian Legend" (closed with the notation "W. Gilmore Simms / Warm Springs, N.C. / September 1842")—a 64-line poem later modified slightly and published under the title "Tzelica, A Tradition of the French Broad" in the January 1845 opening number of *Southern and Western,* a Charleston magazine founded and edited by Simms.

"Tzelica" (or, in the manuscript, "Tselica") bears so little resemblance to the 2,267-line "The Mountain Tramp" that they may be considered separate poems; but the title character, the setting, and the tragic love theme of "The Mountain Tramp. Tselica; a Legend of the French Broad" were already firmly sketched in Simms's mind. Thus, it is obvious that Simms was taking authorial license by implying to Tucker (in the letter cited above) that he had put little time into the composition of "some 1200 lines" for his "Indian tale." "I like the thing," he casually remarked, "probably because it cost me so little effort," a remark belying the fact that he had taken a poetic conception of years' standing and expanded it by more than 1,100 lines. Simms's effort to discount any serious effort on his part in creating his "Indian tale" is even more manifest in a June 1850 letter to Evert A. Duyckinck in which, after summarizing his current literary work, he adds as an afterthought: "I must not forget, however, an unpublished poem, in the octosyllabic, of 12 or 1400 lines, written almost at a bound, in less than a week—an Indian tale called 'Tselica, the Faithful'—a story of the Cherokee. It is yet to undergo the *labor limae*" (*Letters* 3:19–20).

By July 1852—more than two years later—Simms had doubled the length of his poetic Indian saga—still without its eventual title, yet aptly and enthusiastically described in a letter to publisher George Palmer Putnam:

> I have . . . prepared a volume of somewhat novel character, no less than a descriptive and legendary poem—especially descriptive of the rare, little-known & beautiful scenery of our mountain country. The subject, manner and material are all novel. The poem extends to 2500 lines octosyllabic, and would be enriched with copious notes, original and borrowed from such quaint, pleasant old authors as Adair, Bartram, &c. It would make a handsome volume for illustration and with only a couple of good engravings would probably prove attractive as an annual, at a moderate price. As I concieve myself to have been quite successful in the verse, as well as the plan, I should really anticipate considerable success & circulation for it. (*Letters* 6:130–31)

For whatever reasons, neither Putnam nor E. A. Duyckinck* accepted Simms's invitation to publish his Indian poem. It should be noted that American book publishers of the period—when there was no international copyright law to prevent cheap reprints of British authors—were, in general, reluctant to run the financial risk of publishing lesser-known American writers, especially poets. It seems uncharacteristic of Simms, however, that after 1852 he apparently never again seriously sought a publisher.

But more surprising than Simms's inability to find a publisher for "The Mountain Tramp" is the possibility that after about 1850, he never again returned to the composition of the poem. That "The Mountain Tramp" was a poetic work-in-progress makes his neglect of it puzzling; for even though Simms prided himself on "writing precisely as I speak" and acknowledged

---

* In a letter of 10 November 1852 to Duyckinck, Simms (again, without success) tried the same approach with regard to "Tselica" that had failed with Putnam: "If you relish my Poem (Tselica) give me your notion as to propriety of publishing with copious descriptive, legendary, historical & other notes. Such a vol., say 250 pages, with illustrated titles and vignettes from Darley might be a popular book. Eh?" (*Letters* 3:207).

that though he seldom re-wrote "anything for the press," he added a significant "unless it be poetry" (*Letters* 5:400).* Nevertheless, there is no evidence
that the manuscript here published for the first time was ever touched anew
by Simms after he dated it, in his own hand, "December 1849."

☙ The Poem Itself

In one sense, "The Mountain Tramp. Tselica; a Legend of the French Broad"
is two related poems—or a single poem divided into two nearly equal parts
with different but complementary themes. The first part (or "book"), whose
title might well be "The Mountain Tramp," contains twenty-six chapters
totaling 1,117 lines; the second book, with which "Tselica. A Legend of the
French Broad" really begins, has twenty-eight chapters with a total of 1,150
lines.

The first book, "The Mountain Tramp," establishes the atmosphere and the
background for the Indian tale that follows. It is a celebration of the beauty,
the majesty, the bounty, and the joy of nature—a romantic glorification of
the wilderness. A submerged theme hints at what the loss of the wilderness
would mean to one who loves, appreciates, and nurtures it, as the Indian
does—though no Indian actually appears on the scene until the start of the
second book. The feeling of ecstasy and exuberance associated with being one
with nature is the main theme of the first book—a unity of man and nature
that is spiritual in its recognition of the source of life itself.

The second book, "Tselica; a Legend of the French Broad," or what might
simply be called the "Indian tale of Tselica," intensifies the implicit subtheme
of the first book by narrating the violent and passionate tragedy of the vanishing wilderness and the vanishing Indian. The substance—the sacred land
and its native people—has been destroyed, but the spirit survives. Simms's portrayal of the Indian is three-dimensional, with individual character traits that
run the gamut of human emotions and intelligence. Simms's Indians are pic-
tured with realistic balance as being cruel, malignant, jealous, vengeful, and
cannibalistic as well as loyal, brave, loving, generous, and compassionate—
cowardly and superstitious as well as skillful and imaginative—bombastic

---

* In the same letter to A. J. Pickett, dated 18 March 1848, Simms also conceded that "it
would be better" for a writer "whose aim be reputation" to go over the rough "ms.s." not
just once, but "twice or thrice" (*Letters* 5:400).

and barbarous as well as gentle and caring. But as in Faulkner, the implication in Simms is that it is the iron will, the resoluteness of spirit—what might be called "the strength to endure"*—that defines any people.

Though the point of view throughout the poem is that of "the Captain," the otherwise-unnamed gentleman observer, the first book is largely related by his seventy-year-old guide, "A brave old hunter, lithe and strong" (l. 147), who (like Daniel Nelson in "The Two Camps") speaks in the vernacular of the frontier, and knows and loves the wilderness with an emotion comparable to that of Native Americans. In the second book, however, after the old hunter asks his guest, "Hast not heard / the Indian story?" (ll. 1119–20), and "the legend of our guide" (l. 1175) commences, the protagonist takes over as interpreter. Thereafter, weaving "our tale in statelier rhyme" (l. 1190), the omniscient narrator holds forth in a tone more elevated, but in language more inflated and overwrought than that of the colorful, archaic, yet simpler speech of the guide.

⟶ Editorial Principles for Transcribing "The Mountain Tramp"

1. Because of the roughness of Simms's manuscript and the difficulty in interpretting many passages, this poem is an exception to the editorial principle of providing a clear text uncluttered by footnotes other than those of the author. In this case only, the footnotes are those of the editors.
2. The page numbers of the autograph manuscript are placed within the text in brackets [ ]. Brackets are likewise used to indicate the editorial division of the poem into Book One and Book Two.
3. Since Simms, by force of habit, perhaps unconsciously, seems to make some kind of mark at the end of most lines, it is difficult to determine whether or not such marks (frequently only pinpoints) are intended as marks of punctuation. In these instances, when what he has written appears to be a comma (a mark he uses profusely), a comma has been transcribed if so doing does no harm to the meaning or does not, for instance, separate a subject from its verb. Most of the end-of-line marks appear to be simply imprecise dots rather than commas or periods. It is

---

* In the last novel published in Simms's lifetime, *Voltmeier* (1869), the title character— in many ways a personification of Simms—is an iron-willed intellectual who has suffered adversity's sharpest pangs; yet he proclaims in the end: "I have the strength to endure. I have endured!" (212).

often difficult to distinguish between Simms's colons and semi-colons. In all instances, the editors have tried to establish the author's intent and to follow it to the best of their ability. For instance, lines crossed out in the autograph manuscript have not been retained in the printed text.

4. Simms uses both *red man* and *redman* in manuscript; it is regularized here to be two words. Simms traditionally misspells words with *ei* after *c* to read *ie*. These spelling errors have been emended. In order to retain the flavor of the original, however, the editors have chosen not to emend all spelling errors, particularly misspellings of proper nouns (other than *Tselica* and *Ockwallee*) and other words that represent nineteenth-century variants and present no difficulty in comprehension.

5. Simms spells the female protagonist's name both *Tselica* and *Tzelica*. Throughout the poem, the name has been spelled *Tselica* in keeping Simms's intent as expressed in his title. Spelling of the male protagonist's name (occasionally *Ockwalee*) has been regularized to *Ockwallee*.

6. Simms's manuscript fairly consistently uses an ampersand to indicate the word *and*. All of these ampersands have been emended to read *and*.

7. Simms's irregular use of apostrophes has been regularized.

ᗊ *The Mountain Tramp.*

TSELICA; A LEGEND OF THE FRENCH BROAD

[BOOK ONE]

I.

The sun that dries our lowland rills
But warms the Apalachian hills;
And he who droops upon the plain,
By burning skies and airs oppress'd
There wins his manhood back again,   5
And feels new raptures fill his breast.
The sultry breath of lowland skies
Burns never there the heart and eyes;

Title *Tselica:* This may be Simms's transcription of *Tsalagi,* the word the Cherokees used to refer to themselves. Since Tsalagi has no Cherokee etymology, it is thought to have been a loan-word, possibly from the Muskogean *Chelookhookâlke,* "people of a different speech."

The fogs leap from marshy tracts that spread,
And fill the soul with dreams of dread   10
Still cling above the plain, nor dare
The conflict with the mountain air,
Dispersed by winds as wild as those,
That rouse the ocean's maddest throes,
And borne o'er billowy heights that brave   15
The skies more proudly than the wave.
[Page 2]Thither for health, for genial airs,
And generous sports, the heart repairs,
Flings by the load of heavy toil,
The gnawing care for petty spoil,   20
Forgets the cloud, the heat, the gloom,
That crush'd, as with a sense of doom.
And in great dells, where breezes play,
Unflagging, through the summer day.
Cheer'd with fresh draughts of eagle life,   25
The form o'erwearied in the strife
The pallid cheek, the languid eye.
Here gathers health with liberty.
'Till all the soul exults, in sooth,
As with renewal of its youth;   30
The eye and heart, the blood and brain,
Commune in sympathy again.
We gain the mountain tops, and trace
The world's best beauties in her face;
There spread the billowy heights away,   35
A thousand miles, as if in play;
There lie the fields of green below
How pure the sight, how fair the show;
The eagle soars between, and lies,
Poised on his broad expanse of wing,   40
[Page 3]A matchless emblem for the eyes,
That long, like him, to soar and spring;
To gain the wondrous heights which woo,
Ambition, and approve it too;
To rise forever from the earth,   45

As seeking still its place of birth:
Regions of height that sway the sense,
Nor less the soul, with dreams of peace
Forms that with great benevolence,
Look round, and bid the fields increase;   50
And various wonders that the eye
Rejoices as it sees,—the soul,
Thus fitly fashioned by the sky,
Gladdening beneath the strange control.
The mighty stretch of tower, that soars,   55
Forever on and on, a sea
Whose billowy tops seek other shores,
Than those to which our prows are free.
Scooped out below, how like a dream
That o'er its nameless raptures broods,   60
The vale all flowers, with but one gleam,
To lighten up its curtained woods,
A silvery serpent gliding, still,
With scarce the murmur of a rill,
[Page 4]As loth to scare the flow'rs that crave   65
The kisses of its gentle wave.
Or, would your heart a sterner choice,
A scene of strife and grandeur hail,
And hearken to a wilder voice,
Than whispers in that dreamy vale?   70
Then cross yon mighty crags that rise,
As if to bear or breast the skies;
And, hark the crash of streams that leap
In headlong ardour for the deep,
Great flashing forms of white that dart   75
From lofty home, through sheltering groves,
As maddening with a human heart,
Torn by rash doubts, and hopeless loves:—
Broken, dishevelled, far below,
Convulsed and writhing, while their moans,   80
Cries of a never ceasing wo,
Swell, mingling with the mountain tones:—

Mysterious plainings of the wind,
Through pieces of rock, and caverns drear,
Where howls of the cougar to his kind,   85
Where glides the panther, sleeps the bear;—
A world of savage solitude,
Unknown, unwrought and unsubdued;
[Page 5]Terribly beautiful and strange,
Yet full of sweet and pleasing change,   90
Leaving no mood to starve, no dream,
However dark, without its gleam,
And making pictures, scenes for art,
That fill the thought, and soothe the heart.

II.

By toils of study wearied long   95
I fled the city's heat and throng,
And took my way with spirits light
That lighter grew as on I sped
To gain Saluda's mountain height,
And drowse upon his sovereign head.   100
With rifle arm'd, in hunter garb,
I cross'd with joy mine Indian barb,
A neat, light, gay, surefooted steed,
Of certain Andalusian breed,
The gift of Soto's Cavaliers,   105
When first they cross'd their knightly spears,
With Apalachian darts, and felt,
How sharp the stroke the red man dealt!

---

99 *Saluda:* a river and range of mountains in northwestern South Carolina. Here and elsewhere, Simms seemingly intended to add footnotes, but no such footnotes are in the manuscript.

102 *Indian barb:* an Indian horse. The Indians of the Southeast bred several distinguishably different breeds of horses in the eighteenth century, none of which are known to have survived. Almost certainly, they did not come from the Soto expedition, but rather from Spanish horses from Mexico and English horses from Virginia and Charleston. Simms's description of his narrator's horse is inconsistent, however, with eighteenth-century descriptions.

—However wild, I bless'd the deed
Whose issue brought me such a steed;   110
So hardy, swift, so true, so light,
So sleek of limb, so keen of sight
[page 6]So meek at bidding, and so gay,
That eased of toil he still would play,
And when denied all better food,   115
Would always find the canetop good,
Nor, when by straight of travel press'd
Ev'r needed stable for his rest.

III.

We sped, myself and steed, at ease,
Until the tents of men were pass'd;   120
Wild though the scene, 'twas sure to please
Each new one quite unlike the last;
A varied march o'er hill and plain,
Clos'd with the night, begun again,
With dawn; and still the freshening sight,   125
Of wood and vale, in morning's light,
Brought charms to cheer the drooping mood,
And took the sting from solitude.
Our world, the forest paths alone,
It seem'd no other had we known,   130
So natural grew the lengthening way
With fancy ever forth at play,
And not a city care to fling
Its shadows o'er her sunny wing.
Sooth, then, the aspect that I bore,   135
Had mock'd the eye that knew before;
[Page 7]The hunter's shirt, well fringed that flew,
Wide open, as the breezes blew;
Mine Indian legging stain'd with clay,
And mokksens darker still than they;   140
Slouch'd hat of felt, and world of beard,
My gentle city friend had scared,

138 *blew:* Simms wrote *blue,* but his intention was clearly *blew.*

With memories of that brigand lore,
By Radcliffe taught in days of yore.
IV.
But no such doubt oppress'd the guide   145
That met me on Jocassee's side.
A brave old hunter, lithe and strong
Though seventy years had done him wrong,
Had brought him toil, without reward
And left him little save his Bard;—   150
He better loved my savage trim,
As speaking for the man, to him,
Than had I sought him, proudly drest
In city costume, silken vest,
And fashions which we shame to see,   155
Yet wear which leave no motion free,
And fetter manhood till it shapes
The angel monument to the apes.
With honest grasp my hand he shook,—
"You're punctual, Captain, to the book,   160
[Page 8]And now, but make your wishes known,
And all these mountains are your own."
V.
A brave old man, of seventy years,
Scarr'd deeply in the forest strife,
His cheek the panther's totem wears,—   165
That grapple nearly cost him life;
From head to foot, o'er back and breast,
The bear and wolf have left such trace,
As will to life's last hour attest
His matchless trials in the chace;—   170

---

144 *Radcliffe:* Ann Radcliffe (1764–1823), author of the Gothic novels *The Mysteries of Udolpho* (1794) and *The Italian* (1797).
146 *Jocassee:* a mountain and a town in northeastern Oconee County, South Carolina. See story by that title above, 178–96.
147 *hunter:* in Simms's manuscript the word is sometimes capitalized; when referring to the protagonist/character, it has been regularized as *Hunter.*

How quick his hand, how great his skill,
How brave his heart, how firm his will,
What sinews bore him to his prey,
What courage nerved him in the fray.
How keen his sight, how true his aim,   175
How swift his knife, a flash of flame,
As, borne beneath his savage foe,
Half smothered 'neath his shaggy breast,
He felt where first to plant the blow,
Then bade the keen steel do the rest.   180
And now on foot beside my steed,
With equal ease of step and speed,
He climbs the heights, and shows the way
[Page 9]And cheers me at the close of the day,
With promise of supper good and soon.   185
—Be sure I welcomed warm the boon!—
"A short three miles before us now,"
He said— "Behold! Yon mountain's brow,
O'erhangs my cottage; lift your eyes,
And you will see our smokes arise;   190
My girls already know our want,
And, Lord! my larder's never scant:
A venison steak will ease your heart,
If there's a sorrow in that part,
And if it's only in the frame,   195
I reckon the cure is just the same!
We'll give 'em a blast to make 'em hear!"
Then thrice his mellow horn he wound,
A wild, sharp summons, shrill and clear,
That seem'd to shake the hills around,   200
And woke the echoes far and near,
Sent back from each with soft rebound.
Till in a sigh subsides the whole:—
But such a sigh, as if the soul,
Prison'd in every rock, bewail'd   205

178 *shaggy:* Simms first wrote *furry,* then struck through it, and wrote *shaggy.*

The dying notes that late regaled,
And strove itself to make the sound!

VI.

[Page 10]The rock is scaled, the heights are won.
Down, at the moment sinks the sun,
A moment glorious as at dawn,   210
Flush'd ruby red and round, then gone,
Leaving, suffusing distant spires,
The languor of his evening fires
That faintly cheer awhile, then fade
With hills and heights and skies in shade.   215
Then, in their place, another light,
More near is waved before the sight,
Which shows our hunter's home, thrown wide,
His cabin on the Hogback's side;
And at the door, his honest pride,   220
Five stalwart sons, all like their sire,
Well limb'd and never known to tire.
Fearless in any strife, and tried,
In savage fields, with man and beast,
The stillest fiercest at the feast;   225
Could take the trail with any hound,
That ever coursed oe'r hunting ground,
Each with his rifle arm'd, a Fate
To stop the red deer in his bound
The panther, in his leap late,   230
Arrest, and while he writhes in strife,
With his own agony and hate,
[Page 11]Rush in, with sharp and sudden knife,
And 'spite of gnashing foamfleck'd jaws,
The sweep of long and fearful claws,   235

213 Simms's manuscript has a colon (or semicolon) at the end of this line, apparently with the intention of beginning a new clause on the following line (first word, *while*, is struck through). Justification: when Simms changed his mind, he failed to remove the punctuation which was no longer needed.

219 *Hogback:* Hogback Mountain is in the northeastern corner of Greenville County, South Carolina, at the head of the Saluda River.

Pass the keen weapon o'er his throat
And from his carcass rend the coat.

VII.

Such sons of Anak well might glad
The heart of such a guide as mine;
But other children yet he had   240
As fit, in other walks to shine;
His daughters, such ye seldom see,
So fond and fearless—they were three;—
With full and rosy cheeks,—bright eyes
Blue, as if borrowed from their skies,   245
From which they caught their light—a smile
Each word to sweeten, and beguile
The eye, as well as ear, to faith;—
White teeth and rosy lips;—a breath
Like that of flowers;—a motion free   250
And graceful as the bird's a-wing.
To see them spread the board for me
And bring me water from the spring,
I thought of maids of Italy,
And nymphs of Troy. Andromaché,   255
As captive of the Greek, the vase,
[Page 12]Ne'er bore with such a perfect grace.
For proper toils, with willing heart
Begun, pursued, with better teach,
Than all the labour'd laws of art,   260
How best the nameless charm to reach.
The blessing begged, the supper o'er,
The smoking venison well discuss'd,

255 *Andromaché:* in mythology, Andromaché is the daughter of Eëtion, king of Thebes, and the wife of Hector. After the fall of Troy, her son Astyanax was put to death by the Greeks.

263 *discuss'd:* a rare meaning of *discuss* in "to consume (food or drink) enthusiastically." Simms used the same sense of this word in "Indian Sketch" (see above, 128).

Then came the summons to the floor,
The sire would play, and dance we must.   265
Shook the rough rafters then, while swept
The old man's bow his violin;
How swam the girls in grace;—how leapt
The lads—how merrily went the din,
Of rustic pleasure, free from sin   270
As those of angels:—and, with blood
Made glorious with the common mood,
I caught the maiden's outstretched hands,
And whirl'd away to join their bands.
Through circling mazes, forth I sprang   275
As buoyant, with each mellow twang
Of the old violin, while the bow
Went wingèd o'er it, to and fro
As any of that happy brood
That made me happy in their home!   280
Had I a thousand years to roam,
I never shall forget that night,
[Page 13]Of simple, unconstrain'd delight.
That picture, gay but innocent,
Of rustic rapture with content.   285
There, in his oaken chair, the sire,
Sate in the full gleam of the fire,
Drew the swift bow with forest art,
His face displaying all his heart;
So sweet and so benignant;—bless'd   290
With equal sense of joy and rest;—
Eyes shut and chin uplift, and hair,
Thin, streaming from the forehead bare,
Vest open wide, while broad below,
The breast, well bronzed with sun and snow,   295
As if the honest heart beneath
Had nev'r known the need of sheath:
His two dogs at his feet, well tried,

In conflict on that mountain side,
Scarr'd like their master in the strife   300
Yet true, and ready still, with life.

VIII.

That scene, within that rustic hall,
All glowing 'neath the ruddy gleam,
That purpled bright the antler'd wall,
Till all the rafters seem'd aflame;   305
Show'd glittering rifles hung on racks,
And bear and panther skins in packs,
[Page 14]The tools by which the work was done,
The trophy, in the treasures won;—
In groups, the horns and pouches hung   310
From branching antlers hugely spread
Which might, had each possess'd a tongue,
Have told its legend, wild or dread,
Of long and fearful chace, pursuit
Plunged in most savage coverts, where,   315
In equal peril, man and brute,
Might well have felt the pulse of fear;—
And trembled in the wild career,
That brought them to the mountain's edge,
The foaming cataract's dizzy ledge,   320
Where, thundering off from shelving height,
It howls below in rayless night.
But these anon. We shift the scene,
Back to our hall once more. Behold,
How white the canopy and screen,   325
How fair the curtains, fold on fold,
That hide the couches, yet declare
The woman fingers, and her care,
The neat pure tastes, the simple skill,
Most humble yet most lovely still   330

---

314 *chace:* Simms's manuscript has *chase,* but the spelling has been regularized to fit
Simms earlier and later spellings.

319 *edge:* Simms's manuscript has *ledge,* by mistake in anticipation of the following line.

And see the shelves, where gleaming bright,
The homely wares, so clean and white,
Ranged in due order, nay in state,
[Page 15]Pyramidal, of plate o'er plate,
And cup o'er all, with great tureen, 335
The apex—seldom used, I ween!—
Mix'd pictures all around, yet true
To forest need and taste: to these
Add yon great panther's hide in view,
The bright spots outward, flung at ease, 340
Before our Patriarch's couch, the spoil
Of one long day of bloody toil;—
And you've a picture, such as well
May fancy, as the memory spell,
So gay and wild, so free of care, 345
So strange to him the stranger there,
Withal so sweet, as will not part,
While memory lurks from mind or heart!

IX.

We danced till twelve, and then the sire,
Rose up and laid his bow aside; 350
Cast fresh brands on the sinking fire
And threw his little beaufet wide;
Brought forth the honey and the peach,
And Fanny mixed a dram for each,
As skill'd, distilling mountain dews 355
As following up the Dancing Muse.
With temperate joy we gladly quaff'd;
[Page 16]I've seldom swallowed sweeter draught,
But this perchance, was wholly due,
To Fanny's sweetness and her art, 360
Both teaching with an instinct true
How, through the lips to find the heart
She found the way to mine, I wis;

---

352 *beaufet:* from French *buffet* (cupboard).

Mine was the shorter road to bliss,—
I went away with Fanny's kiss! 365

X.

"Now Captain," said to me the Sire,
"I reckon by this time, you tire;
But, as you please; whene'er you'd rest,
Why, there's your bed; it's not the best;
But, I would make an even bet, 370
My rifle 'gainst a reed, you'll lie,
As soundly underneath that net
As under royal canopy.
I reckon England's Queen ha'nt got,
So fine and high a sleeping spot, 375
The sky so fine, the sight so wide,
A hundred miles on every side,
Mountains and vallies, streams and trees,
Such beauty rocks, and such a breeze,
And jist as day begins to break, 380
Such an immortal venison steak.
[Page 17]You'll hear my horse at dawn; then spring
From bed as sprigh as bird a-wing,
And make your appetite so keen,
That it shall slice the meat unseen! 385
Good night!"
"Good night!"
He laid him down
Upon the couch most near my own:
A shed received the boys, but whither 390
The girls had fled, I never knew.
My thoughts awhile pursued them thither,
As well they might, the merry crew!
The sire soon slept, but not for me,
So soon as he had sworn, did sleep 395

---

371 *lie:* Simms originally wrote *sleep* (crossed out), then substituted *lie* to get the (imperfect) rhyme with *canopy.*

379 *beauty:* in the sense of *beautiful* (which would have thrown off the meter).

395 *sworn:* Could Simms have intended *snored* in some form?

With branches of her dewy tree
Bend over, and beside me creep.
I gazed for long around the scene,
So strange and silent, wild, serene,
Watch'd vacantly the glowing fire,   400
Saw the flames sink and then aspire,
Flinging, as flickering to their fall,
Strange shapes and shadows o'er the wall;
That now the Hunter seem'd and now,
[Page 18]The deer with mighty antler'd brow;   405
The mountain's precipice, the rock,
Anon, the cataract, with its shock
Dull sounding in my brain from thought;
Then suddenly, as I drowsed, I caught
The bay of dogs without;—my doze,   410
Fancied the wolf within the close;
And the dogs eager; but the cry
Subsided to a lullaby,
So sweet, that somehow to mine eyes,
Fanny again beside me stood,   415
And bless you, I was flesh and blood,
And my last fancy found my lips
To Fanny's making frequent trips.

XI.

A dawn of mountain sky and sun,
Commencing in mixed blue and bright,   420
Green forests girdling rocks of dun,
And waters flashing far in sight—
Rose up in gladness from the night,
And blessing God that I was born,
In such a world of beauty, forth   425
I leapt at summons of the horn,
To hail below the face of Earth,—
Earth in her loveliness outspread
In verdure glad, by waters fed,
[Page 19]By fountains nourish'd, 'neath blue skies   430

419 Two dots on the manuscript after *mountain* appear to be accidental marks, not a colon.

Made soft, lay sleeping 'neath mine eyes
With not a cloud upon her face,—
Her limbs relaxed, in perfect grace;
No shapeless form, a dreary plain,—
But here a swelling bosom, there,   435
A limb uplifted, soft again,
Subsiding, but to reappear,
In noble height, and lofty brow,
And cove and copse, and stream and dell,
All warming with the sunlight now,   440
And waking 'neath the fiery spell.
Oh! Life! This is to live; to stand
Upon the mountains of the land
To look o'er all to freedom, feel
The sweet winds from the vallies steal,   445
With song of sweet escape, to hear,
The sudden bird note in the ear,
Who sings in very mock of care,
The joys of ignorance, and flies,
Simply because he owns the skies;   450
Nay, cry of beast were not amiss
As speaking for a scene like this,
[Page 20]Which man forbears, where man forgets
The statutes which as snares he sets
For his own soul and senses, when   455
His walks are with his fellow men.
I breathe, I drink the air, I glow
With sense of flight and music; know
How life is felt at last; how wings
Come with the soul that upward springs,   460
And thought breaks shackles; how the heart
May find itself of earth a part,
Yet feel no pain, nor own a Fate,
That drags it down to Hell and Hate.

XII.

That breakfast,—and that venison steak!—   465
Victoria, could you but partake,—
But no! poor girl, your crown is tight

About the brow,—your sceptre's weight.—
Your brilliants,—take off appetite,
The Koh-I-Noor, itself a Fate,   470
Enough to paralyze your state,
Require—that you should breakfast late!—
And not of dishes such as ours,—
"Yet," quoth our Hunter—"By the powers,
Such meat would satisfy a Queen!"   475
I had talked of England's; hence his phrase.—
"Well it's a thing I've seldom seen,
[Page 21]Though living a good smart chance of days.—
A woman master! But every land
Must have its own peculiar ways.   480
The sovereign here that would command,
Must be a man, a strong, brave man,
To do the best that mortal can.
Fight, drive, pursue, nor stop the chace
'Till he has won the game or race.   485
Our law is like the Indian's; he
Who would be chief must prove his skill,
The first to fight, the last to flee,
And take his scalp with right good will.
The woman who here would give the law   490
Must be a soldier, not a squaw,
With a master's soul, to lead in the fray
And win before she can wield the sway.
But that reminds me of work to do.
We must travel the mountains through.   495
See to the dogs and let us tramp
Merrily on, for the Hunter's camp."

XIII.

A brief farewel to our mountain maids,
A hurried squeeze and a parting kiss

---

470 *Koh-I-Noor:* Simms is contrasting the weight and constraints of life in society—perhaps evoking Queen Victoria—with the untrammeled freedom of the American wilderness. It was a breakfast fit for a queen, but the Queen, weighted down by her trappings—e.g., the *Koh-I-Noor*—could not partake.

And down we sped through the rocky shades,   500
And down we peep'd o'er the dark abyss;
Our journey begun, with the rising sun,
[Page 22]Never quite ended when day was done!
O'er mountain path and plain we sped
From Keowee to Caesar's Head;   505
O'er stony ridges now, that, vast,
Lift their bald foreheads to the blast
And mock the feeble growth of trees.
That bitter love the lowland breeze;
Masses of shrubless brown that rise   510
In commerce with the brightest skies,
And on their solemn foreheads wear
The furrows of a nameless year:
Descending now their sides of gloom,
To vales that never fail in bloom,   515
Lock'd from the exploring eye, and known
To hunters and to deer alone;
We stoop to drink at streamlet's side
That, fenced by ramparts steep and wide
Flows on with unanswer'd plaint that knows   520
No change, unless to more repose;
Subsiding, at the last, beneath
Dark fringes of a glittering heath,
Where, sleeping close, its couch is seen
Only in richer wealth of green.   525
Here pause we by the ancient mound
For which no builder yet is found
And muse upon the vanish'd race
[Page 23]That left, without a name, a trace.

505 *Keowee to Caesar's Head:* Keowee was an important eighteenth-century Cherokee town on the Keowee River in northwestern South Carolina. Caesar's Head is a town and a mountain near the North Carolina–South Carolina line.

526 *ancient mound:* There were several small Indian mounds on the Keowee River observed by William Bartram in his *Travels.* Some of them have since been destroyed (David Anderson, *Savannah River Chiefdoms,* 361). The several mounds on the Tugaloo River (Estato, Chauga, and Tugalo) were larger and are better known (ibid., 110, 244).

Our pathway winds; we leave the plain,   530
And win the mountain sides again;
No sterile range of rugged height,
But crown'd with many a sweet delight;
Great oaks for shade; magnolia towers,
Already crown'd with large white flowers,   535
And cedars, ruddy in their green,
Give softness to the solemn scene.
Yet softer fields below that lie,
Persuade from these the yearning eye,
And as we gaze, we fancy bow'rs   540
Of sweet repose for peaceful hearts,
Where it may be, in elder hours,
Some mighty people loved the arts,
And twin'd their shrines with cultured flowers.
Here still the purple Malva shines   545
In strange embrace with rugged vines,
And creepers fond, with blossom's white
Seem languishing, in love with light;—
With faintest tints, a blush that sinks
To pallor by the side of pinks;—   550
White these, in turn, with every jade
To see, in all her flames array'd
[Page 24]Th' Azalea, eager to expand,
And robe with beauty all the land,
Defying rivals, born to shine   555
A crimson sylph beneath the pine.
How gleam and glow as on we move,
New beauties in each forest grove,
What meadowy tracts of varied hue,
Unfold beneath each mountain view;   560
Beds of the strawberry, and bowers
Where vines midst grass veils of flow'rs
Grow wanton in the fond embrace,

---

545 *Malva:* a flower of the Malvacae family, probably *Hibiscus laevis All.*, more common
in the South Carolina piedmont than in the mountains.

With damsels of another race.
And still our onward progress leads   565
Through tracts of sun beloved meads
Each brighter than the last with bloom
That wraps us with the rustic perfume;
Groves of the forest plum and prune
The fruits beneath the smiles of June.   570
Just, on the side which meets the Sun,
Making their purple ripeness on.

XIV.

These children of the sun and air,
So wild yet sweet, so meek yet fair,
But little won our Hunter's eye;   575
His thought was on the sullen bear,
The panther, fierce, the timid deer,
[Page 25] That down in the deeper thickets lie.
Nor did he pause with conscious gaze
In the great forest's giant maze,   580
Nor scan with eyes of mine the range
Of rocks, in blue or brown, that spread,
Vast tier on tier, with aspect strange
With each his crown upon his head;
A mighty conclave;—sovereign heights,   585
Awful, yet clad in soft delights,
Robes wrought fantastically gay,
With flow'rs and shrubs of thousand hue,
And mosses, gleaming through the gray,
And hiding, with mixed green and blue,   590
The rugged seams of rock; each rift
Rejoicing in its own bright gift!
Whole sides of mountain seem aflame,
With robes like those the monarch wears,
Dyed rich with flowers that have no name,   595
Or one unworthy blooms like theirs.

588 Simms first wrote *hues,* then struck through the *s* to assure the rhyme with *blue* (l. 590).

Through groves of great magnificence.
We pass to other heights; yet still
Our vale betrays an outlet thence.—
Rock springs from rock, hill soars o'er hill; 600
A mighty amphitheatre,
Surrounds us, while the barrier walls
Rise up, great ridges circular,
[Page 26] O'er which the glittering waterfalls
Leap desperate, hopeless else to gain, 605
The freedom of that smiling plain.
Yet toil we on to other towers,
Up green and turfy sides that show,
Still other shrubs of scent and flowers,
That make them all like carpets glow. 610
The height is won—, the circle spreads,—
Still other towers above our heads,
Contract our realm: another plain,
Unfolds, to close in rocks again.
A spacious world of green, made gay 615
With one sweet glittering brook, whose play,
When first from off the rocky steeps,
It throws its white arms out and leaps,
Seems that of some glad girl, with robe
All brilliant, to make rich the globe, 620
Scattering her treasures as she flies,
And lost herself, in loving skies.

XV.

Our Hunter smiled to see my trance,
That made me heedless of his word.
He quickly understood the glance, 625
Which show'd how little had I heard;
For well he loved to speak of toils,
Of forest life, its strifes and spoils,
[Page 27]And with shrewd mother wit and sense,
Possess'd strange stores of eloquence, 630
Rough, hardy, wild, and searching thought
With fancies bold and bright unwrought,

That made his phrase a thing of strength,
That fastened on the heart at length.
He gave me silence, when he found   635
My thoughts were in the scenes around,
And not with him; and strove to see,
In scenes but too familiar grown,
The wonders that enchanted me;—
Yet saw but little in the known.   640
The rugged crags o'er which we sped,
With pinnacles of blue o'erhead;
The precipices dark below,
Where still we heard wild waters flow,
In sullen chaunt, but tone subdued   645
As reverent of the solitude;—
Which spell'd my spirit to their mood,
And brought me musings infinite
With all that fancy well could teach,
Leaving the dreaming power alight,   650
Yet taking from the tongue its speech;—
These never touch'd the Hunter's soul,
[Page 28]Appeal'd to neither eye nor ear
O'er fancy held no sweet control
And never moved his thought or fear.   655
The little cascade at our side,
That crouched until ramparts drew nigh
Then leapt, a spectre white and wide,
Scarce met his ear or caught his eye.
But when the valley open'd fair,   660
With lakes of laurel festering there,
Vast tracts of thick, a tangled shade
In gorges of the mountain laid,
Spread far, and sleeping still as death,—
Then blazed his eye, then came his breath,   665
The nature in his heart grew warm,
And lifted proudly soul and form.
He cried—
"There, Captain; look you, there

Is the born dwelling of the bear;   670
Farther than eye can reach, he runs
And feeds and licks his little ones.
For more than twenty miles, you know,
In one great stream, these laurels grow;
Some nine miles wide, I think, they spread,   675
For his, and for the panther's tread.
There, through the day they crouch from sight,
And prowl upon the hills at night.
[Page 29]Oh! It's a world of meat,—to last
When all my generation's pass'd;   680
And, thousand years from now, I guess
'Twill be as now a wilderness;
A mighty harbor for the brute,
Where hunters yet unborn will shoot
And take their skins with just the will   685
That's mine, but with a better skill.
But now, the field is mostly mine,
No rival crosses o'er the line;
I claim as far as eye can see,
And all the country yields to me.   690
The bear that ranges far and wide,
Some day will pay me ham and hide;
And with each sun, this rifle's crack,
Still picks the old buck from the pack.
I've all I want myself, and more,   695
My children share my skill and store,
And they will never want for game,
While strength can shoot, or skill can tame.—
And yet, I sometimes grudge to think,
That, when into the grave I sink,   700
Another foot shall take the trail,
And win, where I perhaps might fail;
Another hunter's eye explore
The thick so sweet to me before;
[Page 30]And dogs of other men shall wake,   705
The sleeping beast in yonder brake!

But what's the use? I've had my day,
A long one too, and full of play;
I reckon, though my life is rough,
I've had my pleasures, quite enough: 710
I've lived in every limb and vein,
In heart and head,—and can't complain,
When the great Captain calls, to lay
My rifle down and leave the prey!—
Put out my boys, and with a will,   715
We'll brush the woods that lie in sight;
While daylight lasts be doing still,
The secret for good sleep at night."

XVI.

O'er rock and valley thus we sped,
For weeks a sylvan life we led,   720
By day we toil'd in earnest chace,
As heedless of the toils as space.
By night we slept beside the stream,
While fires sent up a constant gleam.
We compass'd heights where slept the snow.   725
In caverns, hard congeal'd below.
While, in the smiles of summer glad,
[Page 31]The mountain tops in bloom were clad,—
From height to height, with cry and bound,
We hurried on the panting hound,   730
His bay soon woke the rifle's crack.—
And lo! The spike buck in his track;
We drove the bear to refuge vain
That never gave him home again.
Night found us hollows of the hill,   735
Beside some brightly flashing rill,
Beheld anew the rising pyre,
Of resin, pine and crackling fire;
Our bearskins spread for couch or seat,
We found our steak of venison sweet,   740

732 *spike buck:* a young deer with straight, unbranched antlers.

And group'd around,—our beagles near,—
Keen listeners, never closing ear—
Heard stories full of pride and fear;
Wild hunter legends, strange as true
That haply show what man can do,   745
And what endure, if in his breast,
The soul of courage, stands confess'd.
And so, we slept, the ruddy light
Of fires maintain'd throughout the night,
With watchful dogs whose angry bay   750
Still kept the lurking beast away;
Though ever and anon, we hark
From distant cliff the growl or bark,
[Page 32]A mournful howl, or childlike cry
That tells of wolf or panther nigh,   755
And, sometimes, nearer still, a scream,
That startles from a fearful dream!

XVII.

Then hunting as we sped, we gain
The mighty Apalachian chain,
And every glorious landscape see.   760
In mountains of the Cherokee
To Nequassee from Estato,
From Keowee to Tellico,
The red man's fields, his vallies blest
Their eastern empire to their west,   765
A wondrous waste, a varied wild,

---

762 *Nequassee from Estato:* Estato was an eighteenth-century Cherokee town on the Tugaloo River. Nequassee was an eighteenth-century Cherokee town on the upper Little Tennessee River (near present Franklin, North Carolina). An old trail that connected them lay approximately on modern Highway 441. There is also an Estato Creek that is a headwater for the Keowee River, as well as a town of that name. It is near the Jocassee and Tennessee Rivers. The Mouzon map of 1775 shows "Old Estatohe" on the Tugaloo River, and Estatoe on Upper Estatoe Creek. Likely it is the latter that Simms is referring to.
763 *Tellico:* Tellico was an important Overhill Cherokee town on the Tellico River, a tributary of the Little Tennessee River. Here, as on 762 above, Simms is not describing his narrator's travels, but delineating an area of the Blue Ridge Mountains.

Alternate still that frown'd and smiled,
How soft and wooing in its plains,
How stern in low'ring dark domains!
All these we traversed, pausing long   770
On happy spots, unknown to song,
Which song shall yet enrich, when Time
Shall bare to art this glorious clime!
Then Table Rock, the weird and grey
Beguiled our footsteps many a day,   775
Surveying all from heights, below,
The fair long train of Oolenoe.—
By Toxaway, that garden spot
[Page 33]For wounded hearts, we half forgot
The Hunter's purpose,—Scarce could free   780
Our souls, to 'scape from Jocassee;
And still, we look'd behind to trace,
From distant heights, her virgin grace,
As soft, and full of sweet alarms,
She hides her face in giant arms.   785

XVIII.

We cross at last the mountain range,
From east to western climes we change,
And at our feet at once survey,
The rival waters on their way.
Two kindred founts to drink invite;   790

---

774 *Table Rock:* Table Rock Mountain is a notable peak in northwestern Pickens County, South Carolina.

777 *Oolenoe:* Oolenoe Creek (now Oolenoe River) has some of its headwaters on Table Rock Mountain.

778 *Toxaway:* Toxaway River is a tributary of the Keowee River. It forms the northwestern boundary of Pickens County.

786 In error, Simms repeats the chapter number XVII that he first wrote at l. 781.

789 *The rival waters:* Simms is here describing the transition from streams flowing south and east to the Atlantic Ocean from those flowing north and west into the Tennessee and Mississippi Rivers. He possibly went up Toxaway Creek or Estatoe Creek and over the mountains to the headwaters of the French Broad River. He may have been describing a trail that led up Estatoe Creek, approximately along modern Highway 178.

A green bank lies between; we take
Their separate waters up; unite
And bless the marriage that we make!
We pledge to rival oceans—these,
Two fountains, from that moment part;   795
Pursuing rival distances,
Each hurrying to its ocean mart
Fond tidings to the deeps to bear!—
The Atlantic first the tale shall hear,
The Gulph the last. How wondrous! We   800
[Page 34]Drink from the founts of either sea!—
A realm of rock between! How fraught
The story, with becoming thought!
What legends wild, what marvels sooth,
Lie hidden in this simple truth.   805
What worlds of life domain between
These fountains—What a wondrous scene;
What joys and griefs, what hopes and fears,
What strifes, what triumphs, smiles and tears;—
How bright the future, and how vast,   810
Voluminously dark, the past.
How rich the realm for home and heart,
In spells of song and deeds of art!

XIX.

I guessed the red man's fate, or those,
Who first upon those mountains sway'd,   815
And sank beneath the red man's blows,
Too fiercely savage to be stay'd;
Who left their shrines without a name
Their tombs without a record! Where,
The story of their ancient fame,   820
Their deeds, the Gods they sought in pray'r,
Perchance, in sacrifice! In vain,
The progress o'er each silent fame,
Each sullen mound and ruin'd tow'r.
Oh! For the spell of magic pow'r   825
[Page 35]To burst the casements of the dead,

And bid the sage or hero rise
To tell us, why his people fled
Or how they toil'd and fought, and bled,
And what their triumphs, ere the doom,   830
That shut them in the speechless tomb.
Reveal the story of their prime
When first beneath the march of time
They roved these glorious vales, begirt
By rocks, which were their keepers, men   835
With each but half a head or heart.
All Europe had not entered then!
No voice to answer! All is still.
The echoes die along the hill,
And mock me with my words again!   840
Yet shall the genius of the place
In days of potent song to come
Reveal the story of the race,
Whose native genius now lies dumb.
Yes, Fancy by Tradition led   845
Shall trace the streamlet to its bed,
And well each ancient path explore
The perish'd trod in days of yore.
The rock, the vale, the mound, the dell,
Shall each become a Chronicle.   850
[Page 36]The swift Imagination, borne
To heights of faith and sight supreme
Shall gather all the gifts of morn,
And find for every rock its theme.

XX.

The later race we know. . . . the time   855
The red men fill'd the rock and wood,
The wanderers from another clime,
Who won their way through deeds of blood!
Skill'd in the arts by nature taught
To wing the shaft and barb the bow   860
They toil'd not in the fields of thought
Though stern philosophers I trow.

Severe the school that bade them bear
The ills of life without a tear.
And stern the doctrine that denied   865
The Sachem fame, the warrior pride,
Who, urged by human wants, express'd
The need that hunger'd in his breast;—
Or, when beneath his foeman's knife,
That uttered recreant pray'r for life,—   870
Or, in the chase whose strength was spent
Or, in the fight whose knee was bent,
Or when, with tidings of the fight,
Who sought his allies' camp by night,
[Page 37]And ere his missives well were told,   875
Complain'd of hunger, wet and cold.
A woman, if in strife, his foe
Should give, could not receive the blow,
Or, if undextrously, and dull,
His hand and knife should fail to win   880
The dripping warm scalp from the skull
To trim his yellow mockasin!

XXI.

Our Hunter summons—at his cry
Sent midway from the mountain's side,
The red men vanish from mine eye!—   885
Adown the western slopes we glide
O'er sinuous routes which need a guide;
By rocks and heights whose dark domains
Well hide from man their golden veins;
To vallies scooped from realms of hill,   890
That waste their wealth in fragrance still;
While ever and anon we hear
A joyous murmur take the ear,
Where glimpsing glad, a flash of light,

863–882 An almost identical version of this poem of twenty-two lines is included in *The Yemassee*, 162 [Arkansas Edition].

The Swannanoa clears the height,   895
And still with chaunt of freedom roves
Half hidden, though her guardian groves
With might, a hoarser murmur wakes
The ear—a thrill the valley shakes.
[Page 38]And he who hearkens deems the roar,   900
An ocean striving 'gainst the shore;—
Beheld through dusk, th' illusion grows
As faintly white Tselica shows,
As rushing wild, immersed in foam
All boundless seems her watery home,   905
The giant heights beyond unseen,
As night lets down her dusky screen.

XXII.

But with the dawn, the eager eye
The barrier rocks beyond surveys,
Great mountains soaring to the sky   910
That woo, and yet repel the gaze;
Eternal crags, that castling, keep
Dominion silent o'er the deep.
A wondrous range of rampart—gray
With years, but fearless of decay,   915
And mocking still the sleepless strife
Of waters, raging into life:
That seem, with human pangs to roar,
And writhe in vain against the shore
Whose mighty boulders vainly bar   920
But scatter all their billows far!

XXIII.

We tread with trembling steps beside
The ever vex'd and foaming tide,

895 *The Swannanoa:* the Swannanoa River runs westward to join the French Broad River
at present Asheville, North Carolina.
903 *Tselica:* the poem appears to use Tselica as a name for the French Broad River (as in
the short poem "Tzelica—A Tradition of the French Broad," 1845), and from this point
through chapter XXVI describes a descent along the French Broad River perhaps as far
as Warm Springs (present Hot Springs), North Carolina.

[Page 39]Whose raging waters roar and hiss,
From many a black and wild abyss;   925
While crags o'erhang, that, as we go,
Seem plunging headlong down below
A drear and awful realm, whose sight
Still startles with a strange delight
Of wonder mix'd with dread, and spells   930
The soul with dreams of miracles.
Here warr'd the Titans sure!—They hurl'd
These fragments of a shatter'd world
In conflict with the Gods! They rent
These crags to shake the firmament;   935
Tore wide the Gulph between that lies
To crush their awful enemies,
And in the madness of their ire,
Pour'd from the heart of Earth its fire!
Subdued, at length, and from the steeps   940
Hurl'd down and buried in their deeps,
Here still they rave, and roar, and rage,
With hate, not ages may assuage,
And vainly toss their limbs on high
To brave the Fate they cannot fly!   945
See how the writhing waters flock
As if for conflict, o'er yon rock.
Embrace it long in deadliest fold,
And rage to rend it from its hold!
[Page 40]Methinks yon black'ning masses now,   950
Envelope some dread Titan's brow;
Those swelling waves his limbs conceal—
Behold what horrid strokes they deal;
But foil'd, how madly bound away
As seeking some more easy prey;   955
Hoarse thunders following as they speed,
To cruel fate and nameless deed.
The worst is o'er—and closed the strife,
But still the fury speaks for life
Still the hoarse murmurs tell of Hate   960

That may not be subdued by Fate,—
Of Hate that even more hellish grows
Thus baffled and decreed repose.

XXIV.

As on we glide beneath the steep,
That hangs in terror o'er the deep,   965
What horrid crags impend and throw
Their shadows o'er the path below;
In black batallions still that wait
The summons to the fields of hate,
And ready stand with lifted rock,   970
Poised high to thunder, shock for shock.
And still the waters writhe and moan,
[Page 41]As hosts in deadly strife o'erthrown,
Yet hopeful still of glorious change,
And the sweet bitter, great Revenge.   975
Even like a battle field the plain
Lies piled and crowded with its slain
Wrecks, that shall long survive the storm,
Possess the field and still deform.
What gulphs unfold their gloomy caves,   980
What torrents break in threatening waves,
What forms in flight just pass from view,
What other mightier forms pursue;
Foam tigers leap o'er boulders dark,
And arrowy rushing, lo, the shark.   985
The howl, the shriek, the plaint, the hiss,
Ascend from gulphy fields below;
While hourly shooting the abyss,
New legions to the conflict go:—
And thus for ages, ages, ages,   990
As written on all human pages!

XXV.

With sense of sweet relief, the eye
Looks upward to the opening sky
That weaves its folds of soft white fleece
In token of a reign of peace;   995

Spreads, from the scene of strife, above,
[Page 42]Yet gazes down with eye of love;
Rests, as to soothe and sweeten still,
With blue wing on each sovereign hill,
And from their mighty peaks, flings down,   1000
The sweetest flowers that grace her crown.
They cling about each shatter'd rock
That rests secure from future shock;
Their loving fibres pierce their way
With tender art, to wounds that need   1005
Protection from the noontide ray;—
Their mosses cover those that bleed;—
To broken limbs, with fond embrace,
Cling close, and heal and crown with grace,
Hide the great scars that still deface,   1010
'Till ruin'd tower and desert dome,
With ivied trophies green and glad,
Grow blest and bright, as Beauty's home,
In all her native garlands clad.
How flushes, with crimson moss   1015
Yon castled barbican and towers steep
How glows with greenest robes, the fosse
That circles round yon donjon keep:
And by yon torrents edge, yon stream
That bounds away with headlong flight.   1020
[Page 43]How wild the crimson creepers gleam
In very wantonness of bright;—
The grape, usurper of a shrine,
She never had the power to raise
Drooping with clusters swollen with wine   1025
That bleed in secret sacrifice,
Yet never win from man the praise,
Pleased though the bud alone should prize.
Nor these alone the proofs of peace,
See how the forms of love increase,   1030

1017 *fosse:* a moat or defensive ditch in a fortification, usually filled with water.

How Beauty seizes on the toil
Of war, and finds in wreck her spoil,
And with her spells of love and art
Makes ruin precious to the heart.
Sweet airs of evening woo and guide   1035
To other charms that crown the way.
The rocky cliff, the mountain's side
In fragrant bloom, and blushing sway:
The azalea rises grandly still,
A beacon flame on every hill;   1040
The Malva, with its purple flowers
And gay glad vines and creepers wild
With crowns of teinted white, embowers
The fitting home for fancy's child;
The blushing Rhododendron shares   1045
[Page 44]Her empire with the Cluster Rose.
The Lily of the Valley bares
Her bosom for serene repose.
And still, though Calycanthean grows,
The half imprison'd brooklet roves   1050
To seek its way o'er broken steep,
Bounding, at last, to join the deep,
Through beds of strawberry blooms, that sink
Yet hang above the toppling brink,
Still lifted with each gushing wave,   1055
And soothing where they may not save.

XXVI.

Below, the troubled waters see
The sign of milder dynasty,
And feel the force of gentler skies,
Than those that ruled its fearful rise.   1060
Lapsing from wrath, their future way
Is placed with a benignant sway;
And now a lakelet opens bright,
Reposing sad in summer light.
All are subdued and meekly bless'd   1065
With precious interval of rest.

No chafing billows strive to pour
Their floods in terror 'gainst the shore;
The frowning rocks recede or sink,
Green shrubs and grasses, o'er the brink   1070
[Page 45]Bend fo'w'd, and bless, and gently drink.
Down from the mountain slopes the grove,
Above around beyond might seem,
The home of Happiness and Love,
The Poets and the Painter's dream;   1075
While one fair islet lifts its brow,
The realm of living green below;
Waves flowing smoothly round, and shades,
Within, that seem a realm for maids,
All love and rapture; each with song,   1080
The tides of pleasure to prolong;
While sweet security around,
Flings spells of peace; the soft profound
Of silence, born of whispering flow'rs,
And zephyrs, charming all the hours!   1085

So pure and peaceful all the scene,
The waters fair, the sky serene,
I long to seek the wave, and lave
My panting bosom in the wave;
Swim for the holy islet; rove   1090
Amidst the bow'rs so dear to love,
And dream, if dream I might, of charms,
Kindred with these of nature's grace,
To share my soul, to fill mine arms,
And make me happy with embrace.   1095
[Page 46]Already on the boulders, down
My cap and hunting shirt were thrown,
When promptly interpos'd my guide:
"Woulds't take a demon for a bride?
'Tis here Tselica keeps her home,   1100

1073 *around:* the manuscript has *arround.*

Secure and stern in beds of foam,
Here watches for her lord in vain,
Her lover, by her kindred slain;
And wo, to him who idly braves,
Her passions in these wooing waves!   1105
With arms about his bosom wound,
She deems awhile the lost one found,
But gazing in his face, she grows
The fiercest of the stranger's foes,
Gripes him with deadly grasp, until   1110
The billows choke, the waters chill,
Then flings him from her arms to sink,
Or 'scaped, to perish on the brink;
To perish sure, since never yet
Lived he on whom her hand was set;   1115
Thou little dream'st the fearful rule,
She keeps in yon deceiptful pool!

[BOOK TWO]
XXVII.

"And who's Tselica?"
    "Hast not heard,
The Indian story?"   1120
    "Not a word!"
[page 47]"Then shall you hear; I'm sure you'll say,
It's mighty curious in its way.
I've seen worse stories put in books:—
But here your writer seldom looks,   1125
Yet here might some thing find, to sound
As well as things from foreign ground.
I could, myself, strange legends tell
Of what the Indian tribes befel,
And what our hunters,—since they're gone,   1130
Would chill the hearer's heart to stone;—
Of shapes that walk the woods by night,
And some, that never hide from sight;

1110 *gripes:* grips (nineteenth-century spelling).

And wild enchantments,—curious powers
In rocks and woods and even flowers;   1135
Then sometimes do you hear strange cries,
From forests, and deep gulphs that rise,—
Things, just as wondrous as the lore
That's brought us from thy British shore.
The red man had his miracles   1140
And wizards wrought on him their spells;
His spectres walked, the same as ours,
And numb'd him with their hostile powers;
They charm'd his walks, his bow, his knife,
And chill'd his courage in the strife;   1145
[Page 48]Or, if they loved him gave him charms
That warm'd his heart and nerved his arms,
And made him fleet to stay the deer,
And made him strong to fight the bear,
And warn'd him of the coming fight,   1150
And watch'd his wigwam through the night.
I see you smile; but there's one truth,
That few men ever learn in youth;
And he, whom still you wisest call,
Is yet not wise enough for all.   1155
The red man's God was not so strong,
As his, who did the red man wrong.
But did our God desert him quite,
Ere he put over him the White?—
He had his gods—though weak indeed,—   1160
Yet such as answered to his need,
And spirits, well suited to his race,
Dwelt with him in this very place!"

XXVIII.

"But to Tselica?"
"You shall hear,   1165
While Fergus gets our noonday cheer;—
A steak, my son!"
Our skins we spread
Beneath the grey cliffs butting head,
[Page 49]And while the youth with ready hand,   1170

Prepares and lights the resin brand
And busies with our wild repast,
Our forms beside the stream we cast.
Well pleased, with eager thought and ear,
The legend of our guide to hear— 1175
A sad sweet story, such as might
The heart, in any land, delight,
Of Rapture, happy in its prize,
And Love too dear, too soon that flies,—
Eyes clouded in their brightest noon, 1180
Hopes bann'd and baffled all too soon,
And Hate triumphant in the hour,
When Love exulted most in power!—
A simple tale, and simply told,
Yet worthy of the days of old, 1185
When, though the song was roughly wrought,
'Twas well inform'd by force and thought;
And fashion'd in the simplest dress,
Yet had its charm in tenderness.
I weave our tale in statelier rhyme, 1190
As suiting best a Christian clime,
Supply the garb when aught is nude,
[Page 50]And polish what before was rude,
Yet nothing strip, lest nature fail,
And nothing graft upon the tale. 1195

XXIX.

Of all the tribes that held in fee
These mighty forests, to the sea,
The fiercest was the Muscoghee.
His nature gloomy as the waste
And savage as the beast he chased, 1200
Forever nursing discontent,
His arms on every side he bent;
His sleepless passion was the fight,
And conquest was his sole delight.

1198 *Muscoghee:* the Creek Indians.

Thus did his wild domain increase   1205
And deserts only gave him peace:—
But not before his eye had seen
Tellico's heights and vallies green;
And oft his roving warriors came
To warm its towns with midnight flame.   1210
His boast was ever that he made
The gentler Cherokee afraid;
And truth it is, he sometimes tore
Its frontier towns with besom swore;
Bore off their treasures, slew their brave,   1215
Their children down, as captives drave,
[Page 51]While sadder still, their sweetest maids
Became the trophies of his raids;
Such prize more dear than all the rest,
Since few that saw, but still confess'd   1220
How lovelier far, with loftier grace,
More tall, erect, with sweeter face,
Were damsels of the Cherokee,
Than native maids of Muscoghee.
But one escaped, on whom his eyes   1225
Had fix'd as passion's dearest prize,
The young Tselica. She had grown
The wild flow'r of a forest lone,
Her father's only pride and care,
Surpassing beautiful and fair.   1230
The mico of a town was he.
Below the heads of Tennasee;

1214 *besom swore*: *besom* (OE, ME), a bundle of rods or twigs used for flogging; an instrument for sweeping (Simms used the term also in "The Southern Convention" in 1850); as a verb, *besom* means "to sweep with force." The punishing effect of *besom* is obviously part of Simms's intent, but *swore* used in conjunction with *besom* creates a problem that has not been resolved. Since the manuscript is still in rough form, Simms's final construction was perhaps yet to be decided.

1216 *down*: to the point of defeat or submission.

1231 *mico*: chief.

1232 *Below the heads of Tennasee*: downstream Tennessee River.

A small sweet village, like a nest
Of eaglets, 'neath the mountain's breast,—
Eaglets and doves, together blest,   1235
With union, and a long increase,
'Neath smokes, that, for a hundred years,
Had softly swell'd to heaven in peace,
Nor settled on the vale in tears!
Too sure, in fortunes thus serene,   1240
Kept the fair homes of Euphassee;
Day broke in beauty o'er the scene.
[Page 52]Noon saw its gay festivity;
The young, beneath the patriarch tree,
Disporting fond in dances gay   1245
That whiled the precious hours away,
When watchful Love, with weapon bare,
Had guarded every hill with ire,
Like Lion standing o'er his lair.
That night, the tempest burst in fire   1250
The warriors slumber'd! In surprise,
They open'd but on death their eyes;
In their last agonies survey
Their young, the cruel foeman's prey.
But few escaped. One valiant brand,   1255
Still baffled long the assailing band,
'Till the old mico, with his child,
Found shelter in the mountain wild;
But not before the vivid blaze
The beauty of the maid betrays   1260
To the young chief of Ockwallee;—
His heart from thence was never free.
How well he made his passion known,
In after days, to her alone;
In what disguise her home he sought,   1265

1241 *Euphassee:* a pseudo-Cherokee town name? The Cherokee language has no *f* (i.e.,
ph) sound.
1261 *Ockwallee:* a pseudo-Creek personal name.

And how his sweet persuasion wrought,
The charm on her, that in his soul,
[Page 53]Sway'd ever with supreme control,
The old tradition treasures well,
But needs not now that we should tell!   1270
Enough, he came, he sought, he saw,—
Her heart received from his the law;—
Her sire was in the grave, and she
The last of all her tribe, and free;—
Glad with the stranger chief she flew,   1275
And none their place of refuge knew.
They left the heights of Tennassee;—
There, on yon islet in the stream,
They dwelt, a season sweet, of dream;
Lived for each other, never sigh'd,   1280
For former home and ancient pride,
He glad to leave his world for her,—
Her world, at once, and worshipper!

XXX.

How blest was then that islet home,
All free from care, and yet with cares,   1285
That never suffer thought to roam,
And thought that still each home endears,
Ye well may fancy, when so bright,
Its bloom and blossoms hang in sight,
Shelter'd by crowding trees that grew   1290
To friendly guardians sweet as true,
Their cabin nursed those genial joys,
[Page 54]Whose taste the palate never cloys.
He found in yonder woods his game,
She rear'd about their home the tame;   1295
Their birds made music in the boughs,
And taught, 'twould seem, in human vows,

1278 *islet:* the French Broad and the Tennessee Rivers do in fact have several large, habitable islands.

Grew constant to the cot whose peace,
With every noon still found increase.
Alas! how short the term of bliss!— 1300
The stream that shorts the precipice,
To sleep in gloomy drear abyss,
Not brighter in its headlong flight
Not sooner lost to human sight,
Than that sweet season of delight! 1305

XXXI.

Well Ockwallee his danger knew,
With heights of Cherokee in view,
And if Tselica nursed a care,
'Twas of her kindred, sovereign there,
Sworn foes to all the Muscoghee, 1310
And panting for revenge on him,
Who, at the raid of Euphassee,
Had made their eyes and glories dim.
Still at their parting as he sped,
To rouse the brown deer from his bed, 1315
She counsell'd earnestly his feet
To sly approach, and swift retreat;
[Page 55]And he would take her to his arms,
And strive to soothe her child alarms,
Vow to be watchful, nor in strife. 1320
He still might fly, to peril life;—
Forgetting still the counsel taught
In sweet enjoyment of the charms,
Which then alone supplied his thought
And borne away at last from view, 1325
How would she watch the light canoe,
That bore him from her earnest view,
Until he moor'd the cockle skiff
In shadow 'neath yon jutting cliff
And pass'd himself to groves which still, 1330

1329 *cliff*: the manuscript has *skiff*; this was emended on the theory that Simms repeated *skiff* by mistake from the previous line.

Shroud, as ye can see, each distant hill,—
A hunter famous for his skill,
Not oft he track'd the deer in vain,
The stealthy panther found it ill,
To cross his path upon the plain; 1335
And for his foe, the Cherokee,—
He longed not for the strife, for she,
The woman of his heart, had long
Implored him do her race no wrong.
But ancient lessons still were strong, 1340
And close pursued or roused by pride,
Their bravest had he soon defied,
And slowly yielding, would, at most,
[Page 56]Give back before o'erwhelming host!

XXXII.

That host he found!—With dawn one day 1345
He left this isle in search of prey;
Soon cross'd the stream to yonder steep,
Then hid him in the forest deep.
As was her wont, Tselica stood,
To watch his passage o'er the flood; 1350
Beheld him moor his skiff in shade,
Then steal into the silent glade;
Far as her eye could see, she traced
His pathway through the thickets waste,
Then as from sight she sees him part 1355
Back to her lonely home she goes,
With still a feeling, sick at heart,
As shadow'd by the incoming woes.
A troubling thought, a doubt, a fear,
She knew not what was in her breast, 1360
That kept a busy fluttering there,
And fill'd her with a strange unrest.
Once more she gazed across the stream,
And would have shouted did she deem,
Her cries might reach his distant ear. 1365
Then sought her home to muse and dream,

Of that strange vexing doubt that still
[Page 57]Strove with her thought against her will.
But in her boughs, the cheery bird
Sang ever in notes that seem'd to word   1370
A tale of hope and joy, instead
Of that dim fear on which she fed;
And the sweet strain, reëchoed far,
By other birds, and framed, to war
With every doubt that checks the soul   1375
In progress to its precious goal,
Too soothing or sweet to be denied,
Brought gradual soothing to her fear,
And took the sting at least from care!
Her own song awakens, as her heart,   1380
Feels the cold shadow melt and part,
And sweetly, with a forest strain,
A joyous murmur born to wings,
She answers to the bird again.
But with a tremor still she sings,   1385
As if she deem'd her lover's ear
Hung listening in the coppice near,
And with a chiding still that charms
Complains that he hath fled her arms.

XXXIII.

Even as she sings, her fingers twine   1390
With bead and shell, in gay design,
The aft of gay buckskin, orange dyed,
[Page 58]And weaves with forms of savage pride.
The robe, too gay for eyes of grief,
With broider'd shirt, and figured vest,   1395
Is fashion'd for her Hunter Chief,
And worthy of his manly breast.
She muses on the happy hour,
When o'er his shoulders it is thrown,
And he shall wear the look of power,   1400
And love, she joys to see him own,—
The mico of a savage race,

That yet may never see his face!
These leggins too are wrought for him,
She sees them on each manly limb,— 1405
This baldric o'er his breast shall fall,
With beads adorn'd in waving row;
This turban, with its plumage tall,
Wrought with great pearls, a lovely show;
And mocksens gay, more bright than all, 1410
With stars, and wings of birds, and eyes,
In blue and green and red that glow;—
And thus her secret toil she plies,
To take her Chief with sweet surprise.

XXXIV.

Alas! a sad surprise he knows!— 1415
The woods are crowded with his foes!
Too careless in his courage—gay;
[Page 59]Grown reckless in pursuit of prey,
A hostile eye unseen, has found
Where Ockwallee still hunts alone, 1420
Has group'd the hostile warriors round,
Who count the scalp already won.
The ambush set, they crouch in shade,
Still as the death their souls decree;
Until, the given signal made, 1425
Each starts to life beneath his tree,
With well known cry and battle shout
Then dart they from the covert out,
Wind gradual round the space he holds,
And close him in their fatal folds. 1430

XXXV.

With the first warwhoop of the foe,
The wild halloo from rocks below,
Our hunter braced him for the strife;
Prepared his shafts, and freed his knife,
Loosed tomahawk from sheath, and stood, 1435
A moment ere he sprang away,
Paused in his flight, in thoughtful mood,

As watchful where the danger lay,
Then stoop'd to Earth his ear,—then bore
Still up,—the rugged heights to gain, 1440
Whence with free glance he might explore
The doubtful aspects of the plain.
[Page 60]But soon the guarded rocks betray'd
A foeman on each height array'd,
Whose arrows swift, their watch attest 1445
As thrice they glaze across his breast;—
Foil'd in his course, once more he turns;
His flying step the shingle spurns;
A deeper wood receives him now,—
And lo! a shaft has grazed his brow,— 1450
Sent with too eager hand and aim,
To rouse the victim, not subdue,
It only wakes his soul to flame.—
He stoops—he wings the arrow too,—
And not in vain! His vengeful eye, 1455
Too well perceives his enemy,
And Parthian like, he sends the dart,
While flying to the foeman's heart!
The shriek that follow'd woke his shout,
In fell defiance of the route, 1460
With mingled pride and hate pour'd out.

XXXVI.

But other pathways must he gain
Than these which open to the plain,
For there the track, as well he goes,
Is guarded by the circling foes. 1465
Once more his baffled footstep turns,
[Page 61]To seek the hills above that rise;
But soon, from fearful shout he learns,

1457 *Parthian:* a Parthian shot is a rearward shot by a fleeing mounted archer (so-called from the custom of the ancient Parthian cavalry of shooting arrows while in real or feigned flight).
1458 *flying:* in flight (see note immediately above).

That here again the ambush lies.
Chased with the dangers gathering round,—   1470
They chase the tiger, not confound;—
The shaft that from his bosom drew,
The crimson current as he flew,
But stings him into fond desire
To find new victims for his ire.   1475
He crouches close beside the tree,
As fainting with his hurt;—they see
And bolder grown, with shout and bound,
They rise, on all the rocks around.
Once more the arrow strikes his vest,   1480
And well by sinewy nerve address'd,
Sinks keenly deep within his breast.
Then sprang the ambush'd chief once more,
In flight, now heading for the shore;
Once there, his barque shall bear away,   1485
In safety, from the unequal fray.
As yet, he hath no fear of fate,—
Too warm his blood, too wild his hate,
He may not sink, or yield, until,
His dear revenge hath had its will;   1490
And, with the warwhoop of his race,
He leads his foemen in the chace!
[Page 62]Two victims to his warrior art,
Have sunk in death beneath his dart,
Himself unhurt—for little heed   1495
He gives his wounds of brow and breast,
He feels them not, and though they bleed,
There's glory in a crimson vest!
Could he but strike one other foe,
What rapture would his bosom know!—   1500
He pauses, in the thicket's side,
And harks the signals, far and wide,
North, South, and West—the East alone
Would seem a pathway still his own,
And there the river rolls;—he springs,   1505

As if with eagle power of wings,
And fancies, with a wild delight,
He yet shall 'scape the snare by flight,
For, quite too numerous are the foes
That, still contracting round him close,   1510
For any hope, from single blows.
He speeds awhile in devious ways,
That seem to cheat the foeman's gaze,
Parts the wild forest, on his sight,
The skies, the sun look down in light,   1515
The waters flash within his reach,—
One bound, and lo! he gains the beach.
[Page 63]   XXXVII.
He gains the beach,—and from her isle,
Tselica sees his desperate strait,
Herself conceal'd in groves the while,   1520
With scarce the power to wail her fate,
Already glooming desolate!—
Even at the first, while yet her hands,
Unconscious of the ills so near,
Wove the bright beads in mazy strands,—   1525
When on her senses, full of fear,
The whoop of battle, dread to hear,
Smote with a sudden agony,
A dread presentiment of death,
Arrested speech, suspended breath.   1530
She knows the meaning of that cry,
And from her lap the jewels fall;—
She flings the robe and sandals by,
And flies at last her forest hall,
Lonelier than death, if, in the strife,   1535
He dies, who taught her more than life.
One murmur'd prayer to Manneyto,

1537 *Manneyto:* Simms thought this name referred to of an Algonquin deity and he
assumed that this deity was comparable to the Judaeo-Christian deity and that it was
universally recognized by American Indians.

Broke from her lips as fast she flew;
Still goaded by that wild hallow:
And, by the stream, in covert thick,   1540
She crouch'd, with failing breath and eye,
Brain throbbing wild, heart bounding quick,
As pealed each horrid death whoop nigh.

[Page 64]   XXXVIII.

He gains the banks beneath her eyes,
Ah! wherefore do the waves divide;   1545
Yet soon, if longer thus he flies
He wins a refuge by her side;
'Tis well her strength for speech denies,
Else had she taught the vengeful foe,
How best to deal a double blow;   1550
To tear her thence, from home more blest,
In memories of the raptures known,
Than gather'd to another's breast,
And seated on her people's throne.
Oh! What her agony of grief,   1555
Thus sinking in the thicket's shade,
To see him fly without relief,
To see him die without her aid.
She cannot shriek, she cannot weep,
Her eyes are dry, her heart is chill,   1560
She gazes madly o'er the deep,
And droops and sinks, but gazes still,
With scarce a pulse,—without a will.
He gains the rock beneath whose brow,
His skiff lay hid—the boat is nigh: 1565
His hand is stretched to seize the prow,—
Alas! upstarts the enemy!—
In ambush close, another band,

1547 *stands in safety* is crossed out in the manuscript and replaced with *wins a refuge by;* an unnecessary second *by* is deleted by the editor.

1548 Simms originally wrote *'Twas well that;* he replaced *'Twas* with *'Tis,* and struck out *that* for the sake of meter.

Rise up from shelter of the steep
[Page 65]And dart, with armed and threatening hand,   1570
Between him and the friendly deep.
One cry of rage and baffled hope;—
He may not with their number cope,
Yet in his passions desperate,
He makes the stern resolve to brave,   1575
The worst they offer now of fate,
And will not fly again to save!
Against the rock his form he braced,
His shaft upon the string he placed,
Keenly around he casts his eye,   1580
While peals his slogan on the air
He yet can strike, he can but die,
And still his fate with others share!
This thought restores his native heart,
Renews his strength, rebarbs his dart,   1585
He wooes the conflict, glad to feel,
Or dream, that, in the gripe of death,
His foe shall writhe beneath his steel,
And yield, like him, the forfeit breath.
But with a glance beyond the stream,   1590
Uprises, in his soul a dream,
Of all the hopes and fears that wait,
That bloody strife, and cruel fate.
The islet rose in wealth of shade,
In peace and beauty soft array'd,   1595
[Page 66]And she, its form of loveliness,
Who waits him with her true caress,
The soul of truth and tenderness,
How will she hear the horrid tale,
How linger for his coming long,   1600
And, for wild moan and bitter wail,
Change the sweet burden of her song.
How live, when he who made her life,

Sinks silent in the bloody strife,
How bear the weight of lonely nights,   1605
In place of all their old delights?
He shudder'd as he thought, his eye
Grew dim—he turned again to fly.
"'Tis for Tselica"—muttering low,
"That thus I fly before the foe,   1610
And seek a refuge from their hate,
Which, but for her, with wild embrace,
My soul had sprang, on wing elate,
To grapple in this very place!—
Once more the forest!"   1615
              And he sped,
Close hounded by the vengeful band;
She breathed once more as thus he fled,
Still watching from the other strand,
[Page 67]And wept her blessings on the sand.   1620
Yet still she crouches: still she hears
The war whoop in the shrouding wood;
By fits it rings upon her ears,—
It may be o'er her hero's blood!
Even as the conquering foeman cries,   1625
His note of triumph to the skies,
He gasps in agony,—he dies.
Fierce, full at first, the fearful yell,
Breaks o'er her, like the shriek of hell;
The sound subsides—then rises lone   1630
At distance, sinking to a moan,
That sleeps in silence. It is gone!
XXXIX.
Day sinks—the stars stream out with bright
And tearless eyes, as if no gloom,
No anguish, lay beneath their light,   1635
No death, no savage strife, no tomb!
Night wanes: the pale bright watchers glide,

Each in his pearly barque along,
The great blue deeps, the unbroken tide,
Of ocean-air, as if with song,   1640
Subdued, and soothed to perfect grace
Without one ripple on its face.
[Page 68]That they should smile, that all should glow,
In Heaven, on earth and wave, so fair,
And never feel how vast the wo,   1645
That troubles her who weeps below,
Looks up yet sees no eye to cheer!
Night wanes, and still beside the deep,
Tselica watches shore and steep,
Counts, tearless, every starry beam,   1650
That smiling glides along the stream;
Beholds, with newborn hope, each light,
That kindles soft on distant height
And starts at every sudden sound,
That swells within the gloomy wood   1655
As if some import wild she found,
Some voice renewing strife and blood.
No sleep subdues that night the eyes,
That straining still on rocks and skies,
See nought that soothes or satisfies.   1660
And one by one, the stars depart
The reddening disk of dawn appears,
And still she broods upon her heart,
With dread and dole too deep for tears.
But, as the sun goes up in sight,   1665
She takes new courage from his light,
Resolves to seek her warrior brave,
To find, and if she cannot save,
[Page 69]Embrace his corse, and share his grave!

1647 Simms originally wrote *Looks up and sees no smile to cheer!*
1655 *swells within:* Simms originally wrote *lives in.*

XL.

Day opens bright. The woods are still,   1670
The vapor curls above the hill,
And if the foe hath had his will,
He speeds in triumph far away,
To boast his trophies in the fray.
The winds are whiskt: and if the hoarse   1675
And raging waters, in their course,
Still tell the story of the strife,
That through the rocks first gave them life,
They win no sympathy from flowers,
From shrubs or groves or mountain towers.   1680
These sleep as calmly 'neath the sky,
As if the fires beneath that brood
Had never shot their storms on high,
In earthquake, lava stream and flood.
[Page 70]Down to the stream Tselica glides;—   1685
Well skilled to breast its foaming tides,
To brave their waves with fearless heart,
With eager arms their billows part,
To seek the hollows of the deep
Should hunter rise above the steep,   1690
And float, in effortless repose,
When languid in the billowy strife,
And taste, while round the waters close,
The dream without the toil of life:
No better swimmer might ye see,   1695
'Mongst all the maids of Cherokee;
And now but little thought she gave
To dangers lurking in the wave.
She wins its waters with a bound
Darts through the billows as they rise,   1700
And soon, upon the hostile ground,
She wrings her hair, and lifts her eyes.

1675 *whiskt* (i.e., *whisked*): Simms originally wrote *whisht.*

One moment gazed she thus around,
To heed if lurking foe were near
Then, like the fawn, with heart of fear,   1705
With heavy heart but footstep light,
She seeks the wood, the plain, the height,
And traced the progress of the fight.

XLI.

Through the deep forest steals the breeze,
[Page 71]The Pilgrim of a thousand seas;   1710
His wing the loveliest wilds hath spann'd,
And robb'd the spoils of fairy land;
Borne off from garden realms their bloom,
Brought tribute of their best perfume,
Which, as he speeds, with angel haste,   1715
He flings in bounty to the waste.
This gladdens as he comes, but grows
To deeper sadness as he goes.
One moment ruffles he the bowers,
Of malva, red on rocky towers,   1720
Then fitfully, he glides away
To leave her longing all the day.
Down sweeps he through the gorge, and shakes
The feathery reed tops in the brakes,
Then bounds aloft; a mightier crest,   1725
Bends to th' embrace that makes it blest;
And the great pine, with solemn swing
Sways to the empire of his wing.
The leaves, late turned in summer's hair,
She flings, nor leaves her chaplet bare,   1730
To woo that errant on his way,
And tempt him to a fond delay.
He grasps her offerings glad, but flings
The fluttering trophies from his wings.
[Page 72]They float beneath his breath, then fall,   1735
And earth receives her coronal!

1726 Simms wrote *to* twice; the line has too many syllables for iambic tetrameter.

While he sports with flower and tree,
But never a bondsman will he be,
And, winning all, himself un-won,
The moment of conquest finds him free,— 1740
He flies, and leaves the flowers undone,
Each drooping where she gave her faith,
And silence spread o'er all like Death!
The sun ascends—his sovran beam,
Lights the dark secrets of the stream, 1745
And o'er its gloomy billows flings
A wealth of brilliants such as kings
Might wear on sable in the hour,
When wo is most allied to power.
Unbroken, save by prattling rills, 1750
That murmur down from sloping hills,
The whole wide realm of earth and air,
A more than magic silence fills,
As if the nature, sweet and fair,
Yet own'd some fearful presence there. 1755
So deep the solitude around,
The very silence hast its sound,
And lightest leaf, by breath unstirr'd,
Yet trembling through the air, is heard.
[Page 73]   XLII.
Tselica held her breath to hear, 1760
The very hush seem'd full of fear.
But goaded by the love, whose dread
Of loss, wrought terrors worse than all,
Heedless of self, away she sped
From rocky shore to mountain wall; 1765
With the keen instinct of her race,
The strife's wild progress did she trace;
Here marked the fray'd, or broken bush,
That told of flight and hurried rush;
Here caught the red stain on the leaf, 1770

1744 *sovran:* sovereign.

And trembled with convulsion dread,
Lest from the bosom of her chief,
The crimson token had been shed;
Here track'd the progress, 'till she stood,
Above a very pool of blood,   1775
Now dark and frozen, as was he,
Perchance, from whom it flow'd so free;
Was it her own brave Muscoghee?—
And where his form? Her hopes revive;
He ne'er had yielded while alive   1780
Nor had they borne him dead, away;
His scalp had been sufficient prize,
For the fell victors in the fray,
To wave before their people's eyes.
For hours she speeds, o'er many a league,   1785
[Page 74]She toils in search without fatigue;
Her courage rising as she goes,
To see how well he mock'd his foes.
Through wildest woods, in sinuous flight,
He led them on, with footstep light;   1790
Here, doubling on his track, he sped,
To crouch behind yon boulder's head;
Here shot oblique, as with a will
To gain the steeps of yonder hill.
Then, at its foot swift wheeling flew,   1795
Behind yon coppice hid from view;
And there, with pause awhile, found breath,
And rest and shelter, baffling Death!

XLIII.

But soon they hunt him thence! What need
Each step that mark'd the strife to show?   1800
The Fates had doom'd the chief to bleed,
O'erwhelm'd, not conquer'd, by his foe;
And fearful was his dying blow!
Shaft upon shaft had wounded sore,
And faint, at last, he stood at bay: 1805
Like wolf, that dripping still with gore,

Stops short, and turns with fatal play;
Soon follow'd then the cruel fray.
His back was shelter'd by a tree;
Thence shed his shafts with vengeful flight;   1810
[Page 75]His bloodshot eyes deny to see,—
It is, he feels, his latest fight;—
His proudest could he boast,—but who,
Shall hear again, his war-halloo,
Or list the death song which shall tell,   1815
How long he fought,—how many fell,
Of that despised, pursuing host,
To soothe, and served, his angry ghost.
Not she Tselica!
          From that thought,   1820
His soul new strength and spirit caught;
Five foes have perish'd 'neath his hand,
Which still hath power to use the brand.
His arrows all are sped. His arm
Still wields the tomahawk for harm;   1825
The knife for desperate struggle;—still,
With thoughts like these return the will
With will the hope,—with hope the skill,
And lo! the stratagem! He droops
With forward form—upon his breast,   1830
His head declines—he totters,—stoops,
Sinks on one knee, and seems to rest,
With hand upon the ground!—a dart,
That pierced his side, but fail'd his heart
Moves not his upward gaze!—again,   1835
Another shaft—it brings no pain,
[Page 76]And wakes no seeming consciousness.
To all the fainting chief appears,
No more an object of their fears.
Secure of safety and success,   1840
With wild delight, each eager foe,
Darts forth to deal the deadly blow,
And win the trophied scalp and hair.

They clear the copse, they gain the tree,
They raise the weapon high in air,   1845
But back recoil, for now they see,
The lion rousing from his lair.
With fearful yell, and desperate knife,
The dying warrior starts to life,
Leaps forward to the dread embrace   1850
With all the courage of his race;
His hatchet cleaves the air—a groan—
It crunches through the crumbling bone;
Above the quivering corse he darts
As seeking still for other hearts   1855
With grapple wild, one arm he weaves
About the nearest foeman's neck,
His breast the fatal strike receives,
He offers no defence or check
Content, if in that moment dread,   1860
His own red weapon may be sped,
And he may drag, with tiger hate,
[Page 77]His conqueror down to share his fate:
A shriek! a shout! he feels the foe
Still writhing as he dies below,   1865
And sinks and sees no more, the daze
Of death, o'erspreads the eagle's gaze;
One shout of triumph, and he knows,
No more of mortal fights and foes!

XLIV.

Slowly the conquerors gather near,   1870
Where sleeps the foe whom still they fear,
As dreading, in that grim repose,
Some rare deceipt, some newer guile;
And bare their shafts for other blows,
With one so skill'd in savage wile.   1875
A chief so wondrous swift and bold,
So well by fortune served, so skill'd,
The shaft to wing, the knife to wield,

The wizard of his tribe they hold,
And as around the couchant beast,   1880
Who drowses lightly in his lair,
The hunters' group, with spears in rest,
And deem his moment howl to hear,
So they through forest circuit wide,
Approach with stealthy watch and stride,   1885
And note where prone and stiff he lies,
A victim stretch'd on either side!
[Page 78]Assured at length that life no more
Lurks still beneath the lidded eyes
They crowd around him to explore   1890
That face that still their hate defies.
With scorn and mockery in the glare,
Now upward turn'd the eyeballs stare,
Though glazed by death, yet grim with ire,
As blazing still with mortal fire,   1895
The nostrils wide, the lips compress'd,
Still spoke the courage in his breast
That, to the last, could brave the foe,
Nor seeks to 'scape the fatal blow;
Joyous in thought that life's last hour,   1900
Yet found the foeman in his pow'r,
And the last glimpse of fleeting light,
Betray'd the victim to his sight;
While the last sound that smote his ear,
The warrior-victim's shriek of fear.   1905

XLV.

Down on the fearful form they gaze,
With childlike wonder, mixed with hate;
They scan his deeds with great amaze,
How long he baffled them and fate;
How keen his shaft, how true his aim,   1910

1880 *couchant:* lying down, crouching.

How swift his flight, how dread his blow,
How many warriors, O! the shame,
[Page 79]Had perish'd by this single foe!
With wail and rage they shriek'd the grief
That mourn'd for every slaughter'd chief,   1915
And tramp'd the form, and smote the face,
Of him who wrought them such disgrace;
In madness rent his yellow vest,
Smote with sharp knife, the ample breast,
Tore wide the cell, tore thence the heart,   1920
In bloody morsels this they part,
Each seeks with greedy haste his share,
They grasp, they rend, they rage and tear,
And, as exulting in the taste,
They swallow with remorseless haste.   1925
'Tis thus the savage thinks to gain
The valour of the hero slain,
Partake the soul that made his strength,
And win a fame like his at length!

XLVI.

[Page 80]This done; they join in phrenzied ring,   1930
And dance around the hero slain,
With hellish yell and shriek they sing
The deeds they've done, and those again,
Fed by such lion food of hearts,
Must follow from their arms and arts.   1935
Exulting in their glorious past,
Their future still more glorious grows,
The virtues of their fell repast,
Must make them conquer all their foes.
They joy to think of future blows;—   1940
To paint with savage fancies still,
The bloody stroke, the horrid thrill,
The shout of conquest o'er the dead,
The mangled heart, the bleeding head!—

The horrid food on which they've fed
Has fill'd each soul with hate and hope,
With promise of a fateful spell
'Gainst herds of foes, with skills to cope,
And do for Heaven, the work of Hell!
Fell was the orgy, dread the rite,   1950
Worthy of death, and Hell, and night,
Which kept them till the sun was low,
Still dancing wild, still howling hoarse,
With word of scorn and frequent blow,
[Page 81]Upon the unconscious hero's corse!   1955
With dusk they speed, but ere they go,
They hide the bodies of their slain,
In secret hollows of the plain;
Then, at the last, around they bend
Close crouching o'er the victim now,   1960
To see their chief exulting rend
The scalplock from his lordly brow,
A trophy won at fearful cost,
Yet not unworthy of the lost,
A trophy which to each assures,   1965
Renown, so long as Time endures,
Sung, and in future ages, shown,
When they survive in song alone!—
They pass,—they part—and, up the height,
Leave to the valley death and night!   1970

XLVII.

'Twas there, at length, that stark and cold
Tselica found her hero bold;
How dread the sight, how wild the pain,

1945 *horrid food:* Scalping was practiced in the Southeast in the late prehistoric period and in the colonial historic era. In the sixteenth century, Southeastern Indians were observed dismembering their victims and carrying body parts home as trophies. But ritual cannibalism is not known to have occurred.

It brought alike to soul and brain,
Were more than human speech may tell! 1975
Beside the bloody corse she fell,—
Explored his wounds, unclosed his eyes,
Spoke soft, and fancied soft replies;
Bound up his hurts, and from the spring,
[Page 82]Brought water, o'er his face to fling; 1980
Washed from his breast the blood away,
Kiss'd the red wound, embraced the clay,
And half in hope, and half in fear,
With tremulous whisper, in his ear.—
"'Tis I,—Tselica—Ockwallee,— 1985
Oh! do not hide thine eyes from me;—
Thy foes are gone—the wood is free,—
The boat awaits, and I am near,
Thine own, thy faithfullest, most dear.
Look up, and whisper me again,— 1990
For there's a trouble in my brain,
An icy hand upon my breast,
A pang that will not be repress'd
A death, that is not deathlike rest—
A chill of heart that threats me more 1995
Than all the sorrows dream'd before,
Born of the silence on thy brow,
The hazy depth within thine eyes.
Oh! speak, my hero, answer now,
Bless me with speech,—with sweet replies, 2000
And love, or thy Tselica dies!"

XLVIII.

Long did she doubt, with stubborn will,
The cruel truth that crush'd her still;
[Page 83]'Till all the woman in her soul,
Grew mighty, and escaped control, 2005
And, in the rude conviction taught,
The heart gave up its woes to thought.

1988 Simms originally wrote *awaits us,* but crossed out *us.*

Thus knew she that her life was lone,
Yet made she then no feeble moan
With knowledge of her perfect wo,   2010
The tears at once refused to flow;
The big drops on her chief were dried,
Her grief put on a form of pride;
She rose, and with dilating eye,
Look'd round her as with majesty;   2015
No more her voice in murmurs spoke
To listening echoes grouping round;
No wild complaint of sorrow broke,
The silence of that sad profound.
One husky gasp—one ghastly look   2020
Upon the dead—and then above;
Her form one great convulsion shook,
And then with neither wo nor love,
Within her glance—she fainly stood
As any great tree of the wood,   2025
With soul above that little grief,
That asks of sighs and tears relief!

XLIX.

One passion's loss, must prove the birth,
Of still another, in its place,
[Page 84]Or wo to him who walks the earth   2030
And finds but blankness in its face;
A dark unmeaning vacancy,
As in his heart, before his eye
And vain endurance of this strife,
That leaves no conquering hope to life.   2035
For Love's delirium, sweet and wild,
That bless'd so long, what madness now,
Shall charm that simple forest child,
And soothe the fever of her brow?—
With strength, whose source is in the soul,   2040

2024 *fainly:* gladly, willingly. Simms added *–ly* to *fain* to get the correct meter.
2026 Simms mistakenly wrote *that* twice

Her hero in her arms she bore;
The little islet was her goal.
She reach'd at last the billowy shore,
Then brought she forth, from 'neath the cliff,
Where still it hidden lay, the skiff;   2045
The unconscious chief within she laid,
Her seat beneath his head she made;
Then boldly paddling through the foam,
She sought their happy islet home.
There in that vale of joyous hours,   2050
She'll weave for him anew her flowers,
And teach the mockbird to prolong,
To soothe his ear a wilder song;
[Page 85]Watch—by his couch, through slumber's deep,
And mingle, oh! with happiest skill,   2055
Such music-fancies with his sleep,
As make even sleep with raptures thrill.
Here will she clothe her hero's form,
With robe and sandal, soft and warm,
And barb and wing his shafts so well,   2060
That each shall own a guardian spell,
To make sure passage to the foe,
Yet shield his own from every blow.
Nay, lest the fearful warwhoop rouse,
From sweet repose, her hero spouse,   2065
Herself will use the shaft and knife,
Herself go forth to guard his life;
And take the boat, and cleave the floods,
Supply the venison from the woods,
The fish that haunt the stream,—and lake—   2070
And be the hunter for his sake!
How sweet the thought to guard his rest,
That brought such blessings to her own;
To turn the arrows from his breast,
That warm'd her breast to joy alone.   2075
Ah! She will make her passion known,
By such sweet service as shall move,
His soul to deeper thirst for love,

[Page 86]And she alone such thirst shall shake,

With such delicious draughts, as make, 2080

The drinker thirst afresh, to gain

Such soothing for his pleasant pain.

And thus she dreams in mood as wild

As the boy warrior on his raid;

No more the soft and timid child, 2085

But full of daring, unafraid,

And deeming still that hence, her life,

Must she devote to storm and strife,

To guard with arms her chief's repose

And keep his wigwam 'gainst his foes. 2090

L.

Not strange Tselica's alter'd mood,

To him who knows how in the brain,

With hostile powers prevails the blood,

And leads to madness more than pain;

Or in abrupt convulsion, stills, 2095

The heart, and hushes all its ills!

She was no more the trembling maid

Of storm and strife and change afraid,

Her woman nature perish'd, when,

Her hero flew the world of men! 2100

Once, and the subtle panther's scream,

Had shook her some with terrors drear,

And this same whirlpool in the stream,

[Page 87]To which her skiff is hurrying near,

Had worn to her the look of fear.— 2105

But that was sure a time of dream!

Such terrors now no more affright,

Were but the hostile savage now

To gaze upon that rigid brow,

That eye, that shines with wondrous might, 2110

Or brute, or man, a glance would show,

The soul made eager for the fight!

For she must do and dare she knows,

While lasts the sleep of Ockwallee.

She only may withstand his foes, 2115

With strength through love, to keep him free.
The spell of Heaven is on his breast,
And she must toil that he may rest;—
For her the chase, if need, the strife,
And, till he springs anew to life,   2120
The care that guards his sleep from ill,
The love that warms and watches still!

LI.

While thus she dreams, with fancies wild,
Such as beseem the Indian child,
She heeds not that the waters sway,   2125
Her skiff, a frail and fickle thing,
And bears it from the purposed way
As lightly as the flower of spring.
[Page 88]With eye alone upon her chief,
She marks not how the currents bear,   2130
The little vessel to the reef,
O'er which it safely may not steer.
In that fix'd gaze and mental sleep,
She drifts at random o'er the deep;
The isle for which she turn'd her prow   2135
When first she parted from the shore,
Bright shining with its world of green,
Is dimly now in distance seen;
Smooth was her way at first—but hark,
Rolls the wild torrent 'neath her barque,   2140
That swings it round, and mocks the skill;
That dreaming, steers and paddles still.
Too late she summons strength and will,
Looks back where faint her holy isle,
With sad entreaty seems to smile,   2145
Then down upon the silent form,
That still she fancies breathing warm;
And from the glance new courage takes
From bonds of dream a moment wakes,
And strives once more to turn her prow,   2150
To check its downwards speed amain,

And with new will and vigor now,
The fading isle of green regain;
But as she strives, beneath the wave,
[Page 89]She sees the forms of those, who, slain,   2155
By her bold hero, seek the brave,
Roll through the billowy foam and wave,
And threaten him with kindred grave!
Their giant arms, of swarthy hue,
Rise up, on every side, in view;   2160
They grasp, they shake the little skiff,
And drag it headlong to the cliff.
In vain she smites them with the oar,
They laugh with scorn, they rage, they war;
With fiendish fury wild, they leap   2165
In fearful gambols through the deep,
Hang to the vessel's side, o'erbear
Through foaming gulph and gorge they veer,
Now 'gainst the rocky margin's guide,
Now plunge it headlong down the tide,   2170
Lay bare the gulphs that groan below;
'Till up in heights the surges go,
Roll back and forth, whirl wild and wide
Fling the frail skiff from side to side,
'Till in one howling headlong rush,   2175
They whelm the little barque and crush.

LII.

In that dread moment, ere the wave
Had reach'd and wrapt her sleeping brave,
[Page 90]When from her hand, the paddle torn,
Wrench'd as she deem'd, by foes away,—   2180
And followed by their yells of scorn,
As now exulting o'er their prey;
One glance she gave that isle above,
So dear to blessed hopes and hours;
She next obey'd the voice of love,   2185
That still seemed wooing to its bowers—
And crouching by her hero's side,

She wound him closely to her heart,
Secure, wherever fate betide,
No power should tear their forms apart.   2190
Even as she feels this consciousness,
In spite of terror sure to bless,
The bark is whelm'd;— the torrents sweep
Herself and warrior down the steep
Down, down to the remorseless deep!   2195

LIII.

Then rush'd between a host of foes,
They tear the warrior from her breast;
She clings in vain, her mighty woes,
They mock'd with hate and howls unbless'd.
They bore him from her fond embrace,   2200
They hurl her backward to the shore;
But through the deep she sees his face,
[Page 91]His glance appealing ever more,
With wan entreaty, and she leaps,
From the black rock above the deeps,   2205
And follows—follows fond and fast
The hero she must find at last.

LIV.

She rose no more; but, in her place,
The river knows a form of grace,
A spirit maid, that still pursues,   2210
With dawn and noon, and night the chace,
Nor shrinks from sun, nor dreads the dews,
Still seeking Ockwallee's embrace.
Still haunting every spot she trod—
From where his life blood stain'd the sod,   2215
And from the holy isle above,
Its shady green and sunny grove,
Down to the whirling gulphs below,
That whelm'd them in its mighty flow.
That fearful progress, noon and night,   2220
A sleepless search and ruthless plight,

That fears no dark, and needs no light,
Still finds her eager soul athirst,
And hopeful still as at the first.
Now gazing from the rocks in watch,   2225
That never fails the glimpse to catch,
[Page 92]Of that it seeks, and through the wave,
Still plunging in the hope to save.
Now coursing through the lake above,
Where all is soft, as sleeps the isle,   2230
Where still the brooding soul of love,
Seems through the solitude to smile;
Anon, with wildest passion borne
So fierce the gulph, whose depth of gloom,
Beheld him from her bosom torn   2235
Herself denied to share his doom.
The realm is hers, and dread the night,
She wields o'er all the scene in light,
And he who seeks the stream had best,
Beware, if met upon the way,   2240
She takes him erring to her breast—
He never sees another day.
The fond delusion which persuades
That 'tis her hero's form she sees,
Once gone,—a fury wild pervades   2245
Her soul, and all her beauties freeze,
With deadly chill, instead of charms,
She flings him from her fatal arms
Or gives him sure beneath the wave,
A sunless and a sleepless grave.   2250
Ah! strange that love whose early fruit
Was mild like hers, should bear such fruit.
[Page 93]Strange! that the savage gods should hold,
Such faith—thus kept in spite of hate—
Meet subject for a doom so cold—   2255
Such love unworthy happier fate!
Yet—say the red men—when hath sped

A thousand moons, the penance kept,
And she shall win her warrior's bed,
Where he so long hath lonely slept!—
That then, at her embrace, his heart
Shall from its marble slumbers start,
And they together shall arise,
And find their lodge in Indian skies;
He blest with fields of endless chace;
She ever lovely in his eyes,
And happy in his dear embrace!

2260

2265

APPENDIX 1

ᮐ *Native Americans in the Writings of William Gilmore Simms*

In an effort to put into a convenient format some helpful information concerning Simms's literary uses of the American Indian, the editors have prepared the following chart. Though it is far from definitive, the chart lists significant titles by Simms illustrative of his employment of Indian social groups in a literary context. No attempt has been made to regularize or make consistent Simms's spellings of proper nouns; untitled poems are identified by their first lines without brackets.

If more than one version exists of the same story, all characters listed in the chart may not appear in every version.

	TITLE	CULTURAL, SOCIAL, AND LOCAL GROUPS	INDIAN CHARACTERS
1	"The Adventure of D'Erlach"	Floridian	Oolenoe, *Potanou, *Satouriova
2	"Alphonse D'Erlach"	Apalachian, Auchista, Floridian, Maccou, Ouade, Utina	Unnamed Apalachee princess
3	"The Arm-Chair of Tustenuggee. A Tradition of the Catawba"	Catawba	Conattee, Macourah, Selonee, Tustenuggee ("grey demon of Enoree")
4	"The arrows"—[in *The Yemassee*]	Yemassee [unnamed]	Opitchi-Manneyto (the "black spirit")

* Denotes names that have been identified as having been based on the names of real Indians; others may well be real, but are not identifiable by the editors.

5   "At midnight did the   Choctaw [unnamed]   Oolatibbé [unnamed]
    chiefs convene"
    [in "Indian Sketch"]

6   "Bald-Head Bill   Seminole   Unidentified Indian
    Bauldy"   "queen"

7   "Battle-god Manneyto—"   Yemassee [unnamed]   Battle-god Manneyto
    or "Yemassee War-Hymn"
    [in *The Yemassee*]

8   "The Broken Arrow"   Creek [unnamed]   *McIntosh [the unnamed
    [poem]   "chief"], Mad Wolf,
                                                       *Menawé

9   "The Broken Arrow.   Catawba, Cherokee,   *General William
    An Authentic Passage   Chickasaw, Choctaw,   Mackintosh, *Chilly
    from Unwritten   Creek, Muscoghee,   Mackintosh, Mad Wolf,
    American History"   Seminole   *Menawé, *Opokbyobolo,
                                                       *Pathkiller

10 "Caloya; or, the   Catawba   Caloya, Chickawa, Enefisto
    Loves of the Driver"   (or Richard Knuckles)

11 "Captivity of the   Apalachian, Emola,   Lord of Edelano,
    Great Paracoussi"   Floridian, Potanou   Satouriova, Nia,
                                                       Cubacang, Olata
                                                       Ouvae Utina (or Holata
                                                       Utina, or Olata Utina)

12 "The Cassique of   Accabee, Edisto,   Cassique of Accabee
    Accabee"   Yemassee

13 *The Cassique of Kiawah* Accabee, Cherokee,   Cussoboe, Iawa, Iswattee
                              Chickasaw, Choctaw,
                              Coosaw, Edistoh, Isundigo
                              Floridian, Katahbah,
                              Kiawah, Muscoghee,
                              Ocketta, Savanna, Sewee,
                              Stono, Wadmalah,
                              Westo, Yemassee

14	"The Cherokee Embassage"	Catawba, Cherokee, Chickasaw, Creek, Occonie, Shawnee, Telliquo	Canonjahee, Cenestee, Chulochkolla, Eefistoe, Great Keowee, *Moytoy, *Occonostoto, Sarratahay of Santee, *Skiajagustha, Tonestoi
15	"The Children of the Sun"	Creek, Huspah, Seminole, Yemassee	Anyta, Echotee, Henamarsa, Hillaby, *Huspah, Onea, *Sanuté, Washattee
16	"Chilhowee, the Indian Village"	Cherokee	Only Anglicized names
17	"The Christian Indian"	Mohawk, Narragansett, Pequot	Miona, Wequash
18	"Chronicles of Ashley River"	Yemassee	Redfoot
19	"The 'Coonee-Latee,' or 'Trick-Tongue'" [in *The Yemassee*]	Yemassee	None named
20	"Customs and Peculiarities of the Indians"	Seminole, Yemassee	Matiwan, Occonestoga, *Oceola, *Sanuttee
21	"Dark-eyed Maid of Edisto"	Edisto	None named
22	"Death of King Philip"	Mohegan, Montaup, Narragansett, Nipnet	*King Philip (aka Meta-com), Manitto
23	"Dominique de Gourges"	Apalachian, Floridian	Athoree, Harpaha, Helicopilé, Helmacana, Helmacapé, Holata Cara (Olotocara), Mollova, *Satouriova, Tacatacourou

24	"The Forest Maiden"	Oneida	*Powhatan, *Pocahontas [unnamed]
25	"Haiglar: A Story of the Catawbas"	Catawba, Shawnee	Cunestoga, *Haiglar, Marramatté, Onomatchee
26	"Hear, Opitchi-Manneyto" [in *The Yemassee*]	Savannah, Suwannee, Yemassee	Occonestoga, Opitchi-Manneyto
27	"I go with the long knife" [in *The Yemassee*]	Yemassee [unnamed]	Occonestoga
28	"I hear thee, Opitchi-Manneyto," [in *The Yemassee*]	Yemassee	Opitchi-Manneyto (the "black spirit")
29	"I take from thee the earth of Yemassee—" [in *The Yemassee*]	Yemassee	Occonestoga [unnamed]
30	"I was a wanderer long. . ." [in "The Choctaw Criminal"]	Choctaw	Oakatibbé and Oolatibbé [unnamed], Mewanto
31	"Indian Hunter's Song"	Creek	None named
32	"Indian Serenade"	None named	None named
33	"Indian Sketch"	Choctaw	Mewanto, Oolatibbé
34	"The Indian Village"	Choctaw, Yazoo, Chickasaw	Anglicized names only
35	"Iracana, or the Eden of the Floridian"	Floridian, Olata Utina	Apalou, Athoree, Iracana, Tacadocorou
36	"Is not this a Yemassee?" [in *The Yemassee*]	Yemassee	Occonestoga [unnamed]
37	"It is not the Yemassee" [in the*Yemassee*]	Yemassee	Occonestoga [unnamed]

38	"Jocassée. A Cherokee Legend"	Cherokee, Estatoe (Green Birds), Occonie (Brown Vipers)	Cheochee, Jocassée, Nagoochie
39	"The Last Fields of the Biloxi: A Tradition of Louisiana"	Biloxi, Choctaw	None named
40	"The Last of the Yemassees"	Creek, Yemassee	*Sanuté
41	["League of the Redman"]	Catawba, Cherokee, Coree, Cotheckney, Creek, Matchapango, Mattamasketto, Tuscarora, Yemassee	None named
42	"The Legend of Guernache"	Apalachian, Ouade	Audusta, Maccou, Monaletta
43	"Legend of Missouri: or, the Captain of the Pawnee"	Omaha, Pawnee	Enemoya, Kionk, Missouri, Tanewahakile, Ouanawega-poree
44	"Let the Yemassee have ears" [in *The Yemassee*]	Yemassee	Opitchi-Manneyto, the prophet
45	"Letters from the West"	Choctaw	None named
46	"Logoochie; or, the Branch of Sweet Water. A Legend of Georgia"	Creek, Seminole	Logoochie, Great Manneyto, Opitchi-Manneyto, Satilla
47	"The Love of Mackintosh"	Creek	*Mackintosh
48	"The Love Song of Enemoya"	Omaha	None named

49	"Lucas de Ayllon. A Historical Nouvellette"	Apalachian, Cherokee, Haytian, Mickasukee, Muscoghee, Seminole, Southern, Stono, Yemassee	Chiquola, Combahee, Edelano, Iawa, Kiawah, Maneyto, Ocketee
50	"Mighty is the Yemassee" [in *The Yemassee*]	Edisto, Westo, Yemassee	Opitchi-Manneyto
51	["Mossfoot, the Demon of the Red Man"]	None named	Aboriginal elf, Mossfoot (Logoochie)
52	"The Mountain Tramp"	Cherokee, Muscoghee	Tselica, Ockwallee, Manneyto
53	"The Narrative of Le Barbu: The Bearded Man of Calos"	"people of the Sarropee"	*Barbu, the Iawas, Mico Wa-ha-la, *Olata Utina, Onathaqua, Istakalina
54	"North American Indians"	Cherokee, Coweta, Creek, Seminole	*Gen. McIntosh
55	"Notes of a Small Tourist — No. 6"	Creek	*William McIntosh
56	"Oakatibbe, or the Choctaw Sampson"	Choctaw	Loblolly Jack, Oakatibbe (or Slim Sampson)
57	"An Old Time Story"	Yemassee [unnamed]	Metapah
58	"Pocohontas, A Legend of Virginia"	Virginia Algonquians, Massawomek, Monacan	*Pocahantas, *Powhatan
59	"Sangarrah-me— Sangarrah-me" [in *The Yemassee*]	Yemassee [unnamed]	Occonestoga [unnamed]
60	"Sangarrah-me, Yemassee" [in *The Yemassee*]	Yemassee	Battle-god Manneyto
61	"The Seduction at La Caroline"	Apalachian, Cherokee	Hostaqua, *Olata Utina, Onathaqua, Oolenoe, *Potanou

62	"Severe the school that made them bear" [in *The Yemassee*]	Yemassee [unnamed]	None named
63	"The Sioux Boy; an Indian Legend"	Siouan [unnamed]	
64	"Sketches of Indian Character"	Creek	Big Warrior, *Black Hawk
65	"Song of Philip"	Mohegan, Nipnet, Algonquian, [unnamed]	*King Phillip (aka Metacom), Manitto
66	"The Spectre Chief of Accabee"	None named	None named
67	"A Story of the Old-Time Cherokee" [head-note to "Jocassée"]	Cherokee	None named
68	"The Subaltern's Yarn; or, a Day's Scout in the Florida Campaign"	Creek, Micasukee, Seminole	Micasukee chief, Octtiatchee
69	"That Opitchi-Manneyto!—/ He commands thee for his slave—" [in *The Yemassee*]	Yemassee	Manneyto, Occonestoga [unnamed], Opitchi-Manneyto,
70	"Thlecathcha; or, The Broken Arrow"	Cherokee, Seminole, Sioux, Muscoghee [unnamed]	Thlecathcha, Menawe
71	"Thou that wast a brother" [in *The Yemassee*]	Yemassee	Occonestoga [unnamed]
72	"Thou wast a child of Manneyto" [in *The Yemassee*]	Yemassee [unnamed]	Manneyto, Occonestoga [unnamed]

73	"Thy wing, Opitchi-Manneyto" [in *The Yemassee*]	Yemassee	Opitchi-Manneyto (the "black spirit")
74	"'Tis Opitchi-Manneyto /In Malatchie's ear that cries" [in *The Yemassee*]	Yemassee	*Malatchie, Occonestoga (unnamed), Opitchi-Manneyto
75	"'Tis Opitchi-Manneyto, / Not the prophet, now that that speaks" [in *The Yemassee*]	Yemassee	*Malatchie ("the executioner"), *the good Manneyto, the prophet, Opitchi-Manneyto
76	"The Tryst of Acayama"	None named	Acayama, Panaco
77	"The Two Camps. A Legend of the Old North State"	Cherokee	Lenatewá, Micco Lenatewá Glucco, Oloschottee
78	"Tzelica, A Tradition of the French Broad"	Cherokee	None named
79	*Vasconselos*	Apalachian, Capaha, Chickasaw, Choctaw, Cofachiqui, Floridian, KasKasKia, Mauvilian Seminole, Tomenos, Tula	Chicaza, Chinnabee Himantla, Coçalla, the Great Iawa, Istalana, Micco Tuskina Ithiopolla, Oolena Ithiopoholla, Oolenoe Ifisto, *Patofa, *Tuscaluza, Vitachuco
80	"What is the Seratee?" [in *The Yemassee*]	Seratee, Yemassee	Occonestoga [unnamed]
81	"The Widow of the Chief"	None named	None named, other than in the title
82	"Xanthoxilus, A Shelter from the Sun"	Seminole,	None named

83 *The Yemassee*	Alatanaha, Chareco,	*Sanutee, Choluculla,
	Cherokee, Chickasaw,	Ishiagaska, Tamaita,
	Combahee, Coosaw,	Matiwan, Enoree-Mattee,
	Cussoboe, Estatoe,	*Huspah, Occonestoga,
	Huspah, Seratee, Sewee,	*Mackintosh, Hiwassee,
	Stonoee, Suwannee,	Echotee, Checkamoysee,
	Yemassee	Manneywanto, *Malatchie,
		Chaharattee, Chinnabee,
		*Chigilli

ᕒᕒ *Glossary of Native American Entities*

The following linguistic, cultural, and social entities have been identified in Simms's writings. The numbers following each entry correspond to the works (listed in the preceding chart) in which each entity is mentioned.

Alatanaha Simms probably based this name on the Altamaha River of Georgia. In the sixteenth century, Altamaha was a chiefdom on the middle Oconee River in Georgia. 83

Algonquian (1) A major Native American language family mainly located in the northern plains, around the Great lakes, in the Northeast, and extending into the South to include such languages as Powhatan, Matchapunga, and Shawnee; (2) cultural groupings such as the Virginia Algonquins and the North Carolina Algonquins; (3) a specific group of closely related bands who inhabited the Ottawa Valley and adjacent areas in the first half of the seventeenth century. 65

Apalachian Properly known as Apalachee, this Muskogean-speaking chiefdom was located in and around the Tallahassee area in the sixteenth and seventeenth centuries. 2, 11, 23, 42, 49, 61, 79

Auchista A variant spelling of Audusta (French) or Orista (Spanish), a small sixteenth-century society located on the upper Coosaw River. 2

Biloxi The Biloxi spoke a Siouan language and lived in southern Mississippi. 39

Capaha This is Garcilaso de la Vega's (and Theodore Irving's) apparent misspelling of Pacaha, a chiefdom in northeastern Arkansas. 79

Catawba (1) A language family distantly related to Siouan; (2) in the sixteenth century, a town or small cluster of towns in western North Carolina; (3) in the eighteenth century, a coalescent group of linguistically and culturally diverse peoples living in South Carolina. 3, 9, 10, 14, 25, 41

Chareco Probably a purely fictional group of Indians. 83

Cherokee An Iroquoian-speaking people who lived in the southern Appalachians from southwestern Virginia through eastern Tennessee, the western portion of the Carolinas, into northern Georgia and Alabama. 9, 13, 14, 16, 38, 41, 52, 54, 61, 67, 70, 77, 78, 83

Chickasaw They spoke a Muskogean language closely related to Choctaw and resided principally in northern Mississippi. 9, 13, 14 34, 79, 83

Choctaw They spoke a Muskogean language closely related to Chickasaw. Their towns were located in the southeastern part of Mississippi. 5, 9, 13, 30, 33, 34, 39, 45, 56, 79

Cofachique The preferred spelling is "Cofitachequi," a sixteenth- and seventeenth-century town and chiefdom on the Catawba-Wateree River in South Carolina. 79

Combahee A small group that lived on and near the Combahee River in South Carolina. 83

Coosaw In the sixteenth century, the Cozao (or Kusso) were a town of people on the upper Coosawhatchie River. Survivors later lived around the mouth of the Combahee or Coosaw River. 13, 83

Coree The Coree Indians lived on a peninsula south of the Neuse River in North Carolina and may have been of the Algonquian linguistic family. They joined the Tuscarora in a war against the colonists in 1711; and in 1715 the remnants of the tribe, along with the remaining Machapunga, were assigned to a reservation on Mattamuskeet Lake in North Carolina where they resided until they became extinct. 41

Cotheckney May refer to the inhabitants of the palisaded Tuscarora town and palisade known as Cotechney, located on North Carolina's Neuse River, about the mouth of Contentnea Creek. 41

Coweta One of two principal towns of the lower Creek Indians located on the Chattahoochee River in Georgia. 54 (See also, Creek and Muscogee.)

Creek The Creeks were a coalescence or "confederacy" of linguistically and culturally diverse Indians who formed in the seventeenth and eighteenth centuries. They were the dominant people in what is now Alabama and Georgia. Many of them spoke Muskogean, and those who did are sometimes called Muskogees. 8, 9, 14, 15, 31, 40, 41, 46, 47, 54, 55, 64, 68 (See also, Coweta.)

Cussoboe (or Cusabo) A term applied to several remnant peoples—such as the Combahee, Kusso, Edisto, Etiwaw, Kiawaw, St. Helena, Stono, Wapoo, and Westo Indians—who lived between the Charleston and Savannah Rivers. 83

Edisto (or Orista) A small group who lived in a town between the Broad and Combahee Rivers in the sixteenth century. In the seventeenth century, they occupied the lower Edisto River in South Carolina. 12, 13, 21, 50

Emola A sixteenth-century chief and/or small society located near the mouth of the St. John's River. 11

Estatoe (or Estatoee) A former Cherokee town on the Tugaloo River in upstate South Carolina. 38, 83

Floridian An anachronistic term that Schoolcraft applied to the Apalachee Indians of northern Florida. 1, 2, 11, 13, 23, 35, 79

Haytian The people of Haiti, i.e., Haitians. 49

Huspah Possibly a variant of "Cusabo." 15, 83

KasKasKia The Kaskaskia spoke an Algonquian language and were counted among the Illinois confederacy. They made their home in Illinois along the Mississippi and Kaskaskia Rivers until they were removed west of the Mississippi under a treaty signed October 27, 1832. Theodore Irving equated Casqui, a De Soto–era chiefdom in northeastern Arkansas, with Kaskaskia. 79

Kiawah (also Cayagua) A small group who lived near Charleston Harbor. 13

Maccou Probably a variant of Escamacu, a small group who lived on St. Helena Island, South Carolina. 2

Matchapango (or Machapunga) Indians who spoke an Algonquian language and resided in and around Hyde County, North Carolina. See Coree. 41

Mattamasketto Refers to the inhabitants of the Machapunga town of Matta-muskeet. The town was probably located on Lake Mattamuskeet in North Carolina. 41

Micasukee (or Mikasuki) The name of a group of Seminoles who lived in a town of the same name on the western shore of Lake Miccosukee in Florida. 49

Mohawk The easternmost division of the Iroquois confederation. Their towns were in the valley of the Mohawk River between Schenectady and Utica, New York. 17

Mohegan The Mohegan Indians spoke an Algonquian language and originally occupied most of the upper valley of the Thames River in Connecticut. They are sometimes confused with the Mahican Indians who lived in the valley of the Hudson River in New York. 22

Montaup Simms probably meant this to be the Montauk Indians of central and eastern Long Island. The Montauk spoke an Algonquian language. 22

Muscoghee The modern spelling is "Muskogee." 9, 13, 49, 52 (See also, Coweta and Creek.)

Narragansett An Algonquian-speaking people who occupied most of Rhode Island west of Narragansett Bay. 17, 22

Nipnet (more commonly known as Nipmuc) Indians who lived in central Massachusetts extending into Connecticut and Rhode Island, the Nipnet spoke an Algonquian language. 22

Occonie Oconee was an eighteenth-century Cherokee town on a tributary of the

Keowee River in northwestern South Carolina. They should not be confused with the Creek group by the same name. 14, 38

Omaha The Omaha spoke a Dhegiha Souian language, and their principal home was along the Missouri River in northeastern Nebraska. 43, 48

Oneida A tribe of the Iroquois confederation that occupied the land around Oneida Lake in New York. 24

Ouade A French word for the Guale Indians. It was also the name of one of their chiefs. This group spoke a Muskogean language and lived along the coast of Georgia between St. Andrews Sound and the Savannah River. 2, 42

Pawnee A confederacy of peoples who spoke Caddoan languages, the Pawnee lived principally in the area of the Platte River and the Republican fork of the Kansas River. 43

Pequot The Pequot Indians spoke an Algonquian language and resided in Connecticut and Rhode Island. 17

Potanou In the sixteenth and seventeenth centuries, the Potano Indians spoke a Timucuan language and lived in what is now Alachua County in northern Florida. 11

Powhatan A paramount chiefdom of Algonquian speakers who resided mostly in tidewater Virginia. 22

Sarropee Properly Serrope, a large freshwater lake in southern Florida reported to French Huguenots by two Spaniards (one named Barbu) held captive by the Calusa Indians. Described in René de Laudonnière's narrative of a 1564 voyage. 53

Savanna An anglicized name applied to a group of Shawnee who built a town on the Savannah River, opposite present-day Augusta. 13, 26

Seminole A coalescent group of Muskogean-speaking lower Creeks who immigrated to central Florida after about 1750. 9, 15, 20, 46, 49, 54, 68, 70, 79

Seratee Possibly the Saruti or some other Catawban-speaking people visited by Juan Pardo in 1566–68. 80, 83

Sewee A small group who possibly spoke a Catawban language. They lived along the lower course of the Santee River and coastal South Carolina. 13, 83

Shawnee Several bands of Algonquian-speaking Indians who lived mainly in the Ohio Valley in the late seventeenth and early eighteenth centuries, but who traveled widely. A group of them settled on the Savannah River and later coalesced with the Creeks. 14, 25

Sioux (or Dakota) Siouan-speaking Indians who lived in a territory extending from Wisconsin and Iowa as far westward as Montana and Wyoming. They were one of the dominant peoples of the Great Plains. They are best known today for defeating George Custer. 63, 70

Stono (Simms also has this as Stonoee) A small group of Indians who lived on the coast south of Charleston, South Carolina. 13, 49, 83

Suwannee Fictitious Indians whose name was taken from the Suwannee River in south Georgia and Florida. The name comes from the Mission San Juan de Guacara, later shortened to San-Juanee, then anglicized as Suwannee. 26, 83

Telliquo (or Tellico) A principal eighteenth-century Overhill Cherokee town located on the Tellico River in Tennessee. 14

Tula An Indian province along the Arkansas River in western Arkansas visited by Hernando de Soto's army in 1542. 79

Tuscarora A confederacy of Indians residing on the Roanoke, Tar, Pamlico, and Neuse Rivers in North Carolina. They spoke an Iroquoian language. 41

Utina A group of Timucuan-speakers who resided between the St. John's River and the wetlands at the head of the Santa Fe River in Florida. 2, 11, 35

Wadmalahs Seemingly a fictitious group of Indians named after Wadmalah Island, which is southwest of Charleston, bounded on two sides by the Wadmalah and Edisto Rivers. 13

Westo A group of Indians who migrated from the Northeast and built a town on the Savannah River before the founding of Charleston in 1670. They were aggressive slave-catchers who terrorized the local Indians. 13, 50

Yemassee ("Yamasee" is the preferred modern spelling.) Speaking mainly Muskogean languages, they were a late-seventeenth/early-eighteenth-century coalescence of people on the coast of South Carolina and Georgia. Most of them originated in central Georgia. 4, 7, 12, 13, 15, 18, 19, 26, 27, 28, 29, 36, 37, 40, 41, 44, 49, 50, 57, 59, 60, 62, 69, 71, 72, 73, 74, 75, 80, 83

ᙡ *Cultural, Social, and Local Groups*

William Gilmore Simms could have had no understanding that tremendous discontinuities existed between the sixteenth-century and eighteenth-century Southeast. The names on the landscape of the sixteenth-century Southeast were radically different from those of the eighteenth-century Southeast. Such an understanding has only become possible in the past twenty years with modern research on the travels of Spanish explorers in the sixteenth century and on the activities of Spanish missionaries in the late sixteenth and seventeenth centuries. The native societies of the sixteenth century collapsed, primarily because of Old World diseases, but also because of the colonial programs of various European powers. After this collapse, Native American survivors and their progeny reorganized themselves in the seventeenth century to meet the challenges of the new world order that progressively affected them.

The terminology used to denote different varieties of prestate societies has changed over the centuries. A version of the word *tribe* occurs in middle English, meaning a people claiming descent from a common ancestor, as in the twelve divisions of Israel, claiming descent from the twelve sons of Jacob. Today anthropologists use "tribe" to refer to societies whose constituent groups are based on kinship and which lack hierarchical leadership.

The word *chiefdom* was used in the nineteenth century and earlier to refer to the domain or office of a chief. In the 1950s anthropologists began using the word in a more technical sense to refer to societies intermediate in social complexity between egalitarian bands and states. What distinguishes chiefdoms from tribes is that chiefdoms are commanded by a chief whose succession to office is governed by principles or rules. When Hernando de Soto explored the American Southeast in the sixteenth century he encountered many chiefdoms and in a few places he encountered *paramount chiefdoms*, that is, chiefdoms that had power or influence over other chiefdoms.

After the seventeenth-century population collapse in the Southeast, in many places survivors of the chiefdoms threw in their lot with each other to form *coalescent societies* (sometimes called confederacies) to better withstand competition with colonists from Europe. These coalescent societies included such peoples as the Creeks, Choctaws, Chickasaws, Cherokees, and Catawbas. In the eighteenth century, these coalescent societies were often called *nations,* and to add to the confusion, they were also sometimes called tribes.

Simms got many of his place names and names of societies from eighteenth- and early-nineteenth-century printed sources. Some few he got from sixteenth-century sources, such as René de Laudonnière's account of the activities of French Huguenots in northern Florida and the Georgia and South Carolina coast. He got still others from Theodore Irving's *The Conquest of Florida by Hernando de Soto* (New York: George P. Putnam and Son, 1851). The book by Irving (who was nephew to Washington Irving) was based on his reading of Garcilaso de la Vega's *La Florida del Ynca* and secondarily on the narrative of the anonymous Gentleman of Elvas.

On occasion, Simms uses the names of societies anachronistically, as when he peoples the De Soto expedition with Choctaws and Seminoles, both of whom are from the eighteenth century, or when he peoples the sixteenth-century Ayllon colony with Cherokees, Mikasukees, Seminoles, and Yemassees, all again from the eighteenth century.

✑ Names of Indian Characters

Simms got his names of Indian characters from various sources. Some were from historical documents (e.g., the names Potanou and Satouriova [*sic*] in "The Adventures of D'Erlach").

In sixteenth-century documents, a chief often has the same name as his chiefdom (e.g., Potano was the chief of Potano). Simms assumed without justification that this practice also prevailed in the eighteenth century. Hence, the names of many of the characters in his stories are based on place names. For example, in the story "Jocassée," the names of the characters Jocassée and Nagoochie are based on place names in north Georgia and South Carolina. He used "Occonestoga," based on a Cherokee place name, in several of his stories.

His names from historical sources are not always spelled correctly. In "Satouriova" he substitutes a *v* for an *n*, seemingly a mistranscription. Some names are barely recognizable. For example, is Opokbyobolo in "The Broken Arrow" based on Opothle Yoholo? His names Nia and Cubacang in "The Captivity of the Great Paracoussi" are derived from a single name, Niacubacang.

In some instances, Simms made up Indian-sounding names. This would seem to be the case, for example, with Conattee, Macourah, and Selonee in the story "The Arm-Chair of Tustenuggee. A Tradition of the Catawba."

In several of his stories, Simms has a deity named Manneyto. This is apparently based on the Algonquian concept of *manitou*, a central notion in their religious system. But this word refers not so much to a spiritual being or deity as to a belief in an impersonal sacred property in nature. It is similar to the Siouan concept of *wakanda*. Both concepts have something of the meaning of "sacred," "remarkable," or "wonderful." Such a concept may have existed among Southeastern Indians, but there is little evidence to verify that it did. In any case, there is no justification for using "Manneyto" to refer to a creator god in the Southeast, or for using "Opitchi-Manneyto" to refer to his nemesis, an evil god, or war god. As anthropologists have learned time and time again, when attempting to understand the mentality of people of another culture, it is difficult to avoid imposing one's own conceptions on theirs.

Appendix 2

∽ Emendations in the Text

Listed below are changes made in the copy-text. Numbers refer to page and line of each emendation, e.g. 33.05 indicates page 33, line 5. To the left of the brackets are words or passages as they appear in the copy-text: to the right of the brackets are the changes. Line numbers are from top of page, or from title of selection, whichever is relevant.

Essays and Letters

Sketches of Indian Character

33.05   but] butt

Thle-cath-cha

59.09   remained.] remained,
64.05   Æschylus"] Æschylus:
64.06   The fire] "The fire
64.15   Strath-Ire;—**] Strath-Ire;—"

The Broken Arrow. An Authentic Passage from Unwritten American History

95.08   aids] aides

Literature and Art among the American Aborigines

103 (note) .01   Refusal to emend: Gess] (the historical Sequoyah was also called *Guess*)
108.27   Wetherford] Weatherford

Stories

Logoochie

159.10   than] then

159.29   Refusal to emend: was]   (change would bring subject and verb in agreement)

159.29   Refusal to emend: was]   (same as immediately above)

Jocassée

189.27   deeds] deed

The Arm-Chair of Tustenuggee

201.37   Refusal to emend: missing word
209.28   VI] VII
212.15   VII] VIII
215.06   VIII] IX

Oakatibbé

276.27   Refusal to emend: missing verb

The Legend of Guernache

344.09–10   muscle] mussel
353 (note) .04   Refusal te emend: and] (English word in a French text)
361.37   suspicion's] suspicions

The Narrative of Le Barbu

398.09   dies] dyes
401.08   Refusal to emend: vessels . . . was
402.23   sign.] sign?
408.18   embadey] embedded
410.36   Refusal to emend: thridded] (a valid but archaic English word)
411.21   Myself.] Myself."
414.21   Thus] "Thus

The Spectre Chief of Accabee

428.28   should] shoulder

Poems

[Hear, Opitchi-Manneyto]
451.71   fight] flight

The Last Fields of the Biloxi
483.71   No] Not

The Mountain Tramp

Emendations already accounted for in footnotes to *The Mountain Tramp* are not repeated in this list.

510.213 fires;] fires
512.300 Scar'd] Scarr'd
514.367 I reckon] "I reckon
518.497 camp.] camp."
520.561 strawbery] strawberry
527.778 guarden] garden
527.780 Hunter] Hunter's
527.786 XXVII.] XXVIII.
528.814 XXVIII.] XIX.
529.855 XIX.] XX.
530.883 XX.] XXI.
531.908 XXI.] XXII.
531.922 XXII.] XXIII.
533.964 XXIII.] XXIV.
533.992 XXIV.] XXV.
535.1057 XXV.] XXVI.
536.1071 Refusal to emend: fo'w'd
536.1086 XXVI.:] delete
536.1098 interposes] interpos'd
537.1118 who] who's
543.1328 Refusal to emend : cockle (Simms may have intended coracle)
544.1359 doubt] doubt,
548.1501 thicket] thicket's
552.1613 Refusal to emend: sprang
566.2088 Must be] Must she

Bibliography of the Indian Writings of William Gilmore Simms

This bibliography contains all of Simms's known writings about Native Americans listed chronologically under separate headings: nonfiction, fiction, and poetry. ·If a piece was first published in a periodical, its subsequent book publications by Simms during his lifetime are also listed. With the exception of Simms's letters to Henry Rowe Schoolcraft—never published during the lifetime of Simms—no private correspondence is included. The other guiding principles of the bibliography are:

1. Each entry is listed under the title by which it is best known (usually, but not necessarily, the last published title that has Simms's authority), even if it bore a different title when first published;

2. If a work has been so extensively revised by Simms that it constitutes a new work, both the original publication and publications of the revisions are included, listed separately (for example, "Indian Sketch," "The Choctaw Criminal," and "Oakatibbe, or the Choctaw Sampson" are all listed, under separate entries);

3. Other than as specified above, no effort has been made to include publications of a given work, subsequent to its first book publication, during Simms lifetime; publications subsequent to Simms death are excluded;

4. Certain manuscripts unpublished at Simms's death are included whether or not they have since been published.

ᕲ Essays and Letters

1825

"The Christian Indian." *Album* 1 (27 Aug. 1825): 65–68.

1826

"Letters from the West." *Album* 2 (4 March, 11 March, 1 April, and 20 May 1826): 68–69, 76–77, 100–101, 157–58.

1828

"North American Indians." *Southern Literary Gazette* 1 (Sept. 1828): 31–40.

1831

"Notes of a Small Tourist—nos. 5, 6,7, 8, 9, and 10." Charleston *City Gazette,* 30 Mar., 27 April, 28 April, 30 April, 4 May, 17 May 1831.

1835

"Sketches of Indian Character. Nos. 1 and 2." *Southern Literary Journal* 1 (Oct. 1835): 101–7; 2 (Mar. 1836): 13–17. [Simms's authorship of "No. 2" is highly questionable]

1837–38

"Thle-cath-cha. Being a few passages from Muscoghee History" Chapters 1–5. *Southern Literary Journal* 1 ns (July 1837): 394–97; 3 ns (May 1838): 331–43; 3 ns (June 1838): 427–34; 4 ns (July 1838): 48–55; 4 ns (Sept. 1838): 172–83.

1838

"Customs and Peculiarities of the Indians." *Southern Literary Journal* 4 ns (Dec. 1838): 430–37.

1844

"The Broken Arrow. An Authentic Passage from Unwritten American History." *Ladies' Companion* 20 (Jan. 1844): 110–19.

1845

"Literature and Art among the American Aborigines." *Southern and Western* 1 (March 1845): 153–64; 1:128–47. *Views and Reviews of American Literature, History and Fiction,* 2 vols. (New York: Wiley and Putnam, 1845), 1:128–47.

"The Red Eagle of Muscoghee." *Southern and Western* 2 (Aug. 1845): 119–20.

"Pocahontas: A Subject for the Historical Painter." *Southern and Western* 2 (Sept. 1845): 145–54; *Views and Reviews* (1845), 1:112–27.

Letter of c. 26 Sept. 1845 to Henry Rowe Schoolcraft (collected in *The Letters of William Gilmore Simms,* ed. Mary C. Simms Oliphant, Alfred Taylor Odell, and T. C. Duncan Eaves, 5 vols. [Columbia: University of South Carolina Press, 1952–56] 2:102–3).

1851

Letter of 16 Feb. [1851] to Henry Rowe Schoolcraft (uncollected; published for the first time in this volume).

Letter of 18 Mar. 1851 to Henry Rowe Schoolcraft (collected in *Letters* 3:101–2).

Letter of 8 May 1851 to Henry Rowe Schoolcraft (collected in *Letters* 3:117–18).
Letter of 10 June 1851 to Henry Rowe Schoolcraft (collected in *Letters* 3:129–30).
Letter of 10 June 1851 to Henry Rowe Schoolcraft (collected in *Letters* 3:130).
"History of the Indian Tribes." *Southern Quarterly Review* 4 (July 1851): 245–46
[review of Schoolcraft's *Historical and Statistical Information, respecting the History, Condition and Prospects of the Indian Tribes of the United States* (1851)].

1852

"Schoolcraft's American Indians, and Personal Memoirs." *Southern Quarterly Review* 5 ns (Jan. 1852): 238–39 [review].
Letter of 26 Feb. 1852 to Henry Rowe Schoolcraft (collected in *Letters* 3:166).
Letter of 14 Apr. 1852 to Henry Rowe Schoolcraft (collected in *Letters* 3:176).
Letter of 7 July 1852 to Henry Rowe Schoolcraft (collected in *Letters* 3:186).

ᴄᴡ *Stories and Novels*

1828

"Indian Sketch." *Southern Literary Gazette* 1 (Nov. 1828): 142–49.

1829

"Chronicles of the Ashley River—Nos. 1–6." *Southern Literary Gazette* 1 (15 July, 1 Aug., 1 Sept., 15 Sept., 15 Oct., 1 Nov. 1829): 115–16, 129–30, 176–78, 208–10, 247–52, 278–80.

1832

"Legend of Missouri: or, the Captive of the Pawnee." *New York Mirror* 10 (29 Sept. 1832): 105–6; *The Book of My Lady. A Melange* (Philadelphia: Key & Biddle, 1833; Boston: Allen & Ticknor, 1833), 155–68. *Southward Ho!* (1854), 404–37.
"Haiglar. A Story of the Catawba." *New York Mirror* 10 (6 Oct. 1832): 105–6; *The Book of My Lady* (1833), 126–35.
"A Legend of the Pacific." *New York Mirror* 10 (13 Oct. 1832): 117–18; *The Book of My Lady* (1833), 244–56.

1833

"The Choctaw Criminal." *The Book of My Lady* (1833), 277–90.
"The Children of the Sun." *New York Mirror* 10 (19 Jan. 1833): 225–27; *The Book of My Lady* (1833), 189–211; revised and published as "Onea and Anytea," *Carl Werner, An Imaginative Story; with other Tales of Imagination,* 2 vols. (New York: George Adlard, 1838), 1:209–43.
"An Old Time Story." *Cosmopolitan* 2 (1833): 123–41.

1835

The Yemassee. A Romance of Carolina. 2 vols., New York: Harper & Brothers, 1835.

"The Cherokee Embassage." *Southern Literary Journal* 1 (Dec. 1835): 227–38; *Carl Werner* (1838), 2:175–208.

"Logoochie; or, the Branch of Sweet Water. A Legend of Georgia." *The Magnolia for 1836* (1835), 36–71; *Carl Werner* (1838), 2:83–129.

1836

"Jocassée. A Cherokee Legend." *The Gift for 1837* (1836), 55–82; *Carl Werner* (1838), 2:131–73; *The Wigwam and the Cabin,* 2 vols. (New York: Wiley and Putnam, 1845), 1:209–33.

1840

"The Arm-Chair of Tustenuggee. A Tradition of the Catawba." *Godey's* 20 (May 1840): 193–201; *The Wigwam and the Cabin* (1845), 1:120–48.

1841

"Caloya; or, the Loves of the Driver." *Magnolia* 3 (May, June, July 1841): 222–29, 264–73, 317–24; *The Wigwam and the Cabin* (1845), 2:127–95.

"Oakatibbe, or the Choctaw Sampson." *Family Companion* 1 (Nov., Dec. 1841): 76–82, 163–69; *The Wigwam and the Cabin* (1845), 1:176–208.

1842

"Lucas de Ayllon. A Historical Nouvellette." *Ladies Companion* 17 (May/July/Aug 1842): 36–40, 147–52, 184–90; *The Wigwam and the Cabin* (1845), 2:196–238.

1843

"The Legend of Guernache." *Ladies' Companion* 20 (Nov. 1843): 29–39; *The Lily and the Totem, or The Huguenots in Florida. A Series of Sketches, Picturesque and Historical, of the Colonies of Coligni, in North America, 1562–1570* (New York: Baker and Scribner, 1850), 37–80.

"The Two Camps. A Legend of the Old North State." *The Gift for 1844* (1843), 149–81; *The Wigwam and the Cabin* (1845), 1:37–70.

1845

"The Subaltern's Yarn; or, a Day's Scout in the Florida Campaign." *Southern and Western* 2 (Aug. 1845): 95–105.

"The Sedition of La Caroline." *Southern and Western* 2 (Nov. 1845): 324–32; *The Lily and the Totem* (1850), 166–84.

1850

"The Adventure of D'Erlach." *The Lily and the Totem* (1850), 193–210.

"The Narrative of Le Barbu: The Bearded Man of Calos." *The Lily and the Totem* (1850), 218–50.

"Of the Captivity of the Great Paracoussi—Olata Ouvac Utina, and the War Which Followed Between His People and the French." *The Lily and the Totem* (1850), 263–93.

"Iracana, or the Eden of the Floridian." *The Lily and the Totem* (1850), 294–309.

"Dominique de Gourgues." *The Lily and the Totem* (1850), 414–62.

1852

"The Spectre Chief of Accabee." *Literary World* 11 (31 July 1852): 74–76.

["Mossfoot, the Demon of the Red Man. Larkins' Story"] in "Home Sketches, or Life along the Highways and Byways of the South." *Literary World* 11 (11 Sept., 20 Nov., 11 Dec. 1852): 163–66, 323–24, 378–79.

1853

Vasconselos. A Romance of the New World. New York: Redfield, 1853.

1854

"The Legend of Happy Valley, and the Beautiful Fawn." *Southern Literary Messenger* 20 (July, Aug. 1854): 396–403, 492–503.

["League of the Redman."] *Southward Ho!,* 384–88.

1859

The Cassique of Kiawah[.] A Colonial Romance. New York: Redfield, 1859.

MANUSCRIPT

"'Bald-Head Bill Bauldy,' and How He Went Through the Flurriday Campaign!—A Legend of the Hunter's Camp—; manuscript, South Caroliniana Library. [Note: the now much celebrated story left in manuscript at Simms's death remained unpublished until 1974 when it was included in *Stories and Tales,* ed. John C. Guilds (Vol. V of *The Writings of William Gilmore Simms: Centennial Edition,* Columbia, University of South Carolina Press, 1974), 466–521. Though not primarily an Indian tale, much of the story's ironic satire is aimed at the conduct of United States soldiers in the Seminole War and their stereotyped caricature of the Indian.

ᏟᎳ *Poems*

1826

"The Broken Arrow." Charleston *Courier,* 31 May 1826; *Lyrical and Other Poems* (Charleston: Ellis & Neufville, 1827), 7–9. *The Book of My Lady* (1833), 122–25.

1827

"The Love of Mackintosh." *Lyrical and Other Poems,* 57–59.

"Death of King Philip."* *Lyrical and Other Poems* (1827), 14–17.

"Song of Phillip."* *Lyrical and Other Poems* (1827), 17–21

"The Forest Maiden." *Lyrical and Other Poems* (1827), 80–89; *The Book of My Lady* (1833), 52–59.

"To a Winter Flower, Written in the Creek Nation." *Lyrical and Other Poems* (1827), 97.

"The Wilderness." *Lyrical and Other Poems* (1827), 163–66.

"Indian Hunter's Song." *Lyrical and Other Poems* (1827), 167–68.

"At Midnight."† *Lyrical and Other Poems* (1827), 49–52.

"The Last of the Yemassees." *Early Lays* (Charleston: A. E. Miller, 1827), 65–69; *The Book of My Lady* (1833), 316–19.

"The Green Corn Dance." *Early Lays* (1827), 27–29; *The Book of My Lady* (1833), 257–58.

1829

"Mighty is the Yemassee." *Southern Literary Gazette,* 1 ns (1 Aug. 1829): 130; *The Yemassee* (1835) 1: 188.

1832

"The Sioux Boy; an Indian Legend." New York *Mirror* 10 (15 Sept. 1832): 81; *The Book of My Lady* (1833), 212–13; *Poems Descriptive, Dramatic, Legendary and Contemplative,* 2 vols. (New York: Redfield, 1853; Charleston: John Russell, 1853), 1:321–23.

---

* Simms combined "Death of King Philip" and "Song of Philip" to form a single poem, "Metacom of Montaup," *The Book of My Lady* (1833), 180–88, with only minor revision.
† This poem is included without a title in a footnote to the short story "Indian Sketch" (see above, 131–33). In the footnote, Simms claims that he is the translator, not the author, of "a poem by a native writer upon this subject."

1833

"Metacom and Montaup." *The Book of My Lady* (1833), 180–88.

["I was a wanderer long, and loved the wild,"]. *The Book of My Lady* (1833), 286–90.

1835

"The 'Coonee-Latee,' or 'Trick-Tongue.'" *The Yemassee* (1835) 1:85.

"Yemassee War-Hymn." *The Yemasssee* 2:58.

"The Widow of the Chief." *Southern Literary Journal* 1 (Sept. 1835): 31–32; *Southern Passages and Pictures* (New York: George Adlard, 1839), 225–28.

Selections from *The Yemassee* listed in brackets are untitled poems of various types from that novel: some included in the text of the novel, others serving as epigraphs to chapters; some presented from the point of view of Indian characters, others describing actions of Indians but presented from the narrator's point of view. In a few cases, the Indian themes of these poems are difficult to discern without reading all or parts of the novel.

These untitled poems from *The Yemassee* are not attributed to Simms in James Everett Kibler Jr.'s invaluable compilation, *The Poetry of William Gilmore Simms: An Introduction and Bibliography* (Columbia, S.C.: Southern Studies Program, 1979). The editors of this volume have concluded that the language and style of the poems—and especially their thematic similarity to the chapters in which they appear—identify them as works of Simms that belong on a complete list of his Indian writings.

["And wherefore sings he that strange song of death,"]. *The Yemassee* 1:183.

["Be thy teeth firmly set; the time is come"]. *The Yemassee* 2:50.

["The hunters are upon thee—keep thy pace,"]. *The Yemassee* 1:162.

["A last blow for his country, and he dies,"]. *The Yemassee* 2:190.

["The nations meet in league—a solemn league,"]. *The Yemassee* 1:70.

["Not in their usual trim was he arrayed,"]. *The Yemassee* 1:15.

["The pain of death is nothing. To the chief,"]. *The Yemassee* 1:208.

["A scatter'd race—a wild, unfetter'd tribe,"]. *The Yemassee* 1:9.

["Severe the school that made him bear"]. *The Yemassee* 1:181–82.

["He shouts, he strikes, he falls—his fields are o'er;"]. *The Yemassee* 2:181.

["The storm cloud gathers fast, the hour's at hand,"]. *The Yemassee* 2:124.

["They bind him, will they slay him? That old man,"]. *The Yemassee* 1:202.

["This man is not of us—his ways are strange,"]. *The Yemassee* 1:30.

[——"Ye shall give all"]. *The Yemassee* 1:88

["The arrows—"]. *The Yemassee* 1:104.

["Let the Yemassee have ears"]. *The Yemassee* 1:105.

["What is the Seratee?"]. *The Yemassee* 1:186.

["Hear, Opitchi-Manneyto"]. *The Yemassee* 1:187.

["I take from thee the earth of Yemassee—"]. *The Yemassee* 1:220.

["Sangarrah-me, Yemassee"]. *The Yemassee* 2:59.

["I hear thee, Opitchi-Manneyto—"]. *The Yemassee* 1:104.

["'Tis Opitchi-Manneyto . . . now that speaks"]. *The Yemassee* 1:106–7.

["'Tis Opitchi-Manneyto . . . that cries"]. *The Yemassee* 1:212.

["I go with the long knife"]. *The Yemassee* 1:200.

["Thy wing, Opitchi-Manneyto"]. *The Yemassee* 1:210.

["Is not this a Yemassee?"]. *The Yemassee* 1:211.

["It is not the Yemassee"]. *The Yemassee* 1:212.

["Thou that wast a brother"]. *The Yemassee* 1:218.

["Thou wast a child of Manneyto"]. *The Yemassee* 1:218.

["That Opitchi-Manneyto claims thee"]. *The Yemassee* 1:218–19.

["Sangarrah-me—Sangarrah-me"]. *The Yemassee* 1:206.

1837

"The Indian Village." *Southern Literary Journal* 3 (Jan. 1837): 343–44; *Southern Passages* (1839), 49–53.

1838

"The Tryst of Acayma." *Southern Literary Journal* 3 ns (June 1838): 411–12; *Southern Passages* (1839), 95–97; *Poems* (1853) 1:304–6.

["A Story of the Old-Time Cherokee"]. *Carl Werner* (1838), 2:131.

1842

"Dark-eyed Maid of Edisto." *Magnolia* 1 ns (Dec. 1842): 341; *Areytos: or, Songs of the South* (Charleston: John Russell, 1846), 46.

1845

"Tzelica, A Tradition of the French Broad." *Southern and Western Monthly Magazine and Review* 1 (Jan. 1845): 15–16; *Poems* (1853), 1:324–27.

"Accabee—A Ballad." *Southern and Western* 1 (June 1845): 378–79.

1846

"Indian Serenade." *Areytos* (1846), 30–32.

"Pocahontas, A Legend of Virginia." *Missionary Memorial* (1846), 199–200; *Southward Ho!*, 110–23

1849

"The Cassique of Accabee; A Legend of Ashley River." *The Cassique of Accabee. A Tale of Ashley River. With Other Pieces* (Charleston: John Russell, 1849), 5–38.

1853

"The Last Fields of the Biloxi; A Tradition of Louisiana." Boston *Notion*, 13 Mar. 1841; *Poems* (1853), 1:273–87.

"Love Song of Enemoya, One of the Great War Chiefs of the Omahas." Charleston *Weekly News* 3 ns (16 July 1853); *Southward Ho!* (1854), 414–15.

1858

"Indians Spearing Salmon." *Russell's Magazine* 3 (June 1858): 262.

1867

"Seminole Dogs—Black." Charleston *Courier*, 9 May 1867.

"Xanthoxilus, A Shelter from the Sun." Charleston *Courier*, 9 May 1867.

1868

"Thlecathca; or, the Broken Arrow." *Old Guard* 6 (Nov. 1868): 863–67.

1869

"Chilhowee, the Indian Village." *Old Guard* 7 (Feb. 1869): 148–52.

MANUSCRIPT

"The Mountain Tramp. Tselica; A Legend of the French Broad." Unpublished manuscript, South Caroliniana Library.

Index of Titles

(f) indicates work of fiction, (p) indicates poem, (n) indicates work of nonfiction